THE CAMBRIDGE WOR

\*

VOLUME II

The development of agriculture has oft
most important change in all of human history. Volume II of *The
Cambridge World History* explores the origins and impact of agriculture and agricultural communities, and also discusses issues
associated with pastoralism and hunter-fisher-gatherer economies. To capture the patterns of this key change across the
globe, the volume uses an expanded timeframe from 12,000 BCE
to 500 CE, beginning with the Neolithic and continuing into later
periods. Scholars from a range of disciplines, including archaeology, historical linguistics, biology, anthropology, and history,
trace common developments in the more complex social structures and cultural forms that agriculture enabled, such as sedentary villages and more elaborate foodways, and then present a
series of regional overviews accompanied by detailed case studies
from many different parts of the world, including Southwest Asia,
South Asia, China, Japan, Southeast Asia and the Pacific, sub-
Saharan Africa, the Americas, and Europe.

GRAEME BARKER is Emeritus Disney Professor of archaeology, Senior
Fellow of the McDonald Institute for Archaeological Research, and
Professorial Fellow, St John's College at the University of Cambridge.
He is the author of *The Agricultural Revolution in Prehistory and Prehistoric
Farming in Europe* (Cambridge University Press, 1985).

CANDICE GOUCHER is a professor of history at Washington State
University. With Linda Walton, she published several world history
textbooks, including the second edition of *World History: Journeys from
Past to Present*, and was co-lead scholar on the multimedia project
*Bridging World History*.

*The Cambridge World History* is an authoritative new overview of the dynamic field of world history. It covers the whole of human history, not simply history since the development of written records, in an expanded timeframe that represents the latest thinking in world and global history. With over two hundred essays, it is the most comprehensive account yet of the human past, and it draws on a broad international pool of leading academics from a wide range of scholarly disciplines. Reflecting the increasing awareness that world history can be examined through many different approaches and at varying geographic and chronological scales, each volume offers regional, topical, and comparative essays alongside case studies that provide depth of coverage to go with the breadth of vision that is the distinguishing characteristic of world history.

# THE CAMBRIDGE WORLD HISTORY

\*

## VOLUME II
# A World with Agriculture,
## 12,000 BCE– 500 CE

\*

*Edited by*
GRAEME BARKER
*University of Cambridge*
*and*
CANDICE GOUCHER
*Washington State University*

CAMBRIDGE
UNIVERSITY PRESS

# CAMBRIDGE
## UNIVERSITY PRESS

University Printing House, Cambridge CB2 8BS, United Kingdom

Cambridge University Press is part of the University of Cambridge.

It furthers the University's mission by disseminating knowledge in the pursuit of education, learning, and research at the highest international levels of excellence.

www.cambridge.org
Information on this title: www.cambridge.org/9780521192187

© Cambridge University Press 2015

First published 2015
Paperback edition first published 2017
Reprinted 2018

Printed in the United Kingdom by TJ International Ltd. Padstow Cornwall

*A catalogue record for this publication is available from the British Library*

ISBN 978-0-521-19218-7 Hardback
ISBN 978-1-108-40764-9 Paperback

# Contents

vii

Contents

# Contents

# Figures

# *Maps*

xxi

# Tables

# Contributors

GRAEME BARKER, University of Cambridge
HUW BARTON, University of Leicester
AMY BOGAARD, University of Oxford
PETER BOGUCKI, Princeton University
GYANESHWER CHAUBEY, Estonian Biocentre
TIM DENHAM, Australian National University
TOM D. DILLEHAY, Vanderbilt University
CHRISTOPHER EHRET, University of California, Los Angeles
DORIAN Q. FULLER, University College London
DAPHNE E. GALLAGHER, University of Oregon
CANDICE GOUCHER, Washington State University
RYSZARD GRYGIEL, Museum of Archaeology and Ethnography, Łód
MARTIN JONES, University of Cambridge
SIMON KANER, Sainsbury Institute for the Study of Japanese Arts and Cultures
ELEANOR KINGWELL-BANHAM, University College London
PAUL J. LANE, Uppsala University
GUOXIANG LIU, Chinese Academy of Social Sciences
XINYI LIU, Washington St. Louis University
KEVIN C. MACDONALD, University College London
RODERICK J. MCINTOSH, Yale University
KEN'ICHI OKADA, Archaeological Institute of Kashihara
ALAN K. OUTRAM, University of Exeter
MARIA PALA, University of Huddersfield
DEBORAH M. PEARSALL, University of Missouri
CAMERON A. PETRIE, University of Cambridge
MARTIN B. RICHARDS, University of Huddersfield
CHARLOTTE ROBERTS, University of Durham
GARY O. ROLLEFSON, Whitman College
ALAN H. SIMMONS, University of Nevada, Las Vegas
PEDRO SOARES, University of Minho
ALASDAIR WHITTLE, University of Cardiff
KEN'ICHI YANO, Ritsumeikan University
ZHIJUN ZHAO, Chinese Academy of Social Sciences

# Preface

The Cambridge Histories have long presented authoritative multi-volume overviews of historical topics, with chapters written by specialists. The first of these, the *Cambridge Modern History*, planned by Lord Acton and appearing after his death from 1902 to 1912, had fourteen volumes and served as the model for those that followed, which included the seven-volume *Cambridge Medieval History* (1911–1936), the twelve-volume *Cambridge Ancient History* (1924–1939), the thirteen-volume *Cambridge History of China* (1978–2009), and more specialized multi-volume works on countries, religions, regions, events, themes, and genres. These works are designed, as the *Cambridge History of China* puts it, to be the 'largest and most comprehensive' history in the English language of their topic, and, as the *Cambridge History of Political Thought* asserts, to cover 'every major theme'.

The *Cambridge World History* both follows and breaks with the model set by its august predecessors. Presenting the 'largest and most comprehensive' history of the world would take at least three hundred volumes – and a hundred years – as would covering 'every major theme'. Instead the series provides an overview of the dynamic field of world history in seven volumes over nine books. It covers all of human history, not simply that since the development of written records, in an expanded timeframe that represents the newest thinking in world history. This broad timeframe blurs the line between archaeology and history, and presents both as complementary approaches to the human past. The volume editors include archaeologists as well as historians, and have positions at universities in the United States, Britain, France, Australia, and Israel. The essays similarly draw on a broad author pool of historians, art historians, anthropologists, classicists, archaeologists, economists, linguists, sociologists, biologists, geographers, and area studies specialists, who come from universities in Australia, Britain, Canada, China, Estonia, France, Germany, India, Israel, Italy, Japan, the Netherlands, New Zealand, Poland, Portugal, Singapore, Sweden, Switzerland, and the United States. They include very senior scholars whose works have helped to form the field, and also mid-career and younger scholars whose research will continue to shape it in the future. Some of the authors are closely associated with the rise of world history as a distinct research and teaching field, while others describe what they do primarily as global history, transnational history, international history, or comparative history. (Several of the essays in Volume 1 trace the development of these overlapping, entangled, and at times competing fields.) Many authors are simply specialists on their topic who the editors thought could best explain this to a broader audience or reach beyond their comfort zones into territory that was new.

Reflecting the increasing awareness that world history can be examined through many different approaches and at varying geographic and chronological scales, each volume offers several types of essays, including regional, topical, and comparative ones, along with case studies that provide depth to go with the breadth of vision that is the distinguishing characteristic of world history. Volume 1 introduces key frames of analysis that shape the making of world history across time periods, with essays on overarching approaches, methods, and themes. It then includes a group of essays on the Palaeolithic, covering the 95 per cent of human history up to 10,000 BCE. From that point on, each volume covers a shorter time period than its predecessor, with slightly overlapping chronologies volume to volume to reflect the complex periodization of a truly global history. The editors chose the overlapping chronologies and stayed away from traditional period titles (e.g. 'classical' or 'early modern') intentionally to challenge standard periodization to some degree. The overlapping chronologies also allow each volume to highlight geographic disjunctures and imbalances, and the ways in which various areas influenced one another. Each of the volumes centres on a key theme or cluster of themes that the editors view as central to the period covered in the volume and also as essential to an understanding of world history as a whole.

Volume 2 (A World with Agriculture, 12,000 BCE–500 CE) begins before the Neolithic and continues into later periods to explore the origins of agriculture and agricultural communities in various regions of the world, as well as to discuss issues associated with pastoralism and hunter-fisher-gatherer economies. It traces common developments in the more complex social structures and cultural forms that agriculture enabled, and then presents a series of regional overviews accompanied by detailed case studies from many different parts of the world.

Volume 3 (Early Cities and Comparative History, 4000 BCE–1200 CE) focuses on early cities as motors of change in human society. Through case studies of cities and comparative chapters that address common issues, it traces the creation and transmission of administrative and information technologies, the performance of rituals, the distribution of power, and the relationship of cities with their hinterlands. It has a broad and flexible chronology to capture the development of cities in various regions of the world and the transformation of some cities into imperial capitals.

Volume 4 (A World with States, Empires, and Networks, 1200 BCE–900 CE) continues the analysis of processes associated with the creation of larger-scale political entities and networks of exchange, including those generally featured in accounts of the rise of 'classical civilizations', but with an expanded timeframe that allows the inclusion of more areas of the world. It analyses common social, economic, cultural, political, and technological developments, and includes chapters on slavery, religion, science, art, and gender. It then presents a series of regional overviews, each accompanied by a case study or two examining one smaller geographic area or topic within that region in greater depth.

Volume 5 (Expanding Webs of Exchange and Conquest, 500 CE–1500 CE) highlights the growing networks of trade and cross-cultural interaction that were a hallmark of the millennium covered in the volume, including the expansion of text-based religions and the transmission of science, philosophy, and technology. It explores social structures, cultural institutions, and significant themes such as the environment, warfare, education, the family, and courtly cultures on both a global and Eurasian scale, and continues the examination of state formation begun in Volume 4 with chapters on polities and empires in Asia, Africa, Europe, and the Americas.

The first five volumes each appear in a single book, but the last two are double volumes covering the periods conventionally known as the early modern and modern, an organization signalling the increasing complexity of an ever more globalized world in the last half millennium, as well as the expanding base of source materials and existing historical analyses for these more recent eras. Volume 6 (The Construction of a Global World, 1400–1800 CE) traces the increasing biological, commercial, and cultural exchanges of the period, and explores regional and transregional political, cultural, and intellectual developments. The first book within this volume, 'Foundations', focuses on global matrices that allowed this increasingly interdependent world to be created, including the environment, technology, and disease; crossroads and macro-regions such as the Caribbean, the Indian Ocean, and Southeast Asia in which connections were especially intense; and large-scale political formations, particularly maritime and land-based empires such as Russia, the Islamic Empires, and the Iberian Empires that stretched across continents and seas. The second book within this volume, 'Patterns of Change', examines global and regional migrations and encounters, and the economic, social, cultural, and institutional structures that both shaped and were shaped by these, including trade networks, law, commodity flows, production processes, and religious systems.

Volume 7 (Production, Destruction, and Connection, 1750–Present) examines the uneven transition to a world with fossil fuels and an exploding human population that has grown ever more interactive through processes of globalization. The first book within this double volume, 'Structures, Spaces, and Boundary Making', discusses the material situations within which our crowded world has developed, including the environment, agriculture, technology, energy, and disease; the political movements that have shaped it, such as nationalism, imperialism, decolonization, and communism; and some of its key regions. The second book, 'Shared Transformations?' explores topics that have been considered in earlier volumes, including the family, urbanization, migration, religion, and science, along with some that only emerge as global phenomena in this era, such as sports, music, and the automobile, as well as specific moments of transition, including the Cold War and 1989.

Taken together, the volumes contain about two hundred essays, which means the *Cambridge World History* is comprehensive, but certainly not exhaustive. Each volume editor has made difficult choices about what to include and what to leave out, a problem for all world histories since those of Herodotus and Sima Qian more than two millennia ago. Each volume is arranged in the way that the volume editor or editors decided is most appropriate for the period, so that organizational schema differ slightly from volume to volume. Given the overlapping chronologies, certain topics are covered in several different volumes because they are important for understanding the historical processes at the heart of each of these, and because we as editors decided that viewing key developments from multiple perspectives is particularly appropriate for world history. As with other Cambridge Histories, the essays are relatively lightly footnoted, and include a short list of further readings, the first step for readers who want to delve deeper into the field. In contrast to other Cambridge Histories, all volumes are being published at the same time, for the leisurely pace of the print world that allowed publication over several decades does not fit with twenty-first-century digital demands.

In other ways as well, the *Cambridge World History* reflects the time in which it has been conceptualized and produced, just as the *Cambridge Modern History* did. Lord Acton envisioned his work, and Cambridge University Press described it, as 'a history of the world', although in only a handful of chapters out of several hundred were the principal actors individuals, groups, or polities outside of Europe and North America. This is not surprising, although the identical self-description of the *New Cambridge Modern History* (1957–1979), with a similar balance of topics, might be a bit more so. The fact that in 1957 – and even in 1979, when the last volume of the series appeared – Europe would be understood as 'the world' and as the source of all that was modern highlights the power and longevity of the perspective we have since come to call 'Eurocentric'. (In other languages, there are perspectives on world history that are similarly centred on the regions in which they have been produced.) The continued focus on Europe in the mid-twentieth century also highlights the youth of the fields of world and global history, in which the conferences, professional societies, journals, and other markers of an up-and-coming field have primarily emerged since the 1980s, and some only within the last decade. The *Journal of World History*, for example, was first published in 1990, the *Journal of Global History* in 2005, and *New Global Studies* in 2007.

World and global history have developed in an era of intense self-reflection in all academic disciplines, when no term can be used unselfconsciously and every category must be complicated. Worries about inclusion and exclusion, about diversity and multi-vocality, are standard practice in subfields of history and related disciplines, including archaeology, that have grown up in this atmosphere. Thus as we editors sought topics that would give us a balance between the traditional focus in world history on large-scale political and economic processes carried out by governments and commercial elites and newer concerns with cultural forms, representation, and meaning, we also sought to include topics that have been important in different national historiographies. We also attempted to find authors who would provide geographic balance along with a balance between older and younger voices. Although the author pool is decidedly broader geographically – and more balanced in terms of gender – than it was in either of the Cambridge Modern Histories, it is not as global as we had hoped. Contemporary world and global history is overwhelmingly Anglophone, and, given the scholarly diaspora, disproportionately institutionally situated in the United States and the United Kingdom. Along with other disparities in our contemporary world, this disproportion is, of course, the result of the developments traced in this series, though the authors might disagree about which volume holds the key to its origins, or whether one should spend much time searching for origins at all.

My hopes for the series are not as sweeping as Lord Acton's were for his, but fit with those of Tapan Raychaudhuri and Irfan Habib, the editors of the two-volume *Cambridge Economic History of India* (1982). In the preface to their work, they comment: 'We only dare to hope that our collaborative effort will stimulate discussion and help create new knowledge which may replace before many years the information and analysis offered in this volume.' In a field as vibrant as world and global history, I have no doubts that such new transformative knowledge will emerge quickly, but hope this series will provide an entrée to the field, and a useful overview of its state in the early twenty-first century.

MERRY E. WIESNER-HANKS

# Introduction

## *A world with agriculture*

GRAEME BARKER AND CANDICE GOUCHER

This volume traces the origins of agriculture and the character of early agricultural communities across the world and surveys the development of the more complex social structures and cultural forms that agriculture enabled. Until around 11,500 years ago, when the world's climate changed from the Pleistocene (the 'Ice Ages', a period of dramatic and often abrupt transformations in temperature and precipitation regimes) to our own climatic era termed the Holocene, most of the world's population lived by various combinations of hunting, fishing, and gathering ('foraging'). A few thousand years later many societies in Eurasia, Africa, and the Americas relied wholly or partly on farming for their food. Arguably the most important event in world history, food production has been linked to significant changes in landscapes and populations that eventually supported the rise of urbanism, increasing complexity, and inequality that dominated the planet's history thereafter and enabled human populations to expand from perhaps 6 million at the end of the Pleistocene to over 7 billion today. The processes that led from foraging to farming and herding took thousands of years to unfold globally. Thus this volume necessarily has not only a global perspective but also a very broad chronology to capture the expansive timeframe of the origins and diffusion of agriculture worldwide. Our timeframe is broadly from the beginnings of the Holocene to the beginning of the Common Era, but in some cases the span may be even bigger, as in some parts of the world behaviours that presaged farming went back well into the Pleistocene and in some regions the diffusion and adoption of agriculture continued well into the first millennium CE and even into the second.[1]

The *Oxford English Dictionary* defines agriculture as 'the science and art of cultivating the soil, including the gathering in of the crops and the rearing of

---

1 Graeme Barker, *The Agricultural Revolution in Prehistory: Why did Foragers become Farmers?* (Oxford University Press, 2006).

livestock', and farming as 'the business of cultivating land and raising stock', the mix of science, art, and business in these definitions nicely encapsulating the complex management strategies needed in food production, but also their economic potential. Domestication is commonly used to describe the process by which plants or animals are separated from the natural or wild population to the extent that the individuals within the population lose their ability to survive and produce offspring without human protection and manipulation. At the same time, however, there is increasing recognition that domestication is not a one-way process, and that when plants, animals, and humans are brought into close proximity, domestication has the potential to affect all three parties to the relationship rather than being just a question of humans learning ways to control plants and animals. Pastoralism is defined in the *OED* as 'the practice of keeping sheep, cattle, and other grazing animals', especially in 'the nomadic, non-industrial society that it implies' in a specialized economic system in which people rely mostly on their livestock (i.e. domestic animals) for their food, as opposed to systems of animal husbandry and stock-rearing in which the keeping of livestock is well integrated with, and frequently ancillary to, the cultivation of crops (Chapter 6). Though once thought to be a primitive form of husbandry that preceded plant cultivation, it is now recognized to be more usually a sophisticated economic system on the edge of, and intimately linked to, state-level agricultural societies.

The exploration of a world with agriculture invites a world historical approach. It demands an understanding that is simultaneously both global and local. Many scholars have examined local reverberations of the revolutionary transitions to food production. These often have been site-specific studies by archaeologists, who sometimes have placed their work in a wider context only by considering factors that may have led to the diffusion of agriculture via trade and migration. Until recently few authors have attempted to weave a global perspective. Critical to any broader study of agricultural origins is not only the mapping of expansive regional patterns, but also the interpretation of local ecologies that has framed the understanding of prehistoric behaviour. What continues to confound researchers is the answer to the seemingly simple question of why the advantages of agriculture apparently became obvious to many prehistoric populations in vastly different parts of the world.

## Research traditions

By the middle of the nineteenth century archaeologists were classifying the hunter-gatherer societies of the Ice Ages, the makers of cave art in western

Europe, as Palaeolithic or Old Stone Age, and the first farming societies as Neolithic or New Stone Age. The latter were defined in particular by the first appearance (as then believed) of polished stone tools and pottery along with domestic plants and animals. The British archaeologist Hodder Westropp first coined the term Mesolithic or Middle Stone Age in 1872 (in his *Prehistoric Phases*) to describe the hunter-gatherers in Europe who were living after the Ice Ages, in our own climatic era, but before the development of farming. He described the Mesolithic as the Age of Barbarism when 'man lived as the tiger lives, catching his prey by his superior cunning, strength and pluck' and the Neolithic as the Age of Pastoralism when 'the cow yields him milk and the goat yields him cloth; yet he wins these requisites from them not by murderous cunning but by tender love'.[2] He was one of those who thought that plant husbandry came later, in the Bronze Age, but by the 1880s it was recognized that the beginnings of plant and animal husbandry generally went together, and the Neolithic was defined in these terms. Although the Mesolithic/Neolithic nomenclature was first developed for Europe, the terms were commonly being applied in many other parts of the world in the opening decades of the twentieth century as the frameworks of prehistory were established.

The terminology is widely accepted as unsatisfactory, in particular the term Neolithic, though as with most unsatisfactory terminologies no better alternatives have been proposed. The latter may sometimes be used in the literature as a period descriptor (the 'Neolithic period'), its use in this sense implying that everybody at that time in a particular region practised farming, while the evidence now shows that many people in fact lived by a mixture of farming, hunting, and gathering, or just by hunting and gathering; it may be used sometimes as an economic descriptor, as in the Neolithic Revolution, for example 'Neolithic people' (i.e. farmers) 'lived alongside Mesolithic people' (i.e. hunter-gatherers); it may sometimes be used as a descriptor of a 'package' of material culture, i.e. artefacts such as pottery and polished stone axes but also forms of settlement, houses, burials, etc., as well as domestic plants and animals, leading to descriptions of hunter-gatherers 'adopting part of the Neolithic package'. Clearly it is essential for scholars writing about the beginnings of farming to explain what they mean by Neolithic and how they will use the term, as it is all too easy to slip from one use of the term to another, often unconsciously and sometimes in the same sentence!

2 H. Westropp, *Prehistoric Phases* (London: Bell & Daldy, 1872).

Although he wrote mainly about Southwest Asia (the 'Near East') and Europe, the Australian (but UK-based) prehistorian Gordon Childe remains hugely influential for archaeologists interested in the origins of agriculture. In books such as *Man Makes Himself* (1936) and *What Happened in History* (1942) he proposed that farming probably began as a response by hunter-gatherers to the end of the Ice Ages and beginning of the modern climatic era.[3] Though he was mistaken about the course of climate change in Southwest Asia (he thought that the beginning of the Holocene would have been characterized by the development of aridity, whereas we now know that it got wetter, not drier), the overall argument that hunter-gatherers turned to farming in the context of the changes to the world's climate with the transition from the Pleistocene to the Holocene remains the dominant view for most scholars today. He famously proposed the term 'Neolithic Revolution' to encapsulate the process of changing from foraging to farming, on a par with later revolutions like the Industrial Revolution in its transformational character (even if it took millennia rather than centuries or decades like later socioeconomic revolutions): farming gave people a reliable food supply, in contrast with hunting and gathering, that allowed them to settle down ('sedentism'), build stable communities, and create food surpluses that allowed population numbers to rise and set the stage for the development of cities and states (his 'Urban Revolution').

Childe's ideas about a Neolithic Revolution were in many respects borne out by the explosion of archaeological fieldwork in regions such as Southwest Asia, Central America, and Peru in the 1950s and 1960s. Most of these expeditions represented the beginnings of a new kind of interdisciplinary archaeology involving specialists in archaeological science and ancillary disciplines who collected data sets from the excavated sites such as animal bones and carbonized seeds and other fragments of plants to track the beginnings of, respectively, animal and plant domestication, and to investigate (from sediment cores in the vicinity) fossil pollen and sedimentary indicators of the climatic and environmental contexts in which early farming was practised. Underpinning this work was the collection of organic material such as charcoal for the new dating method of radiocarbon or carbon 14 ($^{14}$C) dating: this allowed archaeologists for the first time to date the sites they were excavating independently of other means, whereas Childe had only been able to date Neolithic sites in Europe, for example, by trying to show

---

3 V.G. Childe, *Man Makes Himself* (London: Watts, 1936), and *What Happened in History* (Harmondsworth: Penguin, 1942).

direct or indirect links in their material culture with pharaonic Egypt, which had dated historical records going back to around 3000 BCE. (The scale of the revolution represented by $^{14}$C dating can be conveyed by the fact that the first dates for the beginnings of the Neolithic in Europe, in Greece, placed the sites at around 6000 BCE, not 3000 BCE!) In Southwest Asia excavations of sites such as Jericho in Israel (by Kathleen Kenyon), Jarmo in Iraq (by Robert and Ann Braidwood), and Ali Kosh in Iran (by Frank Hole and Kent Flannery) showed that by around 8000 BCE, a thousand or so years into the Holocene, people were living in villages of small houses made of packed mud, using polished stone tools (the first Neolithic pottery here was not made until a few thousand years later), growing crops such as wheat, barley, and legumes, and keeping domestic animals such as sheep and goats, pigs, and cattle.[4]

Rather similar 'village farming communities' were revealed by parallel work in other parts of the world, using different mixes of domesticated plants and animals, such as maize and other vegetables in parts of the Americas and rice and pigs in China. In combination, this phase of research indicated that the Neolithic Revolution began in a few 'hearths of domestication', in particular Southwest Asia, China, eastern North America, Central America, Peru, and the African Sahel, and that farming then spread to neighbouring regions, most commonly as a result of a migration by farmers, though in some cases as a result of the adoption of farming by hunter-gatherers coming into contact with farmers.

## Pathways to agriculture

Given that most of the world's population relies on a small number of plants and a smaller number of animals for most of its food, it is easy to assume that the advantages of farming must have been obvious to any prehistoric hunter-gatherers given the opportunity to engage in it. For archaeologists, this assumption received a severe dent in the late 1960s and 1970s from the publication of ethnographic studies of the few remaining

---

4 K. Kenyon, 'Earliest Jericho', *Antiquity*, 33 (1959), 5–9; R.J. Braidwood and B. Howe, *Prehistoric Investigations in Iraqi Kurdistan*, Studies in Oriental Civilization 31 (University of Chicago Press, 1960); F. Hole and K.V. Flannery, 'The prehistory of south-west Iran: a preliminary report', *Proceedings of the Prehistoric Society*, 33 (1967), 147–206; F. Hole et al., *Prehistory and Human Ecology of the Deh Luran Plain*, Memoirs of the Museum of Anthropology 10 (Ann Arbor: University of Michigan, 1969).

populations of present-day hunter-gatherers. Even in the arid Kalahari desert, for example, the small bands of !Kung San people still living there by hunting and gathering were shown not to live an uncertain hand to mouth existence but to enjoy a secure diet of preferred and less attractive emergency foods, and to spend far less time and effort each day securing them than neighbouring subsistence farmers – they spent as much time socializing as they did securing their food supply. The 'downside' was that they needed to stay mobile, not accumulate lots of possessions as everything had to be carried from one campsite to another, and keep their numbers down (as the mother on the move could only carry one baby) so infanticide was not uncommon. Even so, ethnographies such as those of the !Kung San were influential in persuading archaeologists to think about scenarios for the origins of agriculture in which, rather than hunter-gatherers seeing the advantages of agriculture as obvious, external 'push' factors such as climate change or population pressure might have pushed hunter-gatherers into adopting the farming life. More recent thinking has tended to postulate internal 'pull' factors such as social competition or shifts in ideology as possible mechanisms by which hunter-gatherers might have been induced consciously or unconsciously to begin to engage in farming.

Relying on the direct evidence gleaned from the visual analysis of animal bones and seeds, early archaeologists developed limited models for reconstructing the processes of intensification and transformation. Tropical and subtropical regions of the world offered very little in the way of well-preserved sites, particularly in comparison with dry and arid expanses of Eurasia and Africa. Many of these limitations have now been overcome by systematic investigations in the radically different habitats on all continents, employing both traditional studies of cultigens but also analyses of starch residues (a breakthrough for studying the use of root crops such as yams, taro, and sweet potato in tropical regions). Biomolecular techniques have also revolutionized research on the origins and early history of farming, such as using DNA in modern plants and animals and ancient DNA in archaeological bones and seeds to model domestication histories; analysing the isotope chemistry in human and animal bones from archaeological excavations to establish the diets of the living populations and, in some cases, their migration histories; and analysing organic residues attached to artefacts to identify foodstuffs such as cereal residues on the surfaces of stone tools, or traces of milk, milk products, and animal fat (the latter now identifiable to different species) in the fabrics of pottery sherds. The study of the origins and early history of agriculture requires the concerted efforts of a multidisciplinary archaeology and cognate disciplines, and is being enriched by an ever widening array of scientific techniques of analysis and interpretation.

One assumption that has underpinned a great deal of scholarly as well as popular writing about the origins of agriculture has been that it was probably a 'one-way journey of progress' from being a hunter-gatherer to becoming a farmer, a journey with the goal of learning how to domesticate and manage the plants and animals whose products fill our supermarket shelves today. The academic literature is full of models envisaging a step-like sequence of ever more intensive modes of plant and/or animal exploitation, from more or less opportunistic foraging to established systems of farming, much as Hodder Westropp envisaged in 1872. However, there are examples of late Pleistocene and early Holocene hunter-gatherers engaging in subsistence practices that in one form or another presaged the later relationships to the landscape and natural resources within it that we characterize as agriculture; of 'failed' experiments in managing plants and animals that today are regarded as natural weeds in the case of plants or natural game in the case of animals; of hunter-gatherers whose experiments with food production were ultimately unsuccessful moments of intensification, creating temporary farmers and herders, who in time reverted back to foraging and hunting for subsistence.

Like modern scientists, however, some experimenters either unwittingly or intentionally manipulated the genetic make-up of plant and animal populations, selecting for traits and characteristics that were more productive or more pleasing and thus preferred. By complex mixes of historically contingent decision-making, these early food producers altered the ecology of the planet. Their subsistence strategies also represented a revolutionary commitment to specific environmental niches that range from dry Sahel to verdant river valleys. Agricultural success often demanded settled populations, who in turn wrought further changes on their landscapes. Sometimes settling down led to the intensification of plant use and food storage, as transitional systems of food production gave way to full-blown domestication. In the Andes, the domestication of camelids such as llama and alpaca occurred around the same time as *Chenopodium* (quinoa). In Southwest Asia, many farmers living in tell (mound) villages continued to rely on hunted meat. Elsewhere, mixed strategies expanded the domestication of plants together with raising livestock, but the elaboration of these new practices was uneven and uncertain. In many parts of the world the domestication of plants and the onset of cereal agriculture predated the domestication and herding of animals, but the relationship appears to be reversed in Africa (Chapter 18). Perhaps the dominant message from this book is that the global pathways to food production were many and varied.

The development of agriculture was a profoundly human trajectory, bewilderingly complex and often contradictory in its implications. Human and environmental relationships were transformed as the balances recognizable in the Pleistocene shifted in favour of the survival and expansion of human populations at the expense of the rest of the planet during the Holocene. The world with agriculture has secured for the human species its primacy and dominance over the natural world, with all the uncertainties that the industrialized exploitation of selected plants and animals and associated population expansion represent for the sustainable health of the planet. With the development of a world with agriculture, world history became a human story.

The chapters in this volume consist of three kinds, organized into two groups. The first group (Chapters 2–7) takes a series of themes that we selected in order to illustrate some of the wide range of methods and approaches, including non-archaeological as well as archaeological, that we can call on in the study of the origins and diffusion of agriculture. Their authors were encouraged to explore major research questions, and illustrate their particular approaches, at the global scale. For the periods discussed in this volume, archaeology is the primary source of information about material life before the era of written record-keeping, but as the opening chapters following this introduction illustrate, we can also call on subjects as diverse as genetics and linguistics for invaluable insights into past domestication histories and the dispersal of domestic animals and plants, and frequently the movement of people associated with these. The second group of chapters (Chapters 8–23) are archaeology-based, and discuss current understanding of the beginning of agriculture and the character of early agricultural societies on a region-by-region basis, each regional summary (Chapters 8, 10, 12, 14, 16, 18, 20, 22) being accompanied by a case study (Chapters 9, 11, 13, 15, 17, 19, 21, 23) illustrating in more detail a particular archaeological site or set of sites. Part of the rationale for choosing the system of regional summaries and accompanying focused case studies was so that the latter could convey to the non-archaeological reader in some detail the range of data typically making up the 'archaeological record' of a site and to illustrate how archaeologists attempt to draw robust and careful inferences from the observations that they make about it, and the patterns that they detect in it, in ways very different from how the subject is sometimes presented by the popular media as romantic story-telling and speculation unfettered by evidence!

## The contribution of genetics and linguistics

Nothing could illustrate better the formidable contribution of archaeological science to the study of agricultural origins and dispersals than the first of the thematic chapters, on 'archaeogenetics', by Martin Richards and his collaborators Maria Pala, Pedro Soares, and Gyaneshwer Chaubey (Chapter 2). It provides an excellent introduction to the revolutionary collaborations between archaeologists and geneticists and their impact on the spatial and chronological mapping of specific lineages within a species. As early as the 1980s, genetic studies of modern populations, combining information on genealogies, the geographic distribution of lineages, and time depths from calculated mutation rates, began to unravel some of the key questions of prehistory on a truly global scale, including migrations that accounted for the spread of humans out of Africa and across continents. Archaeogenetic research on the Holocene has focused on the persistent questions about the diffusion of farming and herding, especially in Europe, where the combination of inferences from modern population genetic histories and the increasingly robust analysis of ancient DNA in human and animal bones and seeds from archaeological sites have completely retold the old Neolithic narrative. More broadly, the scientific evidence derived from genetic and morphological data emphasizes more than ever the continuous process of the agricultural revolution. In the past decade, along with studies of stable isotopes, archaeogenetics has constituted one of the most promising sources of information about the movements of recent humans and the changes in diet, plants, and animals that shaped their menus and lives.

In Europe the model of 'leapfrogging' colonization movements and assimilation by indigenous hunter-gatherers, taken as the most robust interpretation of current genetics studies, is in accord with current readings of the archaeological record there, as Alasdair Whittle describes in Chapter 22. Europe is fortunate in having a growing data set of ancient DNA to compare and contrast with the modern data. Though interesting insights about domestication histories and dispersals have been drawn from genetic studies of present-day data from the Americas, Africa, and Southeast Asia, it is more difficult than commonly acknowledged to separate signals of Neolithic migrations from the many subsequent migrations of the last few thousand years. In the case of horse domestication processes on the Eurasian steppes, for example, quite apart from the effects of major historical events like the Mongol invasions, millions of horses were moved across the steppes during the course of the twentieth-century world wars and, especially, in the Soviet programme of agricultural collectivization in the 1920s and 1930s. As Chapter 2 concludes, the next phase of research needs to involve the systematic collection of ancient DNA for comparison with the models based on modern data sets.

Chapter 3 takes up the more familiar shared ground of historical linguistics and archaeology, an intersection that emerged in the nineteenth century, and which Christopher Ehret and others have explored for the past three decades.[5] While archaeological evidence can reveal the material life of past communities, linguistics can also document the intangible transformations in technology and ideas. The potential for using language to understand change over time and across space has been mined particularly successfully from the African continent. Like the genetic studies of modern populations, historical linguistics produces a set of lineage relationships that can be interpreted in terms of patterns of historical transformations. The assumption is that when and where such changes took place may be detectable in modern language sets, given that established agricultural systems incorporate new vocabularies to express the technical processes of breeding, herding, and cultivation. Ehret takes the reader through the processes of reconstructing ancestral protolanguages, which may be storehouses for early vocabularies related to agricultural practices. Since language history has been used to trace migrations of speakers, this evidence is also useful for locating origins and mapping the spread of agriculture. Thus it is argued that the dispersal of the proto-Niger–Congo family of speakers (sometimes called the 'Bantu migration') eventually carried farming and herding from West and Central Africa eastwards and southwards across the continent, eventually supplanting many hunting-gathering-fishing communities along the way. Ehret argues for the complementary nature of the two primary sources of evidence, linguistics and archaeology, and suggests new directions for an increasingly global view of the recovery of the origins and diffusion of agriculture. The arguments of linguistic studies are also discussed in several of the regional chapters, though it is clear that some of the earlier linguistic work made overly simplistic assumptions about agricultural origins and dispersals, given how archaeological research is showing that the development of agricultural systems could

---

5  C. Ehret and M. Posnansky (eds.), *The Archaeological and Linguistic Reconstruction of African History* (Berkeley: University of California Press, 1982).

vary enormously in rates of change within as well as between regions and was not necessarily a one-way linear process as the linguistic models some-times assumed.

## Settling down and living together: diet, health, and community

Sedentism, the business of living together in one place for all or most of the year, is known to have developed in some parts of the world in the late Pleistocene, one oft-quoted example being the campsite at Ohalo on the Sea of Galilee in the Jordan valley, dated to around 19,000 years ago, which was probably occupied for several months a year.[6] The same is probably true of some substantial settlements – villages, in effect – sustained just by hunting, gathering, and in particular fishing, for example in resource-rich estuaries on the Atlantic seaboard of Europe.[7] However, while not all societies practis-ing forms of agriculture were sedentary, particularly if they combined these with hunting and/or gathering, a developed commitment to farming in many regions of the world was associated with living together in more or less permanent agglomerated settlements. Chapters 4 and 5 explore the two contrasting faces of such sedentism and associated reliance on diets domi-nated by the domesticates: the impacts respectively on health and social lives.

In Chapter 4 Charlotte Roberts reviews the contribution of scientific techniques clustered under the general term 'bioarchaeology' to examine the impact of agriculture on diet, health, and the human lifespan. Using the macroscopic examination of skeletal material (including teeth), DNA analy-sis, imaging techniques, stable isotopic studies, and other techniques, it has been possible to compare the health, diet, and range of diseases present in pre-agricultural and agricultural communities. The clear conclusion is that farming in permanently settled, densely populated communities was not 'easy street'. Diets did not improve with the transition to agriculture. The pathways to agriculture were littered with problems too numerous to

---

6 M.E. Kislev et al., 'Epipalaeolithic (19,000 BP) cereal and fruit diet at Ohalo II, Sea of Galilee, Israel', *Review of Palaeobotany and Palynology*, 73 (1992), 161–6; D. Nadel and E. Werker, 'The oldest ever brush hut plant remains from Ohalo II, Jordan valley, Israel (19,000 BP)', *Antiquity*, 73 (1999), 755–64.

7 P. Rowley-Conwy, 'Sedentary hunter-gatherers: the Ertebølle example', in G.N. Bailey (ed.), *Hunter-Gatherer Economy in Prehistory* (Cambridge University Press, 1983), 111–26; M. Zvelebil et al. (eds.), *Harvesting the Sea, Farming the Forest: The Emergence of Neolithic Societies in the Baltic Region*, Sheffield Archaeological Monographs 10 (Sheffield Academic Press, 1998).

overlook: refuse disposal, vermin, contamination of water supplies, poor hygiene and sanitation levels, poor harvests, and soil exhaustion frequently resulted in a decline in the variety, quantity, and quality of foodstuffs available. It also turns out that predictable food supplies were not necessarily without nutrient deficiencies, especially in iron, niacin, or vitamins B and C. Other problems emerged with the loss of plant diversity in diets centred on cereals. The repetitive movements embedded in grinding, hoeing, and other activities, together with accidents associated with farming or herding, also took their toll on the bodies of at least some of the prehistoric peoples engaged in early systems of food production. As Akkermans and Schwartz put it somewhat dramatically, 'the Neolithic was . . . a world where life was difficult and people knew they were forever confronted with the Four Horsemen – death, famines, disease, and the malice of other men'.[8] Given the potential disadvantages of living together and relying on a few domesticates for everyday diet, it is not surprising that the development of a commitment to sedentary agriculture was usually not as straightforward as many archaeologists have tended to assume.

For all its negative unintended consequences, however, for many societies agriculture provided the platform for an increasingly coherent, structured, and narrow-based social world that proved remarkably resilient as a social form.[9] In Chapter 5 Amy Bogaard describes the material culture created by agricultural communities, such as field boundaries, rice paddy systems, terracing, and raised beds; biological data such as flora (e.g. crop residues and weeds) and butchered animal bone; and other landscape markers such as funerary monuments. In combination these reveal evidence not only of agricultural decision-making but more generally the social life of early farmers and their 'communities of practice' in different parts of the world. Forms of collective action and culturally specific behaviour (sometimes based on age or gender) can be examined to help us reconstruct the social and physical landscapes as they were transformed by agriculturalists. What emerges from her discussion of 'communities of practice' of farming societies in selected regions (Southwest Asia, Europe, China, Korea, Mesoamerica, and the southwest of North America) is that, though nuclear families emerged as the characteristic residential unit in many regions of the world, and most household farming tended to involve high labour inputs, sedentary village life

---

8 P. Akkermans and G.M. Schwartz, *The Archaeology of Syria: From Complex Hunter-Gatherers to Early Urban Societies (ca. 16,000–300 BCE)* (Cambridge University Press, 2003).
9 J. Robb, 'Material culture, landscapes of action, and emergent causation: a new model of the origins of the European Neolithic', *Current Anthropology*, 54/6 (2013), 657–83.

based on early forms of agriculture could and did take many forms: the emergence of households, compounds, and communally shared spaces differed greatly across Eurasia and the Americas. At the same time, inbuilt in long-term investments in land were issues of ownership and inheritance which provided the seedbed for emergent inequalities.

## Pastoralism and urbanism

The next two chapters have a strong focus on agriculture's propensity for encouraging and sustaining social and economic inequalities, in particular through the acquisition of 'wealth on the hoof' (Chapter 6) and as a part of early urbanism (Chapter 7). Alan Outram describes how, whether keeping a few livestock within a mixed farming system or maintaining large herds and/or flocks in systems of specialized pastoralism, the key limiting factors that have to be solved are access to grazing land and, for times of the year when the natural grazing is insufficient, adequate supplies of fodder. For specialized pastoralists, mobility is invariably the key response, though as Outram describes, this can take many forms, including genuine nomadism and, more commonly, seasonal horizontal or vertical transhumance to move animals between winter and summer grazing. The anthropologist Tim Ingold divided pastoralists in the ethnographic record into three groups: 'meat pastoralists' who, like hunters, exploit animals just for the products of the carcass; 'milch pastoralists' who keep livestock such as cattle, horses, sheep, goats, and llamas not only for meat but also for the 'secondary products' of the live animal such as the power to be ridden or pull equipment, milk, and in the case of sheep their wool; and 'ranchers' who operate within a cash economy.[10] As Outram describes, these categories cannot be imposed on the archaeology of ancient pastoralism in a simplistic way: 'it is key to remember that activities in the past do not always have modern or recent analogues' (Chapter 6). Also, the boundaries between controlled herds and wild populations around them may often be fluid – the modern and ancient DNA of horses, for example, suggests that this has characterized domestic horses on the Eurasian steppes for most of their history, until recent decades in fact. As Chapter 6 describes, the 'secondary products revolution' (the exploitation of horses for riding and pulling light carts or chariots; cattle for pulling ploughs and carts; cattle, sheep, and goats for milk and milk products; sheep for wool; and all of them for their manure), first defined by Andrew

10  T. Ingold, *Hunters, Pastoralists and Ranchers* (Cambridge University Press, 1980).

Sherratt in a brilliant paper in 1981, was clearly a much more complicated process in time and space than he envisaged with the limited data available to him then – the revolution in archaeological science has transformed this branch of archaeology, just as it has the study of health and disease discussed by Charlotte Roberts. Nevertheless, it remains a fundamental step in the development of wealth on the hoof, whether in agricultural societies or specialized pastoralism.

One of the most ubiquitous characteristics of agrarian societies was their impact on the spatial organization of increasingly permanent settlements. Once farmers settled down, populations began to soar and, around the world, both the density and size of communities increased along with the complexity of social structures. Daphne E. Gallagher and Roderick McIntosh (Chapter 7) contend that linking agriculture to urban growth is the necessary consequence of its being at the foundation of our traditional conceptualization of the city (see also Volume 3 in this series). Not only did villages and towns emerge as a result of successful food production, but also large settlements were catalysts for agricultural innovation. However, moving beyond the thinking that agriculture was a simplistic and irreversible driver of societies down the path towards civilization, elite-controlled surplus, and the elaboration of political and social systems, Gallagher and McIntosh remind us that there were many permutations to the relationships between centres and peripheries and urban spaces and their hinterlands. 'The standard narrative that urban zones were highly centralized systems abstracted from [a] hinterland . . . under despotic control', they note, was not the case everywhere, as complex decision-making and control were often negotiated in vastly different points of concentration rather than the agricultural systems of early urban societies simply being the result of top-down decision-making by urban elites. Their Jenne-Jeno case study in the middle Niger valley illustrates how a heterarchically rather than hierarchically organized urban centre was not based on the generation of significant agricultural surplus but relied instead on reciprocal relationships between specialist corporate groups.

## Regional narratives, comparisons, and connectivities

The chapters discussing major world regions provide readers with an outline of the global patterning of research into agricultural practices and their diffusion, and their accompanying case studies illustrate both a typical site or sites from the region discussed in the companion chapter and how archaeologists use the evidence from specific sites to interpret the past. In combination, the geographically based chapters emphasize the variety and limitations of archaeological evidence, with only very well-studied regions such as Europe (Chapter 22) beginning to have sources of data rich enough to provide the first fleeting glimpses of the range of community and individual decision-making involved in the communities of practice associated with agriculture. Whereas the thematic chapters include methods and approaches such as genetics and linguistics that have encouraged (sometimes danger-ously) broad continent-wide, transcontinental, and comparative mappings of the past, the site-specific nature of archaeological research and the environ-ment-specific nature of crop and livestock performance produce contrasting maps of regional domestication histories.

Southwest Asia (the 'Near East') has probably been the greatest focus of scholarly attention in this field of enquiry and remains an influential model for how world historians continue to think about the origins and impact of agriculture. Among the key domesticates here were sheep, goat, cattle, pigs, barley, and the 'primitive' wheats emmer and einkorn. Because of the preservation of evidence in the region's arid conditions and because of the visibility of later achievements based on agriculture (the tell mounds and other monumental architecture of the world's first cities), Southwest Asia remains a remarkably influential region for the theoretical concepts used to examine the Neolithic. Gordon Childe's concept of a Neolithic Revolution encapsulated the notion of revolutionary economic, technological, and social changes accompanying the domestication of wild food resources, but as Alan Simmons (Chapter 8) points out, there is now equally abundant evidence that the Neolithic 'package' sometimes included semi-sedentary villages without agriculture and agriculture without villages. Also, some late Pleistocene ('Natufian') and early Holocene ('Pre-Pottery Neolithic A') 'hunter-gatherers' here were engaging in forms of cultivation and possibly animal management for long periods before their practices altered plants and animals in ways that can be formally recognized as domestication by archaeobotanists and archaeozoologists. Transformations occurred both in the physical landscapes and also in the inner landscapes of people experiencing the transition to agriculture. At the site of 'Ain Ghazal (on the Zarqa River in Jordan), the case study for this region, Gary Rollefson (Chapter 9) suggests substantial changes in the built world of the Neolithic reflected the implications of social changes and ritual practices between the eighth and sixth millennia BCE, evidence of the 'mutual domestication process' mentioned at the beginning of this chapter. Nearly a century of research has created a more flexible package of change in Southwest Asia without removing the primacy of the region in the narrative of agricultural origins, though we have to remember that rather similar environmental conditions favourable to the wheat/barley/sheep/goat mix extended eastwards across the Iranian plateau to Afghanistan and Pakistan and into northwest India as far as the Himalayas, large parts of which have been and remain closed to archaeological fieldwork, so the traditional view that the 'hilly flanks of the Fertile Crescent' (the uplands of the Levant, the Taurus mountains of Turkey, and the Zagros mountains of Iran and Iraq) were an exclusive domestication centre for the cereal/sheep/goat system may turn out not to be entirely true, as already implied by some of the genetic studies of the plants and animals.

Influenced by the assumed primacy of Southwest Asia, it has long been thought that agriculture in South Asia originated with or was influenced by population movements from West Asia. This question of the relative importance of migrations by farmers versus the adoption of domesticates by the indigenous population of hunter-gatherers has been difficult to answer, but in Chapter 10 Eleanor Kingwell-Banham, Cameron Petrie, and Dorian Fuller certainly demonstrate a much more complex set of dynamics for the region's agricultural story than commonly assumed, with at least three clear pathways. The first is the early development of farming in the northwest, with the establishment of permanent settlements such as Mehrgarh in Baluchistan, featured in a case study by Cameron Petrie (Chapter 11), with the full suite of the 'Neolithic package', including Near Eastern-style grain-based breads and mud-brick village architecture, but not (at first) pottery. Genetic evidence confirms multiple clusters of ancestral barley and wild varieties of ancestral einkorn and emmer wheat originating outside the region. Similarly, genetic research on the spread of animals (modern domestic goats and the wild ancestor, the bezoar, as well as cattle and sheep) has produced a complicated picture of both diffusion and possible indigenous innovation (the zebu). Mehrgarh in its later phases also figured prominently in the early history of craft production (pottery, copper metallurgy, and baskets), continuing evidence of the nexus of far-flung economic and social relationships in which such a settlement was located. In the monsoonal Ganges plain of central and northeast India, hunter-fisher-gatherer societies used pottery and ground stone, and wild rice was one of the plants they collected, but people only developed a commitment to rice farming thousands of years later, resulting in large mounded settlements. This region also seems to have been the location of the domestication of the pigeon pea (*Cajanus cajan*). In the savanna regions further south, mobile hunter-gatherers over time integrated the herding of sheep, goats, and cattle into their traditional lifestyles, and domesticated plants such as locally available millets and pulses. The more nuanced interpretations of the evidence call into question the respective roles of trans-regional connections and interactions, on the one hand, and bottom-up local processes of experimentation, on the other.

South Asia also marks one of the world's most important and deep-seated culinary divides, from the tradition of grinding flour, baking bread, and roasting foods that extends from the first farming villages of Southwest Asia to those of northwest India, to the boiling and steaming of grains and other foods characteristic of East Asian methods of food preparation. It is significant in this respect that the first pottery was manufactured by late Pleistocene hunter-gatherers in parts of China far earlier than in most regions of the world, around 18,000 years ago, for boiling fish and plant foods. The reasons for the divide are unclear, but they emphasize how transitions to farming and the addition of domesticates were not simply a matter of calories, economic efficiency, and so on, but also involved matters of cultural norms and taste, a point to which we return in the final section of this chapter. Genetic studies, including those by Xinyi Liu, Dorian Fuller, and Martin Jones (Chapter 12), suggest that there was a protracted process of domestication in a centre or centres in northern China stretching down from the beginning of the Holocene to perhaps around 8000 BCE, a process that included the same kind of 'pre-domestication cultivation' practices now evident with wheat and barley in Southwest Asia. As seen in the case study of Xinglonggou by Xinyi Liu, Zhijun Zhao, and Guoxiang Liu (Chapter 13), domesticated foxtail and broomcorn millets then spread westwards, ultimately across the Eurasian steppes, to Europe. Early domestication processes in northern China also involved pigs, soybeans, and hemp, with changes in the isotope chemistry of pig bones providing nice indirect evidence for the development of a commitment by farmers to millet consumption: millet provided a major food for their pigs after about 4500 BCE, compared with earlier.

Claims for extremely early (late Pleistocene) domestic rice in central and southern China have been made in some of the Chinese literature. However, the analysis of large samples of carbonized seeds and threshing debris collected by the large-scale systematic washing of bulk samples of sediment from excavations (see the illustrations in Chapter 12) has shown that, though morphological changes indicative of incipient domestication can be detected in rice remains by about 4000 BCE, associated with the beginning of paddy technologies, gathering wild rice was just one aspect of Holocene foraging systems that otherwise relied mostly on hunting, fishing, and collecting wild plant foods such as acorns and water chestnuts. The latter were only gradually replaced by rice as a dietary staple by about 3000 BCE. This was also about the time that domestic rice and rice-farming technologies spread south from the Yangtze to the southern provinces of China. By 2000 BCE all five of the legendary 'five grains' described in the Anyang oracle bones of the Shang state (probably broomcorn and foxtail millet, soybeans, wheat or barley, and hemp, though the list varies somewhat) were being grown in China. Wheat and barley, like domesticated sheep, goats, and cattle, probably reached China from the steppes to the west (and originally Southwest Asia and Europe) during the course of the third millennium BCE.

In Japan (Chapter 14), as in China, late Pleistocene hunter-gatherers (here named the Jomon Culture) were making pottery to assist with food preparation, in this case from around 14,000 BCE. The traditional narrative has been that Jomon people practised hunting, fishing, and gathering through much of the Holocene, like Mesolithic people in Europe, with the rich resources of lakes, rivers, forests, and coastlines sustaining more or less permanent villages; and that Yayoi farmers then crossed from Korea and mainland China around 500 BCE, bringing with them wet rice farming and pig husbandry along with a new set of material culture. In fact, as Simon Kaner and Ken'ichi Yano describe, there is increasing evidence that Jomon subsistence sometimes involved an element of cultivation and husbandry of tree fruits such as chestnuts as well as plants like barnyard millet and soybean, and when rice was first introduced into southern Japan *c.* 900 BCE it was incorporated into existing systems of foraging as in China rather than representing a step-change from Jomon foraging, and was practised alongside dry-field agriculture and horticulture of plants such as barnyard millet, broomcorn millet, foxtail millet, barley, pulses, and fruits. Similar arguments are presented for parts of Southeast Asia by Huw Barton in Chapter 16. The case study selected by Ken'ichi Okada (Chapter 15) is the remarkable system of paddy fields he excavated in the pathway of development such as motorway construction in the Nara basin, dating to the early Yayoi period. Whether Yayoi rice farming represented new people, or changes in lifestyles of Jomon 'foragers' (and one argument is that the latter were pre-adapted to taking up rice farming), or a mixture of both, is hotly debated. Certainly once a significant commitment to rice farming developed, it sustained rapid population growth, and by the beginning of the Common Era there were villages over 100 ha in size with perhaps 1,500 residents, sustained by extensive systems of paddy fields irrigated by elaborate networks of canals and managed by elite groups living in separate precincts. Significantly this is the first period where there is wide-spread evidence for inter-communal violence, and, from waterlogged and mineralized residues in cesspits (the aptly named 'toilet archaeology' as described by Kaner and Yano), for a marked increase in the diversity of disease and intestinal parasites.

The first evidence for rice farming in mainland Southeast Asia, as described by Huw Barton (Chapter 16), dates to about 1,000 years after it spread from the Yangtze valley to southern China, and as with Japan the traditional model has been that it was introduced to the new region by migrating Neolithic rice farmers and thence via Taiwan to island Southeast Asia and the wider Pacific region beyond. The fact that many present-day people speak languages belonging to the Austronesian language family has stimulated studies of the possible origin in space and time of these languages, and the dominant model for two or more decades, proposed in the greatest detail especially by Peter Bellwood,[11] has been that Neolithic farmers speaking a proto-Austronesian language spread across the Pacific, taking with them domestic rice and pigs, in the period c. 3000–1500 BCE. As with Jomon 'foraging' in Japan, there is mounting evidence that through the Holocene (and in the late Pleistocene too, on the evidence of sites like Niah Great Cave in Sarawak, Borneo, and Kosipe in the highlands of New Guinea) the indigenous popula-tion of the region was engaged in a variety of 'arboricultural' and 'vegecul-tural' practices, the latter especially with roots and tubers such as taro and sago, sago palms, bananas, and bamboo. (This new knowledge has come especially from the breakthrough in archaeobotanical methodologies that has enabled the recovery of microscopic starch residues, a particular study of Huw Barton, as well as just the macroscopic remains of seeded plants that have traditionally dominated the subdiscipline.) The extraordinary waterlogged site of Kuk in the highlands of New Guinea, as discussed by Tim Denham (Chapter 17), the subject of intensive archaeological fieldwork since Jack Golson began work there in the 1970s, provides a remarkable illustration of the growing evidence in this region for local domestications (such as banana, breadfruit, sugarcane, sago, and associated cultivation technologies) within indigenous systems of arboriculture and vegeculture.

Scholars remain divided about whether a migration of Austronesian farmers best explains the first appearance of domestic rice in island Southeast Asia, or whether it spread by exchange systems which linked

---

11 Peter Bellwood, *First Farmers: The Origins of Agricultural Societies* (Oxford: Blackwell, 2004).

the maritime-oriented communities of the mainland Southeast Asia littoral and island Southeast Asia from the beginning of the Holocene (when an area the size of western Europe was flooded by sea-level rise). What does seem clear from the artefactual and botanical evidence, and from isotope studies of diet change in human skeletal remains, is that, as in China and Japan, there was no sudden switch from foraging (or 'foraging plus' as we might term its integration with arboriculture and vegeculture) to rice farming in either mainland or island Southeast Asia. There appears to have been a long period of active resistance to the new foodstuff, a point to which we return in our Conclusion. The DNA of modern pigs and ancient DNA from pig bones also indicate that domestic pigs did not spread across island Southeast Asia along with rice, but later, and there are indications of some island species of pig being domesticated separately from the main populations of Eurasian pigs. As Huw Barton describes, one recent idea put forward to explain the spread across the region of Neolithic material culture unaccompanied (in most cases) by the domesticates is that there must have been some kind of change in social organization (a rise of elites for example) and belief systems at this time, though what these constituted and why they happened at this time are not clear. As Huw Barton concludes, however, 'Rather than trying to make people fit into entangled concepts like pre-Neolithic pottery-using cultures or pottery-using Neolithic cultures independent of agriculture, or complex hunter-gatherers independent of rice agriculture, we should ignore the contradictions – which are of our own making – and instead explore the diversity for what it is and what it can teach us about the rich complexity of human adaptation in this remarkable part of the world' – and, we would add, what it implies for many aspects of the study of foraging–farming transitions worldwide.

It has been possible to consider the vast sub-Saharan region of Africa as a single entity only because of the paucity of research and, therefore, evidence of early agriculture. In Chapter 18, Paul Lane's discussion of domestication demonstrates the importance of rethinking regional sequences. As in parts of Southeast Asia, the timescales for the spread of domesticates and the commitment to agriculture – often not at all the same thing, as we have seen in other regions – take us from the early Holocene to well into the first millennium CE. Given the dearth of research in many regions, the research agenda has inevitably concentrated on addressing 'what?', 'when?', and 'where?' questions about transitions to farming, with 'how?' and still more 'why?' questions, such as the social and demographic mechanisms involved in the movement of people, crops, and livestock from one region to another, particularly into regions with resident populations of foragers, hardly being addressed, or able to be addressed. What does seem clear so far, and not simply a result of sampling biases, is that animal domestication and pastoralism often (unusually) preceded crop cultivation. The Nile valley's proximity to the Saharan and West Asian domesticates made northeastern Africa an important crossroads. Beginning with the earliest pastoralists (who had probably domesticated local Sahelian cattle by *c.* 6000 BCE), African populations both experimented locally and carried their innovations to new places through migration, trade, and exchange. The cultivation of millet was widespread across the Sahel by *c.* 1500 BCE but, as exemplified by Kevin MacDonald's case study of Dhar Tichitt in Mauretania (Chapter 19), theories of how millet domestication occurred in the Sahel have varied widely. Once thought to have been a locus of cereal domestication, Dhar Tichitt was argued to have demonstrated the impact of decreasing rainfall on foraging populations, who were pushed into an intensified reliance on millet. However, faunal evidence has since demonstrated dispersed hunter-gatherer populations and pastoral activities and the domestic millet grains are present from the time of the earliest inhabitants and even earlier at other sites to the south in Mali and Ghana (*c.* 2500–1900 BCE). This picture is expected to change as research in the vast region of West Africa continues.

The independent domestication of crops happened in more than one locale, such as of the cereal tef in the Ethiopian highlands and cowpea, oil palm, African rice, groundnut, and fonio in West Africa. Also, there are indications of long histories of the management of oil palm and *Canarium*, the incense tree, through the Holocene, rather like the arboriculture and vegeculture of island Southeast Asia. By 500–700 CE we can discern hunter-gatherer communities, farming communities, and pastoralists in different parts of Central Africa, and while the ethnographic record cannot be taken as a simple mirror of the past, since farming and herding systems successfully co-existed in more recent times, their co-existence and combining appear to have been a feature of the spread of domesticates southwards, with evidence that ecological niches were manipulated and modified to suit the needs of farming and herding. The domesticates were present at the Southern Cape by some 2,000 years ago. One of the major debates relating to this spread is whether farming was taken south by Bantu-speaking farmers in a relatively straightforward process of migration, or whether more complex scenarios need to be investigated, as in the case of the Austronesian languages in island Southeast Asia.

Compared with Africa, the beginnings of farming in the Americas, as Deborah Pearsall (Chapter 20) notes, have been the subject of intensive study for decades, though some regions remain far better studied than others. Understanding of the broad geographic range of origins has improved dramatically for some key crops, like the transformation of teosinte into maize, which was domesticated in southern and western Mexico, or the Amazon basin's manioc (cassava), today the staple crops for millions around the world. Plant domestication was characterized by multiple independent domestications throughout the continent. These domestications were often accompanied by the same transformations found in other parts of the world, including reduced mobility and the appearance of villages with pottery and elaborate ritual life. The case study of the Nanchoc valley in Peru by Tom Dillehay (Chapter 21) examines an area where between 7,000 and 4,000 years ago foraging and horticultural groups intensified their adoption of cultigens during a critically arid period. However, environmental change cannot have been a simple forcing agent, because social formations reveal that decision-making strategies, risk management, communal resource use, and technological innovation played key roles in facilitating the movement towards food production – an important general point regarding the role of climate change in agricultural transitions. In turn, agricultural populations expanded into new environments made possible by the successful management of alluvial fan gardening and floodplain exploitation. Thus, new patterns of demographic growth and dynamic ecologies continued to interact even when environmental crises were absent.

In parts of Mesoamerica agricultural regimes transformed landscapes through the employment of irrigation, constructed terracing, fire, modified fields, and canal building. A separate trajectory of plant domestication, of native squash, chenopod, marsh elder, and sunflower, can be discerned from about 3000 BCE in eastern North America. By the time of the European colonial encounters, the cultivation of maize had spread as far north as the Canadian prairies. The controlled use of fire was a common practice, so that, as Deborah Pearsall comments in her chapter, 'By the time of European contact anthropogenic landscapes existed throughout the Americas.'

In contrast to the relatively recent research focus on the Americas and most of Africa, more than a century of research on the development of early farming societies in Europe has produced a surprisingly dynamic view of agricultural origins and the resultant transformations in Neolithic community life and worldview, as described by Alasdair Whittle in Chapter 22, a state of research that in time we must hope will be possible to emulate in other less studied regions of the world. He argues that the time is now ripe for more 'complex, detailed, precise, and regionalized narratives' to move beyond the expectations that once read into the archaeological record a uniform, linear development towards greater complexity and social inequality. Again, the singularity of 'Europe' as a world region is brought into question. Early Neolithic farmers and agricultural origins were vastly different in central, southeastern, and western Europe, Alpine settlements, and the Mediterranean, yet also, as Whittle emphasizes, these were not disconnected worlds. The quality of the evidence in Europe is well demonstrated by Peter Bogucki and Ryszard Grygiel's case study (Chapter 23) of early Neolithic villages at Brześć Kujawski in northern Poland dating to the sixth millennium BCE. The settlements contain both common features (longhouses, rich burials, pottery, and transformed landscapes) and differences reflected in specialized activities (flint manufacture, ground stone and bone tools, decorative jewellery, and copper) and social differentiation. Poor diets, hard labour, and pervasive violence accompanied the mixed strategy of farming and herding activities. The Brześć Kujawski farmers were not isolated from their forager neighbours, but rather lived within a short distance (several days' travel) from each other. Thus, the border between farming and foraging/hunting is likely to have been porous and flexible for a very long time.

There is widespread evidence that initial crop farming was often focused on small gardens rather than extensive fields, but markedly different scenarios for the imposition or adoption of farming can be constructed to portray the dynamics of 6000 BCE and the following millennia during which agriculture diffused from other parts of Eurasia. In this confusion (a welcome feature of the quality of the data set compared with most regions of the world), the common thread discerned by Whittle is the materiality of Neolithic life, which he believes bound people together more than it set them apart. As he comments, 'the range of values held in common by Neolithic people in Europe provided checks and balances against tendencies in the direction of competition, acquisitiveness, and inequality'. Neolithic life was rich in performances and rituals, and using this kind of evidence Whittle demonstrates that Europe is the one region where we can get a sense of early farmers' sense of time, their temporalities of futures, presents, and pasts.

## A world with agriculture

Before 12,000 BCE, the world had few if any signs of agriculture, though plant manipulation may well have a long history stretching back into the late

Pleistocene. Certainly there were no agrarian communities and no pastoral societies. The dramatic increase of world population over the next ten millennia associated with the establishment of agricultural systems (of bewildering variety) provided the foundations for the spread of humans and their achievements to nearly every continent. A world with agriculture was the result of countless individual decisions and intensive experimentation by communities, who committed their energy and labours to the transmission of agricultural knowledge and practices across generations. Despite the bewildering variety of adaptations to agriculture archaeologically visible across world regions, the accumulation of evidence brings the global picture into meaningful focus. Whether mixing food-producing strategies with old traditions or embarking on completely new pathways, these early farmers changed the planet.

At the beginning of the Holocene, a great variety of familiar foods was enjoyed by successful hunter-gatherers and fishing folk in regions defined by narrow ecological niches that were well explored and successfully exploited for millennia. That changed dramatically with the advent of new subsistence strategies that maximized the potential for population growth. Whether the new menu relied on domesticated rice or quinoa, pigs or guinea pigs, diets became cultural elaborations that were ever more focused on intensively cultivated and locally bred food. Food traditions eventually developed around staple crops which, often after much resistance, emerged as the superstars of each culture's diet. Meanwhile, trade and exchange of foodstuffs also eventually contributed exotic flavours to what was found in kitchen gardens and local fields.

One area of science that is transforming the agenda is the analysis of stable isotopes or body chemistry for indicators of diet and movement/migration. There are several examples in this volume of how the technique has given us invaluable insights into dietary regimes at the scale of a community changing from, say, a marine to a terrestrial diet. Change may also have occurred within communities, producing differences based on age and/or gender, and between communities, for example the consequence of marriage partners moving between adjacent villages of foragers and farmers.

In the past archaeologists often assumed that migrating farmers must have been the primary or indeed only process by which domestic animals and plants spread from one region to another, but the growing evidence for different uses of the new resources in adjacent societies, and for extraordinary linkages across huge areas (like phytoliths of bananas, a plant almost certainly first domesticated in New Guinea, turning up in Sri Lanka and West Africa at bafflingly early dates), suggests that things were often not nearly so simple. Certainly the process of 'food globalization' implies social connectivities between neighbouring and far-flung communities that are a priority to investigate in the next phase of research.

The evidence of cases of long-lived resistance to the new foods and to the technologies of their management reminds us of the dangers of projecting our own notions of post-Enlightenment rationality onto the decision-making of prehistoric people. The study of the beginnings of farming has long been characterized by assumptions that economic drivers familiar to us would have played the dominant factor in decision-making, for example in decisions to experiment with or adopt and manage new resources. However, the fact that the diet of the world's population today depends on a very few plant staples does not mean that the same plants were valued from the outset for their capacity to feed people (indeed, to feed more people than existing food sources). Cereals like wheat, barley, sorghum, rice, and maize are all well suited for fermenting into alcoholic drinks, and given the enormous importance of beer-drinking for many ritual events, performances, initiation events, seasonal feasts, social gatherings, etc. in the ethnographic record, several scholars have suggested that this propensity might have been more valued by many hunter-gatherer societies than their suitability to make bread, porridge, or gruel (e.g. Chapter 8, p. 221).

We can well imagine the magic and mystery the new resources may have held for many societies, far removed from the humdrum packets on supermarket shelves in our own world. In fact striking evidence has emerged at some of the earliest sites where 'initial farming' was practised in Southwest Asia that the cereal seeds, the flint sickle blades that would have been used to harvest them, and the grindstones that would have been used to process them are all found in highly ritualized contexts, suggesting that their use involved complex rituals and ceremonies (Chapter 8, p. 240). Dividing the world of the first farmers into a domestic sphere of houses and fields and rational decision-making that we can understand in terms of our own economic models, on the one hand, and irrational beliefs and practices played out in burials, ceremonial monuments, and the like, on the other, is surely unwise even if we cannot begin to investigate the worldviews of early farming societies in most regions of the world with anything of the sophistication that can be applied to the interpretation of the rich European evidence. We need to remember that for many foraging societies, engaging in the cultivation of mysterious and magical new foods may have been at least as much about cultivating social relationships as about increasing calories and filling stomachs.

2

# Archaeogenetics

MARIA PALA, PEDRO SOARES, GYANESHWER CHAUBEY,
AND MARTIN B. RICHARDS

## Introduction: archaeogenetics and phylogeography

Archaeogenetics was described by Renfrew as 'the study of the human past using the techniques of molecular genetics' – involving the collaboration of geneticists with archaeologists, anthropologists, historical linguists, and climatologists. He traced its origins to the pioneering work of Cavalli-Sforza in the 1960s, using classical genetic markers (such as blood groups, etc.). Ammerman and Cavalli-Sforza developed a suite of new approaches, in particular the use of principal component maps, to evaluate the distribution of genetic variation in space. Their results on Europe, in particular, were taken to imply large-scale demic diffusion of farming communities from the Near East with the advent of the Neolithic. The discipline was then renewed in the 1980s by Wilson's work on mitochondrial DNA (mtDNA), as DNA sequencing started to become routine, making it possible for the first time to build genealogical trees of lineages within a species.[1]

The emphasis on developing novel methodologies was extended and deepened as the subject expanded. This is the key to the ongoing controversies in the field, since the analytical approaches are rarely accepted by all practitioners, who hail from widely varied backgrounds. As archaeogenetics went molecular, Wilson and his colleagues developed the *phylogeographic*

---

[1] C. Renfrew, 'Archaeogenetics: towards a population prehistory of Europe', in C. Renfrew and K. Boyle (eds.), *Archaeogenetics* (Cambridge: McDonald Institute for Archaeological Research, 2000), 3–11; A.J. Ammerman and L.L. Cavalli-Sforza, *The Neolithic Transition and the Genetics of Populations in Europe* (Princeton University Press, 1984); L.L. Cavalli-Sforza et al., *The History and Geography of Human Genes* (Princeton University Press, 1994); L.L. Cavalli-Sforza, 'The spread of agriculture and nomadic pastoralism', in D.R. Harris (ed.), *The Origins and Spread of Agriculture and Pastoralism in Eurasia* (London: UCL Press, 1996), 51–69; A.C. Wilson et al., 'Mitochondrial DNA and two perspectives on evolutionary genetics', *Biological Journal of the Linnaean Society*, 26 (1985), 375–400.

approach to molecular marker systems, already emerging in zoology and molecular ecology, applying it to mtDNA variation within the human population. Phylogeography added a genealogical – and therefore also a chronological – dimension to the spatial distribution of genetic markers. Archaeogenetics was again developing its own approaches to data handling, hybridizing techniques borrowed from a variety of disparate disciplines. Voices were raised against this approach, advocating that the new subject should rather be using standard population-genetics methods, which had been developed with quite different questions in mind. This dispute within archaeogenetics has persisted, through various transmutations, to the present day, becoming enmeshed in a rather one-dimensional debate about the scale of Neolithic Near Eastern immigration into Europe which still dominates the subject.[2]

## Phylogeography: the basics

The mtDNA and the male-specific part of the Y chromosome (or MSY) are the two uniparental, non-recombining genetic marker systems, which led the way for genealogical and phylogeographic studies. For both, the genetic material is transmitted down the generations in a single block, along the maternal line of descent for the mtDNA and the paternal for the MSY. As they are passed down, mutations accumulate, highlighting the distinct branches within the genealogy as they appear and leading to the formation of related clusters that we call haplogroups, each of which can trace its descent back to a single common ancestor.

In the early days of the molecular revolution, Avise and colleagues argued that mtDNA was 'not just another molecular marker' because of the exceptional opportunities it afforded for estimating intra-specific gene trees – in themselves an estimate of the genealogy (or 'coalescent tree') of the locus (or stretch of DNA) under study – and detecting geographic patterns in the

2 L.L. Cavalli-Sforza and E. Minch, 'Paleolithic and Neolithic lineages in the European mitochondrial gene pool', *American Journal of Human Genetics*, 61 (1997), 247–51; M. Richards et al., 'Paleolithic and Neolithic lineages in the European mitochondrial gene pool – reply', *American Journal of Human Genetics*, 61 (1997), 251–4; H.-J. Bandelt et al., 'What molecules can't tell us about the spread of languages and the Neolithic', in C. Renfrew and P. Bellwood (eds.), *Examining the Farming/Language Dispersal Hypothesis* (Cambridge: McDonald Institute for Archaeological Research, 2002); M.B. Richards et al., 'Analyzing genetic data in a model-based framework: inferences about European prehistory', in Renfrew and Bellwood (eds.), *Examining the Farming/Language Dispersal Hypothesis*, 459–66; R. Pinhasi et al., 'The genetic history of Europeans', *Trends in Genetics*, 28 (2012), 496–505.

distribution and ages of clusters within the trees.[3] The same soon became true for the MSY as well. Although some population geneticists might disagree, in the age of complete human mtDNA genomes ('mitogenomes') we would argue that this remains true to a surprising extent. Avise was writing in the days of short mtDNA control-region sequences (a few hundred base-pairs from the non-coding part of the mtDNA genome) or slightly higher-resolution restriction maps of the whole-mtDNA genome. Control-region sequences now number more than 150,000, but since about the year 2000 whole-mtDNA genomes have also begun to accumulate, and those publicly available already exceed 15,000.[4] Although many more will be needed in order to address all the issues that archaeogeneticists have been trying to get their teeth into since the 1980s, these are already providing an exquisite degree of resolution of the maternal genealogy. An even greater level of genealogical resolution is starting to appear for the male line of descent,[5] since every new complete human genome includes a complete MSY sequence, ready-made.

As far as the rest of the human genome goes, analytical techniques have barely kept pace so far with the astonishing progress made by sequencing technology, probably because the latter has been driven by medical science and archaeogenetics remains something of a minority (and low-budget) pursuit. The autosomes – the genes in the rest of the genome – are recombined and reshuffled with each other at every generation, and are therefore much more difficult to analyse genealogically than mtDNA and the MSY. Thus although the new level of detail is providing fascinating new portraits of human populations around the world, the flood of new data is often more difficult to interpret in terms of the questions that archaeologists might be interested in, although progress is rapidly being made.

As well as detailed phylogenetic reconstruction and an evolutionary history that broadly seems to reflect that of human populations as a whole, mtDNA retains the edge over other genetic systems in one other way: genetic dating. The so-called 'molecular clock' has been around since the 1960s, and aroused intense controversy from the start. Different parts of the

---

3 J. Avise et al., 'Intraspecific phylogeography: the molecular bridge between population genetics and systematics', *Annual Review of Ecological Systems*, 18 (1987), 489–522.

4 M. van Oven and M. Kayser, 'Updated comprehensive phylogenetic tree of global human mitochondrial DNA variation', *Human Mutation*, 30 (2009), E386–94.

5 W. Wei et al., 'A calibrated human Y-chromosomal phylogeny based on resequencing', *Genome Research*, 23 (2012), 388–95; P. Francalacci et al., 'Low-pass DNA sequencing of 1200 Sardinians reconstructs European Y chromosome phylogeny', *Science*, 341 (2013), 565–9.

genome patently evolve at vastly different rates, rates change along lineages over time, and they are affected by numerous processes that are not particularly well understood, such as selection. Dating any particular region of the genome thus brings numerous challenges. Microsatellites (short repetitive regions in which the number of short tandem repeats varies up and down) have often been targeted, but the mechanisms by which they evolve are poorly understood and there is enormous variation from one to the next. On the other hand, stretches of unique autosomal sequence may have relatively little variation within sequence blocks that have not undergone recombination, since the autosomal mutation rate is very low. For the mtDNA, however, there is a wealth of variation within the non-recombining 16.5 kb (kilo-base) unit, and the effects of selection have been investigated and can be corrected for when estimating time depths, despite some claims to the contrary.[6]

Moreover, the mtDNA has to some extent broken free of its human–chimp split fossil calibration point, by incorporating known ages for island colonizations into the calibration. Although it is more difficult to find suitable archaeological calibration points than is generally appreciated, some do exist that can be used to help refine and corroborate rates calibrated on the human–chimp split (assumed to be around seven million years ago, on the basis of the estimated age of *Sahelanthropus*).[7] Again the high variation in mtDNA helps with this, because better-known relatively recent events, such as the settlement of the Remote Pacific, can be used.[8] Although we still await a full measure of agreement on the mtDNA clock, the consensus is increasingly broad.

Phylogeography utilizes three variables: the reconstructed phylogenetic tree of descent, or genealogy, the geographic distribution of the lineages, and the time depth of various clusters. It is based on the very simple notion that every new variant in a DNA sequence arises by mutation at a particular point in space and time, which can in principle (if not always in practice) be pinned down by examining the distribution of both the lineages descending

---

6  T. Kivisild et al., 'The role of selection in the evolution of human mitochondrial genomes', *Genetics*, 172 (2006), 373–87; P. Soares et al., 'Correcting for purifying selection: an improved human mitochondrial molecular clock', *American Journal of Human Genetics*, 84 (2009), 740–59; F. Balloux, 'The worm in the fruit of the mitochondrial DNA tree', *Heredity*, 104 (2010), 419–20.

7  P. Mellars et al., 'Genetic and archaeological perspectives on the initial modern human colonization of southern Asia', *Proceedings of the National Academy of Sciences*, 110 (2013), 10699–704.

8  P. Soares et al., 'Ancient voyaging and Polynesian origins', *American Journal of Human Genetics*, 88 (2011), 239–47.

from the newly derived sequence and those preceding it in the tree. For example, mutations defining a new genealogical branch of the mtDNA (which we call haplogroup L3) arose around 70,000 years ago in East Africa,[9] and subsequently gave rise to various descendant lineages, two of which are primarily found in non-Africans, throughout the rest of the world. This suggests a dispersal out of Africa which can be dated to around 50,000–60,000 years ago by measuring the mutational variation accumulated on top of each of the founders in each part of the world. This approach forms the basis for 'founder analysis'.[10]

Founder analysis is an attempt to formalize a phylogeographic approach to identifying colonization events, but it exemplifies the approach more broadly. It is not designed for the standard population-genetics scenario of a single large population splitting into two daughters, but for more realistic situations where a minority founder group breaks away from the main (source) population to found a new one (the sink). This is likely to have been the driving process in the dispersal of modern humans around the world, although this assumption needs to be explored in each case. Founder analysis assumes that we can distinguish samples from a source region and a sink region (often on non-genetic grounds), and it then subtracts source from sink diversity as a proxy for arrival times in the sink.

Phylogeographic approaches receive more than their fair share of criticism within population genetics. However, critics often forget that the methodologies have been validated in relatively simple situations where the demographic history is quite well understood, such as Polynesia and southern Africa, and that many scenarios proposed on the basis of mtDNA evidence have subsequently been confirmed by genome-wide analyses – the most obvious being the origins and dispersal of modern humans. A simplistic view of how the analyses are carried out has led to the suggestion that phylogeographic interpretations are essentially 'story-telling' – in contrast to 'more robust' approaches such as 'interpretation of population statistics' or 'explicit modelling of population history'. But while procedures that better estimate the uncertainty of phylogeographic conclusions may be on the way, they have not yet arrived in a form useful for the kinds of question we are interested in here. In fact, as the authors of one major statistical

9 P. Soares et al., 'The expansion of mtDNA haplogroup L3 within and out of Africa', *Molecular Biology and Evolution*, 29 (2012), 915–27.
10 V. Macaulay and M. Richards, 'Mitochondrial genome sequences and phylogeographic interpretation', in *Encyclopedia of Life Sciences*, www.els.net (Chichester: Wiley), doi:10.1002/9780470015902.20843.pub2 (2013).

critique of phylogeographic analyses point out, 'phylogeographic analyses have been a tremendously powerful tool in the analysis of population genetic data' – perhaps, they suggest, because key assumptions (essentially the operation of the founder effect) may in practice have been largely correct.[11]

In any case, exploratory analysis (and even 'story-telling') and hypothesis testing should not be seen as hard-and-fast opposites, and phylogeography has been used to test hypotheses and draw inferences in a number of ways. We advocate an interdisciplinary (and even trans-disciplinary) approach in which hypotheses are evaluated within the framework of models supplied by archaeology, palaeoanthropology, and palaeoclimatology. The improvement in techniques for recovering DNA from archaeological remains can only enhance this approach. Unfortunately, this has so far only been achieved in Europe, on which we therefore focus in order to bring out the underlying methodological issues. We then discuss more briefly a few of the better studied situations in other parts of the world.

## Archaeogenetics of contemporary Europeans

The question of the Neolithic transition in Europe has, alongside that of the origin of modern humans, virtually defined the history of archaeogenetics, from the work of Cavalli-Sforza and his colleagues onwards. They dissected the genetic-geographic patterns with principal components analysis, interpreting the major southeast to northwest gradient of markers in Europe – along the axis of the known gradient of Neolithic radiocarbon dates – as the result of a large-scale demic expansion of Near Eastern populations into Europe with the onset of the Neolithic (Figure 2.1). This led them to strongly emphasize the expanding early farmers at the expense of the indigenous Mesolithic foraging populations, defining the debate in a way that has endured, despite huge and ongoing controversy, ever since.

This fairly simplistic view of the transition was of course challenged by archaeologists, especially those studying the evidence for pre-Neolithic European foragers.[12] However, the first genetic critique came with the advent of DNA studies, and in particular from analyses of mtDNA in the mid-1990s – at that time, focused on just a short segment of the control region. Richards and colleagues estimated that only 10–15 per cent of extant

---

11 R. Nielsen and M.A. Beaumont, 'Statistical inferences in phylogeography', *Molecular Ecology*, 18 (2009), 1034–47.

12 G. Barker, *The Agricultural Revolution in Prehistory: Why did Foragers Become Farmers?* (Oxford University Press, 2006).

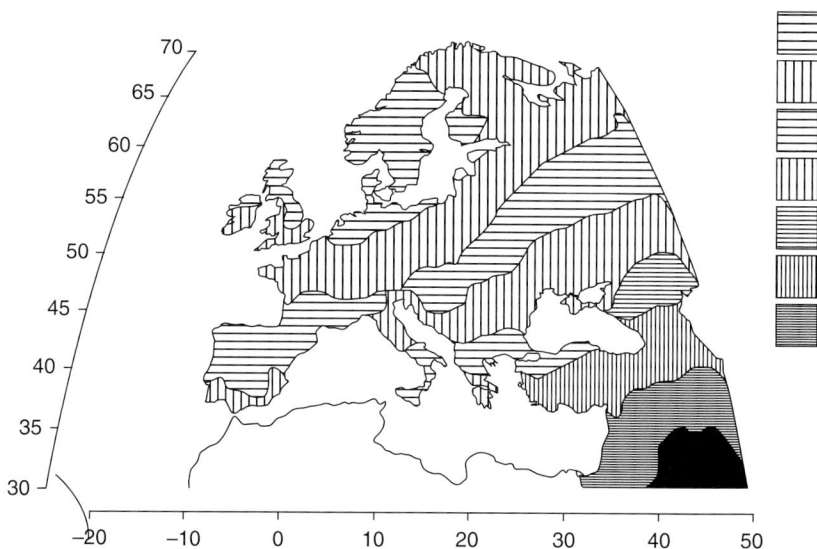

Figure 2.1 Synthetic map of the first principal component of variation in ninety-five classical genetic markers.

mtDNAs had dispersed from the Near East to Europe at the time of the Neolithic, after around 10,000 years ago.[13] Most of the European mtDNAs appeared to have already been established in Europe by this time, among the Mesolithic and preceding Palaeolithic foraging groups scattered across the continent.

This work was bolstered by further studies, involving many more samples, a slightly higher resolution, and a formal founder analysis for which software had been specially developed in the meantime.[14] This resulted in a range for the estimates of extant European mtDNA lineages dating to the Neolithic of 10–22 per cent (Figure 2.2). Meanwhile, Torroni and colleagues had zeroed in on one particular cluster, haplogroup V, tracing its spread from a glacial refuge area in southwestern Europe in the late Glacial period, at the end of the last Ice Age, around 14,000 years ago.[15] Subsequent work focused on several

13  M. Richards et al., 'Paleolithic and Neolithic lineages in the European mitochondrial gene pool', *American Journal of Human Genetics*, 59 (1996), 185–203.
14  M. Richards et al., 'Tracing European founder lineages in the Near Eastern mtDNA pool', *American Journal of Human Genetics*, 67 (2000), 1251–76.
15  A. Torroni et al., 'mtDNA analysis reveals a major late Paleolithic population expansion from southwestern to northeastern Europe', *American Journal of Human Genetics*, 62 (1998), 1137–52; A. Torroni et al., 'A signal, from human mtDNA, of post-Glacial recolonization in Europe', *American Journal of Human Genetics*, 69 (2001), 844–52.

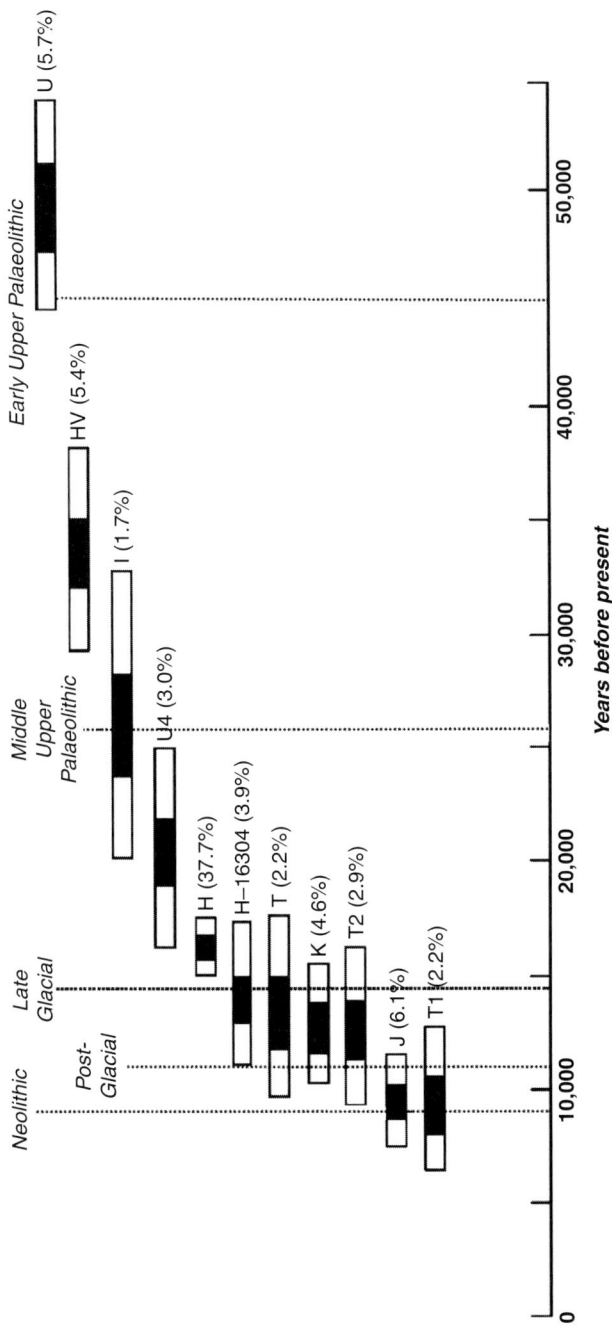

Figure 2.2 Plot of the age ranges of the major mitochondrial DNA founder clusters in Europe, inferred from a founder analysis of control-region sequences and accounting for three quarters of the variation in Europeans. Founder clusters are sets of sequences in the sink population with a common ancestor in a DNA sequence type ('founder type') that has been identified as having migrated from a source (the Near East) into a settled region or sink (Europe), so that the estimate of their coalescence time can serve as a proxy for the timing of the migration. 95 per cent credible regions on the age estimates are shown by white bars and 50 per cent regions by black bars. The founders were identified by a criterion that scaled the amount of variation present in the Near East to the frequency in Europe; under this criterion, the total fraction of lineages arriving with the Neolithic was estimated at approximately 13 per cent, but subsequent work with better-resolving whole-mtDNA sequences suggests that this is likely to have been an over-estimate (see text).

of the clusters within the much more common haplogroups H and U5, suggesting a similar late Glacial ancestry within Europe.[16] Recent simulation studies support this view, suggesting that late Glacial expansions might in fact generate the kind of southeast–northwest gradient patterns seen in the classical markers, and that Neolithic immigration is therefore likely to have been minor, turning the classical picture on its head.[17]

Although often cited as supporting a basically 'indigenist' conclusion, the mtDNA researchers interpreted their results in terms of a pioneer colonization model, with significant Neolithic immigration and leapfrog dispersals across Europe, with a source in the Near East, but ultimately involving widespread assimilation of indigenous forager populations into the resulting gene pool, along similar lines to those proposed on archaeological grounds by Zvelebil and Rowley-Conwy.[18]

The main criticism levelled at the time against the mtDNA work was famously summarized by Barbujani and colleagues as follows: 'suppose that some Europeans colonize Mars next year: If they successfully establish a population, the common mitochondrial ancestor of their descendants will be Palaeolithic. But it would not be wise for a population geneticist of the future to infer from that a Palaeolithic colonization of Mars.' However, founder analysis estimates only the divergence from the founders within the sink region, so this criticism misses its target – provided that the founders can be correctly identified, which is certainly not a trivial issue. Disappointingly, this misunderstanding persists to the present day.[19] Moreover, strictly speaking, the arrival time for any lineage can be at any time on the branch leading

16  A. Achilli et al., 'The molecular dissection of mtDNA haplogroup H confirms that the Franco-Cantabrian glacial refuge was a major source for the European gene pool', *American Journal of Human Genetics*, 75 (2004), 910–18; L. Pereira et al., 'High-resolution mtDNA evidence for the late-Glacial resettlement of Europe from an Iberian refugium', *Genome Research*, 15 (2005), 19–24; K. Tambets et al., 'The western and eastern roots of the Saami – the story of genetic "outliers" told by mitochondrial DNA and Y chromosomes', *American Journal of Human Genetics*, 74 (2004), 661–82; B. Malyarchuk et al., 'The peopling of Europe from the mitochondrial haplogroup U5 perspective', *PLoS ONE*, 21 (2010), e10285.

17  M. Arenas et al., 'Influence of admixture and paleolithic range contractions on current European diversity gradients', *Molecular Biology and Evolution*, 30 (2013), 57–61.

18  M. Richards, 'The Neolithic invasion of Europe', *Annual Review of Anthropology*, 62 (2003), 135–62; M. Zvelebil, 'The social context of the agricultural transition in Europe', in Renfrew and Boyle (eds.), *Archaeogenetics*, 57–79; P. Rowley-Conwy, 'Westward ho! The spread of agriculture from central Europe to the Atlantic', *Current Anthropology*, 52, Supplement 4 (2011), S431–51.

19  G. Barbujani et al., 'Evidence for Paleolithic and Neolithic gene flow in Europe', *American Journal of Human Genetics*, 62 (1998), 488–91; G. Barbujani, 'Human genetics: message from the Mesolithic', *Current Biology*, 22 (2012), R631–3.

to the founder type – and can therefore be substantially older than the divergence time estimated from age of the founder type itself. Thus, ironically (and contrary to the expectations of the critics), some of the founders attributed to Neolithic expansions in this early work might actually have arrived in Europe significantly earlier – as indeed now looks to be the case. Hence this early work seems to have *over*-estimated the Neolithic contribution from the Near East.

In fact, the conclusions from the mtDNA work have been modified in various ways with the advent of whole mitogenome studies. One of the most significant has been the result of freshly calibrating the mtDNA clock. A number of researchers had argued for the time-dependency of the mtDNA rate, but the case was made most cogently by Kivisild and colleagues, who showed that the apparent rate of mtDNA coding sequence evolution slows down as one moves back through the tree, due to the removal of weakly deleterious mutations by purifying selection. This meant that the timing of the more recent coalescent events had tended to be over-estimated. Thus when Soares and colleagues estimated the first whole mitogenome clock rate, they included a correction factor to allow for this effect. Although not affecting conclusions to the extent predicted by some, this new calibration had the curious effect of moving some putative late Glacial mtDNA lineages, previously dating to 13–15 ka (thousands of years ago), into the immediate post-Glacial, or Mesolithic, *c.* 11 ka. Nevertheless, it does not increase the estimated Neolithic contribution. In fact, as a result of the refined genealogical resolution possible for whole-mtDNA lineages, it seems that many of the putative Neolithic lineages (from haplogroups J and T) most probably arrived in Europe from a glacial refuge in the Near East during the late Glacial, reducing the estimated impact of Near Eastern Neolithic lineages on the European mtDNA pool still further, but with major expansions (and most likely dispersals) within Europe during the course of the Neolithic.[20]

Studies of extant Y chromosome (MSY) lineages have proved even more controversial. At around the time of the publication of the mtDNA founder analysis, a major study of MSY variation by Semino and colleagues (including Cavalli-Sforza himself) came to broadly similar conclusions. They estimated a roughly 22 per cent component dating back to Neolithic immigration from the Near East, essentially summing the lineages belonging to MSY haplogroups which are frequent in the Near East. This formula

20 M. Pala et al., 'Mitochondrial DNA signals of late Glacial re-colonization of Europe from Near Eastern refugia', *American Journal of Human Genetics*, 90 (2012), 915–24.

could conflate Neolithic immigration with both more recent and somewhat earlier dispersals of these lineages from the Near East into Europe,
but King and Underhill subsequently correlated high frequencies of these
lineages in Europe with early Neolithic archaeological traditions along
the Mediterranean coast.[21]

Both approaches, however, rapidly came under fire from population
geneticists wielding admixture models.[22] They argued that the MSY results,
in particular, indicated a much higher level of Neolithic Near Eastern ancestry
in Europe – more than 50 per cent, and nearing 100 per cent in the southeast.
The problem here though was the suitability of the admixture approach.
Admixture is designed to measure the contribution of each source population
to a third, hybrid, population formed when the first two mix together, by
comparing the sink variation with that in each source. However, in the case
of Europe in the Neolithic, the model should be somewhat different: part of
one source population (in the Near East) breaks away, and combines with
another (in Europe). As a result, we do not have three distinct populations
to compare: we have to assume that certain populations in Europe (such
as Basques, Sardinians, or Saami) can represent what the variation in the
continent was like before the Neolithic. We also have to assume that there
has been no migration back from Europe into the Near East.

But neither assumption is tenable: we have no pristine representative of
Mesolithic Europe available, and in any case Europe was probably highly
structured in the Mesolithic, so that even if the Basques were a relict of the
southwest they could hardly be used as a proxy for the northeast or southeast, for example. Moreover, mtDNA studies strongly imply that there
has been a huge level of migration from Europe into the Near East over
the last ten thousand years, which would greatly exaggerate the Near Eastern
fraction in an admixture estimate.[23] Finally, admixture studies suffer from the

21 O. Semino et al., 'The genetic legacy of Paleolithic *Homo sapiens sapiens* in extant
   Europeans: a Y chromosome perspective', *Science*, 290 (2000), 1155–9; R. King and
   P. Underhill, 'Congruent distribution of Neolithic painted pottery and ceramic figurines
   with Y-chromosome lineages', *Antiquity*, 76 (2002), 707–14.
22 G. Barbujani and I. Dupanloup, 'DNA variation in Europe: estimating the demographic
   impact of Neolithic dispersals', and L. Chikhi, 'Admixture and the demic diffusion
   model in Europe', both in Renfrew and Bellwood (eds.), *Examining the Farming/
   Language Dispersal Hypothesis*, 421–33, 435–47; L. Chikhi et al., 'Y genetic data support
   the Neolithic demic diffusion model', *Proceedings of the National Academy of Sciences*, 99
   (2002), 11008–13.
23 E.W. Hill et al., 'Y-chromosome variation and Irish origins', *Nature*, 404 (2000), 351–2;
   J.F. Wilson et al., 'Genetic evidence for different male and female roles during cultural
   transitions in the British Isles', *Proceedings of the National Academy of Sciences*, 98 (2001),
   5078–83; S. Rootsi et al., 'Phylogeography of Y-chromosome haplogroup I reveals

weaknesses of the original PC analyses – they do not distinguish different events or tell us *when* the admixture occurred. This is why phylogeographers believe that some kind of founder analysis, however difficult, is a much more appropriate way to estimate the scale of the Near Eastern Neolithic impact. For example, recent work with mtDNA has suggested that at least some of the expansion into Europe from the Near East attributed by Cavalli-Sforza and his colleagues to the Neolithic may in fact have taken place in the late Glacial.

But Y-chromosome phylogeography has not provided definitive answers either. The early picture was of western Europe being peopled after the Ice Age from a southwest refuge area, similar to the model of late Glacial/post-Glacial expansions implied by the mtDNA. However, Balaresque et al. suggested that the microsatellite diversity among these lineages was highest in Anatolia and low in northern and western Europe, and suggested an expansion from east to west in the timeframe of the Neolithic. Although Morelli et al. argued for a much deeper European ancestry and a more recent 'back-migration' into Anatolia, Myres et al. proposed a central European Neolithic LBK (*Linienbandkeramik*) expansion for this lineage. In the end, Busby et al. suggested that the upshot of the debate was that, at present, MSY mutation rates are too poorly understood to resolve the question. However, this should soon change as whole-MSY sequences of sufficient quality for rate calibration purposes and genetic dating become available in sufficient numbers.

The genomic era has, of course, also seen a return in force of autosomal systems, as testing hundreds of thousands of genome-wide SNPs (single-nucleotide polymorphisms) has become routine, and complete genomes start to appear in greater numbers. The first applications of genome-wide scans to European population structure provided the striking image of the plot of the first two PCs mapping almost perfectly onto the geography of Europe.[24] Since these components amount to less than 0.5 per cent of the total variance in the data, however, how this astonishing pattern is to be

distinct domains of prehistoric gene flow in Europe', *American Journal of Human Genetics*, 75 (2004), 128–37; P. Balaresque et al., 'A predominantly Neolithic origin for European paternal lineages', *PLoS ONE*, 8 (2010), e1000285; L. Morelli et al., 'A comparison of Y-chromosome variation in Sardinia and Anatolia is more consistent with cultural rather than demic diffusion of agriculture', *PLoS ONE*, 5 (2009), e10419; N.M. Myres et al., 'A major Y-chromosome haplogroup R1b Holocene era founder effect in central and western Europe', *European Journal of Human Genetics*, 19 (2011), 95–101; G.B. Busby et al., 'The peopling of Europe and the cautionary tale of Y chromosome lineage R-M269', *Proceedings of the Royal Society B*, 279 (2011), 884–92.

24 J. Novembre et al., 'Genes mirror geography within Europe', *Nature*, 456 (2008), 98–101.

interpreted is anyone's guess. More interesting for the question of deep European ancestry has been the development of various 'STRUCTURE-like' algorithms for gathering such data into genetically defined clusters, putatively representing ancestral populations.[25] The clusters are identified by the software, although the number of clusters ($K$) is defined by the user.

Several large published data sets include both Near Eastern and European data.[26] The results broadly indicate (e.g. from $K = 5$ through 10 for a worldwide sample) that European and Near Eastern samples fall into three main genetic clusters (Figure 2.3). The major one present in Europe (shown in black in Figure 2.3) exceeds 75 per cent in northern, western, and eastern Europe (including Basques and Saami), is a minority in the Near East – almost absent from Arabia and about 10 per cent for populations in the vicinity of the Fertile Crescent – but is found at about 25 per cent in northwest (but not northeast) Africans. We can hazard a guess that this cluster has a long-standing ancestry in Europe, given that we know of substantial gene flow from Europe into the Fertile Crescent from the mtDNA evidence. A second cluster (shown in grey) is found in a minority in western (especially Mediterranean) European populations, including Basques and Sardinians (both often thought to have predominantly indigenous ancestry), and is also common across the Near East (focused on the south, including Arabia) and North Africa, but much less so in eastern Europe. The third cluster (shown in white), which is found as a minority across both western and eastern Europeans, is similarly common across the Near East, but more focused on the north, especially the Caucasus and to some extent also the Fertile Crescent, but much less so in Arabia and North Africa, and stretches into Central and South Asia. We can guess that both of these clusters may be indigenous to the Near East, but with southern and western (Mediterranean) and northern and eastern orientations, respectively.

If this interpretation is not too bold, then it suggests that Near Eastern introgression into Europe has varied from less than 10 per cent in the northwest and northeast to around 40 per cent in Italy and the southeast.

25 N.A. Rosenberg et al., 'Genetic structure of human populations', *Science*, 298 (2002), 2381–5.
26 D.M. Behar et al., 'The genome-wide structure of the Jewish people', *Nature*, 466 (2010), 238–42; C. Chaubey et al., 'Population genetic structure in Indian Austroasiatic speakers: the role of landscape barriers and sex-specific admixture', *Molecular Biology and Evolution*, 28 (2010), 1013–24; J.R. Huyghe et al., 'A genome-wide analysis of population structure in the Finnish Saami with implications for genetic association studies', *European Journal of Human Genetics*, 19 (2011), 347–52; M. Pala et al., 'The archaeogenetics of European ancestry', in *Encyclopedia of Life Sciences*, doi:10.1002/9780470015902.a0024624 (2014).

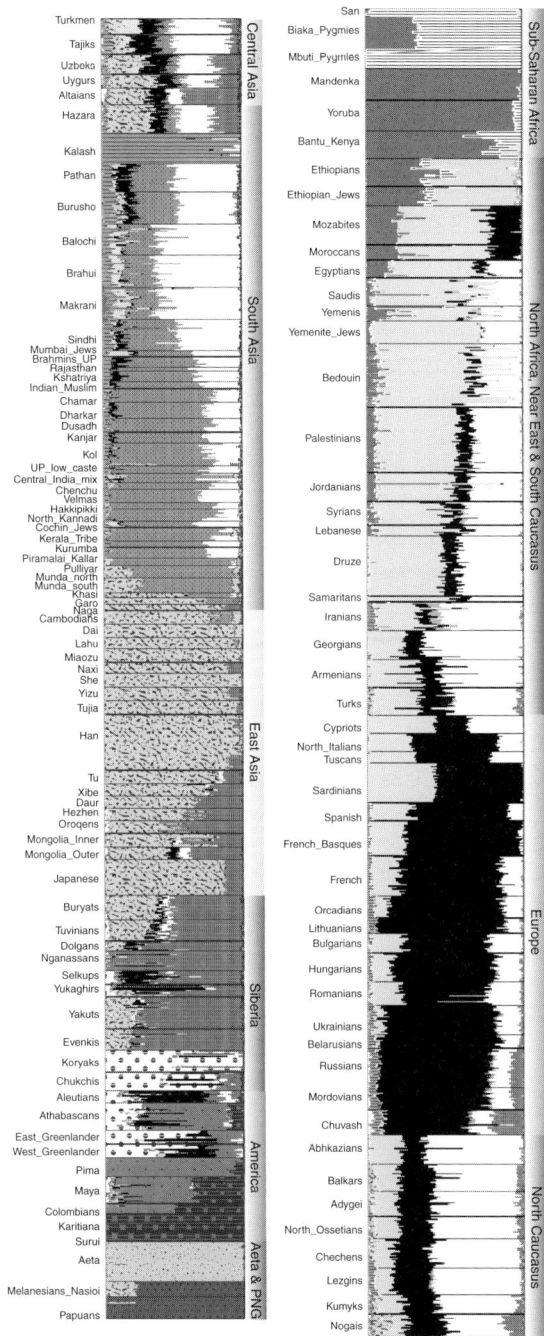

Figure 2.3 Genome-wide SNP ADMIXTURE analysis of global populations. ADMIXTURE is a 'STRUCTURE-like' model-based clustering algorithm that essentially identifies

This would provide a maximum value for genome-wide Neolithic introgression; so the modern autosomal analyses seem to support a very substantial indigenous pre-Neolithic component in the ancestry of most Europeans. Given the mtDNA evidence for late Glacial expansions from the Near East into Mediterranean Europe preceding the Neolithic, however, it is tempting to hypothesize that the second 'Mediterranean' cluster might represent this process, and the third the spread of the Neolithic. If this were correct, the Neolithic Near Eastern contribution to the European autosomal pool would be between virtually zero (in, say, Basques and Sardinians as well as Saami) and about 25 per cent in southeastern Europe and mainland Italy.

It is important to realize, though, that what can be inferred from the modern genetic patterns does not always address the most interesting archaeological questions. In the end, unfortunately, different lines of evidence tell us different things. Even if we assume that about 20 per cent of the modern maternal lineages really do descend from Neolithic newcomers, what does that actually imply in terms of what was going on at the time? Unless it was a simple admixture event, then a 20:80 figure cannot be demographically very meaningful. For example, the people actually crossing into Europe might have numbered only 1 per cent (say) of the population of Europe at that time, but expanded to 20 per cent before (or even after) interacting with the locals. We can explore the alternatives via simulation, to some extent, but choosing between them is another matter. This is where ancient DNA can come into its own.

## Ancient DNA in Europe

Ancient DNA (aDNA) is the final piece of the phylogeographic jigsaw, and has seen a parallel revolution to that in genomics over the past decade – also driven primarily by improvements in technology. The analysis of aDNA has the potential not only to test models built on the basis of modern variation

---

Caption for Figure 2.3 (cont.)

subgroups of genotypes within a sample set with distinctive allele frequencies. Each individual is represented by a narrow vertical column, separated into coloured segments representing the individual's estimated membership fractions for each of $K = 14$ clusters. Black lines separate individuals belonging to different populations. Populations are labelled below the figure, with their broader affiliations above it. We conducted the analysis with a random seed number generator on the linkage-disequilibrium (LD) pruned data set (to remove non-independently segregating alleles) at $K = 2$ to 16. $K = 14$, which had the lowest CV score, is the one shown. All data are from Illumina 610K and 650K chips with 544,193 SNPs; after LD pruning the total number of SNPs was 234,699.

and archaeology, but also to expand upon the details, as alluded to above. Moreover, it opens up questions less accessible to studies of modern variation, such as small-scale movements in later prehistory, and most excitingly of all it can reveal processes that have been erased by time, such as population extinctions.

This new phase of archaeogenetics has once again brought new voices to the debate. If the late 1990s and early 2000s were dominated by discussion of the mtDNA and Y-chromosome results from contemporary populations, and emphasized continuity between Neolithic and Mesolithic populations in Europe, in the years from 2005 onwards ancient DNA took the leading role, and the talk was now of discontinuity.

The game-changer was the work of Haak and colleagues on mtDNA control-region sequences from LBK burials in central Europe.[27] Although 2005 was also the year in which 'next-generation' DNA sequencing technologies were launched, the work of Haak et al. was rather on the careful application and modification of ancient DNA techniques developed over the preceding fifteen years. What was revolutionary about this work was the outcome: that a large fraction of the LBK mtDNA lineages belonged to a cluster, haplogroup N1a, which was vanishingly infrequent in the modern population. This was clearly not the result of a single rare modern contaminant – the N1a lineages represented were quite diverse. At a stroke this both answered doubts about contemporary contamination that had plagued previous ancient human DNA studies and pointed to something completely new.

Although the initial interpretation invoked not discontinuity with the Mesolithic but continuity, this was revised when the researchers began to obtain sequences from Mesolithic and late Palaeolithic samples.[28] The mtDNA variation in contemporary Europeans had led to the prediction that haplogroup U, and especially U5, was likely to have been among the earliest modern human lineages in Europe, in the early upper Palaeolithic. U5b was thought to have expanded from southwestern into northeastern Europe at the end of the last Ice Age, and U4 to have expanded in the eastern European plain at about the same time.[29] The new data from Mesolithic and

27  W. Haak et al., 'Ancient DNA from the first European farmers in 7500-year-old Neolithic sites', *Science*, 310 (2005), 1016–18.
28  B. Bramanti et al., 'Genetic discontinuity between local hunter-gatherers and central Europe's first farmers', *Science*, 326 (2009), 137–40.
29  M.B. Richards et al., 'Phylogeography of mitochondrial DNA in western Europe', *Annals of Human Genetics*, 62 (1998), 241–60; B. Malyarchuk et al., 'Mitochondrial DNA

late Palaeolithic specimens was indeed heavily enriched for haplogroup U, especially U5 and U4, and particularly in eastern Europe, where sixteen samples from Poland, Lithuania, and Russia all belonged to U4 or U5. Mesolithic specimens from Germany also showed a high level of haplogroup U, but with haplogroups J, T, and K also present (although restricted to a single late site regarded as a Mesolithic enclave). Since the lineages in Neolithic central Europe were more diverse, this pattern suggested a sharp Mesolithic–Neolithic discontinuity, with replacement of foraging populations by new populations.

Once again, the striking differences between the Mesolithic samples and modern populations lent credibility to the results. Although the potential for contamination remains significant, the tide seemed to have turned. Even so, despite all the precautions taken, the samples used were museum specimens, often excavated a very long time ago – a risky strategy, because the sources of potential modern human DNA are so ubiquitous that it is virtually impossible to exclude from specimens that have not been excavated in sterile conditions. The presence of identical sequence haplotypes seen in several studies, for example, indicates that we should remain cautious.

Nevertheless, the significance of the results cannot be understated. N1a mtDNAs appear to specifically mark the LBK, and have in fact only been seen in one Neolithic individual outside of central Europe, in a megalithic burial chamber in western France (implying immigration into that region from the LBK zone).[30] The source of the central European Neolithic lineages, however, remains controversial. Although Haak et al. argued for an Anatolian origin, modern N1a lineages in Anatolia are rare and match extant Central and South Asian lineages, whereas the LBK samples all fall within a European subclade, N1a1. A founder analysis of N1a has suggested it may have spread from the Near East into Europe as early as the late Glacial, matching the best estimate for the age of the European-specific subclade of *c.* 17 ka.[31]

These studies of control-region variation have been followed up in even more spectacular fashion by a study of thirty-nine prehistoric central European whole haplogroup H mitogenomes, from the early Neolithic to the Bronze

phylogeny in eastern and western Slavs', *Molecular Biology and Evolution*, 25 (2008), 1651–8.

30  M.F. Deguilloux et al., 'News from the west: ancient DNA from a French megalithic burial chamber', *American Journal of Physical Anthropology*, 144 (2011), 108–18.

31  M.G. Palanichamy et al., 'Mitochondrial haplogroup N1a phylogeography, with implication to the origin of European farmers', *BMC Evolutionary Biology*, 10 (2010), 304; V. Fernandes et al., 'The Arabian cradle: mitochondrial relics of the first steps along the southern route out of Africa', *American Journal of Human Genetics*, 90 (2012), 347–55.

Age.[32] Haplogroup H is both the most common modern European haplogroup, at >40 per cent, and also one of the most poorly resolved at the level of control-region sequences, so whole-mtDNA sequencing is particularly valuable. Again, the nature of the results renders contamination very unlikely to be a significant issue with these data.

Intriguingly, the H lineages appear to become dramatically more diverse from the middle Neolithic (*c.* 6 ka) or late Neolithic onwards, suggesting a change in the gene pool during the course of the Neolithic that might mirror the depletion of N1a. The early Neolithic samples cluster with modern Near Eastern populations and the late Neolithic samples with modern Iberians in PCA, leading the authors to again suggest immigration from the Near East with the early Neolithic and substantial changes thereafter from the southwest. However, such frequency-based analyses are precarious with so few data, and the presence in the early Neolithic of the H1 cluster, which is thought to have spread from Iberia in the Mesolithic,[33] points clearly to assimilation of Mesolithic lineages. Indeed, in the context of the modern distributions, many of the other early Neolithic lineages appear more likely to have a European than a Near Eastern source, with the low diversity perhaps the result of a dramatic expansion from few founders.

The case remains open, but leapfrog migration of Neolithic pioneers from Anatolia into southeastern Europe, with an archaeologically attested pause for an adaptation of farming technology accompanied by assimilation of indigenous populations (carrying, for example, N1a and H lineages), followed then by a rapid expansion into central Europe as the LBK, might well be the best explanation for this pattern.[34] The pioneers would have imported cattle[35] and pigs[36] from the Near East, although the domestic pig lineages (rather like human N1a lineages) were replaced during the middle Neolithic with indigenous animals, in little more than five hundred years. The indigenous

32  P. Brotherton et al., 'Neolithic mitochondrial haplogroup H genomes and the genetic origins of Europeans', *Nature Communications*, 4 (2013), 1764.

33  P. Soares et al., 'The archaeogenetics of Europe', *Current Biology*, 20 (2010), R174–83.

34  M.F. Deguilloux et al., 'European Neolithization and ancient DNA: an assessment', *Evolutionary Anthropology*, 21 (2012), 24–37.

35  C.S. Troy et al., 'Genetic evidence for Near-Eastern origins of European cattle', *Nature*, 410 (2001), 1088–91; C.J. Edwards et al., 'A complete mitochondrial genome sequence from a Mesolithic wild aurochs (*Bos primigenius*)', *PLoS ONE*, 5 (2010), e9255; A. Achilli et al., 'Mitochondrial genomes of extinct aurochs survive in domestic cattle', *Current Biology*, 18 (2008), R157–8.

36  G. Larson et al., 'Worldwide phylogeography of wild boar reveals multiple centers of pig domestication', *Science*, 307 (2005), 1618–21; G. Larson et al., 'Ancient DNA, pig domestication, and the spread of the Neolithic into Europe', *Proceedings of the National Academy of Sciences*, 104 (2007), 15276–81.

pig lineages had spread as far south and east as Armenia by the first millennium BCE.

This would not rule out significant acculturation in central Europe during the early Neolithic. Even if the N1a and some of the H lineages were picked up in southeastern Europe, the remaining LBK lineages are quite diverse, including some of potentially Mesolithic western European origin (like H1). Moreover, simulation studies have suggested that, under realistic demographic parameters for the early Neolithic, the LBK would have had to incorporate a substantial Mesolithic component in order to grow at the archaeologically observed rate.[37] In any event, the virtual lack of N1a (and perhaps also of some of the LBK H lineages) in present-day central European populations suggests that the intrusive LBK populations were subsequently overwhelmed by others, for which the most likely candidates must surely remain their Mesolithic contemporaries, whether local or from elsewhere in Europe. Indeed, direct evidence for late Neolithic assimilation of Mesolithic mtDNA lineages in central Europe has recently been forthcoming.[38] The evidence for the near-extinction of lineages that were common in the early LBK communities is reflected not only in the situation with pig domestication but also in archaeobotanical studies, suggesting that these groups were later replaced.[39] Thus even for central Europe a model of leapfrog pioneer colonization, followed by assimilation of the indigenous hunter-gatherer population, may again be the best explanation for the data. If the replacing populations were intrusive Neolithic populations from elsewhere, their ancestry would in turn be in question.

To clarify the pre-Neolithic picture, we must turn to studies of other parts of Europe, but evidence is thin on the ground (Figure 2.4). Several studies claim to have extracted mtDNA from late Palaeolithic and Mesolithic remains in southwestern Europe. Here, haplogroup H, which is strikingly absent from pre-Neolithic samples to the northeast, appears in several Iberian Magdalenian samples alongside one with U5. U5b has also been identified in three Iberian Mesolithic samples. Although some of these are dubious, for

---

37  P. Galeta et al., 'Modeling Neolithic dispersal in central Europe: demographic implications', *American Journal of Physical Anthropology*, 146 (2011), 104–15.

38  R. Bollongino et al., '2000 years of parallel societies in Stone Age central Europe', *Science*, 342 (2013), 479–81.

39  S. Shennan and K. Edinborough, 'Prehistoric population history: from the late Glacial to the late Neolithic in central and northern Europe', *Journal of Archaeological Science*, 34 (2007), 1339–45; F. Coward et al., 'The spread of Neolithic plant economies from the Near East to northwest Europe: a phylogenetic analysis', *Journal of Archaeological Science*, 35 (2008), 42–56.

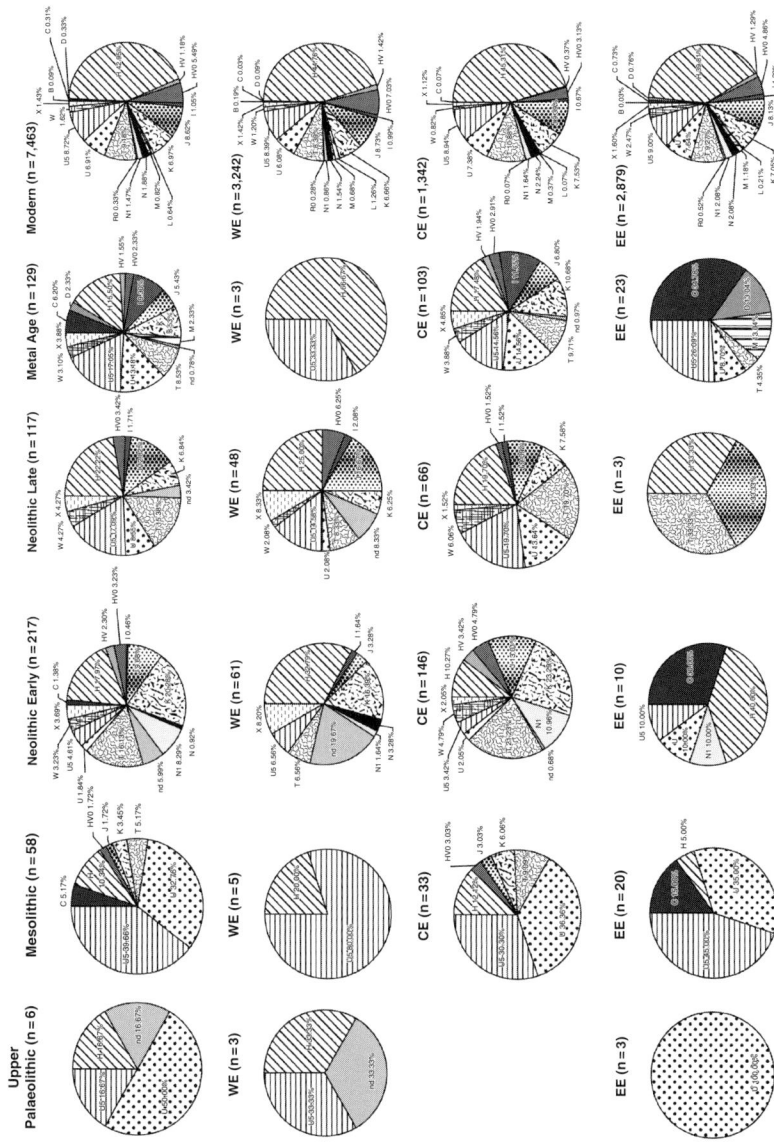

Figure 2.4 Frequencies of mtDNA haplogroups based on ancient DNA from Europe, with comparative contemporary data (April 2014) from the same regions

several reasons, it seems likely that U5 was indeed also present in the south-west before the Neolithic.[40] The presence of H alongside U4 and U5 was also suggested in an earlier study of Portuguese Mesolithic samples,[41] although again we should be cautious of taking these results at face value.

The remainder of the evidence for putative pre-Neolithic lineages comes from northern Europe.[42] Southern Scandinavia only moved into the Neolithic *c.* 6 ka, and hunter-gatherers such as those of the Pitted Ware Culture (PWC, which actually arose after the arrival of the early Neolithic, and is referred to as middle Neolithic) survived alongside farming groups until *c.* 4 ka. About a third of nineteen PWC samples carried U4 (previously inferred on the basis of extant variation to have expanded from the eastern European plain after the last glacial maximum[43]), with slightly fewer U5, some T2, a V, and some unidentified lineages. The authors suggest Neolithic or post-Neolithic population replacement in southern Scandinavia, with the PWC arriving by dispersal from the eastern Baltic, with greater continuity from the Mesolithic to the present day in the eastern Baltic region, where U4 in particular occurs at high frequency. Late Mesolithic Russian remains again carry mainly U (U2 as well as U4 and U5), with a single H and some East Asian lineages. The only earlier upper Palaeolithic remains confidently assigned to mtDNA lineages belong to haplogroups U2, pre-U5, pre-U8b, or other U lineages.[44]

There are few data from the early Neolithic of southwestern Europe, and by the late Neolithic at least, as with central Europe, the pattern appears to be close to the modern distribution. N1a has not been found, even in the earliest Neolithic site samples, and the presence of haplogroup U5 suggests at least some assimilation of Mesolithic populations at even the earliest levels. Some intriguing results have emerged from MSY analyses, where there seem to be high levels of lineages that are currently most common in the Near East. These results might suggest a particularly important role for men in the demographic spread of the Neolithic along the Mediterranean. One of

40 M. Hervella et al., 'Ancient DNA from hunter-gatherer and farmer groups from northern Spain supports a random dispersion model for the Neolithic expansion into Europe', *PLoS ONE*, 7 (2012), e34417; F. Sánchez-Quinto et al., 'Genomic affinities of two 7,000-year-old Iberian hunter-gatherers', *Current Biology*, 22 (2012), 1494–9.

41 H. Chandler et al., 'Using ancient DNA to examine genetic continuity at the Mesolithic–Neolithic transition in Portugal', *Prehistoricas de Cantabria*, 1 (2005), 781–6.

42 H. Malmström et al., 'Ancient DNA reveals lack of continuity between Neolithic hunter-gatherers and contemporary Scandinavians', *Current Biology*, 19 (2009), 1758–62.

43 See footnote 29 above.

44 C. Der Sarkissian et al., 'Ancient DNA reveals prehistoric gene-flow from Siberia in the complex human population history of North East Europe', *PLoS Genetics*, 9 (2013), e1003296; Q. Fu et al., 'A revised timescale for human evolution based on ancient mitochondrial genomes', *Current Biology*, 23 (2013), 553–9.

these has also been found in the Chalcolithic Tyrolean Iceman, where the high-resolution analysis suggested a possible link to (present-day) Corsica or Sardinia, matching the autosomal evidence.[45]

We have summarized the more reliable available published aDNA data in Figure 2.4. Overall, it does not seem that the results to date can justify claims of a huge genetic discontinuity between the Mesolithic and Neolithic across Europe, or that modern Europeans 'derive essentially from those Neolithic migrants', as some have claimed. Suggestions that Mesolithic Europe has 'minimal geographic structure' and that Mesolithic foragers had a 'common origin' are at best premature, and in part based on the citation of dubious reports in several cases. Although some authors seem to disregard population substructure prior to the Neolithic, this ignores both genetic and archaeological evidence suggesting that the Mesolithic European population was the product of late Glacial and early post-Glacial expansions and subsequent fragmentation.[46] However, the patterns that are emerging from the ancient DNA studies are very striking and intriguing. The implication that European populations began to assume their present genetic structure only from the end of the Neolithic is new and exciting,[47] although Figure 2.4 suggests that it does not yet receive clear support from the data outside of the central Europe LBK zone – rather, the overall picture appears to be one of fluctuations in the frequencies of lineages across both space and time, due in part to genetic drift but very likely also due to sampling.

Recent genome-wide analyses of aDNA – technically a further astonishing development – have been interpreted in a similar way, although presently extrapolated from only half a dozen samples. Three PWC samples from Scandinavia most closely resemble modern Finns and Russians, again (as

45 M. Lacan et al., 'Ancient DNA reveals male diffusion through the Neolithic Mediterranean route', *Proceedings of the National Academy of Sciences*, 108 (2011), 9788–91; M.L. Sampietro et al., 'Palaeogenetic evidence supports a dual model of Neolithic spreading into Europe', *Proceedings of the Royal Society B*, 274 (2007), 2161–7; M. Lacan et al., 'Ancient DNA suggests the leading role played by men in the Neolithic dissemination', *Proceedings of the National Academy of Sciences*, 108 (2011), 18255–9; C. Gamba et al., 'Ancient DNA from an early Neolithic Iberian population supports a pioneer colonization by first farmers', *Molecular Ecology*, 21 (2012), 45–56; A. Keller et al., 'New insights into the Tyrolean Iceman's origin and phenotype as inferred by whole-genome sequencing', *Nature Communications*, 3 (2012), 698.

46 C. Gamble et al., 'The archaeological and genetic foundations of the European population during the late Glacial: implications for "agricultural thinking"', *Cambridge Archaeological Journal*, 15 (2005), 193–223.

47 G. Brandt et al., 'Ancient DNA reveals key stages in the formation of central European mitochondrial genetic diversity', *Science*, 342 (2013), 257–61; F.-X. Ricaut et al., 'A time series of prehistoric mitochondrial DNA reveals western European genetic diversity was largely established by the Bronze Age', *Advances in Anthropology*, 2 (2011), 14–23.

with the mtDNA) pointing to an eastern source, whereas a single Neolithic Funnel Beaker Culture sample (dating to *c.* 5 ka, and carrying mtDNA haplogroup H) most resembles southern Europeans. Two Mesolithic samples from Iberia (with identical U5b mtDNAs) appear to fall somewhere between modern central and northern Europeans, and somewhat more distantly from contemporary Iberians.

This might suggest that southern Europe has indeed been reshaped to some extent since late Glacial times by movements from the Near East – perhaps, in part, during the Neolithic – as suggested by mtDNA and Y-chromosome results from modern-day samples – and that the Neolithic involved dispersals from south to north within the continent. Although the major genetic lineages may have been present in Europe since before the Neolithic, their distributions seem likely to have been profoundly reorganized by both long-range and short-range dispersals, by major but regionalized demographic expansions, and by extinctions, such as those of many of the LBK lineages in central Europe. A picture begins to emerge of very diverse histories in different regions, with short-range dispersals ('leap-frog migrations') and episodes of population coalescence in some cases and replacement in others, fitting radiocarbon evidence for short bursts and pauses in the process of Neolithic spread.

Ancient DNA is starting to contribute to the study of other aspects of the spread of farming. For example, present-day Europeans display high levels of lactose persistence (the ability of adults to digest milk sugar) due to the presence of a particular DNA variant, which differs from the variant conferring persistence where it occurs in other parts of the world and most likely rose to high frequencies due to selection in early European dairying populations. One Mesolithic and eight early Neolithic samples from central and northeastern Europe all lacked the persistence variant, supporting the view that dairying had to become embedded in the culture before the variant could be selected.[48] It is likely that this is only the beginning of a dissection of the impact of the spread of farming on the human genome, and vice versa.

## Asia and Africa

Virtually no ancient DNA evidence relevant to the Neolithic transition is available for any other part of the world. Several areas have, however, been

---

48 J. Burger et al., 'Absence of the lactase-persistence-associated allele in early Neolithic Europeans', *Proceedings of the National Academy of Sciences*, 104 (2007), 3736–41; Y. Itan et al., 'The origins of lactase persistence in Europe', *PLoS Computational Biology*, 5 (2009), e1000491.

subjected to intensive study from the perspective of modern human variation, and two in particular include certain checks and balances in the procedure that were lacking in the case of Europe. Both Southeast Asia / Pacific and sub-Saharan Africa are dominated by a single wide-spread language family – Austronesian and Bantu respectively – and both regions underwent recent and well-documented colonization processes at one extreme of the range. The language distributions and archaeological / historical evidence can therefore exert greater discipline upon the genetic models, and provide an independent corroboration for the genetic dating. At the same time, the linguistic evidence in particular has often led to quite simplistic models of demographic expansion across the entire range of the language families,[49] whereas the genetic evidence has suggested a much more complex pattern preceding the final phase of expansion, in the Remote Pacific and southern Africa respectively.

In Southeast Asia, the main focus has been on island Southeast Asia (ISEA) and the Pacific islands, where Austronesian languages have been spoken, but the model of agricultural expansion (fuelled by the development of rice agriculture) ultimately also takes in central and southern China and mainland Southeast Asia. However, by and large, genetic studies have worked from the periphery – beginning with the Remote Pacific and working backwards towards the mainland – because of the relative simplicity of the situation in Oceania. Early studies confirmed the supposition, based on linguistics and archaeology, that genetic diversity was extremely low in the Remote Pacific, as the result of major founder effects in the recent past – in particular generating the so-called mitochondrial 'Polynesian motif', a single lineage spread throughout the Remote Pacific at very high frequencies. The earliest studies saw evidence in this for the consensus farming / language dispersal hypothesis: an expansion from China / Taiwan through Southeast Asia beginning *c.* 6 ka and reaching the Remote Pacific by *c.* 3 ka, largely bypassing New Guinea, which had evolved separately from Southeast Asia for tens of thousands of years. Much genetic work continues to lay the main emphasis on the Pacific, and to interpret the genetic data in these terms.

However, even from the earliest days it was clear that ISEA was much more genetically diverse than Micronesia and Polynesia. Further scrutiny of the mtDNA evidence, and the emergence of MSY evidence as well, indicated that the so-called 'express-train' model of rapid dispersal all the way from

49 J. Diamond and P. Bellwood, 'Farmers and their languages: the first expansions', *Science*, 300 (2003), 597–603.

China/Taiwan was not holding up. Both systems pointed to a major role for eastern Indonesia/Near Oceania (the New Guinea region) as a source for the Remote Pacific islanders. The major proximal source for the mtDNA 'Polynesian motif' appears to be the Bismarck archipelago in the early to mid-Holocene, with a deeper ancestry further back in island Southeast Asia,[50] but also with minor arrivals from ISEA in the late Holocene, preceding the expansions into Remote Oceania. This intertwining of ISEA and the New Guinea region throughout the Holocene renders simplistic admixture accounts that apportion different levels of 'Asian' and 'Melanesian' ancestry to Pacific islanders (often equating the former with 'Austronesian') some-what outmoded, and suggests that archaeological models that emphasize ancient voyaging may have a significant role to play.[51]

Similarly, it seemed clear early on that much of the MSY variation, too, traces to eastern Indonesia/Near Oceania. A minority may derive from Taiwan or Borneo, potentially tracing a male-mediated 'farming/language dispersal' from the north and west, but the details are unclear and similar caveats to those we mentioned with regard to the European studies are appropriate here too.[52] Both mtDNA and some autosomal analyses have suggested, for example, that Taiwan, rather than being a major source for ISEA diversity as suggested by the language distributions, may rather have been largely a recipient for lineages from further south.[53] There are some candidates for minor mtDNA lineages, as well as MSY lineages, that may have transmitted Austronesian languages and/or Neolithic industries through ISEA, but the great majority – including those ancestral to the Polynesian motif – have a deep insular ancestry and appear to have been largely shaped by the sea-level rises accompanying the end of the last Glacial period.[54] The spread of the

50 J.S. Friedlaender et al., 'The genetic structure of Pacific islanders', *PloS Genetics*, 4 (2008).

51 M. Kayser et al., 'Genome-wide analysis indicates more Asian than Melanesian ancestry of Polynesians', *American Journal of Human Genetics*, 82 (2008), 194–8; J.E. Terrell and R.L. Welsch, 'Lapita and the temporal geography of prehistory', *Antiquity*, 71 (1997), 548–72.

52 T.M. Karafet et al., 'Major east–west division underlies Y chromosome stratification across Indonesia', *Molecular Biology and Evolution*, 27 (2010), 1833–44; M. Kayser, 'The human genetic history of Oceania: near and remote views of dispersal', *Current Biology*, 20 (2010), R194–201; M. Kayser et al., 'The impact of the Austronesian expansion: evidence from mtDNA and Y chromosome diversity in the Admiralty Islands of Melanesia', *Molecular Biology and Evolution*, 25 (2008), 1362–74.

53 P. Soares et al., 'Climate change and post-Glacial human dispersals in Southeast Asia', *Molecular Biology and Evolution*, 25 (2008), 1209–18; M.A. Abdulla et al., 'Mapping human genetic diversity in Asia', *Science*, 326 (2009), 1541–5.

54 K.A. Tabbada et al., 'Philippine mitochondrial DNA diversity: a populated viaduct between Taiwan and Indonesia?', *Molecular Biology and Evolution*, 27 (2010), 21–31.

Neolithic and of the Austronesian languages appears to have had a minor impact on population structure and may owe more to the establishment of social networks and spheres of interaction.[55] This pattern of predominantly late Glacial and post-Glacial but pre-Neolithic growth is also seen in Chinese mitogenomes,[56] although a full phylogeographic picture has yet to be worked out.

The pattern in mainland Southeast Asia – where the main language family is Austroasiatic – is rather different from ISEA. There are clear links to southern China, but whether the expansions into Indo-China accompanied the spread of rice farming or the earlier spread of 'coastal Neolithic' hunter-gatherer populations driven by climatic changes remains debatable. It has been suggested that the horticulturalist Senoi of the Malay peninsula are the product of both farmer-dispersals from Indo-China and assimilation of the indigenous people of the peninsula, and may have been the conduit that brought the Austroasiatic languages south. MSY and autosomal patterns suggest that the Austroasiatic languages were spread from mainland Southeast Asia west into India, rather than in the opposite direction as has been suggested. The Indian subcontinent in fact received lineages from both Southeast Asia (mainly on the male side) and Southwest Asia (from both lines of descent), which might possibly signal the diffusion of rice and wheat/barley into the east and west respectively – although work to date suggests that those from the west, at least, may predate the Neolithic.[57]

In Africa, the spread of agriculture through much of the central and southern part of the continent went hand in hand with the dispersal of the Bantu languages from west Central Africa, within the last few thousand years. Rather like in Remote Oceania, the situation in southern Africa is relatively straightforward and reasonably well understood in outline. The indigenous Khoe and San populations speak 'Khoisan' click languages and have traditionally had foraging or herding economies. They have a very characteristic suite of mtDNA and MSY lineages, and highly distinctive autosomal profiles. Bantu-speakers in southern Africa, by contrast, show signs of a maternal founder effect c. 2 ka, and they share many mtDNA and MSY

55 G. Barker and M.B. Richards, 'Foraging–farming transitions in island Southeast Asia', *Journal of Archaeological Method and Theory*, 20 (2013), 256–80.
56 H.X. Zheng et al., 'Major population expansion of East Asians began before Neolithic time: evidence of mtDNA genomes', *PLoS ONE*, 6 (2011), e25835.
57 C. Hill et al., 'Phylogeography and ethnogenesis of aboriginal Southeast Asians', *Molecular Biology and Evolution*, 23 (2006), 2480–91; G. Chaubey et al., 'Peopling of South Asia: investigating the caste–tribe continuum in India', *BioEssays*, 29 (2007), 91–100.

lineages, and an autosomal profile, with Bantu-speakers from across Central Africa.[58]

Again, however, southern Africa lies on the far edge of the Bantu expansion, and the situation further north is much more complex. Bantu-speakers spread both south and east from their core area around west Cameroon/southeast Nigeria, and the eastern stream encountered settled populations with cereal crops in East Africa. Somewhere in this region, or in east Central Africa, they appear to have assimilated new lineages, at least on the maternal line of descent, so that southeast Bantu-speakers have a mixed ancestry including lineages from west Central Africa, East Africa, and southern Africa, with the levels of 'Khoisan' ancestry increasing substantially into southern Africa.[59]

Southwest Bantu-speakers, on the other hand, have a preponderance of Central African lineages barely seen in southeast Bantu-speakers, presumably assimilated in the forest zone of Central Africa by the western stream of dispersal. Intriguingly, these lineages are far more diverse in Bantu-speakers than in Central African forest-dwelling foragers – a counter-intuitive pattern that might imply large-scale assimilation of lineages into the Bantu-speaking groups and heavy losses through genetic drift among the foragers. Similar complexities are evident on the male line of descent, and indeed in the autosomal patterns of, for example, East Africa.[60]

It seems clear that the Bantu dispersals hugely reshaped the genetic landscape of Africa, but as with much of what we have described in this chapter, working out the processes in detail still lies ahead. We have only outlined here some of what we consider to be the more persuasive arguments among what has become a huge and growing area of research, but even so it seems clear that archaeogenetics has barely scratched the surface of its potential.

---

58  D.M. Behar et al., 'The dawn of human matrilineal diversity', *American Journal of Human Genetics*, 82 (2008), 1–11; T. Rito et al., 'The first modern human dispersals across Africa', *PLoS ONE*, 8 (2013), e80031; B.M. Henn et al., 'Hunter-gatherer genomic diversity suggests a southern African origin for modern humans', *Proceedings of the National Academy of Sciences*, 108 (2011), 5154–62; V. Montano et al., 'The Bantu expansion revisited: a new analysis of Y chromosome variation in Central Western Africa', *Molecular Ecology*, 20 (2011), 2693–708; S.A. Tishkoff et al., 'The genetic structure and history of Africans and African Americans', *Science*, 324 (2009), 1035–44.

59  A. Salas et al., 'The making of the African mtDNA landscape', *American Journal of Human Genetics*, 71 (2002), 1082–111.

60  S. Plaza et al., 'Insights into the western Bantu dispersal: mtDNA lineage analysis in Angola', *Human Genetics*, 115 (2004), 439–47; L. Quintana-Murci et al., 'Maternal traces of deep common ancestry and asymmetric gene flow between Pygmy hunter-gatherers and Bantu-speaking farmers', *Proceedings of the National Academy of Sciences*, 105 (2008), 1596–601.

A huge amount of genetic data is pouring out at an accelerating rate, but it is often still treated in quite a broad-brush way. This is in part because of the coarse resolution of genetic studies that have mostly relied on present-day data, where the signals from the Neolithic can be obscured by millennia of subsequent migrations, making nuanced regional studies difficult, but it is beginning to look as if ancient DNA analyses might have the potential to overcome this limitation. Perhaps it is time for renewed collaborations between geneticists and archaeologists in order to refocus the analyses away from the grand narratives of the past and bring the subject down to earth.

# Further reading

Ammerman, A.J. and L.L. Cavalli-Sforza. *The Neolithic Transition and the Genetics of Populations in Europe.* Princeton University Press, 1984.

Avise, J.C. *Phylogeography.* Cambridge, MA: Harvard University Press, 2000.

Bellwood, P. and C. Renfrew (eds.). *Examining the Farming/Language Dispersal Hypothesis.* Cambridge: McDonald Institute for Archaeological Research, 2002.

Bramanti, B., M.G. Thomas, W. Haak, et al. 'Genetic discontinuity between local hunter-gatherers and central Europe's first farmers.' *Science*, 326 (2009), 137–40.

Brandt, G., W. Haak, C.J. Adler, et al. 'Ancient DNA reveals key stages in the formation of central European mitochondrial genetic diversity.' *Science*, 342 (2013), 257–61.

Brotherton, P., W. Haak, J. Templeton, et al. 'Neolithic mitochondrial haplogroup H genomes and the genetic origins of Europeans.' *Nature Communications*, 4 (2013), 1764.

Busby, G.B., F. Brisighelli, P. Sánchez-Diz, et al. 'The peopling of Europe and the cautionary tale of Y chromosome lineage R-M269.' *Proceedings of the Royal Society B*, 279 (2011), 884–92.

Cavalli-Sforza, L.L., P. Menozzi, and A. Piazza. *The History and Geography of Human Genes.* Princeton University Press, 1994.

Deguilloux, M.F., R. Leahy, M.H. Pemonge, and S. Rottiér. 'European Neolithization and ancient DNA: an assessment.' *Evolutionary Anthropology*, 21 (2012), 24–37.

Gamble, C., W. Davies, P. Pettitt, L. Hazelwood, and M. Richards. 'The archaeological and genetic foundations of the European population during the late Glacial: implications for "agricultural thinking".' *Cambridge Archaeological Journal*, 15 (2005), 193–223.

Haak, W., P. Forster, B. Bramanti, et al. 'Ancient DNA from the first European farmers in 7500-year-old Neolithic sites.' *Science*, 310 (2005), 1016–18.

Itan, Y., A. Powell, M.A. Beaumont, J. Burger, and M.G. Thomas. 'The origins of lactase persistence in Europe.' *PLoS Computational Biology*, 5 (2009), e1000491.

King, R. and P. Underhill. 'Congruent distribution of Neolithic painted pottery and ceramic figurines with Y-chromosome lineages.' *Antiquity*, 76 (2002), 707–14.

Lacan, M., C. Keyser, F.X. Ricaut, et al. 'Ancient DNA suggests the leading role played by men in the Neolithic dissemination.' *Proceedings of the National Academy of Sciences*, 108 (2011), 18255–9.

Larson, G., U. Albarella, K. Dobney, et al. 'Ancient DNA, pig domestication, and the spread of the Neolithic into Europe.' *Proceedings of the National Academy of Sciences*, 104 (2007), 15276–81.

Macaulay, V. and M. Richards. 'Mitochondrial genome sequences and phylogeographic interpretation.' In *Encyclopedia of Life Sciences*, www.els.net. Chichester: Wiley. doi: 10.1002/9780470015902.20843.pub2. 2013.

Malmström, H., M.T.P. Gilbert, M.G. Thomas, et al. 'Ancient DNA reveals lack of continuity between Neolithic hunter-gatherers and contemporary Scandinavians.' *Current Biology*, 19 (2009), 1758–62.

Nielsen, R. and M.A. Beaumont. 'Statistical inferences in phylogeography.' *Molecular Ecology*, 18 (2009), 1034–47.

Pala, M., G. Chaubey, P. Soares, and M.B. Richards. 'The archaeogenetics of European ancestry.' In *Encyclopedia of Life Sciences*, www.els.net. Chichester: Wiley. doi:10.1002/9780470015902.a0024624. 2014.

Pala, M., A. Olivieri, A. Achilli, et al. 'Mitochondrial DNA signals of late Glacial re-colonization of Europe from Near Eastern refugia.' *American Journal of Human Genetics*, 90 (2012), 915–24.

Renfrew, C. and K. Boyle (eds.). *Archaeogenetics*. Cambridge: McDonald Institute for Archaeological Research, 2000.

Richards, M. 'The Neolithic invasion of Europe.' *Annual Review of Anthropology*, 62 (2003), 135–62.

Richards, M., V. Macaulay, E. Hickey, et al. 'Tracing European founder lineages in the Near Eastern mtDNA pool.' *American Journal of Human Genetics*, 67 (2000), 1251–76.

Salas, A., M. Richards, T. De la Fe, et al. 'The making of the African mtDNA landscape.' *American Journal of Human Genetics*, 71 (2002), 1082–111.

Semino, O., G. Passarino, P.J. Oefner, et al. 'The genetic legacy of Paleolithic *Homo sapiens sapiens* in extant Europeans: a Y chromosome perspective.' *Science*, 290 (2000), 1155–9.

Skoglund, P., H. Malmström, M. Raghavan, et al. 'Origins and genetic legacy of Neolithic farmers and hunter-gatherers in Europe.' *Science*, 336 (2012), 466–9.

Soares, P., A. Achilli, O. Semino, et al. 'The archaeogenetics of Europe.' *Current Biology*, 20 (2010), R174–83.

Soares, P., L. Ermini, N. Thomson, et al. 'Correcting for purifying selection: an improved human mitochondrial molecular clock.' *American Journal of Human Genetics*, 84 (2009), 740–59.

Soares, P., T. Rito, J. Trejaut, et al. 'Ancient voyaging and Polynesian origins.' *American Journal of Human Genetics*, 88 (2011), 239–47.

Troy, C.S., D.E. MacHugh, J.F. Bailey, et al. 'Genetic evidence for Near-Eastern origins of European cattle.' *Nature*, 410 (2001), 1088–91.

3

# Agricultural origins
## *What linguistic evidence reveals*

CHRISTOPHER EHRET

The first tentative steps towards the deliberate tending of food sources began with the close of the last Ice Age. The new directions in subsistence did not begin in just one region of the world, but rather, between 11,000 and 5000 BCE, peoples in several different distant parts of the globe independently set these developments in motion.

To recover human history in those periods, historians typically rely on the findings of archaeologists. Less often scholars have marshalled a second set of tools, drawing on historical linguistics to advance the knowledge of those early times. Learning about these tools and how to use them is its own full course of study, and so only a short introduction to the key ideas is possible here.[1]

How far back in time can one carry the linguistic investigation of earlier human subsistence practices? That depends on how far back in time the currently available language family reconstructions extend. For some world regions scholars have constructed relatively deep-time linguistic histories. In Africa the linguistic record for the Nilo-Saharan, Niger–Congo, and Cushitic families extends back to the early Holocene era. In other regions of the world the existing reconstructions tend to be of more shallow time depth. Scholars working on the Austronesian language family, for example, and on the Oceanic branch of this family, can take their story back to the later middle Holocene in the island South Asia and Oceanic regions. The reach of the currently available linguistic evidence on early agriculture also extends back to the middle or the later middle Holocene for the Middle East, India, and Mesoamerica.

---

1 C. Ehret, 'Linguistic archaeology', *African Archaeological Review*, 29/2 (2012), 109–30, provides a compact introduction. C. Ehret, *History and the Testimony of Language* (Berkeley: University of California Press, 2011), presents at greater length these methods and how they can be used in the reconstruction of human history, drawing particularly on African case studies.

The essential foundation for the linguistic recovery of history is a systematic reconstruction of the relationships and phonological histories of the families of languages spoken in the regions whose human histories one wishes to investigate. Establishing the foundation is itself arduous and long-term work. But with the framework of language relationship in place, it becomes possible to systematically assess the evidence of language for history.

To say that a certain set of languages are related – that they belong to the same language family – means that they all descend from a single mother language, a *protolanguage*, spoken at some period in the past. Now, language descent is *mitotic*. Like a single-celled organism, a mother language diverges into daughter languages. It does not continue to be spoken alongside its daughters – it *becomes* its daughters. In subsequent eras the daughter languages may in turn become mother languages, or *protolanguages*, by diverging into further daughters. A language diverges into daughter languages over a period of centuries through the gradual accumulation of new words and grammatical features and the loss of old; and unlike the usual outcome of mitosis in single-cell organisms, the protolanguage may undergo divergence into several daughters at once.

Through the application of historical linguistic methods, scholars can uncover the overall succession of divergences that took place in a family of languages over the millennia and, from these findings, construct a family tree of the relationships involved. The key to turning this family tree into a human historical framework is the fact that, in past ages, a language could exist only if there was a society that spoke it. If the community speaking a language lost the sense of separate ethnic identity and was incorporated over time into another society, their language would soon die out. If, in contrast, the communities who spoke a language began to lose their sense of belonging to a common society – for instance, because of divisive internal conflicts, or because some groups moved to new areas, distant from their fellow speakers – they might continue to speak the language. But the changes in lexicon and grammar would be different in the different areas, setting in motion the processes of language divergence. Constructing a family tree of language relationships – a linguistic stratigraphy – therefore depicts not just the lines of language descent among related languages, but the lines of societal descent and divergence among the speakers of those languages down through the millennia.

A key contributor to language change over time is change in the lexicon – changes in the words used for particular things and actions, the addition of new words to the vocabulary, and the obsolescence and loss of other words. People need words for expressing all the aspects of their lives and knowledge, including the things and actions that comprise their economies. Whether they collect or cultivate plants, and whether they hunt or tend their meat sources, people must have the full lexicon necessary to communicate about those activities and the features, ideas, and material items associated with them. To reconstruct the existence of an old root word for a particular activity or thing back to a particular node in the linguistic stratigraphy is to demonstrate that the society speaking the language at that point in time possessed the knowledge connoted by the word. They had or performed or, at the very least, knew of the thing or activity in question.

The presence in a protolanguage of a term for a specific crop or a specific domesticated animal, however, does not by itself demonstrate that the speakers of the protolanguage actually cultivated the crop or herded the animal. The reason is straightforward. Each food plant, once upon a time, before cultivation, would have been collected wild; each domestic animal once was wild. If a protolanguage was spoken within a plant's or an animal's region of origin, its reconstructed term for the plant or animal may well have originally designated the wild plant or animal. The essential diagnostic evidence in such a case would be verbs and nouns that specifically connote or identify the activities of cultivation or herding. For inferring livestock-raising, the strongest indicators of all are breeding terminologies. The case studies of early agricultural vocabulary from around the world provide numerous examples of the application of these various criteria.

Of course, if the protolanguage was spoken in a region distant from where the plant or animal existed in the wild, then the knowledge would have spread to the speakers of that language only because people somewhere else had already begun to cultivate the crop or tend the animal. In that case, one could argue that the speakers of the protolanguage were, at the least, neighbours of people who did cultivate the plant or raise the animal. But their possession of words specifically connoting cultivation or herding would still be important in showing conclusively that they themselves participated in those activities.

One other consideration, cultural *salience*, is also relevant to the historical intepretation of ancient lexicons. If an item had high salience in the culture of a past society, this circumstance can affect word histories in two ways. For one thing, when an item has high cultural salience, the word for the item tends to remain in use over very long periods; only infrequently will people adopt a new term for it.[2] A second indicator of high salience in earlier times can be the existence of a suite of reconstructed secondary words relating to or descriptive of the item. We will encounter examples of both kinds in our considerations here.

Nineteenth-century scholars first put into use the kinds of systematic method that scholars apply today in extracting history from language. The students of this field have since refined and expanded these approaches and applied them to some extent in every continent. In the past two and a half decades a revitalization of this field of scholarly endeavour has taken place, with the methods put to use not just in reconstructing material lifeways of past peoples, but in uncovering deep histories of change and persistence in such non-material areas of culture as political ideas,[3] religious beliefs,[4] gender relations,[5] and kinship systems.[6] The most extensive and detailed applications of language evidence have been in African history[7] and

2  This feature is widely evident from studies in Africa. For an example from the Americas, see B. Berlin et al., 'Cultural significance and lexical retention in Tzeltal-Tzotzil ethno-botany', in Munro S. Edmonson (ed.), *Meaning in Mayan Languages* (The Hague: Mouton, 1973), 143–64.

3  Notably J. Vansina, *Paths in the Rainforests* (Madison: University of Wisconsin Press, 1990), and *How Societies are Born* (Charlottesville: University of Virginia Press, 2004); and D.L. Schoenbrun, *A Green Place, A Good Place: Agrarian Change, Gender, and Social Identity in the Great Lakes Region to the 15th Century* (Portsmouth, NH: Heinemann, 1998).

4  R.M. Gonzales, *Societies, Religion, and History: Central-East Tanzanians and the World they Created, c. 200 BCE to 1800 CE* (New York: Columbia University Press, 2009).

5  C. Saidi, *Women's Authority and Society in Early East-Central Africa* (University of Rochester Press, 2010).

6  E.g. P. McConvell, 'Omaha skewing in Australia: overlays, dynamism, and change', in T. Troutmann and P. Whiteley (eds.), *Crow-Omaha: New Light on a Classic Problem of Kinship Analysis* (Tucson: University of Arizona Press, 2012), 243–60, among other works; C. Ehret, 'Reconstructing ancient kinship in Africa', in N.J. Allen et al. (eds.), *Early Human Kinship: From Sex to Social Reproduction* (Oxford: Blackwell, 2008), 200–31, and 'Deep-time historical contexts of Crow and Omaha systems: perspectives from Africa', in Trautmann and Whiteley (eds.), *Crow-Omaha*, 173–202; P. Hage and J. Marck, 'Proto-Bantu descent groups', and J. Marck and K. Bostoen, 'Proto-Oceanic society (Austronesian) and proto-East Bantu society (Niger–Congo) residence, descent, and kin terms, c. 1000 BC', both in D. Jones and B. Milicic (eds.), *Kinship, Language, and Prehistory* (Salt Lake City: University of Utah Press, 2011), 75–8, 83–94.

7  E.g. C. Ehret, *Southern Nilotic History: Linguistic Approaches to the Study of the Past* (Evanston, IL: Northwestern University Press, 1972), and *An African Classical Age: Eastern and Southern Africa in World History, 1000 BC to AD 400* (Charlottesville: University of Virginia Press, 1998); J. Vansina, *The Children of Woot: A History of the Kuba Peoples* (Madison: University of Wisconsin Press, 1978), *Paths in the Rainforests*, and *How Societies Are Born*; Schoenbrun, *A Green Place, A Good Place*; K. Klieman, '*The Pygmies Were Our Compass': Bantu and Batwa in the History of West Central Africa, Early Times to c. 1900 CE* (Portsmouth, NH: Heinemann, 2003); R.M. Gonzales, *Societies, Religion, and History*; Saidi, *Women's Authority*; R. Stephens, *A History of African Motherhood: The Case of Uganda, 700–1900* (Cambridge University Press, 2013).

in the history of the cultures and settlements of island South Asia and Oceania.[8]

# Africa

Two major originating centres of food production lay in Africa, one in the far eastern Sahara and the other far to the west, in West Africa, along with a probable third centre in the southwestern Ethiopian highlands. With the end of the Younger Dryas, rainfall and climatic belts in Africa south of the Sahara shifted rapidly northward. In the wake of this shift of seasonal rain regimes, tropical steppe and dry savanna vegetation followed northwards into the centre of what previously had been a hyper-arid Sahara. At the same time a countervailing shift of Mediterranean climate took subtropical steppe and grassland southwards, with the two climatic zones meeting midway through the Sahara.[9] In the eastern Sahara, new directions of change first took shape after 8500 BCE, as the delayed spread northwards of tropical steppe flora and fauna reached the middle of the Sahara. In West Africa the first signs of a new human response to these environmental shifts appeared even earlier, by 9500 BCE, in the areas south of the great bend of the Niger.

In the eastern Sahara, two groupings of peoples, the Nilo-Saharans and the Cushites, were primary actors in the transition to herding and cultivation. Unusually in world history, the adoption of livestock-raising preceded crop cultivation among the peoples of these areas. The archaeology and linguistics accord in this implication for the Nilo-Saharans, and the lexical histories indicate the same progression for the Cushites. In the separate West African centre, the prime movers in the changeover spoke languages of the Niger–Congo family, and cultivation preceded the raising of animals.

---

8 R. Blust, 'The prehistory of the Austronesian-speaking peoples: a view from language', *Journal of World Prehistory*, 9 (1995), 453–510, lays out the evidence for the Austronesian language family as a whole. M. Ross et al. (eds.), *The Lexicon of Proto Oceanic: The Culture and Environment of Ancestral Oceanic Society*, vol. 1: *Material Culture* (Canberra: Research School of Pacific and Asian Studies, 1998), sets out in detail the findings for the Oceanic branch of the Austronesian family. Aboriginal Australia has also been relatively well studied: e.g. P. McConvell and N. Evans, *Archaeology and Linguistics: Aboriginal Australia in Global Perspective* (Melbourne: Oxford University Press, 1998); but Australian history prior to the eighteenth century was pre-agricultural and so not directly on topic for this chapter.

9 The spread of vegetation tends to lag behind shifts in rainfall belts, for the simple reason that seeds spread only as far each year as birds, mammals, wind, or water might carry them. And because the connecting links of the food chain are plant-eating animals, the salient faunal shift for human diets follows along with spread of vegetation.

## The Nilo-Saharan linguistic record

The lexicons of subsistence in the first several periods in the history of the Nilo-Saharan language family reveal an extended, stage-by-stage history of shift from food collection to food production. What makes possible the reconstruction of Nilo-Saharan lexical histories is our possession of an extensive, systematic linguistic reconstruction of this family, including morphological aspects as well as phonology.[10]

The family descent tree of the Nilo-Saharan family (Figure 3.1) lays out the succession of language and societal divergences down through the history of the family. Together the lines of linguistic descent identify the major lines of historical transmission of language and culture leading from earlier Nilo-Saharan societies down to the great variety of Nilo-Saharan societies in existence today.[11]

A family tree, like that of Nilo-Saharan, constitutes a *relative* chronology of language and societal history. To link the chronology to an absolute time-scale, one seeks correlative calendar dates, wherever possible, for key nodes on the tree. For early periods the best basis for this kind of correlation is to identify an archaeological sequence in which the developments in material culture parallel in *detailed* fashion the succession of developments in a linguistically reconstructed history. In Figure 3.1 the calendar dates from 10,500 to 6000 BP (before the present), given along the righthand margin for several early nodes on the family tree, rest on just such parallel archaeological and linguistic sequences.[12] We begin with the linguistically attested sequence and then consider the archaeology.

10 C. Ehret, *A Historical-Comparative Reconstruction of Nilo-Saharan* (Cologne: Rüdiger Köppe, 2001); 'Language contacts in Nilo-Saharan prehistory', in H. Andersen (ed.), *Language Contacts in Prehistory: Studies in Stratigraphy* (Amsterdam, PA: John Benjamins, 2003), 135–57; 'A guide to cognate discovery in Nilo-Saharan', in J. Adelberger and R. Leger (eds.), *Language, History and Reconstructions*, Frankfurter Afrikanistische Blätter 18 (Köln: Rüdiger Köppe, 2014), 9–89. For the well-known languages of the family, the sound correspondences are strongly attested. Many uncertainties remain, though, about the numerous still poorly known languages of the family.

11 There is not room enough to include every Nilo-Saharan language and still have a readable figure. So in quite a number of cases one or a few languages have been selected to represent their particular narrower subgroup. Also, the descent lines in this figure for the Nilotic subgroup lead down to the protolanguages of each of its three branches. Nilotic divides in its own complex subordinate family tree, too complex to include; and, as well, the periods of food production history covered here predate the divergence of the Nilotic branches.

12 The one additional date in Figure 3.1, 3000 BP, refers specifically to the long-accepted dating of the Proto-Southern Nilotic society, which rests on a separate detailed archaeological correlation, first laid out in S.H. Ambrose, 'Archaeology and linguistic reconstructions of history in East Africa', in C. Ehret and M. Posnansky (eds.), *The Archaeological and Linguistic Reconstruction of African History* (Berkeley: University of California Press, 1982), 104–57.

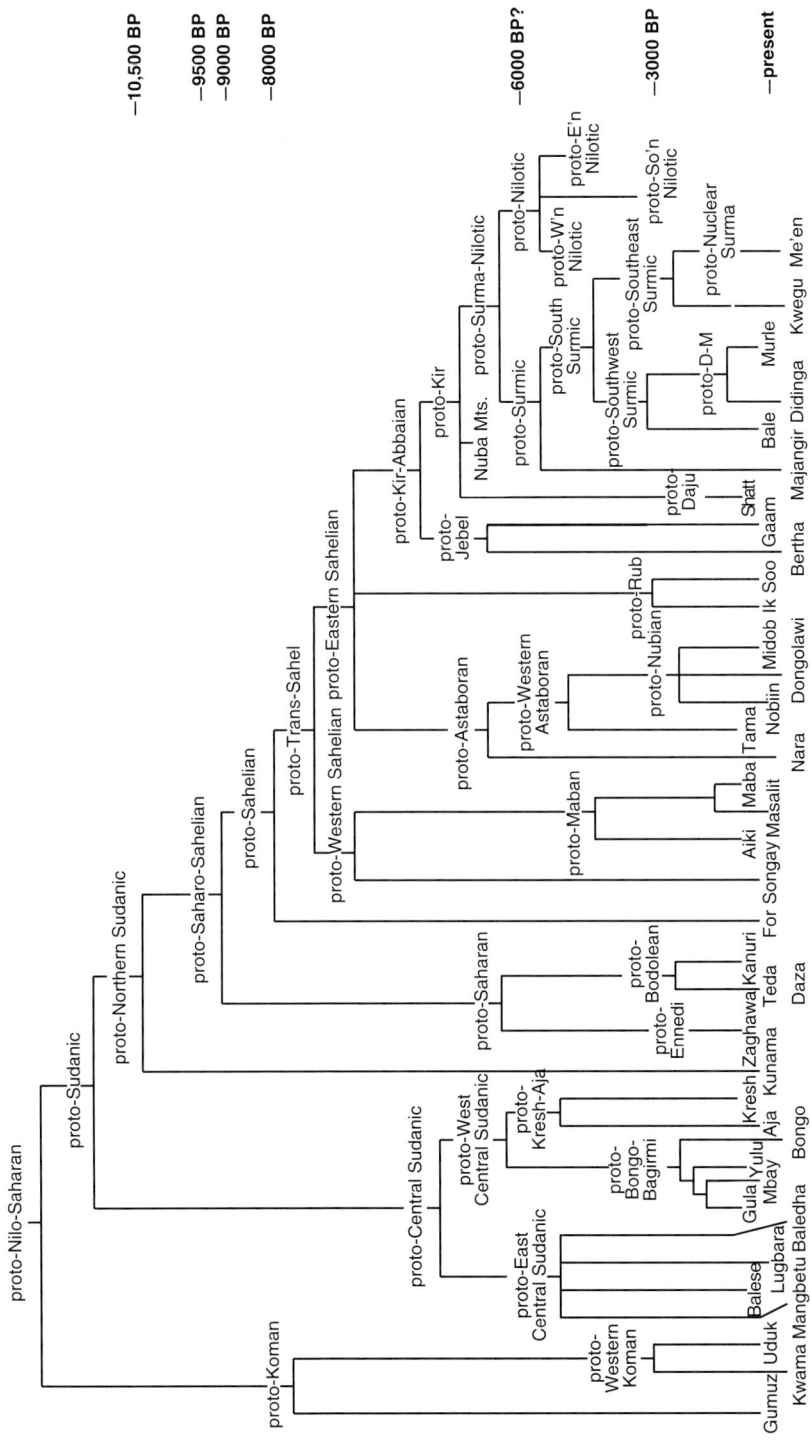

Figure 3.1 Nilo-Saharan linguistic stratigraphy. BP = before the present.

Through the first two periods in the stratigraphic tree, Nilo-Saharan peoples were still food collectors in their economy. The earliest vocabulary indicative of the deliberate manipulation and tending of food resources occurs at the proto-Northern Sudanic node in the tree – in historical terms, during the period represented by the proto-Northern Sudanic stratum in the Nilo-Saharan stratigraphy. The lexical reconstructions have been published previously.[13] But in visualizing how one determines which kinds of word meaning are actually diagnostic of food production and which are not, it may be helpful to look at the relevant reconstructed subsistence lexicon traceable to the proto-Northern Sudanic stratum. Here are those root words, grouped according to what each implies about subsistence:

### Proto-Northern Sudanic subsistence lexicon, not by itself diagnostic of food production

1. *yaayr    'cow' [adds Nilo-Saharan *r noun suffix to earlier PNS *yaay 'meat']
2. *way or *'way    'grain' [not yet known earlier in the family]
3. *keen    'ear of grain' [not yet known earlier in the family]
4. *p'ɛl    'grindstone' [not yet known earlier in the family]

### Proto-Northern Sudanic lexicon diagnostic of livestock-raising

5. *yaaṯ    'to (drive to) water (animals)' [earlier proto-Nilo-Saharan (PNS) *yaa 'drink' plus PNS *ṯ causative suffix, changing 'drink' to 'cause to drink']
6. *sʸuuk    'to drive (animals, to pasture)' [earlier PNS *sʸuu 'lead off, start out' plus PNS *k causative suffix, changing 'start out' to 'cause to start out']
7. *ndʸɔw    'to milk' [PNS *ndʸɔ 'to squeeze' plus PNS *w, focused action suffix]
8. *ɔroh    'thornbush pen' [noun not yet known earlier in the family]

### Other proto-Northern Sudanic new lexicon of material culture

9. *ted    'to make a pot' [verb not yet known earlier in the family]

13 C. Ehret, 'Linguistic stratigraphies and Holocene history in northeastern Africa', in M. Chlodnicki and K. Kroeper (eds.), *Archaeology of Early Northeastern Africa* (Posnan Archaeological Museum, 2006), 1019–55; 'A linguistic history of cultivation and herding in northeastern Africa', in A.G. Fahmy et al. (eds.), *Windows on the African Past: Current Approaches to African Archaeobotany* (Frankfurt: Africa Magna, 2011), 185–208.

Root word 1, for cow, is not in itself diagnostic of food production because wild cattle lived in the early Holocene in the parts of the Sahara inhabited by the Northern Sudanians. Root words 2–4 in similar fashion are not diagnostic of cultivation because they are words just as necessary in a wild-grain-collecting economy as in a grain-cultivating one. Roots 5–8, in contrast, are diagnostic of food production. The first two are verbs for actions explicitly directed at tending and looking after animals. Root 7 connotes an activity possible only with animals that are at least partially tamed and that are used to being in close contact with humans; and root word 8 names a structure in which to keep animals at night to protect them from predators.[14]

So while the word for cow does not by itself require the deliberate tending of livestock, root words 5–8 do. The existence of a word for cow in proto-Northern Sudanic, but no word for any other domestic animal, does, however, identify cows as the animals that the Northern Sudanians had begun to tend. The Northern Sudanians utilized grains for food and ground them into flour, although evidence is lacking that they cultivated the grains. Most interesting for archaeological correlation, they were the possessors and makers of ceramic wares.

In the next two periods in the linguistic stratigraphy, the proto-Saharo-Sahelian and proto-Sahelian eras, additional bodies of root words diagnostic of livestock-raising, and specifically of the raising of cattle, came into use. To the proto-Saharo-Sahelian period can be traced nouns for 'bull' and 'heifer'. A breeding taxonomy, and especially one that distinguishes young female animals that have not yet borne young, is a conclusive diagnostic marker of livestock-raising. An additional noun for the thornbush livestock pen, along with a general verb for the activities of herding animals and an additional verb with the meaning 'to milk', also date to this period.

To the same proto-Saharo-Sahelian period can be dated a major development in residential patterns. Several new nouns in the proto-Saharo-Sahelian language – for an open area within a settlement, for an enclosed yard of a homestead, for round houses, and for a granary – reveal the emergence of larger, sedentary settlements.

By the close of the proto-Sahelian period, the next era in the linguistic stratigraphy, terms for a castrated steer and for a young bull had also become part of the breeding taxonomy, along with a noun that may have applied originally to an outlying cattle encampment, a feature possibly indicative

---

14 Ehret, 'Linguistic stratigraphies'.

of seasonal transhumance. A striking new feature in lexical history at the proto-Sahelian stage was an added new field of livestock meanings. For the first time, terminology relating to both goats and sheep, including generic as well as breeding terms for both animals, came into use. Goats and sheep were not indigenous wild animals of the regions of early Nilo-Saharan peoples, but were domesticated in the Middle East. The presence of terms for these animals indicates that the herding of both of them spread to the Nilo-Saharans at least as early as the proto-Sahelian node in the linguistic stratigraphy. It comports, as well, with the inference that these peoples had begun to domesticate cattle in the previous two eras and thus that the proto-Sahelian communities incorporated sheep and goats into an already evolving pastoral economy (see also Chapter 18).

The linguistic geography of the early stages of Nilo-Saharan divergence, depicted on the family tree (Figure 3.1), favours a location for the proto-Northern Sudanic society in the southern half of the eastern Sahara. On through the proto-Saharo-Sahelian period, these communities mostly likely occupied a wide but still relatively restricted zone of settlement, in areas extending westwards from the Nile towards the Tibesti Range. Following the proto-Sahelian era, however, a vast spreading out of the daughter languages of proto-Sahelian took place, reaching the western edge of the Ethiopian highlands in the east to as far west as modern-day Mali.

These linguistic findings fit in striking detail with the early Holocene archaeological succession of the southern half of the Sahara:[15]

1. 8500–7500 BCE: Pottery-making peoples, who apparently tended cattle in some fashion and lived in relatively ephemeral sites, inhabited parts of the southern eastern Sahara. The best-known finds come from Nabta Playa at the farthest south of modern-day Egypt, but this population also inhabited areas, as yet poorly known, further south and west in northern parts of Sudan and far southeastern Libya.

2. 7200–7000 BCE: A new stage in these developments appears in the same areas, with more significant evidence of cattle and more sedentary, larger settlements with, among other features, granaries and round houses.

15 F. Wendorf and R. Schild, 'Nabta Playa and its role in the northeastern African history', *Anthropological Archaeology*, 20 (1998), 97–123; F. Wendorf and R. Schild (eds.), *Holocene Settlement of the Egyptian Sahara*, 2 vols. (New York: Kluwer Academic/Plenum, 2001–2); R. Kuper and S. Kröpelin, 'Climate-controlled Holocene occupation in the Sahara', *Science*, 313 (2006), 803–7; M. Honegger et al., 'Archaeological excavations at Kerma (Sudan)', *Documents de la mission archéologique suisse au Soudan* (Université de Neuchâtel, 2009).

3. 6400–6000 BCE: The first remains of goats and sheep appear in sites of the region.

4. 6000–4500 BCE: This pastoral economy spreads across a vast expanse of the southern half of the Sahara and the adjacent Sahel zone, extending from the edge of the Ethiopian highlands to as far west as the Hoggar mountains and the great bend of the Niger River in Mali.

Figure 3.2 summarizes the point-for-point fit of the lexical reconstruction of this economic and population history with the Saharan archaeological record.

Recent archaeological work adds a further point of potential correlation. Chemical studies of residues in pots from southern Libya from around 5000 BCE reveal the by-products of processed milk.[16] The lexical histories of terms in Nilo-Saharan for processing milk into ghee or butter place this development in the period following the breakup of the proto-Sahelian society,[17] and thus a date of 5000 BCE is quite in keeping with the milk evidence from pottery in the Sahara. The presence earlier in time of verbs for 'to milk' suggests that milking itself goes back to still earlier stages in the adoption of pastoral pursuits by Northern Sudanian peoples. And that finding raises the question of whether or not milk residues might also be found in eastern Saharan pottery from the eighth millennium, if archaeologists were to undertake this kind of investigation.

Reconstruction of the early Nilo-Saharan subsistence lexicons raises a further issue for future archaeological investigation: the timing of the transition from solely plant food collecting to crop cultivation. The proto-Northern Sudanic language had terms for the utilization of grains as food, but, as far as is known, no terms diagnostic of cultivation. Root words specifically diagnostic of, at the least, protecting and looking after the growth of plant food sources occur for the first time at the next historical stage, in the proto-Saharo-Sahelian language. These include three verbs that always refer to cultivation activities in all later periods in the language family, along with a noun for a cultivated plot (Figure 3.2).[18] The major residential shift to more complex, more sedentary settlements in the later eighth millennium is in keeping with a history in which the first steps towards cultivation took place in that era. The presence of granaries in those sites, along with the occurrence

---

16 J. Dunne et al., 'First dairying in green Saharan Africa in the fifth millennium BC', *Nature*, 48 (2012), 390–4.

17 For this conclusion, see discussion in Ehret, *A Historical-Comparative Reconstruction of Nilo-Saharan*, under Nilo-Saharan root #1118.

18 Ehret, 'Linguistic stratigraphies'.

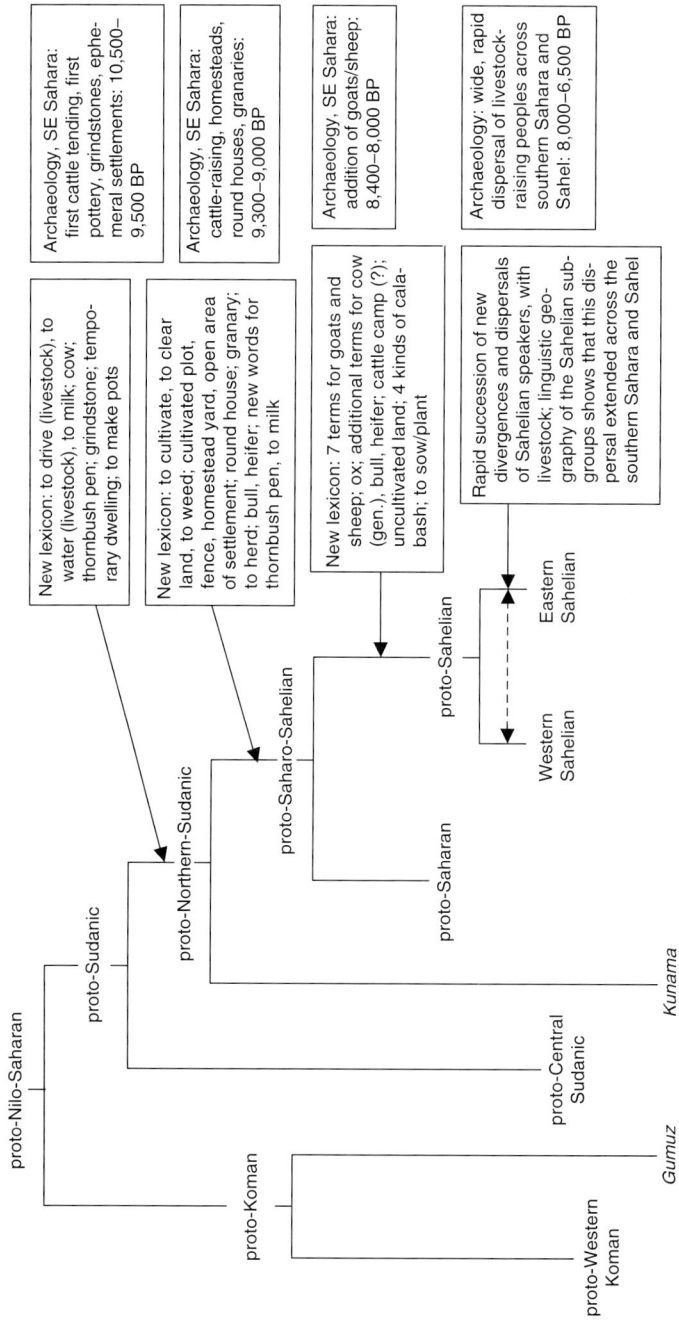

Figure 3.2 Nilo-Saharan family tree: new subsistence lexicon, from proto-North Sudanic to proto-Sahelian periods.

for the first time in the proto-Saharo-Sahelian language of a root word for granary, also favours at least incipient cultivation – although the collection of wild grains, if carried on intensively enough, might also have encouraged the building of granaries.

On the other hand, the available direct evidence from archaeobotany is as yet non-determinative. Archaeologists have recovered sorghum seeds from the late eighth millennium at Nabta Playa, but they are not distinguishable from those of wild sorghum.[19]

Two more verbs for the deliberate tending of plant foods reconstruct to the next stratum in Nilo-Saharan, the proto-Sahelian era. The presence of words for sheep and goats in the proto-Sahelian language dates this period to around 6400–6000 BCE (Figure 3.2). The proto-Sahelian language also had four different terms for melons and gourds.[20] The reconstruction of a cluster of terms for this related set of plants suggests that the plants were culturally salient to the proto-Sahelians and that the first stages in the domestication of this particular suite of crops, botanically of Sudanic African origin, may date to that period also. Thus far, however, direct archaeobotanical evidence confirming or disconfirming these propositions is lacking.

### Herding and cultivation in northeastern Africa

The second major grouping of peoples who participated in the development of food-producing ways of life in the southern eastern Sahara were the early speakers of languages of the Cushitic branch of the Afroasiatic language phylum. The lands of the proto-Cushitic society most probably lay in the mountainous and hilly country of the southern eastern Sahara, east of the Nile and inland from the Red Sea, sometime before 6500 BCE. Following the breakup of the proto-Cushitic society, Cushitic speakers carried their ways of life south and southeastwards, first into Eritrea and along the northern fringes of the Ethiopian highlands and then, following the Ethiopian Rift Valley, southwards through the highlands, with their farthest south outlier, the Southern Cushites, moving into northern Kenya around or just before 3000 BCE.[21] The reasons behind the proposed dates and lands in which

---

19 J.A. Dahlberg and K. Wasilykowa, 'Images and statistical analyses of early sorghum remains (8000 BP) from the Nabta Playa archaeological site in the Western Desert, southern Egypt', *Vegetation History and Archaeobotany*, 5 (1996), 293–9.

20 Ehret, 'Linguistic stratigraphies'.

21 Ehret, 'Linguistic history of cultivation', presents a detailed substantiation of this history, backed up with the Cushitic comparative phonological apparatus for validating the individual lexical reconstructions.

this history took place will become clearer once we have considered the lexical evidence for the proto-Cushitic economy.

The proto-Cushites were already herders of livestock. Their lexicon included two verbs for the herding of animals (*galaal- and *der-) and a noun for a thorn-fenced pen (*dall-), along with terms for cow (*šaʕ-), bull (*yaw-), and bull-calf (*leg-). It possessed, as well, a collective term for goats and sheep (*ʔayz-) and a word for goat (*anaaʕ-) as well as terms for ram/he-goat (*ʔorg-), kid/lamb (*ʔaff-), and young female sheep or goat (*rangan-). Both these sets of evidence, because they include breeding terms and verbs for herding, are directly diagnostic of livestock-raising. In addition, the proto-Cushites possessed a word for the donkey (*ħarle-). But since the Red Sea hills were the ancient heartland of the wild range of donkeys, and because in a few Cushitic languages this term refers to wild equines, it is likely that the proto-Cushites had not yet begun the domestication of the donkey.

Were the proto-Cushites also cultivators of crops? Grains were clearly important in their subsistence: they had two words for sorghum varieties (*ʕag- and harr-), two words for other grains, as yet of uncertain species (*ʕayl-, possibly a Panicum species, and *maʕaar-), and a term for grain prepared as food (*dif-). On the other hand, no terms diagnostic of cultivation have yet been traced back to the proto-Cushitic language, and so for now it seems probable that the proto-Cushites were still collectors of wild grains.[22]

Diagnostic lexical indicators of cultivation turn up, however, at the second node in the Cushitic family tree, proto-Agaw-East-South Cushitic – specifically verbs for cultivating (*ʔibr-/*ʔabr-) and weeding (*ʔarum-) and a noun for a cultivated field (*baayr-). Two new grain terms came into use in that period as well, one apparently for finger millet (*dangaws-/*dingaws-) and the other for tef (*tl'eff-). The fact that both are indigenously domesticated crops of the Ethiopian highlands indicates that adoption of these crops may have proceeded in tandem with the switchover from collection to cultivation of grains. Also, from this period onwards in Cushitic history, terms specifically and always referring to domestic donkeys came into use, suggesting that the domestication of donkeys began also in this era. Figure 3.3 gives the family tree of the early stages of Cushitic divergence and depicts the stratigraphy of the lexical evidence.

When did these stages of agricultural history unfold in the Horn of Africa? Because the archaeology of the crucial regions is as yet little known, there

---

22 See Ehret, *History and the Testimony of Language*, for each of the reconstructed old Cushitic root words presented in the preceding paragraphs.

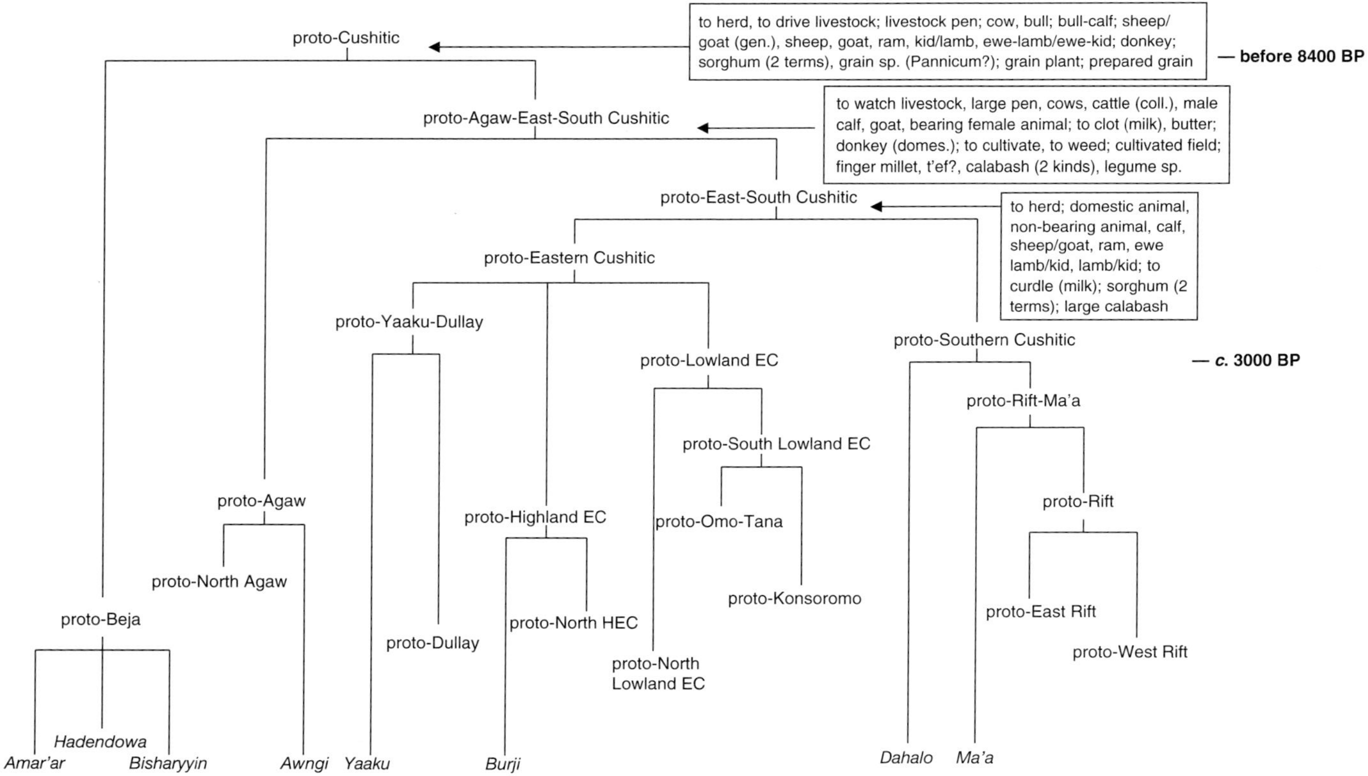

Figure 3.3 The family tree of the early stages of Cushitic divergence.

exist currently just two nodes in the linguistic stratigraphy of Cushitic to which we can assign very rough calendar dates. The more recent dating relates to the history of the Southern Cushites. The early Southern Cushites are generally accepted to have been the makers of the various facies of an archaeological tradition of Kenya known as the Savanna Pastoral Neolithic.[23] The earliest sites of the Savanna Pastoral Neolithic, found in northern Kenya, date to before and around 3000 BCE,[24] thus providing a *terminus ante quem* for the spread of Cushitic peoples southwards through the Rift Valley region of the Ethiopian highlands.

The second Cushitic correlation relates to a much earlier point on the timeline, and it rests on a correlation of archaeological findings with the word histories of two terms for small livestock. Nilo-Saharan peoples, as we discovered from the lexical evidence, fully adopted the raising of goats and sheep by the proto-Sahelian period (see Figure 3.2). The first certain archaeological evidence of the arrival of these animals in the eastern Sahara dates to the centuries 6400–6000 BCE. When the proto-Sahelians began to keep sheep and goats, they adopted their two primary terms for goat, *ay and *nay, from a Cushitic language. Evidently the early Cushites were the intermediaries in the spread of the animal to the Nilo-Saharans.

The sources of those proto-Sahelian words were the two proto-Cushitic root words already cited, *ʔayz- 'goat, sheep' and *anaaʕ- 'goat'. Now, the salient point here is that the borrowed forms of both terms trace, not to proto-Cushitic itself, but to a particular, very early daughter language of proto-Cushitic. The reconstructed proto-Sahelian root word *ay 'goat' derives ultimately from proto-Cushitic *ʔayz-; but its pronunciation reflects the Northern Cushitic version of that root, as attested in the one Northern Cushitic language, Bedauye, that is still spoken today. In ancient Northern Cushitic, proto-Cushitic *z became *y, yielding the modern-day Bedauye general term for small stock, *ay* 'goat, sheep', and thus *ay in the borrowed proto-Sahelian version of the root. Similarly, proto-Sahelian *nay 'goat' shows the phonological changes also seen in Bedauye's regular reflex, *naʔi* 'goat', of proto-Cushitic *anaaʕ-.[25]

23 Ambrose, 'Archaeology and linguistic reconstructions'.

24 See ibid. for a compilation of the relevant dates, uncalibrated. See also J. Barthelme, 'Early evidence for animal domestication in eastern Africa', in J.D. Clark and S.A. Brandt (eds.), *From Hunters to Farmers* (Berkeley: University of California Press, 1984), 200–5; and *Fisher-Hunters and Neolithic Pastoralists in East Turkana, Kenya* (Oxford: British Archaeological Reports, 1985).

25 Ehret, 'Linguistic history of cultivation'; the Medjay of the ancient Egyptian records were apparently a Bedauye people.

The adoption of generic terms for goat by the proto-Sahelians from early Northern Cushitic speakers has two implications, one geographic and the other chronological:

1. The early Northern Cushitic descendants of the proto-Cushites, by the time of the first certain presence of goats and sheep in the eastern Sahara, 6400–6000 BCE, lived nearby to the areas in which the Nilo-Saharan live-stock-raisers of that era resided, most probably in the areas extending eastwards from the Nubian Nile to the Red Sea hills.
2. The divergence of the Northern branch of Cushitic from the rest of Cushitic therefore began no later than the first half of the seventh millennium BCE and very possibly earlier than that, in the eighth millennium.

Goats and sheep, these findings imply, spread from the Middle East south into the regions east of the Nubian Nile, still almost unknown archaeologically, in the first half of the seventh millennium or before.

### Historical background of agriculture in West Africa

Far to the west in Africa lay another major centre of early agricultural innovation. The historical actors in this region spoke languages of the Niger–Congo family, now vastly spread across two thirds of sub-Saharan Africa.[26] Although the full phonological reconstruction of proto-Niger–Congo is a project still in progress,[27] the strength of the lexical and grammatical evidence across the family is such that scholars have no doubts about its validity.[28] The subclassification of the Niger–Congo family (Figure 3.4) reveals that the expansion of the peoples of this family took place over three extended historical stages.

During the first period of expansion, the early descendant societies of the proto-Niger–Congo people spread out across an east–west span of savanna and steppe environments, between roughly 15° N and 20° N, centring on

---

26 G.P. Murdock, *Africa: Its Peoples and their Culture History* (New York: Putnam, 1957), was the first to make the case for an independent West African centre of origin of agriculture in this region.

27 J.M. Stewart, 'The potential of proto-Potou-Akanic-Bantu as a pilot proto-Niger–Congo, and the reconstructions updated', *Journal of African Languages and Linguistics*, 23 (2002), 197–224; and preliminary findings of work currently underway by C. Ehret.

28 K. Williamson and R. Blench, 'Niger–Congo', in B. Heine and D. Nurse (eds.), *African Languages* (Cambridge University Press, 2000), 11–42; D. Nurse et al., *Verbal Categories in Niger–Congo* (St Johns: Memorial University of Newfoundland, 2008), 57–72.

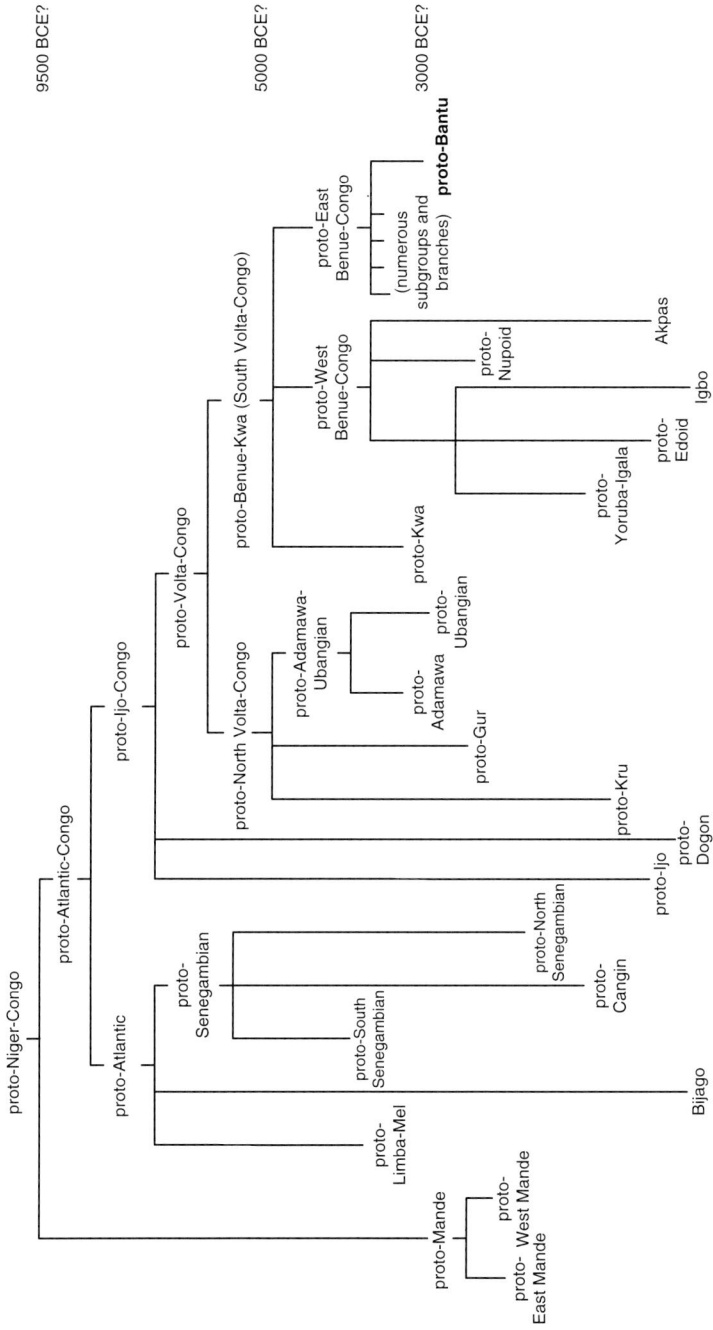

Figure 3.4 The Niger–Congo family tree.

modern-day Mali.[29] Proto-Niger–Congo divergcd, as shown in the Niger–Congo family tree (Figure 3.4), into two daughter languages, each of which in turn became the protolanguage of one of the two primary branches of the family. These branches are Mande and Atlantic–Congo. Proto-Atlantic–Congo, the ancestor language of the latter branch, then diverged into two daughter languages, proto-Atlantic and proto-Ijo–Congo, followed not long after by the divergence of proto-Ijo–Congo into three further daughter languages: a language ancestral to the modern-day Dogon cluster of languages; a language ancestral to the Ijo group; and the protolanguage of the far-flung Volta–Congo branch.

The second extended period of Niger–Congo expansion began with a southwards dispersal of languages of one sub-branch of Volta–Congo, the Benue–Kwa, across a swathe of woodland and rainforest extending between what is now southern Côte d'Ivoire on the west and central Cameroon on the east. Linguists estimate that the Benue–Kwa divergence began roughly around the fifth millennium BCE,[30] several millennia later than the initial Niger–Congo dispersal.

The third major era of Niger–Congo expansion began around the third millennium BCE. The proto-Bantu society, an offshoot of the East Benue–Congo subgroup of Benue–Kwa (Figure 3.4), diversified between 3000 and 1000 BCE into a large number of daughter societies, as Bantu communities migrated successively deeper into the equatorial rainforests of Central Africa.[31] During the same period, peoples of the Ubangian subgroup of Volta–Congo spread eastwards through the Ubangi river basin of the modern-day Central African Republic, with their farthest expansion reaching the far east of that basin as early as the second millennium BCE.[32] A series of subsequent movements of Bantu peoples across East Africa and into south

---

29 For a fuller argument of this case, see C. Ehret, 'Holocene migrations as determined from linguistics in sub-Saharan Africa', in I. Ness and P. Bellwood (eds.), *The Encyclopedia of Global Human Migration*, vol. 1 (Chichester: Wiley-Blackwell, 2013), chap. 13.

30 R.G. Armstrong, *The Study of African Languages* (Ibadan: Institute of African Studies, 1964); Ehret, *History and the Testimony of Language*, chap. 5.

31 B. Heine et al., 'Neuere Ergebnisse zur Territorialgeschichte der Bantu', in W.J.G. Möhlig et al. (eds.), *Zur Sprachgeschichte and Ethnohistorie in Afrika* (Berlin: Reimer, 1977); C. Ehret, 'Bantu expansions: re-envisioning a central problem of early African history', *International Journal of African Historical Studies*, 34/1 (2001), 5–41. C. Ehret, 'Linguistic testimony and migration histories', in J. Lucassen et al. (eds.), *Migration History in World History* (Leiden: Brill, 2010), 113–54, maps the stages of Bantu expansion.

32 D.E. Saxon, 'Linguistic evidence for the eastward spread of Ubangian peoples', in Ehret and Posnansky (eds.), *Archaeological and Linguistic Reconstruction*, 66–77.

Central and southern Africa began in the first millennium BCE and early first millennium CE. This set of expansions rounded out the spread of Niger–Congo languages across the continent.[33]

### Archaeological correlations for early Niger–Congo dispersal

What factors might have set in motion the early Niger–Congo expansions? Current archaeological work in the centre of the West African areas where the Niger–Congo language family most probably originated offers some plausible answers. Excavations at Ounjougou in Dogon country on the Bandiagara escarpment of eastern Mali reveal a major new subsistence strategy and an accompanying major pyrotechnological advance in the tenth millennium BCE. In this region, Erik Huysecom and his colleagues have uncovered an economy based on grain collection, with ceramic technology already in place *before* 9400 BCE.[34] The tools of the societies who brought these innovations into being belong to an early facies of a long-lived archaeological tradition, the West African Microlithic, characteristically found across the early Niger–Congo-speaking regions. The investigators conclude that the people of this cultural horizon based their subsistence on such African grains as fonio (*Digitaria exilis*), which used to grow in extensive and often dense stands in these steppe and dry savanna grassland environments. They propose that the communities of this time and place did not grind their grains into flour, but instead boiled them whole in their pots, and that the invention of ceramic technology was therefore integral to the emergence of this economy.

In keeping with the archaeological expectations, and supporting the conclusion that the makers of these sites were Niger–Congo people, the proto-Niger–Congo (PNC) language did in fact possess a root word **phóndé for the grain fonio.[35] Reconstructing the proto-Niger–Congo consonants and

---

33 For the history of these expansions, see the sources in footnotes 3–5 above.
34 E. Huysecom et al., 'The emergence of pottery in Africa during the tenth millennium cal BC: new evidence from Ounjougou (Mali)', *Antiquity*, 83/322 (2009), 905–17.
35 This root, with a provisional interim reconstruction **pʰóndé, occurs in both the Mande and Atlantic branches as well as in the Dogon branch and in the Ubangian subgroup of the Volta–Congo sub-branch. In the proto-Gbaya (Ubangian) reflex, *fón, the meaning shifted to sorghum; fonio does not grow in the wetter savanna environments in which the Gbaya peoples live. R. Blench, *Archaeology and the African Past* (Lanham, MD: AltaMira Press, 2006), provides a large sample of the reflexes of this root in the Mande and Atlantic languages. C. Ehret, in a review article of this book in the *Journal of African Archaeology*, 6/2 (2008), 259–65, suggests that borrowing spread may account for these terms, but the complex sound change histories in these words, along with the occurrence of this root word far away in the Ubangian branch, much better support Blench's conclusion that this is a very ancient Niger–Congo root word. An additional attestation

vowels is still very much a work in progress; the double asterisk here indicates that pronunciation of the reconstructed root shape is a provisional formulation. Two verbs reconstructed to proto-Niger–Congo indicate an additional possibility: that these early collectors of fonio and other grains may already have been taking measures aimed at enhancing the outcomes of their grain-collecting. One PNC root **k$^h$ɔk$^h$, to judge from its meanings in modern-day languages, denoted the action of clearing away competing plant growth to enhance the growth of favoured food plants.[36] A second PNC verb **ba may have referred more generally to digging up the ground rather than specifically to cultivation, although its reflexes in modern-day languages more often than not refer specifically to agricultural digging.[37]

By the proto-Volta–Congo period (Figure 3.4), the transition to agriculture seems more surely to have been underway. Two new verbs and a noun of specifically agricultural meaning had come into use by that period: a verb **kpa 'to clear a field'; a verb **gbiɛ 'to cultivate'; and a noun **p$^h$ùk$^h$o 'cultivated field'.[38] This period, dating to the sixth millennium BCE or earlier, is as yet poorly known, still lacking sites with determinative evidence of food production. New archaeological work to test these linguistic predictions against the material record is an urgent matter for future work. The earliest staples would likely have been seed crops, such as the grain fonio.

A new stage in the evolution of West African agricultural practices began by no later than the fifth millennium BCE. The archaeological signature of this development is indirect: the adding of ground (and polished) stone axes to the existing West African Microlithic toolkit. This innovation in tool

of this root not included by Blench is Dogon fõ. The alert reader may notice that the English term *fonio* is itself a borrowing of the Fulani language's reflex of this ancient root word.

36 Reflexes of this root include, among others, Serer (Atlantic branch): *khokh* 'to cultivate'; More (Volta–Congo, Gur subgroup): *kó* 'to weed, cultivate'; Benue–Kwa: Edo *kɔ* 'to plant'; and proto-Bantu: *kok-ud-* 'to clear away (vegetation)'.

37 Reflexes of this root include, among others, Busa (Mande branch): *ba* 'to cultivate'; Ngala (Volta–Congo, Ubangian subgroup): *ba* 'to plant seeds'; Day (Volta–Congo, Adamawa subgroup): *va-* 'to cultivate'; and Igbo (Benue–Kwa): *ba* 'to dig, break up soil'.

38 Reflexes of **kpa include Buli (Volta–Congo, Gur subgroup): *kpa* 'to clear ground for new crops, hoe between growing plants'; Ngbaka and Gbanziri (Volta–Congo, Ubangian subgroup): *kpa* 'to weed'; Yoruba (Benue–Kwa): *kpakpa* 'cultivated field'. Reflexes of **gbiɛ include Fon (Benue–Kwa): *gbe* 'to weed'; Yoruba (Benue–Kwa): *agbɛ* 'farmer'; and Ngbaka and Gbanziri (Volta–Congo, Ubangian subgroup): *gbie* 'cultivated field'. Reflexes of **p$^h$ùk$^h$o, all having the meaning 'cultivated field', include More *fuyu*, Dagbani *pua* (Volta–Congo, Gur subgroup); proto-Gbaya *fɔ* (Volta–Congo, Ubangian subgroup); and Brong *vwo*, Twi *afuw* (Benue–Kwa group); this noun derives from a proto-Volta–Congo verb seen in proto-Bantu: *-pùk-* 'to dig up (earth)' and Pambia (Volta–Congo, Ubangian subgroup): *fuwu* 'to hoe a field'.

technology initially took hold across the woodland and rainforest zones from Ghana to Cameroon.[39] Linguistic arguments locate the early expansions of the Benue–Kwa branch of the Niger–Congo peoples in just this span of lands, and date them roughly to this broad period,[40] indicating that the early Benue–Kwa were the likely innovators.

The plausible accompanying development in the crops of farming would have been a shift to two new staples, both indigenous to higher rainfall environments: yams and oil palms. Oil palms were valued not just for cooking oil pressed from their nuts, but for palm wine fermented from their sap. The adoption of these crops would have allowed early Benue–Kwa communities to move from the savannas southwards into the woodland and rainforest environments inland from the West African coasts. Yams and oil palms both require direct sunlight, and stone axes would have enabled the clearing of patches of forest for growing those crops.

After 3000 BCE, cultures with pottery and stone axes, of the kinds associated with the Benue–Kwa peoples, spread southwards from Cameroon into the equatorial rainforest regions of Africa, in keeping both chronologically and in location with the linguistically inferred early migrations of Bantu-speakers. A considerable number of detailed linguistic and other studies have probed the multiple histories of regional and local population movements that spread Bantu languages across a third of Africa, and raised hypotheses about the archaeological reflections of these movements. The evidence strongly suggests that the initial penetration of Bantu-speakers into the equatorial rainforest zone, between 3000 and 1000 BCE, followed river routes.[41] The reconstructed lexicon of proto-Bantu solidly shows that the transition from cultivation to domestication had fully taken place by that period. The proto-Bantu possessed a variety of words for individual crops – native to West Africa, but not native to the areas into which they were expanding – as well as terms for the domestic goat: to cultivate (*-sad-); cultivated field (*-gunda); two species of yam (*-kua and *-pama); black-eyed peas (*-kondɛ); the African groundnut (*-jogo); bottle gourds (*-sopa); oil palm (*-bila and *-ba) and palm oil (*-gadi̧); and goat (*-boli̧) and he-goat (*-bɔkɔ).

Only subsequently did Bantu-speaking communities spread more widely into rainforest areas away from the main rivers, with the last major rainforest expansion, of the Mongo, penetrating up several rivers into the heart of the

39  T. Shaw and S.G.H. Daniells, 'Excavations at Iwo-Eleru, Ondo State, Nigeria', *West African Journal of Archaeology*, 14 (1984), 7–100.
40  Armstrong, *Study of African Languages*; Ehret, *History and the Testimony of Language*, chap. 5.
41  Klieman, *'The Pygmies Were Our Compass'*.

Congo basin between 400 and 1100 CE. Other studies have combined linguistics with the available archaeology, and sometimes with palynology and oral traditions, in constructing regional histories of Bantu expansion beyond the equatorial rainforest, into eastern and southern Africa, in the eras since 1000 BCE.[42]

## Omotic agriculture

One other, apparently separate and independent development of crop cultivation took place in Africa – in the southwestern parts of the Ethiopian highlands, a region of tropical mountain rainforest, broken by deep river valleys – during the period 6000–3000 BCE. The historical actors in this case spoke languages of the Omotic branch of the Afroasiatic language phylum. Their early staple crop was the enset plant, possibly supplemented by indigenous Ethiopian yam species. Enset, which is related to and looks very much like a banana plant, is a very different food source, harvested not for its fruit but for its very large edible corm and inner stem. In his recent work on Omotic agricultural history, Shiferaw Assefa reconstructs the histories of the words not just for the enset plant itself, but for useful parts of the plant, for the stages of growth of the plant, and for the processes and tools of cultivation.[43]

The proto-Omotic language possessed at least two terms for parts of the enset plant, including a term that most probably denoted the edible corm and inner stalk, along with terms for two tools used uniquely in the processing of enset. The earliest known word diagnostic of cultivation traces, however, to the second major era in Omotic history, the proto-North Omotic era, probably around the fourth millennium BCE. This verb, *tokk-, specifically connoted the planting, as opposed to the sowing, of a crop, exactly the kind of activity that enset cultivation involves. The proto-North Omotic language also had terms for each of the four major growth stages of the enset plant, strong indicators of the high cultural salience of this crop.

Assefa shows that several additional elements began to be blended into the Omotic agricultural system during the same era. Terms for cow and sheep, for milking, and for sorghum each trace back to the proto-North Omotic language. The earliest word for sheep appears to be borrowed from a Nilo-Saharan language spoken in South Sudan not far from the early Omotic lands,

42 Ehret, *African Classical Age*; Schoenbrun, *A Green Place, A Good Place*; Gonzales, *Societies, Religion, and History*; Saidi, *Women's Authority*.

43 Shiferaw Assefa, *Omotic Peoples and the Early History of Agriculture in Southern Ethiopia*, unpublished PhD thesis (University of California, Los Angeles, 2011).

and sorghum is likely also to have been an introduction from Nilo-Saharan peoples living immediately west of the southern Ethiopian highlands. Assefa's interpretation is that the early Omotic farmers may particularly have exploited environmental transition zones, cultivating sorghum in fields lower down their mountains, and enset in areas higher up. The regions in which this agriculture arose are almost completely unknown archaeologically as yet, and so Assefa's findings raise a variety of agendas and questions for future archaeological studies.

### Cultivation versus domestication

The African linguistic evidence has implications for a current issue in archaeobotany, and that is the distinction between food production and domestication. By food production is meant the deliberate tending of plants and/or animals. Cultivation of crops and the raising of animals is the first stage of food production. Domestication is a later evolutionary consequence of food production: the processes undertaken in tending food sources themselves affect the evolutionary development of the crops, changing them from their wild into their domestic forms. Plants, for example, best reproduce in nature if their ears or seedpods break easily and scatter the seed. There will always be some plants whose ears or pods do not break as easily as the rest. So, when people harvest plants, they will lose a higher proportion of the more easily scattered seed but retain a greater portion of the less easily scattered seed. Gradually over time, more and more of the seed that people harvest and that they plant back into the ground will be from the seed-retentive plants. In this way human activities over the long run can gradually bring about the genetic evolution of a wild plant into its domesticated form.

But how long does this process take? How long a time can elapse between the point at which people begin to cultivate plants or herd animals and the evolution of the wild forms into archaeologically recognizable domesticated forms? This in-between stage seems frequently to have been a protracted one. Recent studies suggest, for example, that the lag between the first cultivation of grain crops and the full emergence of domesticated forms of those crops may have been as much as 2,000 years, both in the Middle East and in the separate Indian centres of domestication.[44]

In Africa, if one goes by the available archaeology, the lag between the first cultivation of plant foods and the appearance of identifiably domestic forms

---

44 R. G. Allaby et al., 'The genetic expectations of a protracted model for the origins of domesticated crops', *Proceedings of the National Academy of Sciences*, 105/37 (2008), 13982–6.

may have been even more protracted. The great gaps in our archaeological knowledge of Africa are surely part of the explanation for the lack of finds so far of identifiably domesticated plant forms as early as the linguistic evidence indicates. The gaps in the Holocene archaeology of the continent are many and large – for the crucial periods from the tenth to third millennium BCE, and in many of the crucial regions, it is more gap than knowledge. Until recently, as well, work specifically directed towards identifying the material markers of early agriculture was rarely a priority. That has now changed. Nevertheless, because of the immensity of the challenge, it may be a long time before the histories proposed from linguistics can be fully tested against the material record (compare Chapter 18).

But even considering this factor, the delay between the first food production and the development of domesticated forms of the cultivated crops may have been especially long in Africa. One long-term consequence of domestication in the Middle East, for instance, was the development of grain crops with non-shattering ears. But the same factor may not have been crucial among the Nilo-Saharan peoples of Africa. A very old method among Nilo-Saharan cultivators was to harvest grain with a tiny curved blade, clasped between the forefinger and thumb, cutting off each individual grain ear directly into a bag held under it. With this technique, even if the ear shattered easily, few of the grains would be lost, and so the harvesting process would not strongly select for non-shattering ears.

Archaeobotanists have noted a second factor that may have slowed the emergence of domesticated forms in Africa. In many of the areas where cultivation first developed in Africa, the wild varieties of African cultivated grains still grow today in unfarmed land near the fields. In this kind of situation, recurrent interbreeding of wild and cultivated varieties of crops may have taken place for many centuries, slowing the development of changes in seed morphology diagnostic of domestication until long after cultivation was already established. This is, of course, a factor that may have operated in other parts of the world as well.

## Island South Asia and Oceania

Another world region for which scholars have generated major bodies of lexical evidence relating to early agricultural history is island South Asia and Oceania. The evidence from, in particular, the Austronesian language family depicts a complex history of agricultural change across these areas. This history began with the settlement of the speakers of proto-Austronesian on the island of Taiwan in the fifth and fourth millennia BCE. Sometime in the fourth millennium, one descendant society of the proto-Austronesians, the ancestral Malayo-Polynesians, moved southwards from Taiwan, first to the Philippines and then to parts of Indonesia. Still later, after 1500 BCE, peoples of the Oceanic sub-branch of the Malayo-Polynesians scattered far out into the Pacific.[45]

The lexical evidence is clear that the speakers of the proto-Austronesian language were indeed cultivators of rice and other grains and not just intensive collectors. Their possession of a noun specifically connoting seed rice (*bineSiq) is one diagnostic indicator. They also had a word that served as a noun for cultivated garden and a verb for the activity of cultivating it (*qumah); a noun for uncultivated land (*quCaN); and a verb for clearing a field for cultivation (*tebaS). At least two other words diagnostic of cultivation – for fallow field (*talun) and for weeding (*babaw) – trace back to the next era, the proto-Malayo-Polynesian period.[46]

A fascinating feature of Austronesian agricultural history, as revealed in the lexical evidence, is how greatly the focus and content of their agricultural practices changed as the early Austronesian communities spread outwards into new environments. The proto-Austronesians brought to Taiwan an already evolving grain-based cultivating system from the lower Yangtze region. Rice was of high salience in their culture. Their subsistence vocabulary included words specifying the rice plant (*pajay), harvested rice (*beRas), cooked rice (*Semay), rice stalks left standing after harvest (*zaRami), and rice husk (*qeCa). They also knew of at least three varieties of millet (*baCar, *zawa), including foxtail millet (*beCeŋ), already under cultivation in mainland China by that time. In contrast, only a single ancient word for a tuber plant traces back to the proto-Austronesian language, a term specifically for wild rather than domesticated taro (*biRaq).

But when the proto-Malayo-Polynesians moved south into island South Asia, they adopted a whole additional suite of plants, indigenous to the highly tropical environment into which they moved. The proto-Malayo-Polynesians, but not their earlier proto-Austronesian ancestors, possessed words for yam (*qubi) as well as domesticated taro (*tales) and for banana (*punti), sugarcane (*CebuS), breadfruit (*kuluR), sago (*Rambia), and

45  P. Bellwood, 'The origins and spread of agriculture in the Indo-Pacific Region', in D. Harris (ed.), *The Origins and Spread of Agriculture and Pastoralism in Eurasia* (London: UCL Press, 1996), 465–98; see also Harris (ed.), passim.
46  Blust, 'Prehistory of the Austronesian-speaking peoples'; Ross et al. (eds.), *Lexicon of Proto Oceanic*.

coconut (*niuR). And whereas a term for wild pig (*babuy) goes back to proto-Austronesian, a term for the domestic pig (*beRek) traces only to the proto-Malayo-Polynesian stage, suggesting that the adoption of domestic pigs dates to no earlier than around the fifth or fourth millennium among Austronesian-speaking peoples.[47]

The spread of the Oceanic branch of the Malayo-Polynesians into the Pacific brought about still further changes in the inherited agricultural repertoire. The speakers of the proto-Oceanic language were the makers of the Lapita culture of that era. This identification of language with culture rests on an exceedingly great number of detailed, point-for-point correlations between the archaeological record of Lapita material culture and the reconstructed lexicons of proto-Oceanic material culture, from agriculture to fishing to boat-building to houses and residence patterns.[48]

The earliest Lapita sites appeared in the Bismarck archipelago in western Oceania around 1500 BCE. Within the next five hundred years, various descendant communities of the proto-Oceanic speakers began a rapid dispersal outwards into the Pacific. Some groups moved to the nearby coasts of Papua New Guinea, settling among the long-established farming populations of that island. But the major thrust of these expansions went eastwards, to the Solomon Islands and Vanuatu, and then from those island regions both northwards to Micronesia and further eastwards to Fiji, Tonga, and Samoa. Later eras of expansion spread the peoples of the Polynesian subgroup of Oceanic from Samoa to as far east as Easter Island and as far north as Hawaii. These communities continued to cultivate a number of the tropical crops of their proto-Malayo-Polynesian ancestors, among them taro (*talo; PAN *tales), the greater yam (*qupi; PMP *qubi), sago (*Rabia; PMP *Rambia), bananas (*pudi; PMP *punti), breadfruit (*kulaR; PMP *kuluR; also *baReqo), coconut (*niuR), and sugarcane (*topu; PMP *CebuS). They also raised the aerial yam (*p$^w$atik). But most strikingly, they seem to have entirely ceased to grow any of the Asian grain crops, dropping from their crop repertory even the old staple crop of the proto-Austronesians, rice.[49]

---

47  Blust, 'Prehistory of the Austronesian-speaking peoples'.
48  Ross et al. (eds.), *Lexicon of Proto Oceanic*. Ross, Pawley, Osmond, and their colleagues, in their studies of the Oceanic branch, provide a model exercise in the building of a detailed archive of linguistic evidence for all aspects of the history of peoples and their cultures. Their work has now grown to four volumes with a fifth in preparation and a sixth in the planning stage, covering plants, natural environment, and all aspects of non-material culture.
49  Ross et al. (eds.), *Lexicon of Proto Oceanic*, 117–38.

A second body of linguistic resources, of immense potential for the history of agricultural origins across island South Asia and western Oceania but as yet little studied, is the Trans-New Guinea language family. The early speakers of this family of languages were the likely originators of the independent development of agricultural ways of life in New Guinea, underway as long ago as the eighth millennium BCE. How much did the adoption of new tropical crops, such as bananas and taro, by the early Malayo-Polynesian communities who spread from the fourth millennium BCE onwards into island South Asia owe to interactions with those already evolving farming societies? To what extent perhaps also did the knowledge and practices of the foraging peoples who lived in other parts of those island regions contribute to these changes? Where, for example, did the various words for the new tropical plants in proto-Malayo-Polynesian and in the Oceanic subgroup of Malayo-Polynesian come from? Will we be able someday to show that at least some of these terms are loanwords from the Trans-New Guinea family, and thus indicators of the transmission of this knowledge from peoples of that language family?[50]

These matters remain open and fascinating prospects for future research. Reconstructing in detail the histories of agricultural lexicons in the Trans-New Guinea language family, a work still in its infancy, would contribute greatly to this project, as would similarly detailed studies of the other non-Austronesian languages of island South Asia.

For the nearby regions of mainland eastern and southern Asia, on the other hand, the potential contribution of linguistic evidence to the history of agriculture remains mostly unexplored. The Sino-Tibetan family of languages offers an especially complex challenge in these respects because so much more remains to be learned about the internal relationships among the languages of the family and about its ancient vocabulary of subsistence. A recent proposal suggests that the earliest speakers of Sino-Tibetan may have originated in areas close to the eastern end of the Himalaya range as much as 6000 or 7000 years ago. According to this view, they may at first have combined gathering and hunting with the raising of root and tuber crops, but did not cultivate rice, which has usually been the most important crop among Sino-Tibetan peoples in more

---

50 G. Barker and M.B. Richards, 'Foraging–farming transitions in island Southeast Asia', *Journal of Archaeological Method and Theory*, 20 (2013), 256–80, shows just how complex the histories of material change and the demographic processes that lie behind these changes are likely to be; see also Huw Barton, Chapter 16.

recent times.[51] A second Asian language family in which a systematic reconstruction of the ancient lexicon of agriculture remains a future project of great importance is Austroasiatic, which includes such languages as Vietnamese and Khmer in Southeast Asia and the Munda group in eastern India.

## Early agriculture and language in Southwest Asia

The Semitic branch of the Afroasiatic phylum affords an additional case study, similar in the complexity of its evidence to the Austronesian and the several African cases, with relevance to our understanding of the early rise of agriculture in a quite different region, the Middle East. The reconstructed subsistence lexicon of proto-Semitic reveals that a developed, mixed farming economy, with both crops and domestic animals, sustained the proto-Semitic society. A noun for a cultivated field (*ḥaql-) and verbs for cultivation (*ḫrṯ-) and for sowing seed (*ḏrʕ-) certify to the primacy of crop-raising. The proto-Semites raised several grain crops, notably wheat (*ḥinṭ-), emmer (*kunāṯ-), and millet (*duḫn-), along with such subsidiary crops as leeks (*karaṯ-), cucumbers (*ḳVrVʔ-), garlic (*ṯūm-), and cumin (*kammūn-). Their tree crops included figs (*tiʔn-), almonds (*ṯaqid-), and pistachios (*buṭn-), and they also raised grapes (*ʕinab- 'grape'; *gapn- 'grape vine') and made wine (*wayn-) from them. In addition, they herded a variety of domestic animals, as their verbs for herding (*rʕy-) and for watering (*šqy-) livestock, as well as their breeding terminologies, make clear. Their most important animals appear to have been sheep (*ʔimmar-; *raḥil- 'ewe'; *ʕatūd- 'ram (?)'; *lVʔVʔ- 'lamb (?)'; *śaw- 'flock of sheep') and goats (*ʕinz- 'she-goat'; *tayš- 'he-goat'; *ʕuriṭ- 'male kid'; *ʕVnVq- 'female kid'; *śaʔn- 'mixed flock, goats and sheep'). They also raised cows (*liʔ-; *ṯawr- 'bull'; *ʔalp- 'steer') and donkeys (*ḥumār- 'male donkey'; *ʔatān- 'female donkey').[52]

But these findings take us back no earlier than the middle Holocene at the earliest. The proto-Semitic language dates most probably to around 4000 BCE, several thousand years *after* the beginnings of cultivation and

---

51 R. Blench and M.W. Post, 'Rethinking Sino-Tibetan phylogeny from the perspective of North East Indian languages', in N. Hill and T. Owen-Smith (eds.), *Trans-Himalayan Linguistics* (Berlin: de Gruyter, 2013).

52 J. Huehnergard, 'Proto-Semitic language and culture', *The American Heritage Dictionary of the English Language*, 5th edn (New York: Houghton Mifflin Harcourt, 2011), 2066–78; L. Kogan, 'Proto-Semitic lexicon', in S. Weninger (ed.), *The Semitic Languages: An International Handbook* (Berlin: de Gruyter, 2011), 79–258.

animal domestication in Southwest Asia.[53] Are there other possible linguistic resources that might carry this picture further back in time? The Caucasian family of languages, today restricted mostly to the areas around the Caucasus mountains, used to extend from the western edges of Iran through Anatolia, as the written records of the extinct ancient Caucasian languages, Hattic, Hurrian, and Urartian, reveal. Because these areas formed an important part of the originating regions of Middle Eastern agriculture in the early Holocene, the proto-Caucasian agricultural lexicon is a prime candidate for future investigation.[54]

## Mesoamerica

The Americas, and especially Mesoamerica, have been another world region in which recent scholarship has applied linguistic evidence to the study of early agricultural history. In contrast to the wide approach taken in Oceanic history, the linguistic study of early American agriculture has not yet given major attention to the kinds of evidence that are inherently indicative of cultivation, namely the verbs and nouns that specifically connote the carrying out of cultivation. The American work has concentrated on the histories of the terms for individual crops.[55] That approach is problematic because across many parts of Mesoamerica the wild progenitors of the cultivated plants, such as squash and beans, grew in the same lands in which people have cultivated those plants for thousands of years. How can we be sure that the

53  A. Kitchen et al., 'Bayesian phylogenetic analysis of Semitic languages identifies an early Bronze Age origin of Semitic in the Near East', *Proceedings of the Royal Society B*, 276 (2009), 2703–10.
54  A. Militarev, 'The prehistory of a dispersal: the proto-Afrasian (Afroasiatic) farming lexicon', in P. Bellwood and C. Renfrew (eds.), *Examining the Farming/Language Dispersal Hypothesis* (Cambridge: McDonald Institute for Archaeological Research, 2002), 135–50, attributes farming to the proto-Afroasiatic society, but this position cannot be sustained for reasons presented in C. Ehret, 'Applying the comparative method in Afroasiatic (Afrasan, Afrasisch)', in R. Voigt (ed.), *'From Beyond the Mediterranean': Akten des 7. internationalen Semitohamitisten-kongresses* (Aachen: Shaker, 2007), 43–70, and, in greater detail, in Ehret, 'Linguistic stratigraphies'.
55  C.H. Brown has expanded the scope of his investigations to include South American and North American as well as Mesoamerican linguistic evidence for early cultivation, e.g. 'Glottochronology and the chronology of maize in the Americas', in J.E. Staller et al. (eds.), *Histories of Maize: Multidisciplinary Approaches to the Prehistory, Biogeography, Domestication, and Evolution of Maize* (Amsterdam and London: Elsevier Academic Press, 2006), 647–73; 'Prehistoric chronology of the common bean in the New World: the linguistic evidence', in J.E. Staller and M.C. Carrasco (eds.), *Pre-Columbian Foodways in Mesoamerica* (New York: Springer, 2010), 273–89; and 'Prehistoric chronology of squash', in press. See also J.H. Hill, 'Proto-Uto-Aztecan: a community of cultivators in central Mexico?', *American Anthropologist*, 103 (2001), 913–34.

reconstruction of old terms for any particular crop implies cultivation rather than the collection of the wild forms of the crop?

Cecil Brown, a major recent contributor to this field of study, confronts this problem by applying the criterion of cultural salience in studying the lexical histories of three major American crops, maize, squash, and beans. He makes use of the linguistic finding that the words for items of major cultural importance tend to be retained in use over very long spans of time and to be replaced by new words only rarely.[56]

What this approach probably most often brings to light is the historical period in which a crop took on particular cultural salience, that is to say, the period when it became a staple of the diet, rather than the earliest period in which it might have been grown. A crop that gains high cultural salience is most often one that has a history of previous cultivation. So the high salience of a crop tends also to mean that the process of domestication of the plant has already been underway. Its position as a mainstay in the diet means that farmers are selecting, consciously or unconsciously, for plant character-istics that yield more product or require less labour and thus make the plant gradually more and more different from its wild ancestor.

But this kind of evidence does not resolve the question of when the practices of cultivation themselves began. Reconstructing ancient verbs and nouns for the activities of cultivation, which does provide diagnostic information, remains a task still to be systematically undertaken for the Americas. In addition, the studies so far have left aside a great many impor-tant crops domesticated by Native Americans: the pumpkin, perhaps first cultivated as early as 8000 BCE in Mexico; the potato, a primary crop of the separate Andean centre of agricultural innovation; sweet potatoes, peanuts, cassava, and yams from the Orinoco and Amazon lowland centre; and such crops as sunflowers, domesticated 3000–4000 years ago in what is today the southeastern United States.

## India

Essentially the same issues as for the Americas feature in the uses that scholars have made of lexical evidence for early agricultural history in India. India, like Mesoamerica, had multiple centres of early food production, and each major centre can be associated with a different language family. At least three geographically separate major zones of innovation existed:

56 Berlin et al., 'Cultural significance and lexical retention'.

southern India, the Ganges basin, and the region around the middle and lower Indus River. Similarly to work in the Americas, linguistic attention thus far has focused on the evidence of old reconstructed names for particular crops.

The southern Indian core areas extended from Gujarat southwards through central parts of southern India. Early cultivated crops in the northern sector of this zone, in Gujarat, included little millet (*Panicum sumatrense*) and the urd bean (*Vigna mungo*). Further south the early farmers also concentrated on grains and pulses: their early crops would have included browntop millet (*Bracharia ramose*), bristly foxtail millet (*Setaria verticillata*), mung bean (*Vigna radiata*), and horsegram (*Macrotyloma uniflorum*).[57] The languages associated regionally with the southern Indian Neolithic belong to the Central and Southern branches of the Dravidian family.

The names for several of these crops trace back to the common ancestor language of Central and Southern Dravidian, although the insufficient evidence currently available for the North Dravidian branch does not allow the reconstruction as yet of any of these crop terms back still earlier in time to the proto-Dravidian language. As was true for the Americas, the high retention of old crop terms probably suggests that the period of the common ancestor of Central and Southern Dravidian may have been the era in which the crops became fully domesticated and not just cultivated.[58] In the archaeological record, the processes of domestication were well underway by 2000 BCE, and the beginnings of cultivation surely go back much earlier. The main crops were part of the native wild flora before cultivation began, and so reconstructing their early names is not in itself evidence of how much earlier cultivation may have begun. What is now very much needed are reconstructions of verb and noun roots for the activities of cultivation across the Dravidian family. The tending of indigenous zebu cattle is another activity going back to the middle Holocene and perhaps before, and so a historical linguistic study of the lexicons of herding across the family is also a priority.

---

57  D.Q. Fuller, 'An agricultural perspective on Dravidian historical linguistics: archaeological crop packages, livestock and Dravidian crop vocabulary', in Bellwood and Renfrew (eds.), *Examining the Farming/Language Dispersal Hypothesis*, 191–213; and 'Silence before sedentism and the advent of cash-crops', in O. Toshiki (ed.), *Proceedings of the Pre-Symposium of RIHN and the 7th ESCA Harvard-Kyoto Roundtable* (Kyoto: Research Institute for Humanity and Nature, 2006).

58  As Fuller, 'Silence before sedentism', notes, however, it is not yet clear whether the lack of terms reconstructed to proto-Dravidian is due to an actual lack of the terms in the Northern Dravidian branch or simply gaps in the collected data.

A second major region of early cultivation lay in the middle and lower Ganges basin. Before the spread of the Indo-Aryan languages after 1500 BCE, the farming peoples of these areas spoke languages of the Munda branch of the Austroasiatic family.[59] The borrowing of early Munda crop terms in the later Indo-Aryan languages of this region confirms the former much wider presence of Munda speakers in this region.[60] A number of early crops originated there, including cucumber, luffa, and pigeon pea. Most important, it now appears that an independent domestication of Indian rice, separate from the domestication of rice in the Yangtze valley, provided the early staple of this agricultural tradition.[61]

Northwestern parts of the Indian subcontinent constitute the third major region of early cultivation and the earliest region in which domestication took place. The major crops arrived already domesticated, via diffusion across the Iranian plateau from the Middle Eastern origin areas of agriculture, but linguistic studies suggest that the populations that took up the new crops may have been indigenous to the Indus regions rather than intrusive.[62] To the incoming domesticated food resources, these peoples added two new contributions of their own: the raising of indigenous zebu cattle, which they may already have practised before the arrival of the new crops, and the cultivation of indigenous cotton. The lexical evidence, in this case coming ultimately from languages long extinct, reaches us only indirectly, filtered through the Indo-Aryan languages, which are today spoken across the whole region.

Again, in the Indian subcontinent the reconstruction of crop names takes our historical knowledge back to the periods of early domestication, but not to the beginnings of cultivation. In the Ganges basin and in southern peninsular India, the pre-domestication eras of cultivation probably go back another 2,000 or more years beyond where the linguistic evidence yet reaches, and the study of the historical implications of old verbs and nouns

---

59 M. Witzel, 'Early sources for South Asian substrate languages', *Mother Tongue*, special issue (1999), 1–70.

60 A.R.K. Zide and N.H. Zide, 'Proto-Munda cultural vocabulary: evidence for early agriculture', in P.H. Jenner et al. (eds.), *Austroasiatic Studies, Part II* (Honolulu: University of Hawai'i Press, 1976), 1294–334.

61 Fuller, 'Silence before sedentism'.

62 M. Witzel, 'Central Asian roots and acculturation in South Asia: linguistic and archaeological evidence from western Central Asia, the Hindukush and northwestern South Asia for early Indo-Aryan language and religion', in T. Osada (ed.), *Linguistics, Archaeology and the Human Past* (Kyoto: Research Institute for Humanity and Nature, 2005), 87–211.

specifically connoting cultivation, which might open up new knowledge about those times, remains a task still to be pursued.

## Implications of linguistic reconstruction for agriculture in Europe

Finally, the linguistic evidence also affords a quite sharp lesson for the arguments about the agricultural revolution in Europe. First and foremost, the linguistic evidence flatly rules out the possibility that Indo-European-speaking peoples might have introduced agriculture to Europe. The evidence from the Indo-European language family presents two fully fatal objections to this now quarter-century-old proposal.[63]

The first fatal objection has to do with the linguistic reconstruction of technological knowledge and practice. The proto-Indo-European language and society passed through two stages. The early proto-Indo-European stage, or Indo-Hittite stage, came to an end when the ancestral Anatolian-speakers moved away from the rest of the proto-Indo-European communities. The late proto-Indo-European period came to an end several centuries later, when the remainder of the Indo-European communities began to spread out and diverge from each other. The evidence is overwhelming that the late proto-Indo-European communities possessed and used the wheel: their lexicon contained a suite of at least five and possibly six terms relating to wheels. Even the most imaginative special pleading cannot explain away this body of evidence.[64] The number of these root words and the extent of their retention across the family show that wheels and wheeled vehicles were not just known to the late proto-Indo-Europeans, and were not just a salient, but a highly salient, part of their culture.

The possession of wheel technology as a key element of culture shows that the late proto-Indo-European period flat-out cannot date to earlier than the fourth millennium BCE – well after agriculture had already spread far to the west across Europe. Since the Indo-Hittite period preceded the late Indo-European period by no more than several centuries, the lack of words for the wheel at the Indo-Hittite stage, in contrast to their abundance in late proto-Indo-European, indicates a dating of the Indo-Hittite stage to the close of the fifth millennium, towards the end of the pre-wheel era, and a dating of the late proto-Indo-European period to the early or middle fourth millennium.

63 C. Renfrew, *Archaeology and Language: The Puzzle of Indo-European Origins* (Cambridge University Press, 1987).
64 D.W. Anthony, 'Horse, wagon and chariot: Indo-European languages and archaeology', *Antiquity*, 69 (1995), 554–65; and *The Horse, the Wheel, and Language: How Bronze-Age Riders from the Eurasian Steppes Shaped the Modern World* (Princeton University Press, 2007).

The second fatal objection applies the criterion of cultural salience to the proto-Indo-European lexicon of food production. Not one single root word of unambiguous reference to even one of the ancient crops of Middle Eastern agriculture can be reconstructed with certainty to the proto-Indo-European language. Instead, the proto-Indo-European communities (PIE) possessed an abundant domestic animal vocabulary, including even breeding terms, the most diagnostic markers of all for livestock-raising. Along with a collective term for domestic animals in general (PIE *peku-), these ancient root words include terms for sterile domestic animal (PIE *ster-); cow (PIE *guou-); bull (PIE *tauro-); he-goat (PIE *ghaido-); she-goat (PIE *dik-/*dig-); kid (PIE *kaĝo-); sheep (PIE *owi-); (young?) male sheep or goat (PIE *buĝo-: seen in English *buck*); pig (PIE *su-: Latin *sus*; English *sow, swine*; and PIE *porko-*: Latin *porcus*; English *farrow* 'young pig'); and horse (PIE *ekuo-). Even the proto-Indo-European noun for a field (PIE *agro-) originally referred to pasture rather than to cultivated land.

The implications are unequivocal. Cultivated crops lacked cultural salience for the proto-Indo-Europeans. Instead, a variety of domestic animals held first place in their economies and daily lives. The early PIE communities were pastoralists with little or no cultivation, and the late PIE communities of a few centuries later were not only pastoralists, but pastoralists who made and used wheeled vehicles and raised horses along with cows, sheep, goats, and pigs. The proto-Indo-Hittite stage may date to around 4000 BCE or just before, but the wheel-using late proto-Indo-European era cannot be dated earlier than sometime in the fourth millennium BCE. In all the world in the fourth millennium BCE, only on the Pontic steppes did there exist a wholly pastoral economy with highly valued – as their burial customs show – wheeled vehicles. The linguistic testimony puts it beyond reasonable doubt that the far-flung expansions of Indo-European languages began no earlier than the fourth millennium and that they emanated outwards from the lands along the north of the Black Sea.[65]

---

65 As Ehret, 'Linguistic archaeology', points outs – contra T.V. Gramkrelidze and V.V. Ivanov, *Indo-European and the Indo-Europeans: A Reconstruction and Historical Typological Analysis of a Protolanguage and Proto-Culture* (Tbilisi State University, 1984), and 'The early history of Indo-European languages', *Scientific American*, March 1990, 110–16, and R.D. Gray and Q.D. Atkinson, 'Language-tree divergence times support the Anatolian theory of Indo-European origin', *Nature*, 426 (2003), 435–9 – an Anatolian homeland for the ancestors of the Proto-Indo-Europeans is pretty much ruled out by the fact that exceedingly high proportions of the lexicon of the Anatolian branch of Indo-European consist of word borrowings from non-Indo-European languages – notably Hattic, but probably also from other extinct North Caucasian languages, such

So who were the peoples who brought food production to western Europe in the seventh and sixth millennia BCE? The Basque language is the most likely candidate for a surviving descendant of the languages spoken by those early farmers. The alternative hypothesis – that Basque is a survival of a late Palaeolithic hunter-gatherer language – is highly improbable, and here is why: nearly always when farmers spread into regions occupied previously by people who are solely gatherers and hunters, the languages of those foragers in the end die out. The languages die out because the incoming farmers form larger local population groups and because the intrusive farming populations grow more rapidly in numbers as they expand into more and more of the hunter-gatherers' lands. When a language survives the spread of farming peoples, as Basque has, it is normally because the speakers of that surviving language were already themselves farmers. They belonged to communities that were already large enough and numerous enough to compete culturally and demographically with the incoming groups.

## Prospects

As these findings from different parts of the world show, linguistic reconstruction wields a powerful set of tools for revealing the extent and variety of early agricultural knowledge and practice among human societies around the globe. In many cases this kind of study greatly enriches the story that the archaeological record can tell. The findings of linguistic historical reconstruction are essential to identifying the language affiliations of the peoples of earlier times, and its discoveries can, as well, identify new regions and new topics for investigation by archaeologists and archaeobotanists and suggest new agendas to be explored by those disciplines. In addition, tracing the routes of word-borrowing among languages can clarify the directions in which new knowledge spread. The transmission of words for goat and sheep from early Cushites to Nilo-Saharans in the seventh millennium BCE is a striking example.

And linguistic reconstruction is not just a helpmeet for archaeology. The resources of language can fill gaps in historical knowledge that archaeology may not be able or suited to fill. Uncovering the kinship systems of earlier

as Hurrian. This extraordinarily high borrowing rate, together with the fact that the loanwords intrude even into parts of the lexicon in which borrowing only rarely takes place, makes an extraordinarily strong case that the speakers of proto-Anatolian and each of its descendant languages, such as Hittite, Luwian, and Lydian, were *intruders* into the Anatolian regions.

peoples is a prime example. The linguistic record can also supplement the material record where preservation conditions are poor, most especially in the case of tuber crops such as yams and taro, which are rarely preserved in the material record, or for crops cultivated in areas where the environmental conditions limit the preservation of crop remains of any kind.[66] In every part of the world there is still much more to do and so much more that linguistic studies of history can reveal about our common human past.

# Further reading

Anthony, D.W. *The Horse, the Wheel, and Language: How Bronze-Age Riders from the Eurasian Steppes Shaped the Modern World*. Princeton University Press, 2007.

Assefa, S. *Omotic Peoples and the Early History of Agriculture in Southern Ethiopia*. Unpublished PhD thesis. University of California, Los Angeles, 2011.

Bellwood, P. 'The origins and spread of agriculture in the Indo-Pacific region.' In D. Harris (ed.), *The Origins and Spread of Agriculture and Pastoralism in Eurasia*. London: UCL Press, 1996. 465–98.

Blust, R. 'The prehistory of the Austronesian-speaking peoples: a view from language.' *Journal of World Prehistory*, 9/4 (1995), 453–510.

Brown, C.H. 'Glottochronology and the chronology of maize in the Americas.' In J.E. Staller, R.H. Tykot, and B.F. Benz (eds.), *Histories of Maize: Multidisciplinary Approaches to the Prehistory, Biogeography, Domestication, and Evolution of Maize*. Amsterdam and London: Elsevier Academic Press, 2006. 647–73.

'Prehistoric chronology of the common bean in the New World: the linguistic evidence.' In J.E. Staller and M.C. Carrasco (eds.), *Pre-Columbian Foodways in Mesoamerica*. New York: Springer, 2010. 273–89.

Ehret, C. *History and the Testimony of Language*. Berkeley: University of California Press, 2011.

'Linguistic archaeology.' *African Archaeological Review*, 29/2 (2012), 109–30.

'A linguistic history of cultivation and herding in northeastern Africa.' In A.G. Fahmy, S. Kahlheber, and A.C. D'Andrea (eds.), *Windows on the African Past*. Frankfurt: Africa Magna, 2011. 185–208.

'Linguistic stratigraphies and Holocene history in northeastern Africa.' In M. Chlodnicki and K. Kroeper (eds.), *Archaeology of Early Northeastern Africa*. Posnan Archaeological Museum, 2006. 1019–55.

Ehret, C. and M. Posnansky (eds.). *The Archaeological and Linguistic Reconstruction of African History*. Berkeley: University of California Press, 1982.

Fuller, Dorian Q. 'An agricultural perspective on Dravidian historical linguistics: archaeological crop packages, livestock and Dravidian crop vocabulary.' In P. Bellwood and C. Renfrew (eds.), *Examining the Farming/Language Dispersal*

---

66 This, as Brown, 'Prehistoric chronology of the common bean', points out, is the case for beans in wet environments.

*Hypothesis*. Cambridge: McDonald Institute for Archaeological Research, 2003. 191–214.

Ross, M., A. Pawley, and M. Osmond (eds.). *The Lexicon of Proto Oceanic: The Culture and Environment of Ancestral Oceanic Society*, vol. 1: *Material Culture*. Canberra: Research School of Pacific and Asian Studies, 1998.

4

# What did agriculture do for us?
## *The bioarchaeology of health and diet*

CHARLOTTE ROBERTS

Studying data collected from archaeological human remains is of prime importance in archaeology (bioarchaeology); without humans there would be no other archaeological data because our ancestors created the past that we excavate now. They made the pottery, domesticated the animals and plants, built the houses, created societies, developed trade and contacts, and changed the landscape.[1] Therefore, exploring the nature of our ancestors' lives before and after agricultural development, and how agriculture impacted on their existence, necessarily needs to consider relevant evidence seen in their remains. Bioarchaeology is also relevant to understanding the evolution of the human population before urban/city living increasingly became the norm, a continuing and rapid trend we see today.[2] Studies of both past and present hunter-gatherers and agriculturalists show us the advantages and risks to adopting agriculture and leaving the hunter-gatherer way of life behind. Furthermore, there has been, and continues to be, a keen interest in exploring health and dietary changes at the transition to agriculture, along with its intensification, up to the present day. For example, a brief keyword search in May 2013 using 'agriculture' and 'health' revealed 42,858 citations of modern studies on Europe PubMed Central, and 1264 since 1960 in *Social Science and Medicine*; and for ancient studies, 707 since 1918 in the *American Journal of Physical Anthropology*, 148 since 1991 in the *International Journal of Osteoarchaeology*, 192 since 1974 in the *Journal of Archaeological Science*, and 525 since 1960 in *Current Anthropology*. Research in this area, it is anticipated, will remain a strong focus in bio-archaeology.

---

1 C.A. Roberts, *Human Remains in Archaeology: A Handbook*, CBA Practical Handbooks in Archaeology 19 (York: Council for British Archaeology, 2009).
2 United Nations Population Fund, www.unfpa.org/pds/urbanization.htm (accessed May 2013).

## Definitions

It is perhaps necessary to provide three (modern) definitions at this point, for health, diet, and agriculture. Health is defined by the World Health Organization as a state of complete physical, mental, and social well-being and not merely the absence of disease or infirmity.[3] The meaning of well-being (usually viewed as a positive state), however, necessarily has to account for all the attributes of a person's or community's life that may contribute (or not) to well-being; this includes social, economic, psychological, and even spiritual characteristics of a person and the community in which that person lives, not forgetting the state of their health. Diet is defined as the food and drink a person or animal consumes, and agriculture as the science or occupation of cultivating land and rearing crops and livestock. As part of agriculture, domestication of plants and animals also includes deliberate selection and breeding of wild plants and animals. Diet and health are inextricably linked, as the Frenchman Jean Anthelme Brillat-Savarin (1755–1826) indicated when he said 'You are what you eat': 'Tell me what you eat, and I will tell you what you are.' A balanced diet promotes a healthy immune system and mitigates against ill health. Thus, a changing diet with the transition to agriculture could have risks, but also benefits.

## Challenges to health at the transition to agriculture

Through time, up to the present, and as the population of the world has increased, the production of food through farming plants and animals has continued to grow and expand, with increasing intensification of food sources evident.[4] The use of chemical fertilizers and pesticides, improved irrigation systems for crop production, and clearance of land, with all their subsequent impacts on the environment, are well known, as is the effect of intensification of livestock production, which leads to deforestation, factory farming, special feeds, drugs to prevent and treat disease, pollution of land and water from manure, selective breeding, and consequent concerns over animal welfare. Indeed, the World Health Organization has recently reviewed the connections between environmental change, modern agricultural practices, and the occurrence of infectious diseases, finding that there are now 'increased opportunities for contact between humans and the animal

---

3 www.who.int/about/definition/en/print.html (accessed May 2013).

4 N. Middleton, *The Global Casino: An Introduction to Environmental Issues*, 4th edn (London: Hodder Education, 2008).

hosts and reservoirs of pathogens'.[5] Genetic manipulation of crops and animals to produce higher yields is also a concern, and yet advantages of doing so are frequently publicized (e.g. inserting genes into crops to produce a 'natural pesticide', changing the timing for when fruit ripens, and increasing a crop's ability to live in environmental extremes).[6] In recent years there have been escalating campaigns to counteract concerns about how the agricultural industry functions. However, whether the initial move to farming was the result of an increasing population, or instead farming enabled a larger population to be supported, remains a constant debate, as does how detrimental to diet and health farming was and is. Clearly, access to an adequate and good quality food supply was, and continues to be, necessary for everyone to grow normally, and to be healthy and happy. When this is not possible, this is today termed 'food insecurity', and may be caused by a number of factors such as climate change, overpopulation, soil degradation, and conflict.

One of the key questions that has been asked in the past, and continue to be asked, is what happens to demography, diet, and health in populations with the transition to agriculture from hunting and foraging.[7] This first of three transitions is studied alongside two later ones: the second transition, industrialization, which saw a decline in mortality with improved living conditions alongside the development of antibiotics, and a rise in chronic non-infectious diseases such as cardiovascular problems (heart disease and 'strokes') and cancer; and, more recently, the third transition, the re-emergence of infectious diseases and new infections along with resistance to antibiotics. The developing world is of course experiencing the second and third transitions later than developed countries.[8] However, it is well known that socioeconomic, political, and environmental factors all have their part to play in health at these transitions, and ultimately affect the diet people ate and are eating, and their physical and mental health.

---

5  World Health Organization, *Research Priorities for the Environment, Agriculture and Infectious Diseases of Poverty*, WHO Technical Report Series 976 (Geneva, 2013).

6  Middleton, *Global Casino*, 269.

7  See M.N. Cohen, *Health and the Rise of Civilisation* (New Haven, CT: Yale University Press, 1989); M.N. Cohen and G.J. Armelagos (eds.), *Paleopathology at the Origins of Agriculture* (London: Academic Press, 1984; 2nd edn Gainesville: University Press of Florida, 2013); M.N. Cohen and G. Crane-Kramer (eds.), *Ancient Health: Skeletal Indicators of Agricultural and Economic Intensification* (Gainesville: University Press of Florida, 2007).

8  R. Barrett et al., 'Emerging and re-emerging infectious diseases: the third epidemiological transition', *Annual Review of Anthropology*, 27 (1998), 247–71; M. Singer and P.I. Erickson (eds.), *A Companion to Medical Anthropology* (Chichester: Wiley-Blackwell, 2011).

Archaeological human remains capture a snapshot of how people's health was affected by changes in their diet and general way of life with the transition to agriculture when compared to their hunter-gatherer ancestors. It is essential to bear in mind that skeletal evidence for health and welfare in human remains from archaeological sites is the closest we can get to interpreting and understanding this aspect of the past. Being unhealthy and eating an unbalanced diet potentially affects the very function of any society past or present, so bioarchaeology provides key data for answering broader questions about society in a world of agriculture.

Essentially, most studies in bioarchaeology have found that health declines through time, and especially at economic transitions and as society becomes more complex.[9] Indeed, medical anthropological studies (the 'application of anthropological theories and methods to questions of illness, medicine, and healing') have provided bioarchaeology with a wealth of data on the effect of farming on demography and health and have compared health in pre-agricultural and agricultural communities.[10] For example, new diseases appear and fertility and population numbers and density increase with agriculture. As McElroy and Townsend suggest, agricultural communities today do practise controls over population numbers, for example through prolonging breast-feeding, but the young are also 'put to work' early in their lives. Medical anthropology, however, has also shown us that many health problems facing the Western world are not seen in people who have not adopted a 'modern' way of life and do not eat an agriculturally based diet.[11] Evolutionary medicine, which uses an evolutionary perspective to understand why the body is not better designed and why diseases exist, has alerted us to the effects of agriculture on health and emphasizes the benefits and costs of agriculture to the world's population today.[12] Evolutionary medicine, furthermore, 'hypothesizes a mismatch between human biological evolution and health conditions in industrialized societies', but it is notable that few of the ideas promoted have been fully explored in any scientific way.[13] Clearly, bioarchaeology is in a position to exploit both medical anthropology and evolutionary

---

9 See C.A. Roberts and M. Cox, *Health and Disease in Britain: From Prehistory to the Present Day* (Stroud: Sutton, 2003); R.H. Steckel and J.C. Rose (eds.), *The Backbone of History: Health and Nutrition in the Western Hemisphere* (Cambridge University Press, 2002).

10 See A. McElroy and P.K. Townsend, *Medical Anthropology in Ecological Perspective*, 5th edn (Boulder, CO: Westview Press, 2009).

11 W.R. Trevathan et al. (eds.), *Evolutionary Medicine and Health: New Perspectives* (Oxford University Press, 2008).

12 R.M. Nesse and G.C. Williams, *Why We Get Sick: The New Science of Darwinian Medicine* (New York: Vintage, 1994).

13 See Singer and Erickson (eds.), *Companion to Medical Anthropology*.

medicine to understand the past, but it also informs the two disciplines by providing the deep-time perspective in helping us understand the here and now.

This chapter focuses on what kind of evidence can be productively used from human remains to tell us something about a population's diet and health, and to address the questions of how agriculture contributes to our health and diet and how bioarchaeology can help us understand this relationship better. It first describes the nature of bioarchaeology and how and what type of data can be collected, and then the chapter unfolds to consider:

- What kind of diet and health problems face hunter-gatherer and agricultural communities today, and our ancestors at the agriculture transition, and why.
- How they are recognized in human remains and some problems of interpretation.
- Particular health problems and dietary-related conditions that characterize 'diet' and 'living environment'.

The dialogues, necessarily, reach into the archive of biomolecular analyses and primarily, stable isotope analysis as an indicator of diet. The chapter concludes by looking forward to the future.

## Bioarchaeology: principles, methods, and data

### Principles

First, it is imperative that the workings of 'bioarchaeology' are outlined. Bioarchaeology, in the US sense, is the study of human remains, whether they are skeletons (inhumation or cremation burials) or preserved bodies. It is a subdiscipline of archaeology and of physical or biological anthropology, both of which are subfields of anthropology. It encompasses the study of individual skeletons or preserved bodies, and 'populations' of skeletons (or bodies) from all periods of time, and all areas of the world, although the amount of work in this field can be variable across time and space. This depends on many factors, not least whether there is a tradition in bioarchaeology and whether training is available.[14] Likewise some parts of the world preserve human remains better than others (for example, the very cold or dry areas preserve complete bodies), and some funerary rituals can enhance

14 See J.E. Buikstra and C.A. Roberts (eds.), *The Global History of Paleopathology: Pioneers and Prospects* (New York: Oxford University Press, 2012), with reference to the development of palaeopathology, or the study of ancient disease, itself a part of bioarchaeology.

(e.g. burial in crypts inside coffins) or compromise (e.g. burial in acidic soils) the survival of the evidence that is ultimately excavated and analysed. This chapter will focus on the study of skeletal remains, because this is the most common type studied in bioarchaeology.

## Methods and data

Bioarchaeological studies collect a range of data from skeletons from an array of different funerary contexts; the data include primarily the minimum number of individuals represented, the biological sex of the adult skeletons, age at death of both adults and non-adults, and normal (measurements and non-metric traits) and abnormal (disease) variation.[15] In order to understand differences in responses to sociocultural, economic, and political changes in the past using these variables, comparative analyses are done between 'populations' of the same and different time periods and geographic locations. Of note, however, is that not all scholars record the same parameters for skeletons they are studying. This can make comparative analyses impossible.[16]

While the variables described above are collected 'macroscopically' (observation with the naked eye), analytical methods have become more sophisticated, especially in recent years, particularly with the application of stable isotope analysis to answer questions about diet and mobility and ancient DNA analysis to consider disease diagnosis and evolution, relationships between people, and migration.[17] These methods have developed alongside improvements in imaging techniques and histological analysis which have all allowed a nuancing of data previously not possible.[18] Established methods for data collection are recommended and, in the main, are used, and many studies are hypothesis and/or question driven.[19] Most importantly, the data from human remains are always (or should be) placed in context. Understanding

---

15  See Roberts, *Human Remains in Archaeology*, and S. Mays, *The Archaeology of Human Bones*, 2nd edn (London: Routledge, 2010), for more details.

16  See T.A. Rathbun, 'Skeletal pathology from the Paleolithic through the metal ages in Iran and Iraq', in Cohen and Armelagos (eds.), *Paleopathology at the Origins of Agriculture*, 137–67, table 6.1, where a list of studies shows different data sets; and Cohen and Crane-Kramer (eds.), *Ancient Health*.

17  T. Brown and K. Brown, *Biomolecular Archaeology: An Introduction* (Oxford: Wiley-Blackwell, 2011).

18  See R. Pinhasi and S. Mays (eds.), *Advances in Human Palaeopathology* (Chichester: Wiley, 2008).

19  As described in Buikstra et al., *Standards for Data Collection from Human Skeletal Remains*, Arkansas Archeological Survey Research Series 44 (Fayetteville: Arkansas Archaeological Survey, 1994); and M. Brickley and J.I. McKinley (eds.), *Guidelines for the Standards for Recording Human Remains* (Southampton: British Association of Biological Anthropology and Osteoarchaeology, 2004), specifically for Britain.

the archaeological context from which the remains derive is essential for interpretation: this multi-method, multidisciplinary approach to bioarchaeological studies ultimately aims to generate the 'best fit' interpretation for the data collected.[20]

### Normal variation (age, sex, metrical and non-metrical analysis)

Always in the background to such studies is the cautionary approach to interpreting collected data, particularly that relating to health indicators.[21] Additionally, methods may not necessarily be well developed and can have limitations, and one question that always plagues bioarchaeology is whether the population being studied is representative of the living population. It is also not possible to biologically sex non-adult skeletons with any accuracy, although it is more straightforward for adults, depending on completeness of the skeleton. However, ancient DNA analysis can help if the aDNA is preserved in the skeleton.[22] Conversely, assessing age at death of non-adult skeletons using dental development and bone growth produces relatively accurate ages, while for adults the methods available can overage young adults and underage older adults.[23] However, these problems are being addressed by new research, and one hopes that in the future we will have easy to use and reliable methods to place skeletons into age categories beyond '50 years+'. Skeletons are often fragmentary and can be poorly preserved, reflecting the vagaries of different ways of 'disposing' of the dead over time, and regions which enhance or compromise preservation. This affects not only whether it is possible to age and sex a skeleton but also whether 'normal variation' can be recorded via measurements of bones and teeth and recording of non-metric traits.[24] Comparisons of data between populations allow bioarchaeologists to explore differences in size and shape of bones and teeth, including, for example, height as determined from long bone length (stature). It may also be possible to say whether people have a high frequency of inherited 'traits' that either identify them as locally born

---

20 See Roberts and Cox, *Health and Disease in Britain*; S.C. Agarwal and B.A. Glencross, *Social Bioarchaeology* (Chichester: Wiley-Blackwell, 2011).

21 J.W. Wood et al., 'The osteological paradox: problems of inferring health from skeletal samples', *Current Anthropology*, 33 (1992), 343–70; and T. Waldron, *Counting the Dead: The Epidemiology of Skeletal Populations* (Chichester: Wiley, 1994).

22 See Brown and Brown, *Biomolecular Archaeology*.

23 See T. Molleson and M. Cox, *The Spitalfields Project*, vol. II: *The Anthropology: The Middling Sort*, Research Report 86 (York: Council for British Archaeology, 1993), for an example from a documented aged population for eighteenth- to nineteenth-century London.

24 See Roberts, *Human Remains in Archaeology*; Mays, *Archaeology of Human Bones*.

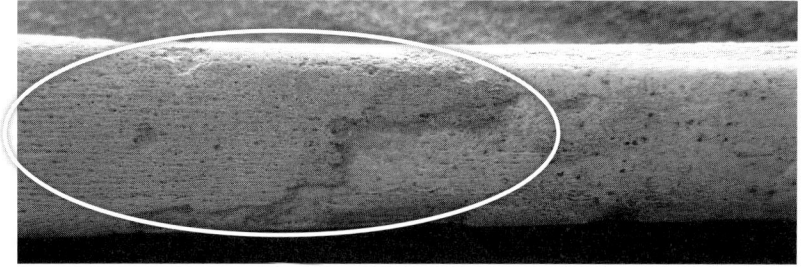

Figure 4.1 Example of bone formation on tibia (lower leg bone).

and raised or highlight them as non-locals with bones and teeth of different sizes and shapes, along with non-metric traits that are not commonly found in the local population. This can of course now be tested using stable isotope analysis.[25]

### Abnormal variation (palaeopathology)

The final class of data collected from skeletons is that which indicates health problems experienced during life. Notwithstanding the limitations to these data, discussed below, it has to be remembered that the health indicators recorded reflect those diseases and traumas experienced over the whole course of a person's life. They are imprinted on the person's bones and teeth as bone formation and destruction, and loss of bone and/or dental tissue in the jaws (Figures 4.1 and 4.2). However, the skeletons of only a small percentage of people will necessarily be affected by disease and trauma because so many diseases (and traumas) affect only the soft tissues of the body. Even diseases that do affect the skeleton may only damage a few per cent of people; for example, the infectious diseases tuberculosis and leprosy only affect 3–5 per cent of untreated people. More often than not when a disease is seen in bones the changes are chronic and healed, indicating a long-standing problem, and the fact that the person survived the acute stages of the disease and did not die from it (strong immune system): they are essentially the 'healthy ones'.[26]

Once the bone changes are recorded, their distribution pattern is examined and compared to clinical data, and possible differential diagnoses are produced. For example, destructive lesions of the spine can occur in tuberculosis, osteoporosis, cancer, fungal diseases, and brucellosis, but their characteristics (and whether there is any other corroborative bone change elsewhere in the

25 Brown and Brown, *Biomolecular Archaeology*.  26 Wood et al., 'Osteological paradox'.

Figure 4.2 Example of bone destruction in vertebrae.

skeleton) will help narrow down the diagnosis. Radiography, histology, and aDNA analysis may help with diagnoses, although they must not be seen as the 'silver bullet'! It should be noted that the skeleton of a person who died of an acute disease will look very similar to that of someone who did not have the disease.[27] Using clinical data it is also possible to map signs and symptoms onto diseases that are recognized in skeletal remains, such that it is possible to build up a hypothetical picture of the 'disease experience' of the individual. However, individuals can react differently to the same disease and not necessarily have the same suite of symptoms. Frequency data are produced for the different disease 'categories' (e.g. infectious, dental, metabolic), and those frequencies compared by age and sex categories, as appropriate and where possible. There may also be comparisons between social statuses and populations of the same or different time periods and geographic regions. Increasingly, the health of our ancestors is considered thematically so that it is possible to explore the effects of living conditions, diet and economy, work, trade, mobility, and access to health care on their experience of disease and trauma. Essentially, bioarchaeological

---

27 See ibid.

studies of health and well-being provide a deep-time perspective on understanding the origin, evolution, and history of disease, which is very relevant to the emerging discipline of evolutionary medicine.

## Hunting, gathering, and farming today

It is much easier to consider the health of contemporary people who hunt and forage or work in agriculture because the data are more accessible and detailed, and ecological factors specific to living hunter-gatherers and agriculturalists can be used effectively to understand the diet they eat and challenges to health they experience. Data from living people can be surprising and can challenge our assumptions about the past.

### Hunter-gatherers

For example, although the general consensus is that fertility rates are low for hunter-gatherers both past and present, Pennington notes that hunter-gatherer total fertility rates are very variable and some of that is because 'virtually all hunter-gatherers . . . are involved economically in one way or another with non-foraging people'.[28] Sexually transmitted diseases are also believed to affect fertility rates. Average age at death is low, as is life expectancy at birth; in a survey of the few studies of hunter-gatherer survival, Pennington notes a maximum in the Ache in Paraguay of thirty-seven years of life for newborns, but twenty-four years for the Agta in the Philippines. With respect to diet and health, which may also be termed 'nutritional ecology' (interaction of diet, physical activity, and pathogenic agents, and their relationship to body composition, development, and function in a particular sociopolitical and natural environment), Cohen noted that people who are classed as hunter-gatherers have lean bodies and occasionally are hungry if resources are not plentiful (e.g. in particular seasons), but they have the ability to move on to find new resources.[29] Although there are great variations between hunter-gatherer groups on the proportions of plant and animal foods that make up their diet, affected by seasonal differences, hunter-gatherers generally have a low calorie and fat (especially saturated) intake and more fibre ingestion, along with higher micronutrient consumption (aided by greater physical activity).[30] Diet is generally well balanced, more varied, and higher in protein

28  R. Pennington, 'Hunter-gatherer demography', in C. Panter-Brick et al. (eds.), *Hunter-Gatherers: An Interdisciplinary Perspective*, Biosocial Society Symposium Series (Cambridge University Press, 2001), 170–204 (178).
29  Cohen, *Health and the Rise of Civilisation*.
30  See Panter-Brick et al. (eds.), *Hunter-Gatherers*.

than a 'farming diet', and in a study in the Kalahari, Truswell and Hanson found no evidence of a poor diet.[31] However, times are changing for living hunter-gatherers who are becoming acculturated and exposed to Western diets, while their natural resources become more challenging to access.

Common health problems of hunter-gatherers are parasitic infection, such as of the blood (malaria) and intestines (e.g. hookworm), and zoonoses (diseases spread from animals to humans), with infectious disease being the most common cause of death. Dental wear and abrasion, periodontal disease, and dental plaque are common, but caries is low. These low-density populations do not favour transmission of density-dependent diseases such as measles, tuberculosis, and influenza. The absence of permanent settlement also prevents the accumulation of waste, and consequent vermin, contamination of water supplies, and associated disease such as cholera. The degenerative diseases, especially associated with old age and Western living, are, overall, rare, but accidents are fairly common and associated with hunting, and hunting can also lead to exposure to zoonoses. Lactose tolerance is generally rare in hunter-gatherers, again illustrating how tolerance has evolved with the transition to agriculture. Hunter-gatherers are overall 'moderately active' but with variation according to the seasons (as for farmers), but not as great as for people practising horticulture or agriculture.[32] It is difficult to know whether hunter-gatherers lived in an ideal world. Considering the contradictory evidence from many studies in bioarchaeology that hunter-gatherers were more healthy than agriculturalists, it is no easy task to make comparisons between past and present ('more or less acculturated') hunter-gatherers, especially with rapid changes to the hunter-gatherer way of life today reflected in changes to the ecosystem and a decline in wild animals to hunt.

### Farmers

Exploring health in agriculturally based populations today as a comparator for the past is similarly fraught with problems because the ways in which agriculture is practised globally vary considerably, from developed to developing countries. The food grown and the domesticated animals kept are diverse, such that each ecological niche, in its broadest sense, will contain multiple facets that in turn affect the quality of the diet and a population's health. Chamberlain notes that agricultural populations have high growth, but that

---

31 A.S. Truswell and J.D.L. Hanson, 'Medical research among the !Kung', in R.B. Lee and I. DeVore (eds.), *Kalahari Hunter-Gatherers: Studies of the !Kung San and Their Neighbors* (Cambridge, MA: Harvard University Press, 1976), 166–95.

32 See Panter-Brick et al. (eds.), *Hunter-Gatherers*.

this is not consistent, and growth is very much related to the carrying capacity of the area.[33] Farmers also have higher fertility, as noted above, which is due overall to having a more settled community and secure food resources. Today some traditional agricultural communities still have practices that limit family size, such as infanticide and abortion, but other practices can lead to high birth rates and, the more people there are, the greater capacity there is for agricultural work to be carried out.[34] For example, if women have children that are born very close to each other chronologically, this does not matter as much as for a hunter-gatherer mother who would have to carry and care for her children between temporary camps and while gathering food. Weaning foods are also readily available in agriculture contexts. Among the many studies of health in agricultural populations today, a range of subject areas is approached but particularly includes occupational risks. For example, respiratory health of farmers has been reported, revealing increased asthma associated with dust inhalation and there are dangers for people practising agriculture in areas where soil may be contaminated and helminth infections associated with contaminated water and crops.

## The implications of farming for people

### Why farm?

As has been discussed above, one question that continues to be debated is why people started farming in the post-Glacial early Holocene, or in the first 5,000 years of the last 10,000. This occurred independently in Africa, Asia, the western Pacific, and the Americas.[35] A number of possible reasons have been suggested: the population increased so more food was needed to feed that growing population (or did agriculture develop to then allow the population to grow?), climate changed and wild animal and plant resources became scarcer, or people essentially wanted a more reliable source of food. However, as is well known, people even today do not necessarily only have agriculture to rely on for their subsistence, as they may also practise pastoralism, or hunt and forage for wild resources, especially in season. The transition to agriculture in the past may also have been over a long time period, with no single subsistence activity

---

33 A. Chamberlain, *Demography in Archaeology*, Cambridge Manuals in Archaeology (Cambridge University Press, 2006).
34 McElroy and Townsend, *Medical Anthropology*.
35 B.D. Smith, *The Emergence of Agriculture* (New York: Scientific American Library, 1995).

predominant, and some people may have preferred to have different subsistence strategies working alongside each other, especially when circumstances made this logical (e.g. extreme weather conditions, harvest failures, etc.). This is the situation in the Levant where the Neolithic Revolution was clearly complex and long term.[36]

### Advances in methods and understanding the agricultural transition in bioarchaeology

Advances in understanding the nature of the agricultural transition and its impact on humans have particularly been seen recently in genetic studies, for example how plants and animals have evolved,[37] and how human genes have adapted and changed. An example of the latter can be seen in lactase. The production of the enzyme lactase in the human body is needed for a person to be able to digest lactose (milk sugar), and therefore with the domestication of animals and the consumption of dairy products this becomes important (lactase persistence). A single nucleotide polymorphism (SNP) in the MCM6 gene encoding lactase (13,910*T) is associated with the ability to digest milk in European populations. Lactase persistence has an approximately 95 per cent prevalence in Europe, but in other areas of the world, south and east of Europe, this frequency declines.[38] Burger et al. have identified lactase-persistent associated genotypes in eight Neolithic (5800–5000 BCE) skeletons and one Mesolithic (2267 ± 116 cal BCE) skeleton from central, northeastern, and southeastern Europe, but the allele most commonly associated with lactase persistence in Europeans was not found.[39] This was interpreted as evidence that it was rare in early European farmers. This type of research shows how advanced methods of analysis can now tell us much more about how people adapted to making a living with agriculture.

### Health, diet, and agriculture

Until more sophisticated analytical methods developed, the key research on the impact of farming on diet and health was the pioneering work of Cohen and Armelagos in which many studies of demography and health in skeletons of people from around the world who had made the transition to farming

---

36  R. Pinhasi and J.T. Stock (eds.), *Human Bioarchaeology of the Transition to Agriculture* (Chichester: Wiley-Blackwell, 2011).
37  See Brown and Brown, *Biomolecular Archaeology*, for some studies.
38  See Trevathan et al. (eds.), *Evolutionary Medicine and Health*.
39  J. Burger et al., 'Absence of the lactase-persistence-associated allele in early Neolithic Europeans', *Proceedings of the National Academy of Sciences*, 104 (2007), 3736–41.

were presented.[40] The work was the outcome of a conference held in 1982 and was a landmark 'event' that has precipitated an abundance of studies since then on health (and diet) at the agricultural transition. The goal of the volume was to compare studies of the economic transition from hunting and gathering to farming. What was consistent was a decline in quality of life following the adoption of farming. Likewise, many of the studies in Cohen and Crane-Kramer document declines in health, this volume showing a similar picture but this time more globally distributed.[41] However, the picture is complex and is not consistent across time or space. Cohen and Crane-Kramer conclude their volume by saying that, 'Overall, evidence of health decline through time is far more common than evidence of stability or improvement' but that 'nothing more than broad generalisations should be expected'.[42] Regional differences will of course reflect a variety of factors, including the location of sites studied (latitude/longitude) and social, cultural, political, and economic factors.

### 'Living environment' and farming: how does life change?

Why might a decline in health be caused by growing food and keeping animals? Fundamental to this question is that the 'Palaeolithic diet' was abandoned with farming, even though the hunter-gatherer lifestyle was, and is, inherent in how the human body has evolved.[43] In effect, a mismatch between human evolution and diet has developed, and remains with us today as we practise an even more sedentary lifestyle and eat against the evolutionary grain.[44] In addition to this, as Cohen suggests, 'human activities can create disease or increase the risk of illness just as surely as medical science reduces the risk'.[45] Nevertheless, people can adapt to changes over generations and longer periods of time, and eventually develop tolerance (or not) and increased metabolic efficiency for staple foods on which they are reliant (see above concerning lactose intolerance). Another example of intolerance to food can be illustrated with regard to gluten, whereby the inability to digest gluten in cereals, and associated coeliac disease, have occurred as farming has developed.[46] The HLA B8 DR3 gene has been associated with gluten intolerance, thereby showing it to be a genetic disorder.

40  Cohen and Armelagos (eds.), *Paleopathology at the Origins of Agriculture*.
41  Cohen and Crane-Kramer (eds.), *Ancient Health*, 343.    42  Ibid.
43  S.B. Boyd Eaton and M. Konner, 'Paleolithic nutrition: a consideration of its nature and current implications', *New England Journal of Medicine*, 312 (1985), 283–9.
44  See Trevathan et al., *Evolutionary Medicine and Health*.
45  Cohen, *Health and the Rise of Civilisation*, 7.
46  See Trevathan et al., *Evolutionary Medicine and Health*.

It is perhaps rather obvious to say that it is very difficult to grow food and keep domesticated animals while 'on the move' so, in the past, permanent housing and settlements became the norm with agriculture, leading to problems of refuse disposal and vermin, contamination of the water supply, poor hygiene and sanitation levels, potential harvest failure and soil exhaustion, and a decline in the variety, quantity, and quality of foodstuffs available. While population density increased, the impact of these changes on everyday life led to consequent increases in infectious disease loads, zoonoses, dental disease, and nutritional deficiency diseases; social inequality also developed. However, there were ways of mitigating the disadvantages farming communities experienced, such as protecting and manipulating crops and storing food.

## Bioarchaeological data and the transition to agriculture

While many studies of the agricultural transition using skeletal remains have found a decline in health, not all studies follow that trend, which suggests that the association is not so easy to understand at first sight. It is therefore instructive to now take a closer look at the indicators that most scholars use to assess health and how a change in any one health indicator can be interpreted in different ways.

In exploring the impact of economically based transitions such as that to agriculture, bioarchaeologists consider a wide range of 'markers' on the bones and teeth of skeletons that are accepted as indicating ill health, and also changes in the shape and size of bones and teeth. It should be stated at the outset that interpretation of these observations is challenging because these normal and abnormal variations may often be attributable to more than one cause. As discussed above, the quality of diet impacts the strength of the immune system, and consequently health. Therefore, evidence of dietary-deficiency-related diseases, and also diseases that are related to the consequences of living in settled communities, are relevant to questions about diet and health in pre- and post-agricultural contexts.

Bearing in mind that abnormal (disease) variation may have both environmental causes, in their widest sense, but also a genetic predisposition, it is sensible to divide the subsistence-related markers of 'normal' and 'abnormal' variation into those specifically related to diet, those related to the 'living environment', and ones that cover both themes. Dental caries, calculus, and attrition, scurvy (vitamin C deficiency), and changes in

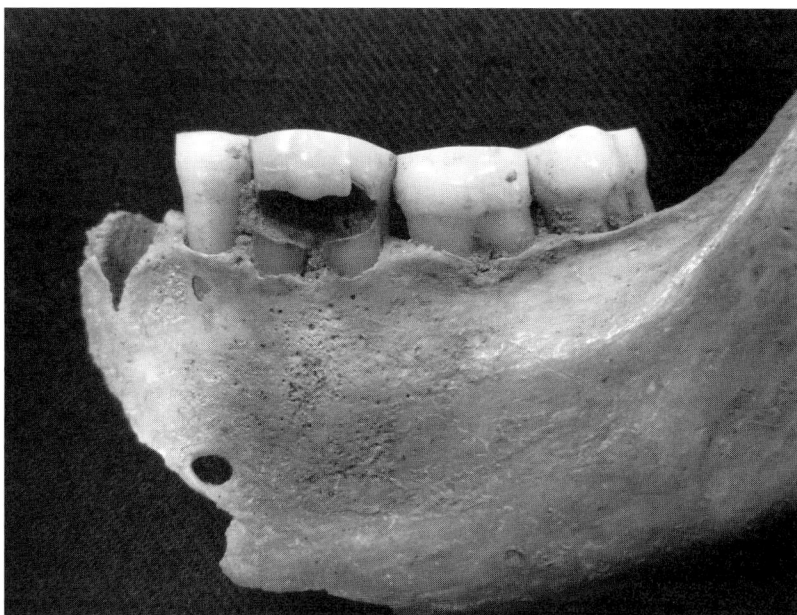

Figure 4.3 Dental caries in first permanent molar tooth.

craniofacial morphology and tooth size ('shape/size change') are specifically relevant to *dietary deficiencies and excess*. Specific (e.g. bacterial) and
non-specific (e.g. respiratory) infections, possible work-related conditions
(e.g. trauma, entheseal changes, changes in biomechanical properties of
bones, joint degeneration), and injuries related to conflict are relevant to
*living conditions*. Both themes may also be characterized by specific demographic profiles, growth retardation (long bone length and attained stature,
Harris lines of arrested growth), enamel hypoplasia, cribra orbitalia, and
porotic hyperostosis.

### Diet: skeletal changes

Dental caries (destruction of the tooth structure) results from an oral environment that is acidic, caused by fermentation of carbohydrates, especially sugars,
by bacteria in plaque (Figure 4.3). Sugars in other foods, beyond starchy
cereals/domesticated plants, may also cause caries, for example honey and
fruit. Caries has been documented to increase in farmers compared to hunter-
gatherers in many studies, but this is not a consistent pattern. For example, in
the Levant, dental caries rates were similar in Natufian hunter-gatherer

people compared to the Neolithic.[47] A further example shows that rice agriculture is apparently not as likely to cause caries as other cereals: in Southeast Asia Tayles et al. found caries did not increase with the adoption of rice agriculture.[48] More recent work also shows no decline in infant dental health with intensification of rice agriculture.[49] Temple and Larsen, furthermore, found no real difference in caries rates between hunter-gatherers and agriculturalists in prehistoric Japan (Jomon and Yayoi, respectively).[50] They suggested that rice was no more cariogenic than other carbohydrate foods consumed by the Jomon. Females in general suffered caries more than men and, with the transition to agriculture, this difference intensifies, being attributed to increased demands on women due to increased fertility.[51]

Of course, extreme dental wear will expose the dentine underlying the enamel and the tooth pulp cavity, predisposing the tooth to caries (and dental abscess), and possible antemortem tooth loss. Dental attrition or wear differs in character from flat (hunter-gatherer) to angled (agriculturalists) but, overall, dental macro- and microwear generally decline with agriculture due to the softer nature of foodstuffs being eaten. However, individual microwear features have been shown to change from the Mesolithic to Neolithic periods. Intensification of agriculture further leads to increased dental disease. Inflammation of the gums (gingivitis) as a result of plaque buildup, and subsequent periodontal disease (inflammation and loss of bone in the jaws), are also exacerbated by the softer carbohydrate foods of a farming community. Dental calculus (calcified plaque) is generally seen in people eating a high protein diet, and thus would be expected to be seen more in hunter-gatherer populations. Unfortunately many studies of the agricultural transition have not systematically recorded calculus, until recently. It is clear, however, that calculus on teeth of archaeological skeletons tends to be ubiquitous regardless of subsistence economy.[52] In recent

---

47 V. Eshed et al., 'Tooth wear and dental pathology at the advent of agriculture: new evidence from the Levant', *American Journal of Physical Anthropology*, 130 (2006), 145–9.
48 N. Tayles et al., 'Agriculture and dental caries? The case of rice in prehistoric Southeast Asia', *World Archaeology*, 32 (2000), 68–83.
49 S.E. Halcrow et al., 'From the mouths of babes: dental caries in infants and children and the intensification of agriculture in mainland Southeast Asia', *American Journal of Physical Anthropology*, 150 (2013), 409–12.
50 D.H. Temple and C.S. Larsen, 'Dental caries prevalence as evidence for agriculture and subsistence variation during the Yayoi period in prehistoric Japan: biocultural interpretations of an economy in transition', *American Journal of Physical Anthropology*, 134 (2007), 501–12.
51 J.R. Lukacs, 'Fertility and agriculture accentuate sex differences in dental caries rates', *Current Anthropology*, 49 (2008), 901–14.
52 See Roberts and Cox, *Health and Disease in Britain*, where prehistoric to post-medieval skeletons all showed calculus.

years dental calculus has been examined in much more detail, in light of developments in biomolecular methods, and these studies have much potential for exploring oral ecology at the transition to agriculture. For example, Adler et al. document a change in the oral flora at the transition to agriculture, albeit with a small sample size.[53] The fact that dental calculus is a common finding on all skeletal remains, and that pathogenic aDNA has now been isolated from it, indicates the potential for its use in answering questions about the past, not only concerning the agriculture transition.

Deficiencies of dietary constituents as a result of agriculture include a range of conditions, some of which can be identified in the skeleton. For example, vitamin C is necessary to absorb iron, so iron deficiency often occurs along with scurvy (vitamin C deficiency), and cereals contain no C, creating the potential for C deficiency. Recognized primarily by a specific patterning of new bone formation reflecting a response to haemorrhaging fragile blood vessels, systematic studies of scurvy in pre- and post-agricultural populations have not yet been done, probably because the diagnostic criteria for skeletons have only fairly recently been published, and many of the synthetic studies on health and the transition to farming were done many years before the late 1990s.[54] Even so, there is little reference to scurvy in Cohen and Crane-Kramer, suggesting that most authors either did not record it, misdiagnosed it, or it was not present.[55] Of course, fresh fruit and vegetables are essential to prevent scurvy and one might imagine that practising agriculture could have led to a decline in their consumption in a less varied diet. Another response of the skeleton to a deficiency in diet is that of osteopenia and subsequent osteoporosis (low bone density), resulting from calcium deficiency. Cereals are a poor calcium source and cereal phytates affect its absorption (as seen for iron).[56] It would be expected, therefore, that these conditions would rise in frequency with the agricultural transition, and a reduction in 'activity' when compared to hunter-gatherers would exacerbate the problem. Osteoporosis is diagnosed in a number of ways, including thinning of the cortical (outer layer) bone, reduced bone mass as seen in the trabecular honeycomb (internal) structure, and fractures of the hip,

---

53 C.J. Adler et al., 'Sequencing ancient calcified dental plaque shows changes in oral microbiota with dietary shifts of the Neolithic and Industrial Revolutions', *Nature Genetics*, 45 (2013), 450–6.
54 E.g. D. Ortner and M. Ericksen, 'Bone changes in infancy in the human skull probably resulting from scurvy in infancy and childhood', *International Journal of Osteoarchaeology*, 7 (1997), 212–20.
55 Cohen and Crane-Kramer (eds.), *Ancient Health*.
56 M. Brickley and R. Ives, *The Bioarchaeology of Metabolic Bone Disease* (London: Academic Press, 2008).

wrist, and spine; a decline in cortical thickness has been found in a number of studies, but diagenesis (post mortem damage) can compromise diagnosis.[57]

Other nutrient deficiencies may also be considered but may or may not be recognized in the skeleton. These include protein deficiency, seen for example in maize, rice, and wheat agriculture, which can lead to growth retardation, as can low zinc levels with wheat consumption. Pellagra (low niacin or vitamin $B_3$) can also occur and is related to maize agriculture. Periodontal disease (non-specific infection), dental caries, enamel hypoplasia, periosteal new bone, osteomyelitis, cribra orbitalia, and cranial pitting have been described as a suite of features associated with this condition.[58] In this study of skeletons representing people with a known diagnosis of pellagra, and people who had general malnutrition at the time of death, in the Raymond Dart twentieth-century documented skeletal collection of South Africans, the frequency of this suite of indicators separated the pellagrous from those with non-specific general malnutrition, but the indicators were not pellagra specific. Finally, and something that will be discussed further below, cribra orbitalia and porotic hyperostosis (porosity in the eye sockets – Figure 4.4 – and on the skull vault, respectively), which appear to rise in frequency with the transition to agriculture, have also been long been associated with iron deficiency as a result of a reliance on low-iron-content cereal crops and inherent phytates.[59] However, ideas have changed as to what causes the bone changes of cribra orbitalia and porotic hyperostosis.

Changes in craniofacial shape (morphology) and tooth size are fairly consistently shown in studies of crania of hunter-gatherers and agriculturalists; the shape of skulls changes and robusticity declines, along with a reduction in jaw and tooth size and crowding of teeth. These changes are again due to the softer nature of the agricultural diet and reflect less demand on the chewing muscles. People who hunted and gathered had long and narrow skulls and those practising farming had shorter and wider skulls,[60] and this suggests that jaws got smaller and could not accommodate the teeth without recourse to crowding and size reduction. An extensive study of tooth size in over 600 individuals, dating from the early upper Palaeolithic to the late Neolithic

57 Cohen and Armelagos (eds.), *Paleopathology at the Origins of Agriculture.*

58 R.P. Paine and B.P. Brenton, 'The paleopathology of pellagra: investigating the impact of prehistoric and historical dietary transitions to maize', *Journal of Anthropological Sciences*, 84 (2006), 125–35.

59 See studies in Cohen and Crane-Kramer (eds.), *Ancient Health*; and Cohen and Armelagos (eds.), *Paleopathology at the Origins of Agriculture.*

60 C.S. Larsen, *Our Origins: Discovering Physical Anthropology* (London: W.W. Norton, 2008).

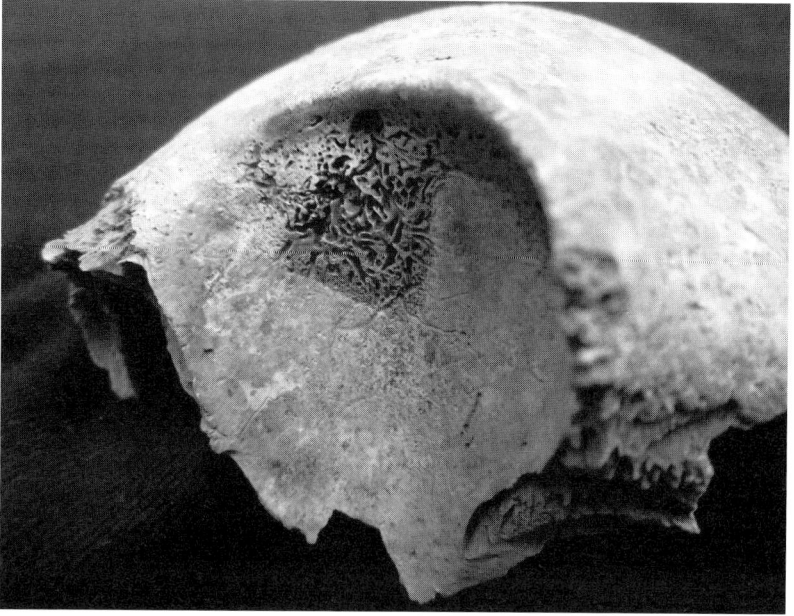

Figure 4.4 Cribra orbitalia in orbit.

across central Europe, found a trend through time to tooth reduction into the early Neolithic, but in the Levant the reduction was much more severe (up to twelve times higher). It was concluded that dental size changes should always be interpreted on an individual basis according to region.[61] Teeth are under genetic control, suggesting tooth size reduction is an evolutionary change, but that under stressful conditions, such as when agriculture was adopted, teeth failed to reach their genetic size potential. This illustrates the importance of considering both genetic and environmental causes for observations of biological changes.

The identification of the type of diet people were eating is also increasingly being accessed through stable isotope analysis. Here carbon and nitrogen isotope values are analysed in teeth and bone to assess the overall components of the diet, for example the relative proportions of marine versus terrestrial resources.[62] Diet at the transition to agriculture has been a large focus of the work to date. For example, Lillie and Richards studied skeletons from late Mesolithic/early Neolithic Ukraine (10,000–4500 cal BCE) and found people

61 See Pinhasi and Stock (eds.), *Human Bioarchaeology*.
62 See Brown and Brown, *Biomolecular Archaeology*.

were eating a hunter-fisher-gatherer diet throughout, with increased fish consumption into the Neolithic period.[63] However, Lubell et al. in their study of Mesolithic and Neolithic sites in western central Portugal (7,240 ± 70 BP to 4,110 ± 60 BP) found that people ate terrestrial and marine foods in the Mesolithic but only terrestrial foods in the Neolithic.[64] It is clear from many studies that the Mesolithic–Neolithic transition in Europe was not a 'one size fits all' situation in terms of stable isotope analyses and skeletal indicators of normal and abnormal variation – there was much variation at the transition to agriculture, remembering that individual people and populations can react differently to the same 'events', as they do today.[65]

### Living environment: skeletal changes

While dietary-related observations of skeletal remains are important for consideration in a world with agriculture, the changes people experienced in how they lived their daily lives are also reflected in their skeletons. The health indicators here relate to poor air quality, population density increases, living with animals, and working on the land. Firstly, respiratory disease (sinus and lung inflammation as a result of infection, allergies, indoor pollution, etc.) may be recognized in facial sinuses and on ribs (Figure 4.5), but it is only recently that scholars have focused on these bones in human remains. This means that it is difficult to assess how common poor air quality was pre- and post-agriculture. However, in a study of a range of hunter-gatherer, rural agriculture and urban populations from North America, England, and Sudan, hunter-gatherers had less sinusitis than rural agriculturalists and urban populations, suggesting hunter-gatherers were exposed to better quality air.[66] Studies of farming communities have also found evidence for respiratory disease, this time on ribs. However, it is important to recognize that rib lesions may be caused by many lung conditions, and until systematic studies of these bone changes are undertaken it is impossible to assess more widely their frequency in hunter-gatherers compared to agriculturalists.

Infections generally need high population numbers and density to enable spread from human to human and then maintain them in the population. At the advent of agriculture, as populations increased, this provided ideal conditions for infection, along with humans living side by side with their animals, often in

---

63  M.C. Lillie and M. Richards, 'Stable isotope analysis and dental evidence of diet at the Mesolithic–Neolithic transition in Ukraine', *Journal of Archaeological Science*, 27 (2006), 965–72.

64  D. Lubell et al., 'The Mesolithic–Neolithic transition in Portugal: isotopic and dental evidence of diet', *Journal of Archaeological Science*, 21 (1994), 201–16.

65  See Pinhasi and Stock (eds.), *Human Bioarchaeology*.

66  Roberts, *Human Remains in Archaeology*.

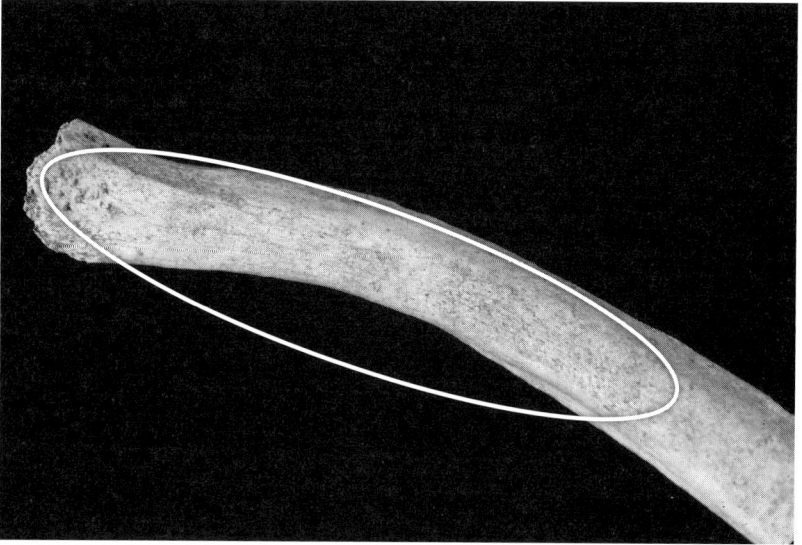

Figure 4.5 Rib with new bone formation on it.

the same living quarters. Depressed immune systems (due to poor quality foods) and poorer living conditions also contributed to make people more susceptible to infectious disease. Specific bacterial infections such as TB (destruction of the spine) are seen to rise with farming, which could be related to both an increasing population density, allowing respiratory droplet spread of the infection from human to human, but also closer contact with tuberculous animals and ingestion of their products.[67] Another bacterial infection, also affecting the spine, but only caught from animals, is brucellosis, which would also be expected in farming communities in the past but, as yet, few reports of evidence in skeletons have been made. However, although these two infections can affect a range of domesticated animals, they can also be seen in wild animals, thus having the potential to infect humans via hunting and butchery activities (although they have generally not been reported in hunter-gatherer populations). The potential threat of zoonoses being transmitted to humans in both hunter-gatherer and agricultural populations is as yet unknown because of the lack of work on the zoonoses in archaeozoology.[68]

Possible work-related conditions have been a focus of studies of health in farmers. Physical activity can ultimately have an impact on bone, and this

67 See Roberts and Cox, *Health and Disease in Britain.*
68 See Buikstra and Roberts (eds.), *Global History of Paleopathology.*

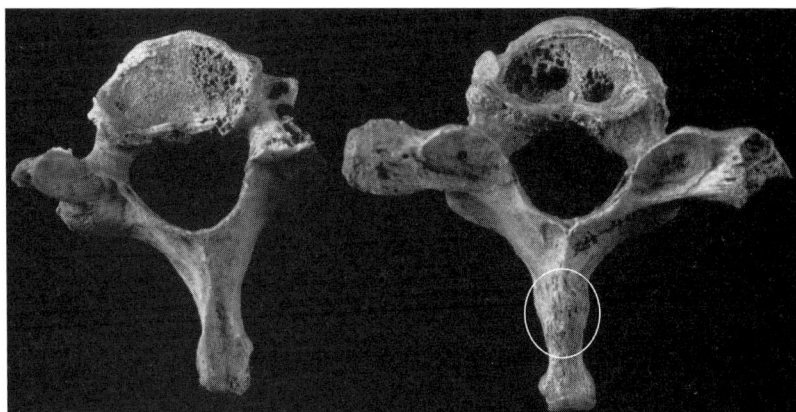

Figure 4.6 Normal vertebra (left) and one with a healed fracture to the spinous process ('clay-shoveller's fracture').

may be seen in a change in size and/or shape,[69] reflecting increasing robusticity. Additionally, entheseal changes, i.e. new bone formation or destruction at muscle, tendon, and ligament attachment sites on bones, degeneration of joints (osteoarthritis), and specific fractures, e.g. of the fifth lumbar vertebra (spondylolysis), and of the spinous process of the lower cervical or neck vertebrae ('clay-shoveller's fracture', Figure 4.6), may also reflect 'activity'. It should be noted that all these bone changes could have other causes beyond physical activity, for example increasing age causes osteoarthritis and entheseal changes (Figure 4.7).[70] Indeed, much discussion has centred on whether it is possible to infer 'occupation' from these bone changes, and scholars have even found non-correlation of skeletal markers with heavy and light manual occupations.[71] Indeed, a recent study of a historically dated skeletal remains from rural agricultural Yorkshire, England, found recorded occupation at the time of death is insufficient to aid in interpretation of entheseal changes.[72] Recent work has highlighted that

69 C.B. Ruff, 'Biomechanical analyses of archaeological skeletons', in M.A. Katzenberg and S.R. Saunders (eds.), *Biological Anthropology of the Human Skeleton* (Chichester: Wiley, 2008), 183–206.

70 R. Jurmain, *Stories From the Skeleton: Behavioral Reconstruction in Human Osteology* (Amsterdam: Gordon and Breach, 1999).

71 G.P. Lopreno et al., 'Categorization of occupation in documented skeletal collections: its relevance for the interpretation of activity-related osseous changes', *International Journal of Osteoarchaeology*, 23 (2013), 175–85.

72 C.Y. Henderson et al., 'Occupational mobility in 19th century rural England: the interpretation of entheseal changes', *International Journal of Osteoarchaeology*, 23 (2013), 197–210.

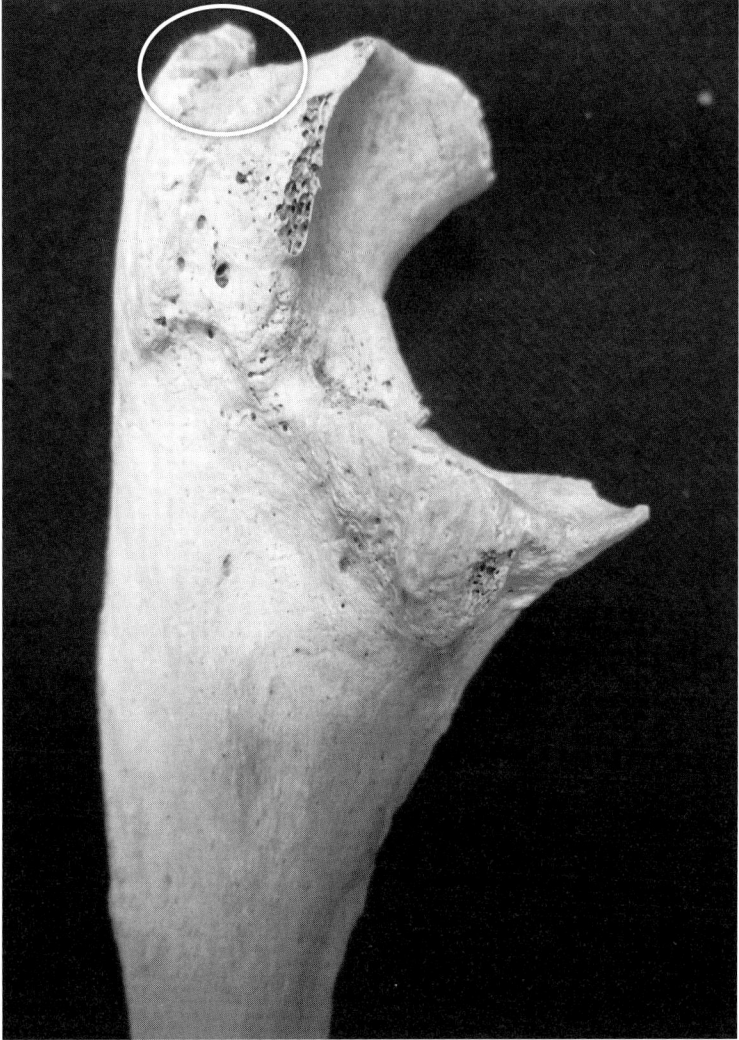

Figure 4.7 Entheseal changes (new bone formation in form of a spur) to end of ulna (forearm bone).

'There are clear problems relating methodology between EC [entheseal changes], occupation and biomechanics'.[73]

73 C.Y. Henderson and F.A. Cardoso, 'Special issue: entheseal changes and occupation: technical and theoretical advances and their applications', *International Journal of Osteoarchaeology*, 23 (2013), 130.

With respect to bone size and shape, hunter-gatherers tend to have more robust bones and prominent muscle attachment sites, and some studies show more circular cross-sections in bones of agriculturalists, reflecting mechanical factors related to greater physical activity in foragers and a reduction in farmers. Logically the frequency of entheseal changes and osteoarthritis would be expected to decline with the adoption of a more sedentary life, such as the adoption of agriculture, and they do, with exceptions which likely reflect local and regional terrain effects.[74] Bridges noted in her study of hunter-gatherers and agriculturalists in Alabama that the former had more osteoarthritis but that differences were not significant statistically.[75] As an extension to this discussion, there are 'activity'-related non-metric traits (Figure 4.8), but it is very challenging indeed to determine whether activity led to the traits or produced an 'environment' conducive to trait development. Using all these kinds of 'bone markers' to assess 'activity' at the transition to farming is fraught with problems, and published data – and interpretations thereof – should not be considered lightly. However, many scholars are now working towards improving recording methods and interpretive tools to better nuance these kinds of data.

Injuries related to accident and conflict at the transition to agriculture also show a mix of rises and declines.[76] While hunter-gatherer populations do show evidence of interpersonal violence, this evidence increases for some groups with the adoption of agriculture, suggesting competition over land.[77] However, the evidence is not consistent. For example, in a study of interpersonal violence at four sites on the Danube (Mesolithic and Neolithic Serbia–Romania), Roksandic et al. found no evidence of an increase in interpersonal violence in the Neolithic.[78] With regard to accidental injuries as a result of daily living, it might be expected that different types of fracture might be experienced by hunter-gatherers and agriculturalists (and vary according to terrain and 'activity'). Indeed, Judd and Roberts found a range of bones fractured in people associated with a medieval farming village in England, with a higher frequency overall when compared to urban

74 See the many papers in Cohen and Armelagos (eds.), *Paleopathology at the Origins of Agriculture*; and Cohen and Crane-Kramer (eds.), *Ancient Health*.
75 P.S. Bridges, 'Degenerative joint disease in hunter-gatherers and agriculturists from the southeastern United States', *American Journal of Physical Anthropology*, 85 (1991), 379–91.
76 Cohen and Armelagos (eds.), *Paleopathology at the Origins of Agriculture*.
77 C.S. Larsen, 'The agricultural revolution as environmental catastrophe: implications for health and lifestyle in the Holocene', *Quaternary International*, 150 (2006), 12–20.
78 M. Roksandic et al., 'Interpersonal violence at Lepenski Vir Mesolithic/Neolithic complex of the Iron Gates Gorge (Serbia–Romania)', *American Journal of Physical Anthropology*, 129 (2006), 339–48.

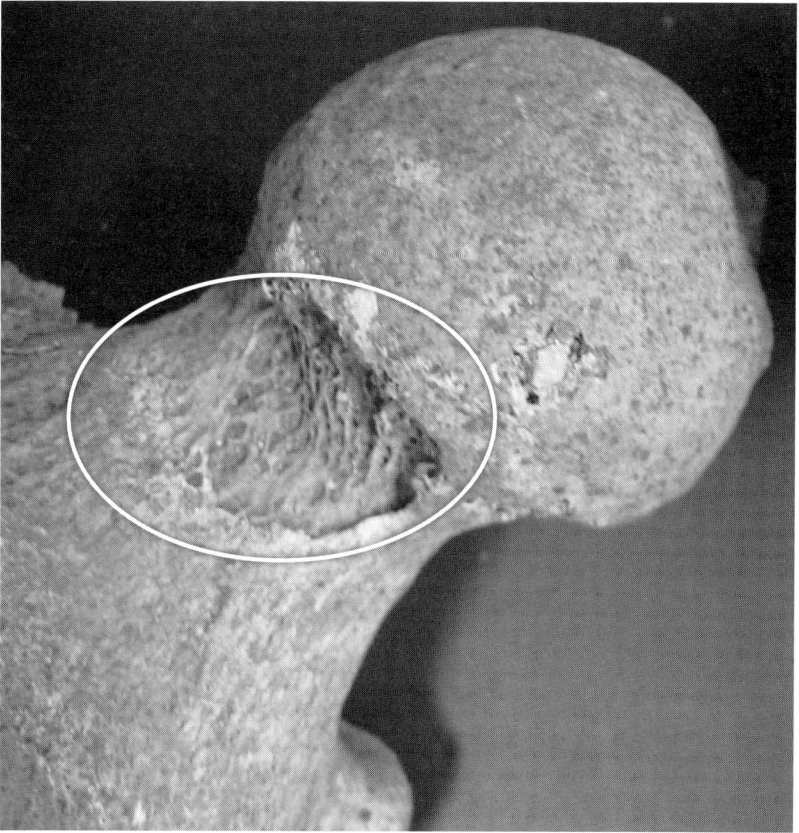

Figure 4.8 Femur (thigh bone) with circumscribed area of destruction (Allen's fossa), possibly related to 'activity'.

populations.[79] Using ethnographic analogy, different possible 'occupations' associated with farming were explored here as potential causes.

### Diet and living environment: skeletal changes

When it comes to skeletal changes potentially reflecting both diet and living environment, demographic profiles, growth retardation, and cribra orbitalia and porotic hyperostosis are relevant. Chamberlain notes that sedentary populations can sustain high fertility rates and, with the adoption of farming, those higher fertility rates are indeed seen, with peak fertility at an earlier

79 M.A. Judd and C.A. Roberts, 'Fracture trauma in a Medieval British farming village', *American Journal of Physical Anthropology*, 109 (1999), 229–43.

age.[80] Reasons for increased fertility include the reduced need to carry dependent offspring around, in contrast to the case for hunter-gatherers, and the fact that food supply increases, and there is a ready availability of weaning foods, and better food security. It has also been shown that people who adopted farming had lower mean ages at death than hunter-gatherers. Growth retardation may be reflected in reduced long bone length when compared to dental age in non-adult skeletons (i.e. bones shorter than they should be for the age of the person), smaller attained stature in adults, Harris lines of arrested growth, and enamel hypoplasia. As there are problems with recording and interpreting Harris lines, including differences in the number of lines counted by different observers but also by the same observer (inter- and intra-observer error), they are not discussed further.

In effect, because farming communities appear to have had poorer diets than their hunter-gatherer forebears, it is therefore not surprising that growth problems are seen to increase with agriculture. Studies in Cohen and Armelagos and Cohen and Crane-Kramer consistently report declines in stature and juvenile growth rates, and increases in enamel hypoplasia, cribra orbitalia, and porotic hyperostosis with agriculture, and later intensification.[81] However, while Meiklejohn and Babb, in their study of stature and long bone length in 68 upper Palaeolithic, 173 Mesolithic, and 467 Neolithic individuals from Europe, found a decline in long bone length from early to late upper Palaeolithic Europe, they detected no change from the late Palaeolithic through to the Neolithic.[82]

Enamel hypoplasia (Figure 4.9), defects in tooth enamel that reflect disruption to the normal growth of the enamel prenatally and in early childhood, has been recorded as correlating with reduced longevity and also caries susceptibility.[83] The former probably accords with the developmental origins hypothesis of Barker.[84] They furthermore have been seen to correlate with infection in the same individual. Enamel hypoplasia has been associated with dietary deficiency and many childhood diseases, but the former cause is considered dominant. Increases in enamel defects have been noted by many with the transition to agriculture. For example, in early

---

80 Chamberlain, *Demography in Archaeology*, 64.
81 See studies in Cohen and Crane-Kramer (eds.), *Ancient Health*; and Cohen and Armelagos (eds.), *Paleopathology at the Origins of Agriculture*.
82 C. Meiklejohn and J. Babb, 'Long bone length, stature and time in the European late Pleistocene and early Holocene', in Pinhasi and Stock (eds.), *Human Bioarchaeology of the Transition to Agriculture*, 153–75.
83 S.M. Duray, 'Dental indicators of stress and reduced age at death in prehistoric Native Americans', *American Journal of Physical Anthropology*, 99 (1996), 275–86.
84 D.J.P. Barker, *The Fetal and Infant Origins of Adult Disease* (London: BMJ Books, 1992).

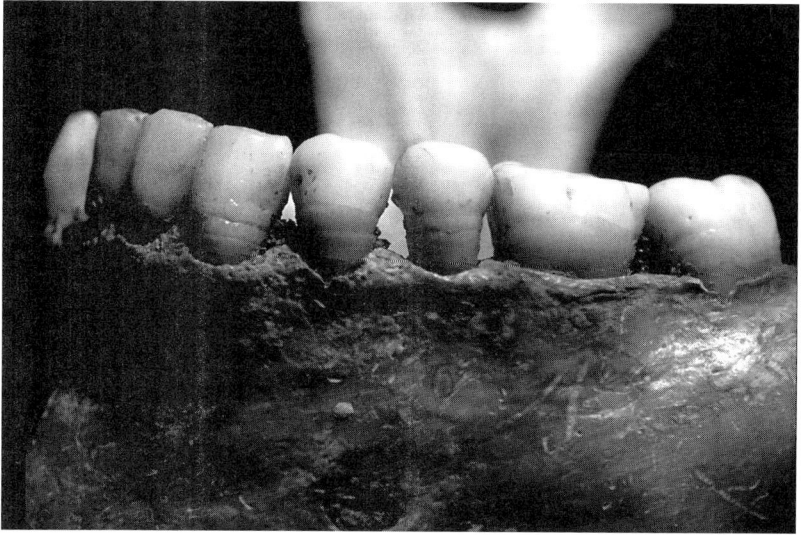

Figure 4.9  Enamel hypoplasia in teeth (lines/grooves).

agricultural Egypt and Nubia enamel hypoplasia was greatest in pastoralist communities but declined with state formation, increased urbanism, and trade.[85] A study of enamel hypoplasia in India has focused on the impact of climatic deterioration on frequency rates, the deterioration having caused a move back to nomadism from farming.[86] Frequency rates declined with this transition, and these were interpreted as indicating a more diverse and protein rich diet, with consequently less physiological stress.

Cribra orbitalia and porotic hyperostosis, as has been discussed above, have long been reported as having higher frequencies in people practising agriculture compared to hunter-gatherer, and as being related to iron deficiency anaemia. However, now these lesions are seen as having a more complex aetiology, suggesting megaloblastic (e.g. caused by a deficiency of vitamin B12, found in high quantities in liver, eggs, shellfish, fish, beef, lamb, and cheese) or haemolytic anaemias such as sickle-cell anaemia and thalassaemia.[87] Iron-poor foods

85 A.P. Starling and J.T. Stock, 'Dental indicators of health and stress in early Egyptian and Nubian agriculturists: a difficult transition and gradual recovery', *American Journal of Physical Anthropology*, 134 (2007), 520–8.

86 J.R. Lukacs and S.R. Walimbe, 'Physiological stress in prehistoric India: new data on localized hypoplasia of primary canines linked to climate and subsistence change', *Journal of Archaeological Science*, 25 (1998), 571–85.

87 P.L. Walker et al., 'The cause of porotic hyperostosis and cribra orbitalia: a reappraisal of the iron-deficiency anemia hypothesis', *American Journal of Physical Anthropology*, 139 (2009), 109–25.

(including cereals) or foods containing phytates (maize and wheat) that inhibit iron absorption, but also high pathogen loads (infection), including parasitic infections, are also believed to be key to development of cribra orbitalia/ porotic hyperostosis.[88] Indeed, infection actually leads the body to withhold iron and make itself iron deficient to prevent pathogens surviving in the body. It has been suggested that while increased pathogen loads can lead to iron deficiency, conversely iron deficiency can prove protective against infection (e.g. in children). Research has also illustrated the synergistic relationship between nutrition and health. In a study that focused on the influence of iron and protein on TB bone changes, it was concluded that these two dietary components could influence whether TB caused bone changes that would be visible in the skeleton.[89] Indeed, there is a strong association between how a bone functions, or does not, and a person's immune system status, which clearly has implications for which abnormalities are visible in skeletal remains and their subsequent interpretations.[90] The association of cribra orbitalia and porotic hyperostosis with the haemolytic (or genetic) anaemias appears to be an adaptive response to malaria. It is highly likely that the occurrence of porotic hyperostosis and cribra orbitalia in studies in some regions of the world will relate to malaria, and it is well known that land clearance for farming, permanent settlements, and stagnant pools of water all allow malarial mosquitoes to flourish.

It should be emphasized that while the suite of 'skeletal markers' recorded to assess diet and health with the transition to agriculture described above is extensive, some scholars concentrate on documenting frequency rates for a smaller subset of these markers, and some diseases are not really considered at all (e.g. the rarer developmental problems, i.e. abnormalities people are born with, and neoplastic conditions (tumours) that can have both genetic and environmental causes).

## Conclusions

Today we live in an agriculturally driven world within a global population that, in general terms, relies on agriculture for its food source. Hunter-gatherers are increasingly being marginalized, so that many become acculturated and 'forced'

---

88 See P. Stuart-Macadam, 'Porotic hyperostosis: a new perspective', *American Journal of Physical Anthropology*, 87 (1992), 39–47.
89 A.K. Wilbur et al., 'Diet, tuberculosis and the palaeopathological record', *Current Anthropology*, 49 (2008), 963–91.
90 See also Wood, 'Osteological paradox'.

by circumstances to adopt an agricultural diet, along with its consequences. The transition to agriculture by our ancestors was challenging and, as today, had benefits and risks. Many of those risks are visibly expressed in their remains and serve as a direct way of assessing diet and health status at and after the transition to agriculture. While there are limitations to bioarchaeology, outlined above, there are numerous studies that have explored the question of quality of life at this transition.

Overall, health declines over time and with the transition to agriculture, as does the quality of the diet, but it is important to note that this interpretation can be very variable. In some studies improvements in health and diet do occur, so assumptions cannot be made with any degree of reliability. Specific conditions in which people lived can lead to very different conclusions about their health, emphasizing the need to consider each site studied on an individual basis. While synthetic studies are becoming more common in bioarchaeology, these studies do highlight that individuals and populations can be variable in their responses to subsistence changes, and there are many potential variables throughout the world over time that will ultimately affect the data interpretation.

In the future, without doubt, bioarchaeological studies will continue to focus on this first epidemiological transition. While macroscopic methods of analysis will be the primary vehicle for data generation, due to low costs, biomolecular analyses will be used more often to explore diet and mobility (especially as costs decline), and ancient DNA analysis will be used more to consider genetic attributes of 'populations', and answer questions about migration relating to the first farmers. Using DNA analysis may also help to unravel those skeletal conditions that have both genetic and environmental components. Teams from different disciplines working holistically to place the data in context, and using 'cutting-edge' analytical methods, will surely nuance our understanding of people in the past living in a world with agriculture.

## Further reading

Agarwal, S.C. and B.A. Glencross. *Social Bioarchaeology*. Chichester: Wiley-Blackwell, 2011.

Barrett, R., C.W. Kuzawa, T. McDade, and G.J. Armelagos. 'Emerging and re-emerging infectious diseases: the third epidemiological transition.' *Annual Review of Anthropology*, 27 (1998), 247–71.

Brickley, M. and R. Ives. *The Bioarchaeology of Metabolic Bone Disease*. London: Academic Press, 2008.

Brown, T. and K. Brown. *Biomolecular Archaeology: An Introduction*. Oxford: Wiley-Blackwell, 2011.

Buikstra, J.E. and L.A. Beck (eds.). *Bioarchaeology: The Contextual Analysis of Human Remains*. London: Academic Press, 2006.

Buikstra, J.E. and C.A. Roberts (eds.). *The Global History of Paleopathology: Pioneers and Prospects*. New York: Oxford University Press, 2012.

Chamberlain, A. *Demography in Archaeology*. Cambridge Manuals in Archaeology. Cambridge University Press, 2006.

Cohen, M.N. *Health and the Rise of Civilisation*. New Haven, CT: Yale University Press, 1989.

Cohen, M.N. and G.J. Armelagos (eds.). *Paleopathology at the Origins of Agriculture*. 2nd edn. Gainesville: University Press of Florida, 2013.

Cohen, M.N. and G. Crane-Kramer (eds.). *Ancient Health: Skeletal Indicators of Agricultural and Economic Intensification*. Gainesville: University Press of Florida, 2007.

Jurmain, R. *Stories From the Skeleton: Behavioral Reconstruction in Human Osteology*. Williston, VT: Gordon and Breach, 1999.

Larsen, C.S. *Our Origins: Discovering Physical Anthropology*. London: W.W. Norton, 2008.

Mays, S. *The Archaeology of Human Bones*. 2nd edn. London: Routledge, 2010.

McElroy, A. and P.K. Townsend. *Medical Anthropology in Ecological Perspective*. 5th edn. Boulder, CO: Westview Press, 2009.

Nesse, R.M. and G.C. Williams. *Why We Get Sick: The New Science of Darwinian Medicine*. New York: Vintage, 1994.

Panter-Brick, C., R.H. Layton, and P. Rowley-Conwy (eds.). *Hunter-Gatherers: An Interdisciplinary Perspective*. Biosocial Society Symposium Series. Cambridge University Press, 2001.

Pinhasi, R. and S. Mays (eds.). *Advances in Human Palaeopathology*. Chichester: Wiley, 2008.

Pinhasi, R. and J.T. Stock (eds.). *Human Bioarchaeology of the Transition to Agriculture*. Chichester: Wiley-Blackwell, 2011.

Roberts, C.A. *Human Remains in Archaeology: A Handbook*. CBA Practical Handbooks in Archaeology 19. York: Council for British Archaeology, 2009.

Roberts, C.A. and K. Manchester. *The Archaeology of Disease*. 3rd edn. Stroud: Sutton, 2005.

Smith, B.D. *The Emergence of Agriculture*. New York: Scientific American Library, 1995.

Steckel, R.H. and J.C. Rose (eds.). *The Backbone of History: Health and Nutrition in the Western Hemisphere*. Cambridge University Press, 2002.

Waldron, T. *Counting the Dead: The Epidemiology of Skeletal Populations*. Chichester: Wiley, 1994.

Wood, J.W., G.R. Milner, H.C. Harpending, and K.M. Weiss. 'The osteological paradox: problems of inferring health from skeletal samples.' *Current Anthropology*, 33 (1992), 343–70.

World Health Organization. *Research Priorities for the Environment, Agriculture and Infectious Diseases of Poverty*. WHO Technical Report 976. Geneva: World Health Organization, 2013.

5

# Communities

AMY BOGAARD

Research into early agriculture often focuses on 'origins': the earliest indications of plant and animal management, and the development of domesticated characteristics that distinguish crops and livestock from their wild progenitors. Understanding the time depth, sequence, and pace of these developments is crucial for assessing how and why particular groups of hunter-gatherers became farmers. Following these transitions, however, it was the social and ecological *consequences* of established agriculture that shaped communities around the world. Just as agriculture altered the physical landscape, so it also reconfigured social landscapes, not least because raising crops and livestock is concerned with a basic human need and form of cultural expression: food.

This chapter surveys the nature of early agricultural communities, focusing on archaeological evidence for the social life of early farmers in different parts of the world. In many ways early agricultural societies are extremely diverse, but underlying this range of cultural forms are striking similarities, suggesting that agriculture tended to constrain and direct social behaviour along certain lines. In a pair of seminal papers, Kent Flannery compared the development of houses and settlements of early farmers in West Asia and Mesoamerica, and found remarkable convergences.[1] Early sedentary settlements often resemble loose clusters of simply constructed huts, such as those occupied by extended family groups of complex foragers or forager-cultivators; ethnographically such settlements feature shared storage facilities. With increasing dependence on agriculture, nuclear families emerged as the characteristic residential unit, occupying separate houses with internal storage facilities. The implication is that the risks and rewards of agriculture

---

1 K.V. Flannery, 'The origins of the village as a settlement type in Mesoamerica and the Near East: a comparative study', in P.J. Ucko et al. (eds.), *Man, Settlement and Urbanism* (London: Duckworth, 1972), 23–53, and 'The origins of the village revisited: from nuclear to extended households', *American Antiquity*, 67 (2002), 417–33.

shifted from the level of the group to the level of the nuclear household. Flannery notes that there are multiple reasons why sharing might tend to become more restricted in early farming communities. First, agriculture raises productivity of land but also variance around average production; second, restricted sharing makes it easier to monitor balanced reciprocal exchanges and to avoid 'cheating'; and third, reduced sharing, restricted land tenure, and increasingly private storage make economic decision-making (at the household level) more flexible.

The word 'community' derives from the Old French/Anglo-Norman *communité*, which in the medieval period could refer to any group of people living in the same place, usually sharing a common cultural and ethnic identity, ranging in scale from monastic bodies to entire populations of nations or states. The *communitas* of classical Latin conveyed an even broader sense of participation, fellowship, joint possession, or use. In this chapter, the term *community* refers not only to people living together in houses and settlements but also to more elastic forms of social cohesion through periodic aggregation and/or exchanges of materials. A relevant concept is that of 'communities of practice', which form around shared interests and are perpetuated through regular participation and exchange of knowledge.[2] The aim here is to consider how early farming and herding regimes con-tributed to the formation or perpetuation of 'communities' at varying social and spatial scales, and to assess how far community 'types' or trajectories of community development can be recognized cross-culturally.

In order to address these issues, the chapter will focus on archaeological evidence for, first, the nature of agricultural practice, and second, forms and scales of collective social action, from residential families to work parties, ritual 'congregations', and broader networks. The chapter will present three pairs of case studies, each comprising a major centre of agricultural origin involving domestication of key cereal crops and an adjacent region of agricultural spread/adoption: West Asia and Europe; China and Korea; and Mesoamerica and the Southwest. While West and East Asian agricultural origins incorporated domestication of animals as well as cereal crops, the establishment of agriculture in Mesoamerica involved a major cereal (maize) but no animal domesticates aside from the dog. Outram (Chapter 6) provides a case study on specialized pastoralist groups in Central Asia that can usefully be compared with the farming societies dealt with here. In the

2 J. Lave and E. Wenger, *Situated Learning: Legitimate Peripheral Participation* (Cambridge University Press, 1991).

final part of the chapter, similarities and divergences among the case studies will be reframed in a concluding discussion on the nature of early agricultural communities.

## Relevant evidence

Inferences on the nature of agricultural practice rely primarily on the bioarchaeological record – broadly comprising organic remains recovered from archaeological contexts – that can be interpreted as evidence of plant and/or animal production and consumption practices. Minimally, this evidence indicates the range of species managed and consumed by early agriculturalists, but ideally it also incorporates variables that reflect further dimensions of agricultural decision-making.

The remains of seed crops, most widely preserved by charring, are often associated in archaeological deposits with the seeds of arable weeds. Weeds are generally an unwanted component of crop fields consisting of species that mimic the crop's growth habit or that can exploit the arable habitat opportunistically. Though certain weed species may also be collected in their own right as edible greens, flavourings, and so on, they compete with crops for space, light, and nutrients, and a major aspect of farming is therefore to reduce weed growth at certain points in the growing season, most intensively by hand-weeding or digging them out. As a diverse group of species, weeds have a range of ecological potentials and requirements; for example, some are large, leafy plants that can outshade competitors and dominate fertile situations, while others are small, slower-growing plants adapted to relatively unproductive conditions. Though hand-weeding or hoeing/digging will reduce weed density and especially remove early-growing species, some form of weed flora often survives to the harvest stage, when farmers cut or strip off the seed-bearing parts of crops and (to varying degrees, depending on harvesting method) collect in weeds as well. Where weed seeds occur with crop remains archaeologically, there is an opportunity to infer the *specific* combination of ecological conditions under which the crop was grown. Though weeds (like crops themselves) were subject to genetic selection through human management of arable habitats, *groups* of species are unlikely to have altered in the same way, and hence archaeological inferences of past crop-growing conditions based on the present-day ecological characteristics of weed groups are relatively robust. Weed-based inferences enable, for example, a crucial distinction between 'shifting' (slash-and-burn) cultivation – involving a few seasons' growth on newly cleared plots prior to abandonment and clearance of new plots – and more permanent forms of farming, with implications for the nature and social scale of land tenure.

The weed-based approach to the inference of crop-growing conditions is relevant to seed crops such as wheat and rice but is of limited usefulness for maize cultivation in the Americas, or for crops grown for their vegetative parts (roots, leaves, etc.), since the harvesting techniques involved are not conducive to the collection of weeds. Other archaeobotanical approaches to the inference of crop husbandry practice include morphological analysis of phytoliths and stable isotope analysis of crop remains. Analysis of phytoliths (the silica casts of cells that form in certain parts of, especially, monocotyledonous plants such as grasses and sedges), for example, can yield information on habitat moisture, since high humidity allows the formation of long 'chains' of silicified cells. Stable isotope analysis of crop material enables inferences about certain aspects of the crop-growing environment, including crop water status (through stable carbon isotope values).

Material culture in the form of 'built' cultivation features, such as field boundaries, raised beds, and rice paddy systems, also provides key insight. Though far less frequently preserved than the remains of crops and associated weeds, such fragments of the arable landscape can provide unique evidence of its scale and spatial configuration (e.g. Chapter 15). Harvesting and tillage implements also offer evidence of particular techniques and 'styles' of farming that were part of cultural identity.

Turning to faunal evidence for the nature of herding practice, the age/sex structure of livestock assemblages (bones and teeth) has implications for culling practices and management goals. Like the approaches to reconstructing crop-growing conditions, these inferences rely on modern comparative studies and uniformitarian assumptions (see Outram, Chapter 6). Other data relevant to animal husbandry practice include evidence for animal housing/penning, such as shed deciduous teeth and stabling deposits. Metrical and/or DNA evidence for interbreeding or lack thereof between domesticated and wild populations of the same species has implications for how closely animals were herded/controlled. Stable isotope analysis of bone collagen and tooth enamel affords direct insight into animal (as well as human) diet and/or mobility.

Inferences on forms of community rely on archaeological evidence of collective action and/or markers of shared identity. Farming practice itself implies 'communities of practice' variously associated with clearance, cultivation, processing, and consumption. Domestic architecture and its associated features and occupation deposits reflect the activities and diversity of co-residential groups. Spatial relationships among residential units and uses of external areas are suggestive of social relationships between neighbouring households. Non-domestic built features such as enclosures or 'public' buildings imply supra-household co-operative effort. Similarities and differences in material culture among households and settlements may highlight social groupings that transcend residential boundaries. Mortuary practices offer another archaeological opportunity to investigate social relationships that may involve intra- or extramural burial, individual or collective interment, or curation/circulation of human remains. Food debris and associated material culture (storage facilities, hearths and ovens, roasting pits, grinding installations, ceramics) are a major source of evidence for social collectivity, shedding light on dining practices and the forms and scales of sharing (and exclusion) they imply. For example, study of ceramic decoration as a means of social identification and communication can be integrated with bioarchaeological evidence for the storage, processing, and consumption of cultivated or collected plants and hunted or herded animals.[3] Forms of collective action are shaped by gender and/or age roles, assessed directly from biological signatures of repetitive activities (leaving traces on the skeleton) and disease or diet (through stable isotope ratios) in sexed/aged individuals, or more indirectly through burial practices, representational evidence, or the spatial distribution of artefacts associated with (potentially age- or gender-specific) activities.

## West Asia and Europe

### West Asia

This region, and in particular the Levant (encompassing modern Jordan, Israel, Lebanon, Syria, and southeastern Turkey), has been the focus of intensive research into early agriculture since the mid twentieth century. The Levant presents great topographical, ecological, and species diversity in a restricted area. Some of the earliest evidence in the world for deliberate burial of the dead relates to the arrival of anatomically modern humans in this region around 100,000 years ago; together with other behaviours indicative of 'investment in place', such as caching of large, non-portable, ground stone tools, the archaeological evidence suggests that sedentary

---

3  M. Pappa et al., 'Evidence for large-scale feasting at late Neolithic Makriyalos, N Greece', in P. Halstead and J. Barrett (eds.), *Food, Cuisine and Society in Prehistoric Greece* (Oxford: Oxbow, 2004), 16–44.

habits (re-)emerged periodically where resources were locally abundant.[4] The archaeological record of the late Epipalaeolithic in West Asia (*c.* 13,000–10,000 cal BCE), coinciding with a period of dramatically increased temperature and precipitation at the end of the last Ice Age (the Bølling/Allerød interstadial), suggests that a 'peak' of sedentary behaviour preceded the emergence of cultivation and herding. Particularly well researched is the archaeology of complex, relatively sedentary hunter-gatherer groups in the southern Levant, characterized by a form of material culture known as 'Natufian' after its initial identification in Wadi en-Natuf by Dorothy Garrod in the 1920s. Subsequent research has established that Natufian 'base camp' sites in relatively resource-rich settings featured substantial, semi-subterranean circular structures of varying sizes; the Natufians buried certain individuals (sometimes with elaborate grave goods) in and around these buildings or in dedicated cemetery areas (often caves). Their settlements were occupied continuously enough to accommodate thriving populations of mice and rats. The Natufians made intensive use of ground stone tools for processing foods, and elaborate carving on some of these items suggests that meal preparation and hospitality were performative and prestigious activities.[5] Pounding and grinding made relatively 'low-ranked' foods such as grass seeds accessible; considerable investment of labour is required to remove husks surrounding edible grains, and such plants are therefore often ranked lower by hunter-gatherers than others (such as certain nuts and tubers) that require less processing and offer a larger calorific return per unit of time invested. The use of pounding and also grinding tools was a key development for territorial hunter-gatherer groups making full use of the resources available in their immediate surroundings. Faunal assemblages vary but the dominant large mammal is generally the gazelle. Groups in other parts of West Asia are less well documented but probably formed part of a broader trend towards greater sedentism that developed in the warmer conditions of the Bølling/Allerød interstadial.

A return to colder, drier climatic conditions during the Younger Dryas stadial (*c.* 11,000–10,000 cal BCE) has been seen as a trigger for the shift from plant gathering to cultivation (sowing, tending, and harvesting) among late Natufian hunter-gatherers, but more recent work on key archaeobotanical

---

4 O. Bar-Yosef, 'From sedentary foragers to village hierarchies: the emergence of social institutions', in W.G. Runciman (ed.), *The Origin of Human Social Institutions* (Oxford University Press, 2001), 1–38.

5 K. Wright, 'The social origins of cooking and dining in early villages of Western Asia', *Proceedings of the Prehistoric Society*, 66 (2000), 89–121.

assemblages suggests that this pivotal development took place later, under the favourable climatic conditions of the early Holocene, in association with an archaeological complex in the Levant known as the Pre-Pottery Neolithic A (PPNA, c. 10,000–8500 cal BCE).[6] Cultivation of wild cereals and pulses is attested alongside a continued focus on gazelle hunting at many sites dating to the tenth and earlier ninth millennia BCE.[7] Indicators of cultivation include the association of 'crops' with assemblages of arable weeds, as well as evidence of storage (including the droppings of house mice that infested stores) and an abundance of wild cereal chaff used as mud-brick temper. Faunal research at sites around the northern end of the Levant, at Hallan Cemi in eastern Turkey and at Zawi Chemi Shanidar in northern Iraq, suggests a roughly contemporary shift in hunting practices among hunter-gatherer groups focused on wild sheep: here culling of prime (2 to 3-year-old) male sheep suggests a strategy for ensuring a steady supply of meat while protecting local populations of females and young.[8] Thus cultivation and 'conservation-oriented' hunting both emerge as solutions to the problem of resourcing semi-sedentary communities during the tenth millennium cal BCE (see also Alan Simmons, Chapter 8).

What was cultivation in this early period like? A major clue is that it did not rapidly lead to 'domesticated' cereals, in which the ripe ear remains intact rather than 'shattering' (the natural seed dispersal mechanism of wild cereals). Experimental sickle-harvesting of wild cereals suggests that shifting cultivation would accelerate domestication; in long-lived, fixed plots, by contrast, the wild form would tend to dominate the 'bank' of seeds residing in the soil until germination.[9] Long-term use of cultivation plots, combined with harvesting of cereals prior to full ripeness (before shattering), would help to explain the persistence of wild forms under cultivation, as would replenishment of seed stocks from wild stands. Burning of a building at Gilgal I, a PPNA site in the lower Jordan valley, preserved concentrations

6  S. Colledge and J. Conolly, 'Reassessing the evidence for the cultivation of wild crops during the Younger Dryas at Tell Abu Hureyra, Syria', *Environmental Archaeology*, 15 (2010), 124–38.

7  S. Colledge et al. (eds.), *The Origins and Spread of Domestic Animals in Southwest Asia and Europe* (Walnut Creek, CA: Left Coast Press, 2013).

8  M.A. Zeder, 'The origins of agriculture in the Near East', *Current Anthropology*, 52, Supplement 4 (2011), S221–35.

9  G.C. Hillman and M.S. Davies, 'Domestication rates in wild wheats and barley under primitive cultivation: preliminary results and archaeological implications of field measurements of selection coefficient', in P.C. Anderson (ed.), *Préhistoire de l'agriculture: nouvelles approches expérimentales et ethnographiques* (Paris: Éditions du Centre National de la Recherche Scientifique, 1992), 113–58.

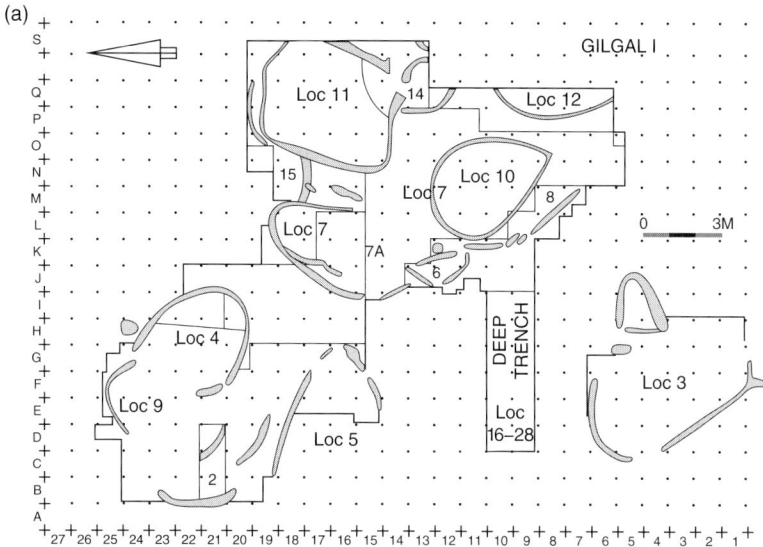

Figure 5.1 Gilgal I, Jordan valley: (a) general site plan; (b) Locus 11, which contained concentrations of flint (black, FL) in the southeast part of the room and multiple baskets (BSK) from which a distinct lithic toolkit and a store of unprocessed wild barley and oats had spilled onto the floor; the floor assemblage also included figurines (F), a charred post-socket (PS) and a charred beam or post (CH).

of wild unprocessed cereals in baskets (Figure 5.1).[10] While the scale of these plant concentrations is substantial, it is small in comparison with later periods, and the dietary importance of 'crops' relative to other plant- and animal-derived foods is unknown. Charred remains of figs from this structure may derive from managed trees, propagated vegetatively.

Cultivation of annual seed crops and management of fruit- or nut-bearing trees must have raised concerns over ownership of land and its produce, and over social status linked to these activities. Indeed, the material culture of the PPNA suggests a fascinating series of social adjustments to the potentials and constraints of food production. In the southern Levant, PPNA architecture is in some ways similar to earlier Natufian forms, featuring circular-elliptical huts and a fluid arrangement of food processing/preparation equipment inside and among clustered dwellings. But settlements tend to be larger and longer lived than in previous periods, and there are new forms of large-scale architectural endeavour, the most famous of which is the tower

10 O. Bar-Yosef et al. (eds.), *Gilgal: Early Neolithic Occupations in the Lower Jordan Valley: The Excavations of Tamar Noy* (Oxford: Oxbow, 2010).

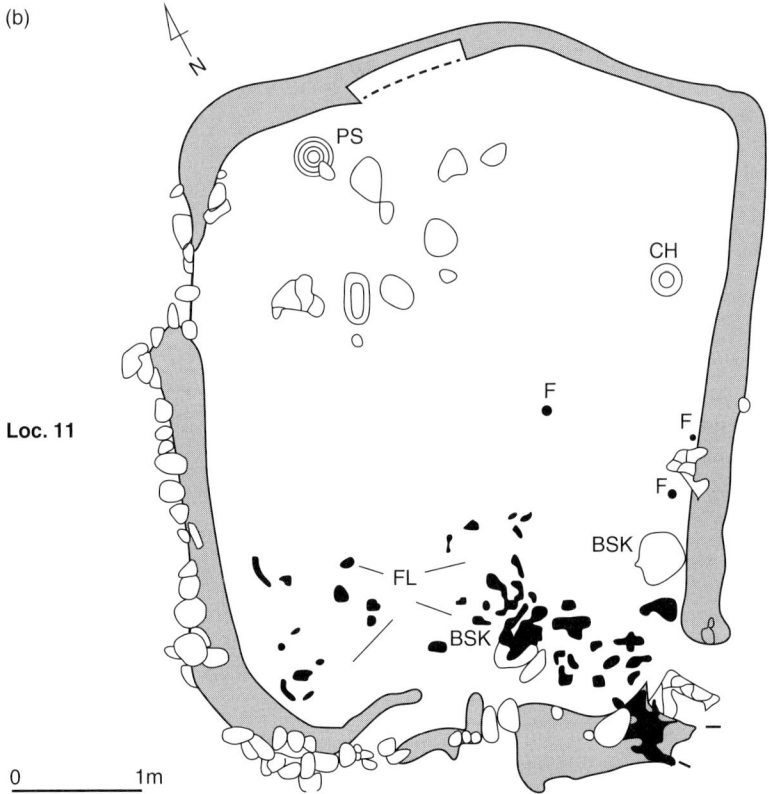

Figure 5.1 (cont.)

at Jericho, originally interpreted as part of a defensive enclosure and subsequently as a ritual monument and/or flood defence. Whatever its precise function(s), the tower is now known to be one of a series of large-scale PPNA structures reflective of communal effort, including a recently excavated large building at Wadi Faynan 16 in southern Jordan[11] and, most spectacular of all, the early monumental enclosures at Göbekli Tepe in southeast Turkey, with massive T-shaped pillars, up to 5.5 metres in height, bearing low and high reliefs of a range of mammals, birds, and insects (Figure 5.2).[12] These animals

11 B. Finlayson et al., 'Architecture, sedentism, and social complexity at Pre-Pottery Neolithic A WF16, southern Jordan', *Proceedings of the National Academy of Sciences*, 108 (2011), 8183–8.
12 K. Schmidt, *Sie bauten die ersten Tempel: das rätselhafte Heiligtum der Steinzeitjäger: die archäologische Entdeckung am Göbekli Tepe* (Munich: C.H. Beck, 2006).

Figure 5.2 Göbekli Tepe, southeast Turkey: (a) aerial view of the main excavation area; (b) Pillar 43 in Enclosure D is one of the most richly decorated.

evidently had totemistic significance for communities in the region, who invested many months of labour to build each enclosure, perhaps in celebration of periodic male initiation rites, before deliberately filling them in. Geophysical prospection of the ground surface across the hill of Göbekli Tepe has detected twenty such enclosures, and T-shaped pillars occur at several other sites in the region.

The public architecture of the PPNA points to a new emphasis on community-wide cohesion and co-operative effort. Such co-ordination may have accompanied other, practical endeavours, such as the clearance and establishment of cultivation plots and hunting of large mammals. Critically, these monuments also posed a powerful counterpoint to divisive social tensions over rights to land and its resources. Flannery's discussion, cited at the outset of this chapter, suggests that agriculture ultimately prompts a shift from sharing and risk-taking at the group/community-wide level to that of a small-scale residential family. The monuments of the PPNA suggest that there were dramatic attempts to *maintain* group-level sharing and cohesion, and this inference is supported by interpretation of anomalous, non-domestic structures on a range of sites in the northern and southern Levant as communal 'store houses' and/or special purpose buildings.[13]

The evidence currently available suggests that cultivation was well established – and that (unconscious) selection for domesticated/non-shattering cereal varieties was well underway in some regions – by the time the earliest clear indications of livestock herding emerge during the mid to late ninth millennium cal BCE, in the early part of the lengthy Pre-Pottery Neolithic B period (PPNB, c. 8500–6500 cal BCE). Though scholarly interest in early animal husbandry regimes has often focused on the emergence of specialized nomadic pastoralism (a later development), it is evident that early herding in West Asia was practised by communities that also farmed. The mixed farming 'package' that crystallized in the course of the long PPNB period – ultimately incorporating sheep, goats, pigs, and cattle, as well as a range of cereals and pulses, plus oil-seed crops – formed a resilient subsistence system. This system facilitated the emergence of the household or residential unit as the locus of storage and basic unit of storage and consumption, albeit in communities that remained tightly knit.

The nature of this early form of established farming, gleaned from a range of sources, provides a detailed sense of the agricultural practices that shaped communities in this period. It appears that disturbance-tolerant weed species become more frequent through the PPNB, suggesting a trend towards more intensive tillage and weeding.[14] Increasingly artificial growing conditions are also broadly implied by the diverse crop spectrum of cereals, pulses, and oil-seed crops that proliferated during the PPNB. The crop suite of the PPNB enabled rotation between crops as a means of breaking disease cycles and maintaining fertility on long-established cultivation plots, while also providing complete dietary protein. In terms of animal husbandry, recent lipid residue evidence suggests that milking and consumption of dairy products go back as far as pottery (and hence probably earlier),[15] but unspecialized 'meat-type' culling patterns and decreasing animal sizes through the Pre-Pottery and later Pottery Neolithic (PN) suggest relatively small-scale herding as a complement to arable farming.

13 G. Willcox and D. Stordeur, 'Large-scale cereal processing before domestication during the tenth millennium cal BC in northern Syria', *Antiquity*, 86 (2012), 99–114.

14 S. Colledge, 'Identifying pre-domestication cultivation using multivariate analysis', in A.B. Damania et al. (eds.), *The Origins of Agriculture and Crop Domestication: Proceedings of the Harlan Symposium* (Aleppo: International Center for Agricultural Research in the Dry Areas, 1998), 121–31.

15 R.P. Evershed et al., 'Earliest date for milk use in the Near East and southeastern Europe linked to cattle herding', *Nature*, 455 (2008), 528–31.

Figure 5.3 Reconstructed MPPNB house, Tell Halula, Syria, showing subfloor burials and rooms at the back for storage.

In several respects the labour investments made in fixed plots of arable land and in animal husbandry are paralleled in the houses of the Levantine PPNB (Figure 5.3), where frequent 'whitewashing' with plaster, fastidious cleaning (and middening), and in some cases elaborate house decoration emerge. 'Investment' extended to the placement of burials under house floors, sometimes with skulls removed for plastering and display prior to reburial. Dedicated storage rooms and facilities are common in PPNB houses, which generally become more spacious and compartmentalized through time. As agricultural practice became more diversified and robust, households turned increasingly inwards in matters of storage, food preparation, and daily meals. Paradoxically, some enormous aggregated villages developed during the late PPN and PN on a scale not seen again until the urban developments of the Chalcolithic-Bronze Age. These 'megasites' suggest that the interests of the supra-household collectivity complicated or derailed inter-household competition and its potential outcomes. Some of these communities included special buildings of various types, the larger of which may have served communal ritual purposes.[16] Neighbourhood or community-wide feasting, particularly involving large animals conducive to sharing/social storage, probably played a key role in mitigating the divisiveness of household storage of staple plant foods.[17] Broader links evidenced

16  G.O. Rollefson, 'The character of LPPNB social organization', in H.D. Bienert et al. (eds.), *Central Settlements in Neolithic Jordan* (Berlin: Ex oriente, 2004), 145–55.
17  K.C. Twiss, 'Transformations in an early agricultural society: feasting in the southern Levantine Pre-Pottery Neolithic', *Journal of Anthropological Archaeology*, 27 (2008), 418–42.

through shared material culture and circulation of valued materials such as obsidian attest to interaction at nested spatial scales across the PPNB 'koine'.

The later PN sites of West Asia reflect more regionalized material culture complexes and interaction spheres. Settlements varied enormously in scale; within the southern Levant, for example, 20 ha 'proto-urban' Sha'ar Hagolan contrasts with tiny hamlets such as Tabaqat al-Buma.[18] Both sites, however, reflect a shift towards greater economic diversification and independence of the residential household. Courtyard-houses at Sha'ar Hagolan appear to have accommodated several nuclear families living grouped in an enclosed compound. Variations on these 'extended-family' compounds emerge through the PN and subsequent Chalcolithic and broadly reflect the diversification of household economic activities, encompassing not only arable and pastoral production but also specialized manufacture of prestige ceramics that were widely exchanged. It is in the context of these large, diversified households that clear indications of lasting social inequalities between families eventually emerge.

Divisions of labour and gender roles in early agricultural West Asia have been discussed partly on the basis of skeletal remains and partly in light of representational evidence, especially anthropomorphic figurines. There are possible indications of female involvement in crop processing at early-farming Abu Hureyra, but wider-ranging analysis of human health and pathology suggests broad similarities between the sexes, with more intensive work during the Neolithic than the Epipalaeolithic.[19] Narrative art of the late PPN and early PN supports the association of male groups with hunting, while large outdoor ovens and grinding installations may reflect the activities of female workgroups. It is notable that PPNB plastered skulls correlate with age rather than gender, the treatment being confined to adults. Early scholarly interpretation of female figurines as evidence of a goddess-worshipping matriarchal society has given way to a growing recognition that early agricultural societies produced a range of female, male, and androgynous images, and that emphasis was placed on longevity, robusticity (even obesity), and survival rather than femaleness or fertility per se.[20] The extended-family compounds and characteristic seated female figurines of later Pottery

18 Y. Garfinkel and M.A. Miller (eds.), *Sha'ar Hagolan 1: Neolithic Art in Context* (Oxford: Oxbow, 2002); E.B. Banning, 'Housing Neolithic farmers', *Near Eastern Archaeology*, 66 (2003), 4–21.
19 J. Peterson, *Sexual Revolutions, Gender and Labor at the Dawn of Agriculture* (Walnut Creek, CA: AltaMira Press, 2002).
20 C. Nakamura and L. Meskell, 'Figurine worlds at Çatalhöyük', in I. Hodder (ed.), *Substantive Technologies at Çatalhöyük: Reports from the 2000–2008 Seasons* (Los Angeles: Cotsen Institute of Archaeology, University of California, 2013), 201–34.

Neolithic complexes such as the Halaf may suggest polygamy and particular value attached to female labour in successful extended-household production. It is plausible that gender and age roles became increasingly specialized as household activities expanded and diversified.

## Europe

Early farming communities in Europe were shaped from the outset by a fully formed 'package' of crop cultivation and livestock herding. Strong traditions of household food storage and preparation emerge in the varied material cultures of Mediterranean Europe, in a climate zone with similar seasonality to that of the West Asian regions where the farming package developed. Farming was taken up on Crete and in mainland Greece from the early seventh millennium BCE, and reached the Iberian peninsula in the earlier sixth millennium cal BCE. Agricultural spread across the continental interior took place through the sixth millennium and featured a distinctive wave of material culture characterized by linear-incised fine-ware vessels (called *Linearbandkeramik* or LBK) and large timber-framed longhouses. LBK settlements range from cohesive 'villages' to loose groupings of longhouses strung out along watercourses. Direct evidence for storage facilities is generally lacking, but final processing of crops for consumption was widespread and probably conducted at the household level, suggesting that each longhouse stored its own produce.[21] The range of crops grown in Neolithic central Europe was narrower than in southern regions, as cultivation of frost-sensitive pulses became impractical, and the resulting decrease in plant-sourced protein likely coincided with more intensive use of animal-derived foods, especially dairy products. Recent genetic evidence suggests that lactose tolerance had not yet developed in the LBK but was likely selected for through use of milk products in central Europe, processed as yoghurt or cheese to make them digestible.[22] In later Neolithic lakeshore settlements of the Alpine foreland (dating from the later fifth millennium cal BCE onwards), the combination of milk-oriented culling patterns and ruminant dairy fat residues on pots provides clear indications of intensive cattle dairying.[23]

---

21 A. Bogaard, *Plant Use and Crop Husbandry in an Early Neolithic Village: Vaihingen an der Enz, Baden-Württemberg* (Bonn: Habelt, 2012).

22 J. Burger et al., 'Absence of the lactase-persistence-associated allele in early Neolithic Europeans', *Proceedings of the National Academy of Sciences*, 104 (2007), 3736–41; M. Salque et al., 'Earliest evidence for cheese making in the sixth millennium BC in northern Europe', *Nature*, 493 (2013), 522–5.

23 J.E. Spangenberg et al., 'Direct evidence for the existence of dairying farms in prehistoric central Europe, 4th millennium BC', *Issues in Environmental and Health Studies*, 44 (2008),

The lakeshore sites of the northern Alpine foreland, with large organic assemblages preserved through waterlogging, provide some of the clearest 'snapshots' of subsistence practice and social life in all of Neolithic Europe. Hornstaad-Hörnle, at the western end of Lake Constance (Bodensee) in southwest Germany, provides a good example, dating to *c.* 3900 cal BCE. The central part of a cluster of over forty small two-room houses, arranged in parallel rows, was destroyed by fire, preserving not only architectural and artefactual remains but also stores of cereal ears, harvested by cutting high on the straw and kept in attic spaces to dry for later processing (Figure 5.4). Weeds associated with the crops indicate productive, well-tilled conditions for crop growth, and provide an example of the kind of labour-intensive, 'garden-like' cultivation that is widely evidenced by arable weed assemblages across Neolithic central Europe.[24] Cleaned cereal grain was kept in small birch-bark containers, and charred food remains suggest that cereals were eaten as coarse porridge or bulgur. The high frequency of cereal bran in human faecal remains in waterlogged detritus layers confirms that cereals were a staple plant food, consumed alongside a variety of wild plants. Crop stores in each house demonstrate that residential families were the fundamental unit of consumption, and artefactual evidence suggests that a similar set of tasks – ranging from hoeing to woodworking and hunting – was carried out by each household, indicating that they were the basic unit of production as well (Figure 5.4). Subtle differences between houses are also evident; one house, for example, grew a wider range of cereals, made regular use of dill (a condiment of eastern Mediterranean origin), and possessed two very rare examples of early copper objects. Recent underwater excavation at slightly later sites on Lake Constance – Ludwigshafen and Sipplingen – has uncovered evidence of 'cult houses' with internal wall paintings including female figures with moulded breasts; one of the structures contained the horn core and fragmentary skull of a wild bull.[25] The implication is that here, too, the

189–200. A. Bogaard, *Neolithic Farming in Central Europe: An Archaeobotanical Study of Crop Husbandry Practices* (London: Routledge, 2004).

24 U. Maier, 'Archäobotanische Untersuchungen in der neolithischen Ufersiedlung Hornstaad-Hörnle IA am Bodensee', in U. Maier and R. Vogt (eds.), *Siedlungsarchäologie in Alpenvorland*, vol. VI: *Botanische und pedologische Untersuchungen zur Ufersiedlung Hornstaad-Hörnle IA* (Stuttgart: Konrad Theiss, 2001), 9–384; Bogaard, *Neolithic Farming in Europe: an Archaeological Study of Husbandry Practices* (London: Routledge, 2004). B. Dieckmann et al., 'Hornstaad – zur inneren Dynamik einer jungneolithischen Dorfanlage am westlichen Bodensee', in A. Lippert et al. (eds.), *Mensch und Umwelt während des Neolithikums und der Frühbronzezeit in Mitteleuropa* (Rahden: Marie Leidorf, 2001), 29–51.

25 H. Schlichtherle, 'Kulthäuser in neolithischen Pfahlbausiedlungen des Bodensees', in A. Hafner et al. (eds.), *Die neue Sicht: Unterwasserarchäologie und Geschichtsbild*, Antiqua 40 (Basel: Archäologie Schweiz, 2006), 122–45.

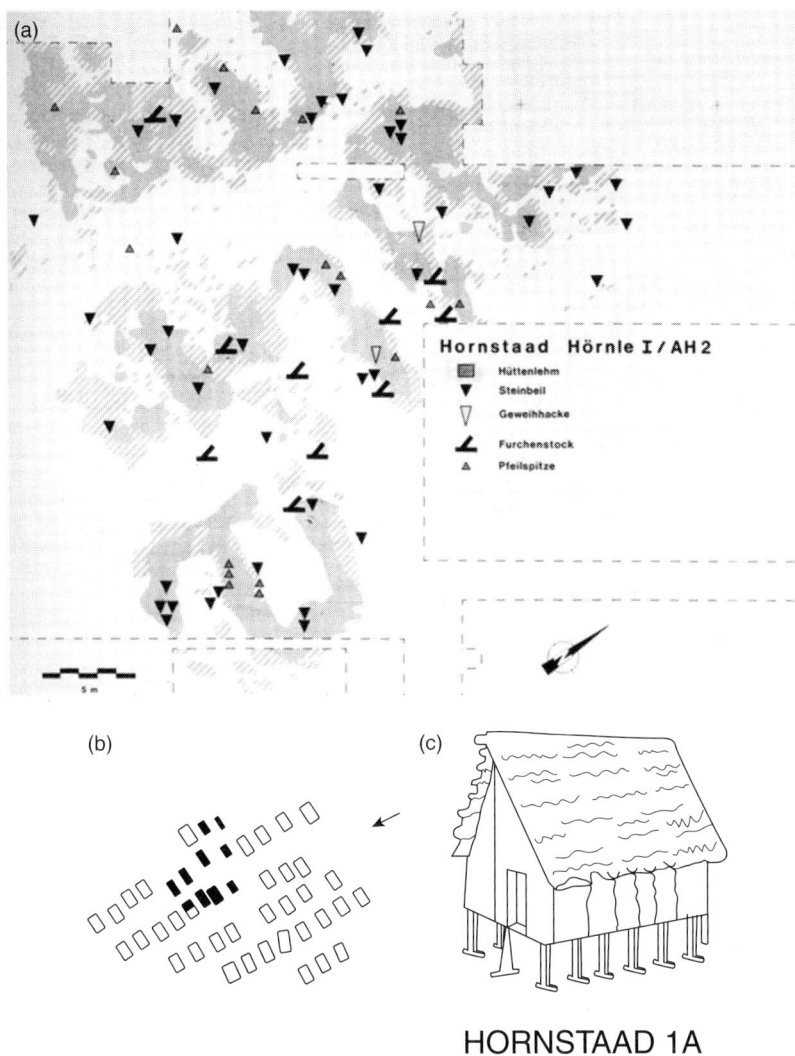

Figure 5.4 Hornstaad-Hörnle, Lake Constance, southwest Germany: (a) plan of the excavated area with distribution of tool types (grey shading = house wall daub); (b) inset of whole site plan and reconstructed house; (c) charred cereal ears from household stores.

modular farming household emerged alongside spaces specifically dedicated to integrative ritual activity.

The beginnings of metallurgy in Neolithic Europe featured spectacular Balkan goldwork, unparalleled in the contemporary metal-working traditions of West

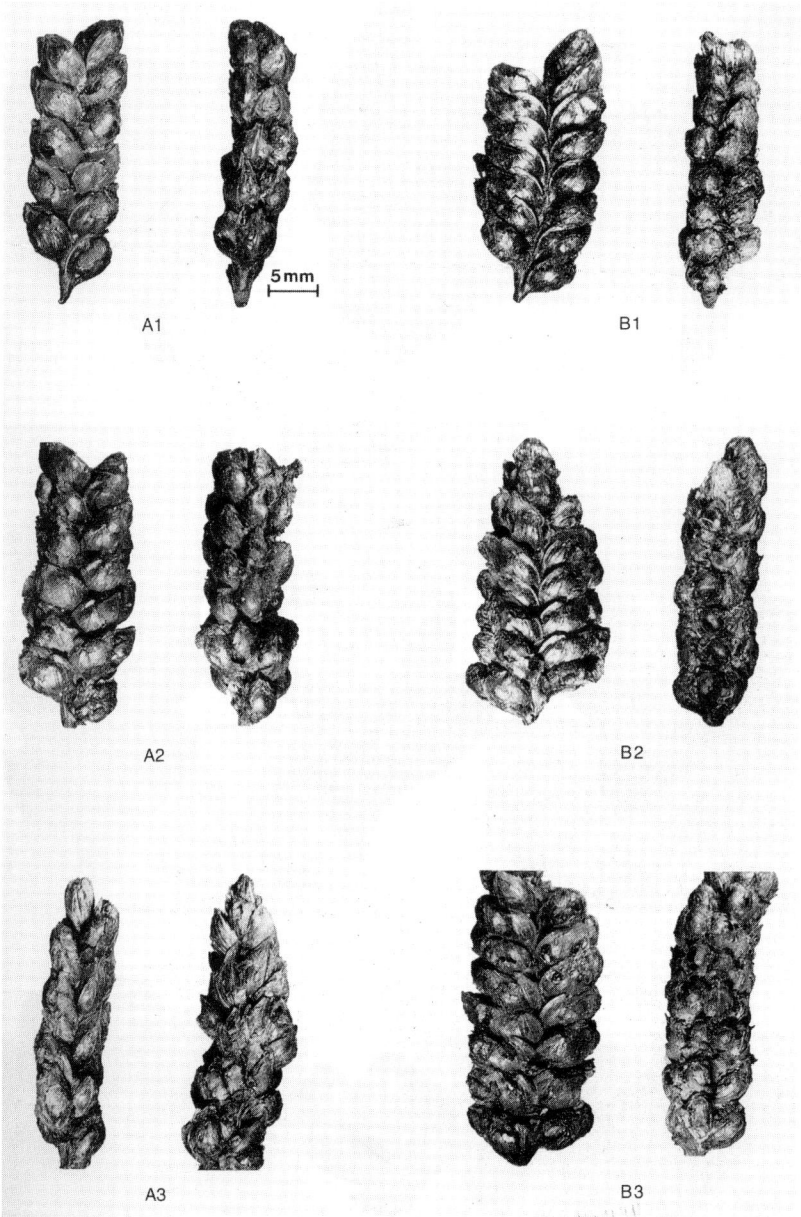

A1

5mm

B1

A2

B2

A3

B3

Figure 5.4 (cont.)

Asia and an ideal medium for emerging concerns over status in early farming communities. These concerns also found expression in early depictions of draught cattle/oxen and of wheeled vehicles, in media ranging from rock carvings in the Alps to paired cattle burials in eastern/central Europe. Ownership of animals and their use as labour-saving devices were major sources of prestige in these small-scale societies. Sharing of meat from slaughtered livestock also conferred social advantage. In the Alpine lakeshore settlement of Arbon Bleiche 3, dating to the thirty-fourth century BCE (the era of the 'Iceman' found in the Öztal Alps 100 km to the southeast), the inhabitants hung the heads of cattle and goats on the outer walls of their houses, perhaps to commemorate the hosting of past feasts.[26] Hunted game also continued to be important in nutritional terms, especially during periods of cooler climate when crop failure was relatively frequent,[27] but in other contexts also as a source of trophies attesting to bravery and prowess among (probably) male hunters.[28]

Skeletal evidence, especially dietary assessment based on stable isotope values, reveals intermittent contrasts between men and women in early European agricultural communities, generally suggesting slightly higher meat consumption by men, presumably in connection with male hunting sodalities.[29] An association of women with food preparation is suggested by the fifth-millennium cemetery assemblage at Trebur on the middle Rhine, Germany, where some adult women were buried with saddle querns for processing grain.[30] Certain forms of supra-household collective action such as hunting were likely structured along gender lines, while others referred to kinship and lineage. The later sixth-millennium longhouse settlement of Vaihingen an der Enz, southwest Germany, was enclosed by a ditch, probably constructed in segments by neighbourhood groups; these groups, in turn, had wider links with distinct regional trading networks.[31]

---

26  S. Deschler-Erb et al., 'Bukranien in der jungsteinzeitlichen Siedlung Arbon-Bleiche 3: Status, Kult oder Zauber?', *Archäologie der Schweiz*, 25 (2002), 25–33.

27  J. Schibler and S. Jacomet, 'Short climatic fluctuations and their impact on human economies and societies: the potential of the Neolithic lake shore settlements in the Alpine foreland', *Environmental Archaeology*, 15 (2010), 173–82.

28  L. Bartosiewicz, 'Plain talk: animals, environment and culture in the Neolithic of the Carpathian basin and adjacent areas', in D. Bailey et al. (eds.), *(Un)settling the Neolithic* (Oxford: Oxbow, 2005), 51–63.

29  C. Dürrwächter et al., 'Beyond the grave: variability in Neolithic diets in southern Germany?', *Journal of Archaeological Science*, 33 (2006), 39–48.

30  H. Spatz, *Das mittelneolithische Gräberfeld von Trebur, Kreis Groß-Gerau*, vol. 1 (Textteil): *Materialhefte zur Vor- und Frühgeschichte von Hessen* (Wiesbaden: Selbstverlag des Landesamtes für Denkmalpflege Hessen, 1999).

31  A. Bogaard et al., 'Towards a social geography of cultivation and plant use in an early farming community: Vaihingen an der Enz, south-west Germany', *Antiquity*, 85 (2011), 395–416.

Ditched enclosures – sometimes but not invariably defensive in nature – are one of the most widely attested forms of 'communal' endeavour across Neolithic Europe. Those that do appear defensive include the Stepleton enclosure at Hambledon Hill, Dorset, and Crickley Hill in Gloucestershire, UK, both dating to the earlier fourth millennium cal BCE. Concentrations of arrowheads and some actual human remains suggest an association with violent conflict. Deadly conflict between early farming communities is further evidenced by discoveries such as the LBK 'mass grave' of over thirty men, women, and children at Talheim, southwest Germany, which probably represents the population of a small settlement killed by a rival community.[32] Forms of communal conflict likely included cattle raids and bride theft.

Larger scales of social interaction are suggested by abundant evidence for movements of materials and artefacts such as stone axes across hundreds to thousands of kilometres, including green jadeitite axes from the Alps that circulated widely within western Europe. While the scale of personal contacts involved in such exchanges could be small, vast regional aggregations of people are also occasionally documented. At the later sixth-millennium BCE ditched enclosure site of Makriyalos near Thessaloniki, Greece, a large pit containing the remains of hundreds of rapidly deposited animal carcasses, serving vessels, and cups suggests massive feasting by a vast regional 'community' incorporating many settlements.[33]

A striking feature of Neolithic material culture along the Atlantic fringes of western Europe are funerary monuments: tombs variously constructed of boulders, smaller stones, earth, and timber that were the focus of burial, often functioning as ossuaries for tens to hundreds of individuals (Figure 5.5). Some of these were (re-)used over many centuries, but their initial construction, concentrated in the fourth millennium cal BCE, relates to the adoption of the mixed farming package. In a way reminiscent of the much earlier monuments of West Asia such as Göbekli Tepe, these dramatic architectural statements seek to advertise and promote a form of 'communal' identity that was to some extent in tension with the logic of small-scale intensive farming. They likely reflect the importance of group endeavours such as the clearance, establishment, and

---

32 J. Wahl and H.G. König, 'Anthropologisch-traumatologische Untersuchungen des menschlichen Skelettreste aus dem bandkeramischen Massengrab bei Talheim, Kreis Heilbronn', *Fundberichte aus Baden-Württemberg*, 12 (1987), 65–193.

33 M. Pappa et al., 'Evidence for large-scale feasting at late Neolithic Makriyalos, N. Greece', in P. Halstead and J. Barrett (eds.), *Food, Cuisine and Society in Prehistoric Greece* (Oxford: Oxbow, 2004), 16–44.

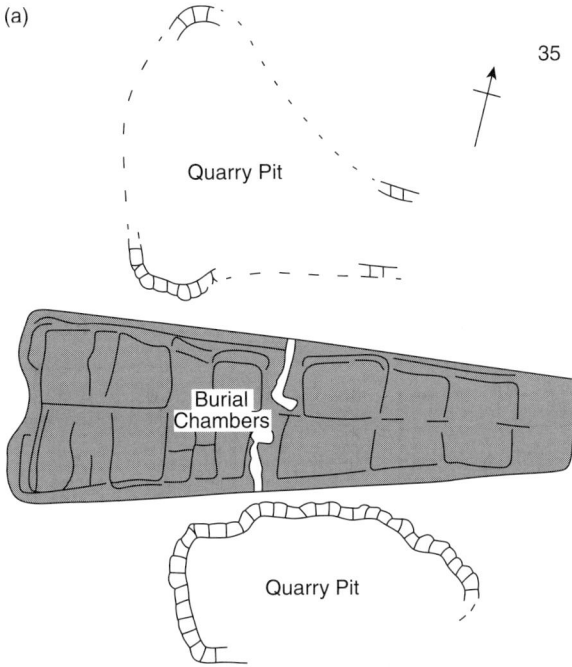

Figure 5.5 The chambered long cairn at Hazleton North, Gloucestershire, UK: (a) plan; (b) disarticulated human remains in the south chamber.

fencing of arable land, co-operative herding/protection of cattle herds, and efforts to perpetuate inter-family obligations over multiple generations.

More broadly, the treatment and representation of the human body provides key insights on the nature of social groupings and categories across Neolithic Europe. Work on anthropomorphic figurines from the Aegean, for example, suggests that female bodies were associated with body decoration such as tattooing in the earlier Neolithic and subsequently with decorative dress and jewellery, and hence material wealth. Female figurines sometimes depict postures emphasizing sexual attributes, while only male figurines are seated on stools.[34] Many figurines depict adults of unspecified gender and, as for West Asian figurines, age was more fundamental than gender in structuring social roles. The emphasis on adult representation coincides in some

34 M. Mina, '"Figurin"' out Cretan Neolithic society: anthropomorphic figurines, symbolism and gender dialectics', in V. Isaakidou and P. Tomkins (eds.), *Escaping the Labyrinth: The Cretan Neolithic in Context* (Oxford: Oxbow, 2008), 115–35, 136–54.

Figure 5.5 (cont.)

regions with distinctive funerary treatment; in Neolithic Greece, for example, adult remains are more often found disarticulated and dispersed than younger age categories, suggesting that eligibility to join the 'community of ancestors' depended on maturity.[35] In these societies practising intensive farming and herding, where production was limited by available labour, it is plausible that full 'personhood' was linked with the capacity to contribute economically (see also Alasdair Whittle, Chapter 22).

---

35 S. Triantaphyllou, 'Living with the dead: a re-consideration of mortuary practices in the Greek Neolithic', in Isaakidou and Tomkins (eds.), *Escaping the Labyrinth*, 136–54.

# East Asia: China and Korea

## *China*

There is a now extensive literature on the domestication of major seed crops – rice and millet – in China, and increasing understanding of the emergence of domesticated pigs and water buffalo, and their role in the establishment of mixed farming systems. The picture that is forming of early established agricultural communities in key regions such as the Yellow (Huanghe) River valley, with evidence of early millet farming, and the Yangtze River valley to the south, where early wet rice cultivation developed, suggests broad convergences with sequences in West Asia and Europe but also telling differences.

A good starting point for consideration of early agricultural practice and its impact on the formation of communities is the late seventh to sixth millennium cal BCE Peiligang culture (and related complexes) with over seventy known sites in the foothills of the loess highlands in the middle Yellow River valley of northern China.[36] Foxtail and broomcorn millet were cultivated by the inhabitants of substantial 1–2 ha villages, with houses ranging from small (2–3 m diameter) circular huts to larger rectangular structures, with storage in pits and ceramic vessels. Domestic pigs, dogs, and chickens may have been kept, and a range of wild plants was gathered and mammals hunted. The deceased were buried in cemeteries separate from living areas. Though long-fallow/slash-and-burn cultivation has traditionally been linked with early farming in both the Yellow River valley and the Yangtze valley, much as with early farming in Europe, this is ecologically implausible.[37] Small grinding slabs may have been used to dehusk millet on a household scale, while examples of boiling and steaming ceramic kits mark the onset of a distinctive East Asian culinary tradition that contrasts with bread-based cuisines of Western Eurasia.[38] Stable isotope analysis suggests that millet was an important component of the human and managed animal diet by the mid sixth millennium cal BCE in northern China.[39]

36  A.P. Underhill, 'Current issues in Chinese Neolithic archaeology', *Journal of World Prehistory*, 11 (1997), 103–60; A. Zhimin, 'Prehistoric agriculture in China', in D.R. Harris and G.C. Hillman (eds.), *Foraging and Farming: The Evolution of Plant Exploitation* (London: Unwin Hyman, 1989), 643–9; K.-C. Chang, *The Archaeology of Ancient China* (New Haven, CT: Yale University Press, 1986).

37  G. Barker, *The Agricultural Revolution in Prehistory: Why did Foragers Become Farmers?* (Oxford University Press, 2006).

38  D.Q. Fuller and M. Rowlands, 'Ingestion and food technologies: maintaining differences over the long-term in West, South and East Asia', in T.C. Wilkinson et al. (eds.), *Interweaving Worlds: Systemic Interactions in Eurasia, 7th to the 1st Millennium BC* (Oxford: Oxbow, 2011), 37–60.

39  P. Atahan et al., 'Early Neolithic diets at Baijia, Wei River valley, China: stable carbon and nitrogen isotope analysis of human and faunal remains', *Journal of Archaeological Science*, 38 (2011), 2811–17.

In terms of domestic architecture, the Peiligang situation suggests a merging of the 'communal compound' and 'modular household' living arrangements in a critical phase when agricultural risks and rewards were rapidly devolved to the small-scale residential family. Recent work suggests that there was a relatively abrupt shift in northern China from mobile hunting and gathering to millet farming, perhaps because small, low-density hunter-gatherer populations could rapidly shift conceptually from a sharing to a private hoarding mentality.[40]

In a roughly similar timeframe, early rice cultivation is attested in the middle and lower Yangtze valley. As in the Levantine PPNA, a lengthy period of cultivation prior to domestication is evident here.[41] Domestic forms were established by the early fifth millennium BCE in the lower Yangtze, and coastal wetland sites of the Hemudu culture indicate that farming was integrated with raising of pigs and probably water buffalo, alongside a broad range of hunting, fishing, fowling, and foraging pursuits. The scapulae of water buffalo were apparently hafted on wooden handles as hoes for thorough tillage of the soil. This labour-intensive form of mixed farming, here focused on wet perennial rice-growing, appears to have had broadly similar social consequences in terms of household production and consumption and ultimate isolation as seen in the West Asian and European sequences above. The earliest preserved paddy-field systems in the lower Yangtze (late fifth millennium) consist of small plots dispersed among houses to allow careful monitoring of water levels (Figure 5.6). The spread of wet rice cultivation from this region – to Korea, Japan, and Southeast Asia (below) – was therefore contingent on the ability to mobilize and maintain high labour inputs. Larger-scale systems of terraced paddy fields in the fourth millennium suggest supra-household labour mobilization, perhaps supported by pig feasting.[42]

Alongside evidence for the rise of the intensive farming household in different regions of China, there are also dramatic statements of communal co-operation and identity. In the middle Yangtze, earthwork enclosures date back to the seventh millennium at Bashidang, where wild rice was probably cultivated, while villages enclosed by ditches with palisades proliferate in the Yellow River valley from the end of the sixth millennium cal BCE.

---

40  R.L. Bettinger et al., 'The origins of food production in North China: a different kind of agricultural revolution', *Evolutionary Anthropology*, 19 (2010), 9–21.
41  D.Q. Fuller et al., 'Presumed domestication? Evidence for wild rice cultivation and domestication in the fifth millennium BC of the lower Yangtze region', *Antiquity*, 81 (2007), 316–31.
42  D.Q. Fuller and L. Qin, 'Water management and labour in the origins and dispersal of Asian rice', *World Archaeology*, 41 (2002), 88–111.

Figure 5.6 Early paddy-field systems at Chuodun, lower Yangtze, China: (a) plan; (b) paddy-field unit showing connecting canals.

## Korea

The earliest evidence of crops in the Korean peninsula appears around 3500 cal BCE, midway through the period of the Chulmun culture (*c.* 5500–2000 cal BCE), which is characterized by pointed-based pottery and semi-subterranean circular pit-houses. Dry-farming of millets, pulses, and other crops was practised alongside a range of intensive foraging activities, including pit storage of acorns, fishing, and hunting.[43] It appears that cultivation initially served to perpetuate a continuation of hunter-gatherer strategies. During the subsequent Mumun period (*c.* 2000–500 BCE), archaeobotanical finds indicate the establishment of wet rice cultivation and continued farming of dry-field crops. Available faunal data are as yet very limited. Water buffalo may have formed part of wet rice farming in the late Mumun, as in the subsequent Three Kingdoms period. Domesticated pig has been reported from Chulmun sites, but the earliest secure evidence dates to the first millennium CE. Preserved fields provide glimpses of actual farming landscapes of the Mumun period and later. In the Nam River valley of south-central Korea, 'dry' (non-paddy) fields with ridges and furrows suggestive of ploughing were uncovered across an area of 1.8 ha; Mumun period houses and hearths nearby yielded crop remains including millets, legumes, barley, and wheat (Figure 5.7).[44] The earliest rice paddy fields also date to the Mumun period. It appears that both dry- and wet-field cultivation of an intensive type was practised in the second to first millennia BCE.

The layout and domestic architecture of Chulmun and Mumun settlements reflect social adjustments to a subsistence spectrum ranging from pre-agricultural sedentary foraging to intensive farming. Excavations along the Han River in the central peninsula included large-scale investigations that provide a sense of changing settlement layouts. An early Chulmun settlement at Amsa-dong contained circular pit-houses, each with a square central hearth edged with river pebbles. Chulmun pit-houses range in size from 3–6 m in diameter and had thatch roofs supported on posts. The Amsa-dong pit-houses were clustered close together, suggesting that external activities were conducted on their periphery. External storage pits and concentrations of large storage pots may reflect supra-household storage.

Later Munun period settlements are often located on hillsides, with riverside land presumably reserved for farming; houses are generally larger than in the Chulmun and vary from circular to rectangular. Some contain multiple

43  S.M. Nelson, *Korean Social Archaeology: Early Villages* (Seoul: Jimoondang, 2004); G.-A. Lee, 'The transition from foraging to farming in prehistoric Korea', *Current Anthropology*, 52, Supplement 4 (2011), S307–29.
44  G.W. Crawford and G.-A. Lee, 'Agricultural origins in Korea', *Antiquity*, 77 (2003), 87–95.

Figure 5.7 (a) Dry-fields and adjacent houses of the Chulmun period at the Pyeonggeodong site, Jinju, South Gyeongsang province, South Korea; (b) plan of dry-field areas and associated houses, hearths, and pit features of the Mumun period, Daepyeong I, Jinju, South Gyeongsang province, South Korea.

Figure 5.7 (cont.)

hearths and might have housed extended families; household clusters with shared storage facilities have also been identified. The hillslope site of Hunamni on the Han River consisted of dispersed rectangular dwellings constructed over several centuries. Household inventories included net weights, projectile points, maceheads, spindle whorls, axe-adzes, semi-lunar reaping knives, and stone swords. Archaeobotanical sampling in one house yielded a range of crops including barley, foxtail millet, and rice.

The establishment of wet rice cultivation in Korea is broadly linked with metallurgy and possibly with use of water buffalo as draught animals. The arrival of this 'package' in the Mulmun period coincides with the proliferation of dolmens (megalithic tombs) across the peninsula, in a development that resonates with the spread of funerary monuments at the opposite end of Eurasia (see above and Figure 5.8). In contrast to the collective burial tradition often linked with the western European monuments, Korean dolmens are generally associated with single burials, and their interpretation has been tied into an account of increasing social disparity. Dolmens often occur in clusters, suggesting that they represented groups of select individuals from nearby communities. Larger settlements tend to be associated with relatively large clusters of dolmens. It is clear that dolmens were much more than the territorial markers of intensive agriculturalists, though in practice that may

Figure 5.8 Dolmen cluster at San 125, Osang-ri village, Naega-myeon subcounty, Gyeonggi province, South Korea.

have been part of their function; they were plausibly a focus of periodic rituals that commemorated the dead while also renegotiating the social landscape of living communities.

## Mesoamerica and the Southwest

### Mesoamerica

Research in the Mexican highlands has established that cultivation of maize and other crops including beans and squashes was combined with diverse foraging practices for several thousand years before sedentary village life developed.[45] As in West Asia and East Asia, therefore, there was a long period during which cultivation was integrated with continued hunting and gathering (see also Deborah Pearsall, Chapter 20).

Sedentary village life emerged in the second millennium cal BCE, the Formative period, and appears to be linked with increased dependence on

---

45 E.M. de Tapia, 'The origins of agriculture in Mesoamerica and Central America', in C.W. Cowan and P.J. Watson (eds.), *The Origins of Agriculture: An International Perspective* (Washington, DC: Smithsonian Institution Press, 1992), 143–71.

maize agriculture. In the Oaxaca valley, Tierras Largas and San José Mogote provide examples of Flannery's village type with rectangular houses and private storage, which he likens to the Levantine PPNB villages of West Asia. At this and other Formative sites, 'household clusters' consisted of wattle-and-daub dwellings, ovens, hearths, and storage pits over an area of around 300 m². These are more dispersed spatially than many PPNB villages and recall varying degrees of household dispersal documented in Neolithic Europe and East Asia. In some cases 'courtyard groups' of houses are apparent, arranged around open activity areas. The implication is that households insulated themselves from risk by sharing it with close neighbours/kin. A more formal version of this arrangement, in the extended family household, developed in the later Formative.

Recent archaeobotanical investigation at Formative sites in lowland Mesoamerica sheds light on how agricultural practice articulated with the development of farming households and sedentary villages. VanDerwarker's analysis of charred plant assemblages from La Joya and Bezuapan on the Gulf Coast of Mexico suggests increasingly intensive infield cultivation of maize through the Formative period, and ridged plots preserved by volcanic ash fall in the terminal Formative directly attest to intensive management.[46] Infield cultivation was accompanied by shifting outfield plots that were increasingly given over to permanent fruit tree arboriculture. The emergence of fields and tree plots as fixed, permanent 'assets' of particular households or groups increased the potential for differential production and wealth. Extreme inequalities were ultimately expressed in the rich burials, monumental architecture, and iconography of later Olmec sites in the region.

Several levels of 'community' are apparent in early agricultural Mesoamerica, from the co-residential household to the courtyard group and the wider village. Mechanisms for maintaining cohesion at the village level apparently involved special or 'public' buildings, attested from the early Formative period onwards. San José Mogote provides a well-known example, with a sequence of buildings on a different orientation to contemporary houses and with crushed bedrock foundations and lime-plastered floors and walls (Figure 5.9). Though their specific function(s) are unknown, they may plausibly have housed ritual activities that served to bind the community together. By analogy with later periods, the powdered lime stored in central pits in these structures was mixed with a sacred plant such as wild

---

46 A.M. VanDerwarker, 'Field cultivation and tree management in tropical agriculture: a view from Gulf Coastal Mexico', *World Archaeology*, 37 (2005), 275–89.

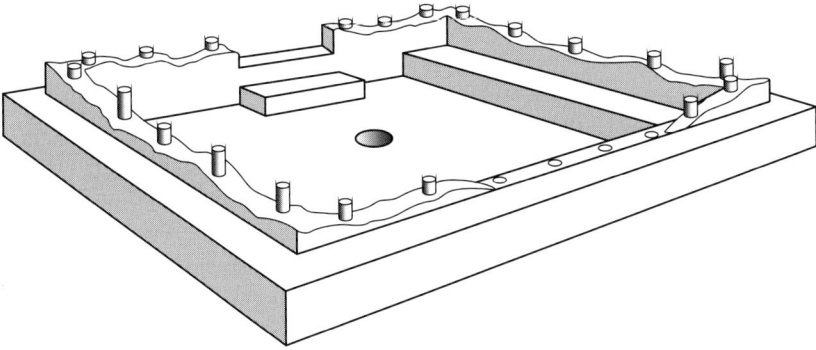

Figure 5.9 Reconstruction of the 'public building' (Structure 6) at San José Mogote, Oaxaca, Mexico.

tobacco, believed to increase male strength.[47] Broader social networks are also evident at San José Mogote: the villagers made magnetite mirrors traded up to 250 km away, and obtained turtle drums, stingray spines, conch shell horns, and armadillo shell for costumes from the coastal lowlands.

Evidence for specialized craft production alongside intensive farming raises questions of labour organization. Attempts have been made to distinguish 'male' and 'female' toolkits and tasks in burial and domestic contexts. While the distributions of features and artefacts on house floors at Tierras Largas, for example, suggest that activities such as cooking and various crafts were spatially distinct, the extent to which these activities were gendered is unclear. As noted above, ethnographic observation of small-scale farming societies suggests that men and women often work alongside each other (e.g. at harvest time), though men may be more closely associated with clearance and women with daily tending, weeding, etc. The grouping of some houses around 'courtyard' areas suggests that inter-household work parties formed around food processing and preparation outdoors. While women arguably presided over such work parties, the 'public' buildings at San José Mogote have been interpreted as 'Men's Houses', where fully initiated men assembled to plan hunting or raiding expeditions, carry out specific rituals, smoke or ingest sacred plants, etc.

47 K.V. Flannery and J. Marcus, *The Creation of Inequality: How our Prehistoric Ancestors Set the Stage for Monarchy, Slavery and Empire* (Cambridge, MA: Harvard University Press, 2012).

## The Southwest

The agricultural sequence in Arizona, New Mexico, Colorado, and Utah centres around the northward spread of maize, beans, and squash from Mesoamerica. From the first occurrences of maize at around 2000 cal BCE, a long phase ensued during which cultivation formed part of a largely hunter-gatherer way of life.[48] An increase in sedentary behaviour and agricultural commitment is evident in the first millennium CE, by which time beans had joined maize and squash. Stable isotope analysis of human remains suggests that maize may have been a dietary staple from as early as 500 BCE in some regions, increasing further in the late first to second millennia CE, but the differential presence of maize remains across sites in different regions of the Southwest suggests that the pace and degree of uptake were variable.[49]

Pit-house settlements of the mid first millennium CE in New Mexico exemplify contrasting social adjustments to farming. At the SU site, in the Mogollon mountains, large pit-houses (on average 40 m²) contained internal storage pits that could accommodate enough staple food to feed a resident family for over a year (Figure 5.10a). The settlement also contained a large number of burials, many of them associated with abandoned houses. All of this evidence suggests year-round occupation and a household mode of production. Many other contemporary sites, however, more closely resemble Flannery's 'communal compound'. At Shabik'eshchee Village in Chaco Canyon, pit-houses are much smaller (averaging 17.8 m²) and storage pits were located in outdoor 'public' areas rather than internally (Figure 5.10b). Wills argues that the inhabitants of the SU site enjoyed greater resource security in a region of higher precipitation, enabling them to pursue the riskier strategy of house-hold production, while those at the Shabik'eshchee Village site adapted their strategies to a drier landscape with more sparsely distributed resources, and so opted for more communal living. Not all resources, however, would be equally susceptible to sharing; ethnographically, meat

---

48  W.H. Wills, 'Plant cultivation and the evolution of risk-prone economies in the prehistoric American Southwest', in A.B. Gebauer and T.D. Price (eds.), *Transitions to Agriculture in Prehistory*, Monographs in World Archaeology 4 (Madison, WI: Prehistory Press, 1992), 153–76; T.A. Kohler, 'News from the northern American Southwest: prehistory from the edge of chaos', *Journal of Archaeological Research*, 1 (1993), 267–321.

49  J.B. Coltrain et al., 'The stable and radio-isotope chemistry of eastern Basketmaker and Pueblo groups in the Four Corners region of the American Southwest: implications for Anasazi diets, origins and abandonments in southwestern Colorado', in J.E. Staller et al. (eds.), *Histories of Maize: Multidisciplinary Approaches to the Prehistory, Biogeography, Domestication, and Evolution of Maize* (Amsterdam and London: Elsevier Academic Press, 2006), 276–87.

Figure 5.10 (a) Plan of the SU site, Mogollon mountains; (b) plan of Shabik'eshchee Village, Chaco Canyon, New Mexico.

from large hunted game is more likely to be shared out than storable plant foods that can be consumed piecemeal.

Archaeobotanical evidence indicates that cultivation took place in a range of lowland and upland contexts, using high-water-table, floodwater, mesa top run-off, or rain-fed techniques. Evidence at some early agricultural sites indicates that maize was grown in an intensive horticultural system. For example, grid-gardens of the ceramic period at the Chama Alcove site in New Mexico used run-off from the mesa top. The swollen state of first-millennium CE maize kernels found in the rock shelter suggests that they were charred soon after harvest, and hence locally cultivated.[50]

Both the mid-first-millennium CE SU site and Shabik'eshchee Village, mentioned above, included unusual buildings interpreted as communal religious or 'public' buildings. Such early examples arguably foreshadow the kivas (circular, masonry-lined subterranean rooms) that played a key role in supra-household ritual integration in later, Pueblo period agricultural communities. As in other

---

50 B.J. Vierra and R.I. Ford, 'Early maize agriculture in the northern Rio Grande valley, New Mexico', in Staller et al. (eds.), *Histories of Maize*, 497–510.

(b)

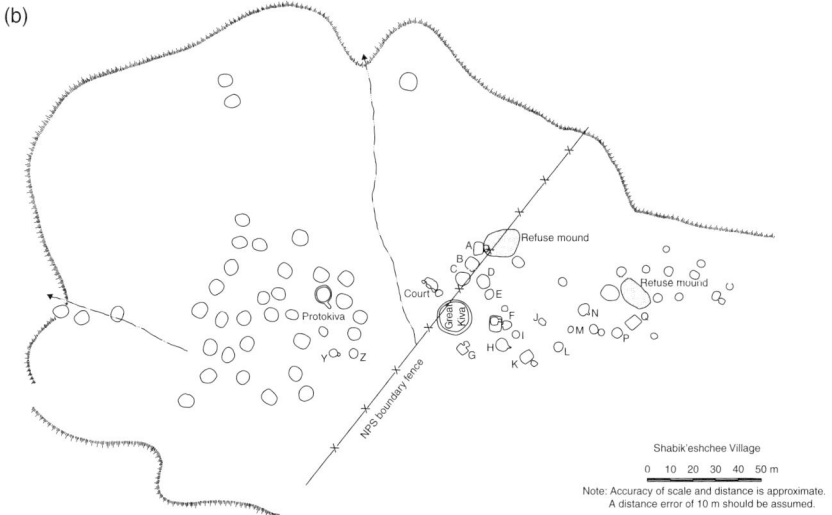

Figure 5.10 (cont.)

regions reviewed above, the atomization of society into productive households was accompanied by new mechanisms for maintaining community cohesion, and regular group rituals likely played a key role.

## Conclusions

Several broad conclusions about the social consequences of early agricultural practice emerge from the regional case studies considered here. In areas with an indigenous agricultural transition (West Asia, China, Mesoamerica), there are extended periods during which cultivation (whether technically 'pre-domestication' or not) was practised by groups displaying some or all of the characteristics that Flannery associates with open, communally oriented compounds; families are distributed across multiple small dwellings, there is much continuity between indoor and outdoor activities, and the external location of storage facilities suggests that they were (at least partially?) shared across the residential group. There is little incentive to increase labour investments in agricultural production; the dietary importance of agricultural produce is often unclear and could be limited.

Communities may eventually atomize into small-scale households that store their own produce for a range of reasons: to avoid sharing with neighbouring non-kin in growing settlements, for example, and/or to gain a socially competitive advantage by increasing production. Early agricultural households, however, tended to remain firmly embedded in broader scales of community, from the neighbourhood group or cluster of houses to the local settlement and wider regional networks for exchanging materials, livestock, and marriage partners.

In West Asia and China, the emergence of household production was quickly linked with the dual pursuits of farming and herding. The addition of herding was attractive for a number of reasons: it provided a means of spreading risk, banking surplus, improving crop-growing conditions (e.g. through manuring), and maintaining a ready source of meat for hosting feasts. The combination of crops and livestock added flexibility and robusticity to household farming, and eventually undermined very dense cohesion among households in early agricultural villages, such as the West Asian 'megasites'.

In regions such as Europe and Korea, to which farming spread from core areas of origin, 'packages' of crops and livestock (the role of the latter being much less certain in Korea) were adopted, and with them the potential for resilient household economies. In Europe the establishment of mixed agriculture was clearly linked with the appearance of distinct residential units storing their own produce. In environmentally marginal circumstances, elements of the 'communal compound' living arrangement re-emerge, underscoring the possibility that risks could be shifted back from the household to community depending on ecological and social conditions.

In Mesoamerica and the Southwest, where herding did not develop, successful households diversified their production in other ways, and the long-term social consequences – such as the Olmec civilization of Mesoamerica and the great houses and kivas of Chaco Canyon in the Southwest – were dramatic. It has been suggested that the absence of animal domesticates, and in particular their 'secondary products' (milk, muscle power, wool/hair), contributed to the collapse of Mesoamerican civilizations when they eventually clashed with European ones.[51] The fundamental significance of herding, however, is that it enabled flexible and resilient household economies to develop and spread relatively rapidly.

In terms of agricultural practice, a striking convergence across the regional case studies is that household farming, when it emerged, tended to involve high inputs of labour per unit area of arable land. Though these regimes took very different forms – from the wet rice paddy fields of East Asia to various

---

51 J. Diamond, *Guns, Germs and Steel: The Fates of Human Societies* (New York: W.W. Norton, 1997).

forms of 'garden-like' agriculture in West Asia and Europe to the ridged plots of Mesoamerica and the grid-gardens of the Southwest – all featured long-term investments in land that would have raised issues of ownership and inheritance. The potentially drastic social impacts of such tensions on wider communities were mitigated in a number of ways, including a degree of co-operative farming within 'neighbourhood groups' of related families, and feasting (especially meat sharing) at varying social scales.

One of the most fascinating aspects of early agricultural communities is the dramatic ways in which they announced themselves through monumental construction, such as the earthwork enclosures that proliferated across Europe and China and the megalithic funerary monuments of Atlantic Europe and Korea. These monuments emerge in early agricultural contexts that placed a whole new emphasis on the value of *labour*. On one level, they are statements about the social feat of large-scale labour mobilization. These achievements are all the more remarkable because they arose in small-scale societies that resisted strong traditions of hereditary leadership and lasting social inequalities. They can thus be read as statements about a carefully maintained obligation to invest labour for the benefit of a wider community, despite (or, rather, precisely because of) the continual burden of attending to the interests of the farming household. Less tangible but equally important to these physical statements of communal effort are the forms of integrative ritual practice that must have been associated with them. Recent cross-cultural research in cognitive anthropology suggests that doctrinal religion, involving frequent, low-intensity ritual (such as weekly visits to the mosque, synagogue, or church), is broadly correlated with dependence on agriculture.[52] Further work is needed to assess how the emergence of agriculture articulated with new forms of ritual practice and potential for large-scale group cohesion.

There has been much discussion of gender roles in early agricultural societies, but direct archaeological evidence is sparse, and the tentative statements offered in the case studies above are largely based on ethnographic analogy and indirect evidence. In a household-based production system, where labour investment was the surest means of safeguarding survival and success, the overriding tendency was presumably for women and men to work together at crucial points in the agricultural calendar, especially harvest time. If anything, therefore, established agriculture might

---

52  Q.D. Atkinson and H. Whitehouse, 'The cultural morphoscape of ritual form: examining modes of religiosity cross-culturally', *Evolution and Human Behaviour*, 32 (2011), 50–62.

tend to promote equality of status, to the extent that standing was based on hard work. Reality could have been far more complex, however, and potentially gendered skills such as hunting and food preparation may well have served to differentiate levels and forms of status in these societies. Activities such as these likely formed the basis of work parties or 'communities of practice' that brought women and men into regular contact with members of other households and forged relationships across the immediate community that cross-cut kin structure. Indeed, it is evident that the rise of the farming household involved not only new concerns with descent / inheritance and the division of labour, but also with the social 'weft' of shared interests and identities that bound households together, involving a range of routine and ritual practices.

# Further reading

Banning, E.B. 'Housing Neolithic farmers.' *Near Eastern Archaeology,* 66 (2003), 4–21.

Barker, G. *The Agricultural Revolution in Prehistory: Why did Foragers Become Farmers?* Oxford University Press, 2006.

Barnes, G.L. *China, Korea and Japan: The Rise of Civilization in East Asia.* London: Thames & Hudson, 1993.

Bar-Yosef, O. 'From sedentary foragers to village hierarchies: the emergence of social institutions.' In W.G. Runciman (ed.), *The Origin of Human Social Institutions.* Proceedings of the British Academy 110. Oxford University Press, 2001. 1–38.

Bogaard, A. *Neolithic Farming in Central Europe.* London: Routledge, 2004.

Bogucki, P. *The Origins of Human Society.* Oxford: Blackwell, 1999.

Bradley, R. *The Significance of Monuments.* London: Routledge, 1998.

Colledge, S. and J. Conolly (eds.). *The Origins and Spread of Domestic Plants in Southwest Asia and Europe.* Walnut Creek, CA: Left Coast Press, 2007.

Colledge, S., J. Conolly, K. Dobney, K. Manning, and S. Shennan (eds.). *The Origins and Spread of Domestic Animals in Southwest Asia and Europe.* Walnut Creek, CA: Left Coast Press, 2013.

Flannery, K.V. 'The origins of the village as a settlement type in Mesoamerica and the Near East: a comparative study.' In P.J. Ucko, R. Tringham, and G.W. Dimbleby (eds.), *Man, Settlement and Urbanism.* London: Duckworth, 1972. 23–53.

'The origins of the village revisited: from nuclear to extended households.' *American Antiquity,* 67 (2002), 417–33.

Flannery, K.V. and J. Marcus. *The Creation of Inequality: How our Prehistoric Ancestors Set the Stage for Monarchy, Slavery and Empire.* Cambridge, MA: Harvard University Press, 2012.

Fuller, D.Q., E. Harvey, and L. Qin. 'Presumed domestication? Evidence for wild rice cultivation and domestication in the fifth millennium BC of the lower Yangtze region.' *Antiquity,* 81 (2007), 316–31.

Fuller, D.Q. and M. Rowlands. 'Ingestion and food technologies: maintaining differences over the long-term in West, South and East Asia.' In T.C. Wilkinson, S. Sherratt, and

J. Bennet (eds.), *Interweaving Worlds: Systemic Interactions in Eurasia, 7th to the 1st Millennia BC*. Oxford: Oxbow, 2011. 37–60.

Hodder, I. *The Domestication of Europe*. Oxford: Blackwell, 1990.

Isaakidou, V. and P. Tomkins (eds.). *Escaping the Labyrinth: The Cretan Neolithic in Context*. Oxford: Oxbow, 2008.

Kohler, T.A. 'News from the northern American Southwest: prehistory from the edge of chaos.' *Journal of Archaeological Research*, 1 (1993), 267–321.

Lave, J. and E. Wenger. *Situated Learning: Legitimate Peripheral Participation*. Cambridge University Press, 1991.

Lee, G.-A. 'The transition from foraging to farming in prehistoric Korea.' *Current Anthropology*, 52, Supplement 4 (2011), S307–29.

Marcus, J. and K.V. Flannery. *Zapotec Civilization: How Urban Society Evolved in Mexico's Oaxaca Valley*. London: Thames & Hudson, 1996.

Nelson, S.M. *The Archaeology of Korea*. Cambridge University Press, 1993.
    *Korean Social Archaeology: Early Villages*. Seoul: Jimoondang, 2004.

Pappa, M., P. Halstead, K. Kotsakis, and D. Urem-Kotsou. 'Evidence for large-scale feasting at late Neolithic Makriyalos, N Greece.' In P. Halstead and J. Barrett (eds.), *Food, Cuisine and Society in Prehistoric Greece*. Oxford: Oxbow, 2004. 16–44.

Peterson, J. *Sexual Revolutions, Gender and Labor at the Dawn of Agriculture*. Walnut Creek, CA: AltaMira Press, 2002.

Plog, S. *Ancient Peoples of the American Southwest*. London: Thames & Hudson, 2008.

Price, T.D. (ed.). *Europe's First Farmers*. Cambridge University Press, 2000.

Schibler, J. and S. Jacomet. 'Short climatic fluctuations and their impact on human economies and societies: the potential of the Neolithic lake shore settlements in the Alpine foreland.' *Environmental Archaeology*, 15 (2010), 173–82.

Staller, J.E., R.H. Tykot, and B.F. Benz (eds.). *Histories of Maize: Multidisciplinary Approaches to the Prehistory, Biogeography, Domestication, and Evolution of Maize*. Amsterdam and London: Elsevier Academic Press, 2006.

Twiss, K.C. 'Transformations in an early agricultural society: feasting in the southern Levantine Pre-Pottery Neolithic.' *Journal of Anthropological Archaeology*, 27 (2008), 418–42.

Whittle, A. *Europe in the Neolithic*. Cambridge University Press, 1996.

Willcox, G. and D. Stordeur. 'Large-scale cereal processing before domestication during the tenth millennium cal BC in northern Syria.' *Antiquity*, 86 (2012), 99–114.

Wills, W.H. 'Plant cultivation and the evolution of risk-prone economies in the prehistoric American Southwest.' In A.B. Gebauer and T.D. Price (eds.), *Transitions to Agriculture in Prehistory*. Monographs in World Archaeology 4. Madison, WI: Prehistory Press, 1992. 153–76.

Wright, K. 'The social origins of cooking and dining in early villages of Western Asia.' *Proceedings of the Prehistoric Society*, 66 (2000), 89–121.

# 6

# Pastoralism

ALAN K. OUTRAM

According to the *Oxford English Dictionary*, pastoralism can be defined as 'the practice of keeping sheep, cattle, or other grazing animals' and 'the nomadic, non-industrial society that this implies'.[1] The first part of this definition is very broad and would include a vast range of mixed farming practices as well as those based principally upon livestock. The second part of the *OED* definition raises some significant questions that will be revisited later in this chapter. To what extent are pastoralists bound to be nomadic? How can we investigate questions of mobility through archaeological research, and are highly mobile societies less visible in the archaeological record? What should we call animal herders in industrial societies, and how do they differ? This chapter, however, focuses on cultures that rely on the herding of animals for the majority of their subsistence, though some discussion of mixed farming regimes is important in setting the scene, in order to identify the origins of some herding practices and to help make comparisons with purely pastoralist economies. The chapter will first deal with key issues affecting the origins of pastoral societies, such as the circumstances of animal domestication, the supply of fodder, and the origins of dairying and wool exploitation. It will then deal with the issue of mobility and how to identify it. These sections will draw attention to the variety of methods that can be used to investigate the nature of pastoral economies and societies. While reference will be made, as appropriate, to pastoralist cultures worldwide, the chapter will focus primarily on Eurasia. The prehistoric sequence in Kazakhstan, in Central Asia, will serve as a case study for the archaeological analysis of the development of pastoral societies, and will also highlight how much research there still is to do.

1 *Oxford English Dictionary Online* (accessed March 2012).

## Pastoralism and the origins of agriculture

When considering the origins of farming, and the domestication of both plants and animals, it is striking that plant domestication and cereal agriculture tend to predate animal domestication and herding in most cases. The three most significant centres of early agriculture are the Near East (wheat, barley), the Far East (rice, millet), and Central America (maize, beans, squash),[2] and all of these areas see plant domestication occur significantly before the exploitation of domestic animals.[3] In the Near East, agricultural 'tell' sites continued to source their meat by hunting wild gazelle for centuries before there was a significant shift towards the herding of goats, sheep, cattle, and pigs.[4] Mixed farming dominates the majority of subsistence economies throughout Eurasia from that point onwards, at least in areas with the highest population densities.[5] Pastoral societies develop within the steppes of Central Asia, the Siberian taiga, Arctic tundra, and some upland and desert zones. In Central and North America, the only significant domestic animals to be exploited were turkeys and dogs, and thus pastoralism is essentially absent throughout prehistory in that region.[6] In South America it seems likely that camelids such as llama and alpaca were domesticated around the same time as *Chenopodium*, in the Andes, and that those two processes were integrally linked.[7] There are a few examples where grazing animals may have been domesticated before, or independently from, plant agriculture. These include reindeer in Siberia, possibly cattle in North Africa, and maybe even horses in Central Asia. While there were events of animal domestication independent to plant agriculture, and there are regions of the world that came to depend principally upon herded livestock for their subsistence, it also seems that plant domestication tended to be first and that mixed farming regimes came to be dominant. It is important to understand why this might be, as it reveals significant differences between mixed farming and pastoralism, and helps us to better understand the needs of pastoralists.

2 G. Barker, *The Agricultural Revolution in Prehistory: Why did Foragers Become Farmers?* (Oxford University Press, 2006).

3 J. Clutton-Brock, *A Natural History of Domestic Mammals*, 2nd edn (Cambridge University Press, 1999); E.J. Reitz and E.S. Wing, *Zooarchaeology*, 2nd edn (Cambridge University Press, 2008).

4 A.J. Legge and P.A. Rowley-Conwy, 'The exploitation of animals', in A.M.T. Moore et al. (eds.), *Village on the Euphrates: From Foraging to Farming at Abu Hureyra* (Oxford University Press, 2000), 423–74.

5 Barker, *Agricultural Revolution in Prehistory*.     6 Reitz and Wing, *Zooarchaeology*, 291–2.

7 L.A. Kuznar, 'Mutualism between *Chenopodium*, herd animals, and herders in the south Central Andes', *Mountain Research and Development*, 13 (1993), 257–65.

The key limiting factor for any society wishing to keep herds of grazing animals is the provision of a secure food supply to livestock. This problem can be overcome in a number of ways. The size of herds can be kept very small, such that their needs are easily satisfied by local vegetation, but this is clearly a very limiting strategy in economic terms. Larger herds can be moved around the landscape in search of good grazing, but such an extensive approach requires free access to significant expanses of land, most likely implying the availability of large territories with very low population densities. If environmental conditions permit, more intensive pasture can be maintained locally, though this, in and of itself, implies significant human modification of natural vegetation for the purposes of maintaining a pastoral economy. All of these strategies are made even more difficult to sustain if there are strong seasonal patterns to weather, such as very cold winters, particularly if there is snow cover, or periods of aridity with little plant growth.

Cereal agriculturalists, on the other hand, generate huge quantities of vegetable biomass as an automatic by-product of plant food production. Only the seeds are eaten by humans, leaving substantial quantities of straw and chaff. Straw can be used for roofing and bedding, and chaff can be burnt as fuel, but these materials are also excellent animal fodder, which can be stored for use during dry seasons or winters. It is hardly surprising that we tend to see early animal domestications occur in areas where fodder is already freely available as a by-product. From the agriculturalists' point of view, the feeding of stock allows the conversion of inedible by-products into protein and fat. The keeping of livestock not only generates more food, but also different types of food, allowing for a higher quality diet. It also allows for the storage of that food supply; the meat will only spoil after the animal is slaughtered. Mixed farmers can also exploit lands unsuitable for plant agriculture for grazing or additional production of fodder, hence allowing further intensification of their livestock production.

It is hard to overstate the importance of fodder and grazing land to herders, and this issue likely impinges heavily on many aspects of a pastoralist's life and culture, most notably on territoriality and mobility. While environment may not determine the culture of pastoralists, it is a constant and strong influence. Most ethnographically observable pastoralist cultures are located in deserts, semi-arid grasslands, uplands, tundra, or high-latitude forests. The majority of these areas are poor or non-viable in terms of large-scale cereal agriculture. The simplest explanation for this is that where cereal agriculture or mixed farming are possible, these modes of subsistence tend to be favoured above pastoralism. They are more efficient, have higher yields, and can support much larger populations. As such, even if a pastoral regime had established itself, it would likely be outcompeted in the long term. Whether high mobility is necessary in all cases or not, pastoralists require extensive territories that cannot be defended easily by force, should they appear attractive to large sedentary farming populations. In prehistory, the picture appears to be similar, with specialist pastoralism only dominating in areas where other forms of agriculture could not succeed. On the face of it, however, there appear to be a few exceptions. The forest steppes of southern Russia and northern Kazakhstan became the bread basket of the former Soviet Union, and remain major producers of wheat today, without need for irrigation, yet these zones were apparently dominated by pastoralists from the Eneolithic through to the rise of the USSR. At least part of the explanation for this lies in the need for appropriately adapted strains of cereal to survive cold winters and short growing seasons, and perhaps a lack of population pressure from surrounding regions. Yet the strength of pastoralism in this agriculturally viable zone still raises questions and warns against overly simplistic models of environmental determinism.

## Specialist pastoralism

Having identified some key differences between mixed farmers and those who live principally from grazing livestock, let us investigate different forms of animal exploitation and pastoralism in economic terms. According to Tim Ingold, in his influential book *Hunters, Pastoralists and Ranchers*, there are four key economic modes in which one can live from herds: as a hunter, a meat pastoralist, a milch pastoralist, or a rancher.[8] A meat pastoralist exploits only the products that can be gained from a dead animal, including meat and fat for food, and hides, bones, and sinew for clothing, tools, and other material culture. Zooarchaeologists define these foods and materials as being 'primary products'. But 'primary products' are also the main concern of any hunter, so what is the difference? Many would see a simple dichotomy between hunters living off wild animals, and pastoralists herding domestic ones, but Ingold sees this slightly differently. The biological definition of a domestic animal is one that has, as a result of human actions, become genetically separated from its wild progenitor species.[9] Under this definition a pastoralist would have to have had sufficient control over animals to prevent interbreeding with wild

---

8  T. Ingold, *Hunters, Pastoralists and Ranchers* (Cambridge University Press, 1980).
9  M.A. Blumler and R. Byrne, 'The ecological genetics of domestication and the origins of agriculture', *Current Anthropology*, 32 (1991), 23–35.

stock. Such a clear separation may hold largely true for some species, such as sheep and cattle, but matters are much more complicated for other animals, pigs and reindeer in particular. If we shift our emphasis away from genetic, biological domestication to think more about economic modes of subsistence within human cultures, we soon come across examples of types of herding that pay scant attention to breeding control, but yet differ significantly from hunting.

Peoples of the northern forests of Siberia essentially herd wild reindeer that breed freely, but they are husbanded nonetheless.[10] Temporary fences are used in some cases to keep herds in a particular area, or the use of salt licks encourages animals to stay nearby. Animals are often captured by lasso and slaughtered near the camp, rather than hunted down and killed with projectiles. Such slaughter will be selective to ensure the continued health of the herd. Some individual reindeer may be captured young and tamed for use in pulling sleds. What defines the pastoralist is their interest in the future progeny of the herd, and the husbandry they employ to promote future viability. There is clearly something of a continuum between pure hunting and meat pastoralism. There are clearly examples of hunters who just take what they want from nature, leading to stress and even extinction of species, others who take care to leave viable herds, and meat pastoralists who aim to ensure future herd health through husbandry, with or without control of breeding. Other reindeer pastoralists will milk tamed or domesticated females, and hence become 'milch pastoralists'.[11]

Zooarchaeologists define milk as a 'secondary product', meaning something that can be repeatedly exploited from a live animal.[12] Another key secondary product is wool, and a less common one is blood. The Maasai pastoralists of central East Africa, among others, extract limited quantities of blood from animals, for use as a protein-rich food, without killing them.[13] The benefits of exploiting secondary products are clear enough. Significant yields of food can be obtained without the need for killing stock. Furthermore, milk can be processed into a wide range of preservable dairy products, allowing for both storage and trade in foodstuffs. Exploitation of wool, accompanied by

---

10 Ingold, *Hunters, Pastoralists and Ranchers.*   11 Ibid.
12 A.G. Sherratt, 'The secondary products revolution of animals in the Old World', *World Archaeology*, 15 (1983), 90–104, and 'Plough and pastoralism: aspects of the secondary products revolution', in I. Hodder et al. (eds.), *Pattern of the Past: Studies in Honour of David Clarke* (Cambridge University Press, 1981), 261–306.
13 K. Århem, 'Maasai food symbolism: the cultural connotations of milk, meat and blood in the Maasai pastoral diet', *Anthropos*, 84 (1989), 1–23.

either weaving or felting technology, produces warm clothing, bedding, and, in case of the use of structures like yurts, housing. It too is a valued trade commodity. A 'milch pastoralist' who exploits secondary products is clearly operating a more intensive economy, much more likely to support larger populations.

The last of Ingold's categories is ranching. Pastoralists exploit their herds as part of their basic subsistence economy. While a limited amount of produce may be traded, perhaps even with neighbouring agriculturalists for grain, the majority of what is produced is for the consumption of the group. Ranchers, however, operate within a cash economy, and the vast majority of what they produce is for sale for money. The ranchers support themselves from that income, not from the animals directly. While the word conjures images of cowboys and beef cattle, in principle Ingold's definition would apply also to modern industrial dairy farms too. Ranching is a feature of the last few hundred years, therefore, and 'meat pastoralism' that is not part of a mixed farming regime is a relatively limited phenomenon in terms of species and geography. 'Milch pastoralism', with exploitation of secondary products, strongly dominates archaeological and ethnographic examples of those who live mainly from grazing herds. When and how did this particular economic adaptation develop?

## Secondary products revolution

In 1981 Andrew Sherratt proposed that a 'secondary products revolution' had taken place in European prehistory that coincided with the introduction of copper and bronze metallurgy, and contributed significantly to the rise of more complex societies.[14] He argued that Neolithic animal exploitation had focused on the use of animals for meat, but by the Chalcolithic (Copper Age) and early Bronze Age there were major shifts occurring in the patterns of animal husbandry, which saw widespread dairying as well as increased use of animal labour for transport and ploughing. This massive intensification of the animal side of mixed farming helped underpin increases in population, changes in patterns of wealth and power, and a movement towards significantly more complex societies. The geographic focus for this revolution was the eastern Mediterranean and Near East, where the economy was strongly based upon mixed farming, but the Chalcolithic/Bronze Age also sees the expansion of significant pastoralist cultures in the eastern European plain and

14  Sherratt, 'Plough and pastoralism'.

Central Asian steppes in the general absence of cereal agriculture.[15] Sherratt was not explicitly arguing that practices such as milking, use of wool, or animal traction were first invented at the same time as copper metallurgy, but more that at that same time the emphasis of economies shifted strongly towards intensive exploitation of secondary products. In order for us to understand the development of prehistoric pastoralism, it is necessary to ask when practices such as milking first developed, and whether the timing of Sherratt's secondary products revolution holds true for all regions and environments within Eurasia.

The 1970s and 1980s saw significant advances in zooarchaeological methods by scholars such as Sebastian Payne and Tony Legge.[16] This body of research established methods for identifying the age and sex ratios of slaughtered animals from the study of animal bones in the archaeological record. Such work allows past herd structures and slaughter patterns to be reconstructed and compared against a number of different husbandry models. When animals are kept for different purposes, it makes economic sense to maintain herds with different sex and age ratios. The following zooarchaeological models were developed through ethnographic observation of traditional farming practices. When keeping animals primarily for dairying, it makes sense to slaughter most males soon after birth, to avoid wasting fodder on them and to prevent them from using up their mother's milk. Only enough males to maintain a breeding population need to be kept. For meat exploitation it is logical to slaughter most males when they reach full size, when they will produce the maximum amount of meat; killing any later will simply result in wasting fodder to no economic advantage. A small number of males are kept for breeding with the females of the herd. For maximizing wool exploitation, all animals can be kept alive while still productive. These are all extreme models, and mixed use can also be identified. It is quite common to see many males slaughtered just before their first winter in order to exploit some meat, but also avoid the need for extra winter fodder. This leaves a selective slaughter pattern that lies somewhere between meat and milk models.

Analyses of faunal assemblages using such methods generally supported Sherratt's view of a secondary products revolution at the start of the Bronze

---

15 P.L. Kohl, *The Making of Bronze Age Eurasia* (Cambridge University Press, 2007), 128.

16 S. Payne, 'Kill-off patterns in sheep and goats: the mandibles from Asvan Kale', *Anatolian Studies*, 23 (1973), 281–303; A.J. Legge, 'Aspects of cattle husbandry', in R. Mercer (ed.), *Farming Practice in British Prehistory* (Edinburgh University Press, 1981), 169–81.

Age, particularly in southeastern Europe, Anatolia, and the Near East. However, the zooarchaeological record also hinted at the possible presence of significant Neolithic dairying in some regions of Europe with a less Mediterranean climate. Early Neolithic Britain was one such region, with cattle dominating faunal assemblages at a number of causewayed enclosure sites. The majority of these cattle bones appear to have derived from adult females.[17] The evidence for the very early slaughter of male calves is absent, but so is evidence for the consumption of meat from juvenile males that have just reached full size. The consumption of mature females suggests the use of dairy cows for meat at the end of their productive lives. Elsewhere, such as the Alpine foreland, patterns of caprine exploitation were more suggestive of a mixed strategy of milk and meat exploitation, rather than meat production alone.[18] Much more recent zooarchaeological analyses, that incorporate methodological advances and consideration of a wider range of herd structures (including significant milking), however, are beginning to suggest that human groups in many regions extensively exploited dairy products during the Neolithic.[19]

A step-change in the study of pastoral economies has been made possible over the last fifteen years or so, as a result of the development of new techniques for identifying chemical residues in archaeological pottery. It is now possible to identify both lipid (fat) and protein residues derived from the milk of ruminant animals.[20] Lipid residue techniques, developed by Richard Evershed's team, have been most useful in the study of early dairying because fats survive very well when absorbed into the fabric of ancient, unglazed pottery. Residues can be commonly found in large proportions of pottery sherds from many thousands of years ago, and it is possible to distinguish the fats of ruminant animals from other species such as pig or horse, and to establish if the ruminant fats derive from meat or milk. Early applications of this method focused upon dairying evidence in Britain, and found that milk residues dominated during the early Neolithic, demonstrating that those

17 Legge, 'Aspects of cattle husbandry'.
18 P. Halstead, 'Like rising damp? An ecological approach to the spread of farming in southeast and central Europe', in A. Milles et al. (eds.), *The Beginnings of Agriculture* (Oxford: British Archaeological Reports, 1989), 23–53.
19 J.-D. Vigne and D. Helmer, 'Was milk a "secondary product" in the Old World neolithisation process? Its role in the domestication of cattle, sheep and goats', *Anthropozoologica*, 42 (2007), 9–40.
20 S.N. Dudd and R.P. Evershed, 'Direct demonstration of milk as an element of archaeological economies', *Science*, 282 (1999), 1478–81; O. Craig et al., 'Detecting milk proteins in ancient pots', *Nature*, 408 (2000), 312.

mature cows from causewayed enclosures probably were from dairy herds.[21] While species proportions fluctuate throughout British prehistory, the lipid residues indicate that milk was a key component of the economy from the earliest farming onwards. More recent studies of Neolithic ceramics from southeastern Europe, Anatolia, and the Near East show that milk residues are present in small proportions in all those regions. However, in northwestern Anatolia, where the environment is more suited to cattle husbandry, a very high proportion of Neolithic pots appear to contain milk residues.[22] The most recent data on the subject suggest that early Neolithic dairying might well be most associated with areas where cattle were most likely to thrive.

The notion of a secondary products revolution remains reasonably valid for some regions, notably Greece and some areas of the Near East, but it is clear that in other environmental zones, particularly more temperate ones, dairying was an important feature of early animal husbandry in the Neolithic. This is important, as it suggests that the innovation of dairying did not require such a long lead-in time, and the problems associated with the intensive exploitation of animals for milk could be overcome more easily than previously suspected. This means that the theoretical ability for people to live principally from milch pastoralism existed much earlier than the obvious establishment of such cultures on the plains and steppes of Eurasia. As a result, we can no longer view the secondary products revolution of the Bronze Age as being an essential prerequisite for such cultures, and we must look elsewhere for explanations for their genesis.

This is not to say that there are not significant barriers to the successful, intensive exploitation of herds for dairy products. It is worth discussing two of these potential barriers: sustaining milk let-down in primitive breeds, and human lactose intolerance. Naturally, animals produce milk for their young, not for us. As such, lactation is designed to stop after their young have been weaned. Millennia of selective breeding have resulted in modern dairy cattle producing much higher yields and prolonged milk let-down in the absence of a calf to feed. Early breeds produce much less milk and tend to stop producing it without stimulus from a calf.[23] On the other hand, if the calf is present, it is consuming much of the milk, rather than us. One way of dealing with this

21 M. S. Copley et al., 'Direct chemical evidence for widespread dairying in prehistoric Britain', *Proceedings of the National Academy of Sciences*, 100 (2003), 1524–9.

22 R.P. Evershed et al., 'Earliest date for milk use in the Near East and southeastern Europe linked to cattle herding', *Nature*, 455 (2008), 528–31.

23 F. McCormick, 'Early faunal evidence for dairying', *Oxford Journal of Archaeology*, 11 (1992), 201–9.

problem is to keep at least one calf alive to stimulate milk let-down, while controlling its consumption to an extent to ensure that enough surplus milk can be harvested for human consumption. Such a method may result in a peak of slaughter of calves shortly after weaning, and before overwintering. Recent zooarchaeological analyses of Neolithic sites in France have indicated that such a practice may well have been in place among early dairy herds in that region. Other sites in France, Italy, and the Balkans, however, display classic milk herd patterns of slaughtering many male calves very young indeed.[24] Without so many calves there is more milk for human use, but how is milk let-down encouraged? First, female calves are unlikely to be slaughtered, but second, ethnography tells us about a number of tricks that can be used to induce milk let-down in primitive cattle breeds. Such practices include tricking the cow with the use of a calf skin, or the stimulus of the cow's vulva by blowing strongly into it, sometimes with the aid of a pipe.[25] It is clear that with a combination of trickery and careful herd management, this problem could be readily overcome prior to significant breed improvement.

As infants, all mammals should be able to digest milk, because they produce an enzyme called lactase which is designed to help break down lactose, the sugar found in milk. However, after weaning, lactase is no longer produced and it becomes difficult to digest milk thereafter. This state is known as lactose intolerance, and, rather than being an unusual condition, it is the default for adult mammals. Lactose intolerance would also have been the normal state for human populations prior to the domestication of animals and the regular exploitation of their milk. Over time, human groups that consume dairy products must have been put under considerable selective pressure to tolerate that foodstuff. Those who could would have a genetic advantage, and the result is the high prevalence of the lactase persistence gene among modern humans. There are, however, a number of racial groups who, no doubt related to their forebears' subsistence economies, have not developed this genetic trait.[26] So, how did dairying become so popular in the first place – when most people were lactose intolerant – and to an extent significant enough to pose selective pressure towards lactase persistence?

24 Vigne and Helmer, 'Was milk a "secondary product"?'
25 K. Ryan, 'Facilitating milk let-down in traditional cattle-herding systems: East Africa and beyond', in J. Mulville and A.K. Outram (eds.), *The Zooarchaeology of Fats, Milk and Dairying* (Oxford: Oxbow, 2005), 96–106.
26 P. Gerbault et al., 'Evolution of lactase persistence: an example of human niche construction', *Philosophical Transactions of the Royal Society B*, 366 (2011), 863–77; I.G. Romero et al., 'Herders of Indian and European cattle share their predominant allele for lactase persistence', *Molecular Biology and Evolution*, 29 (2012), 249–60.

There are a few key facts we need to know about lactose intolerance in order to answer this. First, it is not an allergy that can have potentially fatal consequences. Instead, it is an intolerance that leads to digestive discomfort, and even with that discomfort, however unpleasant, it is still possible to extract nutritional value from milk. Second, milk can be made more digestible through the consumption of processed dairy products rather than raw milk. The biotic and chemical processes involved in the production of fermented drinks, yoghurt, butter, and cheeses all tend to result in the partial breakdown of lactose prior to consumption. As such, it is possible to conceive of a largely lactose intolerant population still deriving much nutrient value from dairy products, while those naturally possessing lactase persistence would be afforded a selective advantage.

With our much increased capability to understand the human genome and extract ancient DNA (aDNA), it has become possible to study the issue of lactase persistence directly. Work in this area is still in its infancy, but the most recent models suggest that the lactase persistence gene may well date back to about 7,500 years ago somewhere in the central European or Balkan region.[27] While this date relates to the earliest animal herding in these regions, studies of aDNA in central and eastern Europe do not indicate that the gene was widespread at this time,[28] and it may not have become prevalent for another thousand years among groups that were particularly dependent upon dairying. This work is still based upon quite small sample sizes, and many regions and periods are yet to be analysed using this aDNA technique. It is becoming clear, however, that while there was a period of milk exploitation by largely lactose intolerant individuals, perhaps aided by use of processed dairy products, the evolution to lactose tolerance was still relatively quick. It is also likely that lactose tolerance was established among mixed farmers in Europe, prior to the expansion of pure pastoralism in the plains and steppes further east. No similar aDNA work has been performed in those regions, so it is still open for us to debate whether pastoralism was an adaptation of local indigenous populations of the steppes, or whether already lactose tolerant groups moved into the area with their domestic herds.

The establishment of African pastoralism and dairying is an even more complex issue. Modern-day Africa is home to many pastoralist groups who

---

27  Y. Itan et al., 'The origins of lactase persistence in Europe', *PLoS Computational Biology*, 5 (2009), e1000491.

28  J. Burger et al., 'Absence of the lactase-persistence-associated allele in early Neolithic Europeans', *Proceedings of the National Academy of Sciences*, 104 (2007), 3736–41.

are dependent upon secondary products.[29] Some of the most notable are the Bedouin and Berbers of North Africa, the Tuareg of the north-central Sahara, the Afar of the Horn of Africa, the Fula people of the Sahel, and a number of cultures in central East Africa, including the well-known Maasai. It is clear that cattle pastoralism was present in Africa well before the development of cereal agriculture.[30] Domestic cattle appear in North Africa every bit as early as in the Near East, but in Africa the cattle come first, while in the Near East sheep and, particularly, goats are arguably the earliest animals to be domesticated.[31] While there is still much room for debate, current genetic studies of African cattle provide some support for a long-held archaeological view that cattle were independently domesticated in North Africa to fill a very particular economic niche in an unpredictable arid environment, where mobile herds could respond better to localized drought than an economy based upon the planting of immovable crops.[32] Later, increased aridity may well have encouraged expansion of this form of economy further south.[33] Human genetic studies also support a separate origin for dairying in Africa, because sub-Saharan Africans appear not to share the same lactase persistence gene as Eurasians, yet they are lactose tolerant.[34] While the genetic basis for lactose tolerance in these populations is yet to be determined, this difference is likely to indicate the indigenous development of dairying rather than an influx of lactose tolerant pastoralists from the Near East. One exception to this are the Berbers, who share the Eurasian gene, perhaps showing a more integrated development of pastoralism and dairying between people in the far north of Africa and Eurasia, or at least later population movement into North Africa.[35]

Other important secondary products, such as wool, have not received quite the same level of recent scientific attention, and as a result we know little more about that topic now than we did thirty years ago. Wild sheep are not particularly woolly, but instead have a more hairy coat made up of coarse 'kemps'. Below the kemp is a soft, warm underwool that is rather short. Over

29  A.B. Smith, *Pastoralism in Africa: Origins and Development Ecology* (London: Hurst, 1992).
30  F. Marshall and E. Hildebrand, 'Cattle before crops: the beginnings of food production in Africa', *Journal of World Prehistory*, 16 (2002), 99–143; and see Paul Lane, Chapter 18.
31  Legge and Rowley-Conwy, 'Exploitation of animals'.
32  A. Beja-Pereira et al., 'The origin of European cattle: evidence from modern and ancient DNA', *Proceedings of the National Academy of Sciences*, 103 (2006), 8113–18.
33  Marshall and Hildebrand, 'Cattle before crops'.
34  S. Myles et al., 'Genetic evidence in support of a shared Eurasian–North African dairying origin', *Human Genetics*, 117 (2005), 34–42; Romero et al., 'Herders of Indian and European cattle'.
35  Myles et al., 'Genetic evidence'.

perhaps thousands of years, domestic sheep were selectively bred to reduce the kemp and increase the amount and length of the underwool. Further breed improvements resulted in higher yields and white rather than brown wool, and prevented unwanted moulting prior to harvesting with shears.[36] Given the current lack of genetic evidence for the geography and timing of such developments in sheep and other wool-bearing animals, we have to rely upon the zooarchaeological identification of wool production herd structures, alongside evidence from the portrayal of animals in art and the rare survival of ancient fabrics. The vast majority of this evidence still supports Sherratt's original suggestion that this secondary product became more important from the Chalcolithic and Bronze Age onwards.[37] This still suggests that woolly sheep were potentially available to the early pastoralists of the Eurasian steppes, and neither caprines nor wool were the focus of early African pastoralism.

## Mobility

The *OED* definition of pastoralism suggests that living from grazing herds naturally implies a nomadic existence. This issue is clearly of key importance in understanding the nature of pastoralist societies, particularly the nature of land tenure and the environments they inhabit. The topic becomes particularly interesting where there was potential for conflict of interest in land use between mobile herders and sedentary agriculturalists. Despite high mobility offering some military advantage in short-term territorial gains, for instance by the Mongol invaders, history appears to suggest that the long-term winners in such conflicts have been settled agricultural groups who defend defined territories, with, most likely, higher population densities. Surviving groups of nomadic pastoralists are only to be found in lands that are marginal or impossible for agriculture. Even then, the scale of their mobility is somewhat curtailed by modern geopolitics. In Africa, groups like the Maasai, Tuareg, and Bedouin are still mobile, but much less nomadic than records show they once were.[38] Kazakh steppe pastoralists were forcibly settled by Soviet interventions, and not just in the agriculturally rich north of Kazakhstan.[39]

---

36 M.J. Ryder, 'Livestock products: skins and fleeces', in Mercer (ed.), *Farming Practice in British Prehistory*, 182–209.

37 Sherratt, 'Plough and pastoralism'.    38 Smith, *Pastoralism in Africa*.

39 M.D. Frachetti, *Pastoralist Landscapes and Social Interaction in Bronze Age Eurasia* (Berkeley: University of California Press, 2008), xiv.

Mongol herders still maintain strong nomadic traditions,[40] as do some groups of reindeer herders, such as the Evenki in Siberia.[41]

Mobility can be classified into two basic types. First, a 'nomadic pastoralist' moves constantly, camping for only relatively short periods in any given area. The economic assumption that underlies such regular movement is that most lands can only support the grazing of animals for a limited period before needing to be left to regenerate. The pattern of movement is also likely to take account of the likely availability of water sources in dry seasons, and more sheltered areas in cold winters. Storage of fodder is rarely practised. Second, 'transhumant pastoralists' tend to move their stock seasonally between two areas of pasture. Most commonly, this involves taking herds into upland pastures during the summer when these areas are free of snow, and returning to a lowland base in winter. This can be regarded as a semi-sedentary way of life, because lowland settlements are often long term and include the construction of immovable houses. The summer residences are temporary encampments and, in some cases, only part of the population travels with the herds into the uplands, so lowland residences might be occupied year round. Such transhumance with livestock is common around the Mediterranean and in Alpine regions among traditional farming econo-mies today and in the recent past.[42] Such groups are, of course, not purely pastoralists, and it is hotly contested whether these transhumant practices date back into prehistory in their familiar form. If one examines ethnographic examples of pastoralism in the Central Asian steppes, both forms of mobility are found. To take Kazakhstan as an example, pastoralists in the central semi-arid steppe zones were certainly fully nomadic, as they remain today in many regions of Mongolia. But in the foothills of upland zones such as the Altai and Tian Shan mountains, they practised transhumance, and ethnic Kazakh groups on the Chinese side of the Tian Shan still do.[43]

Because mobility is fairly ubiquitous among ethnographic examples of pastoralism, there has been a general assumption that prehistoric pastoralists were similarly mobile. While this may be true for the majority of cases, the

40  N. Fijn, *Living with Herds: Human–Animal Coexistence in Mongolia* (Cambridge University Press, 2011).
41  P. Jordan (ed.), *Landscape and Culture in Northern Eurasia* (Walnut Creek, CA: Left Coast Press, 2011).
42  E.g. G. Barker et al., 'Ancient and modern pastoralism in central Italy: an interdisci-plinary study in the Cicolano mountains', *Papers of the British School at Rome*, 59 (1991), 15–88.
43  V.A. Shnirelman et al., 'Hooves across the steppes: the Kazakh life-style', in S.L. Olsen (ed.), *Horses Through Time* (Boulder, CO: Roberts Rinehart, 1996).

assumption could be dangerous. All our ethnographic examples come from environments that are relatively marginal from an agricultural point of view, so these are areas where pastoralists have not faced competition from other cultures. In periods when there were lower populations and less worldwide pressure on land, it is possible to conceive of pastoralists inhabiting richer lands, with higher levels of plant growth and resource predictability. In such circumstances, it may not have been necessary to range so widely, and it may have been possible to concentrate herd movements around a sedentary base. It is key to remember that activities in the past do not always have modern or recent analogues, so assumptions of this type should be avoided.

It is archaeologically very difficult to reconstruct patterns of mobility among ancient pastoralists. Fully nomadic groups will leave extremely ephemeral settlement evidence. In some cases funerary monuments may be much easier to find than domestic structures, but such monuments will tell us relatively little about the pastoral economies of their builders, even if they do inform us about other social matters. Transhumance is much more likely to leave a good archaeological signature, because of semi-sedentary sites, with more substantial domestic structures, and more structured patterns of repeated movement. Zooarchaeologists are relatively accustomed to reconstructing the seasonality of hunting camps, but slaughter patterns within mobile domestic herds are much more likely to relate to global husbandry strategies and, hence, will not mark out the season of site use in the same way as an immediate-return hunting economy will. Advances in isotope science offer a potential solution to this problem. The stable isotopes of oxygen within the atmosphere change with temperature and season. An animal will absorb different ratios of oxygen isotopes from its diet at different times of year. In most of the body this isotopic record is not preserved, but it is preserved in teeth as they grow and form in the jaw of a young animal. If one extracts samples of tooth enamel and analyses them for isotope ratios, then one sees seasonal fluctuation in temperature over the months of growth which that tooth represents.[44] Nomadic or transhumant movement of herds on a seasonal basis will affect those patterns. Furthermore, the tooth profile will also record changing geographic sources of diet over the year. Plants carry isotopic signatures of the geologies they grow on, and these can be reflected in the stable isotope ratios seen in trace metals such as strontium. Movements from one geological zone to another may therefore also show up

---

44 A. Zazzo et al., 'A refined sampling strategy for intra-tooth stable isotope analysis of mammalian enamel', *Geochimica et Cosmochimica Acta*, 84 (2012), 1–13.

in the isotopic analysis of tooth profiles. By combining these two lines of evidence, it is becoming possible to understand animal seasonal movements much more precisely.[45] These methods are still very new, and while they have been demonstrated to work, much larger samples need to be analysed before a clear picture of mobility is established for most early pastoralist societies.

## Case study: prehistoric steppe pastoralism in Kazakhstan

This chapter has, so far, principally discussed the herding of various ruminant animals, but non-ruminant horses are also exceptionally important to many pastoral economies, particularly those in the Eurasian steppes and plains.[46] The following section of this chapter is dedicated to discussing the origins and development of pastoralism in one particular region, as a case study. The region in question is Kazakhstan, where horses play a major role in the story throughout prehistory. There are three major ecological zones within the vast territory of Kazakhstan (Map 6.1). In the north, which borders with southern Siberia, there is 'forest steppe', which is made up of a patchwork of grassland with stands of birch and pine trees. While summers are hot, this region tends not to suffer from drought, and plants remain green for most of the year. It is now home to vast wheat fields that do not generally require irrigation. The central portion of the country is semi-arid steppe, which is relatively treeless. The south is desert steppe, which tends to be treeless and parched in summer. Camels are herded today in this region, as well as cattle, sheep, and goats. The whole of Kazakhstan is subject to a strongly continental climate involving hot summers and long, cold, snowy winters. Large-scale agriculture appears not to have been practised in the country until after the area fell under Soviet control. We do, however, know from ethnographies that Kazakh pastoralists, particularly in the south of the country, did occasionally grow small amounts of millet. The production of millet can be compatible with a fairly mobile lifestyle, and certainly a transhumant one, because it grows and provides a crop so quickly,[47] within a single season.

---

45  E.g. M. Balasse et al., 'The seasonal mobility model for prehistoric herders in the south-western cape of South Africa assessed by isotopic analysis of sheep tooth enamel', *Journal of Archaeological Science*, 29 (2002), 917–32.

46  D.W. Anthony, *The Horse, the Wheel, and Language: How Bronze-Age Riders from the Eurasian Steppes Shaped the Modern World* (Princeton University Press, 2007).

47  M. Jones et al., 'Food globalisation in prehistory', *World Archaeology*, 43 (2011), 665–75.

Millet is also still popular as a crop with some Mongolian pastoralists. Recent work has shown that broomcorn millet was present in southeast Kazakhstan by the end of the third millennium BCE at a site called Begash, in the foothills of the Tian Shan, where transhumance may well have been practised.[48]

In different archaeological traditions, the word 'Neolithic' can refer either to the earliest farming societies, or to societies that used ceramics. In former Soviet countries, it tends to mean the latter. This is the case for the Neolithic of Kazakhstan, where conical-bottomed pots were used, but, as far as one can tell based upon current evidence, the economy was one of hunting, gathering, and fishing, and the stone tool tradition consisted mainly of microblade technology, more akin to the Mesolithic in many regions of Europe. With a few exceptions, settlements are rather ephemeral, and many comprise little more than scatters of material. In the fourth millennium BCE, late phases of Neolithic cultures like the Atbasar of northern Kazakhstan hint at the possible presence of horse, cattle, sheep, and goat at sites, but the remains are fragmentary and not clearly domestic.[49] There remains the possibility of incipient pastoralism, but sample sizes are very low and dating resolution is poor.

North Kazakhstan, in particular, sees a major new phenomenon at around 3500 BCE.[50] Two sister cultures, the Botai and Tersek, see major changes in economic focus, settlement structure, and material culture.[51] Pottery use becomes much more widespread and lithic technologies change totally, shifting from microblades to bifacial flaking and the creation of ground stone tools. A wide range of new bone tool types appears too, mainly made from horse bones. The Botai and Tersek cultures develop sizeable settlements that can have more than one hundred semi-subterranean pit-houses, which represent a significant investment in what must have been, at least, semi-sedentary residences. While metal usage is still very rare, the use of copper is occasionally seen in the region, leading to these cultures being termed Eneolithic. In terms of discussions of pastoralism, however, the

48  M.D. Frachetti et al., 'Earliest direct evidence for broomcorn millet and wheat in the Central Eurasia steppe region', *Antiquity*, 84 (2010), 993–1010.

49  A. Kislenko and N. Tatarintseva, 'The eastern Ural steppe at the end of the Stone Age', in M. Levine et al. (eds.), *Late Prehistoric Exploitation of the Eurasian Steppe* (Cambridge: McDonald Institute for Archaeological Research, 1999), 183–216.

50  M. Levine and A. Kislenko, 'New Eneolithic and Bronze Age radiocarbon dates for north Kazakhstan and south Siberia', in K. Boyle et al. (eds.), *Ancient Interactions: East and West in Eurasia* (Cambridge: McDonald Institute for Archaeological Research, 2002), 131–4.

51  V.F. Zaibert, *Botaiskaya Kultura* (Almaty: KazAkparat, 2009); S.S. Kalieva and V.N. Logvin, *Skotovody Turgaya v Tret'em Tysyacheletii do Nashej Ehry* (Kustanai University, 1997).

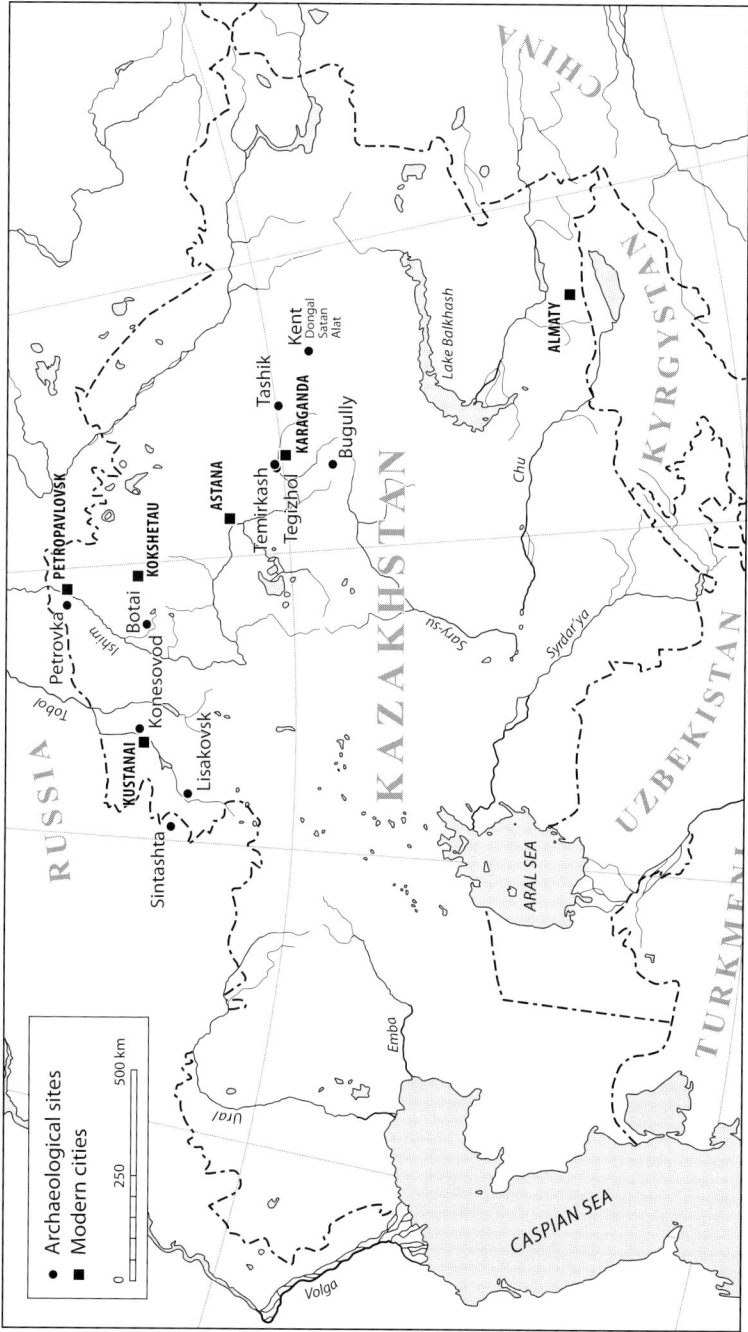

Map 6.1 Central Asia, showing archaeological sites in Kazakhstan.

most significant change is a sudden and extreme focus on the exploitation of horses. Horse bones represent the vast majority of faunal assemblages at all Botai and Tersek sites, and at Botai itself reach 99 per cent.[52] The steppes of Central Asia had a substantial population of wild horses that were also available to earlier prehistoric groups in the region as a prey animal. With Botai, however, one sees a sudden focus on that animal, in conjunction with the arrival of large semi-sedentary villages and significant changes in material culture.

Since Botai was discovered in the early 1980s, there has been considerable academic discussion over whether the horses were being hunted or herded, and whether they were biologically domestic or still wild. Some have argued that there was no clear size change in the animals,[53] and that there was not a clearly managed herd structure for meat production.[54] However, others have argued that the semi-sedentary nature of the settlements and the low frequency of hunting material culture suggests more control of the animal populations.[55] There is no reason to assume the herd was managed specifically for meat, and quite a mixed herd will have been maintained if the animals were used for riding, meat, and even milking. There is also the possibility of the simultaneous exploitation of both wild and domestic stock. This seems like a strange notion, but in fact we know that aurochs (wild cattle) were hunted regularly well into the Bronze Age in much of Eurasia, including Kazakhstan, despite the presence of many domestic cattle that were being exploited for milk (and see also comments on reindeer, p. 165).

It is now becoming increasingly clear that the Botai horses were herded, and probably domestic. Two studies, using different methodologies that examine bone and dental pathologies, have indicated that at least some of

---

52  S.L. Olsen, 'Early horse domestication: weighing the evidence', in S.L. Olsen et al. (eds.), *Horses and Humans: The Evolution of Human–Equine Relations* (Oxford: Archaeopress, 2006), 81–114; M. Levine, 'The origins of horse husbandry on the Eurasian steppe', in Levine et al. (eds.), *Late Prehistoric Exploitation of the Eurasian Steppe*, 5–58; Anthony, *The Horse, the Wheel, and Language*.

53  N. Benecke and A. von den Driesch, 'Horse exploitation in the Kazakh steppes during the Eneolithic and Bronze Age', in M. Levine et al. (eds.), *Prehistoric Steppe Adaptation and the Horse* (Cambridge: McDonald Institute for Archaeological Research, 2003), 69–82.

54  M. Levine, 'Exploring the criteria for early horse domestication', in M. Jones (ed.), *Traces of Ancestry: Studies in Honour of Colin Renfrew* (Cambridge: McDonald Institute for Archaeological Research, 2004), 115–26.

55  Anthony, *The Horse, the Wheel, and Language*; Olsen, 'Early horse domestication: weighing the evidence'; S.L. Olsen, 'Early horse domestication on the Eurasian steppe', in M.A. Zeder et al. (eds.), *Documenting Domestication: New Genetic and Archaeological Paradigms* (Berkeley: University of California Press, 2006), 245–72.

the Botai horses were bitted and harnessed for labour or riding.[56] In 2009 further research indicated that Botai horses had developed more slender legs, like later domestic horses from the region, and, most interestingly, Botai pottery appeared to contain the lipid residues of mare's milk.[57] Mare's milk is not a familiar commodity in most societies, but is still regularly exploited throughout Central Asia and Mongolia, usually consumed as a fermented drink. Furthermore, ancient DNA evidence has also suggested that the date and general region of Botai fit relatively well with genetic evidence for horse domestication.[58] As such, it seems that early pastoralism in Central Asia may have started with the horse, and may have encompassed secondary products as well as primary ones.

It seems likely that by 3500 BCE the people at Botai had some contact with societies closer to the Near East who already had domestic ruminants, so why would this localized development in pastoralism have focused upon horses? Horses were, of course, plentiful in the region, but also, and more importantly, adapted to cold winters. Horses are able to stay out all winter long and are able to clear the ground of snow so that they can continue to graze.[59] There is no need to provide either fodder or shelter. This may well explain the development of this unusually specialized pastoral society, and is also an important factor in understanding later mixed pastoralist regimes in the region. Domestic horses appear to spread across Eurasia during the Bronze Age. While Botai currently represents the earliest clear archaeological evidence for the use of domestic horses, it may not be the earliest or only locus of horse domestication. Mitochondrial DNA studies on modern horse populations seem to suggest that there are quite a number of mares from which domestic horses are descended, which may suggest multiple, independent domestication events. However, Y-chromosome studies in stallions suggest far more restricted lineages in the male line. This hints at a possible trade in domestic stallions from one region of early domestication, which were then bred with local wild mares, either deliberately or by accident.[60]

---

56 A.K. Outram et al., 'The earliest horse harnessing and milking', *Science*, 323 (2009), 1332–5; D. Brown and D. Anthony, 'Bit wear, horseback riding and the Botai site in Kazakhstan', *Journal of Archaeological Science*, 25 (1998), 331–47.

57 Outram et al., 'The earliest horse harnessing and milking'.

58 A. Ludwig et al., 'Coat colour variation at the beginning of horse domestication', *Science*, 324 (2009), 485.

59 L. Koryakova and B. Hanks, 'Horse husbandry among early Iron Age trans-Ural societies', in Olsen et al. (eds.), *Horses and Humans*, 275–87.

60 V. Warmuth et al., 'Reconstructing the origin and spread of horse domestication in the Eurasian steppe', *Proceedings of the National Academy of Sciences*, 109 (2012), 8202–6.

The Botai and Tersek cultures end at the start of the third millennium BCE. There is then very limited settlement evidence until the Bronze Age establishes itself firmly in the region in the very late third millennium. The sites of Sergeevka and Balandino, dating to the mid third millennium, possibly represent transitions from the horse-dominated Eneolithic to a Bronze Age economy more heavily based upon ruminants.[61] There remains a worrying lack of evidence for human use of the steppes during the best part of a thousand years, however. We must ask ourselves whether this is real, or caused by the nature of the archaeological record. It is clear that the Eneolithic cultures were semi-sedentary, and, as such, they left substantial settlements with a palimpsest of domestic debris. If later cultures became truly nomadic, and did not possess any form of monumental culture (the Botai people did not build funerary monuments), then they would be very hard to spot.[62] The absolute dating of even large sites in most of the region is limited, never mind ephemeral scatters of material that might represent nomadic camps. Is this gap real? This example highlights some of the archaeological uncertainties that surround the study of certain possible types of pastoral society.

The next significant development is the Bronze Age Sintashta culture, which dates from about 2100–1800 BCE and is located in the steppe territory between the Ural mountains and the Tobol River. Settlements of this culture, perhaps best represented by the Arkaim settlement, consisted of subcircular fortresses with concentric walls, and spoke-like subdivisions. In the settlement middens of Sintashta and Arkaim the refuse consisted of 60 per cent cattle, 26 per cent sheep/goat, and 13 per cent horse, showing a significant economic shift at this time towards domestic ruminants. However, horse sacrifice was a key component of high-status burials at this time and the richest Sintashta graves contain the remains of chariots. In northern Kazakhstan the Sintashta culture devolved into the Petrovka culture, dating to the first part of the second millennium BCE. Petrovka burials also contain horse sacrifices, horse tack, and chariots, but the number of such burials declines through the period.[63]

The later part of the Bronze Age in central and northern Kazakhstan is dominated by the Andronovo culture. During this period, in the mid second millennium BCE, the economic focus upon the pastoral exploitation of

---

61 Frachetti, *Pastoralist Landscapes*.
62 A.K. Outram et al., 'Horses for the dead: funerary foodways in Bronze Age Kazakhstan', *Antiquity*, 85 (2011), 116–28.
63 Anthony, *The Horse, the Wheel, and Language*; Outram et al., 'Horses for the dead'.

domestic ruminants continues,[64] but Andronovo graves are simpler and are typified by both inhumations and cremations accompanied by ceramics with geometric designs. Animal sacrifices continue, but include a number of different species, particularly dogs, with animals frequently represented by only their heads and feet. The final phase of the Bronze Age (*c.* 1300–900 BCE) in Kazakhstan consists of the Sargary and Begazy-Dandybaevsky cultures. Once again, mixed domestic ruminants dominate in the faunal assemblages, while funerary rites now involve inhumations with relatively modest grave goods comprising ceramics and occasional ornaments.[65]

It is clear that the proportion of horses in assemblages declines in the later part of the Bronze Age, and this pattern is generally maintained in later periods too. However, their proportions remain quite significant, albeit highly variable from one site to another. Lipid residues from ceramics seem to indicate very frequent use of ruminant milk and meat, and much less horse, while herd structures at some sites indicate that cattle might have been the principal source of milk, with sheep and goats managed more for meat supply.[66] This way slaughter for meat can be smaller in scale, producing more convenient meat packages, and maximum dairying productivity can be maintained from cattle. Surveys of faunal records from across Europe and Central Asia indicate that proportions of cattle decrease generally with increased aridity of environments, and this most likely represents a simple issue of ecological adaptation.[67] Horses remain significant for transport and riding to assist in the control of herds, but their adaptation to snow-covered landscapes is still significant because horses not only clear snow for themselves to reach grass but leave clearings in their wake for ruminants that are less adapted to grazing through snow. They reduce risk in hard winters, and their addition to the usual triad of ruminants is therefore much more than cosmetic. The great value of horses to Sintashta and Petrovka cultures is expressed in the way they are buried in kurgans (earth mounds). While this practice does not continue into the later Bronze Age, a study has shown that funerary deposits still contain many more horse bones than settlements do, and that funerary pots contain a much higher proportion of horse residues.[68] Horses perhaps

64 A.K. Outram et al., 'Patterns of pastoralism in later Bronze Age Kazakhstan: new evidence from faunal and lipid residue analyses', *Journal of Archaeological Science*, 39 (2012), 2424–35; Frachetti, *Pastoralist Landscapes*.
65 Outram et al., 'Horses for the dead'.    66 Outram et al., 'Patterns of pastoralism'.
67 R. Bendrey, 'Some like it hot: environmental determinism and the pastoral economies of the later prehistoric Eurasian steppe', *Pastoralism: Research, Policy and Practice*, 1 (2011), 1–16.
68 Outram et al., 'Horses for the dead'.

maintained their relevance to social status and were the food of special feasts. The proportion of horses in assemblages does not vary predictably across this region in the same way as cattle/caprine ratios do.[69] Perhaps numbers of horses relate more to wealth and social standing than to climate?

One of the most significant sites of the final Bronze Age is called Kent, in the central-east region of Kazakhstan. It is an impressively large settlement, with many satellite settlements and associated funerary monuments. Much stone is used in construction, and the settlement has a clear layout and possible piazzas. Despite the general assumption that pastoralists have high levels of mobility, it seems likely that this, and the more significant settlements from the Sintashta, Petrovka, and Andronovo cultures, were transhumant at their most mobile. It will be interesting to see what isotopic studies, of the type outlined above, will reveal about these cultures in the future. Are archaeologists assuming too much about the mobility of past pastoralists from recent ethnographic examples? Are we correctly identifying the traces of truly nomadic peoples?

## Conclusion

This chapter has summarized some of the issues most important to the economies of pastoral societies and has outlined some of the most up-to-date techniques that can be used in studying them. No short chapter could hope to cover the entire range of the subject, throughout the world and throughout all of time, but it is clear from the case study provided here that archaeologists have a very long way to go in fully understanding past pastoralism. Some of the problems are caused by recent geopolitics and the limited access archaeologists have had to certain key regions, and some relate to the more ephemeral nature of the evidence. However, we now have a range of new tools in our analytical armoury that will allow us to tackle fundamental questions of economy, environment, mobility, and migration, and thus to have much firmer underpinnings for our wider understanding of these societies.

## Further reading

Anthony, D.W. *The Horse, the Wheel, and Language: How Bronze-Age Riders from the Eurasian Steppes Shaped the Modern World*. Princeton University Press, 2007.

69 Outram et al., 'Patterns of pastoralism'.

Balasse, M., S.H. Ambrose, A.B. Smith, and T.D. Price, 'The seasonal mobility model for prehistoric herders in the south-western cape of South Africa assessed by isotopic analysis of sheep tooth enamel.' *Journal of Archaeological Science*, 29 (2002), 917–32.

Barker, G. *The Agricultural Revolution in Prehistory: Why did Foragers Become Farmers?* Oxford University Press, 2006.

Bendrey, R. 'Some like it hot: environmental determinism and the pastoral economies of the later prehistoric Eurasian steppe.' *Pastoralism: Research, Policy and Practice*, 1 (2011), 1–16.

Clutton-Brock, J. *A Natural History of Domestic Mammals*. 2nd edn. Cambridge University Press, 1999.

Copley, M.S., R. Berstan, S.N. Dudd, et al. 'Direct chemical evidence for widespread dairying in prehistoric Britain.' *Proceedings of the National Academy of Sciences*, 100 (2003), 1524–9.

Evershed, R.P., S. Payne, A.G. Sherratt, et al. 'Earliest date for milk use in the Near East and southeastern Europe linked to cattle herding.' *Nature*, 455 (2008), 528–31.

Fijn, N. *Living with Herds: Human–Animal Coexistence in Mongolia*. Cambridge University Press, 2011.

Frachetti, M.D. *Pastoralist Landscapes and Social Interaction in Bronze Age Eurasia*. Berkeley: University of California Press, 2008.

Gerbault, P., A. Liebert, Y. Itan, et al. 'Evolution of lactase persistence: an example of human niche construction.' *Philosophical Transactions of the Royal Society B*, 366 (2011), 863–77.

Ingold, T. *Hunters, Pastoralists and Ranchers*. Cambridge University Press, 1980.

Jordan, P. (ed.). *Landscape and Culture in Northern Eurasia*. Walnut Creek, CA: Left Coast Press, 2011.

Legge, A.J. 'Aspects of cattle husbandry.' In R. Mercer (ed.), *Farming Practice in British Prehistory*. Edinburgh University Press, 1981. 169–81.

Marshall, F. and E. Hildebrand. 'Cattle before crops: the beginnings of food production in Africa.' *Journal of World Prehistory*, 16 (2002), 99–143.

Mulville, J. and A.K. Outram (eds.). *The Zooarchaeology of Fats, Milk and Dairying*. Oxford: Oxbow, 2005.

Outram, A.K., A. Kasparov, N.A. Stear, et al. 'Patterns of pastoralism in later Bronze Age Kazakhstan: new evidence from faunal and lipid residue analyses.' *Journal of Archaeological Science*, 39 (2012), 2424–35.

Outram, A.K., N.A. Stear, R. Bendrey, et al. 'The earliest horse harnessing and milking.' *Science*, 323 (2009), 1332–5.

Outram, A.K., N.A. Stear, A. Kasparov, et al. 'Horses for the dead: funerary foodways in Bronze Age Kazakhstan', *Antiquity*, 85 (2011), 116–28.

Payne, S. 'Kill-off patterns in sheep and goats: the mandibles from Asvan Kale.' *Anatolian Studies*, 23 (1973), 281–303.

Reitz, E.J. and E.S. Wing. *Zooarchaeology*. 2nd edn. Cambridge University Press, 2008.

Ryan, K. 'Facilitating milk let-down in traditional cattle-herding systems: East Africa and beyond.' In J. Mulville and A.K. Outram (eds), *The Zooarchaeology of Fats, Milk and Dairying*. Oxford: Oxbow, 2005. 96–106.

Ryder, M.J. 'Livestock products: skins and fleeces.' In R. Mercer (ed.), *Farming Practice in British Prehistory*. Edinburgh University Press, 1981. 182–209.

Sherratt, A.G. 'Plough and pastoralism: aspects of the secondary products revolution.' In I. Hodder, G. Isaac, and N. Hammond (eds.), *Pattern of the Past: Studies in Honour of David Clarke*. Cambridge University Press, 1981. 261–306.

'The secondary products revolution of animals in the Old World.' *World Archaeology*, 15 (1983), 90–104.

Smith, A.B. *Pastoralism in Africa: Origins and Development Ecology*. London: Hurst, 1992.

Vigne, J. D. and D. Helmer. 'Was milk a "secondary product" in the Old World neolithisation process? Its role in the domestication of cattle, sheep and goats.' *Anthropozoologica*, 42 (2007), 9–40.

## 7

# Agriculture and urbanism

DAPHNE E. GALLAGHER AND RODERICK J. MCINTOSH

Cities are rarely part of the narrative of agricultural origins. In most cases, agricultural economies are well established by the time urban centres develop, and if included at all, cities come at the end of the story; the development of an effective, reliable agricultural base has enabled their existence. In contrast, agriculture has been at the foundation of our traditional thinking about cities, from their origins to their abandonments.[1] Scholars such as Wittfogel and Childe originally focused on the power associated with control over agricultural production and products.[2] However, as our archaeological understandings of urban centres have focused increasingly on the experiences of average citizens, rather than the wealthy minority, it has become clear that we must move beyond the standard narratives of elite control, and recognize that decisions about food production and the disposition of agricultural (and pastoral) surpluses were made in particular cultural and environmental contexts, leading to the emergence of the distinctive styles of pre-industrial urbanism that we have documented around the globe. Likewise, the pressures of increasingly large, dense, and sedentary populations (and development of new social and political institutions) spurred agricultural innovation, leading to diverse intensified farming technologies and practices.

In this chapter, we introduce themes relating to agriculture (and food production generally) in urban societies that anticipate discussions in several

---

1 For recent examples, see G.L. Cowgill, 'Origins and development of urbanism: archaeological perspectives', *Annual Review of Anthropology*, 33 (2004), 525–49; J. Marcus and J. Sabloff (eds.), *The Ancient City: New Perspectives on Urbanism in the Old and New World* (Santa Fe, NM: School for Advanced Research Press, 2008); M.L. Smith (ed.), *The Social Construction of Ancient Cities* (Washington, DC: Smithsonian Institution Press, 2003); G. Storey (ed.), *Urbanism in the Preindustrial World: Cross-Cultural Approaches* (Tuscaloosa: University of Alabama Press, 2006).
2 K.A. Wittfogel, *Oriental Despotism: A Comparative Study of Total Power* (New Haven, CT: Yale University Press, 1957); V.G. Childe, 'The urban revolution', *Town Planning Review*, 21 (1950), 3–17.

chapters of Volume 3 of *The Cambridge World History*. The complex relationships between food production (where, by whom, for whom, symbolism), decisions about surplus, exchange, and transport, and power–authority displays around food and agricultural commodities are at the core of comparative archaeological research on early cities. To fully explore these phenomena in diverse urban contexts is not possible here, and consequently we will focus our discussion around the twin questions of the relationships of urban centres to farming practice and to decisions about agricultural production goals and methods. Our discussion will be grounded in a critique of a pervasive historical narrative linking urbanism, surplus production, and hierarchical forms of government. From there, we will examine the relationship of cities and their hinterlands, and explore the environmental, technological, and cultural factors at play in the development and maintenance of urban agricultural systems. We conclude with a case study, Jenne-jeno (Mali), that challenges many of the standard narratives regarding agricultural production in urban societies, in particular the importance of elite-controlled surplus.

## Urban agriculture, surplus, and despotism: historical perspectives

Traditionally, agriculture has been seen not only as a necessary precondition for cities, but also as a source of tension in the rural–urban dynamic (a dynamic which, as we will see, is yet another false dichotomy). For many of the influential early scholars on ancient cities (e.g. Fustel de Coulanges, James Henry Breasted, William Foxwell Albright, Max Weber, Oswald Spengler, Karl Wittfogel, and even Friedrich Engels[3]), life in the (pastoral) countryside was characterized by a certain rectitude or piety not present in the urban centre. Indeed, these constructs have led to a lingering conceptualization of the depraved city elite for whom the downtrodden provide the agricultural surplus that sustains their impious despotism. McIntosh finds an

---

3 N.D. Fustel de Coulanges, *La cité antique: étude sur le culte, le droit, les institutions de la Grèce et de Rome* (Paris: Librairie Hachette, 1864); J.H. Breasted, *Ancient Times – A History of the Early World* (Boston: Athenaeum Press, 1916); W.F. Albright, *Archaeology and the Religion of Israel* (Baltimore, MD: Johns Hopkins University Press, 1956); M. Weber, *The City*, trans. D. Martindale and G. Neuwirth (Glencoe, IL: Free Press, 1958 [1921]), and *Economy and Society: An Outline of Interpretive Sociology*, 3 vols. (New York: Bedminster Press, 1968 [1922]); O. Spengler, *The Decline of the West: Perspectives of World-History*, 2 vols., trans. C.F. Atkinson (New York: Knopf, 1926–8 [1918–23]); K. Wittfogel, *Oriental Despotism: A Comparative Study of Total Power* (New Haven, CT: Yale University Press, 1957); F. Engels, *The Origin of the Family, Private Property and the State* (London: Lawrence & Wishart, 1942 [1884]).

example of the insidious persistence of these narratives in his analysis of the biblical exegetical tradition of Yahwism, which he argues has created certain expectations about not only what should be found in the archaic city, but also the anticipated relationships of various classes of city residents to land, labour, and agricultural production and surplus.[4] These expectations not only obscured the variability in the urban traditions of the Levant, but also helped hide alternative forms of urbanism in places such as West Africa or late Neolithic China when those cities did not display the expected form (tightly nucleated and bewalled with significant investment in monumental architecture).[5]

To one degree or another, all those social thinkers concerned with the early city, each influential in his or her own way, reproduced in their writings a shared concept of the city in which urbanism is fundamentally based in the creation of a new order of human nature forever dedicated to the control of the many by the few, i.e. to hierarchy. This control severs direct relationships with self-sufficient agricultural production, and in the process robs most city residents of their essential freedoms, their connectedness to (kinship-based) community, and, in the Yahwist case, their covenantal relationship with God. These fundamental assumptions of hierarchy – projected onto the circumstances under which cities developed, the organization of agricultural production, and the relationship of surplus both to population rise and to control of people's actions within this new sociopolitical arena – developed in terms of those features of fundamental human values and of people's history that the researchers held as basic or immutable.

These assumptions about the moral life of the pre-industrial city were not only central to the writings of many of these early theorists, but also resonated with their scholarly and educated lay readership. McIntosh argues that one reason may be rooted in Yahwism, which was subscribed to by several generations of biblical scholars and, most importantly, by many social theorists of early city origins. Yahwism is the term both for this historical biblical commentary tradition and for the description of a way of life of the Israelites.[6] The positive values attributed to an idealized, pastoral piety – and the condemnation heaped upon the impious lifestyles of urban dwellers – are

---

4 R.J. McIntosh, 'Western representations of urbanism and invisible African towns', in S. McIntosh (ed.), *Beyond Chiefdoms: Pathways to Complexity in Africa* (Cambridge University Press, 1999), 56–65.

5 R.J. McIntosh, 'Early urban clusters in China and Africa: the arbitration of social ambiguity', *Journal of Field Archaeology*, 18 (1991), 199–212.

6 N.K. Gottwald, *The Tribes of Yahweh: A Sociology of the Religion of Liberated Israel 1250–1050 BCE* (Maryknoll, NY: Orbis, 1979); D.C. Benjamin, *Deuteronomy and City Life* (Lanham:

a dichotomy that underlies much of this once monolithic and still mainstream Old Testament biblical scholarship. A historical critique of this tradition demonstrates clearly why early cities were presented as a dark moral exemplar and why agriculture was incorporated in the same judgment.

In the Yahwist tradition, the clearest commandments of Judaeo-Christian piety strongly influenced interpretations of the Levantine Bronze Age, a period during which early Israelites revolted against the iniquitous and impious cities of the Mediterranean coast. In the period from roughly 1800 to 1200 BCE (and especially after c. 1550), the Bronze Age of the southern Levantine coast ended in a jumble of famine, political turmoil, and plague stories.[7] While modern scholars interpret this chaos as the result of climate change, outside interference by Hittites, Hurrians, Hyksos, and Egyptians, and/or random local political adjustments, for nineteenth- and early twentieth-century Yahweh scholars, later Bronze Age urban culture collapsed as an expression of divine retribution.

Yahweh was signalling not only his extreme displeasure with Canaanite urban culture. He was also offering a covenant to those willing to leave the material security of a centralized urban existence – including, importantly, agricultural surpluses produced by the enslaved or servile members of the towns' populations – for the spiritual fulfilment of a (pastoral) life on the margins, in Yahweh's care. The early city was both the physical seat and the metaphor of all the surpluses (artisan and agricultural), riches, and iniquities that would be lost in the move to the marginal existence of the Judaean hills. Those who elected to pioneer this new relationship with Yahweh would sacrifice the security of city walls, the potential to rise in citadel and temple bureaucracies, and, significantly, the abundant harvests and pastures of the coastal plain. Only by forfeiting these *apparent* advantages would the adherents of this new piety be in a position to become the chosen of an all-powerful God.

In Yahwist exegesis, early cities are characterized as having a particular sociopolitical structure in which the king's power rested upon a centralized, surplus economy supporting the standing army needed both to protect the city from covetous neighbours and to maintain a degree of state terrorism

University Press of America, 1983); V.H. Matthews and D.C. Benjamin, *The Social World of Ancient Israel, 1250–587 BCE* (Peabody: Hendrickson Press, 1993).

7  Gottwald, *Tribes of Yahweh*; Matthews and Benjamin, *Social World of Ancient Israel*, 3–5; A. Mazar, *Archaeology of the Land of the Bible, 10,000–586 BCE* (New York: Doubleday, 1990), 191–300.

within the city walls. This economy depended on the administratively directed labour of an unfree populace, be they *de jure* slaves or the *de facto* servile urban peasantry, making only those relatively few with kinship ties to the monarch free; all others were the king's bondspersons. Thus, according to Yahwist interpretation, city life is equated with absolute submission, absolute loyalty to the monarch's person, an authority that is linked to the exclusive, personal relationship of the despot with the city's god. This is Weber's 'anointed' right to rule at the dawn of *Gottesgnadentum* (the divine right of kings).[8] The state (and all corollary institutions, such as the city – seat of the king) exists as an expression of the relationship of god and monarch, and consequently the monarch's power is absolute. There can be no higher check on the state.

The city as dark moral exemplar (and the underlying unspoken values of covenental piety) are such integral parts of the Western intellectual tradition that we must acknowledge and analyse their influence if we are to understand the history of archaeological investigations of cities, whether in the Levant or elsewhere. Few of the founding scholars who formulated our canon of historical sociology of the early city could have escaped the endless scriptural descriptions of bondage, despotic rule, and urban impiety that came out of Yahwist exegesis. The traditional mistrust of city life was fully subscribed to by the first urban archaeologists,[9] and a conception of primitive urban despotism (standing in stark opposition to the free-will covenant with God and the harsh strictures of the pastoral life on the Judaean hills) drove these scholars' expectations for the kinds of artefact and feature that would serve as signatures for the earliest cities. Layard, preparing to dig Nineveh, could scarcely imagine finding anything of importance that did not reflect this primal state despotism: 'It is very doubtful whether these fortified enclosures contained many buildings besides the royal palaces, and such temples and public edifies as were attached to them.'[10]

Much of the excavation by early archaeologists did focus on temples and palaces, and the foundations of these edifices in control over agricultural surplus consistently figured in the resulting sociopolitical reconstructions. In a typical passage, Weber characterizes the city as the artefact of the will of a despot and as an arena for a pre-existing, exploitative economy and social structure based around control of agricultural labour:

---

8 Weber, *Economy and Society*, vol. 1, 241–3.   9 McIntosh, 'Early urban clusters', 202.
10 A.H. Layard, *Discoveries in the Ruins of Nineveh and Babylon* (London: John Murray, 1953), 639–40.

Chinese, Mesopotamian, Egyptian, and occasionally even Hellenistic war-lords founded cities, relocated them, and settled in them not only voluntary immigrants, but also human livestock rustled from here and there as needed and opportunity dictated. This was most pronounced in Mesopotamia, where the forced settlers first had to dig the canal which made possible the construction of the city in the desert. As the prince with his official administrative apparatus in such cases remains the absolute master, no municipal association can develop.[11]

Here, the population, the 'human livestock', is supremely unfree. They are units of (often agricultural) labour, trapped by an authority based in a despotic covenant with the city deity. Wittfogel is even more blunt in his functionalist assessment of the social structure of early urban centres:

> Unlimited control over the labor power of their subjects enabled the rulers of Sumer, Babylon, and Egypt to build their spectacular palaces, gardens and tombs.[12]

For Wittfogel, farming in the arid lands of Mesopotamia, home of the earliest cities in the world, inherently demanded large-scale government organization to establish and maintain the essential networks of irrigation canals and to co-ordinate the specialists engaged in manufacture and long-distance trade of items not immediately available to the farmer. These 'hydraulic' methods of social control (permanent surrender by the many of their labour and essential freedoms to a few, whether secular princes or temple bureaucracy) provided the despot with the capacity to build monumental structures within the city (defences, roads, palaces, temples, tombs), which preserve as enduring memorials to the authority of the rulers. Most importantly in Wittfogel's causal sequence, cities (i.e. the physical expression of the despotic ideology) can only appear subsequent to a profound social reordering: 'A governmental apparatus capable of executing all these hydraulic and non hydraulic works . . . could be used wherever the egalitarian conditions of a primitive tribal society yielded to tribal or no-longer tribal forms of autocracy.'[13] The city, then, is the product and the instrument of a new order of society, based not upon consensual rule, but upon the domination and oppression of the people by an aberrant hereditary monarchy of the rich and labour-controlling elite.

Thus the intellectual underpinnings of the standard narrative – in which agricultural production not only enables larger urban populations than were

---

11 Weber, *Economy and Society*, vol. III, 1244–5.   12 Wittfogel, *Oriental Despotism*, 39.
13 Ibid.

supportable by the hunting/gathering way of life, but also necessitates water management and landscape manipulation that can only be accomplished under a stringently hierarchical form of government – have their foundations in Yahwist assumptions of the immorality of urban despots and, by extension, urban society. While this standard narrative has maintained a subtle influence, modern archaeological research in what we now understand to be a multitude of heartlands of cities around the world challenges this unimodal conception of the relationships between agriculture, labour, surplus, and political control (Volume 3).

## Agriculture and the urban hinterland

In exploring the role of agriculture in early urbanism, we need a working definition of that new mode of settlement, the city, that emerged out of the previous landscape of (often undifferentiated) villages, hamlets, and more or less mobile camps of seasonal passage. Most definitions coalesce around a common set of themes: a relatively large population size and density, a population engaged in diverse tasks providing services for residents and non-residents, and, in many cases, the existence of spatial features such as an urban core.[14] However, given our emphasis on agriculture, we require a robust conception of 'hinterland', one that allows us to link the urban core to its agricultural foundation.

For some scholars, particularly those who emphasize the many similarities of cities throughout human history, the concept of hinterland becomes intertwined with industrial and post-industrial mega-plexes of the modern era, in which there is a significant spatial dissipation of what would have been considered 'urban' activities in the pre-industrial era.[15] These approaches, while useful in drawing connections within the shared urban experience of ancient and modern peoples, are functionally challenging for archaeologists actively reconstructing ancient landscapes who wish to determine the relationship between an urban core and its surrounding territory. It is for this reason that we engage the useful heuristic of city/hinterland, utilizing this dichotomy to expose the pairing as an intertwined whole. These linkages are central to the dynamic interplay of agriculture (specifically, decisions about production and disposal of surplus) and early urbanism (understood as an

14 Marcus and Sabloff (eds.), *The Ancient City*, 12–20.
15 N. Yoffee, 'Making ancient cities plausible', *Reviews in Anthropology*, 38 (2009), 264–89.

interplay of several dimensions of demographics and cities as arenas for the negotiation of authority in emergent, highly unstable, complex societies).

Given this centrality of hinterland in our agriculturally focused analysis, we take as our definition one drawn from Trigger and modified by us, characterizing the city as a large and heterogeneous settlement supported by, and providing a variety of services and manufactures to, a wider hinterland.[16] Implicit in this definition is the two-way exchange in which commodities (agricultural products, raw materials), objects (e.g. manufactured goods such as ceramic or metal objects), and even practices (construction styles, religious cults, etc.) flow between the centre and the periphery. While this exchange will occur in both directions (and among hinterland communities) for each of these classes, in general there is an expectation that commodities will be traded to cities while goods and practices will spread from cities. Likewise, there is an assumption that there will be some relationship between the 'distance' (whether characterized by length, travel time, social connections, or otherwise) of a community from the focal city and the intensity of exchange. These presumptions create challenges for archaeological visibility, as the movement of goods is frequently easier to track than the movement of consumables. This can in some cases lead to circular attempts to define a city–hinterland space when the size of the urban 'catchment' is estimated by the number of residents who need to be sustained and the urban demographics are presumed to be a function of the rural sphere of influence.

Trigger provides us with not only a useful definition, but also an important distinction in characterizing cities' relationships with their hinterlands.[17] He argues that most pre-industrial urban societies can be divided into city-states and territorial states, with each having a distinct set of characteristics. City-states are small political entities that typically consist of just the city and a small surrounding territory. As they are frequently more defensive in orientation (being often located in regions populated by multiple competing polities), and since their agricultural catchment is usually directly adjacent to the urban centre, these cities frequently include a high proportion of resident farmers, and it is not unusual for them to incorporate substantial fields within the city walls. For example, early Mesopotamian cities were known for their orchards, and some estimates suggest (perhaps

---

16 R.J. McIntosh, *Ancient Middle Niger: Urbanism and the Self-Organizing Landscape* (Cambridge University Press, 2005), 192, after B. Trigger, 'Determinants of growth in pre-industrial societies', in P. Ucko et al. (eds.), *Man, Settlement and Urbanism* (London: Duckworth, 1972), 577.

17 B. Trigger, *Understanding Early Civilizations* (Cambridge University Press, 2003), 92–119.

optimistically) that as much as two thirds of 'urban' space was in fact farmland or gardens.[18] In contrast, territorial states encompassed numerous cities within comparatively secure territories. As a result, their populations were less heavily urbanized, with more farmers living in rural settlements and an elite that was frequently more isolated from the general population. Cities in each of these categories create different on-the-ground expectations for interaction, cohesion, and urban–hinterland boundaries.

Trigger's distinction focuses on the macro scale, but at the level of the individual farmer, the urban–hinterland distinction becomes more complex. Early urbanites not only had, in many cases, substantial garden plots in or near their residences (even within territorial states), but may have left the city on a daily or even seasonal basis to cultivate near or distant fields. Within kin groups, members of the same nuclear family could be distributed between residing in an urban household, cultivating a seasonally occupied farmstead, and tending to a mobile herd of livestock. Likewise, a rural household could send members to urban markets, to apprentice with urban craftsmen, or to fulfil military and/or labour obligations administered through an urban centre. This process becomes even more multifaceted when 'family' is expanded to include people with whom urban residents maintained long-term relations of reciprocity, usufruct, or fictive kinship.

The problems of distinguishing the city spatially from its hinterland are likewise challenging on the ground. While some cities, such as Teotihuacan, may in general conform to the ideal of a centre surrounded by farmland, others, such as the classical Mayan centres, have farmland integrated throughout.[19] Recent studies have even found agricultural terracing between ceremonial pyramids, and field systems were organized not around the central urban core, but rather around households that are distributed in an increasingly diffuse arrangement as you move from the urban centre.[20]

Even more intriguing are the cities of the ancient Yoruba kingdoms of Nigeria.[21] These settlements consist of complex arrangements of earthen walled enclosures, spread in some cases over tens of kilometres, such that

18 M. van de Mieroop, *The Ancient Mesopotamian City* (Oxford University Press, 1997), 82–3.
19 W.T. Sanders et al. (eds.), *Urbanism in Mesoamerica* (University Park: Pennsylvania State University Press, 2003).
20 A.F. Chase and D.Z. Chase, 'Scale and intensity in Classic period Maya agriculture: terracing and settlement at the "garden city" of Caracol, Belize', *Culture & Agriculture*, 20 (1998), 60–77.
21 A.L. Mabogunke, *Yoruba Towns* (Ibadan University Press, 1962); B. Agbaje-Williams, 'Yoruba urbanism: the archaeology and historical ethnography of Ile-Ife and Old Oyo', in A. Ogundiran (ed.), *Precolonial Nigeria: Essays in Honor of Toyin Falola* (Trenton, NJ: Africa World Press, 2005), 215–40; A. Ogundiran, 'Four millennia of cultural history in

it is often difficult to distinguish an urban core from a hinterland. This landscape is reflective of the extensive agricultural practices of these societies, where many of the inhabitants of political centres practised agriculture both in fields adjacent to settlements and in others further away. Given the extensive nature of agricultural practice, there are complex histories of villages, towns, and cities moving or being moved by political centres, further complicating the process of identifying the 'urban core'.

New technologies are increasingly aiding archaeologists in documenting the spatial networks of these urban centres. While classic, low-tech methods like pedestrian survey are still among the most thorough methods of locating archaeological sites within an urban catchment, this form of research is inherently limited in scale. In contrast, remote sensing technologies, including aerial photos, satellite images, and LiDAR, allow archaeologists to rapidly identify various human constructions, including habitation sites and agricultural infrastructure, over very large areas.[22] For example, Jason Ur has used satellite images to document the numerous radial paths extending from third-millennium BCE cities in the upper Khabur basin (Syria),[23] demonstrating the intensity of movement from urban centres to farm and pastureland, and utilized the particular properties of soil on human-occupied sites (anthrosols) to remotely identify habitation sites in a systematic and comprehensive manner over the entire region.[24] In the densely forested region of Mesoamerica, archaeologists are increasingly using LiDAR (a technology that analyses reflected light from a laser) to literally see through the trees and rapidly create detailed topographic maps of the ground surface.[25] These maps have revealed significant investment in agricultural terracing and allowed scholars to more accurately analyse the distribution and density of the small residential groups around which most agricultural fields were located.

These expanded archaeological data sets on urban–hinterland relationships have both increased our ability to challenge the standard narrative and illustrated its persistence. The Yahwist conception of the impious

Nigeria (ca. 2000 BC–AD 1900): archaeological perspectives', *Journal of World Prehistory*, 19 (2005), 152–4.

22  D.C. Comer and M.J. Harrower, *Mapping Archaeological Landscapes from Space* (New York: Springer, 2013).

23  J. Ur, 'CORONA satellite photography and ancient road networks: a northern Mesopotamian case study', *Antiquity*, 77 (2003), 102–15.

24  B.H. Menze and J. Ur, 'Mapping patterns of long-term settlement in northern Mesopotamia at a large scale', *Proceedings of the National Academy of Sciences*, 109 (2012), 778–87.

25  A.F. Chase et al., 'Geospatial revolution and remote sensing LiDAR in Mesoamerican archaeology', *Proceedings of the National Academy of Sciences*, 109 (2012), 12916–21.

urban centre in opposition to a rural countryside does not allow for the extensive flow of people and ideas between city and hinterland, nor for the direct involvement of urban residents in agricultural or, particularly, pastoral production. However, we are still left with the despot in control of a large agricultural surplus, an idea which was elaborated in Weber's conceptualization of pre-industrial cities as 'consumer' cities.[26] For Weber, the power of urban elites derived from extraction of wealth from the hinterland, and the overall urban economy was oriented towards the interests of a small group of wealthy consumers. In a sense then, our theoretical conception of a city–hinterland dichotomy aligns with his fundamental conceit distinguishing the urban elite from the general populace, and under a consumer city paradigm, the interaction with and investment in the hinterland documented archaeologically could simply demonstrate close control by an extractive power. Therefore, we must examine not only the integration of agricultural practice into the urban landscape, but also the integration of agricultural decision-making.

## Administration, control, and negotiation in agricultural decision-making

Under the Yahwist model, the ruler controls agricultural production in an authoritative top-down fashion. Decision-making is highly centralized in hierarchical government, and the means and modes of production are dictated to a bonded labour force. While that may have been the case in a few highly despotic settings, in most early cities different decisions were not only made at different levels, but they were also negotiated through complex webs of potential authority relationships.[27] In all cases, however, early cities were grappling with the same fundamental question: How do you reliably feed a large population in a sustainable fashion? While there is a tendency to focus on a basic assessment of carrying capacity and yields, the systems of social, political, and economic obligations that enable any given farming system are as crucial to its success as choosing the right irrigation method or crop variety. Here we will explore the environmental, technical, and social constraints on decision-making, and how both the availability of information and variability in cultural norms could empower and restrict the authority of various constituencies.

---

26 Weber, *The City*, 68–9.   27 Smith (ed.), *Social Construction of Ancient Cities*, chap. 1.

While certain limitations can be overcome through the use of technology (see below), aspects of the local environment, including precipitation, day-length, temperature, humidity, and soil quality, dictate the types of crop that are easiest to grow and the types of animal that are easiest to keep. Farmers and herders must consider not only the average conditions, but also the typical fluctuations. Some environments, like the savannas of West Africa, have extremely high interannual variability, such that annual precipitation amounts will not reach the mean four out of five years.[28] In addition, many early cities had to cope with periods of climate change, i.e. persistent changes in 'normal' local conditions.[29]

To reconstruct the ancient environments in which these early urban agricultural systems operated, archaeologists draw on a wide range of data from a diversity of disciplines.[30] For example, scholars will often work with palaeoclimatologists to determine the variability and trends in local climates, utilizing a variety of methods, each of which has both particular settings in which it is appropriate or possible and limitations in terms of its spatial and temporal resolution.[31] For example, tree-rings can be used to develop an annual record of precipitation but only for a fairly local area in places with arid climates and/or long-lived trees. In contrast, while ice cores are useful for reconstructing general global trends over long periods (in some cases more than 750,000 years), they have limited temporal and spatial resolution.

For the archaeologist interested in the limitations of environments for farmers and herders, resolution is crucial, as decisions will often be made based on local or at most regional information. The farmers themselves, who are generally the most familiar with the conditions of any given field, may curate and exchange information, which may also be collected and pooled at the regional level. Many of the so-called 'managerial' models of hierarchical political formations focused on this process of assembling and processing information in order to enact and manage well-formed agricultural strategies.[32]

---

28 K.M. Baker, *Indigenous Land Management in West Africa: An Environmental Balancing Act* (Oxford University Press, 2000).
29 A. Rosen, *Civilizing Climate: Social Responses to Climate Change in the Ancient Near East* (Lanham, MD: AltaMira Press, 2007).
30 E.J. Reitz and M.L. Shackley, *Environmental Archaeology*, updated edn (New York: Springer, 2012).
31 T.M. Cronin, *Paleoclimates: Understanding Climate Change Past and Present* (New York: Columbia University Press, 2010).
32 H.T. Wright, 'Recent research on the origin of the state', *Annual Review of Anthropology*, 6 (1977), 379–97.

While perhaps limited by their local environments, most urban agricultural systems are characterized by their technologies (here taken broadly to include crop varieties, animal breeds, irrigation systems, fertilization practices, tools, and other farming/herding techniques). These technologies are utilized for a variety of purposes: to increase the land under cultivation, to increase the yield of a given area, to decrease the labour required to produce a certain harvest, or to increase the reliability of the agricultural system. Regardless of how well adapted any particular set of agricultural technologies is to the local environment, or how stable the typical conditions are, there is still always an inherent risk of crop or herd failure.

In a 2011 review, Marston summarized the diversification and intensification strategies early urban agriculturalists utilized to buffer the risk in their systems.[33] Diversification strategies are those that spread risk over space and time. Early urban centres almost always grew multiple varieties of multiple crops and/or multiple breeds of domestic animals and regularly included hunted or gathered foods in their diet (in many cases from managed 'wild' populations). To take advantage of local microclimates and small-scale variation, spatial diversification through fragmenting fields (particularly in areas with patchy rainfall or susceptibility to flooding) and animal transhumance was common, as was establishing reliable trade relationships such that, if necessary, food could be obtained from outside the region. Temporally, within a given year, crops could to a certain extent be spaced to allow for successive harvests (or in certain climates year-round harvests), a practice that also relieved labour bottlenecks. Finally, many early urban centres stored significant quantities of staple foods. While there were often strong sociopolitical goals associated with this stockpiling, these stores also served the practical function of bridging bad years. While the ability to store a particular crop varied depending on local environment and crop variety, technologies such as parching, ventilation, and domestic cats could extend storage life. It should be noted that storage doesn't necessarily imply a large warehouse: even in urban centres storage could take place at the household level, and long-lived livestock such as cattle may be considered storage on the hoof.

In contrast to diversification, intensification strategies increase production per unit of land. However, as Marston points out, it is useful to expand the definition to include strategies that increase both the labour input and

---

33 J.M. Marston, 'Archaeological markers of agricultural risk management', *Journal of Anthropological Archaeology*, 30 (2011), 190–205.

land under cultivation in order to significantly improve expected yields. Numerous well-known agronomic strategies such as multiple weedings, mulching and other forms of fertilization, crop rotation, irrigation, and terracing require significant effort, but can pay off not only in improved yields but also in maintaining the productivity of a given field over an extended period of time. While many of these practices can easily take place at the scale of a single homestead, larger intensification projects, notably extensive irrigation networks, are often assumed to have implications for labour and hierarchical control.

As described above, despotic control of labour necessary for irrigation is at the heart of Wittfogel's conceptualization of early cities as extractive in nature, and many scholars working in more current frameworks have likewise assumed that this type of labour-intensive capital investment in agricultural productivity would have required both centralized management and an elite-driven impetus to increase harvests. However, as Erickson points out, historical and ethnographic analyses of large-scale irrigation networks have found that locally organized and controlled systems are often more productive, efficient, and stable and the mere occurrence of irrigation or other labour-intensive agricultural infrastructure in conjunction with urbanism does not necessitate top-down management and control.[34] This is not to say that urban elites did not frequently leverage irrigation networks for wealth and political gain, but rather that this process must be demonstrated rather than assumed.

Both diversification and intensification strategies are inevitably linked to questions of growth and sustainability. Most cities experience net growth over the course of their occupation, and agricultural systems generally increase their capacity with increased investment in extensive or intensive strategies. This is expected since, as Boserup famously argued, in response to increasing population pressure on agricultural resources, farmers will respond by innovating and working harder (eventually for diminishing returns).[35] In contrast, the Weberian extractive economy model lies at the other extreme, arguing that production will rise at a more rapid pace than population growth in order to maximize the surplus of the wealthy elite.

34 C.L. Erickson, 'Intensification, political economy, and the farming community: in defense of a bottom-up perspective of the past', in J. Marcus and C. Stanish (eds.), *Agricultural Strategies* (Los Angeles: Cotsen Institute of Archaeology, University of California, 2006), 334–63 (340).

35 E. Boserup, *The Conditions of Agricultural Growth: The Economics of Agrarian Change under Population Pressure* (University of Chicago Press, 1965).

However, both Boserup and Weber assume that farmers will expend the least effort possible, and neither approach allows for the many household- and community-level motivations to intensify and increase agricultural pro- duction in the absence of an external stimulus (be it population pressure or a powerful despot).[36]

Regardless of the particularistic circumstances of growth in agricultural production around an urban centre, agricultural practices must be sustainable if the city is to persist. Just as success in agricultural production has been tied to the origins and growth of urban settlements, the abandonment of urban centres is likewise often attributed to problems in the agricultural system.[37] These problems, which may include declining yields, population growth outpacing agricultural capacity, or outright crop failure, are often broadly attributed to the effects of climate fluctuations, unsustainable farm- ing practices, or, most frequently, a combination of the two.

Climate fluctuations, and in particular severe multi-year droughts, can have a significant impact on agricultural production. However, not all droughts lead to urban abandonment, and in many cases urban centres have previously weathered severe droughts or other natural disasters.[38] Likewise, the technol- ogies and practices discussed above can buffer the impact of interannual fluctuations such that severe drought can affect some urban centres more severely than others. In contrast, 'overfarming' (intensive utilization of soil leading to a long-term loss of fertility through processes such as erosion or salinization) is more frequently seen as evidence of unsustainable practices. However, recent research has demonstrated that characterizing an agricul- tural system as unsustainable is challenging in the context of the changing social and environmental conditions that often accompany city abandonment, particularly since these other factors may prevent the development of tech- nological solutions.[39]

While the 'collapse' of urban societies is frequently a research focus, the archaeology of early cities in practice speaks more broadly to questions of sustainability in agricultural systems. Many cities known primarily through archaeology were occupied for hundreds or thousands of years. Thus in cases

---

36  K.D. Morrison, 'The intensification of production: archaeological approaches', *Journal of Archaeological Method and Theory*, 1 (1994), 111–59.

37  J.A. Tainter, 'Archaeology of overshoot and collapse', *Annual Review of Anthropology*, 35 (2006), 59–74.

38  G.M. Schwartz and J.J. Nichols (eds.), *After Collapse: The Regeneration of Complex Societies* (Tucson: University of Arizona Press, 2006).

39  P.A. McAnany and N. Yoffee (eds.), *Questioning Collapse: Human Resilience, Ecological Vulnerability, and the Aftermath of Empire* (Cambridge University Press, 2010).

like Mesopotamia, where the rich soils were eventually rendered infertile due to salinization related to intensive irrigation, there is perhaps as much to learn from the several thousand years of successful intensive farming as from the eventual agricultural problems. Likewise, many of the cities of classical antiquity, such as Athens and Rome, maintained sustainable agricultural systems such that their surrounding territories are still farmed today.[40]

Within these contexts of sustainable production, it is essential to realize that cultural practices and goals fundamentally shape the ways in which agriculture is carried out in different times and places. Stone has discussed the importance of considering what he terms 'social technology' in analysing agricultural systems, notably the ability of an individual or group within a given society to motivate labour resources.[41] Local economic needs, political goals, and systems of obligation (or in the case of the Yahwist perspective, coercion) ultimately dictate production methods and objectives.

The organization of labour in urban settings, according to the standard narrative, derives from the direct managerial control of a stratified ruling class. This highly centralized model of political/economic organization, while potentially characterizing some time periods in archaeological and historical examples, is not in fact common in ancient political systems.[42] We now know that urban centres are typically characterized by diverse populations holding both competing and shared goals who can control aspects of the economic system, regardless of whether the political apparatus is highly centralized.[43] For example, Mesopotamian cities varied over time in the organization of production, with some periods in which centralized bureaucratic systems were in control and others in which competing labour groups, notably the kin-based *oikos*, owned and managed agricultural land.[44] While in both situations agriculture functioned as an important political/religious/economic tribute, in the former it was a top-down means of control, while for the *oikos* it was a potential avenue to political power. Similarly, among the Yoruba, with their diffuse urban zones incorporating significant agricultural production, the urban centre can be modelled as a

40 G. Kron, 'Food production', in W. Schiedel (ed.), *The Cambridge Companion to the Roman Economy* (Cambridge University Press, 2012), 156–74.

41 G.D. Stone, *Settlement Ecology: The Social and Spatial Organization of Kofyar Agriculture* (Tucson: University of Arizona Press, 1996), 193–4.

42 R.E. Blanton and L. Fargher, *Collective Action in the Formation of Pre-modern States* (New York: Springer, 2008).

43 A. Smith, *The Political Landscape: Constellations of Authority in Early Complex Polities* (Berkeley: University of California Press, 2003); Blanton and Fargher, *Collective Action*.

44 S. Pollock, *Ancient Mesopotamia: The Eden that Never Was* (Cambridge University Press, 1999), 78–148.

'macrocosm of an extended family compound', with complex networks of social relations and obligations characterizing the system.[45] Kin groups appear to have had the ability to access land in areas both close and peripheral to their residential spaces, creating cross-cutting social connections. There is little evidence that this agricultural production was managed by the elite (whose power and prestige are thought to have been derived from religious authority and access to trade goods rather than surplus), and even some construction of the extensive earthworks may have been controlled at the local level. It is interesting in this discussion of urbanism that the most centralized agricultural economy that could be used to support parts of the standard narrative is one, ancient Egypt, that was not highly urbanized.

Contributing to understanding the past and present diversity in the organization of agricultural labour in urban settings has been an increasing realization of the fallacy that settlement hierarchies imply control hierarchies.[46] Rather, researchers throughout the world have begun to recognize that most complex societies and urban environments have heterarchical elements and include multiple nodes of power and decision-making that play a dynamic role in the political process.[47] These groups and/or individuals, who may be fluidly ranked depending on the circumstances, can range from kin-based organizations of agricultural production, competing elite class groups, republics characterized by more market-based systems, etc., rather than a single concrete stratified elite that abstracts individuals from their labour.

In conclusion, the role of agriculture in urban settings is constrained by local environments, enabled by technological innovation and practices, and controlled by cultural values. While production can be organized in a top-down fashion and surplus may be funnelled to a small elite, this scenario is the exception rather than the rule. In practice, agriculture is intensively negotiated, with different social segments manipulating production in diverse ways. While these negotiations may take place within a framework of classic power relations, they illustrate that within the context of very complex systems, such as the agricultural networks supporting early urban centres, a constricted, abstracted decision-making apparatus is rare. We will

---

45  Ogundiran, 'Four millennia of cultural history', 154.
46  C.L. Crumley, 'Heterarchy and the analysis of complex societies', in R.M. Ehrenreich et al. (eds.), *Heterarchy and the Analysis of Complex Societies* (Arlington, VA: American Anthropological Association, 1995), 1–5.
47  McIntosh (ed.), *Beyond Chiefdoms*; Blanton and Fargher, *Collective Action*; Ehrenreich et al. (eds.), *Heterarchy*.

now turn our attention to a case study which exemplifies the alternative ways in which agricultural production can be organized in an urban context, and the attendant implications for the structure of urban society.

## Case study: Jenne-jeno (Mali)

Unrecognized by the archaeological community until the late 1970s, Jenne-jeno rises 7 m high over Mali's middle Niger floodplain, a tell that would not be out of place in Mesopotamia. Within 4 km are seventy tells in total, apparently all occupied contemporaneously; many were founded simultaneously with Jenne-jeno (within centuries of the BCE/CE transition) and most were likewise abandoned at the same time, around 1400 CE.[48] The Jenne-jeno urban complex, encompassing not only the site itself but the other tells in its cluster, provided urban services and manufactures to a vast region far exceeding the city's immediate agricultural hinterland. In practice, the site was part of a dense urban landscape: in the 55,000 km$^2$ of the seasonally inundated middle Niger floodplain there are many hundreds of similar mounds.

The site of Jenne-jeno, reinforced by the urban complex, provides evidence of multiple occupations, multiple manufacturing areas, and multiple 'identity groups' as indicated by a great diversity of contemporaneous burial practices. After some thirty-five years of controlled stratigraphic excavations at some twenty-two units spread over the 33 ha area of the site, we can model how occupational and identity diversity burgeoned from the relatively simple (although already 20 ha) community at the time of its founding in the third century BCE. What subsistence and productive forces might have been behind the emergence and evolution of this clustered urbanism? While clearly arising from the complex dynamics of interactions between multiple corporate groups (i.e. self-identified groups that held real or symbolic property in common), the question of precisely how sociopolitical processes are mapped onto/create this spatial configuration remains a focus of research.

While several of the mounds in the Jenne-jeno urban complex have been excavated (albeit most with only small test units), a more comprehensive picture emerges from the systematic documentation of surface artefacts (ceramics, net weights, iron-working debris, etc.) and features (burials, house foundations, etc.) from every site in the complex. These studies have

48  R.J. McIntosh, *The Peoples of the Middle Niger: The Island of Gold* (Malden, MA: Blackwell, 1998), and *Ancient Middle Niger*.

identified numerous anomalous concentrations of certain artefacts or features, compared to the range and relative proportions at Jenne-jeno itself, that reveal numerous specialized activities concentrated at different locales.[49] While unambiguous evidence of activities focused on perishable foods and commodities is elusive in surface contexts, there is strong evidence of mutual exclusivity, or near-exclusivity, of activities such as hunting of aquatic mammals and snakes, certain styles of fishing, and weaving. The spatial focus of tasks is most apparent for iron-smelting. This is a dirty, hot, and noisy activity that also leaves a strong material signature in the form of furnace bases, tuyeres, and slag. Due in part to its transformative nature, iron-smelting has been locally associated with the production of highly dangerous occult power in the historical and modern eras, and likely during the occupation of Jenne-jeno as well. Through the Jenne-jeno sequence we see the migration of smelting from the focus site to multiple satellites.

Overall, a concentration of activities continues to be the best explanation for the non-uniform, non-random distribution of surface and stratified artefacts in the Jenne-jeno urban complex. This is not surprising, as specialized quarters are a common feature of global urban settlements, although at Jenne-jeno these specialists are not only dispersed over a large area, but also maintain spatially discrete loci of both activity and residence. It is in attempting to reconstruct the political meanings of this arrangement that Jenne-jeno truly begins to challenge the standard narrative.

Susan McIntosh has analysed in detail the numerous ways in which Jenne-jeno does not fit the standard model for emerging 'archaic' urbanism.[50] While the site and urban cluster conform to many familiar expectations (nucleation, population growth, increasing scale, internal differentiation), it is lacking many others (subsistence intensification, clear vertical stratification, public monuments). Given our focus on the role of agriculture, we will concentrate here on the question of subsistence intensification.

As described above, the positive relationship between large-scale nucleation (as we have at Jenne-jeno) and intensification is a frequent element of

---

49 R.J. McIntosh and S.K. McIntosh, 'Early urban configurations on the middle Niger: clustered cities and landscapes of power', in Smith (ed.), *Social Construction of Ancient Cities*, 103–20.

50 S.K. McIntosh and R.J. McIntosh, 'Cities without citadels: understanding West African urbanism', in T. Shaw et al. (eds.), *The Archaeology of Africa: Foods, Metals and Towns* (London: Unwin Hyman, 1993), 622–41; S.K. McIntosh (ed.), *Excavations at Jenné-jeno, Hambarketolo, and Kaniana (Inland Niger Delta, Mali), the 1981 Season* (Berkeley: University of California Press, 1995); S.K. McIntosh, 'Modeling political organization in large-scale settlement clusters: a case study from the inland Niger delta, Mali', in McIntosh (ed.), *Beyond Chiefdoms*, 66–79.

the standard narrative. Given the population of the urban cluster, agricultural production would of necessity increase. However, as Jenne-jeno demonstrates, expansion in an urban context need not include such markers as large infrastructural improvements, top-down hierarchical control and co-ordination, or significant production of surplus. Rather, the evidence from the site suggests diversified strategies and co-operative co-ordination among subsistence specialists combined to reliably and sustainably meet the needs of the urban population.

When the southern floodplains of the middle Niger opened up to permanent occupation in the last centuries BCE, those who took advantage were mixed agriculturalists–pastoralists–fisherfolk who, millennia earlier, occupied the similar riverine/lacustrine environments of the progressively desiccated Sahara to the north. They brought with them already domesticated African rice (*Oryza glaberrima*) and were likely involved in its diversification into at least forty-two varieties characterized by differences in germination period and tolerance of depth of flooding.[51] In addition to rice, pearl millet (*Pennisetum glaucum*) and sorghum (*Sorghum bicolor*) are in evidence throughout the 1,500-year sequence (if in a distinctively minority status). These grains were likely grown in conjunction with rice as part of a flood recession (decrue) system that took advantage of the seasonal fluctuations of the Niger and Bani rivers.[52] In addition to grains, residents likely cultivated many regionally domesticated vegetables, including melons, okra, and garden egg. While these are generally less visible in the palaeoethnobotanical record, a few seeds from a melon or bottle gourd were identified at the site. Wild plants (many of which are managed/protected/cultivated) are a standard element of diets in the West African savanna today, a practice which appears to have been common at small villages and urban centres alike during Jenne-jeno's occupation. At the urban complex, there is clear evidence for harvesting of a wild millet (*Brachiaria ramosa*), and several other wild plants, including multiple grasses, that could have been collected were also identified. Interestingly, there is little evidence from excavations for the exploitation of useful trees such as baobab, jujube, and various palms, all of which are contributors to the diet today.[53]

51 J. Gallais, *Le delta intérieur du Niger: étude de géographie régionale*, Mémoires de l'Institut Fondamental d'Afrique Noir 79 (Dakar: Institut Fondamental d'Afrique Noir, 1967).

52 J.R. Harlan and J. Pasquereau, 'Décrue agriculture in Mali', *Economic Botany*, 23 (1969), 70–4.

53 S.K. McIntosh, 'Paleobotanical and human osteological remains', in McIntosh (ed.), *Excavations at Jenné-jeno*, 348–53.

Likewise, inhabitants of the Jenne-jeno urban cluster exploited a mix of domestic and wild animals. Cattle, sheep, and goats were herded, including at least some breeds that would have moved seasonally between the inland Niger delta and surrounding regions, and chickens would have been kept close to households. In addition, residents hunted wild animals found in floodplain environments, including reedbuck, bushbuck, hartebeest, kob, and waterfowl, and fished extensively.[54]

The most interesting subsistence story of Jenne-jeno is that during the 1,500-year uninterrupted occupation, while population and settlement size grew dramatically, there is little change in this diverse, generalized subsistence economy. There is no evidence that farming of secondary grain crops, i.e. millet and sorghum, was expanded, nor that efforts were made to increase the yields of the intensively exploited *Brachiaria ramosa*. Overall, the contributions of wild resources appear to have remained stable over the course of the occupation (with the possible exception of kob, which does decrease in frequency). This stability is a testament to the careful management of these plants and animals, as given the increased and more nucleated population one would expect their contributions to decline in favour of agricultural production. Most significantly, there is no evidence for experimentation with the water control and irrigation systems frequently utilized in floodplain environments. Instead, farmers employed resilient techniques well suited to the morphologically and pedologically diverse middle Niger and to high interannual variation in the timing and levels of rainfall and floods. Overall, the subsistence system was aimed at producing reliable yields in uncertain conditions rather than maximizing return.[55]

As Susan McIntosh notes, at a logistical level the local methods for avoiding significant intensification during a period of rapid population growth are relatively straightforward:

> For the most part, they maximized production through the development of specialized subsistence niches linked by exchange and interdependence, maintaining wild resources as a significant element of diversification within otherwise specialized economies. For flood rice cultivation, part of this diversification-within-specialization strategy was avoidance of increased labor inputs to single, fixed plots.[56]

---

54 K.C. MacDonald, 'Analysis of the mammalian, avian, and reptilian remains', and W. van Neer, 'Analysis of the fish remains', both in McIntosh (ed.), *Excavations at Jenné-jeno*, 291–318 and 319–47.

55 S.K. McIntosh, 'Conclusion: the sites in regional context', in McIntosh (ed.), *Excavations at Jenné-jeno*, 360–98.

56 McIntosh, 'Modeling political organization', 73.

However, the implications of these strategies for urban organization are profound and indicative of how this society was structured and how that structure reflected a long evolution of production and exchange strategies.

Clustering at the Jenne-jeno urban cluster (and in the multitude of other clustered cities and village-clusters of the middle Niger) appears to have been a solution to the problem of how different specialist corporations might maintain and display their distinct identities, while at the same time having immediate access to other providers of needed goods and services and access to those to whom they themselves provided materials. These specialist corporate groups may have been self-defining in terms of subsistence (as one sees locally today in the Nono rice farmers, the Bambara millet growers, the Bozo swamp fisherfolk, the Somono deep channel fishers, or the Peul cattle herders)[57] or in terms of craft or artisan skills. Key to the arrangement is the development, in this highly unpredictable landscape, of the expectation of access to the goods and services of other groups in time of need.

One must at the same time address the linked sociopolitical question: Who monitors or controls the exchange of those manufactures and services? In the case of the Jenne-jeno urban cluster, we appear to have an exchange system that functioned organically through the relations of reciprocity forged among corporate groups. If corporate groups were defined unambiguously, along with expectations and rules of reciprocity, including consequences if the rules were transgressed, the urban system would not have required a vertically hierarchical control structure – which in fact we do not see. Rather, corporate ownership of individual mounds by members of an occupationally defined or kin group is established by the archaeological data indicating near-exclusivity of occupational debris at each of the satellite sites. Did risk-management 'cause' this mixed and flexible subsistence, that in turn 'caused' this unusual clustered urbanism? Or did a tolerant acceptance of others (defined by their subsistence and artisanal pursuits) 'cause' a robust risk-sharing landscape, 'accelerated' by the flooding of displaced Saharans into the floodplain of the middle Niger? At this stage in our research it is impossible to untangle causation from correlation to any convincing degree. What is clear is that this intertwined system of dependency did not require the production of significant agricultural surplus, but rather maximized reciprocal relationships within the context of a heterarchically organized urban centre.

---

57  McIntosh, *Ancient Middle Niger*.

# Conclusion

In this chapter, we have explored the complex relationship between agriculture and urbanism, from its central role enabling the development of larger and denser settlements over time, to varying strategies and choices in agricultural practice. These are based in diverse sociopolitical systems, where power and authority dynamics influence the relations between the city and agriculture, with many urban centres in constant negotiation as to the degree of central or dispersed control in agricultural decisions. These varying systems expose the problems with concepts of urban–rural and urban–hinterland division, but remind us of the dynamism of ancient urban societies throughout the globe. These modern understandings of the relationship between urbanism and agriculture continue to erode long-held beliefs – the standard narrative – that urban zones were highly centralized systems abstracted from their hinterland, which provided agricultural products for the city under despotic control.

# Further reading

Blanton, R.E. and L. Fargher. *Collective Action in the Formation of Pre-modern States.* New York: Springer, 2008.

Boserup, E. *The Conditions of Agricultural Growth: The Economics of Agrarian Change under Population Pressure.* University of Chicago Press, 1965.

Childe, V.G. 'The urban revolution.' *Town Planning Review*, 21 (1950), 3–17.

Cowgill, G.L. 'Origins and development of urbanism: archaeological perspectives.' *Annual Review of Anthropology*, 33 (2004), 525–42.

Fisher, C.T., S.J. Leisz, and J.F. Weishampel. 'Geospatial revolution and remote sensing LiDAR in Mesoamerican archaeology.' *Proceedings of the National Academy of Sciences*, 109 (2012), 12916–21.

Heckenberger, M.J., J.C. Russell, C. Fausto, et al. 'Pre-Columbian urbanism, anthropogenic landscapes, and the future of the Amazon.' *Science*, 321 (2008), 1214–17.

Kron, G. 'Food production.' In W. Schiedel (ed.), *The Cambridge Companion to the Roman Economy.* Cambridge University Press, 2012. 156–74.

Marcus, J. and J. Sabloff (eds.). *The Ancient City: New Perspectives on Urbanism in the Old and New World.* Santa Fe, NM: School for Advanced Research, 2008.

Marcus, J. and C. Stanish (eds.). *Agricultural Strategies.* Los Angeles: Cotsen Institute of Archaeology, University of California, 2006.

Marston, J.M. 'Archaeological markers of agricultural risk management.' *Journal of Anthropological Archaeology*, 30 (2011), 190–205.

McAnany, P.A. and N. Yoffee (eds.). *Questioning Collapse: Human Resilience, Ecological Vulnerability, and the Aftermath of Empire.* Cambridge University Press, 2010.

McIntosh, R.J. *Ancient Middle Niger: Urbanism and the Self-Organizing Landscape*. Cambridge University Press, 2005.

McIntosh, S.K. 'Modeling political organization in large-scale settlement clusters: a case study from the inland Niger delta, Mali.' In S.K. McIntosh (ed.), *Beyond Chiefdoms: Pathways to Complexity in Africa*. Cambridge University Press, 1999. 66–79.

Menze, B.H. and J.A. Ur. 'Mapping patterns of long-term settlement in northern Mesopotamia at a large scale.' *Proceedings of the National Academy of Sciences*, 109 (2012), 778–87.

Morrison, K.D. 'The intensification of production: archaeological approaches.' *Journal of Archaeological Method and Theory*, 1 (1994), 111–59.

Ogundiran, A. 'Four millennia of cultural history in Nigeria (ca. 2000 BC–AD 1900): archaeological perspectives.' *Journal of World Prehistory*, 19 (2005), 133–68.

Pollock, S. *Ancient Mesopotamia: The Eden that Never Was*. Cambridge University Press, 1999.

Redman, C.L. *Human Impact on Ancient Environments*. Tucson: University of Arizona Press, 1999.

Rosen, A. *Civilizing Climate: Social Responses to Climate Change in the Ancient Near East*. Lanham, MD: AltaMira Press, 2007.

Sanders, W.T., A.G.M. de Escobar, and R.H. Cobean (eds.). *Urbanism in Mesoamerica*. University Park: Pennsylvania State University Press, 2003.

Smith, A. *The Political Landscape: Constellations of Authority in Early Complex Polities*. Berkeley: University of California Press, 2003.

Smith, M. (ed.). *The Social Construction of Ancient Cities*. Washington, DC: Smithsonian Institution Press, 2003.

Stone, G.D. *Settlement Ecology: The Social and Spatial Organization of Kofyar Agriculture*. Tucson: University of Arizona Press, 1996.

Storey, G.D. (ed.). *Urbanism in the Preindustrial World: Cross-Cultural Approaches*. Tuscaloosa: University of Alabama Press, 2006.

Trigger, B. *Understanding Early Civilizations*. Cambridge University Press, 2003.

Turner, B. and J. Sabloff. 'Classic period collapse of the Central Maya lowlands: insights about human–environment relationships for sustainability.' *Proceedings of the National Academy of Sciences*, 109 (2012), 13908–14.

van de Mieroop, M. *The Ancient Mesopotamian City*. Oxford University Press, 1997.

Weber, M. *The City*, trans. D. Martindale and G. Neuwirth. Glencoe, IL: Free Press, 1958 [1921].

  *Economy and Society: An Outline of Interpretive Sociology*. 3 vols. New York: Bedminster Press, 1968 [1922].

Wittfogel, K.A. *Oriental Despotism: A Comparative Study of Total Power*. New Haven, CT: Yale University Press, 1957.

Zeder, M.A. *Feeding Cities: Specialized Animal Economy in the Ancient Near East*. Washington, DC: Smithsonian Institution Press, 1991.

## 8

# Early agriculture in Southwest Asia

### ALAN H. SIMMONS

When V. Gordon Childe[1] coined the term 'Neolithic Revolution', he may have had no idea how enduring it would be. This transition from hunting and gathering economies to those based on agriculture was one of the most significant and transformational events in human history, affecting virtually every sphere of human society since its inception through to the present day. Perhaps because of this, the Neolithic defies easy definition. Certainly it was an economic transformation that involved the domestication of wild food resources and the establishment of permanent communities. It is not that simple, however, since there were at least semi-sedentary settlements in the Near East and other regions prior to domestication. Conversely, domesticated plants initially occur in some places, such as parts of the American Southwest, without the development of villages.[2] Thus, a flexible range of behaviour is embedded in the concept of 'Neolithic'. Ultimately, the most significant impacts of the Neolithic dictated a change in how humans interacted with each other and the environment. Thus, the Neolithic was an economic transformation, but not so much of *what* was domesticated, but rather of *how* people used and viewed food. This required technological and social innovations, all of which comprise the 'Neolithic package'.

The oldest documented Neolithic cultures occur in the 'Fertile Crescent' of Southwest Asia, more commonly known as the 'Near East' (Map 8.1).[3] While future research may ultimately yield an even older Neolithic, it has been best and

---

1 V.G. Childe, *Man Makes Himself* (London: Watts, 1936).
2 S. Fish and P. Fish, 'Comparative aspects of paradigms for the Neolithic transition in the Levant and the American Southwest', in G. Clark (ed.), *Perspectives on the Past: Theoretical Biases in Mediterranean Hunter-Gatherer Research* (Philadelphia: University of Pennsylvania Press, 1991), 396–410.
3 G. Barker, *The Agricultural Revolution in Prehistory: Why did Foragers Become Farmers?* (Oxford University Press, 2006); S.F. McCarter, *Neolithic* (New York and London: Routledge, 2007); A.H. Simmons, *The Neolithic Revolution in the Near East: Transforming the Human Landscape* (Tucson: University of Arizona Press, 2007).

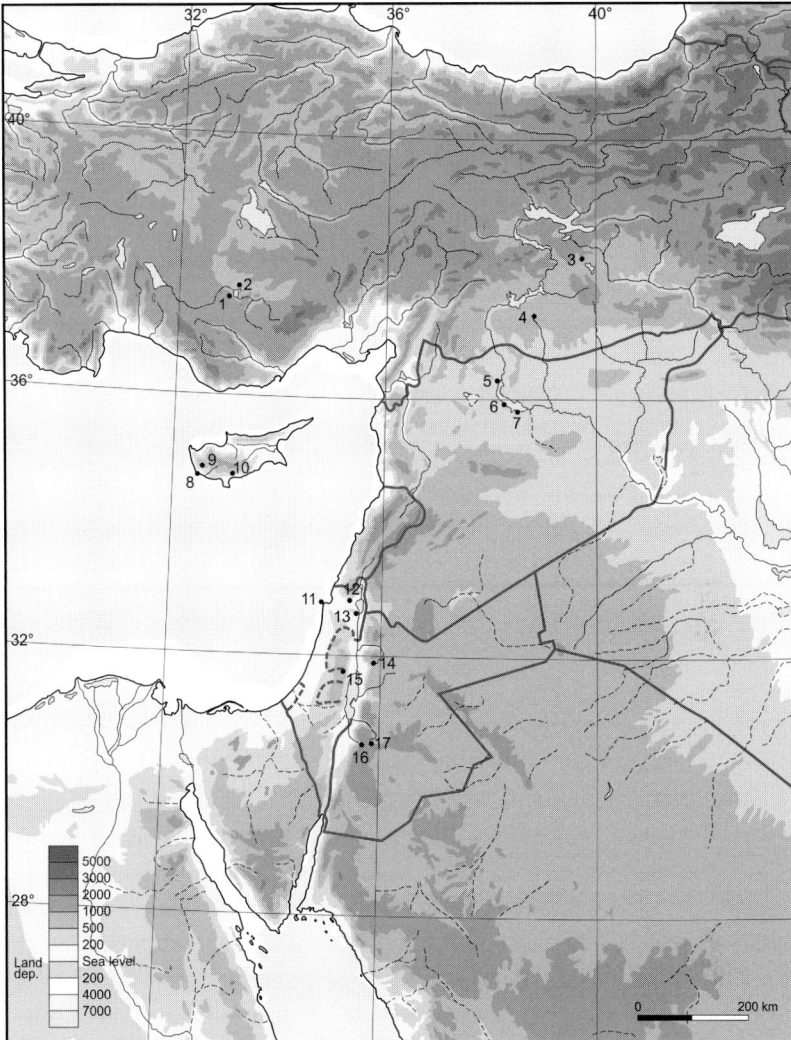

Map 8.1 Near East showing principal archaeological sites mentioned in Chapter 8: 1. Suberde; 2. Catal; 3. Cayonu; 4. Godeckli; 5. Jerf el Ahmar; 6. Mureybat; 7. Abu Huyera; 8. Mylouthkia; 9. Ais Yiorkis; 10. Shillourokambos; 11. Atlit Yam; 12. Kfar Hahoresh; 13. Shar HaGolan; 14. Ain Ghazal; 15. Jericho; 16. Wadi Feinan; 17. Ghwair I.

most thoroughly studied in this region. One reason for this is that much of Western culture derives from the Near East, so much of the early development of European and American archaeology focused on this area. My usage of 'Near

East' in this chapter is a broad one, and includes the intensively studied Levantine region, as well as Mesopotamia and Anatolia, or modern Iran, Iraq, and Turkey.

I use the term 'Neolithic' as follows. It is defined by both a timeframe and similarities in material culture. The definition, however, becomes a bit fuzzier after chronology and material culture. For example, my conception of 'Neolithic' can include people who largely remained hunters and gatherers economically, but adopted Neolithic material culture and interacted with villagers. This is reflected, for example, in arid parts of the southern Levant, where some Neolithic peoples were mobile hunter and gatherers, at least part of the year.[4] While these 'marginal' Neolithic people were present, however, the bulk of Neolithic populations lived in permanent villages and subsisted largely on humanly manipulated resources.

In this chapter, I provide an overview of the Near Eastern Neolithic in the context of several co-related themes: environment and climate, Near East-specific theories on the Neolithic, the economic nature of the Neolithic, issues of sedentism and the nature of the first villages, trends in material culture, newly developed social orders, regional cores and the expansion of the Neolithic, consequences of Neolithic lifestyles, and contemporary and future research trends. Before addressing these themes, however, a few words are necessary on terminology and chronology.

## The basics: history of research, terminology, and chronology

The Near Eastern Neolithic was first documented during archaeology's formative development and some of the considerable diversity in terminology is a result of the academic and national backgrounds of the variety of scholars involved in these early studies. Here, I have retained the traditional Neolithic phraseology, realizing that it is not always used in every region of the Near East. This begins with the Natufian, an important pre-Neolithic period in which much of the framework for subsequent developments occurred. The Natufian is divided into early and late phases. It is followed by two broad periods, the Pre-Pottery Neolithic (PPN), and the Pottery Neolithic (PN). The PPN, which in many ways represents the florescence of the Near Eastern Neolithic, is commonly divided into the Pre-Pottery Neolithic A, B, and C (PPNA, PPNB, PPNC). Many subdivide the PPNA into the Khiamian and Sultanian,[5] although

---

4  Simmons, *Neolithic Revolution*, 127–8.
5  O. Bar-Yosef, 'Earliest food producers – Pre-Pottery Neolithic (8000–5000)', in T. Levy (ed.), *The Archaeology of Society in the Holy Land* (London: Leicester University Press, 1998), 190–204.

there is debate as to whether or not the Khiamian is a distinct entity.[6] For the PPNB, it is typical to use subphases that include early, middle, and late PPNB. The PPNC is relatively recent, having been defined during excavations at the Jordanian mega-site of 'Ain Ghazal.[7] The PN is usually divided into PNA and PNB, although there is regional variability. These terms were popularized by Kathleen Kenyon's research at Jericho, and remain enduring.

The first discoveries of Neolithic materials were made prior to World War I by colourful early archaeologists such as T. E. Lawrence and Sir Leonard Woolley. While these initial discoveries demonstrated that there was an intermediate stage between the Palaeolithic and the great urban cultures of the Near East, little else was known.[8] More serious Neolithic studies began in the 1920s, especially in the southern Levant, and certainly the most significant milestone was at the biblical site of Jericho where in the 1930s John Garstang established a stratified Neolithic sequence. Kenyon's subsequent excavations in the 1950s documented a large, elaborate, and long-lived Neolithic community that provided a still widely used base for defining the Neolithic.[9] A consequence of the early studies at Jericho, however, was that it came to be identified as the type site for the Neolithic, an unfortunate occurrence since Jericho is quite distinct from most other Neolithic sites.

To the north, Robert Braidwood and other scholars were also document-ing Neolithic sites. After World War II, research accelerated, and of parti-cular importance was Braidwood's pioneering interdisciplinary work at Jarmo and other Iraqi sites. Indeed, Braidwood and Kenyon were fre-quently involved in colourful exchanges about whose Neolithic sites were 'more important'. Also significant was the research of Mellaart and others in Turkey, especially at important sites such as Çatalhöyük, Suberde, and Çayönü. These studies greatly expanded our knowledge of the Neolithic outside of what had become a perceived Levantine Neolithic core. Unfortunately, political considerations, especially in Iran and Iraq, have hampered a continuation of research into these very important areas.

---

6 Y. Garfinkel, 'Critical observations on the so-called Khiamian flint industry', in S. Kozlowski and H.G. Gebel (eds.), *Neolithic Chipped Stone Industries of the Fertile Crescent and their Contemporaries in Adjacent Regions* (Berlin: Ex oriente, 1996), 15–21.

7 A.H. Simmons et al., ' 'Ain Ghazal: a major Neolithic settlement in central Jordan', *Science*, 240 (1988), 35–9; and see Chapter 9.

8 A. Moore, 'The development of Neolithic societies in the Near East', in F. Wendorf and A. Close (eds.), *Advances in World Archaeology*, vol. IV (New York: Academic Press, 1985), 1–69.

9 K. Kenyon, *Digging Up Jericho* (London: Benn, 1957).

Table 8.1  Chronology for the Near Eastern Neolithic.

| Phase | Conventional (uncalibrated) BP | Calibrated BP |
|---|---|---|
| Natufian | c. 12,800–10,200 | c. 15,000–12,000 |
| PPNA | c. 10,500–9,200 | c. 11,700–10,500 |
| PPNB | c. 9,500–7,900 | c. 10,500–8,700 |
| PPNC | c. 7,900–7,500 | c. 8,600–8,250 |
| PN | c. 8,000–6,100 | c. 9,000–6,900 |

*Note* some potential overlap between PPNC and PN; in the Levant, a beginning of around 7,500 BP is often used for the PN.

Likewise, but for other reasons, it is only recently that the elaborate and expansive Turkish Neolithic has come into clearer focus.[10] Research in the Levant has also greatly expanded, documenting numerous Neolithic communities more modest than Jericho, providing a more balanced perspective. Despite the ever-changing political climate in the Near East, contemporary research is both refining and, in some cases, rewriting our comprehension of the Neolithic, especially with discoveries from Jordan, Turkey, and Cyprus.

The chronology of the Near Eastern Neolithic is supported by numerous radiocarbon determinations. While there is regional variation and overlap, Table 8.1 lists the general chronological framework. The following thematic discussion incorporates, as appropriate, data from each phase.

## Environmental context

The Near East covers a large area and is a remarkably varied landscape. Today much of it is environmentally degraded, but 12,000 years ago it was substantially different. The end of the Pleistocene and the beginning of the Holocene were times of dramatic climatic and temperature fluctuations, resulting in the expansion and contraction of favourable environments suitable for early farming. Many of these changes occurred rapidly, and would have had human consequences over generations. Accordingly, there has been considerable discussion of whether climatic or environmental variables were causal factors for the Neolithic, or whether it was a purely cultural

---

10  M. Özdoğan and N. Başgelen (eds.), *Neolithic in Turkey: The Cradle of Civilization* (Istanbul: Arkeoloji Sanat Yayınları, 1999).

phenomenon. Specifically, debate has focused on whether the Neolithic developed under favourable or adverse conditions.

Refinements in precise environmental reconstruction methods have greatly assisted in addressing this issue. For example, detailed analyses of speleothems (stable isotopic records obtained from cave deposits) from Soreq Cave in Israel provide very specific palaeoenvironmental data for much of the Neolithic.[11] Other lines of evidence include GISP2 Greenland ice core studies, pollen cores in Greece, Turkey, and the Levant, Negev snail isotope variability, low Dead Sea levels, and geochemistry from Lake Van, Iran.

Based on such studies, it appears that the first experimentations with relatively substantial sedentary living, but not agriculture, started during the early Natufian under optimal post-Glacial conditions (although semi-sedentism is likely at earlier Epipalaeolithic sites such as Ohalo[12]). The subsequent dramatic cooling and drying of the Younger Dryas (*c.* 11,000–10,000 BP) may be partially linked to the general dispersal of many late Natufian groups to a more mobile settlement pattern. During the early Neolithic, however, environmental conditions were optimal, often better than those prevailing today. While some lingering Younger Dryas conditions likely persisted into the early PPNA, much of this period correlates with a warming trend resulting in expanded and food-rich Mediterranean woodland and forest steppes and the increase of lakes and ponds, presenting new opportunities for human exploitation. The PPNB enjoyed only slightly less favourable climatic conditions. By *c.* 9,000 BP a Mediterranean climatic regime was apparently well established in the Levant (and likely elsewhere in the Near East). Landform changes occurred as well. At the onset of the Holocene, the coastal plain was considerably larger than at present, but a gradual rise in sea levels reduced it, with its modern configuration occurring around the Chalcolithic.

Around 8,200–8,000 BP a brief but severe deterioration occurred, of a magnitude comparable to the Younger Dryas, resulting in an abrupt aridification in many parts of the world. This is important since it may roughly correspond to the end of the PPN, and could have been a causal variable. There are, however, some concerns relating to the variable use of calibrated and uncalibrated years for this event, and it could have occurred *after* the

---

11  M. Bar-Matthews et al., 'Late Quaternary paleoclimate in the eastern Mediterranean region from stable isotope analysis of speleothems at Soreq Cave, Israel', *Quaternary Research*, 47 (1997), 155–68.

12  D. Nadel (ed.), *Ohalo II – a 23,000 Year-Old Fisher-Hunter-Gatherers' Camp on the Shore of the Sea of Galilee* (Haifa: Hecht Museum, 2002).

beginning of the PN.[13] In any event, during the PN, environmental conditions approximated those of today.[14]

## Theories on why the Neolithic occurred

The Neolithic Revolution was recognized as a major cultural event even during the early years of archaeology. As the discipline proceeded from an emphasis on excavation and culture history towards theoretical explanations for past human behaviour, many scholars postulated a variety of reasons why the Neolithic occurred. Here I provide a limited discussion of Near Eastern-specific models that have had an impact on theoretical insights into the origins of domestication.

One of the first models was Childe's classic, environmentally oriented formulation often known as the 'oasis propinquity theory'.[15] This assumes that major climatic change at the end of the Pleistocene caused the drying of broad areas and forced plants, animals, and humans to congregate in oases and river valleys. People rapidly realized that some animals and plants were more useful than others, and eventually domesticated these. Childe's model was widely embraced at the time, although it lacked much empirical data. This was partially rectified by Robert (and Linda) Braidwood's interdisciplinary field-based investigations in Iraq that set out to explicitly test the oasis hypothesis. Braidwood believed there was a 'nuclear zone' for domestication in the foothills of the Zagros mountains. Hence, his model is often referred to as the 'hilly flanks' model. A pioneering component of Braidwood's investigations was the incorporation of a wide range of scientists from the biological and earth sciences. Braidwood viewed food production as the culmination of increasing human specialization, a natural result of cultural evolution.[16]

In light of archaeological data that have accumulated over the past several decades, it is easy to refute many earlier models. For example, the oasis propinquity model is too simple for the facts. There is no evidence of drastic or catastrophic climatic changes in the early Neolithic; furthermore, most early sites do not occur in major river valleys and oases (Jericho is an exception). Likewise, despite using actual archaeological data, Braidwood's hilly flanks model cannot be strongly supported, primarily because the

---

13 Simmons, Neolithic Revolution, 40–4, 185.
14 A. Rosen, Civilizing Climate: Social Responses to Climate Change in the Ancient Near East (Lanham, MD: AltaMira Press, 2007).
15 Childe, Man Makes Himself.
16 R. Braidwood, 'The agricultural revolution', Scientific American, 203 (1960), 130–41.

earliest Neolithic sites are not located in the foothills. Nonetheless, these early models were first attempts to understand why the Neolithic occurred, and certainly have historical significance.

With the advent of processual, or 'new', archaeology, many scholars turned their attention to explanatory, if often conflicting, models. Many used the Near East as their primary data source. Typically, processual models are variants on themes of broad spectrum subsistence, population growth and expansion, resource stress, climatic change, or combinations of these. Most involve the interplay between agricultural intensification, environmental change, land use, and sedentism. A basic premise was that larger populations led to agriculture, and not the reverse. This was contrary to many older views that essentially saw domestication as coming first, leading to population increase. Based on current data, however, it is likely that, in the Near East at least, sedentism and population increase during the early Natufian ultimately created the need for agriculture.

One of the earliest processual models was that of Louis Binford, who argued that once early Natufians became sedentary in favourable Mediterranean environments, populations increased, as did aridity, placing new stresses on expanding populations and forcing some groups to 'bud off' into more marginal areas.[17] These groups then used previously under-exploited resources, such as wild cereals, resulting in domestication.

Around the same time, Kent Flannery proposed a 'broad spectrum subsistence' model in which a wide variety of resources were used at the end of the Epipalaeolithic, leading to population growth.[18] Wild cereals were considered second or third choice foods but their chief benefit was that they could support higher populations and thus people began to specialize more, domesticating them. Flannery felt that farming represented a decision to work harder and eat less desirable foods, and thus people likely adopted agriculture not because they wanted to but rather because they were forced to. Flannery also proposed a model for the origins of villages in both the Near East and Mesoamerica that was more reliant upon social factors based on communal sharing that gradually evolved into nuclear families.[19]

17 L. Binford, 'Post Pleistocene adaptations', in S. Binford and L. Binford (eds.), *New Perspectives in Archaeology* (Chicago: Aldine Press, 1968), 313–41.

18 K. Flannery, 'Origins and ecological effects of early domestication in Iran and the Near East', in P. Ucko and G. Dimbleby (eds.), *The Domestication and Exploitation of Plants and Animals* (Chicago: Aldine Press, 1969), 73–100.

19 K. Flannery, 'The origins of the village as a settlement type in Mesoamerica and the Near East: a comparative study', in P. Ucko et al. (eds.), *Man, Settlement and Urbanism* (London: Duckworth, 1972), 23–53.

There are numerous other processually oriented Near Eastern models that rely on population increase, resource stress, and environmental variables. Likewise, with the advent of 'post-processual archaeology' there have been a number of models emphasizing social causation. Neither processual nor post-processual approaches have escaped criticism. For example, Henry argued that many processually oriented models generally did not fit the archaeological data.[20] Social and post-processual models have also been challenged, with Smith effectively dismantling many as 'fact-free'.[21] Likewise, Cauvin's 'symbolic revolution' concept has been criticized, even by post-processual archaeologists.[22] While Cauvin's model may have considerable merit as an intellectual concept, it, too, is not well supported by empirical archaeological data. It, and some more recent works,[23] also seem to implicitly assume that somehow pre-Neolithic peoples were not quite fully modern in their mental capabilities, a concept out of tune with much current anthropological thought.

Despite some well-deserved criticisms, much is currently known about the transition to food production and its consequences. Smith notes that several interdisciplinary technological innovations have advanced the search for why domestic economies were adopted.[24] These include refinements in dating, better environmental data, searching for relationships between domesticates and their wild progenitors at the molecular level using 'molecular archaeology', and DNA analyses for genetic 'fingerprinting'.

Thus, while there is no consensus on the emergence of agriculture, many feel that there is a core of recurring traits.[25] These include sedentism, storage facilities, high population density, high resource diversity, appropriate harvesting and processing technology, and suitable potential domesticates.

---

20 D. Henry, *From Foraging to Agriculture: The Levant at the End of the Ice Age* (Philadelphia: University of Pennsylvania Press, 1989).

21 B. Smith, 'The transition to food production', in G. Feinman and T.D. Price (eds.), *Archaeology at the Millennium: A Sourcebook* (New York: Kluwer Academic/Plenum, 2001), 199–229.

22 J. Cauvin, *The Birth of the Gods and the Origins of Agriculture*, trans. T. Watkins (Cambridge University Press, 2000 [1994]); for criticism, see I. Hodder, 'Symbolism and the origins of agriculture in the Near East', *Cambridge Archaeological Journal*, 11 (2001), 107–12.

23 T. Watkins, 'Household, community and social landscape: maintaining social memory in the early Neolithic of Southwest Asia', in M. Furbolt et al. (eds.), *As Time Goes By? Monumentality, Landscapes, and the Temporal Perspective* (Bonn: Habelt, 2012), 23–44.

24 B.D. Smith, *Emergence of Agriculture* (New York: Scientific American Library, 1995).

25 B. Hayden, 'An overview of domestication', in T.D. Price and A.B. Gebauer (eds.), *Last Hunters, First Farmers: New Perspectives on the Prehistoric Transition to Agriculture* (Santa Fe, NM: School of American Research Press, 1995), 273–99.

Other possibly significant factors include competition, ownership of produce and resource localities, changes in climate or vegetation, and population pressure. These variables all continue to influence theoretical concepts of the Neolithic.

## Examining agriculture and domestication

In the Near East, key domesticates included sheep, goats, cattle, pigs, barley, emmer wheat, and einkorn wheat. Lentils, peas, chickpeas, bitter vetch, flax, broad beans, and rye were also domesticated, although they were of less importance.[26] There are many technical issues and difficulties associated with determining what, exactly, a domestic plant or animal looks like compared to its wild counterpart, and how this can influence definitions of the Neolithic. Much recent discussion revolves around determining what exactly is meant by 'domestication'. We know that certain morphological changes ultimately differentiated domestic species from their wild predecessors, but perhaps more important is the concept that many species were *used* in a domestic sense prior to these changes. Several researchers now believe that the criteria for determining domestication must be re-evaluated and that several species may have been 'anthropologically' domesticated even if morphological changes had not yet occurred.[27]

The Natufians practised an array of economic options and were complex foragers. Despite the broad spectrum nature of Natufian adaptations, however, specialized exploitation, especially of gazelle, produced the majority of protein. The situation is less clear with plant resources, although many Natufian groups appear to have harvested wild cereals on a seasonal basis. While some Natufian groups may have practised some forms of cultivation, there is no evidence that they domesticated plants or animals, with the apparent exceptions of the dog and rye cereal.

Overall, trends observed during the Natufian continued into the PPNA, and, at least at larger sites, intensive cultivation of plants and specialized

---

26 D. Zohary, 'Domestication of the Neolithic Near Eastern crop assemblage', in P. Anderson (ed.), *Prehistory of Agriculture: New Experimental and Ethnographic Approaches* (Los Angeles: Cotsen Institute of Archaeology, University of California, 1999), 42–50.

27 E. Asouti and D.Q. Fuller, 'A contextual approach to the emergence of agriculture in Southwest Asia: reconstructing early Neolithic plant-food production', *Current Anthropology*, 54 (2013), 301–5; J.D. Vigne et al., 'New archaeological approaches to trace the first steps of animal domestication: general presentation, reflections and proposals', in J. Vigne et al. (eds.), *First Steps of Animal Domestication* (Oxford: Oxbow, 2005), 1–16.

hunting supported the population base. Importantly, however, there is still no clear evidence for morphological domesticates, beyond the dog and rye. The PPNA economic (and social) pattern is emerging as much more complex than previously believed, and exhibits considerable geographic variation. For example, at northern sites, cattle and caprovines (sheep and goats) were hunted, and pig husbandry at Hallan Çemi in Anatolia has been suggested, although this has been disputed.[28] In the central and southern regions, gazelle were the dominant species exploited. And, we now know that some PPNA people had expanded to the Mediterranean island of Cyprus, introducing wild cereal cultivation and hunting wild boars.[29]

Both animal husbandry and agriculture became firmly established during the PPNB, although wild resources continued to be used. Confirmed domesticates vary regionally. For animals, a major change is that caprovines replace gazelle. Most evidence points to animal domestication occurring after plant domestication and many researchers agree that initial domestication of primary animal species occurred in the northern Levant and southeastern Turkey, rather than in the southern Levant.[30] The Levantine Corridor, a link between the northern and southern portions of the Fertile Crescent, likely served as a natural route for introducing these to the south. During the PPNB, there was an increasing dependence on herding of goats and, especially, sheep, and, to the north, cattle and pigs were important. Many animals were bred for primary resources (meat) and secondary ones (milk, hair, fertilizer, traction). The domestication of some species also has implications for the development of pastoralism and it is likely that classic Near Eastern patterns of pastoral nomadism and village life – the 'desert and the sown' – became established.

Marine resources also may have been important at coastal sites. While substantial data are lacking, Neolithic underwater sites such as Atlit-Yam in Israel provide rare glimpses into this element. The establishment of fishing economies based in coastal villages has implications not only for adding dimension to our knowledge of Neolithic economic practices, but also for exploration of the Mediterranean islands.[31]

---

28 M. Rosenberg et al., 'Hallan Çemi, pig husbandry, and post-Pleistocene adaptations along the Taurus–Zagros arc (Turkey)', *Paléorient*, 24 (1998), 25–41; J. Peters et al., 'Early animal husbandry in the northern Levant', *Paléorient*, 25 (1999), 27–47.

29 J.D. Vigne et al., 'First wave of cultivators spread to Cyprus at least 10,600 y ago', *Proceedings of the National Academy of Sciences*, 109 (2012), 8445–9.

30 J. Peters et al., 'Early animal husbandry in the northern Levant', *Paléorient*, 25 (1999), 27–47.

31 E. Galili et al., 'The emergence of the Mediterranean fishing village in the Levant and the anomaly of Neolithic Cyprus', in E. Peltenburg and A. Wasse (eds.), *Neolithic Revolution: New Perspectives on Southwest Asia in Light of Recent Discoveries on Cyprus*, Levant Supplementary Series 1 (Oxford: Oxbow, 2004), 91–101.

While the PPNB witnessed a rich and diverse economic base, during the PPNC available data indicate a more restricted dietary breadth. This pattern continues into the PN, where economic strategies were almost entirely dependent on domesticated grains and pulses and the management of either tamed or domesticated animals. Typically, domesticates are represented by fewer species than they were during the PPN. Towards the end of the PN, olive oil production may have begun in the southern Levant, and there is evidence for dairying activities. In Mesopotamia, there is limited evidence of irrigation, which had not been well documented previously.[32]

There are also suggestions that beer-brewing and wine-making began during the PN, if not earlier. Although direct evidence is limited, ceramic residue analysis from the Iranian PN site of Hajji Firuz Tepe (c. 7,000 BP) suggests that the vessels contained wine (possibly both red and white), and contextual evidence at the site suggests relatively large-scale production and consumption. Even more recent research hints at beer-brewing at PPN Göbekli Tepe. The use of alcohol has tremendous implications with regard to social relations, status, leisure time, ritual, prestige, and even use as psychopharmacological substances.[33]

The PN economic pattern is essentially what Butzer and others have characterized as the basic Mediterranean agrosystem, consisting of grain and legume cultivation, tending of various vegetables and condiments, orchard crops, and livestock.[34] It is likely that this basic pattern became established during the PN and that an agropastoral economy existed that became more and more dependent on a smaller number of domesticated resources. Changes in processing and cooking brought about by the incorporation of ceramics undoubtedly influenced this pattern and aided in the increased use of secondary products. In addition, pastoral nomadism played an increasingly important economic and social role.

---

32 E.B. Banning, 'Ceramic Neolithic: late or Pottery Neolithic', in P. Peregrine and M. Ember (eds.), *Encyclopedia of Prehistory*, vol. VII: *South and Southwest Asia* (New York: Kluwer Academic/Plenum, 2002), 40–55.

33 O. Dietrich et al., 'The role of cult and feasting in the emergence of Neolithic communities: new evidence from Göbekli Tepe, south-eastern Turkey', *Antiquity*, 86 (2012), 674–95; S. Katz and M. Voigt, 'Bread and beer: the early use of cereals in human diet', *Expedition*, 28 (1986), 23–34; P. McGovern, *Ancient Wine: The Search for the Origins of Viniculture* (Princeton, NJ and Oxford: Princeton University Press, 2003).

34 K. Butzer, 'Ecology in the long view: settlement histories, agrosystemic strategies, and ecological performance', *Journal of Field Archaeology*, 23 (1996), 141–50.

# Sedentism, the first villages, and Neolithic material culture

Traditional hallmarks of the Neolithic are sedentary village life and a rich material culture. And yet, what 'sedentism' really means is much debated. Indeed, an age-old question is a variant on the adage 'What came first – the chicken or the egg?', here expressed as 'What came first – sedentism or domestication?' In the Near East, this issue appears resolved by the presence of at least semi-sedentary Natufian communities that did not have domesticated resources. It is important to note that there is an enormous range of site types throughout both the Natufian and the Neolithic that reflect a sliding scale of sedentism. These range from artefact scatters, ritual centres, villages, and 'mega-sites' (see Chapter 9).

Some early Natufian groups lived in small villages or hamlets. Although there are a few exceptions, most structures are interpreted as domestic dwellings. Less elaborate and more mobile adaptations over a larger geographic area occurred in the late Natufian. The exception to this appears to be large middle Euphrates Syrian villages such as Abu Hureyra or Mureybat during the equivalent of both early and late Natufian. Natufian architecture is typically characterized by semi-subterranean structures, usually circular or semicircular, and most are usually 3 to 6 m in diameter. At Abu Hureyra, however, the first structures are complex, multi-chambered pit-dwellings, followed by above-ground timber-and-reed huts. While most Natufian sites with architecture contain only a few structures, their solid construction and the fact that structures are often grouped together in small clusters suggest that they qualify as 'villages' or as small hamlets.[35]

Sedentism is better established during the PPNA, and some sites are much larger than their Natufian predecessors. Large villages likely housed hundreds of people, but smaller hamlets and sites of limited activity also occurred. Domestic architecture is varied, although the basic form of dwellings continues to be circular or oval, but not semi-subterranean. In the north, some PPNA structures are rectangular or subrectangular. Some structures are quite large, up to 5–8 m in diameter. At Mureybat, one structure has traces of a painted fresco decoration, ranking as among the earliest uses of art that is integral to architecture. PPNA Jericho stands out from many other sites in size and duration, estimated at some 10 acres and including over twenty-five building levels.

---

35 O. Bar-Yosef, 'The Natufian culture in the Levant: threshold to the origins of agriculture', *Evolutionary Anthropology*, 6 (1998), 159–77.

Figure 8.1 View of the Round Tower at Jericho, 8000 BCE.

There are also examples of non-domestic PPNA architecture. For example, at Tell Abr 3 and Jerf el Ahmar in Syria and Wadi Feinan 16 in Jordan, a few structures may have been communal buildings.[36] Wadi Feinan 16 particularly stands out due to its overall small size and remote location. Even more dramatic non-domestic architecture occurs at two PPNA sites. The large stone tower (Figure 8.1) and walls at Jericho have long stood out from contemporary sites. Although Kenyon believed that the tower and associated walls were built for defence, Bar-Yosef argued that the wall system was linked

---

[36] T. Yartah, 'Tell 'Abr 3, un village du Néolithique précéramique (PPNA) sur le moyen Euphrate: première approche', Paléorient, 30 (2004), 141–58; S. Mithen et al., 'An 11,600-year-old communal structure from the Neolithic of southern Jordan', Antiquity, 85 (2011), 350–64.

to the diversion of flash floods and that the tower might have been a shrine.[37] Ronen and Adler believe that the entire wall and tower complex were magical, perhaps used to protect the settlement from dangerous 'evil spirits'.[38]

By far the most impressive and unique site, however, is Göbekli Tepe in Turkey. This is a huge locality, approximately 22 acres, with a depth up to 15 m, that was occupied during both the PPNA and PPNB. There is limited indication of domestic daily life at the site, and it has been interpreted as both a ritual site and a regional meeting place for the exchange of goods and ideas. Its excavators believe that it was built not by true Neolithic people but rather by a predominantly hunter-gatherer society.[39] This conclusion is supported by the lack of domesticated plants or animals. This, however, could be too strong an interpretation. The lack of domesticates does not necessarily mean that Göbekli Tepe's occupants were hunters and gatherers, especially during its later PPNB occupation. Rather it could simply imply that whatever function the site had did not require domesticates during its use. Additionally, Banning has questioned the ritual significance of Göbekli Tepe.[40] Regardless of interpretation, there is no denying Göbekli Tepe's impressive architecture. Several large (10–30 m in diameter) concentric circular or oval stone enclosures containing carved upright stelae or pillars form the site. The elaborate motifs (Figure 8.2) primarily include animals, often life-size, as well as human arms and landscape portrayals. The enclosures were completely buried by presumably intentional backfilling.

Distinctive architecture is a PPNB hallmark. Many sites have spectacularly preserved architecture, often standing to three or more metres. The past two decades have witnessed several detailed analyses of this architecture as a way of understanding social organization, household composition, economic patterns, site and regional patterning, and the relationship between domestic and non-domestic architecture.[41]

37 O. Bar-Yosef, 'The walls of Jericho: an alternative interpretation', *Current Anthropology*, 27 (1986), 157–62.
38 A. Ronen and D. Adler, 'The walls of Jericho were magical', *Archaeology, Ethnology and Anthropology of Eurasia*, 2 (2001), 97–103.
39 O. Dietrich et al., 'The role of cult and feasting in the emergence of Neolithic communities', *Antiquity*, 86 (2012), 674–95; S. Scham, 'The world's first temple', *Archaeology*, 61 (2008), 22–7; K. Schmidt, 'Göbekli Tepe, southeastern Turkey: a preliminary report on the 1995–1999 excavations', *Paléorient*, 26 (2001), 45–54.
40 E.B. Banning, 'So fair a house: Göbekli Tepe and the identification of temples in the Pre-Pottery Neolithic of the Near East', *Current Anthropology*, 52, Supplement 4 (2011), S619–60.
41 E.B. Banning, 'Houses, households, and changing society in the late Neolithic and Chalcolithic of the southern Levant', *Paléorient*, 36 (2010), 45–83.

Figure 8.2 One of the carved columns from Göbekli Tepe.

Figure 8.3 PPNB architecture at Ghwair I, southern Jordan.

The PPNB witnessed the development of architectural complexity, and villages often consisted of multi-room rectangular structures. The major innovation from the PPNA to the PPNB is the change from circular or oval structures to well-formed rectangular rooms (Figure 8.3), resulting in a pattern still observed today at small Near Eastern villages (Figure 8.4). Despite this, however, some PPNB settlements, especially in the arid regions, consisted of circular architecture. While there is overall architectural continuity throughout the PPNB, there is regional and chronological variation, and changes occurred during the late PPNB, especially at the megasites, where the number of rooms in structures often increased, but their size decreased. Many PPNB structures are elaborate, and some of the two-storey units often contain internal stairways. Generally, structures are linked into room-blocks, frequently forming an almost 'condominium' morphology. The floors of many structures were made of high quality plaster, often painted. Burials often occurred beneath these floors. A notable activity during much of the PPNB was extensive 'remodelling' of individual structures.

Figure 8.4  The modern village of Dana, near Ghwair I in southern Jordan, as an analogy for a PPNB village.

In addition to domestic architecture, there is considerable evidence for non-domestic structures with communal or ritual significance. There also are examples of elaborate non-residential sites. Non-residential architecture includes distinctive buildings both within and outside of settlement boundaries. These often differed from residential structures in that they were larger and had different artefact compositions, suggesting use for either ritual or community-wide purposes. Sometimes, non-domestic buildings were incorporated into residential units.

Specialized PPNB sites that lack residential architecture include Kfar Ha-Horesh in Israel, a site apparently constructed primarily for mortuary purposes.[42] As with the PPNA, Göbekli Tepe is perhaps the most dramatic example of a non-residential site. Some non-domestic sites that likely do not relate to symbolic behaviour occur in the arid zones. These are desert-kites,

42  N. Goring-Morris, 'Life, death and the emergence of differential status in the Near Eastern Neolithic: evidence from Kfar Ha-Horesh, lower Galilee, Israel', in J. Clarke (ed.), *Archaeological Perspectives on the Transmission and Transformation of Culture in the Eastern Mediterranean* (Oxford: Oxbow, 2005), 89–105.

linear stone features usually interpreted as elaborate game drives used in gazelle hunting.[43]

Architectural data for the PPNC is more limited than for the PPNB, with most data coming from 'Ain Ghazal. At that site, there was considerable re-use of late PPNB domestic structures, with two primary house plans. One consists of small rectangular structures, while the other includes semi-subterranean pier and cell houses. A major change is in the use of plaster flooring, which deteriorated in quality, perhaps due to ecological reasons. Non-residential architecture at 'Ain Ghazal includes a massive but low wall that probably separated courtyard areas and a walled street.[44]

Kenyon's initial characterization of the PN as retrogressive has influenced generations of scholars. She interpreted circular structures in the PN levels at Jericho as either dwellings or quarries for mud-brick material. This contributed to the image of PN peoples as partially nomadic and no longer constructing substantial architecture. We now know that this is an incorrect perception. Indeed, it was during the PN that some of the largest Neolithic sites in the Near East were constructed, perhaps the most famous of which is Çatalhöyük in Turkey, although substantial villages were also present in the Levant.

PN architecture generally is characterized by single- or multiple-roomed rectangular buildings, although round structures also occur, as at Jericho. Gypsum or lime plaster is often used for flooring, but not as frequently as during the PPNB. Most structures range from 10 to 30 m$^2$, and some multi-room buildings were two-storey.[45] There is considerable geographic variation in architectural and village layouts. Perhaps most distinctive is the 'agglutinative plan' layout of large settlements in central Turkey, which appear to represent original Anatolian creations. These sites were large agglomerations that were very tightly packed together. At Çatalhöyük, approximately every other room was some sort of domestic sanctuary containing frescoes and sculpted figures, as well as burials. Often, the wall art depicts headless human corpses. The inclusion of sanctuaries within domestic structures further blurs the distinction between public and private architecture.

In the southern Levant, many sites reinforced Kenyon's original characterization of the ephemeral nature of the PN. More recent excavations,

---

43  A. Betts, 'The Pre-Pottery Neolithic B period in eastern Jordan', *Paléorient*, 15 (1989), 147–53.

44  G. Rollefson, 'Changes in architecture and social organization at 'Ain Ghazal', in H.-G. Gebel et al. (eds.), *The Prehistory of Jordan II: Perspectives from 1997* (Berlin: Ex oriente, 1997), 287–307; and see Chapter 9.

45  Banning, 'Ceramic Neolithic'.

however, have shown considerable architectural variability that contradicts Kenyon's original characterizations. For example, renewed excavations at Shaar Hagolan in Israel have documented extensive and elaborate rectangular architecture, including a new pattern – the courtyard house built along streets and alleys – as well as large structures interpreted as communal buildings.[46]

At 'Ain Ghazal, substantial architecture during the early PN occupation consists of large (*c.* 9 × 5 m) rectilinear houses that had mud floors and contained multiple rooms, and a large apsidal structure, remodelled from a late PPNB structure, that is interpreted as a public building. Other architecture includes courtyard or compound walls, and continued use and remodelling of a large wall originally constructed during the PPNC. Towards the end of the site's final occupation, however, there is evidence for temporary structures, possibly tents, replacing the more permanent facilities.[47]

## Trends in material culture

With the establishment of true sedentary settlements came an increasingly complex array of material and ritual culture. Natufian hallmark artefacts are microliths, often produced in a wide range of specific types and occurring in remarkably high densities at many sites. Microlithic tools usually account for 40 per cent or more of assemblages, and many were likely used as composite tools, hafted into bone or wood shafts. Most of the raw material used in chipped stone manufacture was relatively local, although imported Anatolian obsidian is occasionally found. Typical tools include geometric microliths known as lunates. Other tools, both microlithic and larger, include triangles, burins, perforators, end scrapers, core scrapers, picks, choppers, and backed bladelets and blades, some of which show sickle polish ('glossed pieces').[48] Projectile points are absent, at least as distinct aerodynamically shaped and typologically identifiable entities. Specific frequencies of tools may indicate regional traditions and functional and chronological differences.[49]

Natufian ground stone tools are especially significant, particularly regarding economic parameters and implications for sedentism. They are diverse and elaborate, often occurring in large numbers, especially at bigger sites.

46 Y. Garfinkel et al., *'Sha'ar Hagolan 1: Neolithic Art in Context* (Oxford: Oxbow, 2002).
47 Rollefson, 'Changes in architecture'.   48 Bar-Yosef, 'Natufian culture in the Levant'.
49 A. Belfer-Cohen and N. Goring-Morris, 'The late Epipaleolithic as the precursor of the Neolithic: the lithic evidence', in Kozlowski and Gebel (eds.), *Neolithic Chipped Stone Industries*, 217–25.

These include a large variety of portable and not-so-portable items, such as mortars and pestles and numerous more specialized artefacts, including a unique type of deep mortar that is often hollowed through, referred to as 'stone pipes'. Some ground stone artefacts also show stylistic or artistic efforts.

Other artefacts reflect an elaborate bone craftsmanship. Outstanding examples include sickle handles, some of which are decorated with animal representations. Shell artefacts, some coming from a considerable distance, also occur, and personal ornamental artefacts are abundant. Portable naturalistic and schematic figurines made on bone and limestone are also relatively common. These objects are primarily zoomorphic rather than human representations.[50]

In many ways, PPNA material culture resembles that of the Natufian, especially in maintaining primarily microlithic chipped stone assemblages and in the continuation of a rich ground stone industry. Artefact density is high and varied, and there is considerable regional variation. Tools include lunates and sickle blades; small projectile points now occur. Axes and polished celts also are present at many sites.

As would be expected in sites with an increased dependence on plant foods, a variety of ground stone artefacts is especially abundant during the PPNA. Some are engraved with geometric or meander patterns, a continuation from the Natufian. Particularly impressive is an array of engraved and carved artefacts from Jerf el Ahmar in Syria, which features intricately engraved stone vases, animal figurines, including birds of prey, geometrically decorated grooved stones, and small oval stones engraved with animal motifs on one side and numerous dots on the other.

There is a large array of non-stone items, typical of village life. For example, the bone industry is rich and varied. There is also limited evidence for basketry technologies. The PPNA has a large variety of artefacts with images. As with the Natufian, these include incised stones and cobbles, but more significant are animal and human figurines. In contrast to the Natufian, human figurines, primarily female, become more common, while animal representations are virtually unknown. Cauvin feels that the 'animal kingdom' is represented in the PPNA by the bull, not so much in figurines but by cattle skulls buried in houses or incorporated into features.[51] He attributes

---

50 Bar-Yosef, 'Natufian culture in the Levant'; F. Valla, 'The first settled societies: Natufian (12,500–10,200 BP)', in Levy (ed.), *Archaeology of Society*, 169–87.

51 Cauvin, *Birth of the Gods*, 25–33.

this pattern to the beginning of a new religion exemplified by the dualism of 'the goddess and the bull'. Not all researchers, however, agree that most PPNA figurines are female; rather, many are ambiguous or are dual-gendered representations.[52]

The PPNB is very rich in material culture. There is more known about PPNB chipped stone than about that of any other Neolithic period. In general terms, the microlithic aspect nearly disappears and assemblages are blade-dominated, with frequent usage of naviform cores. This standardized technology resulted in a large variety of well-made tools, including very diverse projectile points, sickle blades, drills, borers, knives, scrapers, and burins.

Ground stone vessels are finer and more diverse than in the PPNA. Platters are a PPNB innovation, and handstones and querns are common. Many milling tools are larger than their PPNA counterparts and must have permitted cooks to process more food. Some grinding slabs were essentially immovable. Other ground implements include palettes, bowls, axes or celts, probable gaming boards, and many items of personal ornamentation, such as stone bracelets. Other vessels were made of cordage, basketry, wood, stone, plaster ('white wares'), and early versions of pottery. Plaster vessels, sometimes incised and painted, are more complex than stone vessels. The presence of many such artefacts has considerable social implications with regard to leisure time and individual personae.[53] Other PPNB artefacts include a remarkable array of bone tools and stone and shell jewellery. It is, however, in the ritual and symbolic realm that the PPNB stands out, where tokens, masks, plastered human skulls, statues, and figurines have been recovered. Most notable are the striking human statues from 'Ain Ghazal (see Figure 9.8).[54]

Finally, an important technological contribution of the PPNB is a sophisticated pyrotechnology: the application of high temperatures to manufacture plaster from limestone. Plaster was used for a variety of purposes, especially for floor and wall finishes, sculpture, and the production of vessels.[55]

PPNC assemblages become less standardized and there are some major changes in chipped stone technology.[56] There are changes in raw material

52 D. Schmandt-Besserat, 'A stone metaphor of creation', *Near Eastern Archaeology*, 61 (1998), 109–17.

53 E.B. Banning, 'The Neolithic period: triumphs of architecture, agriculture, and art', *Near Eastern Archaeology*, 61 (1998), 188–237; K. Wright, 'The social origins of cooking and dining in early villages of western Asia', *Proceedings of the Prehistoric Society*, 66 (2000), 89–121.

54 Simmons et al., ' 'Ain Ghazal', 36.   55 Banning, 'Neolithic period', 204–5.

56 G. Rollefson, 'Neolithic chipped stone technology at 'Ain Ghazal, Jordan: the status of the PPNC', *Paléorient*, 16 (1993), 119–24.

preferences and a reduced emphasis on naviform core technology. Smaller and lighter projectile points are another PPNC characteristic. Little is known of the ground stone technology, but overall it reflects a continuation of the late PPNB.

During the PN, ceramics obviously become important components. It has been thought that ceramics may have initially served ceremonial functions rather than purely utilitarian ones. Ceramics initially appear in the Levant with reasonably sophisticated quality, leading earlier researchers to believe that they were imported from the north. Newer studies, however, show that local people were fully capable of developing their own ceramics.[57] Gopher does not believe that the addition of ceramics was a dramatic qualitative change, since working plaster and clay occurred during the PPN.[58] Limited amounts of ceramics, probably experimental, have been recovered from PPNB and PPNC contexts, and of course the statuary of 'Ain Ghazal, as well as white wares, clearly shows a knowledge of working with a plastic medium. There is considerable variability in ceramics, which occur in both decorated and undecorated forms and in crude and finer wares. Some of the earliest ceramics were handmade and include a variety of forms. Regional variation is substantial.

Chipped stone continues to be a major element. Often, the expedient character first observed during the PPNC continues into the PN. The technology is now dominated by flakes rather than blades. A variety of projectile points and sickles also occurs, but points are not as common as they were during the PPNB. A de-emphasis on hunting may be one reason for this. Heavy bifacial tools are important. Ground stone continues to be important throughout the PN, not surprisingly given the emphasis on farming.

Non-stone items include a variety of utilitarian artefacts, such as spindle whorls. Stamp seals also occur in some contexts.[59] Perhaps the most 'famous' type of PN artefact, however, is the remarkably varied anthropomorphic figurine, of stone (sometimes incised) or clay, which many researchers believe had symbolic significance, often related to fertility. These are most famously represented as so-called mother goddess figurines at Çatalhöyük and elsewhere. In the southern Levant, the best examples of imagery come from Shaar Hagolan. Here, two major groups of imagery artefact occur: incised stones and clay figurines. The clay figurines include women and men.

---

57 Banning, 'Neolithic period'.
58 A. Gopher, 'Early pottery-bearing groups in Israel: the Pottery Neolithic period', in Levy (ed.), *Archaeology of Society*, 205–25.
59 Banning, 'Ceramic Neolithic'; Gopher, 'Early pottery-bearing groups'.

These are often characterized as highly stylized figurines, usually of large, obese females. The eyes are the most prominent feature and are often called 'coffee bean eyes' or 'cowrie shell eyes', harking back to a much earlier PPNB use of these shells in some plastered skulls. Others interpret the eyes as cereal grains, date pits, or even vulvae. Several figurines are quite remarkable, with minute details. Another category is shaped phalli of stone or clay.[60]

## A new social order: community and ritual elaboration

Domestication and settled village life transformed the fabric of society. During the Neolithic, several societal and ideological changes occurred that set the stage for subsequent developments: the elaboration of ritual behaviour, of household and community structure, of equalitarian vs. non-equalitarian behaviours, and of feasting activities. Much of this is reflected in the rich material culture of the Neolithic, as described above. Increasingly, research is focusing on this intriguing yet elusive dimension of Neolithic life. While it can be difficult to document ritual and ideology in the archaeological record, recent studies have indicated that these elements were far richer in the Neolithic than originally believed.[61]

In the Natufian, there is limited evidence to suggest substantial social ranking, but some degree of status differentiation is likely, particularly at large sites. Burials, especially during the early Natufian, are often multiple and elaborate, and contain grave goods, while during the late Natufian these patterns disappear and are replaced by single interments. Some researchers feel that mortuary patterning may reflect achieved status, rather than more formal ascribed status and social stratification.[62]

It is clear that, during the PPNA, major social reorganizations were required for those inhabiting both larger villages such as Jerf el Ahmar and smaller settlements such as Wadi Feinan 16 in order to cope with expanding populations and the need for communal activities associated, minimally, with cultivating wild plants and the construction of public works. One aspect of this is in mortuary practices, which continued trends started in the late

---

60  A. Gopher and E. Orrelle, 'Yarmukian imagery', within Gopher, 'Early pottery-bearing groups in Israel', 222–3.

61  Asouti and Fuller, 'Contextual approach'; Dietrich et al., 'Role of cult and feasting'; Watkins, 'Household, community and social landscape'.

62  B. Byrd and C. Monahan, 'Death, mortuary ritual, and Natufian social structure', *Journal of Anthropological Archaeology*, 14 (1995), 251–87.

Natufian, and included ritualized decapitation after burial beneath house floors. This pattern becomes even more formalized during the PPNB. Burials do not indicate individual social status, but may reflect communal hierarchies. Other evidence for ritual behaviour during the PPNA includes a change to human female figurines from the zoomorphic figurines that were common in the Natufian. Cattle skulls were incorporated into some structures. Architecture also shows increasing complexity. This includes large-scale works at Jericho, the massive complex at Göbekli Tepe, and the larger communal structures at domestic sites, all of which suggest large-scale ritual activity. These communal and monumental PPNA structures hint at social experimentation in which community might have been more important than economy.[63] Long- and short-distance trade were also components of PPNA society, indicating that individual communities did not exist in cultural vacuums; indeed, it is now apparent that trade networks also involved maritime travel to Cyprus. Aspects of trade were undoubtedly regulated by social rules, although there is only limited evidence for hierarchically structured society.

Given the large-scale nature of many PPNB communities and the presence of public or communal structures, relatively complex social organization can be inferred.[64] Many researchers believe that the PPNB was characterized by the formation of nuclear families as the basis for household economy and group interaction.[65] Byrd has argued that Neolithic villages were characterized by more restricted social networks for sharing and consumption and by more formalized mechanisms for community-wide integration.[66] Ideology appears to have focused on the memory of individual family members. Critical to farmers, of course, is the issue of land ownership.

The PPNB is rich in symbolism. Some scholars view the Neolithic as essentially a religious revolution,[67] while others see it as an increasing elaboration of society in which symbolism played an important, although not overwhelming, role. Regardless of specific interpretations, there is no doubt that PPNB people had a rich ritual life, reflected by an abundance of symbolic items, mortuary practices, and ritual sites. There is also increasing

---

63 Mithen et al., 'An 11,600-year-old communal structure'.
64 I. Kuijt (ed.), *Life in Neolithic Farming Communities: Social Organization, Identity, and Differentiation* (New York: Kluwer Academic/Plenum, 2000).
65 Flannery, 'Origins of the village', and 'The origins of the village revisited: from nuclear to extended households', *American Antiquity*, 67 (2002), 417–33.
66 B. Byrd, 'Public and private, domestic and corporate: the emergence of the Southwest Asian village', *American Antiquity*, 59 (1994), 639–66.
67 Cauvin, *Birth of the Gods*.

evidence that feasting and dancing likely played major roles in integrating Neolithic life.[68]

Whether PPNB societies were egalitarian or hierarchically structured is debated. Mortuary data have often been used to infer social status and Kuijt argues that there is some degree of social differentiation in the form of cranial deformation, skull plastering and painting, and the select use of secondary skull removal and caching.[69] It is likely that, at least in larger communities, there was some degree of communal leadership, at least for certain regulatory roles.

The PPNB world was widespread, and considerable evidence exists for trade and other social interactions across essentially the entire Near East and Cyprus.[70] With both domestic economies and sedentary villages now firmly established, it is likely that radical social transformations characterized much of PPNB society. The existence of PPNB 'interaction spheres' is likely, and it was during this time that regionalism became more pronounced, and that ethnically distinctive populations perhaps emerged.

The PN, too, was a time of considerable change, particularly in some regions. In the northern reaches of much of the Near East, developments continued the elaboration first seen during the PPN. Earlier researchers proposed a 'Great Neolithic Gap' between the PPN and the PN. This now, however, is largely rejected, since the PPNC and the PN show an unbroken linkage. In some areas there may have been a period of late PPN abandonment, but this was soon followed by substantial PN communities. In the north, many of these were on a cultural trajectory that led to the development of some of the world's first urban societies. Other regions, particularly the southern Levant, were more marginalized and peripheral, although earlier claims of cultural deterioration are unsubstantiated. While parts of the southern Levant did not reach the elaboration seen elsewhere, this may reflect an efficient re-adaptation to new conditions rather than a cultural regression.

Despite the existence of these large communities, social organization still appears to be primarily at the household level. Likewise, there are few data to

68 Dietrich et al., 'Role of cult and feasting'; Y. Garfinkel, *Dancing at the Dawn of Agriculture* (Austin: University of Texas Press, 2003); K. Twiss, 'Transformations in an early agricultural society: feasting in the southern Levantine Pre-Pottery Neolithic', *Journal of Anthropological Archaeology*, 27 (2008), 418–42.

69 I. Kuijt, 'Keeping the peace: ritual, skull caching, and community integration in the Levantine Neolithic', in Kuijt (ed.), *Life in Neolithic Farming Communities*, 137–64.

70 T. Watkins, 'Putting the colonization of Cyprus into context', in Peltenburg and Wasse (eds.), *Neolithic Revolution*, 23–34; M. Zeder, 'The origins of agriculture in the Near East', *Current Anthropology*, 52, Supplement 4 (2011), S221–35.

indicate highly structured social stratification. Mortuary patterns represent a change from the PPNB, especially in the abandonment of post-mortem decapitation and in the way in which infants are treated. Ritual or symbolic behaviour is expressed especially through elaborate figurine imagery, particularly of corpulent females. The PPNB interaction sphere appears to have been replaced by more regionally distinctive cultures. Overall, the PN may be characterized as an adaptation of local settlements with strong tribal ties, forming a pattern that has endured in the Near East over several millennia.[71]

## Regional cores and the expansion of the Neolithic

The Near East is a huge area, exhibiting considerable diversity. And yet, due to an abundance of research, much of our knowledge on the Neolithic comes from the Levant, often leading to a Levantine primacy model. There were, however, other regional centres in Anatolia and the 'interior' Near East (primarily Iran and Iraq), all pointing to the diversity of the Near Eastern Neolithic.[72] The nature of interaction between these, however, is unclear.

Though the Neolithic spread to other regions, such as Europe, it owes its genesis to the Near East. There are several 'demic vs. diffusion' issues associated with this expansion, and we now know that old models are too simplistic. The transmission is often thought to have been through Anatolia,[73] but marine routes also have been suggested,[74] and nowhere is this more in evidence than in Cyprus.

The Mediterranean islands were until recently considered peripheral to the Neolithic. Traditionally it was believed that colonization of most of the islands occurred during the late Neolithic, with Cyprus having the earliest colony, the Pre-Pottery Khirokitia culture, commencing some 2,500 years later than the earliest mainland Neolithic. Once established on the islands, it was thought, the Neolithic did little to advance itself there, showing few mainland parallels and contacts, and rapidly developing into isolated, idiosyncratic island-adapted entities.

The past twenty years, however, have revolutionized our understanding of the early occupation of the Mediterranean islands. Previous reports of

---

71 Banning, 'Ceramic Neolithic'; Simmons, *Neolithic Revolution*, 226–8.
72 T. Watkins, 'Supra-regional networks in the Neolithic of Southwest Asia', *Journal of World Prehistory*, 21 (2008), 139–71.
73 J. Diamond and P. Bellwood, 'Farmers and their languages: the first expansions', *Science*, 300 (2003), 597–603.
74 C. Broodbank, 'The origins and early development of Mediterranean maritime activity', *Journal of Mediterranean Archaeology*, 19 (2006), 199–230.

Figure 8.5 Cypro-PPNB 'Ais Giorkis, Cyprus.

early, pre-Neolithic occupations on the islands are generally not well documented, although recent claims for pre-*Homo sapiens* on some islands are provocative if as yet unverified.[75] For the Neolithic, though, Cyprus is increasingly playing a major role. A few key sites there now document both a late Epipalaeolithic presence contemporary with the Natufian, and newly defined early Neolithic occupations (both PPNA and Cypro-PPNB) that are as early as those on the Levantine and Anatolian mainlands (Figure 8.5). Actual permanent colonization appears to have occurred during the Cypro-PPNB.[76] We now know that Cyprus was not peripheral to the Neolithic Revolution, but rather a central part of it. It is now clear that multiple trips between Cyprus and the mainland occurred. This emerging research on Cyprus has reoriented how archaeologists view island colonization, early seafaring abilities, domestication processes and accompanying social changes, and the spread of the Neolithic from its mainland cores.

While major domesticates such as caprines and pigs formed a significant part of the Cypriot Neolithic diet, cattle were thought to have been absent. New data, however, indicate a pattern of early cattle introduction, although this usage apparently ceased after the earliest Neolithic. The

75 A.H. Simmons, *Stone Age Sailors: Paleolithic Seafaring in the Mediterranean* (Left Coast Press, 2014).

76 A.B. Knapp, 'Cyprus' earliest prehistory: seafarers, foragers and settlers', *Journal of World Prehistory*, 23 (2010), 79–120.

reasons for this are not clear, and could be related to economic, ritual, or ecological variables.[77]

The early Neolithic of Cyprus demonstrates a significant level of continuous interaction between the island and the mainland. It is conceivable that Cyprus could have served as a staging ground for further expansion from the mainland. This new research is requiring a dramatic reinterpretation of the diffusion and migration of Neolithic peoples, the emergence of the 'Mediterranean fishing village', and its possible role in transporting people and resources to Cyprus.[78]

## Neolithic consequences

While much research attention has focused on Neolithic origins, far less discussion has been on the consequences of the Neolithic. There have, however, been more numerous recent discussions of these consequences, both positive and, especially, negative. Ecological and social consequences, such as over-exploitative land use practices, increases in diseases, and sanitation issues associated with village life, likely accelerated during the Neolithic. For example, Akkermans and Schwartz paint a rather disheartening view of village life during the Neolithic:

> Settlements . . . were undoubtedly heavily polluted with . . . rotting organic matter and human waste . . . The refuse would have attracted vermin, as well as the diseases they carried with them. Flies and mosquitoes transmit fecal-oral infectious and other illnesses; rats bring hemorrhagic fevers; wild dogs and other carnivores carry rabies; and wild cats bring toxoplasmosis . . . diseases became constant . . . Clearing . . . the land near ponds and streams . . . may have encouraged the spread of tetanus, malaria, and schistosomiasis. Stock rearing may have been another major source of human disease . . . The Neolithic was . . . a world where life was difficult and people knew that they were 'forever confronted with the Four Horsemen – death, famine, disease, and the malice of other men'.[79]

This likely is an overstatement, but certainly village living brought with it several unanticipated consequences. Strangely, one thing that does seem clear is that despite increasing populations, and social complexity and stresses, Near

---

77  A.H. Simmons, 'Until the cows come home: cattle and early Neolithic Cyprus', *Before Farming* (on-line version), 2009/1, article 5.
78  Galili et al., 'Emergence of the Mediterranean fishing village'.
79  P. Akkermans and G.M. Schwartz, *The Archaeology of Syria: From Complex Hunter-Gatherers to Early Urban Societies (ca. 16,000–300 BC)* (Cambridge University Press, 2003), 78–9.

Eastern Neolithic people were apparently reluctant to resort to extreme violence. There is a general lack of evidence indicating community-wide violence during the Near Eastern Neolithic. This is in sharp contrast to the later Neolithic in Europe, where violence was common.[80] Perhaps this is a testament to the efficiency of the social organization that had been forged. Given the duration of many Neolithic settlements, the advantages of living in them must have outweighed the disadvantages.

## Contemporary and future trends

Despite over one hundred years of investigation, there are still many things not known about the Neolithic, although these are constantly being refined to ever more precise problems. For example, pinpointing geographic origins of specific domesticates, understanding how they came to form Neolithic 'packages', and tracing their diffusion to other areas are topics of current investigation. Much recent research has also addressed the complex issue of social structure and organization, but gaps remain. In particular, there is a lack of understanding of hierarchy, leadership roles, and, especially, 'invisible' personalities, particularly with regard to gender and childhood. Neolithic ideology and ritual have been at the forefront of much recent research, but interpreting these in a realistic fashion remains a challenge. More precision is required in establishing criteria for fully evaluating degrees of sedentism. Despite enormous leaps in dating methods, there are still pressing issues relating to the Neolithic. One is simply in arriving at a consistent use of either calibrated or radiocarbon years. This is complicated by the fact that portions of the Neolithic fall within the calibration 'wiggles' and 'flat spots' that make interpretation particularly difficult. Recent research has also helped redefine the ever-expanding Neolithic world. It is now clear that there were multiple Neolithic 'cores' throughout the Near East, and future research must focus on placing new discoveries into a broader pan-Near Eastern framework. Furthermore, data from Cyprus indicate a considerable expansion of Neolithic communication and seafaring skills. Continued investigations there will clarify early colonization strategies, and stimulate the search for similar developments on other islands.[81]

80 J. Guilaine and J. Zammit, *The Origins of War: Violence in Prehistory* (Oxford: Blackwell, 2005).
81 N. Phoca-Cosmetatou (ed.), *The First Mediterranean Islanders: Initial Occupation and Survival Strategies* (Oxford University School of Archaeology, 2011); M. Zeder,

Other refinements will be directed at better definition of the nature of Neolithic interactions. This will involve the difficult issue of assessing core / periphery relationships and specific tribal or even 'ethnic' entities and their spread. In this context, detailed analyses of burial data and attempts to conduct DNA studies will be of immense importance. Thus, there remain many tasks at hand. These include broad-scale synthetic regional analyses, as well as more mundane tasks of establishing further 'base-line' data to characterize individual sites and artefact assemblages in both well-documented areas and less-documented regions of the Near East. Additionally, future trends need to focus on shedding 'new light' on the big-picture perspective,[82] and to include the types of research envisioned by Asouti and Fuller,[83] using multiple lines of evidence to investigate all aspects of the Neolithic. This will include incorporation of contextual data on numerous elements and a realization that the Neolithic is more than an economic transition. Rather, food production and consumption was an integral component of community interaction and ritual 'performance'.

Finally, there is an important issue not yet addressed: protecting the fragile heritage that Neolithic peoples left to the modern world. The antiquities services of most Near Eastern countries have limited budgets, and preservation funds tend to be devoted to large, impressive sites belonging to periods later than the Neolithic. At the time many sites were excavated, preservation and conservation were not major issues. Even today, with limited research funds, these issues tend to be short-changed, and funding for preservation was always limited. There is no ready answer to this dilemma. Certainly one obvious solution is simply not to excavate any more until sufficient funding for preservation can be obtained. While not conducting any new excavations and instead focusing on previously excavated materials is an attractive option, there is much to be learned from new excavations. Certainly this is a major challenge for future research.

## Conclusion

The development of domestic economies was one of humankind's major milestones. Had this not happened, the modern world, for better or worse,

'Domestication and early agriculture in the Mediterranean basin: origins, diffusion, and impact', *Proceedings of the National Academy of Sciences*, 105 (2008), 11597–604.
82  T. Watkins, 'New light on Neolithic revolution in South-west Asia', *Antiquity*, 84 (2010), 621–34.
83  Asouti and Fuller, 'Contextual approach'.

simply would not exist. This phenomenon is best represented by the Near Eastern Neolithic, and considerable insights have been achieved in addressing how and why it occurred. At the same time, the Near Eastern Neolithic has contributed substantially to the broader development of contemporary archaeological theory.

Many scholars of the Neolithic now talk about the domestication not only of plants and animals, but also of the landscape and of people themselves.[84] This tacitly assumes that with the advent of the Neolithic nothing was 'natural' any more. While not belittling the undisputed success of hunting and gathering for most of humankind's existence, without the security and surplus provided by food production, subsequent cultural achievements, manifest in the development of urban cultures in the Near East and elsewhere, but ultimately culminating in contemporary society, would never have occurred.

## Further reading

Asouti, E. and D.Q. Fuller. 'A contextual approach to the emergence of agriculture in Southwest Asia: reconstructing early Neolithic plant-food production.' *Current Anthropology*, 54 (2013), 299–345.

Banning, E.B. 'The Neolithic period: triumphs of architecture, agriculture, and art.' *Near Eastern Archaeology*, 61 (1998), 188–237.

Barker, G. *The Agricultural Revolution in Prehistory: Why did Foragers Become Farmers?* Oxford University Press, 2006.

Bar-Yosef, O. 'The Natufian culture in the Levant: threshold to the origins of agriculture.' *Evolutionary Anthropology*, 6 (1998), 159–77.

Bar-Yosef, O. and R. Meadow. 'The origins of agriculture in the Near East.' In T.D. Price and A.B. Gebauer (eds.), *Last Hunters, First Farmers: New Perspectives on the Prehistoric Transition to Agriculture*. Santa Fe, NM: School of American Research Press, 1995. 39–94.

Bellwood, P. *First Farmers: The Origins of Agricultural Societies*. Oxford: Blackwell, 2005.

Binford, L. 'Post Pleistocene adaptations.' In S. Binford and L. Binford (eds.), *New Perspectives in Archaeology*. Chicago: Aldine Press, 1968. 313–41.

Braidwood, R. 'The agricultural revolution.' *Scientific American*, 203 (1960), 130–41.

Cauvin, J. *The Birth of the Gods and the Origins of Agriculture*, trans. T. Watkins. Cambridge University Press, 2000 [1994].

Colledge, S. and J. Conolly (eds.). *The Origins and Spread of Domestic Plants in Southwest Asia and Europe*. Walnut Creek, CA: Left Coast Press, 2007.

Colledge, S., J. Conolly, K. Dobney, K. Manning, and S. Shennan (eds.). *The Origins and Spread of Domestic Animals in Southwest Asia and Europe*. Walnut Creek, CA: Left Coast Press, 2013.

84 P. Wilson, *The Domestication of the Human Species* (New Haven, CT: Yale University Press, 1988).

Diamond, J. and P. Bellwood. 'Farmers and their languages: the first expansions.' *Science*, 300 (2003), 597–603.

Flannery, K. 'Origins and ecological effects of early domestication in Iran and the Near East.' In P. Ucko and G. Dimbleby (eds.), *The Domestication and Exploitation of Plants and Animals*. Chicago: Aldine Press, 1969. 73–100.

Garfinkel, Y. *Dancing at the Dawn of Agriculture*. Austin: University of Texas Press, 2003.

Henry, D. *From Foraging to Agriculture: The Levant at the End of the Ice Age*. Philadelphia: University of Pennsylvania Press, 1989.

Hodder, I. 'Symbolism and the origins of agriculture in the Near East.' *Cambridge Archaeological Journal*, 11 (2001), 107–12.

Kuijt, I. (ed.). *Life in Neolithic Farming Communities: Social Organization, Identity, and Differentiation*. New York: Kluwer Academic/Plenum, 2000.

McCarter, S.F. *Neolithic*. New York and London: Routledge, 2007.

Mellaart, J. *The Neolithic of the Near East*. London: Thames & Hudson, 1975.

Özdoğan, M. and N. Başgelen (eds.). *Neolithic in Turkey: The Cradle of Civilization*. Istanbul: Arkeoloji Sanat Yayınları, 1999.

Price, T.D. and O. Bar-Yosef (eds.). *The origins of agriculture: new data, new ideas*. Special edition of *Current Anthropology*, 52, Supplement 4 (2011).

Simmons, A. *The Neolithic Revolution in the Near East: Transforming the Human Landscape*. Tucson: University of Arizona Press, 2007.

Simmons, A., I. Köhler-Rollefson, G. Rollefson, R. Mandel, and Z. Kafafi. ''Ain Ghazal: a major Neolithic settlement in central Jordan.' *Science*, 240 (1988), 35–9.

Smith, B.D. *The Emergence of Agriculture*. New York: Scientific American Library, 1995.

Twiss, K. 'Transformations in an early agricultural society: feasting in the southern Levantine Pre-Pottery Neolithic.' *Journal of Anthropological Archaeology*, 27 (2008), 418–42.

Vigne, J.D., F. Briois, A. Zazzo, et al. 'First wave of cultivators spread to Cyprus at least 10,600 y ago.' *Proceedings of the National Academy of Sciences*, 109 (2012), 8445–9.

Watkins, T. 'New light on Neolithic revolution in South-west Asia.' *Antiquity*, 84 (2010), 621–34.

Wilson, P. *The Domestication of the Human Species*. New Haven, CT: Yale University Press, 1988.

Zeder, M. 'Domestication and early agriculture in the Mediterranean basin: origins, diffusion, and impact.' *Proceedings of the National Academy of Sciences*, 105 (2008), 11597–604.

'The origins of agriculture in the Near East.' *Current Anthropology*, 52, Supplement 4 (2011), S221–35.

# 9

# 'Ain Ghazal, Jordan

GARY O. ROLLEFSON

## Chronology

'Ain Ghazal was not founded until almost a thousand years after the onset of agriculture, but because of the local ecological combinations and the persistent presence of water (the permanent stream of the Zarqa River and the copious spring of 'Ain Ghazal itself), it continued to exist as a permanent settlement until around 5750 BCE[1] or perhaps even later.[2] This long duration of constant occupation – approximately 2,500 years – is one of the most important aspects of 'Ain Ghazal's archaeology, for it reveals how the residents of 'Ain Ghazal adapted themselves to the changing environment, changes that were strongly driven by the unwitting actions of the people of 'Ain Ghazal themselves. This long period of time witnessed four major developments in how the inhabitants of 'Ain Ghazal lived their daily lives and can be broken down into the following periods:

- Middle Pre-Pottery Neolithic B (MPPNB) 8500–7500 BCE
- Late Pre-Pottery Neolithic B (LPPNB) 7500–6900 BCE
- Pre-Pottery Neolithic C (PPNC) 6900–6400 BCE
- Yarmoukian Pottery Neolithic 6400–5500 BCE

## Site size and setting

The oldest layers occur atop sterile red clay, and it appears that 'Ain Ghazal began as a small village about 2 ha in area (Figure 9.1). The lucrative

---

1 The dates mentioned in this chapter are expressed as calibrated radiocarbon dates, reflected by the use of the uppercase 'BCE' referent.
2 Z. Kafafi et al., ''Ain Ghazal revisited: rescue excavations October and December–January 2011–2012', *Neo-Lithics*, 2/12 (2012), 21–9; cf. G. Rollefson et al., 'Neolithic cultures at 'Ain Ghazal, Jordan', *Journal of Field Archaeology*, 19 (1992), 443–70.

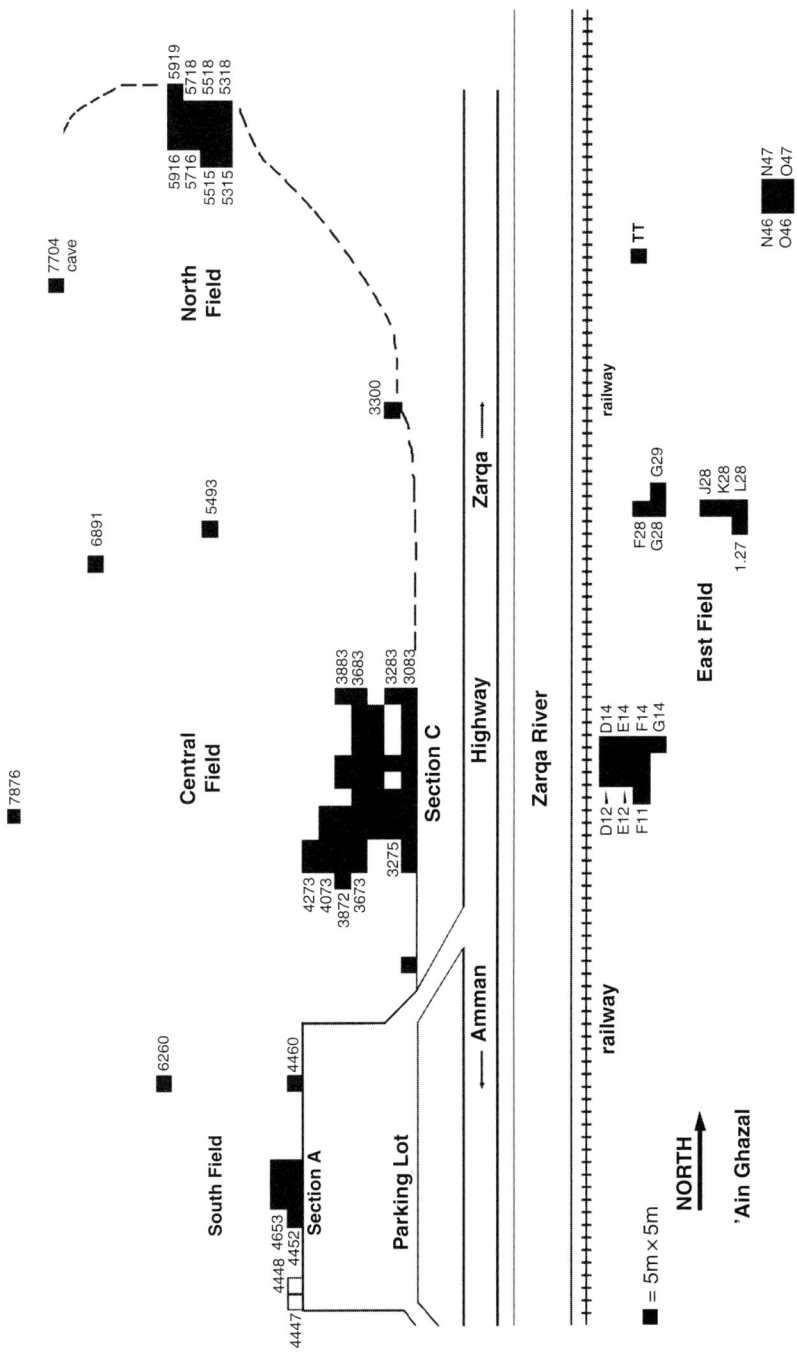

Figure 9.1 Schematic plan of excavated units at 'Ain Ghazal on the western (top) and eastern banks of the Wadi Zarqa (Zarqa River).

combination of environmental conditions allowed a rapid MPPNB population growth, and within a thousand years as many as 600–750 people lived together in a compact community that covered 5 ha.

The end of the MPPNB in the southern Levant was a tumultuous one, and there were severe disturbances in the settlement pattern of the region.[3] Wholesale abandonment of farming villages in Israel and the Jordan valley began around this time, and many of the dislocated populations sought refuge elsewhere, probably often in highland Jordan. Near the beginning of the LPPNB, 'Ain Ghazal underwent a virtual population explosion, altogether doubling in size within a couple of generations to *c.* 10 ha and reaching almost 15 ha on both the eastern and western sides of the Zarqa River by 7000 BCE;[4] by this time more than 2,500 people lived at 'Ain Ghazal. Other huge PPNB 'mega-sites' were founded in Jordan and southern Syria.[5] During this period of rapid population growth, social and economic organization changed dramatically, and while not reaching 'urban' status, 'Ain Ghazal and its neighbours left the simple egalitarian village behind.

After the constant pressure on the land around 'Ain Ghazal during the MPPNB and LPPNB periods, it is not surprising that the quality of life for the townspeople began to decline. The East Field appears to have been deserted as a residential area by the beginning of the PPNC, and on the western side of the Zarqa housing density fell dramatically at the beginning of the seventh millennium. With the onset of the Yarmoukian Pottery Neolithic, the size of 'Ain Ghazal continued to contract; furthermore, houses were very far apart, and it is likely that the population fell to levels of the early MPPNB. Eventually, the fields around 'Ain Ghazal had simply played out, and farming was no longer a reliable means to support a family. The last vestiges of Neolithic presence at 'Ain Ghazal are some circular tent foundations of pastoral nomads of the late Yarmoukian period (Figure 9.2).

3 G. Rollefson, 'Local and regional relations in the Levantine PPN period: 'Ain Ghazal as a regional center', *Studies in the History and Archaeology of Jordan*, 3 (1987), 29–32, and 'The character of LPPNB social organization', in H.-D. Bienert et al. (eds.), *Central Settlements in Neolithic Jordan* (Berlin: Ex oriente, 2004), 145–55; H.G.K. Gebel, 'Central to what? The centrality issue of the LPPNB mega-site phenomenon in Jordan', in Bienert et al. (eds.), *Central Settlements in Neolithic Jordan*, 1–19.

4 G. Rollefson, 'Neolithic 'Ayn Ghazal in its landscape', *Studies in the History and Archaeology of Jordan*, 6 (1997), 241–4.

5 H.G.K. Gebel and G. Rollefson (eds.), *Neo-Lithics*, 2/97 (1997).

Figure 9.2 The circular structure at the top of the photo is a late Yarmoukian tent foundation, a remnant of a visit to 'Ain Ghazal by sheep/goat pastoralists; the stone feature at the centre of the photo is a walled 'street', originally constructed by LPPNB or PPNC residents, but used into the Yarmoukian period as well.

## The changing environment at 'Ain Ghazal

The fragility of the ecosystem in the southern Levant is well documented for the past fifteen millennia,[6] and the area around 'Ain Ghazal never recovered from an environmental calamity that began around 9,500 years ago while the settlement was enjoying its greatest florescence: unending overgrazing and deforestation for construction and fuel turned the surrounding countryside into a virtual extension of the steppe immediately to the east.[7]

The environmental evidence comes principally from faunal remains. Animal bones give us our best indication of the local vegetational zones

---

6 E.g. B. Weninger et al., 'Abrupt climate forcing observed at early Neolithic sites in southeast Europe and the Near East', in H. Todorova et al. (eds.), *In the Steps of James Harvey Gaul*, vol. II: *The Struma/Strymon River Valley in Prehistory* (Sofia: Gerda Henkel Stiftung, 2007), 7–28; G. Rollefson, 'Slippery slope: the late Neolithic rubble layer in the southern Levant', *Neo-Lithics*, 1/09 (2009), 12–18.

7 G. Rollefson and K. Pine, 'Measuring the impact of LPPNB immigration into highland Jordan', *Studies in the History and Archaeology of Jordan*, 10 (2009), 473–81.

and how this mosaic of plant communities changed through time. In the MPPNB period more than fifty species show that the immediate area surrounding 'Ain Ghazal included woodland, steppe, riverine forest gallery, wooded parkland, desert ecological zones, and even standing water.[8] Of all of the animal species, one provided approximately half of the remains: the goat, which was domesticated in the MPPNB.[9]

By the LPPNB the great diversity of animals had declined considerably, and in the PPNC the number of species had dwindled to around fifteen, testimony to the degraded environment around the settlement.[10] Gone were the woodland-related animals and most of the birds, and it is clear that by the beginning of the seventh millennium hunting had declined in its importance: 50 per cent of the meat had been procured this way in the MPPNB, and at only around 10 per cent, meat from wild animals probably served more as a source of variety in the diet than as a principal component of meals in the Yarmoukian period.[11] The people at 'Ain Ghazal compensated for the loss of protein from wild animals by widening the range of domesticated animals, with sheep in the LPPNB, pigs in the PPNC, and cattle by the beginning of the Yarmoukian, if not earlier.

## Social organization

The relationships among people in the 'Ain Ghazal settlement (and with other communities in the area) changed dramatically during the town's existence. Much of our information comes from the kinds of structures that the people built, but symbolic behaviour and post-mortem treatment of the town's residents are also important sources.

---

8  I. Köhler-Rollefson et al., 'The fauna from Neolithic 'Ain Ghazal', in A. Garrard and H.G. Gebel (eds.), *The Prehistory of Jordan: Status of Research in 1986*, British Archaeological Reports – International Series 396 (Oxford: British Archaeological Reports, 1988), 423–30; I. Köhler-Rollefson and G. Rollefson, 'The impact of Neolithic subsistence strategies on the environment: the case of 'Ain Ghazal, Jordan', in S. Bottema et al. (eds.), *Man's Role in the Shaping of the Eastern Mediterranean Landscape* (Rotterdam: Balkema Press, 1990), 3–14 (4); I. Köhler-Rollefson et al., 'A brief note on the fauna from Neolithic 'Ain Ghazal', *Paléorient*, 19 (1993), 95–8.

9  I. Köhler-Rollefson, 'Proto-élevage, pathologies and pastoralism: a post-mortem on the process of goat domestication', in H.G. Gebel et al. (eds.), *The Prehistory of Jordan, II: Perspectives from 1997* (Berlin: Ex oriente, 1997), 557–65.

10  G. Rollefson and I. Köhler-Rollefson, 'The collapse of early Neolithic settlements in the southern Levant', in I. Hershkovitz (ed.), *People and Culture in Change*, British Archaeological Reports – International Series 508 (Oxford: British Archaeological Reports, 1989), 73–90.

11  Köhler-Rollefson et al., 'Brief note on the fauna'.

Figure 9.3 The western room of an MPPNB house from the Central Field at 'Ain Ghazal; the eastern room (at the top) was almost completely removed by bulldozers during the construction of the highway in the 1970s. The remains of twelve individuals were buried beneath the floors of this structure.

## Architectural inferences

In the earliest part of 'Ain Ghazal's development, the village was compactly organized, with houses built in very close proximity to each other along the west bank of the Zarqa River. The 'nearest neighbour' distribution of the houses suggests that closeness of the dwellings was probably associated with kinship: some houses were built so near to each other that a person could not walk between them, but such groups of houses were separated from other clusters by several metres.

MPPNB house sizes throughout the Levant, including 'Ain Ghazal, indicate that the dwellings were occupied by single-family units of parents and unmarried children, a common arrangement in current subsistence agricultural societies (Figure 9.3). The clumping of houses suggests that, although these families were independent in terms of economic production and consumption, the practice of familial sharing was the norm in times of shortfall, and the possibility certainly can't be excluded that contributing to households outside the cognate group was a normal practice during calamitous periods for some single families or a cluster of related families.

Figure 9.4 The badly damaged building in the upper right third of the photo represents the ground floor of a two-storey building that caught fire and was thoroughly destroyed in the later LPPNB period. Reconstruction of the floor plan suggests that three or four families probably inhabited the structure. The circular feature in the plaster floor at upper right is a hearth.

After some 1,000 years of environmental degradation, many of the farming villages in the Jordan Valley and Israel were abandoned, and those families that emigrated to 'Ain Ghazal precipitated an eruptive expansion on the western bank of the Zarqa River as well as the establishment of a new neighbourhood across the river, straining 'Ain Ghazal's social system. During the LPPNB phase a new social order evolved: two-storeyed buildings of considerable size (up to twice the floor plan of the MPPNB for the ground floor alone) are clearly documented (Figure 9.4). The importance of these two-storey buildings is that the common nuclear family household of the MPPNB had developed, in some cases at least, into extended family units during the LPPNB.[12] Instead of the independent economic units of the MPPNB, by the latter half of the eighth millennium closely related families had consolidated, whereby nuclear family units pooled their labour and consequent resources into a common store to be shared by the participating cognates and their spouses.[13]

Shortly after the beginning of the seventh millennium, sociocultural alterations caused major changes in social structure, especially visible in architectural forms. For the first time two distinct versions of domestic buildings appeared, and the functional probabilities are telling. The first, or 'normal', building reverted to the nuclear family situation, with parents and unmarried children living in a small single-room house of c. 15 m², although the associated walled courtyard was the scene of important daily activities.[14] Notably, the walled courtyard around a domestic house made its first appearance during the PPNC period at 'Ain Ghazal, although walled courtyards were associated with the LPPNB 'shrines' (see below).

The new architectural phenomenon was the 'corridor building', a semi-subterranean storage feature that was probably associated with families who lived at 'Ain Ghazal only during a part of the yearly round (Figure 9.5a). During the rainy season in the autumn/winter until the end of the harvest in May/June, these families would have been in the steppe and desert areas with the herds of sheep and goats, returning to 'Ain Ghazal when the water and vegetation in the eastern regions had disappeared.[15]

By the beginning of the Yarmoukian period, the PPNC partial separation of the 'Ain Ghazal population into permanently settled farming and mobile pastoral groups was evidently concluded. The earlier phases of the Yarmoukian presence are once again uniform in terms of the kinds of dwelling, suggesting that the pastoral element was no longer an integral part of the 'Ain Ghazal community. Single-family structures dominated again (Figure 9.5b), and nuclear family independence is emphasized by the relative

---

12 It is possible, of course, that many nuclear families remained independent and lived in more modest dwellings during the LPPNB at 'Ain Ghazal, but we have found no clear evidence of this. So far, LPPNB excavations throughout Jordan, at least, have found only large, complex houses that more closely fit the extended-family scenario.

13 G. Rollefson, 'Developments in social organization at Neolithic 'Ain Ghazal based on changes in architecture', in Gebel et al. (eds.), *Prehistory of Jordan, II*, 287–307.

14 G. Rollefson and I. Köhler-Rollefson, ''PPNC adaptations in the first half of the 6th millennium BC', *Paléorient*, 19 (1993), 33–42 (36).

15 Rollefson and Köhler-Rollefson, 'PPNC adaptations'.

Figure 9.5 (a) A PPNC 'corridor building', with the entrance at bottom centre; a flagstone ramp leading down (from top towards the bottom) is at left. (b) At lower right is a Yarmoukian 'longhouse' with at least three rooms, measuring *c.* 4 × 9 m. A small oval 'kitchen' outhouse occurs at left centre; just above the asterisk at upper left is a PPNC house.

isolation of houses in the extensive courtyards, where neighbours were probably at least 15 m away.[16]

## Ritual inferences

But it is in the ritual sphere that social differences within families and larger kinship units, and in the community in general, are most emphatically demonstrated. Burials, for example, argue for at least three different 'sorts' of people:

1.  'Special' people. Although they were once considered 'typical burials' for the MPPNB,[17] it is now indisputable that the people buried beneath house floors were anything but 'typical'.[18] A good example of this is the situation for one house, where the remains of twelve individuals were found beneath the complex sequence of floor replacements, renovations, and remodelling (Figure 9.3) that took place over some four hundred years. This reflects a burial about every thirty-three years. If we assume that families consisted of the parents and three to four children who lived to maturity, we are missing at least four to five (80 per cent or more) of the burials for each generation, which is a strong argument that the subfloor burials represent people with extraordinary status (Figure 9.6a). The age of the people buried beneath house floors ranges from juvenile to more than fifty years, and since there are both males and females, the selection rules for this post-mortem distinction remain unknown.[19]

2.  The second group of people consists of those family members who were not buried beneath house floors. What happened to them is simply not known; one might surmise a 'cemetery' outside of the settlement, but after more than a century of Neolithic excavations, no such PPNB burial ground has been found anywhere in the Levant.

3.  The third disposal method is the 'trash burial', named after the circum-stances that suggest some people were actually 'discarded' in refuse dumps. These interments invariably included the skull intact with the skeleton, and the presence of rubbish in the burial, as well as the postures of the skeletons, indicates that these people received the least respect of all

---

16  Z. Kafafi and G. Rollefson, 'The 1994 season at 'Ayn Ghazal: preliminary report', *Annual of the Department of Antiquities of Jordan*, 39 (1995), 15–16.

17  G. Rollefson, 'The 1983 season at the early Neolithic site of 'Ain Ghazal', *National Geographic Research*, 1 (1985), 44–62 (55).

18  H.-D. Bienert et al., 'Where are the dead?', in Bienert et al. (eds.), *Central Settlements in Neolithic Jordan*, 157–75.

19  Ibid., 169–75.

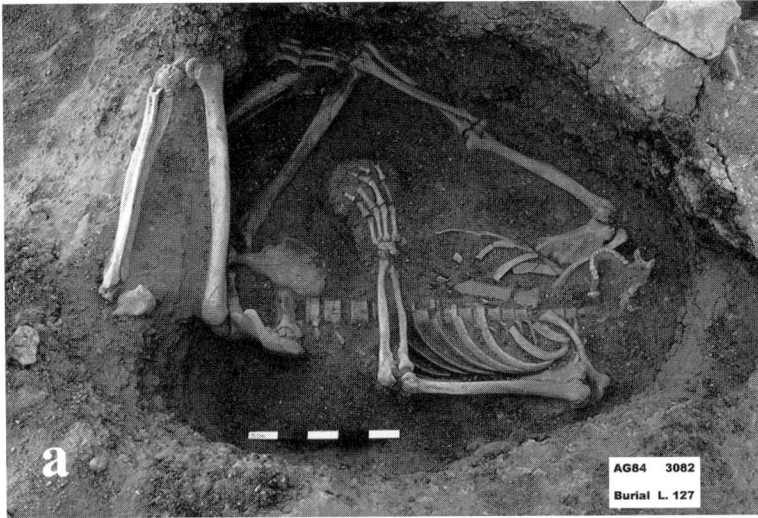

Figure 9.6 (a) An MPPNB subfloor burial whose skull was removed, and the body then re-covered with dirt and a new plaster floor; (b) a 'trash burial' from the later MPPNB period. Contrast the 'cleanliness' of the soil in (a) with the inclusions of charcoal, stony rubble, and broken animal bones around the skeleton in (b).

at death, a possible reflection of their social status when they were alive (Figure 9.6b).[20]

If being buried beneath a house was a signal of primary social distinction, there was still another difference that set some family members apart from others. This involves the intriguing concentration on the skull. All subfloor burials were decapitated in the sense that the body was placed beneath the floor, and after a suitable time for the flesh to decay, the burial pit was re-opened in order to remove the head, leaving the lower jaw behind (Figure 9.7; cf. Figure 9.6a). What happened to the skulls afterwards was variable, for reasons that we don't understand at present. The practice of skull separation and special treatment certainly did not carry over into the PPNC period, and there are some reasons to think that perhaps this practice was already abandoned before the end of the LPPNB in the southern Levant. We have no certain evidence of special skull treatment from 'Ain Ghazal during the LPPNB, but the frequent presence of burials with intact skulls at LPPNB Basta suggests that in southern Jordan, at least, skull removal had come to an end by the last quarter of the eighth millennium.[21] Nevertheless, skull removal seems to have enjoyed continued and vigorous celebration in the Damascus area at sites such as Tell Ramad and Tell Aswad.[22]

For the Yarmoukian period, we have only one burial from 'Ain Ghazal, placed in the corner of an abandoned house, suggesting that burial within the community limits had lost all social distinctions.[23]

## Statuary

If the plastering of skulls of some family members might have had some relationship with ancestral veneration in the MPPNB,[24] it is highly likely that the stunning plaster statuary from 'Ain Ghazal is an extension of the ancestral

---

20 Infant burials (i.e. less than *c.* fifteen months old at death) are a separate phenomenon and should not be used in calculating these burial rates. See G. Rollefson, 'Ritual and ceremony at Neolithic 'Ain Ghazal (Jordan)', *Paléorient*, 9 (1983), 29–38, and 'Neolithic 'Ain Ghazal (Jordan): ritual and ceremony II', *Paléorient*, 12 (1986), 45–52. See also G. Rollefson, 'Ritual and social structure at Neolithic 'Ain Ghazal', in I. Kuijt (ed.), *Life in Neolithic Farming Communities* (New York: Kluwer Academic/Plenum, 2000), 163–90 (170).

21 H. Nissen et al., 'Report on the excavations at Basta 1988', *Annual of the Department of Antiquities of Jordan*, 35 (1991), 17–19; M. Berner and M. Schultz, 'Demographic and taphonomic aspects of the skeletons from the late Pre-Pottery Neolithic population from Basta, Jordan', in Bienert et al. (eds.), *Central Settlements in Neolithic Jordan*, 241–58.

22 H. de Contenson, *Ramad: site Néolithique en Damascène (Syrie) au VIIIe et VIIe millénaires avant l'ère Chrétienne* (Beirut: Institut Français d'Archéologie du Proche-Orient, 2000); D. Stordeur and R. Khawam, 'Les crânes surmodelés de Tell Aswad (PPNB, Syrie): premier regard sur l'ensemble, premières réflexions', *Syria*, 84 (2007), 5–32.

23 Kafafi et al., ' 'Ain Ghazal revisited', 22.    24 Bienert et al., 'Where are the dead?', 169–70.

Figure 9.7 MPPNB skull from 'Ain Ghazal showing the delicate modelling of the plaster coating

cult that characterized the central Levant.[25] Two caches of plaster statuary were recovered from 'Ain Ghazal and the 'cosmetic' treatment of the faces of statues and busts closely mirrors that of the plastered skulls.[26] While oral tradition is a strong medium of memory in many societies, tracing pedigrees

25  E.g. J. Garstang, 'Jericho: city and necropolis, fifth report', *Liverpool Annals of Archaeology and Anthropology*, 23 (1935), 143–84; K. Kenyon, *Archaeology in the Holy Land* (London: Ernest Benn, 1979).

26  Rollefson, 'Ritual and ceremony at Neolithic 'Ain Ghazal (Jordan)', and 'Neolithic 'Ain Ghazal (Jordan): ritual and ceremony II'; C. Grissom, 'Statue cache 2', in D. Schmandt-Besserat (ed.), *Symbols at 'Ain Ghazal*, vol. III, 'Ain Ghazal Excavation Reports (Berlin: Ex oriente, 2013), 247–336; K. Tubb and C. Grissom, ' 'Ayn Ghazal: a comparative study of the 1983 and 1985 statuary caches', *Studies in the History and Archaeology of Jordan*, 5 (1995), 437–47; D. Schmandt-Besserat, 'The plastered skulls', in Schmandt-Besserat (ed.), *Symbols at 'Ain Ghazal*, 215–42.

beyond many generations can develop into the establishment of mythical ancestors, which is what we assume the statuary to represent (Figure 9.8).

## Ritual buildings

Several structures have been unearthed at 'Ain Ghazal that clearly were not used as domestic dwellings: at least four from the LPPNB period and one from the Yarmoukian period. In addition, it is possible that three more LPPNB buildings served in some non-domestic way. So far, all of the MPPNB structures excavated at the town appear to have been normal houses.

Two or probably three different sorts of non-domestic building are known from the latter half of the eighth millennium BCE (LPPNB). The apse buildings (one from the East Field, one from the Central Field, and one or two from the North Field), named after the curved ends of one of the rectangular buildings, are much smaller (*c.* 7.5 m² interior floor space) than normal houses at 'Ain Ghazal for any of the occupational periods (Figure 9.9a).[27]

There are two circular cult buildings or 'shrines' (Figure 9.9b) from the North Field, and both are smaller than the apsidal structures (less than 5 m² each), and in this diminutive area the focus on the central hole and the character of the subfloor channels, the rare geometry, and the multiple reflooring episodes are all strong points to claim that the circular buildings were specially dedicated to cult activity associated with a particular kinship unit.[28] The cult activity undertaken in these smaller buildings may relate to ancestral veneration, a practice that may have become more private after the emergence of 'Ain Ghazal's megasite status.[29] In view of larger cultic buildings (see below), we prefer to call the smaller apsidal and circular buildings 'shrines' to indicate a lower rank in a hierarchy of ritual buildings.

The remaining two ritual structures, which we term 'temples', are located in the East Field across the Zarqa River from the main settlement (Figure 9.10). In contrast to domestic structures from the PPNB (both middle and late), both buildings have unplastered dirt floors. The presence of three 'standing stones', altars, and hearths surrounded by seven stones all point decidedly to structures

27  G. Rollefson et al., 'The Neolithic village of 'Ain Ghazal, Jordan: preliminary report on the 1988 season', *Bulletin of the American Schools of Oriental Research*, Supplement 27 (1990), 95–116 (fig. 12).
28  G. Rollefson and Z. Kafafi, 'The 1993 season at 'Ain Ghazal: preliminary report', *Annual of the Department of Antiquities of Jordan*, 38 (1994), 20–3.
29  G. Rollefson, 'Blood loss: demographic stress and religious revolution in Neolithic 'Ain Ghazal, Jordan', in M. Benz (ed.), *The Principle of Sharing: Segregation and Construction of Social Identities at the Transition from Foraging to Farming* (Berlin: Ex oriente, 2010), 183–202.

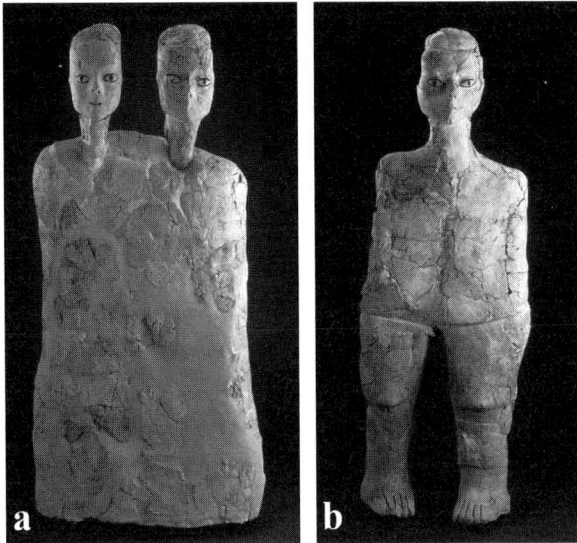

Figure 9.8 (a) One of three two-headed plaster busts from the cache excavated from 'Ain Ghazal in 1985 (height 95 cm); (b) one of two free-standing statues from the 1985 statue cache at 'Ain Ghazal (height 115 cm)

devoted to ritual activity. The two temples are separated by about 100 m, and while one has been dated to 7015 ± 131 BCE, its temporal relationship to the other remains unknown.[30]

While the smaller apsidal buildings may have served individual corporate kinship groups to perform traditional rituals, the larger temples served the entire community to weld together social groups who otherwise threatened to split the settlement apart due to competition for scarce resources such as farmland and pasturage.[31] How this new ritual system operated is not known, but there may have been some special religious societies whose membership cross-cut kinship affiliations, sodalities whose objectives were to perform ritual duties and feasts that benefited all of the population rather than just segments of it.[32]

All of the Yarmoukian structures investigated so far appear to have been regular dwellings for nuclear families. However, one apsidal building in the

---

30 G. Rollefson and Z. Kafafi, ' 'Ain Ghazal excavations 1996', *Biblical Archaeologist*, 59 (1996), 238, and ' 'Ain Ghazal: ten seasons of discovery', *ACOR Newsletter*, 8 (1996), 1–3; G. Rollefson, ' 'Ain Ghazal (Jordan): ritual and ceremony III', *Paléorient*, 24 (1998), 43–58, and 'Blood loss'.
31 Rollefson, 'Ritual and social structure'.    32 Rollefson, 'Blood loss'.

Figure 9.9 (a) An apsidal building originally constructed in the LPPNB period but later cleared and re-used by Yarmoukian residents at 'Ain Ghazal (*c.* 4.5 × 3.5 m); (b) a circular 'shrine' in the North Field at 'Ain Ghazal. The circular shape (2.5 m diameter) is the fourth phase of use, which began as an apsidal building.

Figure 9.10 (a) View to the north of an LPPNB temple built high on the slope of the East Field. The standing stones are at top centre (the middle stone is tumbled over) and the red plaster hearth right centre. A burned clay 'floor altar' lies just to the left of the standing stones. (b) The temple at the south end of the East Field was built above an earlier LPPNB house (lower third of the photo). The altar is against the rear (eastern) wall, in front of which is an unpainted plaster hearth.

Central Field from the LPPNB period was excavated and re-used by the Yarmoukians (Figure 9.9a). The exclusive presence of Yarmoukian fine-ware cups and small bowls and the absence of any coarser domestic pottery suggest that the oval-ended building served some public purpose, although the lack of any diagnostic artefacts (other than pottery) or features makes it difficult to suggest what that purpose might have been. The ritual sphere of the Yarmoukians is poorly known at 'Ain Ghazal, and there is no reason to suggest that the apsidal structure served as anything but a meeting place, perhaps for village council meetings.

## Further reading

Betts, A.V.G. *The Later Prehistory of the Badia. Excavations and Surveys in Eastern Jordan*, vol. II. Oxford: Oxbow, 2013.

Byrd, B. *Early Village Life at Beidha, Jordan: Neolithic Spatial Organization and Vernacular Architecture*. Oxford University Press, 2005.

Garfinkel, Y., D. Ben-Shlomo, and N. Korn. *Symbolic Dimensions of the Yarmukian Culture: Canonization in Neolithic Art*. Sha'ar Hagolan 3. Jerusalem: Hebrew University Institute of Archaeology, 2010.

Garfinkel, Y., D. Dag, H. Khalialy, et al. *The Pre-Pottery Neolithic B Village of Yiftahel: The 1980s and 1990s Excavations*. Berlin: Ex oriente, 2012.

Gebel, H.G.K., H.J. Nissen, and Z. Zaid (eds.). *Basta. II: The Architecture and Stratigraphy*. Berlin: Ex oriente, 2006.

Rollefson, G. 'The greening of the badlands: pastoral nomads and the "conclusion" of Neolithization in the southern Levant.' *Paléorient*, 37/1 (2011), 101–9.

Simmons, A., G. Rollefson, Z. Kafafi, et al. 'Wadi Shu'eib, a large Neolithic community in central Jordan: final report of test excavations.' *Bulletin of the American Schools of Oriental Research*, 321 (2001), 1–39.

Stordeur, D. and R. Khawam. 'Les crânes surmodelés de Tell Aswad (PPNB, Syrie): premier regard sur l'ensemble, premières réflexions.' *Syria*, 84 (2007), 5–32.

# Early agriculture in South Asia

ELEANOR KINGWELL-BANHAM, CAMERON A. PETRIE,
AND DORIAN Q. FULLER

Vast tracts of the landscape of modern South Asia are covered in fields and farmlands. In the northwest, cultivation of wheat and barley watered by winter rains predominates. In the east, the low-lying land is covered in a blanket of rice watered by summer rains, while in the south coconut groves play a highly important role in agricultural economies. Within this expanse there is a small but scattered population for whom agriculture has had a limited role, and though marginalized, hunter-gatherer groups have played important parts in the socioeconomy since prehistory.[1] Additionally, shifting cultivators and nomadic pastoralists have co-existed alongside settled agriculturalists since, and undoubtedly before, written records began. The interplay of all of these groups is hard to characterize in prehistory, particularly in the Neolithic where evidence is limited to a handful of material and environmental remains. This makes it hard to pinpoint when and where agriculture began in the subcontinent. Indeed, the prehistory of South Asia is uniquely muddled and the mixing of traditions has been one of its hallmarks. Domesticates from South Asia, East Asia, Africa, and Southwest Asia were all introduced to various parts of the subcontinent at different times and all played a part in the development of local agricultural communities. While archaeological investigations into the origins of agriculture in South Asia are not as developed as those in other areas (see Chapter 8 on Southwest Asia and Chapter 22 on Europe in this volume), generations of work have shed light on independent domestications and agricultural developments across this region.

In general, the natural ecology of much of the subcontinent is characterized by the yearly monsoons that bring the majority of annual rainfall in as

---

1 K.D. Morrison and L.L. Junker (eds.), *Forager-Traders in South and Southeast Asia* (Cambridge University Press, 2002), 1–20.

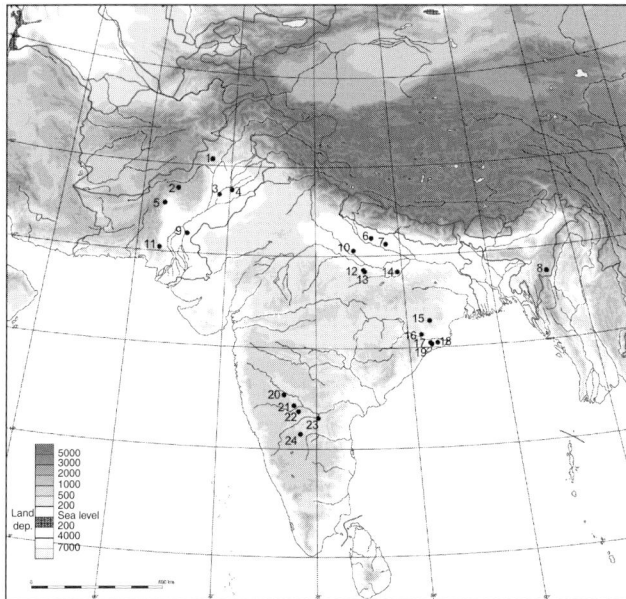

Map 10.1  South Asia showing principal sites mentioned in the text: 1. Sheri Khan Tarakai; 2. Rana Ghundai; 3. Jalipur; 4. Harappa; 5. Mehrgarh; 6. Tokwa; 7. Lahuradewa; 8. Napachik; 9. Kot Diji; 10. Damdama; 11. Amri; 12. Koldihwa; 13. Mahagara; 14. Senuwar; 15. Kuchai; 16. Salabhdihi; 17. Gopalpur; 18. Golbai Sasan; 19. Bajpur; 20. Kodekal; 21. Budihal; 22. Watgal; 23. Utnar; 24. Sanganakallu.

little as two weeks, heavily influencing socioeconomic life. Early agricultural communities in many areas may have been severely hindered by the monsoon. The stark seasonal variability created in some regions would have made adapting to settled life incredibly difficult. Alongside inherent issues such as the increase in disease associated with living in close proximity to livestock, regular flooding episodes and/or drought would have had to be overcome. Nevertheless, the Neolithic in South Asia, as elsewhere, was an era of change in which food production tended to replace foraging, sedentism increased over mobility, and population density tended to increase. The Neolithic period, and how it is defined chronologically, varies by region in South Asia, beginning by *c.* 7000 BCE in some areas, or by 3500–2500 BCE in others. By the end of the Neolithic, sedentism was present in many parts of the subcontinent, pottery production was nearly universal, and some textile production and metallurgy had been established. This period continued in many areas up to *c.* 1000 BCE, with the direct transition to what was in effect an Iron Age. A distinct Bronze Age is only recognized in the Indus valley region and is associated with the rise and decline of the urban Indus civilization. It has also been suggested that it was during the Neolithic that much of the basic linguistic geography of the subcontinent is likely to have been established, including the regional distributions of Dravidian, Munda, and Indo-Aryan language families.[2]

While there remains debate over the extent to which early farming was brought about by the immigration of farmers, adoption of domesticates by local hunter-gatherers, or local domestication processes from wild forms, it is clear that patterns of agricultural origin were regionally varied across South Asia. Domesticates included those that were derived from indigenous wild species, as well as those introduced from elsewhere, especially those from West Asia. Key field crop plants that were native domesticates of South Asia include several millets (*Brachiaria ramosa*, *Echinochloa frumentacea*, *Panicum sumatrense*, *Paspalum scrobiculatum*, and *Setaria pumila*), pulses (*Cajanus cajan*, *Macrotyloma uniflorum*, *Vigna mungo*, *Vigna radiata*, and *Vigna aconitifolia*), sesame and cotton (*Gossypium arboreum* and *Sesamum indicum*), and possibly taro (*Colocasia esculenta*).[3] In addition, water buffalo and zebu cattle were animal domesticates indigenous to the subcontinent (Table 10.1).[4]

This chapter summarizes the archaeological evidence for the Neolithic and early food production across South Asia, with a focus on four major macro-regions (Table 10.1; Figure 10.1) with distinct chronological sequences, crop ecologies, and cultural traditions:

1. the northwest, including the greater Indus valley
2. the Gangetic plains
3. eastern India
4. savanna India

It has been argued that each of these areas developed early agricultural practices and 'Neolithic'-type societies independently.[5] Nevertheless, within any of these macro-regions it is plausible that a mosaic of multicentric origins took place, such

2 F.C. Southworth, *Linguistic Archeology of South Asia* (London: Routledge-Curzon, 2005); D.Q. Fuller, 'Non-human genetics, agricultural origins and historical linguistics in South Asia', in M. Petraglia and B. Allchin (eds.), *The Evolution and History of Human Populations in South Asia* (Netherlands: Springer, 2007), 393–443; F.C. Southworth and D.W. McAlpin, 'South Asia: Dravidian linguistic history', in I. Ness and P. Bellwood, *The Encyclopedia of Global Human Migration*, vol. 1 (Chichester: Wiley-Blackwell, 2013).
3 D.Q. Fuller, 'Agricultural origins and frontiers in South Asia: a working synthesis', *Journal of World Prehistory*, 20 (2006), 1–86.
4 R.H. Meadow and A.K. Patel, 'Prehistoric pastoralism in northwestern South Asia from the Neolithic through the Harappan period', in S. Weber and W. Belcher (eds.), *Indus Ethnobiology: New Perspectives from the Field* (Lanham, MD: Lexington, 2003), 65–93.
5 Fuller, 'Agricultural origins and frontiers', and 'Finding plant domestication in the Indian subcontinent', *Current Anthropology*, 52, Supplement 4 (2011), S347–62.

Table 10.1 The animals and plants of South Asia that may have been domesticated and the areas in which their domestication may have occurred; numbers in brackets refer to the regions shown in Figure 10.1.

| Common name | Latin name | Area of earliest appearance in the archaeological record |
| --- | --- | --- |
| **Animals** | | |
| Pig | *Sus scrofa* | A genetically separate lineage in India? |
| Water buffalo | *Bubalus bubalis* | Northwest, lower Indus; more than once? (1) |
| Zebu cattle | *Bos indicus* | Northwest, Indus (1) |
| **Food crops** | | |
| Browntop millet | *Brachiaria ramosa* | South India (4) |
| Cucumber | *Cucumis sativus* | North/northwest India? (multiple origins?) (2, 1?) |
| Horsegram | *Macrotyloma uniflorum* | South India and northwest (1, 4) |
| Kodo millet | *Paspalum scrobiculatum* | India |
| Little millet | *Panicum sumatrense* | Western India (Gujarat, Punjab) |
| Melon | *Cucumis melo* | Northern India (additional origins in East Asia, and possibly Egypt) (2) |
| Moth bean | *Vigna aconitifolia* | North India? |
| Mung bean | *Vigna radiata* | South India and northwest (1, 4) |
| Pigeon pea | *Cajanus cajan* | East India: Orissa (3) |
| Rice (*indica* subspecies) | *Oryza sativa* subsp. *indica* | North India: middle Ganges (2) |
| Sawa millet | *Echinochloa frumentacea* | Secondary rice weed, north India? (2?) |
| Sesame | *Sesamum indicum* | Northwest, Indus (1) |
| Urd bean | *Vigna mungo* | Western India (Gujarat) |
| **Textile crops** | | |
| Tree cotton | *Gossypium arboreum* | Northwest, Indus (1) |
| Cylindrical luffa | *Luffa cylindrica* | Northern India (additional origins in East Asia, and possibly Egypt) (2) |
| Jute | *Corchorus olitorius, Corchorus capsularis* | North/northwest India? (2, 1?) |

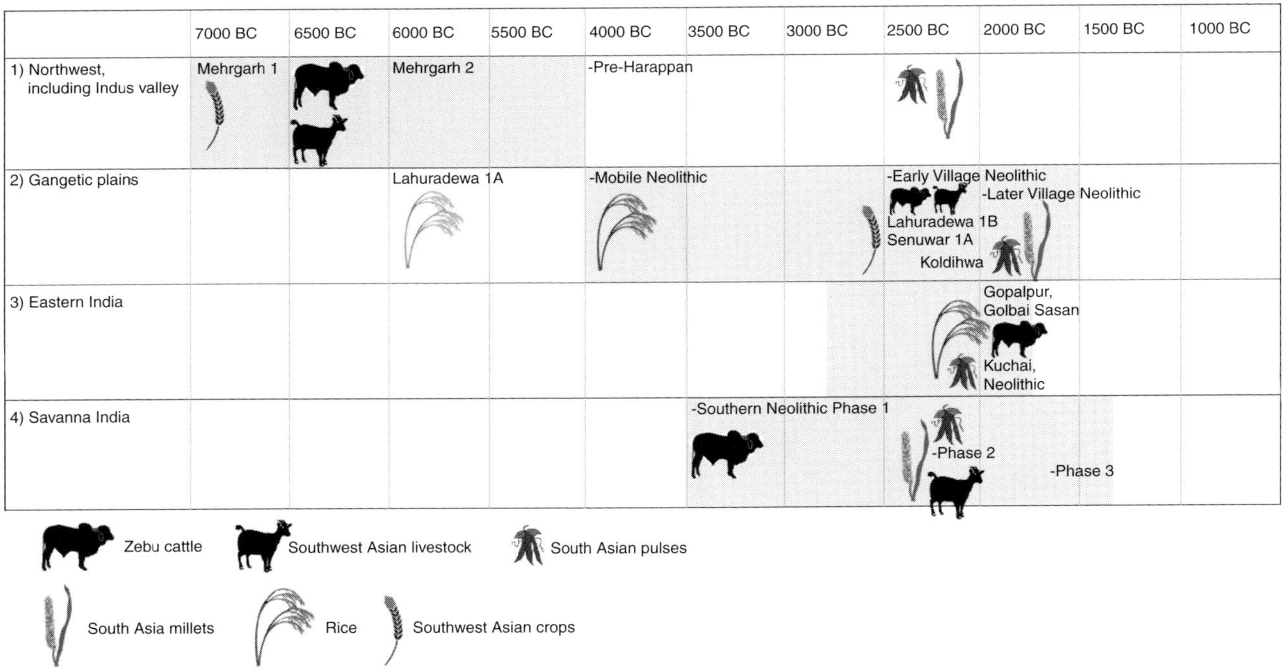

| | 7000 BC | 6500 BC | 6000 BC | 5500 BC | 4000 BC | 3500 BC | 3000 BC | 2500 BC | 2000 BC | 1500 BC | 1000 BC |
|---|---|---|---|---|---|---|---|---|---|---|---|
| 1) Northwest, including Indus valley | Mehrgarh 1 | | Mehrgarh 2 | | -Pre-Harappan | | | | | | |
| 2) Gangetic plains | | | Lahuradewa 1A | | -Mobile Neolithic | | | -Early Village Neolithic<br>Lahuradewa 1B<br>Senuwar 1A<br>Koldihwa | -Later Village Neolithic | | |
| 3) Eastern India | | | | | | | | | Gopalpur,<br>Golbai Sasan<br>Kuchai,<br>Neolithic | | |
| 4) Savanna India | | | | | | -Southern Neolithic Phase 1 | | -Phase 2 | | -Phase 3 | |

Legend:

Zebu cattle

Southwest Asian livestock

South Asian pulses

South Asia millets

Rice

Southwest Asian crops

South Asian crops

Figure 10.1 Timeline of the South Asian Neolithic, focusing on the areas mentioned in the text and showing the approximate time that various crops and livestock enter the archaeological record.

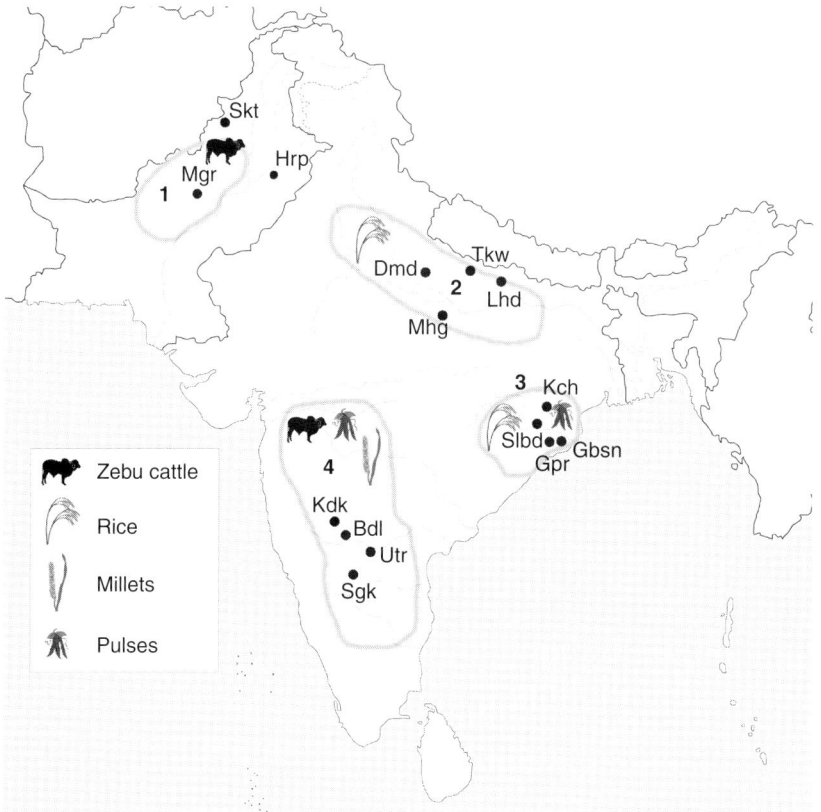

Map 10.2 Map of South Asia showing the areas mentioned in the text, the main sites mentioned in the text, and the South Asian species that most represent the early agriculture of each area (key: Skt = Sheri Khan Tarakai, Hrp = Harappa, Mgr = Mehrgarh, Dmd = Damdama, Tkw = Tokwa, Lhd = Lahuradewa, Mhg = Mahagara, Kch = Kuchai, Slbd = Sulabhdihi, Gpr = Gopalpur, Gbsn = Golbai Sasan, Kdk = Kodekal, Bdl = Budihal, Utr = Utnur, Sgk = Sanganakallu). 1: the northwest including the greater Indus valley; 2: the Gangetic plains; 3: eastern India; 4: savanna India.

as the suggested independence in crop origins in Saurashtra (Gujarat) versus that in the southern Deccan (Karanataka), or between the Indo-Gangetic divide and upper Ganges (Punjab / Haryana / western Uttar Pradesh) versus the middle Ganges (eastern Uttar Pradesh / Bihar). Even so, it is clear that in many areas agricultural societies only emerge in the archaeological record with the influx of agricultural elements from other parts of the subcontinent and beyond. Within the subcontinent as a whole, there have been differing and conflicting directions for the diffusion of cultivation.[6] For example, the evidence from the Gangetic plains suggests that a South Asian agriculture spreading from east to west met a Southwest Asian agriculture spreading broadly west to east. These contrasting patterns have encouraged some efforts at modelling the interaction of multiple currents of agricultural and demographic spread.[7] This review will focus on the current evidence that constrains the chronology of origins, the biogeography of origins, and the main trends in settlement–subsistence systems (Figure 10.2).

## Northwestern South Asia

The earliest agriculture in South Asia can be found along the western tributaries of the Indus River, at aceramic settlements like Mehrgarh (see Chapter 11 on Mehrgarh). Here, Southwest Asian crops, sheep, and goats have been discovered dating back to the seventh millennium BCE. This occurs in the context of aceramic Neolithic Mehrgarh, which was a modest sized and apparently sedentary village. The precise date at which the Neolithic begins here remains poorly established, with 7000 BCE being a widely cited supposition.[8] The transition to Mehrgarh period II and the ceramic Neolithic appears to be well dated to around c. 6000 BCE, which is approximately coincident with the 8.2 ka event. This climate event saw an increase in aridity across the area, which is likely to have been a factor that led to the development of agriculture. For this period of >6000 BCE up to c. 4000 BCE, Mehrgarh remains essentially unique in providing details of subsistence and a continuous sequence of occupation, as no other contemporary sites have been systematically excavated. By c. 4000 BCE, smaller Neolithic villages are known to have existed throughout the western borderlands, including the

---

6 Fuller, 'Agricultural origins and frontiers', and 'South Asia: archaeology', in Ness and Bellwood, *Encyclopedia of Global Human Migration*, vol. I.

7 E.g. N. Patterson et al., 'Genetic structure of a unique admixed population: implications for medical research', *Human Molecular Genetics*, 19 (2010), 411–19; C. Lemmen and A. Khan, 'A simulation of the Neolithic transition in the Indus valley', in L. Giosan et al. (eds.), *Climates, Landscapes, and Civilisations*, Geophysical Monograph 198 (Washington, DC: American Geophysical Union, 2013), 107–14.

8 Fuller, 'Agricultural origins and frontiers', and 'Mehrgarh Neolithic: the updated sequence', in C. Jarrige and V. Lefèvre (eds.), *South Asian Archaeology 2001*, 2 vols. (Paris: Éditions Recherche sur les Civilisations, 2005), vol. I, 129–41; C.A. Petrie et al., 'The investigation of early villages in the hills and on the plains of western South Asia', in C.A. Petrie (ed.), *Sheri Khan Tarakai and Early Village Life in the Borderlands of North-West Pakistan: Bannu Archaeological Project Surveys and Excavations 1985–2001*, Bannu Archaeological Project Monographs 1 (Oxford: Oxbow, 2010), 7–28.

Bannu basin, and these settlements re-emphasize the importance of domesticates of Southwest Asian derivation.[9]

There are perhaps as many as nineteen aceramic Neolithic sites (the Kili Gul
Muhammad phase) that have been identified in western Pakistan,[10] though
some of the identifications are speculative (e.g. Rana Ghundai) and at least
some sites listed as being villages have in fact previously been identified as
Mesolithic/hunter-gatherer sites on the basis of the lithics found on the surface,
and are effectively undated (e.g. Gul Shah Tup, Nekumshakh, Tup Takhtikhel,
and Yarak in the Bannu region[11]). It is entirely feasible that some of the
Mesolithic sites that have been identified were in fact used contemporaneously
with the period I occupation at Mehrgarh and other likely and reputed
aceramic sites. Furthermore, given the evidence for continuity in hunter-
gatherer subsistence in other parts of the subcontinent in later millennia
(e.g. at Bagor, Adamgarh, and Tenmalai[12]), it is also possible that some hunter-
-gatherer subsistence may have occurred in later phases in the borderlands and
other parts of western South Asia. Surveys in upper and lower Sindh have
identified an abundance of sites that are characterized by a microlithic assemblage that is distinct from the Mehrgarh, Amri, Kot Diji, and Harappan
assemblages,[13] but again the precise dates of these sites are not clear.

These early village sites were often situated on large alluvial fans, and such
fan environments were also favoured by early farmers in various parts of
West Asia, including many on the plains of southern Iran, such as the
settlements at Rahmatabad and Shah-Maran/Daulatabad.[14] It is possible
that the adaptation of farming practices to such specific ecological conditions
may have been a factor in the distribution of such early villages and the

9 Petrie (ed.), *Sheri Khan Tarakai*, 7.
10 G. Possehl, *Indus Age: The Beginnings* (Philadelphia: University of Pennsylvania Press,
1999), figs. 4.14 and 4.28, table 4.13.
11 F. Khan et al., 'Prehistoric and protohistoric settlements in Bannu district', *Pakistan
Archaeology*, 23 (1988), 99–148 (102); F. Khan et al., *Explorations and Excavations in Bannu
District, North-West Frontier Province, Pakistan, 1985–1988* (London: British Museum, 1991),
21–2.
12 D.K. Chakrabarti, *India: An Archaeological History: Palaeolithic Beginnings to Early
Historical Foundations* (Delhi: Oxford University Press, 1999), 99, and *The Oxford
Companion to Indian Archaeology: The Archaeological Foundations of Ancient India* (Oxford
University Press, 2006), 97.
13 E.g. P. Biagi, 'The Mesolithic settlement of Sindh (Pakistan): a preliminary assessment',
*Praehistoria*, 4–5 (2003–4), 195–220, and 'New discoveries of Mesolithic sites in the Thar
desert (upper Sindh, Pakistan)', in E. Olijdam and R.H. Spoor (eds.), *Intercultural
Relations between South and Southwest Asia: Studies in Commemoration of E.C.L. During
Caspers (1934–1996)* (Oxford: Archaeopress, 2008), 78–85.
14 C.A. Petrie and K.D. Thomas, 'The topographic and environmental context of the
earliest village sites in western South Asia', *Antiquity*, 86/334 (2012), 1055–67 (1057).

pattern seen in the dispersal of farming practices, where specific habitats were preferentially chosen (essentially a form of habitat tracking), consistent with a dispersal of at least some farmers from Southwest Asia.

Cereals present in the aceramic Neolithic (naked six-row barley, domestic hulled six-row barley, wild and domestic hulled two-row barley, domestic emmer, domestic einkorn, and a free threshing wheat) represent several of the 'founder crops of Southwest Asian agriculture',[15] though no pulses have been found in these early levels. The presence of some modern wild barley in parts of Pakistan and Afghanistan has fuelled speculation that there may have been local domestication at or near Mehrgarh.[16] Recent genetic research on barley suggests multiple origins, including an eastern barley group that differs from the Levantine and main European barleys, and could have originated in Iran or somewhere further east.[17] However, an archaeological sequence documenting a domestication process is lacking and the crop package that dominated the Indus region during the third millennium BCE is West Asian in character (pulses, flax, wheat, and barley) with a limited indigenous South Asian component. This points to the predominance of this early crop dispersal from the west.[18]

The faunal assemblage of earliest Mehrgarh is dominated by wild species, including gazelle, wild sheep, deer, wild buffalo, wild cattle, and goats, which are the second most common species after gazelles.[19] However, significant numbers of goat kids in burials and the remains of relatively small subadult or adult animals in rubbish deposits is consistent with kill patterns in domestic herds and indicates that domesticated goats were present from the earliest levels. Over the course of the aceramic Neolithic, sheep and cattle increasingly came to dominate the faunal assemblage and the animals represented decrease in size, which is a common marker used

15 D. Zohary, 'The mode of domestication of the founder crops of Southwest Asian agriculture', in D.R. Harris (ed.), *The Origins and Spread of Agriculture and Pastoralism in Eurasia* (London: UCL Press, 2006), 142–58.

16 C. Jarrige et al. (eds.), *Mehrgarh: Field Reports 1975–1985 from Neolithic Times to the Indus Civilization* (Karachi: Department of Culture and Tourism, Government of Sindh, Pakistan, in collaboration with the French Ministry of Foreign Affairs, 1995), 63ff.; Possehl, *Indus Age*.

17 P.L. Morrell and M.T. Clegg, 'Genetic evidence for a second domestication of barley (*Hordeum vulgare*) east of the Fertile Crescent', *Proceedings of the National Academy of Sciences*, 104/9 (2007), 3289–94.

18 Fuller, 'Agricultural origins and frontiers', and 'Finding plant domestication'.

19 R.H. Meadow, 'Notes on the faunal remains from Mehrgarh, with a focus on cattle (*Bos*)', in B. Allchin (ed.), *South Asian Archaeology 1981* (Cambridge University Press, 1984), 34–40, and 'Animal domestication in the Middle East: a revised view from the eastern margin', in G.L. Possehl (ed.), *Harappan Civilization: A Recent Perspective*, 2nd rev. edn (New Delhi: Oxford University Press, 1993), 295–320; Meadow and Patel, 'Prehistoric pastoralism'.

to identify domestication.[20] Sheep genetics, however, appear to preclude an independent South Asian domestication of sheep, unless a population domesticated in the east was replaced more recently by imported breeds.[21]

In this northwestern region there are a few taxa that are plausibly local domestications that broadened the agricultural economy. The most important of these was undoubtedly zebu cattle (*Bos indicus*), which has long been argued to be a local domestication at or around Mehrgarh between *c.* 7000 and 4500 BCE.[22] This is important because cattle dominate most faunal assemblages throughout the subcontinent, and they may all derive ultimately from this domestication process with the incorporation through hybridization of additional wild genetic lineages. In addition, Mehrgarh provides early evidence for the exploitation and probable cultivation of Indian tree cotton (*Gossypium arboreum*), which was to become important in Bronze Age and later textile production.[23] Water buffalo (*Bubalus bubalis*) and sesame (*Sesamum indicum*) are further domesticates that had been added to subsistence regimes certainly by 2500 BCE in at least some parts of the Indus region.

There appear to have been a number of distinct stages in the transition from mobile hunter-gatherer subsistence to sedentary farmer-herder subsistence, the subsequent dispersal of the agropastoral subsistence economy based on wheat, barley, sheep, goats, and cattle, and the progressive sophistication in craft production in western South Asia.[24] At a fundamental level, this process was characterized by a diffusion of practices into South Asia via the Iranian plateau or Afghanistan, initially into western Pakistan. The precise pattern of this process is, however, unclear. It is not readily apparent whether there was demic diffusion, involving movement of agropastoralist populations; cultural diffusion, involving the adoption of agropastoralism by populations previously using other subsistence strategies; or nuanced combinations of the two. A disjunction in the physical anthropological record at Mehrgarh and differing

20 R.H. Meadow, 'The origins and spread of agriculture and pastoralism in northwestern South Asia', in Harris (ed.), *Origins and Spread of Agriculture*, 390–412.
21 S. Hiendleder et al., 'Molecular analysis of wild and domestic sheep questions current nomenclature and provides evidence for domestication from two different subspecies', *Proceedings of the Royal Society B*, 269 (2002), 893–904.
22 Meadow, 'Animal domestication'; S. Chen et al., 'Zebu cattle are an exclusive legacy of the South Asia Neolithic', *Molecular Biology and Evolution*, 27/1 (2010), 1–6.
23 C. Moulherat et al., 'First evidence of cotton at Neolithic Mehrgarh, Pakistan: analysis of mineralized fibers from a copper bead', *Journal of Archaeological Science*, 29 (2002), 1393–401; D.Q. Fuller, 'Domestication, diffusion and the development of agricultural villages: a study of the south Indian Neolithic', in E.R. Raven (ed.), *South Asian Archaeology 1999* (Groningen: Egbert Forsten, 2008), 143–58.
24 E.g. G.L. Possehl, *The Indus Civilization: A Contemporary Perspective* (Walnut Creek, CA: AltaMira Press, 2002), 30–40; Petrie et al., 'Investigation of early villages'.

phylogenetic signatures in lentils could suggest two waves of diffusion/migration, with the second around 4500 BCE.[25] Evidence for long-range trade in exotic raw materials such as lapis lazuli clearly indicates that long-range contacts were maintained over several millennia, so there should be no doubt that this earliest phase of village occupation in South Asia was one where mobility of people and ideas could be widespread.

The transition to the use of fired ceramics *c.* 6000 BCE saw a number of other important and dramatic socioeconomic changes for the inhabitants of early villages in the northwest. Along with evidence for the first fired ceramic vessels, we see the first substantial mud-brick buildings, clear indications that specific craft activities were being carried out, and a marked development of the agricultural subsistence economy of the inhabitants.[26] Ceramics were slab-built and, as they do in West Asia, represent a change in food processing to focus on grinding and clay-oven baking, a contrast to other parts of Neolithic India.[27] Notable changes are evident in the subsistence economy in period IIA at Mehrgarh, including the almost complete replacement of wild animals with domesticates, the majority of which were cattle (over 50 per cent of the assemblage), with lesser numbers of sheep and goats.[28] There were also increases in the number of settlements, the size of settlements, and the settled area over the preceding phase.[29] However, the raw treatment of the data may have masked a range of possible dynamics. For instance, as noted above, it is entirely possible that groups subsisting wholly or principally by hunting and gathering persisted in the borderlands and other parts of western South Asia after the appearance of ceramics. New villages may thus have been established in regions that did not previously have them.

During the fourth millennium BCE, there were further significant socioeconomic developments for the early village societies living in the western parts of the subcontinent. It is during this period that there is the clearest evidence for the initial spread of the wheat-, barley-, sheep-, goat-, and cattle-based agropastoralist subsistence economy into different parts of the hill, piedmont, and plain zone along the edge of the borderlands, and ultimately into the Indus plains themselves.[30]

25  Fuller, 'South Asia: archaeology'.
26  Meadow, 'Origins and spread of agriculture'; Jarrige et al. (eds.), *Mehrgarh: Field Reports*, 62ff.
27  D.Q. Fuller and M. Rowlands, 'Ingestion and food technologies: maintaining differences over the long-term in West, South and East Asia', in T.C. Wilkinson et al. (eds.), *Interweaving Worlds: Systemic Interactions in Eurasia, 7th to the 1st Millennia BC* (Oxford: Oxbow, 2011), 37–60.
28  Meadow, 'Faunal remains from Mehrgarh', and 'Origins and spread of agriculture'.
29  Possehl, *Indus Age*.
30  Petrie et al., 'Investigation of early villages'; Petrie and Thomas, 'Topographic and environmental context'.

In terms of what we understand about the relative and absolute chronology of early village sites in western South Asia, it appears that it was only after the expansion of wheat-, barley-, sheep-, goat-, and cattle-based pastoralism into southern and northern Baluchistan and also southern Khyber Pakhtunkhwa that settlements practising agropastoralism appeared on the Indus plains. Settlements such as Rana Ghundai (Loralai) and Periano Ghundai (Zhob) appear to have been settled before Sheri Khan Tarakai (Bannu basin) and Jhandi Babar A (Gomal plain), which share a similar material assemblage and were in turn earlier than settlements on the plains.[31] Our understanding of the earliest village settlements on the Indus plain comes from excavations at Jalilpur and Harappa,[32] and the Cholistan survey,[33] during which a total of ninety-nine sites characterized by Hakra ware ceramics were identified (including fifty-two that were interpreted as camp sites and forty-five as settlement sites, and two where there is evidence for craft production) with a suggested four-tiered site-size hierarchy. Hakra ware ceramics include the first wheel-thrown ceramics in the region, alongside handmade wares. At Harappa this period is recognized as the Ravi phase (3300–3000 BCE) and is succeeded by the early Harappan period that culminated in the transition to the mature urbanism of the Harappan era around 2600–2500 BCE.

Unanswered questions remain about the possibility of a separate early food-producing tradition of the upper Punjab, Haryana, and the Indo-Gangetic divide. Evidence from several sites in northwestern India indicates the presence of crops that were absent from Baluchistan and Khyber Pakhtunkhwa. There is the possibility of a local transition to crop cultivation based on indigenous monsoon taxa, such as millets (*Panicum sumatrense*, *Setaria pumila*, and *Setaria verticillata*) and pulses (*Vigna mungo* and *Macrotyloma uniflorum*).[34] In both Rajasthan and Saurashtra in Gujarat, the local Mesolithic tradition gave way to ceramic-producing cultures around 3500 BCE. These are usually classed as 'Chalcolithic' cultures, due to the early availability of copper and links to the Indus region. Current evidence points

---

31 Petrie et al., 'Investigation of early villages'; K.D. Thomas et al., 'Early village sites in the Gomal plain', in Petrie (ed.), *Sheri Khan Tarakai*, 379–98; Petrie and Thomas, 'Topographic and environmental context'.

32 M.R. Mughal, 'A summary of excavations and explorations in Pakistan (1971 and 1972)', *Pakistan Archaeology*, 8 (1972), 117–24; J.M. Kenoyer and R.H. Meadow, 'The Ravi phase: a new cultural manifestation at Harappa', in M. Taddei and G. De Marco (eds.), *South Asian Archaeology 1997* (Rome: Instituto italiano per l'Africa e l'Oriente, 2000), 55–76.

33 M.R. Mughal, *Ancient Cholistan: Archaeology and Architecture* (Rawalpindi: Ferozsons, 1997).

34 Fuller, 'South Asia: archaeology'.

to the dominance of West Asian-derived winter cereals and pulses with some input from the indigenous crops of 'inner' monsoonal India at these settlements.[35] Unfortunately data are only available from the era of the Indus civilization (after 2600 BCE) but they may point to an Indian savanna agriculture, quite different from the winter-crop wheat/barley traditions of the contemporary Indus valley. While this provides an argument for a local Neolithic tradition with local plant domestications, it is not empirically documented and remains undiagnosed on the ground in terms of sites or material assemblages. It is also unclear whether this tradition should be seen as connected to the southern Deccan development of farming (see below), especially as both regions share the same introduced livestock complex.

## The Gangetic plains

Towards the middle Ganges plains there is clear evidence of a strongly indigenous Neolithic tradition, which included the development of rice cultivation and eventual sedentism. There remains room for debate as to whether or not true village farming (sedentism, with domesticated crops and animals and an agriculture-dominated economy) developed on its own or only after influences from wheat–barley–sheep–goat systems of the greater Indus region, but there is clear evidence for a unique rice-based Neolithic.

The first evidence for rice in South Asia comes from the site of Lahuradewa, one of the most important in the subcontinent.[36] The site also potentially provides evidence for the earliest ceramics in South Asia. Lahuradewa is in eastern Uttar Pradesh, situated on an oxbow pond of a former Ganges tributary. The smaller tributaries, and oxbow ponds, would have lent themselves to fishing, which is likely to have been a major resource of Mesolithic and Neolithic alike in the middle Ganges region. Lahuradewa may have been occupied as early as c. 9000 BCE, but certainly by c. 7000–6000 BCE, which is confirmed by a direct date on rice (*Oryza* sp.) at c. 6400 BCE. Rice grains and chaff have been recovered from the early deposits, suggesting that rice was harvested at this site. Rice-type phytoliths and an increase in grass-type pollen

35  M.D. Kajale, 'Palaeobotanical investigations at Balathal: preliminary results', *Man and Environment*, 21/1 (1996), 98–102; see also A.K. Pokharia et al., 'Archaeobotany and archaeology at Kanmer, a Harappan site in Kachchh, Gujarat: evidence for adaptation in response to climatic variability', *Current Science*, 100/12 (2011), 1833–46; and Fuller, 'Finding plant domestication'.
36  R. Tewari et al., 'Preliminary report of the excavation at Lahuradewa, district Sant Kabir Nagar, U.P. 2001–2002: wider archaeological implications', *Pragdhara*, 13 (2002/3), 37–68; R. Tewari et al., 'Early farming at Lahuradewa', *Pragdhara*, 18 (2008), 347–73.

found in a pollen core were dated to *c.* 6000 BCE,[37] and it is therefore not surprising that the mound has been heralded as a very early rice farming site, perhaps rivalling those of the Yangtze, China, for the first domestic rice. However, it is not agreed that the rice from Lahuradewa was actually domestic, and the degree of sedentism at the site is unclear.

Recent synthesis of the genetics and archaeology of rice suggests that the *indica* subspecies of domesticated rice associated with this region is not a truly independent domesticate. Instead, it shared key domestication mutations with East Asian *japonica* rice. This indicates that early hybridization between a fully domesticated *japonica* and wild-type (but managed or cultivated) proto-*indica* created the domestic *O. s. indica*.[38] That proto-*indica* was under management is implied by the preservation of traits that would not have survived if introduced into truly wild populations on the Ganges plains. Instead human management of wild rice habitats and resowing would provide a context in which domestication traits from *japonica* could have been successful. This is supported by the archaeological evidence from Lahuradewa and by micro charcoal found in a core taken from Lahuradewa Lake.[39] The burning of vegetation, which produced increased levels of micro charcoal *c.* 7200 BCE, may have occurred as part of a wild rice management routine where rival vegetation was burnt to provide weed-free locations in which to grow rice.

Lahuradewa is an unusual site in that it provides evidence from the very early Neolithic to the Chalcolithic. Equally unusual is that radiocarbon dates from the site push back the antiquity of early rice harvesting to at least *c.* 6400 BCE. However, much like Mehrgarh, there are no other known sites in this area with such an antiquity. Instead the majority of secure radiocarbon dates for the early layers of Neolithic settlements, including Jhusi, Koldihwa, and Tokwa, fall around 2500–2000 BCE, contemporary with Lahuradewa period IB.[40] During this period wheat, barley, lentil, sheep/goats, and zebu cattle begin to appear in the archaeological record. These would have crossed into the Gangetic plains from the northwest, via the Indus civilization.

---

37  M.S. Chauhan et al., 'Pollen record of Holocene vegetation, climate change and human habitation from Lahuradewa Lake, Sant Kabir Nagar district, Uttar Pradesh, India', *Man and Environment*, 34 (2009), 88–100.

38  D.Q. Fuller and L. Qin, 'Water management and labour in the origins and dispersal of Asian rice', *World Archaeology*, 41/1 (2009), 88–111; D.Q. Fuller et al., 'Consilience of genetics and archaeobotany in the entangled history of rice', *Archaeological and Anthropological Sciences*, 2/2 (2010), 115–31; Fuller, 'Finding plant domestication'.

39  Chauhan et al., 'Pollen record of Holocene vegetation'.

40  E. Harvey, 'Early agricultural communities in northern and eastern India: an archaeobotanical investigation', unpublished PhD thesis (University College London, 2006).

After 2000 BCE south Indian crops were adopted into the agriculture of the area, including browntop millet, horsegram, and mung bean. This points to trade contacts across the Vindhyas hills to the Deccan in the south, distinct from the more obvious cultural connections upriver towards the Indus. In summary we have three phases: a proto-*indica* rice Neolithic or Neolithic-Mesolithic (Lahuradewa phase IA, 7000–2500 BCE), a formative Village Neolithic (Lahuradewa phase IB, 2500–2000 BCE), and an established Village Neolithic/Chalcolithic (Lahuradewa phase 2, 2000–1000 BCE), after which there was a transition to the Iron Age. Earlier dates have been proposed for the beginning of the formative Village Neolithic, *c.* 5000–4000 BCE; however, these primarily come from mixed charcoal samples (with the inherent issues of the Old Wood Effect) and/or from disturbed deposits.[41]

Early permanent agricultural settlements in the Ganges grew wheats and barley and reared sheep/goats and cattle. By *c.* 2500–2000 BCE rice is found at many sites, including Damdama, Senuwar, and Mahagara.[42] This period marks a major agricultural development to a double-cropping system, with summer crops (wheats, barley, etc.) and winter crops (rice, etc.) grown in the same year. Culturally this period shows a classic developed Neolithic society. Pottery includes cord-impressed ware, and stone tools include polished celts and quern stones. The sites of Koldihwa, Senuwar, and Narhan, among others, provide evidence for thatched wattle-and-daub buildings, and burnt lumps of clay with the impressions of reeds and/or bamboo give an indication of the types of building material used. These structures tended to be circular, for example at Tokwa, with internal hearths, and were often encircled by post holes.[43] Perhaps the clearest evidence for the importance of double-cropping comes from these buildings, which have rarely been found prior to it. The need, and indeed the ability, to stay in one location to take advantage of the seasonal flooding of the Ganges and its plains arose with rice.

41 Fuller, 'Finding plant domestication'; V.D. Misra, 'Beginnings of agriculture in the Vindhyas (north-central India)', and J.N. Pal, 'Recent excavations at Tokwa: fresh light on the early farming culture of the Vindhyas', both in L. Gopal and V.C. Srivastava (eds.), *History of Agriculture in India, up to c. 1200 AD* (New Delhi: CSC for the Project of History of Indian Science, 2008), 19–30 and 48–69.

42 Damdama: K.S. Saraswat, 'Plant economy of early farming communities at Senuwar', in B.P. Singh (ed.), *Early Farming Communities of the Kaimur*, vol. II (Jaipur: Publication Scheme, 2004), 416–535; M.D. Kajale, 'Some initial observations on palaeobotanical evidence for Mesolithic plant economy from excavations at Damdama, Pratagarh, Uttar Pradesh', in N.C. Ghosh and S. Chakrabarti (eds.), *Adaptation and Other Essays* (Santiniketan: Visva Bharati Research Publications, 1990), 98–102. Senuwar: Saraswat, 'Plant economy'. Mahagara: Harvey, 'Early agricultural communities'.

43 V.D. Misra et al., 'Excavation at Tokwa: a Neolithic–Chalcolithic settlement', *Pragdhara*, II (2000/I), 59–72.

In a similar vein to the rest of South Asia, we have clear evidence for the continuation of aceramic Mesolithic cultures into the Neolithic in this region. Damdama, for example, was occupied up to 2000 BCE, Lekhahia provides a date of *c.* 2100 BCE, and Sarai-Nahar-Rai and Mahadaha of *c.* 1000 BCE.[44] These sites often have shallow archaeological deposits, indicating seasonal occupation, but some of the latest dates could be plagued by intrusive material. Circular structures with hearths and burnt plaster floors have been discovered at Damdama, Mahadaha, and Sarai-Nahar-Rai, but perhaps more excitingly a significant number of human burials were also found.[45] Zooarchaeological assemblages are dominated by deer and gazelle,[46] and archaeobotanical assemblages show a reliance on wild foods, including rice.[47] Taken as a whole, the middle Ganges region displays a particularly protracted transition from the exploitation of wild rice (after 7000 BCE) to fully sedentary agropastoral villages by around 2000 BCE, alongside persistent pockets of hunter-gatherer-fisher Mesolithic cultures. Once intensive rice production was established, however, during the second millennium BCE, the population grew rapidly and social complexity ultimately emerged during the period of Iron Age urbanism that took place in the middle of the first millennium BCE.

## Eastern India

The nature of early Neolithic societies in eastern India has been less well studied than other parts of the subcontinent. However, there is a growing corpus of information from various streams of evidence available in the

---

44 Harvey, 'Early agricultural communities'; J.N. Pal, *Archaeology of Southern Uttar Pradesh: Ceramic Industries of Northern Vindhyas* (Allahabad: Swabha Prakashan, 1986).

45 U.C. Chattopadhyaya, 'Settlement practices and the spatial organisation of subsistence and mortuary practices in the Mesolithic Ganges valley, north-central India', *World Archaeology*, 27/3 (1996), 461–76; J.R. Lukacs, 'Mesolithic hunters and foragers of the Gangetic plain: summary of current research in dental anthropology', *Dental Anthropology News Letter*, 6/3 (1992), 3–8; J.R. Lukacs and J.N. Pal, 'Mesolithic subsistence in north India: inferences from dental attributes', *Current Anthropology*, 34/5 (1993), 745–65; J.N. Pal, 'The Mesolithic phase in the Ganga valley', in K. Paddayya (ed.), *Recent Studies in Indian Archaeology*, Indian Council of Historical Research Monograph Series 6 (Delhi: Munshiram Manoharlal, 2002), 60–80; G.R. Sharma et al., *Beginnings of Agriculture (Epi-Palaeolithic to Neolithic): Excavations at Chopani-Mando, Mahadaha, and Mahagara* (Allahabad: Abinash Prakashan, 1980); R.K. Varma et al., 'A preliminary report on the excavations at Damdama (1982–1984)', *Man and Environment*, 9 (1985), 45–65.

46 U.C. Chattopadhyaya, 'Researches in archaeozoology of the Holocene period (including the Harappan tradition in India and Pakistan)', in S. Settar and R. Korisettar (eds.), *Indian Archaeology in Retrospect*, 4 vols. (New Delhi: Indian Council of Historical Research, 2002), vol. III, 365–422.

47 Harvey, 'Early agricultural communities'; Kajale, 'Some initial observations'.

archaeological literature. The recovery and examination of environmental evidence, vital to understanding transitions to farming, are limited in this area. Therefore the trajectories of change leading to the establishment of agricultural communities are, at this stage, still largely suppositions. However, the nature of Neolithic society and intriguing patterns within the data can still be examined. Discussion will focus on the state of Odisha (formerly Orissa), which appears to have had a distinct Neolithic culture in which subsistence was primarily based on rice, pulses, wild animals, and cattle.

Only a few archaeological sites in this area have been radiocarbon dated. What dates we have suggest that the Neolithic began around 2500 BCE, but these dates largely come from later deposits of Neolithic–Chalcolithic sites, leaving the earliest levels undated.[48] The beginning of the Neolithic in this area is often placed at 3500 BCE[49] on the basis of typological similarities with other, better-dated parts of South Asia. The results of several regional surveys and excavations indicate that there are two main settlement types present in the eastern Neolithic. The first of these, the Upland tradition, can be found in the foothills and uplands. The sites are very shallow with few archaeobotanical and zooarchaeological remains. They are often identified through lithic and pottery scatters and appear to represent seasonal camps. The second tradition, of the coastal plains of Odisha, is characterized by mounded settlement sites up to 8 m high, from which both archaeobotanical and zooarchaeological material has been recovered.

Our best evidence for early farmers in east India comes from the coastal plain settlements, which have been referred to as the Eastern Wetlands tradition: Khameswaripali, Golbai Sasan, and Gopalpur.[50] The large settlement mounds of Golbai Sasan and Gopalpur have been systematically excavated and submitted to full archaeobotanical analysis. The mounds are around 150–200 m in diameter and up to 8 m high. Scant evidence for structures in the Neolithic, in the form of floor layers and occasional post holes, suggests roughly oval hut dwellings. Red-ware and grey-ware ceramics

---

48  Harvey, 'Early agricultural communities'; E. Harvey et al., 'Early agriculture in Orissa: some archaeobotanical results and field observations on the Neolithic', *Man and Environment*, 31/2 (2006), 21–32.

49  See R.N. Dash, 'The Neolithic culture of Orissa: a typo-technological analysis', in K.K. Basa and P. Mohanty (eds.), *Archaeology of Orissa*, vol. 1 (New Delhi: Pratibha Prakashan, 2000), 201–21.

50  P.K. Behera, 'Excavations at Khameswaripali – a proto historic settlement in the middle Mahanadi valley, Orissa: a preliminary report', *Pragdhara*, 11 (2000/1), 13–34. On the original excavations, see B.K. Sinha, 'Golbai: a protohistoric site on the coast of Orissa', and S.K. Kar, 'Gopalpur: a Neolithic–Chalcolithic site in coastal Orissa', both in Basa and Mohanty (eds.), *Archaeology of Orissa*, 322–55 and 368–91.

were recovered from both sites, as were bone tools and several celts. Detailed macrobotanical and phytolith analyses have provided much of the information about the type of agriculture practised in the east Indian Neolithic. In this region agricultural production was dominated by rice, with approximately 50 per cent of the crop remains recovered from each site identified as rice grains.[51] The sites are situated on alluvial soils close to seasonally flooded rivers, and rice grains, rice-type phytoliths, and spikelet bases have all been recovered from the very earliest levels. Other crops include pulses (horsegram and pigeon pea), plus a few small millets (browntop millet and *Setaria* sp.). This diet was largely based on rice and beans complemented by livestock meat. Cattle rearing and possible pig rearing occur by the Chalcolithic, but probably also took place in the Neolithic. Pig rearing is of particular interest as modern genetic data indicate that Indian pigs and wild boar are highly distinct from those elsewhere in Asia,[52] and that pig bones are generally rare on sites elsewhere in Neolithic–Chalcolithic South Asia. Faunal remains also demonstrate hunting, with wild species such as chital deer and nilgai appearing in the archaeological record.[53] Chalcolithic levels provide evidence for fishing in the form of bone harpoons and marine fish remains; however, similar remains have not been found from Neolithic levels.

Of key interest to archaeologists studying early crop cultivation is the discovery of pigeon pea (*Cajanus cajan*) at both Gopalpur and Golbai Sasan. While both the frequency and ubiquity of finds were low, it appears likely that this was a cultivar domesticated within the region.[54] Wild progenitors of pigeon pea are present in the Eastern Ghats today and it is likely that their range was slightly broader in the past, though still centred on the Eastern Ghats. The eastern Neolithic therefore appears to have an independent, local domestication of a pulse crop. The east Indian Neolithic has been considered as a possible area for the management or cultivation of native wild rices, but recent work has challenged this theory. The earliest rice in this region is found alongside domestic-type spikelet bases (around 70 per cent of the identifiable spikelet base assemblage, which is expected in domesticated

---

51 Harvey, 'Early agricultural communities'; E. Kingwell-Banham, conference poster, 'An Indian domestication of rice? The story from Orissa, East India, and the development of rice cultivation systems', International Union for Quaternary Research, Bern (2011), and 'Rice and language across Asia', Cornell University (2011).

52 G. Larson et al., 'Patterns of East Asian pig domestication, migration, and turnover revealed by modern and ancient DNA', *Proceedings of the National Academy of Sciences*, 107/17 (2010), 7686–91.

53 S.K. Kar et al., 'Explorations at Gopalpur, district Nayagarh, coastal Orissa', *Man and Environment*, 23/1 (1998), 107–14.

54 Harvey, 'Early agricultural communities'.

populations), and morphometric data suggest that most rice grains are consistent with domesticated populations.[55]

In addition, there is some evidence for fruit and nuts at Gopalpur and Golbai Sasan. Citrus-type peel has been found in deposits at Gopalpur and unidentified nutshell fragments have been recovered from both sites. Whether the nuts were collected from wild trees or represent some form of arboriculture is not clear, but it is likely that tree species were managed to some extent at this time. Indeed, citrus trees are native to a belt that runs across the Himalayas. Therefore the presence of citrus-type peel in this area may indicate the movement by people of trees across the subcontinent and the early stages of arboriculture. The movement of economically valuable tree species, such as citrus, could be used to track shifting cultivation by providing a *terminus ante quem*.[56] In this case it is rather late, *c.* 1500 BCE, but the evidence provides a glimpse of a usually unobserved activity. Elsewhere in India wood charcoal evidence for citrus and mango wood outside the expected wild range dates from *c.* 1400 BCE onwards, pointing to the mid second millennium BCE as the era when fruit tree arboriculture became established in much of India.

The small, ephemeral sites of the foothills, such as Bajpur, Banabasa, and Kuchai, have little or no archaeological remains outside of lithic scatters.[57] Several have Mesolithic and Neolithic layers (often identified through the presence of pottery sherds), indicating continuity of at least some groups during the transition to agriculture in this region. The almost total lack of archaeobotanical evidence has been taken to indicate the seasonal nature of these settlements. It seems that they are temporary camps, possibly occupied by hunter-gatherers or shifting cultivators, or perhaps specialists involved in lithic production.[58] The environment in which they are located could have been used for agriculture. However, there is what appears to be a cultural demarcation in the landscape of Neolithic east India that separated settled agriculturalists from more mobile groups.

55 Fuller et al., 'Consilience of genetics'; Harvey, 'Early agricultural communities'; Kingwell-Banham, 'Indian domestication of rice?'
56 E. Kingwell-Banham and D.Q. Fuller, 'Shifting cultivators in South Asia: expansion, marginalisation and specialisation over the long-term', *Quaternary International*, 249 (2012), 84–95.
57 Harvey, 'Early agricultural communities'; K.K. Basa et al., 'Neolithic culture of Pallahara, central Orissa', in Basa and Mohanty (eds.), *Archaeology of Orissa*, 264–84.
58 P.K. Behera, 'Neolithic culture complex of Bonaigarh, Orissa', in Basa and Mohanty (eds.), *Archaeology of Orissa*, 222–63; D.Q. Fuller, 'Agricultural origins and frontiers in South Asia: a working synthesis', *Journal of World Prehistory*, 20 (2006), 1–86.

It is possible that people using these upland sites consumed tubers and gourds (various *Cucurbitaceae*), which are more ephemeral in the archaeological record. Both can be pit-roasted, removing the need for pottery, of which there is very little at these sites. Unfortunately, both are hard to identify archaeobotanically and are less likely to be preserved than cereal grains. More work needs to be done before we can truly begin to develop hypotheses about the subsistence regimes at these sites; however, both taro and yams are found in wild forms in Odisha and it is possible that these are wild progenitor species.

One of the richer streams of evidence on the Neolithic societies of east India comes from stone tool analysis. In particular, several production sites have been located in the Sundargarh district of Odisha.[59] Here Neolithic sites are concentrated in areas of dolerite rock with which most tools were made. The site of Sulabhdihi shows evidence for the mass production of celts and a smaller-scale production of flakes, blades, and other tools. This site is situated close to a tributary of the Brahmani River and is comprised of four huge mounds of production waste measuring up to 3 m high and 160 m across. The majority of tools recovered were in a semi-finished state, suggesting that they would have been transported to other locations before completion, perhaps settlement sites. Dolerite tools have been found at a variety of settlements across east India and, while this may be due to the ubiquity of the material, the size of the production site indicates that there may have been extensive stone tool trade networks during this time. Early farmers in this region may have been engaged in large-scale lithic manufacturing, an activity which may have occurred during the winter season. No winter crops have been recovered from Neolithic sites in Odisha, indicating that cultivation activities did not take place during this season. Perhaps farmers moved to the temporary camps, of the Upland tradition, to engage in lithic production. Or perhaps the Upland tradition represents a co-existing, more mobile society, in which case it would be interesting to explore the interaction dynamics between both groups.

While evidence is relatively thin on the ground, it is clear that east India had a unique and complex Neolithic society. It is certainly one that deserves further investigation. The interplay of farmers and mobile groups is particularly interesting, as is the domestication of the native wild pigeon pea.

Although there is little archaeological evidence for the Neolithic cultures of northeast India and Bangladesh, the region deserves brief discussion. It is

---

59 Behera, 'Neolithic culture complex of Bonaigarh'.

worth flagging that recent genetic work on rice identifies the *aus* rices, which include several landraces of Bangladesh and northeast India, as being as genetically distinct from other *Oryza sativa* types as *indica* is from *japonica*.[60] Although conventionally classified morphologically as *indica*, genetic data suggest these represent a third group, plausibly from a separate domestication somewhere in this region.[61] It has often been proposed that this area saw an influx of tools, pottery traditions, and agricultural plants and animals from Southeast Asia.[62] Unfortunately, to date we do not have the data to securely back up this hypothesis. Evidence for a Neolithic in this area is thin on the ground. In general, Neolithic sites are situated in elevated positions, on hilltops and high ground. Archaeological deposits are often shallow and less than 1 m deep. Several sites have been excavated and have revealed Neolithic stone tools and corded pottery. Pottery of particular interest comes from the site of Napachik, Manipur, in the form of tripod legs. Tripod vessels are characteristic of ceramic traditions in China,[63] and the Neolithic cultures in this region should perhaps be seen in the context of Chinese and Southeast Asian Neolithic traditions rather than those of the Indian subcontinent. However, currently available radiocarbon dates from this area only go back to around 0 CE, making the Neolithic here a continuing mystery.

## Savanna India

The case for a truly independent origin of agriculture in South Asia is strongest in the southern peninsula of India. Here we have clear evidence for the domestication of crops from local wild progenitors, including millets and pulses. Although the dates for early agriculture are significantly later than those in the north, *c.* 2800 BCE compared to *c.* 6000 BCE in Pakistan, the

---

60 A.J. Garris et al., 'Genetic structure and diversity in *Oryza sativa* L', *Genetics*, 169/3 (2005), 1631–8; K.L. McNally et al., 'Genomewide SNP variation reveals relationships among landraces and modern varieties of rice', *Proceedings of the National Academy of Sciences*, 106/30 (2009), 12273–8.

61 Fuller, 'Finding plant domestication'.

62 M. Hazarika, 'A recent perspective on the prehistoric cultures of northeast India', in M. Rajput (ed.), *Understanding North East India: Cultural Diversities, Insurgency and Identities* (New Delhi: Manak, 2011), 30–55; C.F.W. Higham, 'Languages and farming dispersals: Austroasiatic languages and rice cultivation', in P. Bellwood and C. Renfrew (eds.), *Examining the Farming/Language Dispersal Hypothesis* (Cambridge: McDonald Institute for Archaeological Research, 2002), 223–32; G. van Driem, 'The trans-Himalayan phylum and its implications for population prehistory', *Communication on Contemporary Anthropology*, 5 (2011), 135–42.

63 Fuller and Rowlands, 'Ingestion and food technologies'.

difference in agricultural systems is sufficient to preclude outside influence. In this area, incorporating Karnataka, Andhra Pradesh, and northwest Tamil Nadu, over 200 Neolithic sites have been excavated, producing one of the richest collections in South Asia. Of these, around 50 per cent are ashmounds, denominating this the 'ashmound tradition'.[64] These are mounds of ash and vitrified material, generally burnt cattle dung as well as cultural artefacts and animal bone, the largest of which span up to 5,000 $m^2$ and are 10 m high.

The earliest dates for the Neolithic of south India come from the sites of Kodekal, Utnur, and Watgal and date the earliest Neolithic settlements to c. 3000 BCE (Southern Neolithic phase 1a).[65] These sites have occupation levels with ceramics, but no ashmounds and very few plant or animal remains. Dates from Budihal, Brahmagiri, Piklihal, and Utnur, among others, place the start of Southern Neolithic phase 1b at around 2500 BCE. This phase saw the emergence of ashmounds as well as herding of cattle, sheep, and goats. However, there is no evidence of domesticated crops. By 2200 BCE (Southern Neolithic phase 2), village sites such as those at Sanganakallu and Tekkalakota appear across the hilltops of the southern peninsula and evidence for crop plants emerges. By 1800 BCE (Southern Neolithic phase 3), ashmounds cease to be used, although village sites continue to be occupied, in some cases with continuous occupation up to the Megalithic period, c. 1400–1200 BCE.[66]

Unlike the rest of India, where early agriculture was synonymous with cereal farming, southern agriculture appears to have taken an alternative route via pastoralism. Cattle, sheep, and goat bones have been recovered from the earliest deposits at nearly every excavated ashmound.[67] The majority of ashmounds are situated in the driest parts of the peninsula, on a granitic geology with sandy soils, and fewer in the better-watered black soils in adjacent areas. These areas today remain relatively uncultivated. This settlement pattern can be seen to reflect the relative unimportance of crops to the

---

64 K. Paddayya, 'The problem of ashmounds of southern Deccan in the light of the Budihal excavations, Karnataka', *Bulletin of the Deccan College Post-Graduate and Research Institute*, 60–1 (2001), 189–225; F.R. Allchin, *Neolithic Cattle-Keepers of Southern India: A Study of the Deccan Ash Mounds* (Cambridge University Press, 1963).

65 D.Q. Fuller et al., 'Dating the Neolithic of south India: new radiometric evidence for key economic, social and ritual transformations', *Antiquity*, 81 (2007), 755–78.

66 B. Allchin and R. Allchin, *The Rise of Civilisation in India and Pakistan*, South Asian edn (New Delhi: Cambridge University Press, 1996); Fuller et al., 'Dating the Neolithic'; R. Korisettar et al., 'Bhramagiri and beyond: the archaeology of the southern Neolithic', in Settar and Korisettar (eds.), *Indian Archaeology in Retrospect*, vol. I, 151–237.

67 Korisettar et al., 'Bhramagiri and beyond'.

early mobile pastoralists occupying this area.[68] The growth of agricultural settlements after 2000 BCE indicates both sedentism, with increasing cultivation, and also the resilience of indigenous cultivation systems against an environmental aridification trend.[69]

Radiocarbon dating shows that ashmounds generally grew over a relatively short timeframe of around 100–200 years. At the end of their lives they were either abandoned or succeeded by sedentary village sites. Some of the abandoned ashmounds were subsequently restarted, leading to larger accumulations over extended periods, but consisting of multiple, discrete 100–200-year episodes. For example, Kudatini and Palavoy show abandonment periods within their sections and the accumulation of natural soils.[70] Why these ashmounds were re-established, while others were abandoned or developed into sedentary villages, remains unclear.

The role of the ashmounds, whether purely symbolic or utilitarian, is not really known. The preservation of cattle hoof prints within some ashmounds suggests that they were large cattle pens, at least initially. However, as mounds developed they became somewhat 'monumental' in their own right. For example, at Budihal, upper layers indicate that the dung was layered in deliberate patties.[71] Visually, these large burning mounds of dung would have been incredibly striking and visible from across large tracts of the landscape, both foci for large social gatherings and iconic features in the landscape that signified past events.[72] The importance of seasonal gatherings in facilitating trade, marriage arrangements, and the genetic mixing of cattle herds can all be considered. However, the existence of these mounds tends to imply that some widespread ethnographically documented uses of cattle dung, such as manure for agricultural fields, were not being widely practised. Therefore it is probably no accident that agricultural diversification and intensification are evidenced from the era when ashmounds were in decline.

Ashmounds, located in the lower plains, have frequently been found in the vicinity of hilltop settlement sites dating to the same period. Only a few of these settlements have been excavated, and it is from these that the

68 P.G. Johansen, 'Landscape, monumental architecture, and ritual: a reconsideration of the south Indian ashmounds', *Journal of Anthropological Archaeology*, 23 (2004), 309–30.

69 C. Ponton et al., 'Holocene aridification of India', *Geophysical Research Letters*, 39/3 (2012), L03704.

70 Allchin, *Neolithic Cattle-Keepers*; Fuller et al., 'Dating the Neolithic'.

71 K. Paddayya, 'The ashmounds of south India: fresh evidence and possible implications', *Bulletin of Deccan College Post-Graduate and Research Institute*, 51–2 (1991–2), 573–626.

72 N. Boivin, 'Landscape and cosmology in the south Indian Neolithic: new perspectives on the Deccan ashmounds', *Cambridge Archaeological Journal*, 14/2 (2004), 235–57; Johansen, 'Landscape, monumental architecture, and ritual'.

majority of the archaeobotanical remains of crops come. The nature of the interaction between these types of site has not been comprehensively investigated, but it has been suggested that these were seasonal encampments of a transhumant segment of society. They might have come to these sites near permanent hill villages in the post-harvest period of winter, allowing animals to graze stubble and add to field fertility, and exchanging animal products for crop produce.[73] More isolated ashmounds have been interpreted as dry-season social gathering sites, perhaps near the borders between tribal territories.[74]

Once agricultural crops begin to appear in the archaeological record, it is at habitation sites on the hilltops overlooking the plains that they are found. It seems likely, therefore, that the hilltop sites were the centres from which most crop farming took place. The key feature of this farming is that it was based on native plants. The staple crops of the southern Neolithic were two small millets (*Brachiaria ramosa* and *Setaria verticillata*) and two pulses (*Macrotyloma uniflorum* and *Vigna radiata*). The wild progenitors of these species were likely present in the local environment in the woodlands and forest margins of the Deccan and Western Ghats. The small millets are still fairly common in the riverine zones and savannas of the region and frequently appear as weeds within millet fields. Because of this, *Brachiaria ramosa* has even earned the nickname 'illegal wife of little millet' (*Panicum sumatrense*) in several parts of India. The route to domestication for these species appears incredibly protracted. It is not until around 1000 BCE that we begin to see domestic-sized *Vigna radiata* grains within the archaeological record, showing that the morphological changes that we expect to occur during domestication did not materialize until the early Historical period. This may, however, be misleading and it is likely that the plant developed non-dehiscent pods and lost its seed dormancy period before this – both markers of domestication.[75]

By 1900 BCE some of the sites indicate the adoption of winter crops from the north (wheat, barley, grass pea), while by 1500 BCE the agricultural systems had diversified, with summer crops from elsewhere. The late Neolithic adoptions included pigeon pea (*Cajanus cajan*) from Odisha[76] and

---

73 D.Q. Fuller et al., 'Southern Neolithic cultivation systems: a reconsideration based on archaeobotanical evidence', *South Asian Studies*, 17 (2001), 149–67.

74 E.g. Boivin, 'Landscape and cosmology'.

75 D.Q. Fuller and E. Harvey, 'The archaeobotany of Indian pulses: identification, processing and evidence for cultivation', *Environmental Archaeology*, 11/2 (2006), 219–46.

76 Ibid.

crops of African origin: hyacinth bean (*Lablab purpureus*), pearl millet (*Pennisetum glaucum*), sorghum (*Sorghum bicolor*), and finger millet (*Eleusine coracana*),[77] although none of the latter displaced the indigenous millets as staple grains. Cotton, flax, and fruit tree aboriculture also probably date from this period.[78]

The ecological background to the movement of the native species from their natural environment into manmade contexts has been explored, and it has been suggested that as the area became more arid in the late Holocene, forests retreated and food resources, including pulses and millets, from the forest margins became scarce.[79] This scarcity encouraged people to manage wild stands of edible plants, which increased their productivity, eventually leading to an entangled relationship between plants and humans that gave rise to domesticated crops.[80] For early farmers in this area, the comparative availability of wild foods would have reduced reliance on cultivated, or managed, plants. As aridity increased, these foods were less available, perhaps contributing to the diversification of agriculture seen *c.* 2000–1400 BCE. Expanding the range of cultivated crops creates a buffer against detrimental environmental variants, such as drought. Where one crop might fail, another, the insurance crop, will succeed. In addition finger millet can be stored for a very long period of time with little loss of grain, a characteristic exploited in the risk-avoidance strategies of societies living in arid and semi-arid environments today.

## Conclusion

In very general terms the development of the Neolithic in South Asia followed the classic pattern of the 'Neolithic Revolution'. It saw the establishment of permanent settlements for the first time, the creation and adoption of agricultural practices, and the development of pottery manufacturing. Most of the trademarks of the Neolithic, such as ceramics, sedentism, livestock, and textiles, were present at the end of the period. However, precisely

77 D.Q. Fuller and N. Boivin, 'Crops, cattle and commensals across the Indian Ocean: current and potential archaeobiological evidence', *Etudes Océan Indien*, 42–3 (2009), 13–46.
78 E. Asouti and D.Q. Fuller, *Trees and Woodlands of South India: Archaeological Perspectives* (Walnut Creek, CA: Left Coast Press, 2007); D.Q. Fuller, 'Domestication, diffusion and the development of agriculture villages: a study of the south Indian Neolithic', in Raven (ed.), *South Asian Archaeology*, 143–58.
79 Asouti and Fuller, *Trees and Woodlands*.
80 D.Q. Fuller et al., 'Cultivation as slow evolutionary entanglement: comparative data on rate and sequence of domestication', *Vegetation History and Archaeobotany*, 21/2 (2012), 131–45; Fuller et al., 'Consilience of genetics'.

when these elements were first incorporated into the archaeological record varied between regions and did not occur all at once. The South Asian Neolithic therefore needs to be seen as a protracted transformation episode. Just as improved archaeobotanical evidence for crop domestication processes,[81] where it is available, points to a protracted evolutionary transition from wild to domesticated plants, so too the cultural elements of the Neolithic developed and became interlinked gradually and by differing pathways in different regions. One of the factors that contributed to this was that agriculture co-existed with foraging in many areas and for a very long time.

Nevertheless, within South Asia we can identify at least three major pathways to the developed Neolithic package. In the northwest (Baluchistan), sedentism, cereal farming, and livestock pastoralism evolved early on. This followed a model similar to that of Southwest Asia, in which grain-based breads were central to food traditions, substantial mud-brick buildings were built, and ceramics developed as a later addition. In the Ganges plains we see very early ceramics used by wetland foragers, akin perhaps to some of the East Asian late Pleistocene traditions,[82] but in this case co-existing with persistent 'Mesolithic' aceramic hunters. Here rice cultivation emerged slowly, with commitment to agriculture, domesticated rice, livestock, and sedentism developing perhaps 5,000 years after the initial elements of the Neolithic are first seen (like ceramics and ground stone). In the savannas of India, best documented in the southern Deccan, pastoralism was incorporated into a seasonal mobile savanna and woodland seed-gathering tradition. It may be that this tradition expanded from the Thar desert margin southwards after the adoption of sheep, goats, and cattle from across the Thar desert to the west (Fuller's 'Savanna corridor' hypothesis[83]). But if so, it is still the case that potting traditions (based on coiled ceramics), local plant domestications, and the development of the ashmound tradition were largely indigenous innovations in the southern Deccan. Eastern and northeastern India remain too poorly documented for the transition to be characterized in terms of comparative origins.

---

81 Fuller et al., 'Cultivation as slow evolutionary entanglement'; D.Q. Fuller et al., 'Convergent evolution and parallelism in plant domestication revealed by an expanding archaeological record', *Proceedings of the National Academy of Sciences* (2014), doi:10.1073.
82 See e.g. Fuller and Rowlands, 'Ingestion and food technologies'; Y. Kuzmin, 'Two trajectories in the Neolithization of Eurasia: pottery versus agriculture (spatiotemporal patterns)', *Radiocarbon*, 55/2 (2013), 1304–13.
83 Fuller, 'Finding plant domestication'.

Taken on a global scale, South Asia provides two major pathways into agriculture from primary hunter-gatherers, in the Ganges and south India. But current evidence suggests that, more frequently than not, agriculturalists moved into a new area or local foragers adopted elements of the Neolithic from elsewhere. A diverse range of domesticates and food production practices can be seen in the Neolithic Indian subcontinent. Ultimately this diversity came to support one of the largest concentrations of dense human population of any world region, accounting for 15–20 per cent of the global population today on just 2.73 per cent of global landmass.

## Further reading

Allchin, B. and F.R. Allchin. *The Rise of Civilisation in India and Pakistan*. Cambridge University Press, 1982.

Allchin, F.R. *Neolithic Cattle-Keepers of South India: A Study of the Deccan Ashmounds*. Cambridge University Press, 1963.

Basa, K.K. and P. Mohanty (eds.). *Archaeology of Orissa*, vol. 1. New Delhi: Pratibha Prakashan, 2000.

Boivin, N. 'Landscape and cosmology in the south Indian Neolithic: new perspectives on the Deccan ashmounds.' *Cambridge Archaeological Journal*, 14 (2004), 235–57.

Fuller, D.Q. 'Finding plant domestication in the Indian subcontinent.' *Current Anthropology*, 52, Supplement 4 (2011), S347–62.

'South Asia: archaeology.' In I. Ness and P. Bellwood (eds.), *The Encyclopedia of Global Human Migration*, vol. 1. Chichester: Wiley-Blackwell, 2013.

Many of Fuller's articles can be found online at www.ucl.ac.uk/archaeology/people/staff/fuller

Johansen, P.G. 'Landscape, monumental architecture, and ritual: a reconsideration of the south Indian ashmounds.' *Journal of Anthropological Archaeology*, 23 (2004), 309–30.

Meadow, R.H. 'The origins and spread of agriculture and pastoralism in northwestern South Asia.' In D.R. Harris (ed.), *The Origins and Spread of Agriculture and Pastoralism in Eurasia*. London: UCL Press, 1996. 390–412.

Morrison, K.D. and L.L. Junker (eds.). *Forager-Traders in South and Southeast Asia: Long-Term Histories*. Cambridge University Press, 2002.

Petrie, C.A. (ed.). *Sheri Khan Tarakai and Early Village Life in the Borderlands of North-West Pakistan: Bannu Archaeological Project Surveys and Excavations 1985–2001*. Bannu Archaeological Project Monographs 1. Oxford: Oxbow, 2010.

Possehl, G.L. *The Indus Civilization: A Contemporary Perspective*. Walnut Creek, CA: AltaMira Press, 2002.

Settar, S. and R. Korisettar (eds.). *Indian Archaeology in Retrospect*. 4 vols. New Delhi: Indian Council of Historical Research, 2002.

Singh, P. *Neolithic Cultures of Western Asia*. London and New York: Seminar Press, 1974.

Tewari, R. et al. *Pragdhara*, 19 (2008/9). (This is the most recent issue of *Pragdhara*. Each issue includes excavation reports and archaeological papers from across India, and from the Palaeolithic to Historical periods.)

Weber, S.A. and W.R. Belcher (eds.). *Indus Ethnobiology*. Lanham, MD: Lexington, 2003.

# Mehrgarh, Pakistan

CAMERON A. PETRIE

Mehrgarh is the best-known early village site in South Asia, and presents the earliest evidence for sedentary occupation, agriculture, and pastoralism thus far discovered.[1] The site has played a key role in discussion of the date and dynamics of the adoption of agriculture in the subcontinent, but as Kingwell-Banham et al. review in Chapter 10 in this volume, there was more than one South Asian Neolithic. The shift to farming occurred in a number of discrete regions in the subcontinent, and each process was enabled and constrained by various factors, including differences in the distribution of plant and animal species suitable for domestication, seasonal rainfall patterns, and local environmental conditions. Mehrgarh is particularly significant as it prompts discussion about the degree to which the origins of early farming and pastoralism in western South Asia were the product of indigenous processes, and also about the role played by plant species, animal species, and possibly also populations moving into South Asia from elsewhere, particularly West Asia.

Mehrgarh lies at the foot of the Bolan Pass at the northern end of the Kacchi plain in Baluchistan, Pakistan, and this chapter will review the Neolithic and Chalcolithic period occupation at the site. The Kacchi plain lies in the transition

---

1 C. Jarrige et al. (eds.), *Mehrgarh: Field Reports 1974–1985 from Neolithic Times to the Indus Civilization* (Karachi: Department of Culture and Tourism, Government of Sindh, Pakistan, in collaboration with the French Ministry of Foreign Affairs, 1995); J.-F. Jarrige et al., 'Mehrgarh Neolithic: the updated sequence', in C. Jarrige and V. Lefèvre (eds.), *South Asian Archaeology 2001*, 2 vols. (Paris: Éditions Recherche sur les Civilisations, 2005), vol. I, 129–41; J.-F. Jarrige et al., *Mehrgarh: Neolithic Period – Seasons 1997–2000* (Paris: Éditions de Boccard, 2013); J.-F. Jarrige, 'Mehrgarh Neolithic: new excavations', in M. Taddei and G. De Marco (eds.), *South Asian Archaeology 1997* (Rome: Instituto italiano per l'Africa e l'Oriente, 2000), 259–83; J.-F. Jarrige, 'Mehrgarh Neolithic', *Pragdhara*, 18 (2008), 135–54; J.-F. Jarrige and C. Jarrige, 'Premiers pasteurs et agriculteurs dans le sous-continent Indo-Pakistanais', *Palevol*, 5 (2006), 463–72; also R.H. Meadow, 'The origins and spread of agriculture and pastoralism in northwest South Asia', in D.R. Harris (ed.), *The Origins and Spread of Agriculture and Pastoralism in Eurasia* (London: UCL Press, 1996), 393.

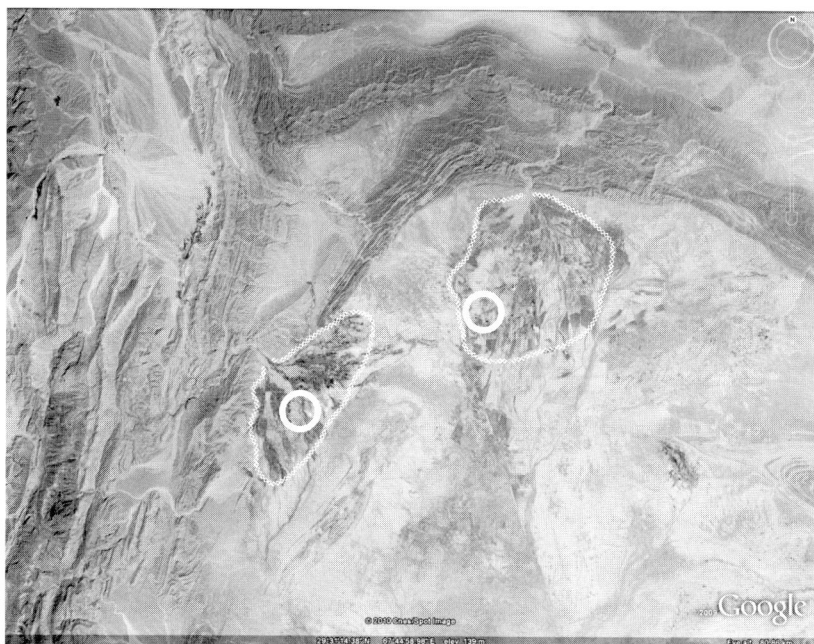

Figure 11.1 Google Earth™ image showing the location of Mehrgarh (circled to left) in relation to the location of the later Pirak (circled to right), each site lying on a separate alluvial fan.

zone between the Indus plains and the Iranian plateau, and is essentially an alluvial fan produced by the erosive action of the Bolan River (Figure 11.1).[2] Mehrgarh was excavated by the French Archaeological Mission to Pakistan in 1974–86, 1997, and 2000 under the direction of J.-F. and C. Jarrige. This review draws heavily on the project's publications.

Mehrgarh is perhaps best referred to as an archaeological complex, as it is comprised of several separate areas of occupation spread over a c. 4 km stretch of the right bank of the Bolan River, covering an area of 300 ha (Figure 11.2). Sedentary occupation here was displaced episodically, such that the use of individual areas appears to have been largely sequential. The occupational sequence has been divided into eight major phases (I–VIII), which span the period from c. 6000–2000 BCE, though it has been suggested that the site was first occupied as early as c. 7000 BCE. This review will outline

2 C.A. Petrie and K.D. Thomas, 'The topographic and environmental context of the earliest village sites in western South Asia', Antiquity, 86 (2012), 1055–67.

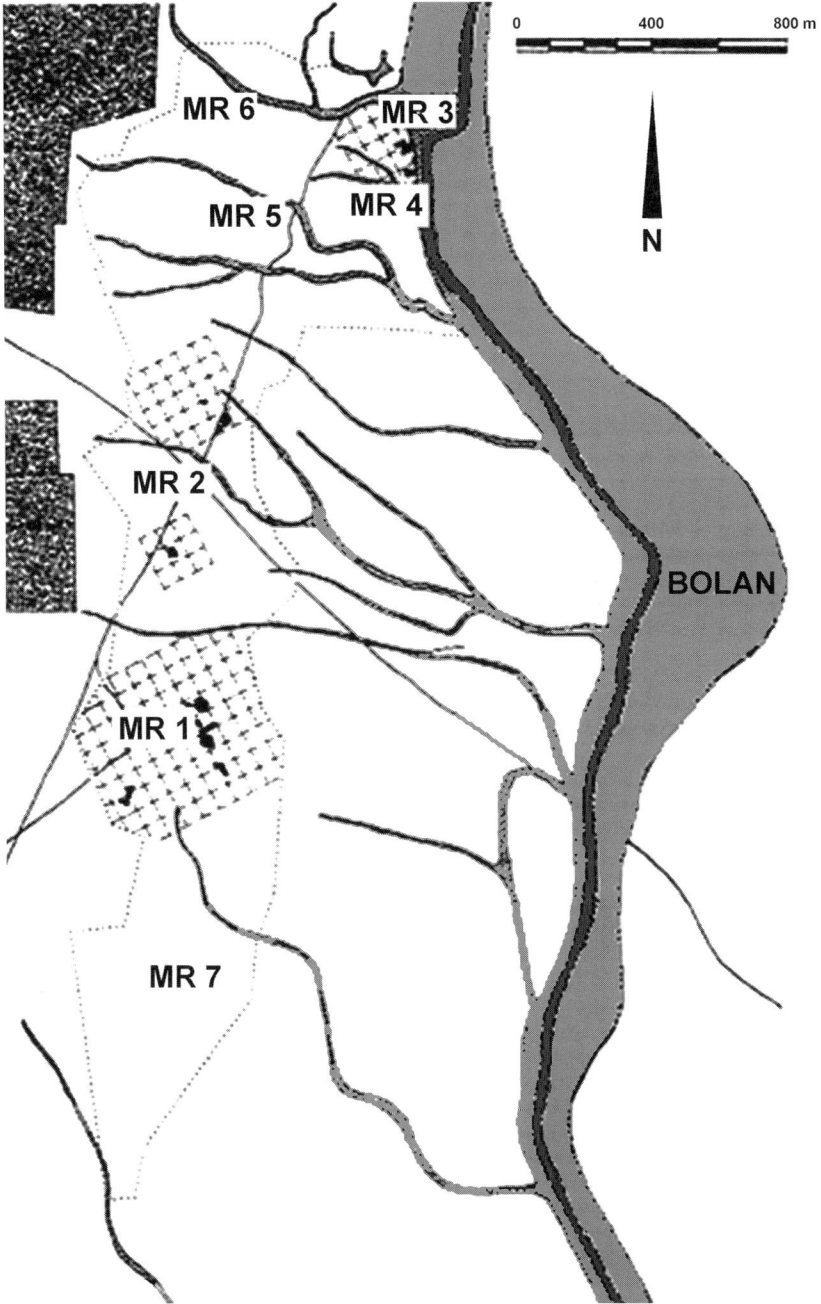

Figure 11.2 Map of Mehrgarh showing the location of excavated areas in relation to the course of the Bolan River.

the 'Neolithic' occupation at the site, which is divided into three phases (periods I, IIA, and IIB); and will also discuss the phases of 'Chalcolithic' occupation: periods III, IV, and V.[3]

Throughout its history, Mehrgarh did not exist in isolation, and material evidence demonstrates that its inhabitants interacted with populations in the hills and piedmonts of the Sulaiman Range, which form the western borderlands of the subcontinent, and populations on the Iranian plateau proper to the far west.[4] It nonetheless remains the most comprehensively investigated early village settlement in Baluchistan and the surrounding regions.

## Aceramic early villages in South Asia

There are outstanding questions about the processes that led to the establishment of the first sedentary villages like Mehrgarh. The rise and dispersal of farming practices in South Asia likely must have seen the displacement of pre-existing mobile hunter-gatherer populations, the conversion of these populations to an agricultural lifestyle, and/or their co-existence with settled populations.

### Life at Mehrgarh period I

The earliest occupation at Mehrgarh was exposed in area MR 3 and comprises 7 m of stratified deposits made up of the remains of nine separate building phases.[5] These levels are ostensibly aceramic, though they contain fired ceramic figurines and remains of asphalt-covered baskets. The earliest period I levels are characterized by a barley-dominated agricultural economy, with the evidence for cereal exploitation primarily coming from grain impressions and charred remains preserved in mud bricks. Naked six-row barley (*Hordeum vulgare*) makes up more than 90 per cent of the seeds and

---

3 Jarrige et al. (eds.), *Mehrgarh: Field Reports*, 56–7, fig. 3; Jarrige et al., 'Mehrgarh Neolithic', 130; Jarrige et al., *Mehrgarh: Neolithic Period*; C. Jarrige, 'Human figurines from the Neolithic levels at Mehrgarh (Balochistan, Pakistan)', in U. Franke-Vogt and H.-J. Weisshaar (eds.), *South Asian Archaeology 2003* (Aachen: Linden Soft, 2005), 27–37 (27); Jarrige and Jarrige, 'Premiers pasteurs et agriculteurs'; Jarrige, 'Mehrgarh Neolithic'; J.G. Shaffer, 'The Indus valley, Baluchistan, and Helmand traditions: Neolithic through Bronze Age', in R.W. Ehrich (ed.), *Chronologies in Old World Archaeology*, 3rd edn, 2 vols. (University of Chicago Press, 1992), vol. I, 441–64 (443, 452ff.), vol. II, 425–46 (fig. 6).

4 See Chapter 10 in this volume.

5 Jarrige et al. (eds.), *Mehrgarh: Field Reports*, 57; Jarrige et al., 'Mehrgarh Neolithic: the updated sequence', 131, fig. 2; Jarrige et al., *Mehrgarh: Neolithic Period*; Jarrige, 'Mehrgarh Neolithic: new excavations'; Jarrige, 'Human figurines'; also Shaffer, 'Indus valley', vol. I, 454; G.L. Possehl, *Indus Age: The Beginnings* (Philadelphia: University of Pennsylvania Press, 1999), 464.

impressions identified, while domestic hulled six-row and wild and domestic hulled two-row barley were also present, and very low proportions of domestic emmer, domestic einkorn, and a free threshing wheat were attested.[6] The faunal assemblage for period 1 is dominated by wild species, including gazelle, goats, sheep, deer, buffalo, and cattle, though significant numbers of goat kids in burials and the remains of relatively small subadult or adult animals in trash deposits indicate that behaviourally domesticated goats were exploited from the earliest levels.[7] The earliest inhabitants of the site thus appear to have engaged in hunting in combination with the cultivation of domesticated crops and keeping of domesticated animals. Mehrgarh period 1 appears to have been at least partly contemporaneous with the earliest aceramic levels at the site of Kili Gul Muhammad, which is situated in the Quetta valley, at the other end of the Bolan Pass.[8]

The earliest structures at Mehrgarh are predominantly made of mud or mud brick, and comprise small cell-like rooms that have hearths and occupation deposits containing stone and bone tools.[9] J.-F. Jarrige et al. have long noted that there are clear similarities in craft products, architecture, and agricultural practices between Mehrgarh and the earliest Neolithic sites in the central and northern Zagros in Iran, which until recently were the closest aceramic sites known to the west (see below). Jarrige et al. have, however, also argued that diffusion from west to east is unlikely, and favour parallel developments achieved by populations that had indirect contact through groups living in the intervening regions.[10]

---

6 L. Costantini, 'The beginning of agriculture in the Kachi plain: the evidence of Mehrgarh', in B. Allchin (ed.), *South Asian Archaeology 1981* (Cambridge University Press, 1984), 29–33; Jarrige et al. (eds.), *Mehrgarh: Field Reports*, 63–4; Jarrige et al., *Mehrgarh: Neolithic Period*; Meadow, 'Origins and spread of agriculture', 393–5.

7 R.H. Meadow, 'Early animal domestication in South Asia: a first report of the faunal remains from Mehrgarh, Pakistan', in H. Härtel (ed.), *South Asian Archaeology 1979* (Berlin: Dietrich Reimer, 1981), 143–79, 'Notes on the faunal remains from Mehrgarh, with a focus on cattle (*Bos*)', in Allchin (ed.), *South Asian Archaeology 1981*, 34–40, 'Faunal exploitation in the greater Indus valley: a review of recent work to 1980', in J. Jacobson (ed.), *Studies in the Archaeology of India and Pakistan* (New Delhi: American Institute of Indian Studies, and Oxford & IBH Publishing, 1986), 46–64, 'Animal domestication in the Middle East: a revised view from the eastern margin', in G.L. Possehl (ed.), *Harappan Civilization: A Recent Perspective*, 2nd rev. edn (New Delhi: Oxford University Press, 1993), 295–320, and 'Origins and spread of agriculture', 402ff.; Jarrige et al., *Mehrgarh: Neolithic Period*.

8 Shaffer, 'Indus valley', vol. 1, 453; Jarrige et al., 'Mehrgarh Neolithic: the updated sequence', 64.

9 Jarrige et al., 'Mehrgarh Neolithic: the updated sequence', fig. 1; Jarrige et al., *Mehrgarh: Neolithic Period*; Shaffer, 'Indus valley', vol. 1, 443.

10 Jarrige et al. (eds.), *Mehrgarh: Field Reports*, 65; Jarrige et al., *Mehrgarh: Neolithic Period*.

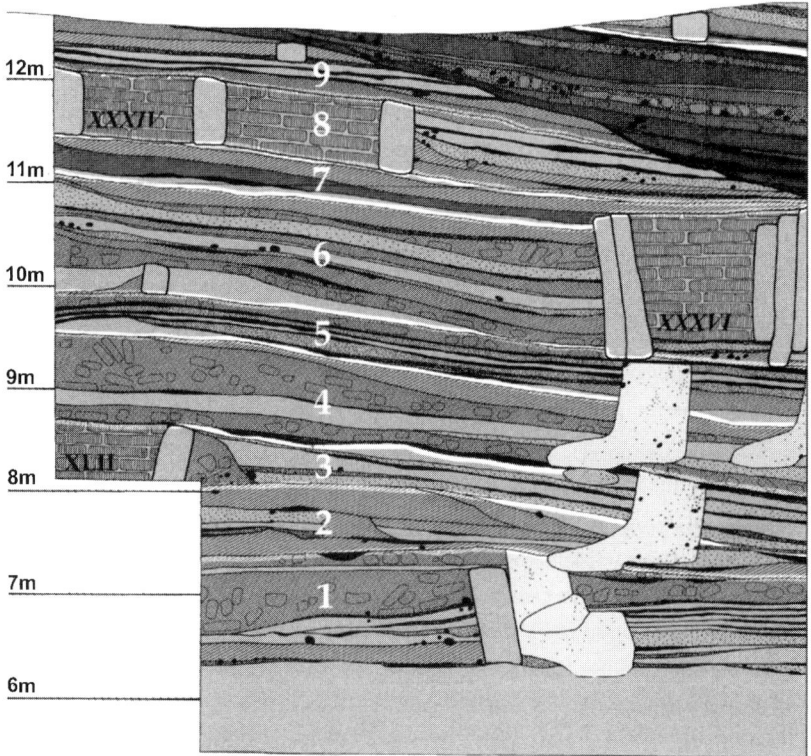

Figure 11.3 Reproduction of the section along the river adjacent to MR 3 South, showing alternating levels of occupation and grave pits.

### Relative and absolute dating of the Kili Gul Muhammad phase

The protracted sequence of occupation attested in the period I deposits at MR 3 has been used to suggest that the earliest occupation at the site might have begun *c.* 7000 BCE, or even earlier in the eighth millennium.[11] A critical piece of evidence used to support a more extended chronology for the sequence of aceramic levels at MR 3 is the depth of the stratigraphy in this part of the site (Figure 11.3). The period I occupation at Mehrgarh was, however, not continuous in any one area of MR 3 and new structures appear to have then been erected adjacent to older ones. Abandoned structures were filled with

---

11 Jarrige, 'Mehrgarh Neolithic: new excavations', 280–3; Shaffer, 'Indus valley', vol. I, 453; Meadow, 'Animal domestication in the Middle East', and 'Origins and spread of agriculture', 393; Jarrige et al., 'Mehrgarh Neolithic: the updated sequence', 141; Jarrige, 'Human figurines', 27; Jarrige and Jarrige, 'Premiers pasteurs et agriculteurs'.

rubbish while they were collapsing, and graves containing single or multiple inhumations of adult and subadult individuals were excavated into the accumulating debris.[12] These burials often contained young goats and/or a range of artefacts, some of which were manufactured from raw material not available locally, such as marine shell, lapis lazuli, and turquoise (Figure 11.4).[13] It is notable that the grave pits do not cut through mud-brick walls, suggesting that the decaying walls were still visible when the graves were being dug. When the newly built structures were subsequently abandoned, the earlier decaying walls were levelled and new structures were erected in the original area. Jarrige et al. have drawn on modern ethnographic observations on the longevity of unbaked mud-brick structures to suggest that each of these occupation phases is likely to have been thirty to forty years in duration.[14] Although a range of variation is to be expected, this estimate is likely to be broadly accurate when taking an average of the duration of multiple phases. The eighteen phases of period I occupation might thus reasonably be expected to span between 540 and 720 years.

Although an early date is claimed for Mehrgarh period I, it is not supported by an unambiguous sequence of absolute dates. In fact, the range of extant radiocarbon dates from period I is problematic and cannot be used to outline a clear absolute chronology, so relative indicators are typically used instead. There were very few charred seeds preserved in period I deposits, and the preservation of charcoal in the earliest levels is poor, and both of these factors may have contributed to the inconsistent radiocarbon determinations for this period.[15] There have been several modifications to the phasing of the period I deposits, and they were initially divided into IA aceramic and IB ceramic levels,[16] and it is not yet clear how this revision affects the available absolute dating evidence.

J.-F. Jarrige's estimate of thirty to forty years for the life of a mud-brick building suggests that the eighteen structural phases of Mehrgarh period I may have spanned up to c. 720 years, assuming continuous occupation throughout the period. Given that period IIA is dated by secure radiocarbon dates spanning c. 5470–4700 BCE (see below), then it is possible that the aceramic occupation at Mehrgarh began in the very late seventh millennium

12 Jarrige et al., 'Mehrgarh Neolithic: the updated sequence', 132.
13 Shaffer, 'Indus valley', vol. I, 443–4; Jarrige et al., *Mehrgarh: Neolithic Period*.
14 Jarrige et al., 'Mehrgarh Neolithic: the updated sequence', 132.
15 Jarrige et al., 'Mehrgarh Neolithic: the updated sequence'; Jarrige and Jarrige, 'Premiers pasteurs et agriculteurs'; also Meadow, 'Origins and spread of agriculture', 393; Jarrige, 'Mehrgarh Neolithic: new excavations', 281.
16 Jarrige et al., 'Mehrgarh Neolithic: the updated sequence', 130.

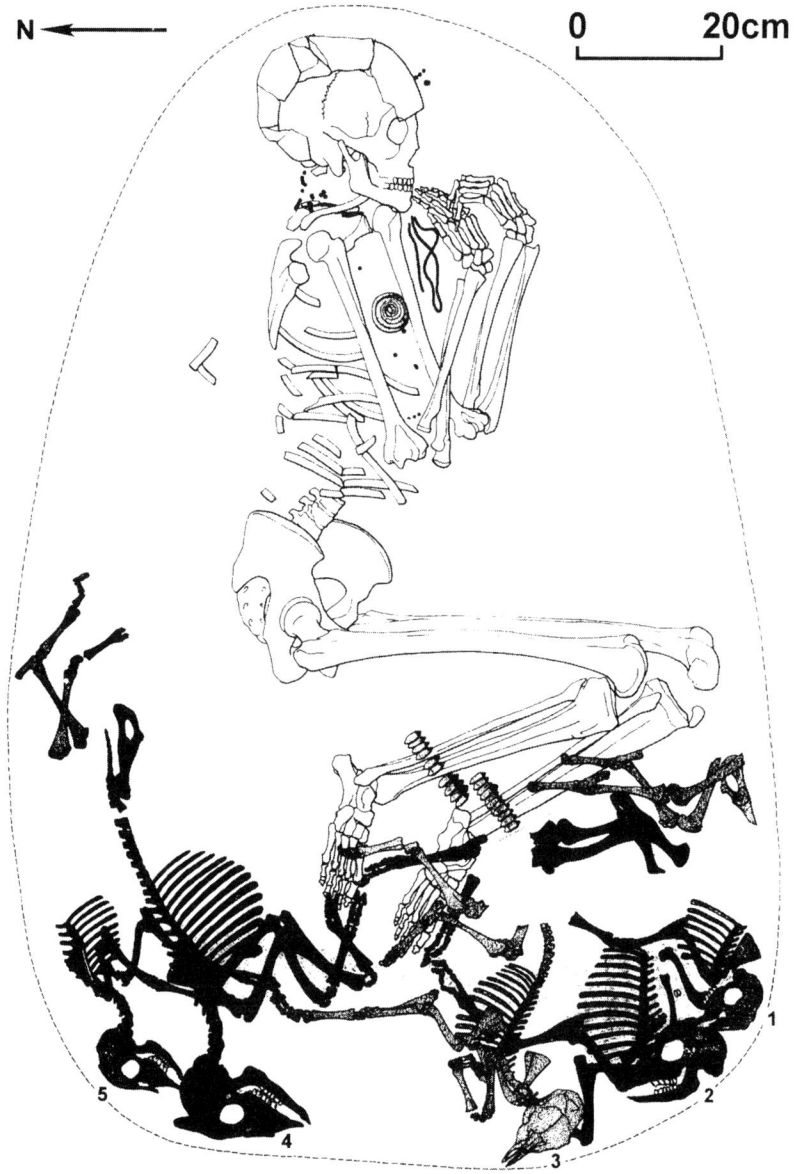

Figure 11.4 Plan of Burial 287, Mehrgarh period I.

BCE, though this assumes that the end of period I and the beginning of period IIA are coeval. However, based on the stratigraphy exposed in the Bolan River profile, it has been suggested that there may have been a substantial gap between the period I and period IIA occupation layers,[17] so it is likely that the date for the establishment of Mehrgarh period I will only be determined accurately through a future radiocarbon dating programme.

### Domestication: local, imported, or both?

The cereals present in Mehrgarh period I (naked six-row barley, domestic hulled six-row barley, wild and domestic hulled two-row barley, domestic emmer, domestic einkorn, and a free threshing wheat) represent several of the founder crops of Southwest Asian agriculture, though notably none of the pulse domesticates have been attested. Zohary and Hopf have shown that the Fertile Crescent is the centre of the distribution of wild barley, but report what have been interpreted as 'weedy forms' in Afghanistan and the areas of Baluchistan that are close to Mehrgarh.[18] While this distribution makes it possible that barley might have been domesticated locally, Meadow has noted that the truly wild forms found in Mehrgarh period I deposits could be field weeds, and pointed out that wild barley is not identified in any post-period I deposits there or elsewhere in South Asia.[19]

Genetic evidence indicates that barley landraces in Greater Asia fall into two genetically distinct clusters, one with an origin in the Levant and the other somewhere to the east of the Fertile Crescent, possibly in the Zagros foothills or even further east.[20] This eastern genetic group appears to have contributed the most to the genetic diversity of barley in regions stretching from Central Asia to the Far East, suggesting that all of the samples that have

17 Jarrige et al. (eds.), *Mehrgarh: Field Reports*, 60; Jarrige et al., 'Mehrgarh Neolithic: the updated sequence', 130.

18 D. Zohary and M. Hopf, *Domestication of Plants in the Old World*, 3rd edn (Oxford University Press, 2000), 54, maps 4 and 5; also D.Q. Fuller, 'Neolithic cultures', in D.M. Pearsall (ed.), *Encyclopedia of Archaeology* (New York: Academic Press, 2008), fig. 5.

19 Meadow, 'Origins and spread of agriculture', 395; though see also Jarrige et al. (eds.), *Mehrgarh: Field Reports*, 63ff.

20 P.L. Morrell and M.T. Clegg, 'Genetic evidence for a second domestication of barley (*Hordeum vulgare*) east of the Fertile Crescent', *Proceedings of the National Academy of Sciences*, 104 (2007), 3289–94 (3291); T.A. Brown et al., 'The complex origins of domesticated crops in the Fertile Crescent', *Trends in Ecology and Evolution*, 24 (2009), 103–9 (107); G. Jones et al., 'DNA evidence for multiple introductions of barley into Europe following dispersed domestications in Western Asia', *Antiquity*, 87 (2013), 701–13; also F. Salamini et al., 'Genetics and geography of wild cereal domestication in the Near East', *Nature Reviews Genetics*, 3 (2002), 429–41; D. Saisho and M.D. Purugganan, 'Molecular phylogeography of domesticated barley traces expansion of agriculture in the Old World', *Genetics*, 177 (2007), 1765–76.

been analysed from these areas share a similar genetic identity. The two domestication clusters were not entirely independent, however, and Jones et al. have shown that this eastern group made a genetic contribution to the flowering-time adaptation of the cultivated barley types found in Europe.[21] The presence of early village sites in the western Zagros, such as Jarmo and Ali Kosh, has led to the suggestion that this region might be the source of this eastern genetic group of barley, but Morrell and Clegg have noted that as Mehrgarh also lies at the easternmost range of wild barley, a local domestication there is possible.[22] While not necessarily disagreeing with this proposal, Salamini et al. and Saisho and Purugganan have hypothesized that the eastern variant of barley is partly due to the genetic influence of strands in the Himalayas.[23] This evidence is far from conclusive when it comes to the situation in South Asia, largely because these analytical projects have used very few accessions from areas to the east of the Fertile Crescent, and no samples taken from the critical zones of modern Afghanistan and Pakistan, so the role of Mehrgarh in the domestication of barley remains unclear.

In contrast to barley, Mehrgarh is located well outside the distribution of the wild progenitors of both domesticated einkorn and emmer wheat, which are limited to the Near Eastern arc or the Fertile Crescent.[24] Given that wild varieties of these grasses do not occur further east than the central-western Zagros, it is likely that domesticated varieties of both crops were introduced to the rest of the Iranian plateau and the regions beyond to the north and southeast. It can only be presumed that the domesticated strands found in period I deposits at Mehrgarh were imported into Baluchistan at some point, either by incoming populations bringing seeds with them, or local populations obtaining seeds from afar through exchange.[25]

As with barley, there have been recent attempts to characterize the ancient genetics of wheat, although much of this research has focused on Europe. Analysis of diploid goat grass (*Aegilops tauschii*) and hexaploid wheat (*Triticum*

---

21 H. Jones et al., 'Population-based resequencing reveals that the flowering time adaptation of cultivated barley originated east of the Fertile Crescent', *Molecular Biology and Evolution*, 25 (2008), 2211–19 (2211).

22 Morrell and Clegg, 'Genetic evidence', 3291; also Brown et al., 'Complex origins', 107.

23 Salamini et al., 'Genetics and geography'; Saisho and Purugganan, 'Molecular phylogeography'.

24 Zohary and Hopf, *Domestication of Plants*, 35, 44, maps 1 and 3; also Meadow, 'Origins and spread of agriculture', 395.

25 Cf. D.R. Harris, 'The origins and spread of agriculture and pastoralism in Eurasia: an overview', in Harris (ed.), *Origins and Spread of Agriculture*, 552–73 (563); Meadow, 'Origins and spread of agriculture', 395; D.Q. Fuller, 'Agricultural origins and frontiers in South Asia: a working synthesis', *Journal of World Prehistory*, 20 (2006), 1–86 (22ff.).

*aestivum*) suggests that hexaploid wheat is likely to have originated in south-east Turkey or northern Syria, in the heartland of the Fertile Crescent,[26] which supports the suggestion that domesticated wheat was introduced to Mehrgarh. Nevertheless, as with barley, a clearer impression benefiting from genetic analysis of wheat will require the analysis of more samples from the subcontinent.

Given the likelihood that the various species of wheat seen in Mehrgarh period 1 were introduced into Baluchistan, there is certainly a possibility that domesticated barley was introduced as well. However, the apparent absence of pulses in the earliest levels at Mehrgarh might indicate that the entire range of Southwest Asian founder crops did not arrive in South Asia at the same time, and in fact, it is still not precisely clear when pulses did arrive.[27] The pattern of crop adoption at Mehrgarh has implications for our understanding of how the Southwest Asian founder crops moved around. These crops in Southwest Asia have often been described as a 'package', but the evidence from Mehrgarh suggests that they did not necessarily spread as such to other regions. The earliest domestic cereals being used at Mehrgarh may thus represent the first of several sets of crops introduced from Southwest Asia and elsewhere.

As noted above, the faunal assemblage for Mehrgarh period 1 is dominated by wild species, though behaviourally domesticated goats were likely present from the earliest levels. Detailed genetic research on the spread of domesticated animals has primarily focused on the diffusion of domesticated species out of the Fertile Crescent westwards into Europe. In contrast, the dynamics that were in operation to the east of the central-western Zagros are poorly understood. Analysis of mitochondrial DNA from modern domestic goats and bezoar (the wild ancestor) collected from across the entire distribution range of the bezoar, including numerous samples from Pakistan, has shown

26  R.J. Giles and T.A. Brown, 'GluDy allele variations in *Aegilops tauschii* and *Triticum aestivum*: implications for the origins of hexaploid wheats', *Theoretical and Applied Genetics*, 112 (2006), 1563–72.
27  Meadow, 'Origins and spread of agriculture', 396; M. Tengberg, 'Crop husbandry at Miri Qalat Makran, SW Pakistan (4000–2000 BC)', *Vegetation History and Archaeobotany*, 8 (1999), 3–12; D.Q. Fuller, 'Harappan seeds and agriculture: some considerations', *Antiquity*, 75 (2001), 410–14, 'An agricultural perspective on Dravidian historical linguistics: archaeological crop packages, livestock and Dravidian crop vocabulary', in P. Bellwood and C. Renfrew (eds.), *Examining the Farming/Language Dispersal Hypothesis* (Cambridge: McDonald Institute for Archaeological Research, 2003), 191–213 (193), 'Indus and non-Indus agricultural traditions: local developments and crop adoptions on the Indian peninsula', in S.A. Weber and W.R. Belcher (eds.), *Indus Ethnobiology: New Perspectives from the Field* (Lanham, MD: Lexington, 2003), 343–96 (350), and 'Agricultural origins and frontiers in South Asia', 20.

there is no haplotype in the modern population that could have been domesticated in the east of the Iranian plateau or regions further east.[28] Of the two centres of domestication identified, the one stretching across the central Iranian plateau to the southern Zagros contributed relatively little to modern mtDNA, while the other stretches from the central to the northern Zagros and into eastern Anatolia, and is the zone that appears to be the centre of origin for all modern domestic goats. Naderi et al. state unequivocally that goats were not domesticated in the area of the Indus valley, and that their results suggest that the early Neolithic goats found in the subcontinent most likely came to the region from over 1,000 km to the west.[29] These results have dramatic ramifications for claims that Mehrgarh was an independent centre of goat domestication, and it will be important to analyse ancient samples from the site, as it is possible, though perhaps unlikely, that the modern populations sampled by Naderi et al. may in the intervening millennia have completely replaced an ancient population domesticated in South Asia.

Sheep and cattle increasingly came to dominate the faunal assemblage over the course of period 1 at Mehrgarh, and the animals decreased in size, which is a common marker used to identify domestication.[30] Genetic studies carried out in the 1980s suggest, however, that all modern domestic sheep appear to have come from a single Southwest Asian ancestor (*Ovis orientalis*), and this is supported by more recent genetic research using mtDNA and chromosomal analysis.[31] These findings preclude an independent South Asian domestication of sheep, unless more recently imported breeds completely replaced a population domesticated in the eastern regions. Given the apparent definitiveness of the genetic evidence, it may be most parsimonious to accept that the domesticated sheep exploited by the Mehrgarh 1 population were introduced into the subcontinent.

The evidence for cattle, in particular *Bos indicus*, is quite different. MtDNA analysis has shown that there is a marked genetic distinction between humpless (taurine) and humped (zebu) cattle (zebu-specific alleles), which, taken in conjunction with the zooarchaeological analysis of the bones from

28  S. Naderi et al., 'The goat domestication process inferred from large-scale mitochondrial DNA analysis of wild and domestic individuals', *Proceedings of the National Academy of Sciences*, 105 (2008), 17659–64.

29  Ibid., 17663.   30  Meadow, 'Origins and spread of agriculture', 403.

31  H.-P. Uerpmann, 'The origins and relations of Neolithic sheep and goats in the western Mediterranean', in J. Guilane et al. (eds.), *Premières communautés paysannes en Méditerranée occidentale* (Paris: CNRS, 1987), 175–9; S. Hiendleder et al., 'The complete mitochondrial DNA sequence of the domestic sheep (*Ovis aries*) and comparison with the other major ovine haplotype', *Journal of Molecular Evolution*, 47 (1998), 441–8.

Mehrgarh, indicates that the zebu was domesticated from wild stock locally in South Asia, or possibly eastern Iran.[32] MtDNA research focusing only on South and East Asian zebu has suggested that the most likely centre of domestication was the Indus valley, *c.* 6000 BCE,[33] and the faunal remains from Mehrgarh may attest to this process occurring there.

Taken as a whole, the bioarchaeological evidence thus suggests that the earliest inhabitants of Mehrgarh engaged in hunting and gathering in combination with the cultivation of domesticated crops and the exploitation of some domesticated animals. Although there is some zooarchaeological and genetic evidence for domestication taking place locally (e.g. zebu), it now appears that the majority of the constituents of the agropastoral economy exploited at Mehrgarh in period I were imported domesticates (wheat, goats, sheep, and possibly barley). This reconstruction implies that there were long-range interactions between the inhabitants of the relatively small number of known aceramic settlements spread through the borderlands of South Asia and across the Iranian plateau. Nevertheless, the variation between the domestic plant and animal species used at Mehrgarh period I and those seen at aceramic sites further to the west suggests that there may not have been a simple process of transferring a complete or packaged subsistence economy from one region to another; rather, it was both complex and nuanced.

### Long-range links and dispersals in the aceramic Neolithic

Until recently, the closest known aceramic Neolithic sites to Mehrgarh lay over 1,500 km to the west in the central Zagros (Ganj Dareh, Tepe Abdul Hossein, Jarmo, and Tepe Guran), and in lowland Susiana (Ali Kosh, Chogha Bonut, and Chogha Mish). New aceramic sites have, however, now been found in south-west and southeast Iran (Tappeh Rahmatabad, Tell-e Atashi), which have added significantly to our understanding of the distribution of aceramic Neolithic settlements.[34] Radiocarbon dates from Tappeh Rahmatabad suggest

---

32  R.T. Loftus et al., 'Evidence for two independent domestications of cattle', *Proceedings of the National Academy of Sciences*, 91 (1994), 2757–61; Meadow, 'Origins and spread of agriculture', 403; D.E. MacHugh et al., 'Microsatellite DNA variation and the evolution, domestication and phylogeography of taurine and zebu cattle (*Bos taurus* and *Bos indicus*)', *Genetics*, 146 (1997), 1071–86; C.J. Edwards et al., 'Taurine and zebu admixture in Near Eastern cattle: a comparison of mitochondrial, autosomal and Y-chromosomal data', *Animal Genetics*, 38 (2007), 520–4; S. Chen et al., 'Zebu cattle are an exclusive legacy of the South Asia Neolithic', *Molecular Biology and Evolution*, 27 (2010), 1–6.

33  Chen et al., 'Zebu cattle'.

34  R. Bernbeck et al., 'Rahmatabad: dating the aceramic Neolithic in Fars province', *Neo-Lithics*, 1 (2008), 37–9; O. Garazhian, 'Darestan: a group of Pre-Pottery Neolithic (PPN) sites in south-eastern Iran', *Antiquity*, 83/319 (2009), Project Gallery.

that the aceramic Neolithic villages in Fars were later than those in the central-western Zagros, so it would appear that there is no specific reason why the date for the establishment of Mehrgarh should be sought through direct parallels with the earlier central-western Zagros sites.

Evidence for trade bringing exotic raw materials such as lapis lazuli to Mehrgarh indicates that long-range contacts were maintained over several millennia, so there should be no doubt that this earliest phase of village occupation in South Asia was one where people and ideas could be spread widely. While several of the domesticated plant and animal species seen at Mehrgarh in period I were not domesticated locally, it is not yet possible to establish whether we are looking at cultural diffusion, where farming was adopted by local foragers, demic diffusion, where farmers moved onto the Kacchi plain from elsewhere, or some combination of the two processes taking place in tandem.

It appears that Mehrgarh period I was at least partly contemporaneous with the earliest levels at Kili Gul Muhammad, and the latter's location at the top of the Bolan Pass implies that its inhabitants interacted with the people living at Mehrgarh, possibly in the form of transhumance, as and when the seasons demanded.[35] Possehl identified a total of nineteen other aceramic Neolithic sites in the western borderlands of South Asia, though not all of these were permanent settlements.[36] The earliest sedentary populations in South Asia thus appear to have been relatively small, and to have favoured specific ecological zones for the establishment of their settlements. In this earliest stage, it is likely that sedentary populations co-existed with hunter-gatherers, and at least at Mehrgarh, it appears that the initial farming populations also engaged in hunting.

## Early ceramic production at villages in South Asia

Mehrgarh period IIA saw the appearance of the earliest known fired ceramic vessels in South Asia, the first substantial mud-brick buildings, clear indications of specific craft activities, and a marked development of the agricultural subsistence economy of the settlement's inhabitants.[37] The period IIA

---

35 Shaffer, 'Indus valley', vol. I, 453; Possehl, *Indus Age*, 442ff., table 4.10; also Jarrige et al. (eds.), *Mehrgarh: Field Reports*, 64.
36 Possehl, *Indus Age*, figs. 4.14 and 4.28, table 4.13; Chapter 10 above.
37 Meadow, 'Early animal domestication in South Asia', and 'Origins and spread of agriculture', 403; Shaffer, 'Indus valley', vol. I, 453; Jarrige et al. (eds.), *Mehrgarh: Field Reports*, 62ff.

deposits at MR 3 were superimposed above those of period I, so the nature of the transition between the two periods is unclear.

### The origins and development of ceramic production at Mehrgarh

Fragments of small numbers of handmade bowls and jars made using chaff-tempered clay and formed through the use of a sequential slab construction technique and baskets were found in period IIA at Mehrgarh.[38] Similar pottery was seen at Kili Gul Muhammad (Burj Basket-Marked ware).[39] The fact that evidence for the formative stages of this technology is present suggests that the technology of producing pottery may have developed locally at Mehrgarh in response to the need for containers more efficient than asphalt-covered baskets. This technology is, however, closely related to the widely dispersed soft-ware tradition that is evidenced all over the Iranian plateau during the sixth millennium BCE.[40] Later-period IIA levels were also exposed in MR 4, and are characterized by the appearance of a small number of red-ware sherds with relatively fine walls that were produced using the same ceramic production technology seen at MR 3, although the use of an iron-rich slip is occasionally evident.[41]

It is not yet clear how the early use of ceramics at Mehrgarh fits into the pattern of dispersal of ceramic use across the southern and northern parts of the Iranian plateau, which has been interpreted as a clear instance of migration and colonization from west to east.[42] From later phases and millennia,

---

38  P.B. Vandiver, 'The production technology of early pottery from Mehrgarh', in Jarrige et al. (eds.), *Mehrgarh: Field Reports*, 648–61 (649–51); also Jarrige et al. (eds.), *Mehrgarh: Field Reports*, 61; Possehl, *Indus Age*, 464–5.

39  W.A. Fairservis, *Excavations in the Quetta Valley, West Pakistan* (New York: American Museum of Natural History, 1956).

40  P.B. Vandiver, 'Sequential slab construction: a conservative Southwest Asiatic ceramic tradition, c. 7000–3000 BC', *Paléorient*, 13 (1987), 9–35; C.A. Petrie et al., 'Ceramic vessels from Sheri Khan Tarakai', in C.A. Petrie (ed.), *Sheri Khan Tarakai and Early Village Life in the Borderlands of North-West Pakistan*, Bannu Archaeological Project Monographs 1 (Oxford: Oxbow, 2010), 71–193; C.A. Petrie, '"Culture", innovation, and interaction across southern Iran from the Neolithic to the Bronze Age (6500–3000 BC)', in B. Roberts and M. Vander Linden (eds.), *Investigating Archaeological Cultures: Material Culture, Variability and Transmission* (New York: Springer, 2011), 151–82.

41  Vandiver, 'Production technology', 650–1; also Jarrige et al. (eds.), *Mehrgarh: Field Reports*, 62.

42  D.R. Harris and C. Gosden, 'The beginnings of agriculture in western Central Asia', in Harris (ed.), *Origins and Spread of Agriculture*, 370–89; L.R. Weeks et al., 'The Neolithic settlement of highland SW Iran: new evidence from the Mamasani district', *Iran*, 44 (2006), 1–31 (24); D.R. Harris, *Origins of Agriculture in Western Central Asia: An Environmental-Archaeological Study* (Pittsburgh: University of Pennsylvania Museum of Archaeology and Anthropology, 2010).

there is clear evidence that pottery production at Mehrgarh became more standardized and more refined at an earlier stage than it did in areas further west, and there is also evidence that ceramic technological developments in Baluchistan impacted on the production technologies of eastern Iran.[43] If various aspects of ceramic production technology developed indigenously in Baluchistan, then the overall similarities in the approach to production make it likely that the earliest potters at Mehrgarh were interacting with potters living on the Iranian plateau. This reinforces the likelihood that there was a significant degree of interaction and perhaps even interdependence between the early village populations across a wide geographic area.

In addition to the appearance of pottery vessels, Mehrgarh period IIA saw an increase in the size of the settled area, and there is evidence for the construction of storage structures for grain, although the buildings are still relatively small and compartmented. The burials of period IIA were all associated with a mud-brick wall or platform, and grave goods included stone tools, ceramic vessels, red ochre, and strings of beads made from marine shell, turquoise, lapis lazuli, and other non-local stones.[44]

There were notable changes in the types of ceramics being used by the inhabitants of Mehrgarh during period IIB. A fine ware with little chaff temper and a fine paste that has been fired to a higher temperature were introduced and these appear together with coarse-ware vessels. By the end of period IIB, the ceramic vessels began to be decorated with simple motifs that developed into more complex motifs executed on a red slip in period III.[45] White-fired steatite beads and a small number of copper objects also appear.[46]

## A developing subsistence economy

There are notable changes evident in the subsistence economy in Mehrgarh period IIA, including the almost complete replacement of the wild animal component of the diet with domesticates, the majority of which were cattle

---

43 Vandiver, 'Production technology', 652; B. Mutin, 'Cultural dynamics in southern Middle-Asia in the fifth and fourth millennia BC: a reconstruction based on ceramic traditions', *Paléorient*, 38 (2012), 159–84, and 'Ceramic traditions and interactions on the south-eastern Iranian plateau during the fourth millennium BC', in C.A. Petrie (ed.), *Ancient Iran and its Neighbours: Local Developments and Long-Range Interactions in the Fourth Millennium BC*, British Institute of Persian Studies Archaeological Monographs Series 3 (Oxford: Oxbow, 2013), 253–75.

44 Shaffer, 'Indus valley', vol. I, 454; Jarrige et al. (eds.), *Mehrgarh: Field Reports*, 61; Jarrige et al., *Mehrgarh: Neolithic Period*.

45 Shaffer, 'Indus valley', vol. I, 454; Vandiver, 'Production technology', 650–1; Jarrige et al., *Mehrgarh: Neolithic Period*.

46 Jarrige et al. (eds.), *Mehrgarh: Field Reports*, 67; Jarrige et al., *Mehrgarh: Neolithic Period*.

(over 50 per cent), and lesser numbers of sheep and goats. Meadow has argued that this progressive increase in numbers of cattle and the synchronous decrease in their size provide robust support for a local domestication at Mehrgarh.[47]

### Dating the Burj Basket-Marked phase (Mehrgarh IIA–IIB)

It has been suggested that Mehrgarh periods IIA and IIB cover the whole of the sixth millennium BCE, but radiocarbon determinations securely date period IIA to c. 5470–4700 cal BCE, and period IIB to c. 4700–4000 cal BCE.[48] Possehl has argued that the chronology for all of the early village phases (Kili Gul Muhammad/Mehrgarh I and Burj Basket-Marked/Mehrgarh IIA–IIB phases) has not been established through the use of reliable radiocarbon determinations.[49]

Although there is evidence for increases in the number of settlements, the size of settlements, and the area settled after the appearance of ceramics, it is entirely possible that there were still some non-sedentary populations subsisting wholly, or principally, by hunting and gathering in the borderlands and other parts of western South Asia. Petrie and Thomas have pointed out that many of the newly sedentary settlements are situated on alluvial fans, which goes some way to reinforcing a model where specific ecological niches were being preferentially selected by farming groups moving into new areas, rather than one where populations expanded in existing locales.[50] Fans are beneficial ecological niches, but they are also restricted in their size and carrying capacity, thereby limiting the size of populations that could be supported in each location.

## Further technological developments at villages in South Asia

### Increasing sophistication in ceramic production at Mehrgarh

Excavations in the uppermost levels at MR 4 and MR 2 revealed evidence for increasing sophistication of the ceramic decoration repertoire during

---

47  Meadow, 'Early animal domestication in South Asia', 'Notes on the faunal remains from Mehrgarh', and 'Origins and spread of agriculture', 403; Shaffer, 'Indus valley', vol. I, 454.
48  Jarrige et al. (eds.), *Mehrgarh: Field Reports*, 63; Jarrige, 'Mehrgarh Neolithic: new excavations', 280–3; Jarrige, 'Human figurines', 27; Shaffer, 'Indus valley', vol. I, 453–4; Meadow, 'Origins and spread of agriculture', 393.
49  Possehl, *Indus Age*, 446.
50  Petrie and Thomas, 'Topographic and environmental context'.

Mehrgarh period III (cf. Kili Gul Muhammad periods II and III, and Possehl's Togau phase).[51] New fine wares appear together with coarse chaff-tempered pottery that is nonetheless hard and well-fired (Burj Basket-Marked ware). The finer vessels show signs of the introduction of the tournette to the production process, where vessels have signs of circumferential strokes on the exterior and banded decoration, and towards the end of this phase finger-impressed wares are also attested.[52] These clear changes to the ceramic industry suggest that there was a significant intensification and evolution of production activities, including the use of non-plastic clay as temper (Nazim Hard Clay), and also the development of considerable skill in fixing coloured pigments and maintaining particular body colours through firing techniques that created alternating oxidizing and reducing conditions.[53]

### The appearance of metal artefacts at Mehrgarh

Fragments of copper rods and pins are attested in Mehrgarh period III deposits, as well as crucible fragments with melted copper ore adhering, providing explicit evidence of local copper production.[54] These discoveries have led to this phase being described as the beginning of a Chalcolithic period at the site, though this terminology is not applicable for all contemporaneous settlements in the region. Areas with evidence for lapidary craft and shell-working were also exposed at Mehrgarh, suggesting that these industries were developing locally. The increased use of non-local stone types suggests that the earlier patterns of communication and interaction were continuing. Craft activities appear to have been carried out in specific areas at the settlement, separate from habitation areas.

### Dating Mehrgarh period III (Togau phase), population dispersal, and nascent regionalism in the hills and piedmonts

Mehrgarh period III (Togau phase) is dated to *c.* 4000–3500 BCE, and Possehl has identified a total of 119 possible Togau phase sites (including Kili Gul

---

51 Fairservis, *Excavations in the Quetta Valley*, 365–7; Shaffer, 'Indus valley', vol. I, 454; Jarrige et al. (eds.), *Mehrgarh: Field Reports*, 68; also B. de Cardi, 'Excavations and reconnaissance in Kalat, West Pakistan: the prehistoric sequence in the Surab region', *Pakistan Archaeology*, 2 (1965), 86–182, and *Archaeological Surveys in Baluchistan, 1948 and 1957*, no. 8 (London: Institute of Archaeology, 1983); Possehl, *Indus Age*, 490.
52 Vandiver, 'Production technology', 651; Shaffer, 'Indus valley', vol. I, 454; Jarrige et al. (eds.), *Mehrgarh: Field Reports*, 250, fig. 5.14.
53 Jarrige et al. (eds.), *Mehrgarh: Field Reports*, 71; Shaffer, 'Indus valley', vol. I, 454; also R.P. Wright, 'Fine ware traditions at Mehrgarh', in Jarrige et al. (eds.), *Mehrgarh: Field Reports*, 662–71.
54 Jarrige et al. (eds.), *Mehrgarh: Field Reports*, 72; Shaffer, 'Indus valley', vol. I, 454.

Muhammad III, Sur Jangal I–II, Surab II, Rana Ghundai I–II, the early levels at Periano Ghundai, and the initial phases at Sheri Khan Tarakai and Jhandi Babar). This marks a dramatic increase in the sedentary population of western South Asia and indicates that there were significant changes in the patterns of settlement during this period (estimated aggregate settled area: 295 ha).[55] In general, there are similarities in Togau phase ceramics across an area stretching from southern Baluchistan to southern Khyber Pakhtunkhwa. This indicates that there was interaction between the populations of those areas via northern Baluchistan, and there is also the possibility that they shared ideologies and ways of life.

### The development of polychrome ceramic decoration

Period IV and V deposits at Mehrgarh revealed evidence for polychrome ceramic decoration (Kechi Beg ware), alongside the coarse and fine wares being used in previous periods, and wet wares also appear, and Jarrige et al. have argued that the development of polychromy was a local phenomenon.[56] Seals made from terracotta, bone, and steatite also appear during periods IV and V, and the range of flint tools declined, suggesting an increase in the importance of copper tools. There were also changes in the way that storage and craft activities were organized and the locations where they were carried out in the settlement.[57] Mehrgarh IV and V appear to correspond with Kili Gul Muhammad IV, Damb Sadaat I, Surab III, late Sur Jangal III, Rana Ghundai III–IV, and also possibly Dabar Kot and Periano Ghundai, which all share a growing sophistication in ceramic production technology. Although copper artefacts dating to this phase have been discovered at Mehrgarh, they have not yet been attested at other sites in Baluchistan.

### Dating the Kechi Beg phase (Mehrgarh periods IV–V)

Various date ranges have been put forward for Mehrgarh periods IV and V, ranging from c. 3500–3000 cal BCE to c. 3800–3200 cal BCE,[58] but there are no well-stratified radiocarbon dates from sites in northern Baluchistan, so the

---

55 Shaffer, 'Indus valley', vol. I, 454; Jarrige et al. (eds.), *Mehrgarh: Field Reports*, 69; C.A. Petrie et al., 'Chronology of Sheri Khan Tarakai', in Petrie (ed.), *Sheri Khan Tarakai*, 343–52; C.A. Petrie et al., 'The investigation of early villages in the hills and on the plains of western South Asia', in Petrie (ed.), *Sheri Khan Tarakai*, 7–28; Possehl, *Indus Age*, tables 4.19, 4.20, figs. 4.43, 4.44.

56 Jarrige et al. (eds.), *Mehrgarh: Field Reports*, 75.

57 Shaffer, 'Indus valley', vol. I, 455; Jarrige et al. (eds.), *Mehrgarh: Field Reports*, 71–6.

58 Shaffer, 'Indus valley', vol. I, 455; G.L. Possehl, *The Indus Civilization: A Contemporary Perspective* (Walnut Creek, CA: AltaMira Press, 2002), 29.

proposed date ranges are based entirely on relative ceramic parallels. The protracted early village phase at Mehrgarh thus appears to extend throughout the sixth, fifth, and much of the fourth millennia BCE.

## Conclusion

The site of Mehrgarh exemplifies the distinct stages in the transition from a subsistence system based largely on mobile hunter-gathering to one based on sedentary farmer-herding, the subsequent dispersal of the agropastoral subsistence economy based on wheat, barley, sheep, goats, and cattle, and the progressive sophistication in craft production in western South Asia. At a fundamental level, the excavations at Mehrgarh demonstrate that this protracted process was characterized by a complex interplay between a range of local developments and the diffusion of various plant and animal species, and their associated practices, into western South Asia. It is, however, clear that the inhabitants of this settlement played a major role in the origins of farming practices in South Asia, the domestication of the zebu, and the development of a range of technological innovations in pottery production and lapidary craft and metal-working that would ultimately go on to have a dramatic impact on the populations of the Indus plains and the Indo-Iranian borderlands.

## Further reading

Costantini, L. 'The beginning of agriculture in the Kachi plain: the evidence of Mehrgarh.' In B. Allchin (ed.), *South Asian Archaeology 1981*. Cambridge University Press, 1984. 29–33.

Fairservis, W.A. *Excavations in the Quetta Valley, West Pakistan*. New York: American Museum of Natural History, 1956.

Fuller, D.Q. 'Agricultural origins and frontiers in South Asia: a working synthesis.' *Journal of World Prehistory*, 20 (2006), 1–86.

'Harappan seeds and agriculture: some considerations.' *Antiquity*, 75 (2001), 410–14.

'Indus and non-Indus agricultural traditions: local developments and crop adoptions on the Indian peninsula.' In S.A. Weber and W.R. Belcher (eds.), *Indus Ethnobiology: New Perspectives from the Field*. Lanham, MD: Lexington, 2003. 343–96.

'Neolithic cultures.' In D.M. Pearsall (ed.), *Encyclopedia of Archaeology*. New York: Academic Press, 2008. 756–68.

Harris, D.R. *Origins of Agriculture in Western Central Asia: An Environmental-Archaeological Study*. Pittsburgh: University of Pennsylvania Museum of Archaeology and Anthropology, 2010.

'The origins and spread of agriculture and pastoralism in Eurasia: an overview.' In D.R. Harris (ed.), *The Origins and Spread of Agriculture and Pastoralism in Eurasia*. London: UCL Press, 1996. 552–73.

Jarrige, C. 'Human figurines from the Neolithic levels at Mehrgarh (Balochistan, Pakistan).' In U. Franke-Vogt and H.-J. Weisshaar (eds.), *South Asian Archaeology 2003*. Aachen: Linden Soft, 2005. 27–37.

Jarrige, C., J.-F. Jarrige, R.H. Meadow, and G. Quivron (eds.). *Mehrgarh: Field Reports 1974–1985 from Neolithic Times to the Indus Civilization*. Karachi: Department of Culture and Tourism, Government of Sindh, Pakistan, in collaboration with the French Ministry of Foreign Affairs, 1995.

Jarrige, J.-F. 'Mehrgarh Neolithic.' *Pragdhara*, 18 (2008), 135–54.

Jarrige, J.-F., C. Jarrige, and G. Quivron. 'Mehrgarh Neolithic: the updated sequence.' In C. Jarrige and V. Lefèvre (eds.), *South Asian Archaeology 2001*. 2 vols. Paris: Éditions Recherche sur les Civilisations, 2005. vol. i, 129–41.

Jarrige, J.-F., C. Jarrige, G. Quivron, and L. Wengler. *Mehrgarh: Neolithic Period – Seasons 1997–2000*. Paris: Éditions de Boccard, 2013.

Meadow, R.H. 'The origins and spread of agriculture and pastoralism in northwest South Asia.' In D.R. Harris (ed.), *The Origins and Spread of Agriculture and Pastoralism in Eurasia*. London: UCL Press, 1996. 390–412.

Mutin, B. 'Cultural dynamics in southern Middle-Asia in the fifth and fourth millennia BC: a reconstruction based on ceramic traditions.' *Paléorient*, 38 (2012), 159–84.

Petrie, C.A., J.R. Knox, F. Khan, K.D. Thomas, and J.C. Morris. 'The investigation of early villages in the hills and on the plains of western South Asia.' In C.A. Petrie (ed.), *Sheri Khan Tarakai and Early Village Life in the Borderlands of North-West Pakistan: Bannu Archaeological Project Surveys and Excavations 1985–2001*. Bannu Archaeological Project Monographs 1. Oxford: Oxbow, 2010. 7–28.

Petrie, C.A. and K.D. Thomas. 'The topographic and environmental context of the earliest village sites in western South Asia.' *Antiquity*, 86 (2012), 1055–67.

Possehl, G.L. *Indus Age: The Beginnings*. Philadelphia: University of Pennsylvania Press, 1999.

Shaffer, J.G. 'The Indus valley, Baluchistan, and Helmand traditions: Neolithic through Bronze Age.' In R.W. Ehrich (ed.), *Chronologies in Old World Archaeology*. University of Chicago Press, 1992. vol. i, 441–64, vol. ii, 425–46.

Tengberg, M. 'Crop husbandry at Miri Qalat Makran, SW Pakistan (4000–2000 BC).' *Vegetation History and Archaeobotany*, 8 (1999), 3–12.

Vandiver, P.B. 'The production technology of early pottery from Mehrgarh.' In Jarrige et al. (eds.), *Mehrgarh: Field Reports 1974–1985*. 648–61.

Wright, R.P. 'Fine ware traditions at Mehrgarh.' In Jarrige et al. (eds.), *Mehrgarh: Field Reports 1974–1985*. 662–71.

Zohary, D. and M. Hopf. *Domestication of Plants in the Old World*. 3rd edn. Oxford University Press, 2000.

## 12

# Early agriculture in China

XINYI LIU, DORIAN Q. FULLER, AND MARTIN JONES

China's vast landmass ranges across contrasting ecological extremes, from tropical in the south, to sub-Arctic in the north, and alpine in the west (Map 12.1). Seventy per cent of this landmass is composed of mountains, plateaux, and hills, and over a substantial part of the country, particularly the continental interior, the availability of water is critical. These features have led to an agriculture that is diverse in its crop ecology, elaborate in its management of water, and at its most intense in the lowlands in the east of the country.

In the west, the cloud capture and montane glaciers provide a critical source of water, feeding China's two longest rivers, the Yangtze and the Yellow River. The Yangtze runs approximately 6,500 km to the sea at Shanghai, through hilly regions into swampy lowlands, along its course draining a fifth of China's land surface. The Yellow River runs approximately 5,500 km through the loess plateau towards the Bohai Sea. The lower reaches of those two rivers frame the northern and southern borders of China's most productive stretch of lowland, the Central Plain, the arena within which much of the history of Chinese civilization has played out. These two rivers have an enduring association with important staple cereals: the Yangtze with rice, and the Yellow River with the Asian millets (broomcorn and foxtail).

Their catchments also include the loci of the domestication of these cereals, but at some remove from lower reaches and plains in which their cultivation subsequently became the most intense. The earliest archaeological sites for the millets are in the middle reaches of the Yellow River in the loess plateau, and also along the foothills that arise at some considerable distance from the river itself. Long before the water in the valley bottom could be effectively managed, the capture of run-off in foothills and elevated locations was critical to the emergence of northern agriculture. The earliest sites for rice are in the middle and lower Yangtze as well as in the Huai River just to the north. These early rice locales are associated with docile minor

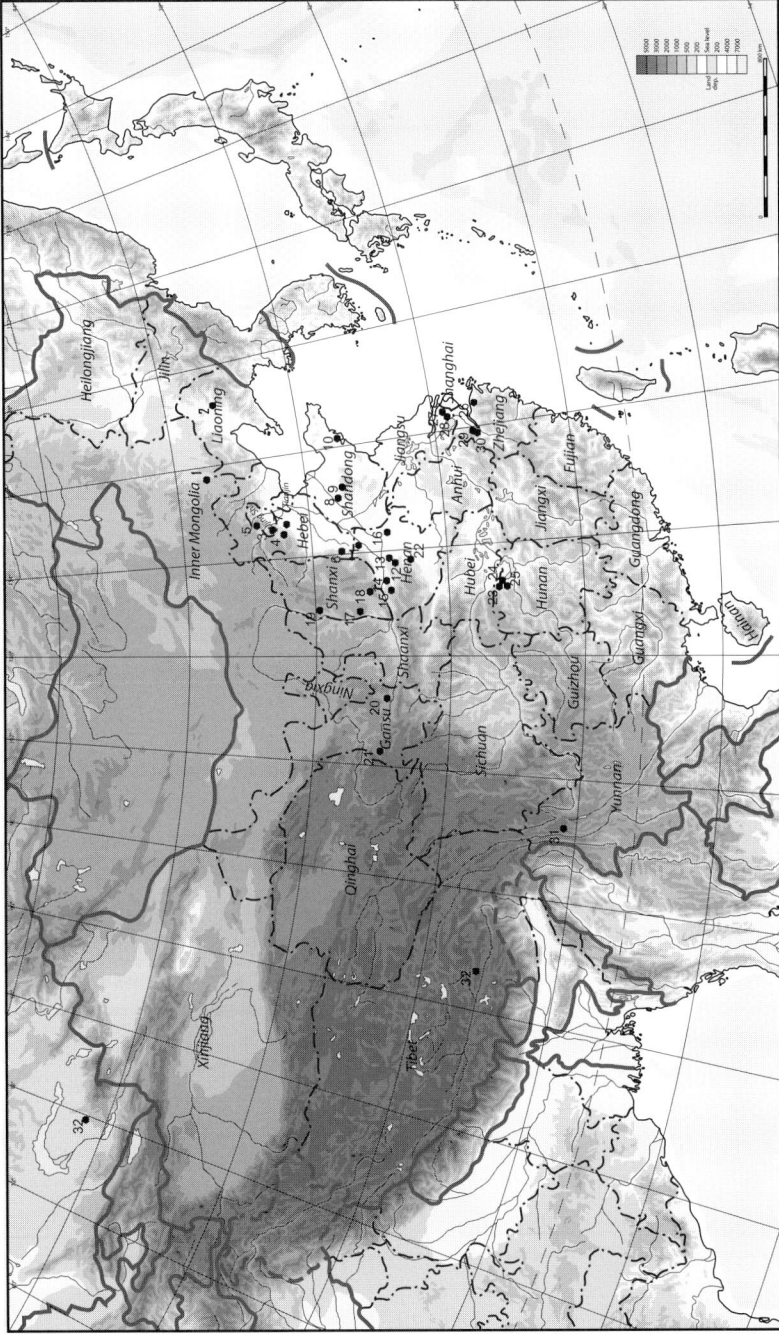

Map 12.1 China showing principal regions and sites mentioned in the text. Key for the map: 1. Xinglonggou; 2. Xinle; 3. Zhoukoudian; 4. Nanzhuangtou; 5. Donghulin; 6. Cishan; 7. Taixi; 8. Yuezhuang; 9. Daxinzhuang; 10. Zhaojiazhuang; 11. Anyang; 12. Peiligang; 13. Shawoli; 14. Wuluoxipo; 15. Erlitou; 16. Xishuipo; 17. Shizitan; 18. Xiachuan; 19. Liulin; 20. Dadiwan; 21. Linjia; 22. Jiahu; 23. Pengtoushan; 24. Chengtoushan; 25. Bashidang; 26. Hemudu; 27. Chudun; 28. Caoxieshan; 29. Mojiashan; 30. Maoshan; 31. Haimenkou; 32. Changguogou; 33. Begash.

tributaries and the wetlands of distal floodplains where cultivation could be more easily managed. By the second millennium BCE, the agrarian management had extended downstream, and the high energy of the main rivers was moderated by irrigation management of increasing scale and complexity. This practice emerges in the documentary record of the first millennium BCE in the form of substantial hydraulic projects associated with named engineers, such as Sunshu Ao (sixth century), Ximen Bao (fifth century), and Li Bing (third century).[1]

To the north of this principal arena of Chinese agriculture, the Central Plain is flanked by the Gobi desert, and beyond that a belt of steppe that continues westwards across Eurasia. Ecologically, both regions are constrained by water scarcity and the severity and length of the winter season. They have nonetheless been of considerable cultural and agricultural significance. For several episodes of China's past, the northern communities have held political sway over the south, and their mobility has facilitated the appearance in China of a range of animals of importance to agriculture, such as the horse and camel, and probably also sheep, goats, and taurine cattle. These mobile peoples around the northern and western fringes of China also facilitated the transfer of crops into and out of China.

The ten millennia of the Holocene in which agriculture has expanded is also a time in which the environment has undergone some change. A key dynamic element is the monsoonal system, comprising a warm, wet summer monsoon, and a cold, dry winter monsoon. The summer monsoon brings water from the Indian and Pacific Oceans onto much of the south and east of China and has a powerful ameliorative effect on the intrinsic aridity of the continental interior. The winter monsoon drives the movement of aeolian dust from the Gobi desert to the loess plateau. The sensitivity of that monsoonal system to fluctuations in the relative temperatures of land and ocean has rendered it the most variable part of the physical environment, critically affecting the water availability in many parts of China, particularly towards the south and east. In western China, the westerlies are the stronger determinants of water availability. A widespread consequence of these combined factors is a drier earlier Holocene and a wetter mid-Holocene, followed by a return to aridity. The timing of the moister mid-Holocene varies according to location in China, particularly in relation to the monsoons. In the loess plateau, for example, it runs from c. 8,500 BP to c. 5,000 BP, in other

---

1 F. Bray and J. Needham, *Science and Civilisation in China*, vol. VI: *Biology and Biological Technology*, Part II: *Agriculture* (Cambridge University Press, 1984).

words following the earliest episodes of cultivation but facilitating the spread and establishment of domestication, while predating the episode of food globalization discussed below.

## History of research

The study of plant and animal remains in China is as old as archaeology itself. Both were analysed in 1928 during the excavation of Zhoukoudian Cave where skeletal remains of *Homo erectus*, known as 'Peking Man', were recovered.[2] They were also both studied during the 1931 excavation of Anyang, believed to be one of the Shang dynasty capitals. The subsequent development of archaeology in China in many ways mirrors the changing social and political discourse of the twentieth century. Archaeological results are often used to justify social and political theories, whether nationalism or communism. Various authors have noted a close relation between Chinese archaeological practice and the building of national identity in the first half of the twentieth century and then subsequently the Marxist framework of history in the second half.[3]

Between 1949 and 1979 the People's Republic was organized under a centralized socialist power system. As in the Soviet Union, archaeological thinking was framed within a theory of linear social evolution. Publications on ancient agricultural systems in this period tended to focus upon relations of production and class struggle. A notable example is Guo Moruo's (1972) hypothesis on three stages of the development of Chinese societies: primary, slavery, and federalist society, relating to the archaeological records of Neolithic, Early Bronze Age, and Late Bronze Age.

In 1979, a more relaxed political atmosphere following the end of the Cultural Revolution and the implementation of economic reforms stimulated developments in all aspects of Chinese archaeology. More broadly, economic reform also opened China's doors to the world. Scholarly exchange between China and Western countries was actively encouraged, and Western archaeological methods and theories introduced. The number of articles dealing with prehistoric agriculture multiplied. In the 1980s, two periodicals were launched for publications of articles related to agriculture, *Nongye Kaogu* (Agricultural Archaeology) and *Gujin Nongye* (Ancient and Modern Agriculture).

---

2 X. Chen, *Zhongguo Shiqian Kaoguxue Shi Yanjiu: 1895–1949* (*The History of Prehistoric Archaeology in China: 1895–1949*) (Beijing: Sanlian Shudian [Joint Publishing], 1997).

3 X. Liu and M.K. Jones, 'When archaeology begins: the cultural and political context of Chinese archaeological thought', *Bulletin of History of Archaeology*, 18 (2008), 25–7.

Figure 12.1 Flotation to retrieve carbonized plant remains at Liulin, Shanxi province; Zhijun Zhao in the middle

Prior to the late 1990s, archaeobotanical data were sporadically collected without systematic use of flotation strategies (washing soil from excavations to retrieve organic remains: Figure 12.1). The documentation of archaeological plant remains was focused upon taxonomic identification. Chinese archaeobotany (the study of plant remains from archaeological excavations) was initiated at the turn of the 1990s, primarily inspired by international encounters. In 1986, following his visit to the University of Cambridge, Huang Qixu published an article in *Nongye Kaogu* introducing the flotation system that had been developed in the late 1960s and 1970s by Eric Higgs's group working on the early history of agriculture.[4] A subsequent account was published in the same journal by Xiong Haitang describing his observations during the visit to Nagoya University in Japan. This method was then applied in Liluo in 1992, an excavation led by the Chinese Academy of Social Sciences. Meanwhile, flotation machines modified from that originally designed by Patty Jo Watson in America (the SMAP type) were brought to East Asia by Toronto archaeobotanist Gary Crawford, first to Japan and Korea and subsequently to China. The last two decades have witnessed the widespread application of systematic flotation and the rapid development of archaeobotanical studies. Beijing archaeobotanist Zhijun Zhao (Figure 12.1) has played a pivotal role in encouraging the application of flotation in China. Zhao in 2011 reported on flotation-based archaeobotany at more than 80 archaeological sites across China: about 7,000 soil samples had been processed, and a significant quantity of charred plant remains recovered.[5] This rapid growth in archaeobotanical evidence has been accompanied by qualitative improvements in the analysis and interpretation of such evidence.

## Deep-seated culinary traditions of the East: boiling and steaming

Compared to other regions of the world, a striking feature of East Asian archaeology is the early date at which ceramics are found. Current evidence places pottery in the Yangtze region back some 18,000 years, with ceramics nearly as old in parts of Siberia and Japan, while in northern China ceramics were being made by the start of the Holocene 12,000 years ago.[6] These early ceramics were associated with hunter-gatherers, who used them for boiling fish and plant foods. By contrast, in Southwest Asia ceramics develop relatively late, *c.* 8,500 years ago, millennia after the beginnings of cultivation and

4 E.S. Higgs (ed.), *Papers in Economic Prehistory* (Cambridge University Press, 1972).
5 Z. Zhao, 'New archaeobotanic data for the study of the origins of agriculture in China', *Current Anthropology*, 52, Supplement 4 (2011), S295–304.
6 E. Boaretto et al., 'Radiocarbon dating of charcoal and bone collagen associated with early pottery at Yuchanyan Cave, Hunan province, China', *Proceedings of the National Academy of Sciences*, 106 (2009), 9595–600; Y.V. Kuzmin, 'Two trajectories in the Neolithization of Eurasia: pottery versus agriculture (spatiotemporal patterns)', *Radiocarbon*, 55 (2013), 1304–13.

domestication. While the Pre-Pottery Neolithic cultures of Southwest Asia made extensive use of querns for flour production and constructed clay ovens (tandoors) for baking bread and roasting foods (see Chapter 8), Neolithic China elaborated forms of ceramic vessel for boiling, steaming, and serving.[7]

So, in Western Asia early crops were processed for a flour-focused food system. While grinding stones were used in prehistoric China, boiling and steaming of grains and other foods appear to have been and remained the predominant East Asian methods for preparing foods. This contrast had consequences for the selection of grain quality features, with gluten proteins being selected in Western Eurasia for bread-making properties and starch properties being more variably selected in East Asian cereals, such as rice, millets, and even wheat varieties. It is clear that cooking traditions have persisted as distinctive and contrasting in China (and East Asia) as opposed to Southwest, Central, or South Asia.[8]

The ultimate expression of the East Asian culinary selection of grain quality is found in the sticky (or 'glutinous') cereals, including sticky rice and sticky millets. This stickiness is conferred by mutations to the waxy gene which reduce the amylose form of starch and increase the amylopectin form. Cereals with this trait, the glutinous rice, millets, and maize, are largely exclusive to East and Southeast Asia, defining what has been referred to as the 'glutinous endosperm starch' culture area.[9] That this trait has evolved in parallel in several species and multiple times in some of these, such as foxtail millet, points to a strong cultural preference since prehistory in at least part of China.

## Beginnings in the north: from millets to soybean and hemp

Two types of millet, broomcorn (*Panicum miliaceum*) and foxtail millet (*Setaria italica*: Figure 12.2), are believed to have originated in northern

---

7  D.Q. Fuller and M. Rowlands, 'Towards a long-term macro-geography of cultural substances: food and sacrifice traditions in East, West and South Asia', *Chinese Review of Anthropology*, 12 (2009), 1–37.

8  D.Q. Fuller and M. Rowlands, 'Ingestion and food technologies: maintaining differences over the long-term in West, South and East Asia', in T.C. Wilkinson et al. (eds.), *Interweaving Worlds: Systematic Interactions in Eurasia, 7th to the 1st Millennia BC* (Oxford: Oxbow, 2011), 37–60.

9  G. Eriksson, 'The waxy character', *Hereditas*, 63 (1969), 180–204; S. Sakamoto, 'Glutinous-endosperm starch food culture specific to Eastern and Southeastern Asia', in R. Ellen and K. Fukui (eds.), *Redefining Nature: Ecology, Culture and Domestication* (Oxford: Berg, 1996), 215–31.

Figure 12.2 Foxtail millet field in Aohan, near the Xinglonggou site

China. While these species are referred to by different names in Chinese in the past and present, the most common names are respectively *shu* and *su*. These were the staple calorie sources of the developed Neolithic in central China (the Yangshao, Dawenkou, and Longshan traditions), as well as the staple grains during the Shang and Zhou dynasties.[10]

The wild ancestor of foxtail millet is *Setaria viridis*, which is an annual grass widely distributed over a large part of East Asia. However, determining its original wild range and habitat is complicated by its proclivity for anthropogenic habits, both as an arable weed and as a volunteer on roadsides, probably including feral populations that derive genetically from the crop. (Indeed *S. viridis* is a widespread weed in North America where it was introduced through European plant translocations in the past few hundred years.) Nevertheless, probable primary habitats can be found in natural disturbed settings such as upper floodplains, including along the Yellow River and its many tributaries.

The wild progenitor for broomcorn millet, by contrast, remains debated. A candidate, at least in morphological terms, is provided by *Panicum miliaceum var. ruderale*, inferred as the wild progenitor by some scholars.[11] These *ruderale* types are widespread as weeds from eastern Europe to East Asia, but are

---

10 Bray and Needham, *Science and Civilisation in China*, 3–8.
11 D. Zohary and M. Hopf, *Domestication of Plants in the Old World*, 3rd edn (Oxford University Press, 2000).

unknown from non-anthropogenic habitats, making them plausibly feral. In contrast to foxtail millet, wild populations in likely primary habitats are unknown, although we expect them to have occurred in the drier north of the loess plateau and the Chinese steppe.

It remains the case that our knowledge about how the domesticated forms of broomcorn and foxtail millet evolved from their wild ancestor is limited. Unlike in the case of rice, wheat, or barley, archaeological data on the loss of seed dispersal, a key domestication trait, are lacking. Nevertheless, in most seed crops an increase in grain size evolved alongside the non-shattering trait.[12] This is one proxy that has shown potential for the Chinese millets. It has been noticed that millet grains show a gradual increase in size and change in shape over the Neolithic period. This has led scholars to speculate that the broomcorn millet (Figure 12.3) from the early Neolithic sites such as Xinglonggou (discussed in Chapter 13) is intermediate in caryopsis size and shape between modern domesticated and wild forms, and therefore

Figure 12.3 Carbonized remains of millet from Xinglonggou, dating to 7700 cal BCE.

12 D.Q. Fuller et al., 'Convergent evolution and parallelism in plant domestication revealed by an expanding archaeological record', *Proceedings of the National Academy of Sciences*, 111 (2014), 6147–52.

represents an early stage of domestication.[13] The increase of grain size and change of shape also appear to be associated with the increasing proportions of millet grains among archaeobotanical assemblages in northern China. Although the timing and process of millet domestication remain to be resolved, the above evidence would suggest that the domestication of millet and the development of early cultivation systems in northern China were a protracted process. Recent genetic research has clarified the geographic relationships of broomcorn millet.[14] While SSR microsatellite studies accommodate both a single (northern Chinese) origin and a dual origin across Eurasia, studies of loci affecting the 'waxy gene' (for grain 'stickiness', see above) are more concordant with an origin in a single region of northern China and a westward spread from there.

Two terminal Pleistocene sites on the loess plateau in Shanxi province have provided residue evidence and tool use-wear evidence for pre-agricultural plant use. Starch granules from Shizitan (*c.* 12,700–11,600 BP) have been identified for a range of plants including acorns (*Quercus* sp.), beans (*Vigna* sp.), tubers (*Dioscorea* sp.), and panicoid grasses.[15] The *Panicoideae* is the subfamily in which both broomcorn and foxtail are placed. In a separate account of the use-wear on grinding implements from Xiachuan (*c.* 23,900–16,400 BP), archaeologists have observed various patterns that may have resulted from different pounding and grinding movements.[16] One of those patterns appears to be similar to those for the grinding of moistened grains with soft husks. None of these data is directly associated with macro-fossil evidence for millet, but they nevertheless indicate the use of post-harvest processing techniques that would be appropriate for incorporating grains in the diet. Prior to the domestication of millets, the development of ceramic vessels suitable for boiling offered another possible method of preparing these hard seeds for consumption.

---

13 Z. Zhao, 'Cong Xinglonggou yizhi fuxuan jieguo tan Zhongguo beifang zaoqi nongye qiyuan wenti (Addressing the origins of agriculture in North China based on the results of flotation from the Xinglonggou site)', *Dongya Guwu*, 12 (2004), 188–99.

14 H.V. Hunt et al., 'Genetic diversity and phylogeography of broomcorn millet (*Panicum miliaceum* L.) across Eurasia', *Molecular Ecology*, 20 (2011), 4756–71; H.V. Hunt et al., 'Waxy phenotype evolution in the allotetraploid cereal broomcorn millet: mutations at the GBSSI locus in their functional and phylogenetic context', *Molecular and Biological Evolution*, 30 (2013), 109–22.

15 L. Liu et al., 'Paleolithic human exploitation of plant foods during the last glacial maximum in North China', *Proceedings of the National Academy of Sciences*, 110 (2013), 5380–5.

16 L. Liu and X. Chen, *The Archaeology of China: From the Late Paleolithic to the Early Bronze Age* (Cambridge University Press, 2012).

Turning from the Pleistocene to the early Holocene, the archaeobotanical record for millet in northern China is clearer. Alongside records of charred grains, evidence from phytoliths and starch granules has moved back the earliest published dates associated with millet by two millennia. This comes from a range of sites in Hebei province, including Nanzhuangtou, Donghulin, and Cishan. The earliest date in a published claim is currently in the eleventh millennium BCE. In the case of foxtail millet, processing of *Setaria italica* and/ or *S. viridis* by the start of the Holocene at Donghulin, Beijing (*c.* 7500 BCE), and Nanzhuangtou, Hebei (*c.* 9500 BCE), has been inferred from recent starch grain studies.[17] In the case of *Panicum miliaceum*, the earliest published claims relate to phytoliths from the site of Cishan, retrieved from pits in stratigraphic section.[18] While morphological identification as *Panicum miliaceum* may be plausible, the wild form cannot be ruled out. AMS radiocarbon dates on associated pit sediments range between 8500 and 7500 BCE.

The earliest macrofossil evidence dates to the turn of the seventh/sixth millennia BCE. Several localities report charred broomcorn and foxtail millet grains from prior to 5000 cal BCE.[19] They include Xinglonggou in Inner Mongolia; Xinle in Liaoning; Yuezhuang in Shandong; Donghulin in Beijing; Cishan in Hebei; Peiligang, Shawoli, and Wuluoxipo in Henan; and Dadiwan in Gansu.

A striking feature of the geographic distribution of the millet sites in this period is their concentration along the margins of the loess plateau and the Inner Mongolian plateau. To the east of these plateaux lie northern China's two major alluvial plains, the Huabei plain (the North China plain) and the Dongbei plain (the Northeast plain). A chain of low mountains, broadly running northeast–southwest, extends over some 2,500 km along the boundary between the plateaux and the floodplains. The pre-5000 BCE millet sites listed above are all situated on foothills and share a similar relationship to the mountain chain. Beyond this mountain chain, other early millet sites are situated in the same relationship with mountains, as for instance Dadiwan in relation to the Qinling mountains and Yuezhuang to the Yitai mountains.

The common feature of those millet sites is their recurrent location at a position above the nearest river course, at the break of slope between the

17  X. Yang et al., 'Early millet use in northern China', *Proceedings of the National Academy of Sciences*, 109 (2012), 3726–30.

18  H. Lu et al., 'Earliest domestication of common millet (*Panicum miliaceum*) in East Asia extended to 10,000 years ago', *Proceedings of the National Academy of Sciences*, 106 (2009), 7367–72.

19  X. Liu et al., 'River valleys and foothills: changing archaeological perceptions of North China's earliest farms', *Antiquity*, 83 (2009), 82–95.

uplands and the softer sediments of the foothills, at points where rainwater can be captured in freely draining fertile plots.[20] Although involving different sediment types and different landform histories, this distribution resonates with the alluvial locales of early farming sites in Southwest Asia. That pattern, described as 'geological opportunism' by Claudio Vita-Finzi and 'catchment farming' by Andrew Sherratt, chimes with the millet landscapes of northern China.[21]

An enigmatic feature of the records for broomcorn millet is its apparent occurrence on both sides of the Old World. During the sixth and fifth millennia BCE, some twenty sites from Europe and the Caucasus report broomcorn millet identified to species level.[22] However, direct radiocarbon dating of grains of European broomcorn millet has indicated that at least some, and possibly all, of these 'early' records are spurious (i.e. intrusions of recent-age seeds into Neolithic layers). The date at which Asian millets reached Europe remains a matter for enquiry and confirmation.

Useful as they are for establishing geographic patterns and chronology, the contribution of millet to the diet is difficult to infer from recorded quantities of archaeological grain, sensitive as they are to archaeological site formation processes (the intrusion problem mentioned above). The dietary contribution of millets is more effectively approached through palaeodietary analyses of stable isotope measurements from bone. A growing body of human stable isotopic values indicates that consumption of $C_4$ crops (which in this region we presume to derive from broomcorn and/or foxtail millet) became common in all regions of northern China from 5000 cal BCE onwards.[23] However, the earlier isotopic pattern is more variable, both between sites and between individual consumers. Among human skeletal remains from the five cultures reporting millet pre-5000 BCE, one is consistent with no millet consumption and two are consistent with a mix of $C_4$ and $C_3$ consumption.[24] In only one of the five pre-5000 BCE cultures, Xinglongwa, does the carbon isotope signal indicate millet consumption on a significant scale (see Chapter 13).

20  Liu et al., 'River valleys and foothills'.
21  C. Vita-Finzi, 'Geological opportunism', in P.J. Ucko and G. Dimbleby (eds.), *The Domestication and Exploitation of Plants and Animals* (London: Duckworth, 1969), 31–4; A.G. Sherratt, 'Water, soil and seasonality', *World Archaeology*, 11 (1980), 313–30.
22  H.V. Hunt et al., 'Millets across Eurasia: chronology and context of early records of the genera *Panicum* and *Setaria* from archaeological sites in the Old World', *Vegetation History and Archaeobotany*, 17 (2008), 5–18.
23  E. Lightfoot et al., 'Why move starchy cereals? A review of the isotopic evidence for prehistoric millet consumption across Eurasia', *World Archaeology*, 45 (2013), 574–623.
24  X. Liu et al., 'The earliest evidence of millet as a staple crop: new light on Neolithic foodways in North China', *American Journal of Physical Anthropology*, 149 (2012), 238–90.

Turning our attention from the east of Eurasia to the west, although the archaeobotanical record for this period includes millet taxa, stable isotopic studies have demonstrated that Neolithic Western Eurasian diets were largely based on $C_3$ resources. The consumption of $C_4$ crops here is not isotopically demonstrated until the Bronze Age (1500–1100 BCE) in Italy and the Iron Age (800–400 BCE) in central Europe, and it was never as prominent as it was in Neolithic northern China.[25]

In summary, the published records of archaeological grain finds have suggested an expanded reliance on millets throughout northern China by c. 5000 BCE. Prior to this, although many archaeological cultures are recorded as using millet to some degree, there is only one, Xinglongwa, in which millet constitutes a significant component of the carbon diet.

Neolithic peoples did not live by millet alone, and over the course of the middle Neolithic, additional domesticates came to contribute to the diet, including pigs, soybeans, and hemp seed. On the basis of available archaeological finds, the earliest evidence of use, if not cultivation, of soybeans is in central China, south of the Yellow River and in the Yellow River basin, rather than in the northeast. Quantities of glycine have been found, for example, at Jiahu, dating to the later seventh millennium BCE.[26] Soybeans at Jiahu have a small seed size. Changes in seed size suggesting domestication are evident between 3650 and 1450 BCE.[27] Korean archaeological soybeans follow roughly the same chronological trajectory as that of the Yellow River region, which could link these two regions into a single domestication pathway, or two closely parallel pathways. By contrast, an earlier and independent domestication in Japan is indicated by middle Jomon soybeans from Shimoyakebe.[28]

Hemp (*Cannabis sativa*) has served as both an oilseed and a fibre crop in early China, in addition to its drug uses. It was well established as an edible seed crop and drug by the time of early Chinese written sources.[29] Although its original wild distribution is unclear, Li (1983) regarded it as being a native of the open environments of the semi-arid loess highland of northern China,

25  Lightfoot et al., 'Why move starchy cereals?'
26  Z. Zhao, 'Flotation results from the Jiahu site, Wuyang county of Henan', in Z. Zhao (ed.), *Paleoethnobotany: Theories, Methods and Practice* (Beijing: Academy Press, 2010), 108–18.
27  Fuller et al., 'Convergent evolution'.
28  G.A. Lee et al., 'Archaeological soybean (*Glycine max*) in East Asia: does size matter?', *PLoS ONE*, 6 (2011), e26720.
29  H.L. Li, 'An archaeological and historical account of cannabis in China', *Economic Botany*, 28 (1974), 437–48, and 'The origin and use of cannabis in Eastern Asia: linguistic-cultural implications', *Economic Botany*, 28 (1974), 293–301.

in addition to wild populations that persist across Central Asia.[30] Genetic evidence seems to support distinct western and eastern domestications in Asia.[31] Archaeobotanical finds have been few but include Majiayao culture Linjia, Gansu (*c.* 4,700 BP), Shang dynasty Taixi, Hebei (*c.* 3,500 BP), and Daxinzhuang, Shandong (*c.* 3,500 BP).

Pigs were the domesticated animal par excellence of early China. Recent zooarchaeological work using geometric morphometrics (computerized modelling of animal size) points to a central Chinese domestication. Indeed, pig teeth from Jiahu (9,000–8,000 BP) on the Huai River group with domestic pigs, close to those from the Yangshao period site of Xishuipo.[32] Stable isotopes from the bones of domestic pigs allow detection of when they become a major consumer of millets, plants that wild boar are unlikely to consume in any quantity. Millet consumption by pigs implies that they were either being pen-fed or else consuming scraps from the human kitchen or latrines of millet-eaters. Barton et al. documented how Yangshao-era pigs (after 4500 BCE) at Dadiwan ate millet in contrast with pigs of the early Dadiwan period (5500 BCE).[33]

## Beginnings in the south: early rice farmers of the Yangtze basin

It has been posited for some decades that rice farming (Figure 12.4) originated in the Yangtze basin. From the discovery during the 1970s excavations of substantial quantities of rice at the Neolithic waterlogged site of Hemudu (7,000–6,300 BP; Figure 12.5), to discoveries in the 1990s on middle Yangtze sites such as Pengtoushan and Bashidang, the Yangtze region has featured at the start of most accounts of rice origins.[34] There has long been an archaeological

---

30 H.L. Li, 'The domestication of plants in China: some ecogeographical considerations', in D.N. Keightley (ed.), *The Origins of Chinese Civilization* (Berkeley: University of California Press, 1983).

31 K.W. Hillig, 'Genetic evidence for speciation in cannabis (*Cannabaceae*)', *Genetic Resources and Crop Evolution*, 52 (2005), 161–80.

32 T. Cucchi et al., 'New insights into pig taxonomy, domestication and human dispersal in island South East Asia through molar shape analysis: the *Sus* remains from Niah, and Lobang Kudih caves in Sarawak', *International Journal of Osteoarchaeology*, 19 (2009), 508–30.

33 L. Barton et al., 'Agricultural origins and the isotopic identity of domestication in northern China', *Proceedings of the National Academy of Sciences*, 106 (2009), 5523–8.

34 D.J. Cohen, 'The beginnings of agriculture in China: a multiregional view', *Current Anthropology*, 52, Supplement 4 (2011), S273–93; G. Crawford et al., 'Houli culture rice from the Yuezhuang site, Jinan', *Dongfang Kaogu*, 3 (2006), 247–51; C. Higham, 'East Asian agriculture and its impact', in C. Scarre (ed.), *The Human Past: World Prehistory and the Development of Human Societies* (London: Thames & Hudson, 2005), 234–63.

Figure 12.4 Rice field in Zhejiang province.

Figure 12.5 The Neolithic site of Hemudu.

and genetic case to be made for the separate origins of *indica* domesticated rice in India,[35] although it now appears that distinct early cultivation practices in India were enhanced by hybridization with introduced domesticated rice forms from East Asia around 4,000 years ago.[36]

Analyses of phytoliths recovered from Pleistocene caves on the southern margins of the Yangtze basin have also led to suggestions of Pleistocene rice domestication in the region,[37] although clear criteria for determining either cultivation practices or morphological domestication of rice have been lacking. Instead what is evident is that, from 18,000 BP, mobile hunter-gatherer societies in the Yangtze region developed ceramics as a novel form of post-harvest food processing,[38] with more sedentary forager villages occurring from around 9,000 BP. Although wild rice was present from at least 15,000 BP, it is unclear how significant this was for these hunter-gatherer systems. More recent improvements in archaeobotanical recovery have indicated that rice domestication was underway during, and only completed after, the Hemudu cultural phase in the lower Yangtze valley, i.e. 7,000–6,000 BP.[39] This points to a start of cultivation in this region of *c.* 10,000–9,000 years ago; in the middle Yangtze valley it could have begun somewhat earlier but may represent a parallel process to the lower Yangtze. Indeed, sites on the Huai River and other northern tributaries of the Yangtze, such as the Han River, could indicate additional centres of early rice cultivation. Evidence for the very earliest cultivation and the start of the rice domestication process remains obscure: current archaeological evidence makes the end of the domestication process clear, rather than its beginnings.

It has also become clear from recent archaeobotanical studies that rice cultivation emerged in the context of broad spectrum foraging focused on the

---

35 D.Q. Fuller, 'Fifty years of archaeobotanical studies in India: laying a solid foundation', in S. Settar and R. Korisettar (eds.), *Indian Archaeology in Retrospect*, 4 vols. (New Delhi: Indian Council of Historical Research, 2002), vol. III, 247–363.

36 D.Q. Fuller, 'Pathways to Asian civilizations: tracing the origins and spread of rice and rice cultures', *Rice*, 4 (2011), 78–92; D.Q. Fuller and L. Qin, 'Declining oaks, increasing artistry, and cultivating rice: the environmental and social context of the emergence of farming in the lower Yangtze region', *Environmental Archaeology*, 15 (2010), 139–59; and see Chapter 10.

37 Y. Yasuda and J.F. Negendank, 'Environmental variability in East and West Eurasia', *Quaternary International*, 105 (2003), 1–6; Z. Zhao, 'The middle Yangtze region in China is one place where rice was domesticated: phytolith evidence from the Diaotonghuan Cave, northern Jiangxi', *Antiquity*, 72 (1998), 885–97.

38 Boaretto et al., 'Radiocarbon dating'.

39 D.Q. Fuller and L. Qin, 'Water management and labour in the origins and dispersal of Asian rice', *World Archaeology*, 41 (2009), 88–111; Fuller and Qin, 'Declining oaks'; D.Q. Fuller et al., 'Consilience of genetics and archaeobotany in the entangled history of rice', *Archaeological and Anthropological Science*, 2 (2010), 115–31.

collection of tree nuts, especially acorns of various oak species, and wetland nuts, especially water chestnuts (*Trapa natans*) and foxnuts (*Euryale ferox*). Besides gathering and storing these nuts, increasingly sedentary societies began to manage the shallow freshwater wetland margins for the production and planting of perennial wild rice (*Oryza rufipogon sensu stricto*). Freshwater fish were also heavily exploited in these environments. In the Hangzhou Bay region, the Kuahuqiao and Hemudu cultures had villages of post-built long-houses, suggestive of large extended household groups, continuing a tradi-tion already evident at the earlier sedentary forager village of Shangshan (10,000–8,500 BP). In the middle Yangtze Pengtoushan culture, houses included mainly large ovoid huts with sunken floors, perhaps for smaller groups. There were just a few rectilinear buildings, with rectilinear architecture becoming more standard during the subsequent Daxi period (6,500 years BP). Rice increasingly supplemented nuts and gradually displaced them as a dietary staple over the course of perhaps 2,000 to 3,000 years. During this same period rice evolved domestication traits – adaptations to being cultivated and harvested – including loss of wild-type seed dispersal, a key trait for documenting domes-tication archaeologically, but also increasing grain size and by inference such traits as closed panicles, increased seed number, erect growth habit, and increased annuality.

The growing quantity of archaeobotanical evidence, as well as sites with preserved field systems, allows the reconstruction of early cultivation sys-tems. Rice was initially managed along wetland margins that were expanded to control water depth, possibly through dry season burning and clearance as well as soil preparation. From the period at which rice remains display clear domestication traits, around 6,000 years ago, artificial field systems are evident, for example in the lower Yangtze region, east of Taihu Lake, at the sites of Chuodun and Caoxieshan.[40] These early fields consisted of small dug-out, ovoid puddle fields in the order of 1–2 m in diameter (Figure 12.6). This technology indicates small-scale but intensive management of rice, in which soils could be fertilized, water readily drained, and harvests easily secured. This is also associated with smaller houses, perhaps indicative of nuclear families. At Chengtoushan in the middle Yangtze, features inter-preted as belonging to elongated fields following natural contours and defined by raised banks (*c.* 2.7 m wide and over 20 m long), in the context of associated archaeobotany, are suggestive of shallow-water, wet rice

---

40 Fuller and Qin, 'Water management'.

Figure 12.6 Field systems at Chuodun, dating to 4000 cal BCE.

cultivation.[41] Houses were also elongated and rectangular, more permanent, and suggestive of larger households than those of earlier Bashidang and Pengtoushan.

By about 6,000 years ago (the Daxi period in the middle Yangtze and the late Majiabang in the lower Yangtze), domesticated rice had become established as the key dietary staple for Neolithic societies, and the basis in subsequent centuries for the emergence of increasing social complexity and population growth. In the middle Yangtze valley the increased productivity and reliance on rice supported the growth of population, as reflected in the scale of the third-millennium BCE settlements of the Qiujialing and Shijiahe cultures. In the lower Yangtze, Liangzhu society (3300–2300 BCE), with its centres of urban character, elaborate jades, and other craft objects, was supported by intensively cultivated landscapes of rice. The central site of Liangzhu included impressive city walls, canal systems for transport, artificial platforms for occupation, and elite burials (such as the Mojiashan site). The nearby site of Maoshan has yielded extensive paddy-field systems that would be familiar to a modern rice farmer, with long walkways and embankments defining

---

41 Ibid.; H. Nasu et al., 'Land-use change for rice and foxtail millet cultivation in the Chengtoushan site, central China, reconstructed from weed seed assemblages', *Archaeological and Anthropological Sciences*, 4 (2012), 1–14.

Figure 12.7 Paddy-field systems at Maoshan dating to 4700–4200 cal BCE

square to rectilinear fields that could be irrigated from local streams (Figure 12.7). Pigs, melons, and bottle gourds are the only other clearly documented domesticates aside from rice. Cultivation of fruit trees like persimmon and peach, and fibre crops like ramie and mulberry for silkworms, is also probable. The first preserved textiles come from Liangzhu contexts and indicate production of ramie and silk, but spindle whorls suggest that textile traditions extend back to the early rice cultivators of Kuahuqiao and Hemudu, as well as the Neolithic middle Yangtze.

The established rice agriculture of the later Neolithic of the Yangtze provided the basis for the spread of agriculture further south, to the southern provinces of Fujian, Guangdong, and Guangxi. The arrival of rice in these regions took place around 5,000–4,500 years ago.[42] Foxtail millet also spread, at least to Guangxi, pointing towards the middle Yangtze as the source region, as millets were unknown in the lower Yangtze. This is supported by material culture parallels as well.[43] From southern China rice and millet

42 T.L.D. Lu, 'Prehistoric coexistence: the expansion of farming society from the Yangzi River to western South China', in K. Ikeya et al. (eds.), *Interactions Between Hunter-Gatherers and Farmers: From Prehistory to Present* (Osaka: National Museum of Ethnology, 2009), 47–52.

43 C. Zhang and H.-C. Hung, 'The emergence of agriculture in southern China', *Antiquity*, 84 (2010), 11–25.

had spread further to mainland Southeast Asia by 4,000 years ago.[44] Prior to the arrival of rice, there is evidence for the consumption of starchy foods, such as palm starch, bananas, arrow root, and Job's Tears, although it is unclear whether any of these were cultivated, as opposed to gathered.[45] Once adopted, rice cultivation probably remained limited for some time, with evidence for population growth, and agricultural impacts on the wider landscape evident in erosional signatures in offshore ocean sediments, only from around 500 BCE.[46]

Unlike in northern China, with its two millets, there was no complementarity of crops in the basic subsistence of the Neolithic Yangtze, nor were any secondary crops of importance added to the subsistence suite, as soybean was in the north. This is in contrast with the diversity of crops domesticated in Southwest Asia or parts of South Asia, which included multiple cereals and legumes (see Chapter 10). The first two to three millennia of farming in the Yangtze basin focused almost exclusively on rice, although there is evidence for small-scale cultivation of adopted foxtail millet in the middle Yangtze. There is also the possibility that the mint 'shiso' (*Perilla frutescens*) and melon (*Cucumis melo*) were cultivated at Chengtoushan from the Daxi period, although we lack clear morphological evidence of domestication.[47] While agriculture in the Yellow River region diversified through secondary domestications (e.g. soybean, hemp) and adoptions (e.g. wheat, rice) and developed an ideology of diversity (the 'five grains' tradition discussed below), early Yangtze agriculture was single-mindedly about rice. Agriculture eventually diversified in the region, especially after 4,000 years ago as the Yangtze was drawn into the orbit of the states that emerged along the Yellow River, and crops such as wheat and soybean spread to the south.

## Influence from the west: from wheat to wheels

The same general era which witnessed the florescence and decline of several regional complex societies of the advanced Neolithic was also the period when central China came into contact via trade with Central Asia, facilitating the adoption of domesticates and other technology from the west. Uncertainty remains over how early broomcorn millet appears in Western Eurasia as well

---

44  C. Castillo, 'Rice in Thailand: the archaeobotanical contribution', *Rice*, 4 (2011), 114–20; and see Chapter 16 below.
45  X. Yang et al., 'Sago-type palms were an important plant food prior to rice in southern subtropical China', *PloS ONE*, 8 (2013), e63148.
46  D. Hu et al., 'Holocene evolution in weathering and erosion patterns in the Pearl River delta', *Geochemistry, Geophysics, Geosystems*, 14 (2013), 2349–68.
47  Nasu et al., 'Land-use change'.

as the east. From the third millennium BCE, however, the presence of Chinese millets beyond China was paralleled by the eastwards spread of crops and livestock, notably wheat and barley, and cattle and sheep, into China. This era has been referred to as one of Bronze Age globalization,[48] and in the north-western parts of India and Pakistan as a 'Chinese Horizon', as several plants of Chinese origin appear to have arrived around or just after 4,000 years ago, including millets, japonica rice, peach, apricot, and hemp.[49] An important Central Asian site with evidence relating to these Old World crop dispersals is Begash in Kazakhstan, with direct dates on wheat and broomcorn millet that fall between 2450 and 2150 cal BCE.[50]

Within China, wheat mostly dates from 2000 BCE onwards, although earlier dates are known. A single radiocarbon date from the Zhaojiazhuang site in Shandong province places bread wheat in China at 2500–2270 cal BCE,[51] currently the oldest record of a Southwest Asian crop in China.[52] During the course of the Han dynasty the adoption of rotary querns allowed the development of flour foods like noodles and buns.

This same period provides the first clear evidence for domesticated sheep, goats, and cattle, which were also likely introduced from the west around 4,500 years ago.[53] Unlike in Western and Central Asia (including Xinjiang) or India, there are no ethnographic or historical traditions of major reliance on dairying these animals in central China.[54] During the course of the second millennium BCE, other technologies moved eastwards across the continent, including bronze metallurgy by c. 2000 BCE and horses, wheels, and chariots by 1200 BCE.[55]

48 N. Boivin et al., 'Old World globalization and the Columbian exchange: comparison and contrast', *World Archaeology*, 44 (2012), 452–69; M.K. Jones et al., 'Food globalization in prehistory', *World Archaeology*, 43 (2011), 665–75.

49 D.Q. Fuller and N. Boivin, 'Crops, cattle and commensals across the Indian Ocean: current and potential archaeobiological evidence', *Etudes Océan Indien*, 42–3 (2009), 13–46.

50 M.D. Frachetti et al., 'Earliest direct evidence for broomcorn millet and wheat in the Central Eurasia steppe region', *Antiquity*, 84 (2010), 993–1010.

51 G. Jin et al., 'Wheat grains are recovered from a Longshan cultural site, Zhaojiazhuang, in Jiaozhou, Shandong province', *Cultural Relics in China* (2008).

52 Z. Zhao, 'Eastward spread of wheat into China: new data and new issues', in Q. Liu and Y. Bai (eds.), *Chinese Archaeology*, vol. IX (Beijing: China Social Press, 2009), 1–9.

53 D.Q. Fuller et al., 'Across the Indian Ocean: the prehistoric movement of plants and animals', *Antiquity*, 85 (2011), 544–58.

54 F.J. Simoons, 'The traditional limits of milking and milk use in Southern Asia', *Anthropos*, 65 (1970), 547–93; W. Yan, 'Zhongguo shiqian daozuo nongye yicun de xin faxian (New discoveries of paddy rice agriculture in prehistoric China)', *Jianghan Kaogu*, 3 (1990), 27–32.

55 K.M. Linduff and J. Mei, 'Metallurgy in ancient Eastern Asia: retrospect and prospects', *Journal of World Prehistory*, 22 (2009), 265–81.

The second millennium BCE sees a substantial increase in evidence of Southwest Asian crops in China as well as in Central Asia.[56] During this period, wheat and barley are frequently reported from dated contexts in western China, including in Gansu and Qinghai provinces and Xinjiang and Tibet autonomous regions.[57] Evidence from western Yunnan at the site of Haimenkou and in southern Tibet at Changgougou (on the Yarlung Tsangpo River) indicates the presence of wheat and/or barley by perhaps as early as *c.* 1400 BCE, but certainly by *c.* 1000 BCE.[58] This early episode of food globalization, linking east to west through crop exchanges, is mirrored in the south by increased contacts between the Yangtze, southernmost China (Lingnan), and Southeast Asia, by which rice and millets spread southwards.

## Conclusion: the 'five grains' and their origin

Agriculture plays a vital role in modern China, employing millions of people and feeding 20 per cent of the world's population. The Chinese word for 'food' or 'meal' is *fan*, which denotes a cereal food such as boiled rice or millet porridge. For those who eat in a Chinese way, *fan* is essential to everyday life; only *fan* will satisfy hunger.[59] This emphasis upon plant crops in the East contrasts with the importance accorded to livestock in the West. In Europe grain production has repeatedly been integrated with animal husbandry in a system of mixed farming. In China, farming has concentrated upon grain production throughout the historical period, and may have done the same in prehistory. Up until recently, the Chinese diet has largely been vegetarian, a pattern undergoing fundamental change in recent years.

China ranks first among nations in cereal output, primarily producing rice, broomcorn millet, foxtail millet, wheat, barley, maize, potatoes, and peanuts. The cultivation of those crops is consequent upon several episodes of global agricultural exchange between different parts of the Old World, and between

---

56 A. Betts et al., 'The origins of wheat in China and potential pathways for its introduction: a review', *Quaternary International*, 30 (2013), 1–11; R. Flad et al., 'Early wheat in China: results from new studies at Donhuishan in the Hexi Corridor', *The Holocene*, 17 (2010), 555–60; N.F. Miller, 'Agricultural development in western Central Asia in the Chalcolithic and Bronze Age', *Vegetation History and Archaeobotany*, 8 (1999), 13–19; Zhao, 'Eastward spread of wheat into China'.

57 Betts et al., 'Origins of wheat in China'; Zhao, 'Eastward spread of wheat into China'.

58 J. d'Alpoim Guedes et al., 'Moving agriculture onto the Tibetan plateau: the archaeobotanical evidence', *Archaeological and Anthropological Sciences*, 6 (2014), 255–69.

59 Bray and Needham, *Science and Civilisation in China*, 3–8.

the Old World and the New. Maize, potatoes, and peanuts originating from the New World were introduced into China in the sixteenth and seventeenth centuries following the European discovery of America. Southwest Asian crops, notably wheat and barley, were adopted into Chinese farming systems in the third and second millennia BCE, as a key component of trans-Eurasian exchange. Parallel prehistoric exchanges between East, Southeast, and South Asia and North Africa have also recently been documented. Many such exchanges conversely brought Chinese domesticates to other regions of the world.

The earliest textual evidence of multiple cropping comes from a Shang dynasty oracle bone from Anyang. This script arguably contains evidence for rotation of autumn-sown wheat or barley and spring-sown millets. Such evidence resonates with a recurrent theme of intensively farmed landscapes in various parts of Eurasia, including Mesopotamia and the Indus valley during the third and second millennia BCE. For example, accounts of Mesopotamian farming systems on cuneiform clay tablets depict estate-based agriculture combining an early harvest of autumn-sown barley and a later harvest of spring-sown millet and oilseeds.

Legendary accounts of the invention of agriculture by Shennong (the divine farmer) credit him with first cultivating *wugu*, 'five grains', and teaching people how to sow them. The lists of 'five grains' vary and very often include such grains as hemp and sesame that are principally used for oils and flavouring. One list in the *Classic of Rites*, a manuscript ascribed to Confucius in the sixth and fifth centuries BCE, comprises broomcorn and foxtail millet, soybeans, wheat or barley, and hemp. In another version of *wugu*, hemp is replaced with rice. Stories of Shennong's 'five grains' are often mythologically charged. Sometimes the crops themselves were regarded as sacred; at other times their cultivation was regarded as the source of agrarian society and civilization itself.

The Anyang oracle bones include characters which may be ascribed to the five grains. Recent advances in archaeobotany and the increasing application of flotation in China have enriched our knowledge of grain production in prehistory. By 2000 BCE, all of the legendary 'five grains' were in evidence at sites in central China, in Henan and eastern Shaanxi provinces. Recent excavation at Erlitou, presumed to be the capital city of the first Chinese dynasty (Xia), yielded charred remains of broomcorn and foxtail millet, rice, soybeans, wheat, and hemp. This list is concordant with the two versions of the 'five grains', completing a chain that links mythology, text, archaeology, and the contemporary world of Chinese agriculture.

# Further reading

Barton, L., S.D. Newsome, F.-H. Chen, et al. 'Agricultural origins and the isotopic identity of domestication in northern China.' *Proceedings of the National Academy of Sciences*, 106 (2009), 5523–8.

Boaretto, E. et al. 'Radiocarbon dating of charcoal and bone collagen associated with early pottery at Yuchanyan Cave, Hunan province, China.' *Proceedings of the National Academy of Sciences*, 106 (2009), 9595–600.

Bray, F. and J. Needham. *Science and Civilisation in China*, vol. vi: *Biology and Biological Technology*, Part ii: *Agriculture*. Cambridge University Press, 1984.

Flad, R., S. Li, X. Wu, and Z. Zhao. 'Early wheat in China: results from new studies at Donhuishan in the Hexi Corridor.' *The Holocene*, 17 (2010), 555–60.

Frachetti, M.D. et al. 'Earliest direct evidence for broomcorn millet and wheat in the Central Eurasia steppe region.' *Antiquity*, 84 (2010), 993–1010.

Fuller, D.Q. 'Pathways to Asian civilizations: tracing the origins and spread of rice and rice cultures.' *Rice*, 4 (2011), 78–92.

Fuller, D.Q., T. Denham, M. Arroyo-Kalin, et al. 'Convergent evolution and parallelism in plant domestication revealed by an expanding archaeological record.' *Proceedings of the National Academy of Sciences*, 111 (2014), 6147–52.

Fuller, D.Q. and M. Rowlands. 'Towards a long-term macro-geography of cultural substances: food and sacrifice traditions in East, West and South Asia.' *Chinese Review of Anthropology*, 12 (2009), 1–37.

Hillig, K.W. 'Genetic evidence for speciation in cannabis (*Cannabaceae*).' *Genetic Resources and Crop Evolution*, 52 (2005), 161–80.

Hunt, H.V., M.G. Campana, M.C. Laws, et al. 'Genetic diversity and phylogeography of broomcorn millet (*Panicum miliaceum* L.) across Eurasia.' *Molecular Ecology*, 20 (2011), 4756–71.

Hunt, H.V., M.V. Linden, X. Liu, et al. 'Millets across Eurasia: chronology and context of early records of the genera *Panicum* and *Setaria* from archaeological sites in the Old World.' *Vegetation History and Archaeobotany*, 17 (2008), 5–18.

Hunt, H.V. et al. 'Waxy phenotype evolution in the allotetraploid cereal broomcorn millet: mutations at the GBSSI locus in their functional and phylogenetic context.' *Molecular and Biological Evolution*, 30 (2013), 109–22.

Jones, M.K., H.V. Hunt, E. Lightfoot, et al. 'Food globalization in prehistory.' *World Archaeology*, 43 (2011), 665–75.

Kuzmin, Y.V. 'Two trajectories in the Neolithization of Eurasia: pottery versus agriculture (spatiotemporal patterns).' *Radiocarbon*, 55 (2013), 1304–13.

Lee, G.A., G.W. Crawford, L. Liu, Y. Sasaki, and X. Chen. 'Archaeological soybean (*Glycine max*) in East Asia: does size matter?' *PLoS ONE*, 6 (2011), e26720.

Lightfoot, E., X. Liu, and M.K. Jones. 'Why move starchy cereals? A review of the isotopic evidence for prehistoric millet consumption across Eurasia.' *World Archaeology*, 45 (2013), 574–623.

Liu, L. and X. Chen. *The Archaeology of China: From the Late Paleolithic to the Early Bronze Age*. Cambridge University Press, 2012.

Liu, X., H.V. Hunt, and M.K. Jones. 'River valleys and foothills: changing archaeological perceptions of North China's earliest farms.' *Antiquity*, 83 (2009), 82–95.

Liu, X., M.K. Jones, Z. Zhao, G. Liu, and T.C. O'Connell. 'The earliest evidence of millet as a staple crop: new light on Neolithic foodways in North China.' *American Journal of Physical Anthropology*, 149 (2012), 238–90.

Vita-Finzi, C. 'Geological opportunism.' In P.J. Ucko and G. Dimbleby (eds.), *The Domestication and Exploitation of Plants and Animals*. London: Duckworth, 1969. 31–4.

Yang, X., Z. Wan, L. Perry, et al. 'Early millet use in northern China.' *Proceedings of the National Academy of Sciences*, 109 (2012), 3726–30.

Zhao, Z. 'New archaeobotanic data for the study of the origins of agriculture in China.' *Current Anthropology*, 72 (1998), 885–97.

# 13

# Xinglonggou, China

XINYI LIU, ZHIJUN ZHAO, AND GUOXIANG LIU

Several hundred sites belonging to the period between 7000 and 5000 cal BCE have been identified in China's northeast and north-central regions.[1] Archaeologists have associated this wealth of sites with the mid-Holocene climatic optimum, as the warm and wet conditions of monsoonal China enabled settlements to flourish.[2] Most sites are situated in mountainous basins or near hills or at the base of mountains.[3] These sites are characterized by structures which could be interpreted as 'dwellings', storage pits, burials, and sometimes by ditched enclosures. Pottery vessels and grinding stones are prevalent in this period. Polished stone tools increase in proportion over time, but chipped stones and microliths continue to be found. It has been widely accepted that these settlements and material assemblages represent the initial development of sedentary life in China. Spreading from Daxinganling to the Taihang and Funiu mountains north to south, and from Yitai to the Qinling mountains east to west, these settlements constitute the 'early Neolithic' in northern China.

Alongside the use of other plants and animals, many of those early Neolithic sites are believed to have been associated with the cultivation of two types of millet: broomcorn millet (*Panicum miliaceum*) and foxtail millet (*Setaria italica*), referred to as *shu* and *su* in Classical Chinese (see Chapter 12). Collection of small grain grasses, including millet, may be traced back to the terminal Pleistocene (between about 15,000 and 11,500 years ago) and may well have been a part of the broad spectrum subsistence during the upper

---

1 L. Liu and X. Chen, *The Archaeology of China: From the Late Paleolithic to the Early Bronze Age* (Cambridge University Press, 2012).

2 Z.S. An et al., 'A synchronous Holocene optimum of the East Asian monsoon', *Quaternary Science Reviews*, 19 (2000), 743–62.

3 X. Liu et al., 'River valleys and foothills: changing archaeological perceptions of North China's earliest farms', *Antiquity*, 83 (2009), 82–95.

Palaeolithic (which dates from about 40,000 years ago).[4] Turning from the Pleistocene to the early Holocene, it has been suggested on the basis of phytolith and starch residue evidence that broomcorn and foxtail millet were already in use in northern China prior to 7000 BCE.[5] Nonetheless, the most abundant macrofossil evidence of broomcorn and foxtail millet is found in association with the early Neolithic sites post-7000 BCE.

Drawing on typological lineages of ceramics, archaeologists group the early Neolithic sites into a number of types of material culture.[6] These are: the Xinglongwa-Xinle culture in the Xiliao region, the Cishan-Beifudi culture in Hebei, the Houli culture in Shandong, the Peiligang culture in Henan, and the Baijia-Dadiwan culture in eastern Gansu and western Shaanxi. Recent advances using flotation systems in China (see Figure 12.1) have revealed dozens of millet assemblages from sites belonging to all five culture groups.[7]

The sites of the Xinglongwa culture are distributed to the southeast of the Daxinganling mountains, in a hilly area that is often referred to in the literature as Liaoxi region, which is mostly in present-day Chifeng in the Inner Mongolia Autonomous Region. Xinglongwa sites are also found in western Liaoning province and northern Hebei. The culture constitutes an early stage in the prehistoric sequence in Chifeng, where there are at least six local subcultures forming a chronological sequence: Xiaohexi (7000–6200 cal BCE), Xinglongwa (6200–5400 cal BCE), Zhaobaogou (5400–4500 cal BCE), Hongshan (4500–3000 cal BCE), Xiaoheyan (3000–2400 cal BCE), and lower Xiajiadian (2200–1600 cal BCE).[8] About a hundred sites of the Xinglongwa culture have been found and dozens of them have been excavated. Well-known sites include Xinglongwa and Xinglongou in Aohan, Baiyinchanghan in Linxi, Nantaizi in Keshiketeng, and Chahai in Fuxin.[9] Among them, Xinglonggou is the most frequently referenced, on account of its rich materials, structured residential patterns, and important early millet finds.

---

4 L. Liu et al., 'Plant exploitation of the last foragers at Shizitan in middle Yellow River valley China: evidence from grinding stones', *Journal of Archaeological Science*, 38 (2011), 3524–32.

5 H. Lu et al., 'Earliest domestication of common millet (*Panicum miliaceum*) in East Asia extended to 10,000 years ago', *Proceedings of the National Academy of Sciences*, 106 (2009), 7367–72; X. Yang et al., 'Early millet use in northern China', *Proceedings of the National Academy of Sciences*, 109 (2012), 3726–30.

6 Liu and Chen, *Archaeology of China*.  7 Liu et al., 'River valleys and foothills'.

8 D. Guo, 'Hongshan and related cultures', in S.M. Nelson (ed.), *The Archaeology of Northeast China* (London: Routledge, 1995), 147–81.

9 X. Li, *Development of Social Complexity in the Liaoxi Area, Northeast China* (Oxford: Archaeopress, 2008).

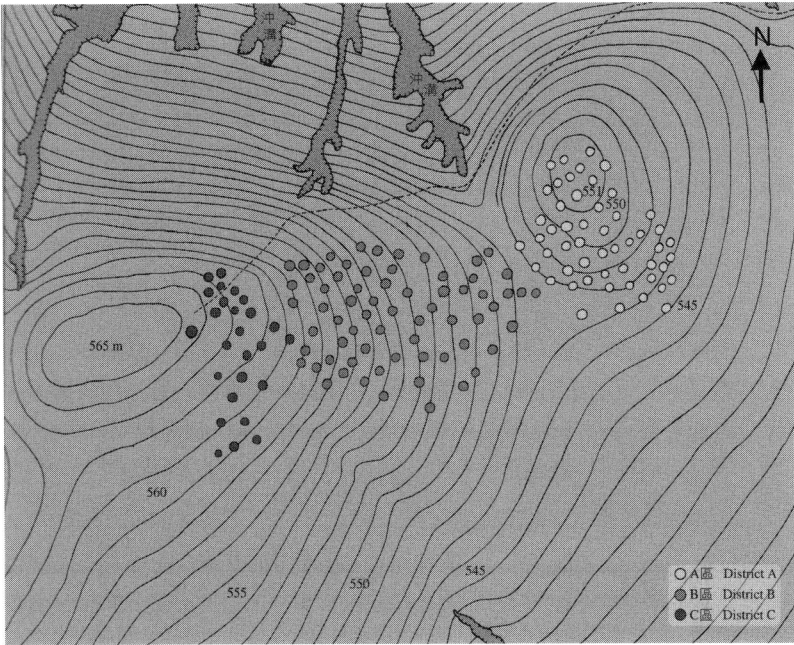

Figure 13.1 Post-excavation plan of Xinglonggou I. Each dot represents a 'pit structure'.

Xinglonggou was discovered in 1982. During the survey of 1998, a joint team from the Institute of Archaeology, Chinese Academy of Social Sciences, and the Aohan Banner Museum, Chifeng, recognized three localities, belonging respectively to the early Neolithic Xinglongwa culture, the middle/late Neolithic Hongshan culture, and the Bronze Age lower Xiajiadian culture.[10] Before the excavation, rows of house plans were discernible on the ground's surface. These house plans were particularly distinct after ploughing. In total, 145 house plans were identified, all aligned in rows running northeast–southwest. In 2001–3, targeted excavations were conducted, uncovering an area of over 5,600 m$^2$ (see Figure 13.1).[11]

Excavations revealed house plans from every period of occupation. They can be divided into three phases and three localities (Xinglonggou I, II, and III

---

10 H. Yang et al., 'Neimenggu Aohan Qi Xinglonggou Xinshiqi shidai yizhi diaocha (Survey on a Neolithic site in Aohan, Inner Mongolia)', *Kaogu*, 88 (2000), 810–28.

11 G. Liu et al., 'Neimenggu Chifeng shi Xinglonggou yizhi 2002–2003 nian de fajue (Excavation at the Xinglonggou site between 2002 and 2003 in Chifeng, Inner Mongolia Autonomous Region)', *Kaogu*, 92 (2004), 579–83.

hereafter). Among the three localities, Xinglonggou I is materially the richest. Abundant debris was found on the 'floors', including tools, ornaments, ceramic vessels, potsherds, animal bones, and occasionally human bones. Many materials may indeed relate to agricultural activities and food processing. For example, grinding debris, such as slabs, hand tools, mortars, and pestles, constitute an important part of household activities. There were also large numbers of microliths, used as blades for notched bone knives and fish spears.

A flotation programme at Xinglonggou I yielded more than 1,500 charred grains of broomcorn millet, together with about 20 grains of foxtail millet.[12] Direct radiocarbon analysis indicates that the broomcorn millet dates to *c.* 7,700 cal BP.[13] It constitutes one of the earliest records of millet in northern China and the oldest directly dated millet so far. Stable isotopic analysis has revealed that early Neolithic humans living at Xinglonggou I consumed millet as their staple food.[14] The following account considers five distinct aspects of Xinglonggou Neolithic lives in association with millet agriculture: landscape, material culture, settlement, production, and consumption. While our ultimate focus is the period of the early Neolithic, we shall introduce this discussion with a consideration of chronological change in the prehistoric ways of life.

## Landscape

The three localities of Xinglonggou are all on the left bank of the Mangniu River to the north of the Qilaotu mountains. The early Neolithic settlement, Xinglonggou I, is situated on a sloped loess accumulation on the second terrace of the river (Figure 13.2). The advantage of such a location to early farmers was its spatially constricted but highly productive soils that accumulate in the catchments of springs and seasonal streams. At those locations, until very recently, a small-scale horticultural version of what is generally known as 'catchment farming' has largely been practised. As the East Asian monsoon reached its Holocene maximum, the flow of water was

12 Z. Zhao, 'Zhiwu kaoguxue jiqi xin jinzhan (Achievements of palaeoethnobotanical study in China)', *Kaogu*, 93 (2005), 522–9.

13 Z. Zhao, 'New archaeobotanic data for the study of the origins of agriculture in China', *Current Anthropology*, 52, Supplement 4 (2011), S295–304.

14 X. Liu et al., 'The earliest evidence of millet as a staple crop: new light on Neolithic foodways in North China', *American Journal of Physical Anthropology*, 149 (2012), 238–90.

Figure 13.2 Xinglonggou 1, looking northwest.

more substantial than today. Vegetation growth was constrained by the seasonality of water flow from springs and streams, favouring annual grasses. The composition of the resulting grassy stands could be modified by selective clearance. This would in particular be true on northern slopes, because on the southern foothills the fluvial dynamic would be higher, favouring deep-rooted perennials. Such a dynamic is still visible today: Figure 13.3 illustrates a northern foothill in Chifeng where two weedy forms of millet, *Setaria viridis* and *Panicum miliaceum var. ruderale*, are flourishing in the uncultivated area alongside the cultivated fields of broomcorn millet and maize.

Xinglonggou 1 is one of a number of early Neolithic sites in this region situated in such a location: Xinglongwa, Baiyinchanghan, Chahai, and Nantaizi, for example, are all located on the slope of north-facing foothills. This is in contrast to sites of the late Neolithic Hongshan period and the Bronze Age lower Xiajiadian period, which are typically situated closer to the courses of rivers. No early Neolithic sites are found on a flat valley floor, and few are found on the higher mountains far from major rivers. Twelve of the

Figure 13.3  Cultivated fields of maize and weedy millet near Xinglonggou.

sites from the Xinglongwa period are located on upland slopes, typically more than 40–50 m above river channels.[15]

It appears that the dynamic between the Holocene hydrological system in Chifeng and the Quaternary loess accumulation is the key to understanding the human occupation systems of different episodes in prehistory. A geoarchaeological study has hypothesized three stages of the development of the Chifeng riverine system in relation to locations of Neolithic and Bronze Age sites.[16] The initial development of the fluvial system in southern Chifeng dates to between 6000 and 4500 BCE. During this period, the landscape was dominated by loess slopes and loess plains between hills and young rivers. Early Neolithic anthropogenic deposits of the Xinglongwa culture are often situated on top of the Quaternary loess accumulation. As the fluvial system developed, a significant downcutting happened between 4500 and 2000 BCE,

15  Chifeng International Collaborative Archaeological Research Project, *Nei Menggu dongbu quyu kaogu diaocha jieduan xing baogao* (*Regional Archaeology in Eastern Inner Mongolia: A Methodological Exploration*) (Beijing: Science Press, 2003).
16  Z. Xia et al., 'Geomorphologic background of the prehistoric cultural evolution in the Xar Moron river basin, Inner Mongolia', *Acta Geographica Sinica*, 55 (2000), 329–36.

forming the second terrace of the rivers. Many late Neolithic anthropogenic activities of the Hongshan period are found on the alluvial sediments of this terrace, indicating that they are younger than the formation of the terrace. A subsequent downcutting after 2000 BCE formed the first terrace of the rivers. The Bronze Age cultural layers of the lower Xiajiadian period are often found either on the first terrace or on top of the Holocene loess deposits of the second terrace. Although the model is based on the integration of wider geographic surveys, the topographical relations of Xinglonggou I, II, and III are broadly in accord with it. The same topographical preference is observed at a number of other early Neolithic sites across northern China and further resonates with the geographic settings of early agricultural sites in Southwest Asia:[17] in the Jordan valley, for example, Claudio Vita-Finzi observed a similar three-stage development of site locations and noted the 'geographic opportunism' of the first farmers there.[18]

## Material assemblage

In some respects the early Neolithic communities of China occupying similar topographical locations formed a network, their interconnections demonstrated both by the rare but diagnostic materials like jade that passed between them and by their sharing of a common typology in objects such as pottery vessels and stone tools, as indeed their shared cultural name, the Xinglongwa culture, indicates. Their ceramic vessels are simple in form and dominated by the bucket-shaped pot.[19] They are sand tempered, brownish in colour, and made with the coiling method. Typical decorations on pots consist of belts of net-patterns, zigzag patterns, mat impressions, 'V' shape patterns, and point impression zones from top to bottom. The tool assemblage consists of both refined bone tools and stone tools.[20] The former include awls, needles, spoons, and notched knives and notched fish spears embedded with microlithic blades. Stone tools include chipped stone hoes, spades, and knives. There are also a large number of microliths, as blades for notched bone knives and fishing spears. Grinding stones, such as slabs, handstones, mortars, and pestles, constitute an important part of the tool assemblage.

Various studies have explored the functions of the grinding tools and grinding activities at these sites. A physical anthropological study of human

---

17 Liu et al., 'River valleys and foothills'.
18 C. Vita-Finzi, 'Geological opportunism', in P.J. Ucko and G. Dimbleby (eds.), *The Domestication and Exploitation of Plants and Animals* (London: Duckworth, 1969), 31–4.
19 Li, *Development of Social Complexity*.    20  Ibid.

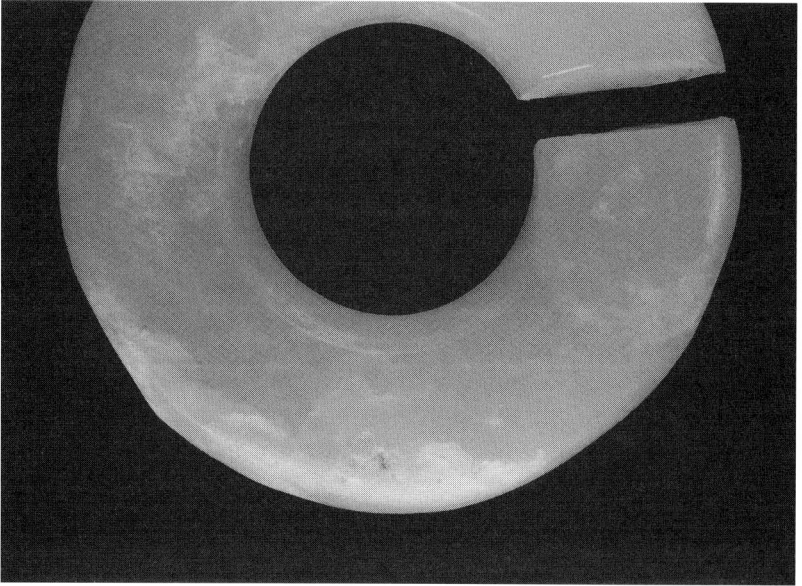

Figure 13.4 Early Neolithic jade slit ring from Xinglonggou 1.

skeletons from Xinglongwa culture sites suggests that young females had deformed knees, probably resulting from prolonged kneeling while using grinding stones.[21] Residue analyses of grinding stones from Baiyinchanghan and Xinglonggou have revealed that these tools were indeed used for processing plants, including yams, acorn, and many types of grass.[22]

Xinglonggou has also provided one of the oldest records of jade objects in China (Figure 13.4). There are many types, including slit rings (the most abundant type), scoop-shaped objects, arcs, tubes, axes, adzes, and chisels. The material, colour, and social significance of the Xinglonggou jade have been discussed by numerous authors.[23] All Xinglonggou jades were made of nephrite, chalcedony, and other soft rock materials.[24] To make such jade objects, various procedures needed to be performed, including percussion, pecking, grinding, sawing, drilling, scraping, and mirror polishing. Traces left

---

21 B.D. Smith, 'Diet, health, and lifestyle in Neolithic North China', unpublished PhD thesis (Cambridge, MA: Harvard University, 2005).

22 Liu and Chen, *Archaeology of China*, 130.

23 H. Yang et al., *The Origin of Jades in East Asia: Jades of the Xinglongwa Culture* (Centre for Chinese Archaeology and Art, Chinese University of Hong Kong, 2007).

24 Ibid., 275–98.

on different types of jades indicate that the shape and size of the object affected the choice of technique. Sometimes more than one technique was employed on the same part of the object: the slits of the slit rings, for example, show differences in the processes by which they were cut, with evidence of both string-sawing and blade-sawing.[25]

In terms of mineral choice for making the ornaments, there appears to have been a colour preference for yellow-green nephrite. More than fifty nephrite jade objects have been recovered from Xinglongwa cultural sites, including many from Xinglonggou, and they are all yellow-green. The choice of this colour is interesting in its distinctness in relation to the colours of local minerals. The latter consist of chalcedony, marble, pyrophyllite, talc, and jasper, materials that were mostly red, black, or white. To date, no nephrite has been found in the Liaoxi region, the nearest nephrite mine being in Xiuyan in Liaoning province, a few hundred miles from Xinglonggou, and its material is yellow-green. It has therefore been suggested that the jades of the Xinglongwa culture were the result of long-distance exchange networks.[26] The original colour of the raw material of Xiuyan nephrite, however, would have been hard to recognize, as the cortex is covered with various false colours hiding the jade's true colour from the collector: it would only have been exposed when the rock was broken up.

Although the preference for green-yellow stone can be traced back to the Palaeolithic in East Asia, scholars have called for caution in automatically assuming that high value was attributed to jade of this colour at Xinglonggou and other Xinglongwa sites. It has been argued that gradations of value were not pronounced during the Xinglongwa period and that the evidence is not strong that the jades themselves were graded in value, whereas in later periods some of the types that exist in Xinglongwa contexts certainly developed into symbolically charged objects.[27]

## Houses, burial, and settlement

The locality of Xinglonggou I is one of the few completely excavated settlements in early Neolithic China with well-preserved settlement plans. As with many sites in northeastern China of the period, Xinglonggou I comprises rectangular pit-based structures. The settlement was divided into three

25 Ibid.  26 Ibid.

27 R. Flad, 'Xinglongwa jades and genesis of value in northeast China', in C. Deng and G. Liu (eds.), *The Origins of Chinese Jade Culture: Xinglongwa Jades Research and Catalogue* (Chinese University of Hong Kong Press, 2008), 224–34.

Figure 13.5 Rows of early Neolithic 'pit structures' at Xinglonggou 1.

different sectors during its early phase of occupation, each with about fifty or fewer pit structures, all aligned in rows. Most Xinglongwa cultural sites are surrounded by a ditched enclosure, yet Xinglonggou itself has no such structure. The 2001–3 excavations exposed 145 of those pit structures over an area of 5,600 m², aligned northeast–southwest in closely packed rows (Figure 13.5).

The ground plans of the pit structures range between 30 and 80 m² in extent. Some studies interpret them as residential dwellings.[28] Others call for caution about intuitive assumptions that house-like structures are invariably habitations and suggest that such structures could have been used for non-domestic purposes such as preparing food, storage, or communal gathering.[29] Each pit structure contained an orderly arrangement of four to six post holes, often laid out symmetrically on the northeast and southwest sides of an

28  G. Liu, 'Xinglonggou yizhi diyidian dian fajue huigu yu sikao (Rethinking the excavation of Xinglonggou 1)', Neimenggu Wenwu Kaogu, 2 (2006), 8–30.

29  G. Shelach, 'Economic adaptation, community structure, and sharing strategies of households at early sedentary communities in northeast China', Journal of Anthropological Archaeology, 25 (2006), 318–45.

Figure 13.6 Animal skulls in the western part of 'pit structure' F5 at Xinglonggou I.

intermediate hearth. Deer and pig skulls were found in some of the pit structures; some were perforated, arranged in clusters (Figure 13.6), and placed on the 'floor'.[30] Excavation also produced artefacts of pottery, stone, jade, bone, tooth, and shell, and ornamental plaques made from human skulls, mostly also placed on the 'floor' of the pit structures. Many pit structures contained human burials, a feature known from other Xinglongwa cultural sites, such as Xinglongwa, Baiyinchanghan, and Chahai.[31] At Xinglonggou I, 28 out of 145 pits yielded burials inside the pit structures.

Although the focus of the excavation between 2001 and 2003 was the early phase of Xinglonggou occupation (Xinglonggou I), excavations were also carried out in 2003 at Xinglonggou II and III.[32] Xinglonggou II is a late Neolithic settlement of the Hongshan period, and Xinglonggou III is a Bronze Age settlement of the lower Xiajiadian period. Archaeological investigations have primarily focused on the monumental architecture and large cemeteries of those two periods. Up until now we have had only limited

30  Liu, 'Xinglonggou yizhi'.
31  G. Liu, 'Xinglongwa wenhua jushi zangsu zai renshi (Rethinking residential burials of the Xinglongwa culture)', *Huaxia Kaogu*, 1 (2003), 43–51.
32  Liu et al., 'Excavation at Xinglonggou site between 2002 and 2003'.

knowledge about the settlement patterns of ordinary villages in the Hongshan and lower Xiajiadian periods, and together with other recent studies, Xinglonggou II and III provide an attempt to understand ordinary lives in, respectively, the late Neolithic and Bronze Age.

At Xinglonggou II, excavations exposed four rectangular pit structures and thirty-one storage pits over an area of 1,500 m². The settlement was surrounded by a ditched enclosure. Although the pits are external to the pit structures, it may be assumed that those 'houses' owned storage facilities. For example, nine storage pits were found surrounding the 'house' F7, and seven were found outside F8. Each 'house' has a fireplace in the centre. Excavation produced artefacts of pottery, stone, and shell, mostly from the pits. In a subsequent excavation in 2012, a terracotta statue was recovered (Figure 13.7).

The area excavated at Xinglonggou III is smaller than the other two localities. Three pit structures were recovered from 250 m². The settlement was again surrounded by a ditched enclosure, which has been interpreted by the excavators as a genuinely defensive structure. Among the three pit structures, only F1 was well preserved. On the northeastern side of the 'house', a 'fire channel' was also recovered, which the excavators interpret as a heating system.

One of the key differences of settlement pattern between the three localities of Xinglonggou is in the relation between houses and storage. As demonstrated by Flannery and Plog, the way storage facilities are distributed within a site and among the domestic structures is a good indication of economic strategies and the type of access people had to economic resources.[33] In Xinglonggou I, storage pits were normally located outside pit structures and evenly distributed in each sector, so their contents may well have been shared among members of the community. There is no evidence, however, for the exchange of goods between sectors. Various authors have suggested that the kinds of settlement seen in the Xinglongwa culture were units of landholding, economic production, redistribution, and ceremonial activity.[34] Contrasting with Xinglonggou I, Xinglonggou II

---

33 K.V. Flannery, 'The origins of the village as a settlement type in Mesoamerica and the Near East: a comparative study', in P.J. Ucko et al. (eds.), *Man, Settlement and Urbanism* (London: Duckworth, 1972), 23–53, and 'The origins of the village revisited: from nuclear to extended households', *American Antiquity*, 67 (2002), 417–33; S. Plog, 'Agriculture, sedentism, and environment in the evolution of political systems', in S. Upham (ed.), *The Evolution of Political Systems: Sociopolitics in Small-Scale Sedentary Societies* (Cambridge University Press, 1990), 177–99.

34 W.M. Yan, 'Neolithic settlements in China: latest finds and research', *Journal of East Asian Archaeology*, 1 (1999), 131–47; L. Liu, *The Chinese Neolithic: Trajectories to Early States* (Cambridge University Press, 2004).

Figure 13.7 Terracotta statue recovered at Xinglonggou II.

probably presents a situation in which households had their own storage facilities, and seems to be akin to what Plog calls 'restricted sharing', where resources are shared among members of the household but much less between different households.[35] If so, 'restricted sharing' seemingly intensified in the

35 Plog, 'Agriculture, sedentism, and environment', 190.

347

Bronze Age. While the excavation of Xinglonggou III was relatively small in scale, drawing from other recent excavations of lower Xiajiadian settlements it has been proposed that each lower Xiajiadian settlement may have been a sociopolitical unit within an overarching political structure.[36] However, each may have had the economic means to sustain itself, with each enclosure within the site representing a family household. Most of those enclosures also have one or two small circular installations built of stone and identified by the excavators as 'granaries'.[37]

The change of settlement pattern in Xinglonggou during its three phases of occupation resonates with that of a number of other sites in northern China. From the early to late Neolithic, villages across northern China experienced a development from shared storage facilities and relatively uniform dwelling size to the formation of large multi-family households. As Peterson and Shelach put it, from the early Neolithic onwards, decisions regarding economic activities were no longer made by the whole residential community, but rather at the household level.[38] Such an arrangement is typical of societies in which risk is assumed at the level of the family. By the Bronze Age, people were living in more compact settlements, the internal organization of which suggests an increase in the intensity of inter-household interaction.

In summary, somewhere between the early and late Neolithic, villages in Chifeng appear to have been organized according to 'restricted sharing' as defined by Plog, characterized by restricted land tenure and growing privatization of storage. In Flannery's terms, from Xinglonggou I to II and continuing in Xinglonggou III, there was a shift in risk from the village collective to individual nuclear families. In this context, we can imagine that there was widespread pooling and sharing of food at Xinglonggou I, with an acceptance of risk and reward being shared by the group as a whole, and plant food storage and animal husbandry taking place communally, beyond the secure perimeter of each dwelling space. By contrast, in Xinglonggou II and III

---

36  G. Shelach, *Leadership Strategies, Economic Activity, and Interregional Interaction: Social Complexity in Northeast China* (New York: Kluwer Academic/Plenum, 1999), and 'Violence on the frontiers? Sources of power and socio-political change at the easternmost parts of the Eurasian steppes during the early first millennium BCE', in B.K. Hanks and K. Linduff (eds.), *Social Complexity in Prehistoric Eurasia* (Cambridge University Press, 2009), 241–71.

37  Z. Guo and C. Hu, 'Neimenggu Chifeng shi Sanzuodian Xiajiadian xiaceng wenhua shicheng yizhi (Sanzuodian: a site with stone fortifications from the lower Xiajiadian period, in Chifeng, Inner Mongolia)', *Kaogu*, 95 (2007), 17–27.

38  C.E. Peterson and G. Shelach, 'Jiangzhai: social and economic organization of a middle Neolithic Chinese village', *Journal of Anthropological Archaeology*, 31 (2012), 265–301.

societies display a more 'closed' site plan, one which has either widely spaced household units or closed-in eating and storage areas.[39]

## Millet production inside and outside the settlement

How people managed the resources available to them is one of the fundamental issues that every study of an early sedentary community must address. In the following sections we discuss food production and consumption in the context of the social spaces of Xinglonggou I, II, and III, in order to address how staple crops were produced, processed, and distributed among members of the community, and consumed or manipulated to acquire status or wealth.

Although the focus of the flotation programme directed by Zhijun Zhao at Xinglonggou was the early Neolithic occupation of the site, samples were also taken from Xinglonggou II and III, representing the first systematic flotation programme in China. The flotation at Xinglonggou I yielded more than 1,500 charred grains of broomcorn millet (see Figure 12.3), together with about 20 of foxtail millet. The broomcorn millet was directly radiocarbon dated to c. 7,700 cal BP. Both broomcorn and foxtail millet were recovered from Xinglonggou II and III.

As the progenitor of broomcorn millet (*Panicum miliaceum*) is unknown, our knowledge about how the domesticated form of broomcorn was selected from its wild ancestor is relatively limited. It has been noticed, however, that millet grains from three localities of Xinglonggou show a gradual increase in size and change in shape over time. Zhao has observed that the broomcorn millet from Xinglonggou I is intermediate in caryopsis size and shape between modern domesticated and wild forms, and therefore represents an early stage of domestication.[40] On a broader geographic scale, broomcorn millet grains recovered from various sites across northern China also show a gradual increase in size over time.[41] This process of morphological change had been associated with the relative increase of foxtail millet and decrease of broomcorn millet in assemblages.

---

39  X. Liu, 'Food webs, subsistence and changing culture: the development of early farming communities in the Chifeng region, North China', unpublished PhD thesis (University of Cambridge, 2010).

40  Z. Zhao, 'Cong Xinglonggou yizhi fuxuan jieguo tan Zhongguo beifang zaoqi nongye qiyuan wenti (Addressing the origins of agriculture in North China based on the results of flotation from the Xinglonggou site)', *Dongya Guwu*, 12 (2004), 188–99.

41  Liu and Chen, *Archaeology of China*, 85.

Turning from the remains of the crops themselves to the accompanying plant taxa, millet grains from Xinglonggou I account for only 15 per cent of all grains recovered by flotation. A great quantity of *Cerastium glomeratum* (*Caryophyllaceae*) and *Astragalus* sp. (*Leguminosae*) was identified from Xinglonggou I. More than 50 per cent of seeds identified from Xinglonggou I belong to these two species. *Cerastium glomeratum* is an annual herb widely distributed in China, often appearing on foothill landscapes in northern China. *Amaranthus* spp. (*Amaranthaceae*) and *Chenopodium* spp. (*Chenopodiaceae*) were also common within Xinglonggou I assemblages. All four genera occur as weed infestations of crops today.[42] Some nine species of *Amaranthus* and eight species of *Chenopodium* are reported as common weeds. *Chenopodium album* is reported as one of the major weeds infesting the fields of crops in northern China.[43] All these species produce edible grains maturing roughly at the same time as millet, suggesting that the field system at Xinglonggou I was quite different from our notion of an agricultural or horticultural field today. In Xinglonggou II, millet accounts for an even lower proportion of all identifiable plant remains. A great number of fruits and nuts were recovered by the flotation, including *Pyrus betulaefolia*, *Prunus armeniaca*, *Quercus* sp., *Corylus heterophylla*, and *Juglans mandshurica*. Contrasting with the patterns of Xinglonggou I and II, in Xinglonggou III crops predominate in flotation samples. Apart from broomcorn and foxtail millet, charred soybean was recovered.

The majority of the carbonized evidence from Xinglonggou I was recovered from houses. An interesting feature of these assemblages and the site in general was the absence of chaff – either free chaff or chaff attached to grains. The grains were all recovered as clean caryopses. This reverses the pattern from later sites in this region, such as Sanzuodian, a large lower Xiajiadian period site contemporaneous with Xinglonggou III. In Sanzuodian, more than 5,500 charred grains of broomcorn millet and about 5,000 foxtail millet grains were identified from 102 samples.[44] Millet remains were recovered from almost every house, from floor areas and the space between the two concentric walls of the house. Moreover, there was plentiful evidence for millet chaff, and millet grains were found in association with fragments of lemma and palea of broomcorn millet as well as with fragments of broken millet embryos. Both constitute evidence of the de-husking stage of millet processing.

42 S. Qiang, *Zacao Xue* (Beijing: Zhongguo Nongye Chubanshe, 2003).  43 Ibid.
44 Liu, 'Food webs'.

These differences may reflect changes in the social organization of crop processing. In the Bronze Age lower Xiajiadian period, the routine processing activities took place inside 'households', where de-husking was probably carried out in a piecemeal manner. As suggested by ethnographic observations, in such a scenario, both the products and the by-products of those activities have a higher probability of reaching household fires and therefore entering archaeological contexts as charred botanical material. The house structure of this period, consisting of a 'dwelling' and 'granary' enclosed by narrow stone walls, formed an enclosure within which food was shared between members, with the substantial stone boundaries separating the sharing of food from other 'households'. In short, there was a boundedness of production and consumption at the family level. By contrast, the crop evidence from Xinglonggou I implies a rather different organization of settlement life, involving the participation and co-operation of a larger community: the grains had been fully threshed beyond these core units, indicating that the processing activities had happened somewhere else beyond the settlement core.

## Millet consumption

All species of millet photosynthesize through the Hatch-Slack or $C_4$ pathway. During photosynthesis, $C_4$ plants discriminate against atmospheric $^{13}CO_2$ less than $C_3$ plants, yielding higher $\delta^{13}C$ values than $C_3$ plants (approximate mean values of $-12.5‰$ and $-26.5‰$ respectively), with no overlap. In the northern latitudes of Eurasia the only indigenous domesticated $C_4$ crops are broomcorn and foxtail millet. The consumption of millet grains consequently generates an isotopically characteristic $C_4$ signature in human and animal bone collagen. Stable carbon isotopic measurements of human and animal skeletal samples can thus be used to infer levels of millet consumption across space and time.

Systematic isotopic research was carried out in Chifeng. Human and animal skeletal specimens from a range of sites, including Xinglonggou I, II, and III, were selected for isotopic analysis.[45] The results indicate that substantial millet consumption by humans in Chifeng began at Xinglonggou I. Although the isotopic values do not directly inform us about the domestication process, of which we still have a limited understanding, the significant dietary input of millet in Xinglonggou I indicates that millet was certainly

---

45 Liu et al., 'Earliest evidence of millet'.

used as a staple food. Throughout the Neolithic and into the Bronze Age in Chifeng, the proportion of $C_4$ foods in the diet increased. The absence of strongly $C_4$ isotopically labelled animals in the early Neolithic indicates that the $C_4$ signal in humans of that period was not derived from the consumption of animals fed on millet, but from humans directly eating millet. In the Bronze Age, the $C_4$ signal in humans may be interpreted as derived from increased consumption of either millet or animals fed on millet, since the contemporaneous animals also have a $C_4$ signal.

# Further reading

Flad, R. 'Xinglongwa jades and genesis of value in northeast China.' In C. Deng and G. Liu (eds.), *The Origins of Chinese Jade Culture: Xinglongwa Jades Research and Catalogue*. Chinese University of Hong Kong Press, 2008. 224–34.

Hanks, B.K. and K. Linduff (eds.). *Social Complexity in Prehistoric Eurasia*. Cambridge University Press, 2009.

Li, X. *Development of Social Complexity in the Liaoxi Area, Northeast China*. Oxford: Archaeopress, 2008.

Liu, L. *The Chinese Neolithic: Trajectories to Early States*. Cambridge University Press, 2004.

Liu, L. and X. Chen. *The Archaeology of China: From the Late Paleolithic to the Early Bronze Age*. Cambridge University Press, 2012.

Liu, X., H.V. Hunt, and M.K. Jones. 'River valleys and foothills: changing archaeological perceptions of North China's earliest farms.' *Antiquity*, 83 (2009), 82–95.

Liu, X., M.K. Jones, Z. Zhao, G. Liu, and T.C. O'Connell. 'The earliest evidence of millet as a staple crop: new light on Neolithic foodways in North China.' *American Journal of Physical Anthropology*, 149 (2012), 238–90.

Peterson, C.E. and G. Shelach. 'Jiangzhai: social and economic organization of a middle Neolithic Chinese village.' *Journal of Anthropological Archaeology*, 31 (2012), 265–301.

Shelach, G. 'Economic adaptation, community structure, and sharing strategies of households at early sedentary communities in northeast China.' *Journal of Anthropological Archaeology*, 25 (2006), 318–45.

Yang, H., G. Liu, and C. Deng. *The Origin of Jades in East Asia: Jades of the Xinglongwa Culture*. Centre for Chinese Archaeology and Art, Chinese University of Hong Kong, 2007.

Zhao, Z. 'New archaeobotanic data for the study of the origins of agriculture in China.' *Current Anthropology*, 52, Supplement 4 (2011), S295–304.

# 14

# Early agriculture in Japan

SIMON KANER AND KEN'ICHI YANO

## A diversity of foodways

At first glance, the modern Japanese agricultural landscape appears to be dominated by rice paddies, laid out in regimented grids across the lowlands that comprise around a fifth of the entire landmass of Japan, and tightly packed into mountain valleys and coastal terraces wherever slope and aspect permit. Even in the urban sprawl that now constitutes such a dominant part of the modern Japanese landscape, dense housing is punctuated by the occasional paddy field. This ubiquitous presence of the rice paddy and the associated importance that rice farming has assumed in Japanese mentalities, however, mask a diversity of cultivation practices and intensive relationships with plants and animals other than rice that extends back millennia before the first paddy field was constructed in the archipelago. Yet rice agriculture and the practices it requires are still by many considered to have shaped the development of early Japanese society. Rice farming is celebrated as central to Japanese heritage: the terraced paddy fields of the Noto peninsula are put forward as a Globally Important Agricultural Heritage System, and the region also boasts the oldest rice ball from Japan, 2,100 years old, from Sugitani Chanobatake in Ishikawa prefecture.[1] The constitution of paddy fields themselves affects the nature of the archaeological record.[2] In this chapter we will track the development of agrarian societies in Japan and consider the ways in which the relationship between rice farming and other

Except in the chapter title, Japanese personal names are given in Japanese order (family name, given name). Macrons have been omitted throughout.

1 http://isp.unu.edu/news/2011/sado-noto-farm-methods-listed-as-giahs.html (accessed 21 June 2014); I.K.M.B. Senta, *Yachi Sugitani iseki gun* (*The Yachi Sugitani Site Group*) (Kanazawa, 1995); J.J. Ertl, 'Revisiting village Japan', unpublished PhD thesis (University of California, Berkeley, 2007), 201–13.

2 G.L. Barnes, 'Paddy field archaeology', *Journal of Field Archaeology*, 13 (1986), 371–9, and 'Paddy fields now and then', *World Archaeology*, 22 (1990), 1–17.

foodways contributed to the broader social and cultural developments in the archipelago up to 500 CE.

The Japanese archaeological sequence from the end of the Pleistocene to 500 CE is divided into three chronological periods. The Jomon begins with the appearance of ceramics around 14,000 BCE, and is named after the Japanese term for the cord-marking by which the majority of Jomon ceramics are distinguished.[3] Broad-based foraging replaced large-game hunting in the early stages of the Jomon, including a degree of plant domestication and cultivation. The Yayoi period begins with the appearance of wet rice agriculture in northern Kyushu and the introduction of metallurgy around 900 BCE and is named after the locality in Tokyo where Yayoi-style pottery was first identified.[4] The Kofun period begins with the construction of the first monumental mounded tombs around 250 CE.[5] During this period the first state-level societies developed in the archipelago, accompanied by large-scale land development for agriculture and the centralized control of agricultural surpluses. This all took place in the context of the introduction of Buddhism along with other aspects of Chinese civilization from the East Asian continent in the sixth century CE, including writing, urban architecture, and systems of governance.

It has long been thought that Japanese traditional culture was based on rice cultivation, associated with many rituals and religious ideas. The first centralized government in the seventh century distributed paddy fields to the male population and collected taxes in the form of rice.[6] The origin of rice cultivation has therefore become a central problem for understanding Japanese culture, economy, and society. There are, however, a series of other important grains traditionally grown in Japan, including barley, wheat, buckwheat, beans, and millets, and they supplemented rice especially in mountainous areas or in famine. The study of the history of Japanese agriculture has focused

3 S. Kaner, 'The western language Jomon', in G.L. Barnes (ed.), *Hoabhinhian, Jomon, Yayoi and Early States: Bibliographic Reviews of Far Eastern Archaeology* (Oxford: Oxbow, 1990), 31–62; T. Kobayashi, *Jomon Reflections: Forager Life and Culture in the Prehistoric Japanese Archipelago* (Oxford: Oxbow, 2005).

4 M. Hudson, 'From Toro to Yoshinogari: changing perspectives on Yayoi period archaeology', in Barnes (ed.), *Hoabhinhian, Jomon, Yayoi and Early States*, 63–112; K. Mizoguchi, *The Archaeology of Japan: From the Earliest Rice Farming Villages to the Rise of the State* (Cambridge University Press, 2013).

5 J.E. Kidder, *Himiko and Japan's Elusive Chiefdom of Yamatai: Archaeology, History and Mythology* (Honolulu: University of Hawai'i Press, 2007).

6 W.W. Farris, *Population, Disease and Land in Early Japan 645–900* (Cambridge, MA: Harvard University Press, 1995).

on the cultivation of these potential staple plant foods. Domesticated animals played only a limited role in Japanese farming.

This chapter discusses the origin and development of rice cultivation in Japan, while reviewing the evidence for the cultivation of other kinds of plant food. Rice cultivation in paddy fields appeared around 900 BCE, but there is an ongoing debate about the role of other cultivated plants, dry-field crops, and their status as staple foods, in the preceding Jomon period, possibly involving slash-and-burn agriculture. This diversity of trajectories towards agrarian society in Japan forces us to question the inevitability of the spread of farming lifeways, and to give weight to the ways in which a diversity of subsistence practices was implicated in the establishment and reproduction of traditions of social and ritual practice relating to agriculture in the archipelago.[7]

## The history of research into agricultural origins in Japan

Although Yayoi-style pottery was first identified at a location adjacent to the University of Tokyo campus in 1888, the significance of the Yayoi period in Japanese history was not recognized till the 1910s. In 1925 Yamanouchi Sugao discovered the imprint of a rice grain in the surface of a Yayoi pot, and in 1936

---

7 C.M. Aikens and T. Akazawa, 'Fishing and farming in early Japan: Jomon littoral tradition carried on into Yayoi times at the Miura caves on Tokyo Bay', in C.M. Aikens and S.N. Rhee (eds.), *Pacific Northeast Asia in Prehistory: Hunter-Fisher-Gatherers, Farmers and Socio-political Elites* (Pullman: Washington State University Press, 1992), 3–12; P. Bleed et al., 'Between the mountains and the sea: optimal foraging patterns and faunal remains at Yagi, an early Jomon community in southwestern Hokkaido, Japan', *Arctic Anthropology*, 26 (1989), 107–26; G. Crawford, 'The transitions to agriculture in Japan', in A.B. Gebauer and T.D. Price (eds.), *Transitions to Agriculture in Prehistory*, Monographs in World Archaeology 4 (Madison, WI: Prehistory Press, 1992), 312–20; M. Nishida, 'The emergence of food production in Neolithic Japan', *Journal of Anthropological Archaeology*, 2 (1983), 305–22; Y. Sato (ed.), *Jomon nogyo wo toraenaosu (Recapturing Jomon Agriculture)*, Science of Humanity Bensei 14 (Tokyo: Bensei Shuppan, 2002); H. Shitara, *Jomon shakkai to Yayoi shakkai (Jomon Society and Yayoi Society)* (Tokyo: Keibunsha, 2014); H. Shitara et al. (eds.), *Shokuryo no kakutoku to seisan (Production and Acquisition of Foodstuffs)*, Yayoi jidai no kokogaku 5 (Archaeology of the Yayoi Period 5) (Tokyo: Doseisha, 2011).

many wooden agricultural implements were discovered at Karako (from 1977 known as Karako-Kagi) in Nara. Although these discoveries led Japanese archaeologists to believe that paddy-field agriculture began in the Yayoi period, it was not until the middle of the twentieth century that the first prehistoric farming settlement with associated paddy fields was excavated, at Toro in Shizuoka prefecture, dating to the late Yayoi period.[8] In 1978 the oldest known paddy fields from Japan were discovered at Itazuke in Fukuoka prefecture (Figure 14.1). Over the following decades, more than 200 examples of ancient paddy fields have been discovered along with a rich material culture and evidence for settlement structure and pattern, discoveries that permit sophisticated discussion of the nature of early agricultural society in the Japanese archipelago.[9] For much of the twentieth century, discussions about the nature of agrarian society in ancient Japan were structured in terms of Marxist-inspired ideas of historical materialism and modes of production. Although the explicit use of these ideas has been critiqued, social and cultural change during this period, and associated developments in agricultural technology, continue to be interpreted using a framework of contradictions. Much of the material culture of the Yayoi period in Japan has its origins on the East Asian continent, and cross-dating with the historical sequence in ancient China has traditionally been very important. In recent years extensive programmes of radiocarbon dating have resulted in a major reassessment of the dating of the beginning of the Yayoi period.[10]

Discoveries at Yoshinogari in Saga prefecture have been instrumental in revising the representation of the Yayoi period. While Toro provided images of a self-sufficient small-scale farming community, Yoshinogari is evidence of an urban form with a high level of social organization (Figure 14.2).[11]

8 W. Edwards, 'Buried discourse: the Toro site and Japanese national identity in the early postwar period', *Journal of Japanese Studies*, 17 (1991), 1–23.
9 R. Takahashi, 'Symbiotic relations between paddy-field rice cultivators and hunter-gatherer-fishers in Japanese prehistory: archaeological considerations of the transition from the Jomon age to the Yayoi age', in K. Ikeya et al. (eds.), *Interactions Between Hunter-Gatherers and Farmers: From Prehistory to Present* (Osaka: National Museum of Ethnology, 2009), 71–98.
10 S. Fujio, *(Shin) Yayoi jidai (The (New) Yayoi period)* (Tokyo: Yoshikawa bunkan, 2011); S. Shoda, 'Radiocarbon and archaeology in Japan and Korea: what has changed because of the Yayoi dating controversy?', *Radiocarbon*, 55 (2010), 421–7.
11 M. Hudson and G. Barnes, 'Yoshinogari: a Yayoi settlement in northern Kyushu', *Monumenta Nipponica*, 46 (1991), 211–35.

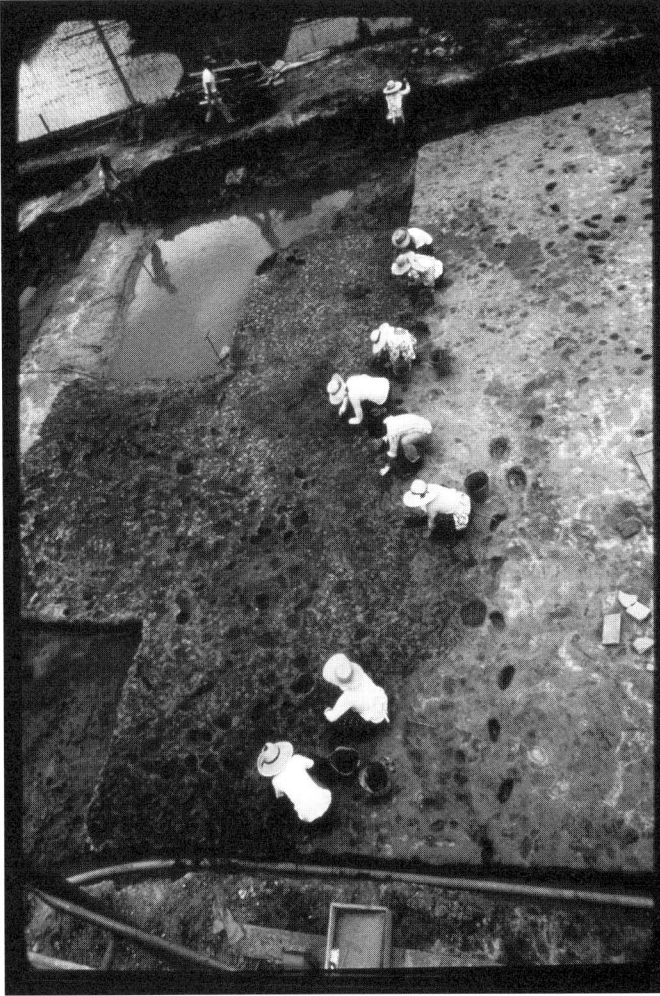

Figure 14.1 Excavations of early Yayoi rice paddies at Itazuke, Fukuoka prefecture, revealed the footprints of some of the earliest known rice farmers in the Japanese archipelago.

## From resistance to resilience: the significance of Jomon cultivation in the history of early Japanese agriculture

For many, the commencement of the Yayoi period, over the last decade redated from 300 BCE to the start of the first millennium BCE, represents the

Figure 14.2 Material culture associated with early rice farming: Yayoi pottery from Itazuke, Fukuoka prefecture, stone reaping knives from Yoshinogari, Saga prefecture, and wooden agricultural tools from Sasai, Fukuoka prefecture.

start of a distinctly Japanese archaeology, with the appearance of rice farming, the identification of elements of later Shinto cults and beliefs, the first mentions of Japan in historical documents,[12] and the arrival of people who were to mix with Jomon people to become the ancestors of most modern Japanese populations, speaking languages akin to modern Japanese.[13] Yayoi culture, based on rice farming, is often regarded as replacing the hunter-gatherer, aboriginal, Jomon cultures that preceded it, cultures that are traditionally not regarded as directly ancestral to present-day Japanese.

In the face of this dominant view, however, from early on some Japanese archaeologists, such as Oyama Kashiwa in the 1910s and 1920s and Fujimori Eiichi in the 1950s and 1960s, argued for some form of incipient farming

---

12 Kidder, *Himiko*; M. Soumare, *Japan in Five Ancient Chinese Chronicles* (Fukuoka: Kurodahan Press, 2009).

13 M. Hudson, *The Ruins of Identity: Ethnogenesis in the Japanese Islands* (Honolulu: University of Hawai'i Press, 1999).

before the advent of wet rice agriculture. They were supported by prominent scholars from other disciplines, such as the botanist Nakao Sasuke, the philosopher Ueyama Shunpei, and the geographer Sasaki Takaki, whose ideas underpinned the theory of cultivation in the Jomon as part of what was regarded as the 'laurel forest culture', named after the major forest zone that extends across southwestern Japan into the East Asian mainland. Although this theory, which has influenced ideas of Japanese identity, remains problematic in terms of archaeological proof, recent years, however, have seen a rehabilitation of Jomon culture as something much more connected to modern Japan than previously recognized.[14] Jomon populations are now regarded as having developed a very successful, resilient series of adaptations to living in the archipelago that secured their continuation for over ten millennia. These adaptations included ecological engineering based on effective understanding of the potential offered by a wide range of plants and animals, and terrestrial, riverine, and marine resources. Nuts, beans, grains, and very likely starchy tubers, along with a range of mammals (in particular boar and deer), fish, and shellfish, were utilized for food, while animal bone, plant fibres, and resins such as lacquer were central to the material culture repertoire.[15]

There are suggestions of a degree of manipulation and interference, including swidden agriculture, with some species indicative of cultivation and husbandry, on occasion resulting in some genetic modification, notably chestnuts.[16] The presence of grains, including rice, is attested from the middle Jomon, with impressions of rice grains being found on sherds of pottery.[17] Fujimori Eiichi was among the first to propose a theory of Jomon cultivation in the 1950s,[18] around the same time that Okamoto Taro was arguing for the

14  M. Hudson, 'Foragers as fetish in modern Japan', in J. Habu et al. (eds.), *Hunter-Gatherers of the North Pacific Rim* (Osaka: National Museum of Ethnology, 2003), 263–74; S. Kaner, 'Jomon revelations: what the prehistoric Japanese did for us', *Proceedings of the Japan Society*, 150 (2014), 129–42.

15  R. Pearson, 'Debating Jomon social complexity', *Asian Perspectives*, 46 (2007), 361–88; S. Noshiro and M. Suzuki, '*Rhus verniciflua* stokes grew in Japan since the early Jomon period', *Japanese Journal of Historical Botany*, 12 (2004), 3–11; H. Obata, *Tohoku ajia kominzoku shokubutsugaku to Jomon nogyo (Northeast Asian Palaeoethnobotany and Jomon Agriculture)* (Tokyo: Doseisha, 2009).

16  Y. Sato et al., 'Evidence for Jomon plant cultivation based on DNA analysis of chestnut remains', in Habu et al. (eds.), *Hunter-Gatherers*, 187–98.

17  M. Nakazawa, 'Examining Jomon cultivation from seed impressions on pottery', in S. Kaner et al. (eds.), *Origins of Agriculture: Challenging Old Orthodoxies, Championing New Perspectives* (Cambridge: McDonald Institute for Archaeological Research, forthcoming).

18  E. Fujimori (ed.), *Jomon noko (Jomon Agriculture)* (Tokyo: Gakuseisha, 1970).

recognition of the artistic merits of Jomon pottery.[19] In the absence of actual cultivated plant remains from Jomon sites, which were only discovered after his work, Fujimori interpreted large numbers of chipped stone axes from Chubu and Kanto as hoes for plant cultivation, which he backed up with circumstantial evidence, including changes in lithic assemblages, site size, and site location, and evidence for rituals.

This longer-term understanding of the development of rice agriculture in Japan is demanding a redefinition of the debate about the origins of agriculture in Japan, and resonates with a revised view of Japanese history which seeks to de-emphasize the significance of rice farming as the predominant lifestyle in the archipelago until the advent of industrialization.[20] In the new model, rice farming is seen as one component of a diverse complex of ways of procuring and producing food, rather than being a clear break with what had gone before, a foreign import resisted by native hunter-gatherers. It was something for which Jomon lifeways were 'pre-adapted', perhaps explaining why agriculture spread across much of the archipelago relatively rapidly.[21] It is quite possible that Jomon foragers were experimenting with rice themselves, or that rice was being imported and consumed even if not grown. The early AMS dates on rice grains from Kazahari in Aomori prefecture, dating to 900 BCE, just around the time when the first paddies were being constructed at the other end of the archipelago, indicate that Jomon people were exercising a degree of choice over their adoption of this new superfood.[22]

Gary Crawford, in recent surveys of early agriculture in Japan, argues that the Jomon should be considered neither as hunter-gatherers nor as agriculturalists as traditionally defined. Instead, he suggests that debates around the nature of Jomon subsistence be moved away from arguments around whether the relationship between people and plants in the Jomon should

---

19 S. Kaner (ed.), *The Power of Dogu: Ceramic Figures from Ancient Japan* (London: British Museum Press, 2009).

20 Y. Amino, *Rethinking Japanese History* (Ann Arbor: Center for Japanese Studies, University of Michigan, 2012); G. Crawford, 'The Jomon in early agricultural discourse: issues arising from Matsui, Kanehara and Pearson', *World Archaeology*, 40 (2008), 445–65.

21 T. Akazawa, 'Cultural change in prehistoric Japan: receptivity to rice agriculture in the Japanese archipelago', in F. Wendorf and A.E. Close (eds.), *Advances in World Archaeology* (New York: Academic Press, 1982), 151–211; K. Yano, 'The introduction of wet rice cultivation into western Japan and its Jomon precursors', in Kaner et al. (eds.), *Origins of Agriculture* (forthcoming).

22 C. D'Andrea, 'The dispersal of domesticated plants into north-eastern Japan and early agriculture in Japan: research since 1999', in T. Denham and R. White (eds.), *The Emergence of Agriculture* (London: Routledge, 2007), 154–74; K.C. Twiss, 'Problems of culture change in the late and final Jomon', *Indo-Pacific Prehistory Association Bulletin*, 21 (2001), 30–6.

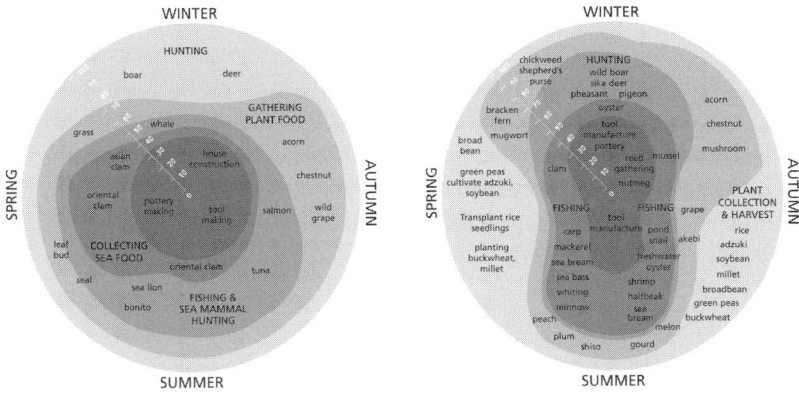

Figure 14.3 The Jomon (left) and Yayoi (right) annual 'calendars' of subsistence activities.
Left: Jomon calendar; right: Yayoi calendar.

be classified as foraging or collecting, or farming, to understanding the ways in which Jomon people engaged in 'plant husbandry' during their niche construction, and had an impact on their surrounding environment. This idea is familiar in Japan through the work of Nakao Sasuke, who proposed 'semi-cultivation' in the Jomon. Such behaviours included 'annual plant encouragement and probably management', and probably the indigenous domestication of barnyard millet and soybean, as well as the cultivation of bottle gourd, hemp, perilla, and adzuki bean.[23] Other possible Jomon cultigens include barley, buckwheat, burdock, rice, and shiso mint. Crawford also argues that Jomon subsistence should be understood in the context of broader 'resource production', which makes sense given that plants were certainly exploited for more than just their dietary value, notably lacquer and timber. Many of these resources continued to be exploited through the Yayoi period (Figure 14.3).

One area of archaeological methodology that continues to constrain understanding of early plant use in Japan is the very limited use of flotation to recover plant remains.[24] There is, however, increasing evidence for plant cultigens identified in the fabric of Jomon pots.[25] Further new lines of investigation include the identification of starch grains on grinding tools, in

23 Crawford, 'Jomon in early agricultural discourse', and 'Advances in understanding early agriculture in Japan', *Current Anthropology*, 52, Supplement 4 (2011), S331–45.

24 Crawford, 'Advances in understanding', 5; J. Habu, *Ancient Jomon of Japan* (Cambridge University Press, 2004), 59–60.

25 Nakazawa, 'Examining Jomon cultivation'.

research being undertaken by Shibutani Ayako and others.[26] An increase in the excavation of waterlogged sites from the Jomon, beginning with Torihama in Fukui prefecture in the 1970s[27] and more recently including sites such as Aota, Niigata prefecture, and Shimoyakebe, Tokyo, has produced additional evidence for intensive plant use, so that many archaeologists since the 1980s have accepted that cultivation and some domestication did take place before the appearance of paddy fields in northern Kyushu. Although the importance of intensive relationships with plant foods during the Jomon is now recognized, however, most scholars still argue against agriculture as such during the Jomon.[28]

Isotopic analysis of human remains is also proving fruitful in terms of understanding diversity and change in Jomon and Yayoi diets, suggesting differential regional and temporal patterning in the amount of $C_3$ and $C_4$ plants and animals consumed, and marine versus terrestrial foodstuffs, as well as differences in the diets of men and women.[29] New research into the chemical composition of food crusts on pottery is also beginning to cast light on the way ceramics were actually being used in the preparation of food as early as 16,000 years ago.[30]

## The development of agricultural settlements and landscapes

### Initial Yayoi: the introduction of paddy technology and the earliest farming settlements

Although even before World War II Japanese archaeologists thought that Yayoi people cultivated rice, one of the reasons the discoveries at Toro

---

26 Y. Kudo (ed.), *Jomonjin no shokubutsu riyo* (*New Perspectives on the Plant Use of Jomon People*) (Tokyo: Shinizumisha, 2014).
27 See Nishida, 'Emergence of food production'.
28 Habu, *Ancient Jomon of Japan*, 60; J. Habu and M. Hall, 'Climate change, human impacts on the landscape and subsistence specialisation: historical ecology and changes in Jomon hunter-gatherer lifeways', in V.D. Thompson and J.C. Waggoner (eds.), *The Archaeology and Historical Ecology of Small Scale Societies* (Gainsville: University Press of Florida, 2013); Kobayashi, *Jomon Reflections*; A. Matsui and M. Kanehara, 'The question of prehistoric plant husbandry during the Jomon period in Japan', *World Archaeology*, 38 (2006), 259–73.
29 B. Chisholm, 'Paleodiet studies in Japan using stable isotope analysis', *Bulletin of the International Jomon Culture Conference*, 1 (2004), 25–34; L.G. Friedman, 'What is Yayoi? Isotopic investigations into the Jomon–Yayoi transition in western Japan', unpublished PhD thesis (University of Cambridge, 2012); M. Yoneda et al., 'Isotopic evidence on inland-water Jomon population excavated from the Boji site, Nagano, Japan', *Journal of Archaeological Science*, 31 (2004), 97–107.
30 S. Kaner, 'A potted history of Japan', *Nature Digest*, 10 (2013), 30–1.

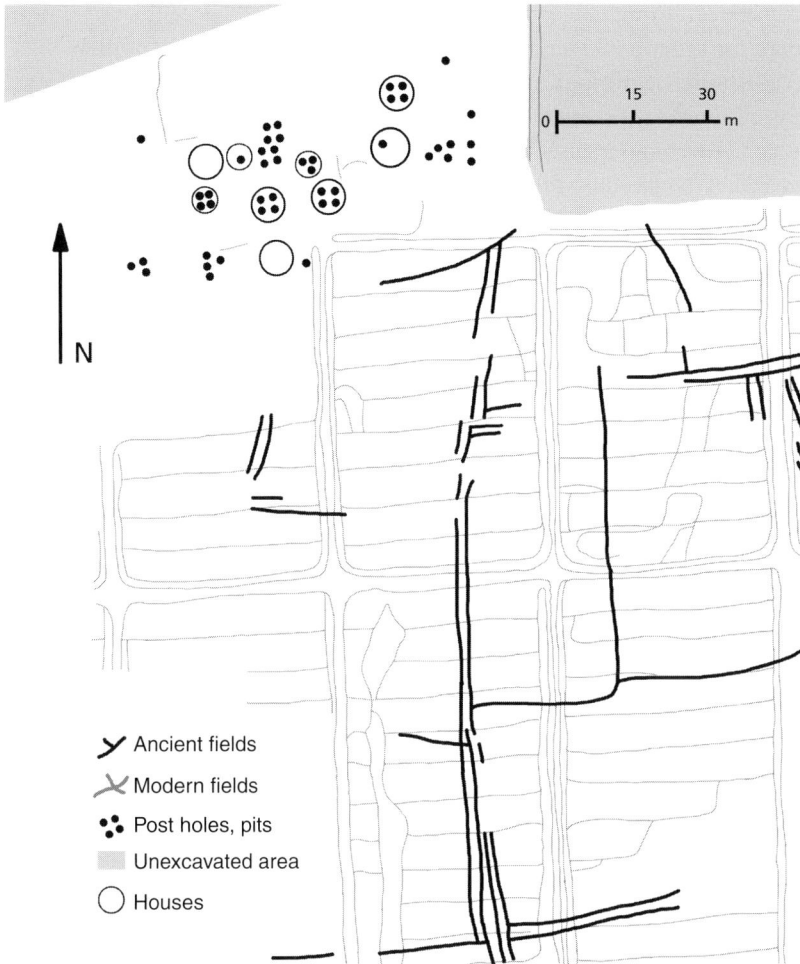

Figure 14.4 Plan of Toro, a late Yayoi farming village in Shizuoka prefecture.

(Figure 14.4) caused such a sensation was that for the first time archaeology was able to demonstrate the great antiquity of the technology of rice farming. The range of artefacts discovered was recognizable to what was still a predominantly agricultural population. This happened at the end of World War II, just as the traditional Japanese study of the past was freed from the long dependence on the acceptance of the quasi-historical narratives set out in the eighth-century *Kojiki* and *Nihon Shoki* and the imperial ideology as propagated through these works – changes which enabled for the first time in Japan the unfettered investigation of everyday life in the ancient past.[31]

The presence of rice agriculture was originally inferred through a new set of tools, unlike those used by Jomon peoples. The agricultural tools required by paddy farming include rice-reaping knives, originally made of stone but eventually replaced by the late Yayoi with iron, for which raw material was imported from the continent. Wooden tools included different types of hoes, with wide, narrow, rounded, and composite blades, some with the blade attached at an oblique angle, and others with forked ends, probable plough blades, fragments of spades and picks, and objects for processing the rice, including pounders.

A number of routes for the arrival of rice farming into northern Kyushu have been proposed (see Map 14.1). Kazuo Miyamoto argues that farmers from the Korean peninsula, where paddy rice was being grown from about 1500 BCE, migrated across the Tsushima Straits into northern Kyushu in search for new land for agriculture, prompted by cooler climatic conditions which may have impacted on the productivity of farming on the peninsula, where larger settlements had already developed and a degree of social differentiation was being expressed through the burial of elites. Miyamoto argues for a series of such migration events, the most significant coinciding with a cooler climatic phase between 850 and 700 BCE, associated with the undecorated pottery recognized as the Yu'usu style in Kyushu.[32]

One of the earliest known paddy fields in Japan was discovered at Nabatake in Saga prefecture. Located in the bottom of a small valley, this paddy required no artificial irrigation. Within a relatively short time, however, paddies that required irrigation were being constructed at Itazuke, a short distance to the northeast of Nabatake. Although the whole area was not excavated, the paddies at Itazuke are thought to extend across an area some 400 × 80 m, just below a ditch-enclosed settlement area. The paddies were divided into segments by low banks, 10 cm high. Water was supplied via a canal which ran along the edge of the upper terrace, on which the settlement area was located, with a series of dams and outlets controlling the flow of water to the paddies below.

---

31 Edwards, 'Buried discourse'.
32 K. Miyamoto, *Nogyo no kigen o saguru: ine no kita michi* (*Searching for the Origins of Agriculture: The Route Rice Came By*) (Tokyo: Yoshikawa Kobunkan, 2009), and 'The East Asian contexts for the origins of agriculture in Japan', in Kaner et al. (eds.), *Origins of Agriculture* (forthcoming).

Map 14.1 Japan showing the principal sites mentioned in the chapter: 1. Yagi; 2. Kakinoshima B; 3. Sannai Maruyama; 4. Sunazawa; 5. Kazahari; 6. Taretabagi; 7. Jizoden; 8. Kutsukata; 9. Aota; 10. SugitaniChanobatake; 11. Yashiro; 12. Hidaka; 13. Kuroimine; 14. Mitsudera; 15. Shimoyakebe; 16. Otsuka and Saikachido; 17. Torihama; 18. Asahi; 19. Toro; 20. Aoya-Kamijichi; 21. Hoenzaka; 22. Uryudo; 23. Ikeshima-Fukumanji; 24. Daikai; 25. Karako-Kagi; 26. Hyakkendawa; 27. Ama; 28. Ikegami-Sone; 29. Doigahama; 30. Haranotsuji; 31. Itazuke; 32. Nishijinmachi; 33. Nabatake; 34. Etsuji; 35. Hie-Naka; 36. Kuma-Nishida; 37. Yoshinogari.

The first rice farming communities such as Etsuji and Itazuke on the Fukuoka plain were enclosed by ditches. A number of settlements dating to this initial Yayoi stage have been identified in northwestern Kyushu. Polished stone reaping knives were found at the settlement of Etsuji, which was occupied by rice farmers in an area with considerable evidence for Jomon activity.[33] The site exhibits an interesting combination of Jomon and Yayoi features. Although no settlements that can be considered actual colonies from Korea have been found to date, new house types, similar to those found on the Korean peninsula, were constructed, along with V-sectioned ditches enclosing settlement areas. Burial areas were spatially distinct from residential areas. The ceramics used in these new settlements, however, remained of the indigenous variety, arguing against the presence of migrants, and for the adoption of certain aspects of continental culture by some of the residents of northern Kyushu.

### Early Yayoi

The next phase in the development of agricultural landscapes began around 500 BCE (the start of the early Yayoi period), when rice farming villages began to appear in many parts of western Japan as the technology of paddy agriculture spread across western Honshu, along the coasts of the Japan Sea and the Inland Sea. During the early Yayoi period the number of settlements increased markedly, new hamlets fissioning off from older, established ones, probably due to population increase facilitated by the stability of food supply afforded by rice farming. Many of these settlements, although the majority were newly established, reflecting the need for particular locational attributes, also exhibit traces of Jomon culture, suggesting that they were being established by, or in conjunction with, the local populations. Akazawa Takeru was among the first to argue that the Jomon populations of western Japan were to an extent pre-adapted to taking up rice farming. These new farming communities were relatively small, often enclosed by ditches and comprising just a few pit-buildings and a raised-floor storage granary. Examples include the Hyakkengawa-Sawada settlement in Okayama prefecture, where the Jomon tradition of burying the dead within the residential area continued, and Daikai in Hyogo prefecture, where Jomon-type stone tools, including polished stone bars, were found within a ditch-

---

33 Mizoguchi, *Archaeology of Japan*, 55–66.

enclosed farming settlement.[34] The Kawachi plain in modern-day Osaka began to be settled, but the low-lying topography meant that the early occupations of sites such as Ama and Uryudo were susceptible to flooding.[35] Paddy fields also began to be constructed in inland basins, as at the Nakanishi-Akitsu complex in the Nara basin, separated from the Osaka plain by a range of mountains.[36] This period also saw the establishment of a number of sites that were to develop into major centres during the subsequent middle Yayoi, including Ikegami-Sone in Osaka[37] and Karako-Kagi in Nara.[38]

Other domesticated plants that regularly occur on Yayoi period sites include millet (barnyard millet, *Echinochloa utilis*, Japanese *hie*; broomcorn millet, *Panicum miliaceum*, Japanese *kibi*; and foxtail millet, *Setaria italica*, Japanese *awa*); barley (Japanese *omugi*), although this does not become common until the Kofun period; and pulses, including adzuki beans, pea, and soybean. A number of fruits were imported from the continent, including apricot, melon, peach, pear, and plum. Nuts, including acorns, chestnuts, and walnuts, continued to be exploited from the Jomon period. The presence of these plants demonstrates that dry-field agriculture and horticulture were practised from the beginning of the Yayoi period in conjunction with paddy rice farming.[39]

## Middle Yayoi

Entering the middle Yayoi, larger villages developed, comprising a cluster of hamlets, each from several to tens of dwellings with shared storage facilities and public areas. Mizoguchi and others argue for the existence of some form of social organization that cross-cut a number of such villages, akin to clans or sodalities, forming larger-scale inter-settlement descent groups. Towards the end of the middle Yayoi, large regional centres appeared at key locations on the coastal plains in Kyushu, serving as centres of production, distribution, and ritual activity. At Sugu in Fukuoka, for example, some estimates suggest

---

34 Ibid., 86–7.

35 C.M. Aikens and T. Higuchi, *The Prehistory of Japan* (New York and London: Academic Press, 1982).

36 See Chapter 15 below on the Nara basin.

37 L.A. Hosoya, 'Sacred commonness: an archaeobotanical approach to Yayoi social stratification: the "Central Building Model" and the Osaka Ikegami site', in K. Ikeya et al. (eds.), *Interactions*, 99–178.

38 J. Oksbjerg, 'Religious imagery of middle Yayoi settlements', unpublished PhD thesis (University of London, 2009).

39 G. Crawford, 'East Asian plant domestication', in M. Stark (ed.), *Archaeology of Asia* (Oxford: Blackwell, 2006), 77–95; Crawford, 'Advances in understanding'; Hudson, 'From Toro to Yoshinogari', 75–7.

that as many as 1,500 people lived in an agglomeration comprising some 40 to 50 hamlets extending over 200 ha.

Following the period of rapid growth in the early Yayoi, the number of settlements remained relatively stable during the middle Yayoi. Karako-Kagi in the Nara basin is one of the most famous examples of central settlements. Oksbjerg describes how by the start of the middle Yayoi, a dual settlement system was established in the Kinki region, with large moated centres of craft production (such as Karako-Kagi) and smaller farming hamlets. Although Karako-Kagi has been excavated many times since the 1940s, only two pit-houses have been discovered, along with many post holes amid the patch-work of the many small-scale excavations that have taken place there, suggest-ing that these large moated sites may have functioned as centres of production, exchange, and ceremonial activity as much as residential centres.[40] There is also evidence for large structures, perhaps akin to a $17 \times 7$ m building discovered in 1995 at the Yayoi 'city' of Ikegami-Sone in Osaka prefecture. Karako-Kagi, the earliest known agricultural settlement in the Nara basin, was established in the early Yayoi, at the same time as the initial agricultural settlement of the Osaka plain. In the first phase of occupation, three individual settlements, each measuring between 150 and 300 $m^2$, formed around a central natural depression. Each settlement comprised a cluster of five or six pit-houses and was enclosed by a series of ditches. Between phases II and III, in the first half of the middle Yayoi, this complex of ditches was deliberately filled in and replaced by a much larger, single moat, up to 10 m wide and 2 m deep. This was followed by the further digging of a series of concentric moats, eventually creating a ditched zone up to 200 m wide, along with a series of internal ditches which divided up the enclosed area. An episode of catastrophic inundation occurred at the end of the middle Yayoi, after which ditches were redug on a reduced scale at the start of the late Yayoi. These ditches were then again filled in at the end of the late Yayoi, and the settlement continued to function, though without moats, during the early Kofun period. Although clear evidence for residential occupation following the enclosure of the whole site remains elusive, traces of large buildings have been identified, along with remains of bronze casting (including for bronze bells), and stone (notably for rice-reaping knives), woodworking, weaving, and ceramic production. Large quantities of pottery imported from other regions of western Japan attest to the central nature of Karako-Kagi. The site also functioned as a ceremonial ritual centre, as indicated by the large number of pottery sherds with incised pictures, with the deliberate deposition

40 Oksbjerg, 'Religious imagery', 70–82.

of large quantities of ceramic vessels in ditches and around wells, often rapidly followed by the intentional filling in of the ditches. The site also produced quantities of animal bones that had received special attention, including boar and deer bones that appear to have been used for purposes of divination.

By the turn of the millennium, 'substantial portions of the major flood-plains in western Japan were covered by paddies watered by sophisticated irrigation systems. The latter often consisted of large irrigation canals and/or triangular-sectioned dams of substantial scale constructed by compositing logs across small rivers.'[41] Excavated examples include Hyakkengawa in Okayama and Ikeshima-Fukumanji in Osaka. Despite the scale and complexity of these facilities (that at Hyakkengawa is over 1 km in length), the way in which the water was divided indicates that paddies and their irrigation systems were a device well suited to communal egalitarianism.

By the end of the late Yayoi, these major centres were enclosed, and individual residential zones divided by ditches, sometimes on a massive scale. Some of these settlements, such as Hie-Naka in Fukuoka prefecture, which extended over 100 ha in area, were almost urban in character. These large settlements also had huge cemeteries whose catchments clearly transcended individual residential groupings: over a thousand burials were excavated at Kuma-Nishida, some set out in a linear fashion, suggestive of descent groups or moieties. Despite the scale of some of these settlements, however, there is no evidence for any clear social hierarchies, for example overtly rich individual burials or elite-precinct-type compounds as are found later.

The middle Yayoi also witnessed considerable increase in population in the eastern part of Honshu, with some larger centres appearing. Hidaka in Gunma prefecture and the deeply buried paddies at Yashiro in Nagano prefecture are examples of rice-farming communities in inland parts of central Honshu. Large settlements and settlement clusters developed around the Kanto region, one of the most famous being the moated settlement of Otsuka and associated cemetery of ditched burial enclosures at Saikachido, in Kanagawa prefecture (Figure 14.5).[42] Rice paddies had already appeared in northern Honshu, for example at Tareyanagi and Sunazawa in Aomori prefecture.[43] These fields were used for several decades before being abandoned. Paddies at Kutsukata 4 km inland from the Pacific coast in Miyagi prefecture were inundated by a huge tidal wave, which left lenses of marine sand across the site.

41 Mizoguchi, *Archaeology of Japan*, 186.   42 Aikens and Higuchi, *Prehistory of Japan*.
43 Y. Kuraku, *Suiden no kokogaku* (*The Archaeology of Paddy Fields*) (Tokyo University Press, 1991).

Figure 14.5 Ditch-enclosed Yayoi settlement at Otsuka Kanagawa prefecture.

## Late Yayoi

The beginning of the late Yayoi witnessed some marked changes. While in some areas, especially in central and eastern Japan, the number of settlements increased, elsewhere there were significant declines, possibly related to political changes on the continent disrupting the flow of imported prestige goods, and to

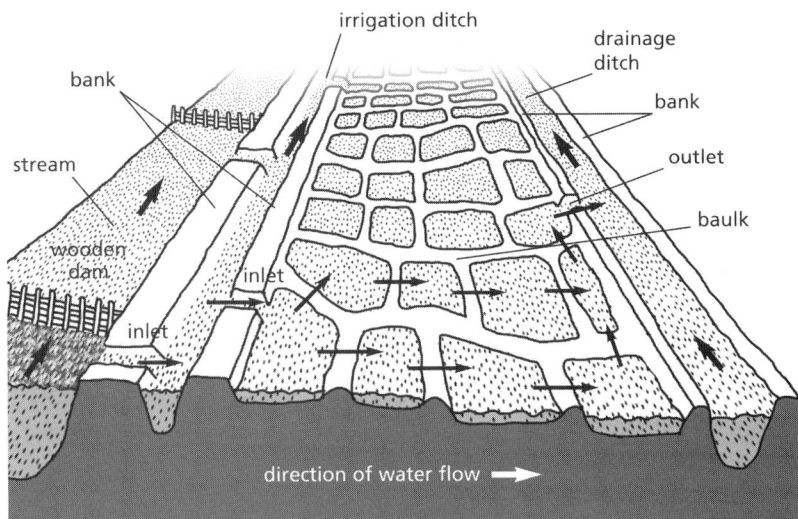

Figure 14.6 Yayoi period paddy fields from Osaka.

another cold spell, adversely affecting productivity. Many small settlements were abandoned altogether, with a greater degree of aggregation in the established regional centres in northern Kyushu, and a series of larger hilltop settlements appear in the Kinki region, especially around Osaka Bay.[44] One of the regional centres that survived in Kinki was Karako-Kagi in the Nara basin.

The scale of paddy complexes and the associated infrastructure required for effective irrigation increased, in turn demanding new levels of management. Large-scale irrigation facilities are present in various parts of Japan, notably Osaka, and at sites such as Hyakkengawa in Okayama and Naka-Kunryu in Fukuoka (Figure 14.6). At Toro, for example, some fifty paddies, the largest of which was about 2,000 m$^2$ in area, extended over 70,000 m$^2$, irrigated by wide canals and possibly farmed in collaboration with the inhabitants of nearby settlements.[45] The organization of labour needed to support rice production on this scale required significant collaboration, and it appears that ritual practices may have been employed to reassert the egalitarian ethos. About this time, however, new forms of settlement and burial began to appear which suggest that social status was for the first time ascribed rather than just achieved. Residential compounds segregated from the

44 T. Arbousse Bastide, *Les structures d'habitat enclos de la protohistoire du Japon (période de Yayoi 350 BC–300 AD)* (Oxford: Archaeopress, 2005).
45 Mizoguchi, *Archaeology of Japan*, 190–1.

ordinary dwelling areas began to appear, sometimes with exclusive storage facilities. These elite residential precincts begin to be constructed at the same time as individual burial compounds, with children receiving the same special funerary treatment as adults, replacing the large communal burial facilities.

The site of Yoshinogari in Saga prefecture provides a clear example of a large late Yayoi settlement.[46] Yayoi settlement in this area extends back to the early Yayoi, and during the middle and late Yayoi a very large settlement developed covering some 25 ha in total, enclosed by a moat that was in places 7 m wide and 3 m deep. Large parts of Yoshinogari have been reconstructed as a historical park, and visitors today gain a strong impression of this Yayoi town divided into a number of sectors by internal ditches and palisades, including cemeteries and an elite residential compound. Over 100 pit-buildings from the middle to late Yayoi were excavated and the population is estimated to have been between 1,000 and 1,500 people at any one time. In the northwestern part of the inner moated sector was located an elite residential compound, with pillared buildings and pit-buildings. A series of pillared watchtowers, each estimated as originally being 10 m in height, overlooked the settlement from the inner moat. Such towers are described in the third-century CE Chinese historical document, the *Wei Zhi*. In addition, the remains of a number of large raised-floor storehouses were found: a cluster of thirty such buildings was located outside the main fortifications. The largest were 5 × 6.5 m in area, much larger than normal Yayoi raised-floor buildings.

Large numbers of burials were also found at Yoshinogari, most notably a large oval burial mound, 40 m long and 30 m wide, estimated to have had an original height of between 4 and 5 m, dating to the end of the early Yayoi and the beginning of the early middle Yayoi. This mound contained a series of jar burials, with bronze daggers and glass beads that originated on the East Asian mainland. Elsewhere over 2,500 other burials, including jar burials, pit burials, wooden coffins, and cists, have been excavated from at least twelve cemetery areas. Some of those interred died a violent death, as attested by headless bodies and individuals with arrowheads and sword fragments. Shell bracelets evidence trade and exchange of commodities across a wide area, as far as the Ryukyu islands southwest of Kyushu, and Hokkaido to the north. Fragments of linen and silk were recovered from some of the burials, silkworm cocoons having been introduced from southern China by the end of the early Yayoi. Enormous quantities of artefacts included numerous stone reaping knives, axes, chisels, grinding stones, querns, and spindle whorls, and from the middle

46 Hudson and Barnes, 'Yoshinogari'.

Yayoi, large numbers of iron tools, including arrowheads, axes, knives, sickles, and spade-shoes. Bronze-working was also undertaken at the site, and a number of stone moulds were discovered. Rice agriculture was the major subsistence activity. The production of sufficient surplus to fill the large-scale storage facilities mentioned above would have required large areas of rice paddy, as discussed further below. Dog, deer, boar, and pig bones and shells indicate that hunting and shellfish gathering were undertaken, especially during the earlier phases of occupation.

## Kofun period: agriculture and state formation

The fifth and sixth centuries saw the arrival from the continent of a new generation of agricultural technology which facilitated unprecedented land development for farming. Iron bits on ploughs began to be used in the fourth century CE, and in the fifth century a new type of U-shaped iron shoe to fit on the end of the blade of a hoe made turning the soil much easier, especially in dry upland areas. From this time it seems that draught animals – cattle and horses – were increasingly used to prepare the ground for farming.[47]

The eruption of Mount Haruna in Gunma prefecture in the middle of the sixth century CE, however, covered the surrounding landscape in up to 2 m of pumice and ash, and excavations since the 1980s have uncovered an exceptionally well-preserved landscape with complete farming communities, complementing the evidence for elite residential compounds and burial facilities at Mitsudera I and Hodaka. Discoveries at Kuroimine have revealed exceptionally well-preserved remains of buildings, including dwellings and cow-sheds, storage structures with raised floors, possible rice seedbeds, and irrigated rice paddies (Figure 14.7).[48] The buildings and other facilities were connected by footpaths and the residential units were enclosed by brushwood fences. At least eight such units measuring 30 × 40 m were uncovered, along with one much larger house.

By the fifth century CE, the storage and control of agricultural surpluses were transformed. The remains of massive centralized storage facilities have been discovered at Hoenzaka in Osaka prefecture and Narutaki in Wakayama prefecture.[49] At Hoenzaka, it is estimated that the sixteen large storehouses,

47 R. Pearson (ed.), *Ancient Japan* (Washington, DC: Arthur M. Sackler Gallery; Tokyo: Agency for Cultural Affairs, 1992).

48 H. Tsude, 'Kuroimine', in Pearson (ed.), *Ancient Japan*, 223–5.

49 H. Tsude, 'Early state formation in Japan', in J.R. Piggott (ed.), *Capital and Countryside in Japan, 300–1180: Japanese Historians Interpreted in English* (Ithaca, NY: East Asia Program, Cornell University, 2006), 13–53 (33–5).

(a)

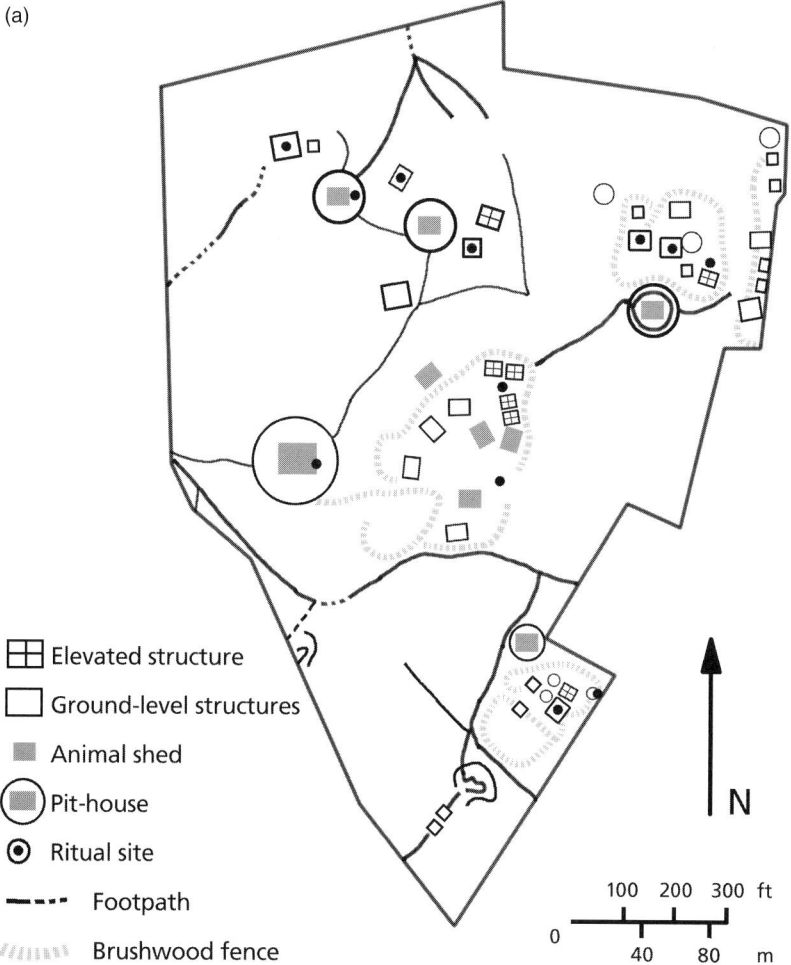

Elevated structure

Ground-level structures

Animal shed

Pit-house

Ritual site

Footpath

Brushwood fence

100   200   300 ft

0

40    80    m

N

Figure 14.7 Plan of the sixth-century farmstead at Kuroimine, Gunma prefecture:
(a) Kuroimine western area; (b) Kuroimine eastern area.

each up to 90 m² in area and greatly exceeding the scale of storehouses in contemporary settlements, had an overall capacity of some 37,000 *koku* of rice, or 189,000 bushels. Accepting that such huge storage facilities may also have held other important commodities (iron, salt, textiles), and drawing on early historic tax records, Tsude suggests that the area of paddy required to yield such amounts would be in the region of 400,000 acres.[50]

50  Ibid., 52, note 44.

(b)

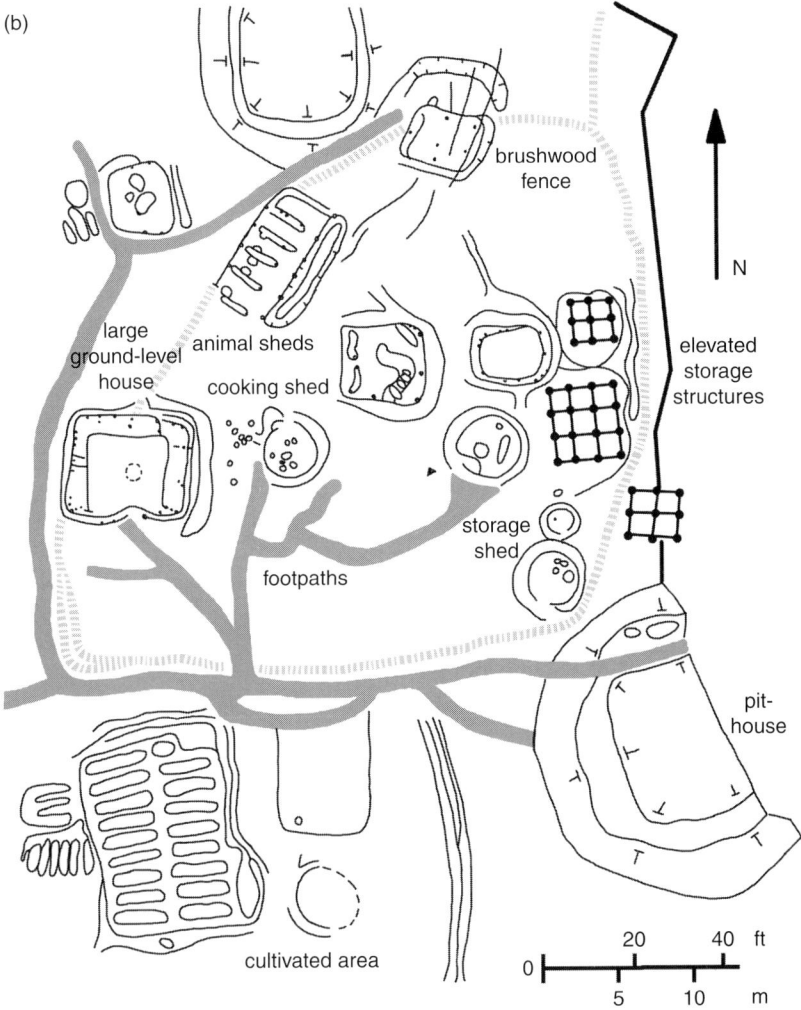

brushwood fence

N

large ground-level house

animal sheds

cooking shed

elevated storage structures

storage shed

footpaths

pit-house

cultivated area

20    40  ft

0

5    10   m

Figure 14.7 (cont.)

The fifth century also saw a number of civil engineering projects on a new, massive scale. These included the largest of the keyhole-shaped tombs in which paramount leaders were interred. One estimate suggests that 6.8 million man days were required for the construction of the largest of all the tombs, Daisen in Osaka prefecture, traditionally assigned to the fifth-century Emperor Nintoku, at 486 m in length the largest tomb in Japan and one of the largest funerary monuments from the ancient world. Other large-scale projects included the new development of cultivated land, and associated irrigation canals, such as that at Furuichi Omizo, 2 km long and 20 m wide.[51] Large-scale land development such as this is thought to have been directed by chiefs and rulers living in spatially distinct residential enclosures such as that found at Mitsudera.

## Early agrarian society in Japan and the social implications of paddy rice farming

Discussions of the social and cultural significance and consequences of paddy rice agriculture during the Yayoi period are becoming increasingly sophisticated, based on the large amounts of information generated through the high levels of archaeological investigation carried out in advance of land development since the later twentieth century across Japan. The routine practices involved in growing rice in paddy fields, from the construction of the paddies themselves, and the control of the water supply essential to the successful harvest, to the post-harvest storage and processing, structured everyday life for most Yayoi people.[52]

Rice agriculture supported massive population increase, and in certain places, most notably northern Kyushu and the Kansai region around Osaka Bay during parts of the Yayoi period, supported very large settlement agglomerations up to 100 ha in area with up to 1,500 residents. These regional centres developed at key locations in the Yayoi landscape, central nodes in networks along which flowed commodities including metal-work and fine stone, information, and people wanting access to the most advantageous points in those networks. Paddy rice farming, however, also depended heavily on a high degree of social co-operation, community cohesion, and reciprocity which, until towards the end of the Yayoi period, meant that there was a resistance to the development of inherited social hierarchies.

All of this occurred in a context of environmental unpredictability, with low-lying settlements and paddies regularly being inundated by floods, which had a devastating effect on local carrying capacity. The tensions generated through large populations living in close proximity to each other, the competition for limited supplies of high-value commodities, and the threat of flood or failed harvest, were in part mediated by an ideological framework, described by Mizoguchi as the 'Yayoi myth'. One expression of this myth is found in the depictions on a small number of the bronze bell-shaped objects known as

51 Ibid., 35, 37.    52 Hosoya, 'Sacred commonness'; Mizoguchi, *Archaeology of Japan*, 186–92.

*dotaku*, which were deposited near agricultural areas during much of the Yayoi period, interpreted by Kobayashi Yukio as representing an epic story celebrating rice farming. Some of these *dotaku* depict people and creatures in scenes of an intermediary nature that can be interpreted as representing the transformation from nature to culture. This transformation from nature to culture is expressed through the change from rice seed to food, which becomes a metaphor for the reproduction of Yayoi society: the death and regeneration of rice grains being linked to the death and regeneration of human beings and the community, in what Mizoguchi terms the 'Yayoi structuring principle'.

As well as transforming the worldview of the people engaged in rice farming, paddy-field agriculture was associated with major changes in social organization, facilitating for the first time the division of society in terms of inherited social differences. This process took several centuries and, until the late Yayoi period, an egalitarian principle was enacted through residential practices, with no evidence of the spatial segregation of elites, and reproduced through communal burial rites. Northern Kyushu, where wet rice farming was first introduced, followed a somewhat different trajectory to other areas, with elites being interred in distinct burial areas or mounds from the end of the early Yayoi. Though the power of these elites was played out through competition and warfare, the success of Yayoi farming depended mainly on social cohesion and co-operation, ensuring the management and maintenance of the infrastructure of paddies and irrigation systems, without which the elites could not survive.

The tensions inherent in Yayoi society, which included high-density populations living in close proximity and gradually increasing competition over land, resources, and commodities, were not always resolved peaceably. There is evidence for violence, including headless burials and individuals apparently killed with arrows and swords. The defences at many later Yayoi settlements, and the move to upland locations, indicate raiding and fighting. The earliest accounts of Japan in the Chinese chronicles refer to violent disturbances during the third century CE, out of which emerged regional leaders such as Queen Himiko who ruled with her brother over a country known as Yamataikoku. Mark Hudson has argued that 'the need for warfare and social cohesion was negotiated through the ritualization of war and its association with hunting'.[53] Deer are the most common animal to appear in Yayoi art, on bronze bells and pottery sherds, and are interpreted as representing spirits of the land in

---

53 M. Hudson, 'Rice, bronze and chieftains: an archaeology of Yayoi ritual', *Japanese Journal of Religious Studies*, 19 (1992), 139–90 (149).

agricultural rituals. In another manifestation of the Yayoi 'myth', Hudson suggests a metaphorical connection between these depictions of deer controlled by hunting, and the control of rice through agriculture, and the control of society through warfare.

These disturbances were part of a broader set of changes in the third century CE that saw new forms of burial and greater control over the production of important resources, including bronze and iron. Large, centralized settlements developed, some supported by trade, and others depending on increasingly intensive paddy agriculture. There is some evidence of stone weights from Yayoi sites, interpreted as further evidence for market-based trade.

## Changing relations with animals

During the Jomon period, wild boar played an important role in both subsistence and ideology. A degree of animal husbandry is suggested by the presence of boar bones at Jomon sites in Hokkaido and on islands off the Pacific coast of Honshu, beyond their natural range. Although deer bones are regularly found in Jomon shell middens, they are barely represented in Jomon material culture, while ceramic figurines of boar are relatively common.[54] Work by Koike Hiroko on faunal assemblages suggests that at certain times and places during the Jomon, there was considerable hunting pressure on larger wild animals, as well as on shellfish.[55] Populations may have become depleted, with the result that the relatively sedentary populations of larger Jomon settlements had to depend more on fish, small animals, and especially plants. These findings are backed up by more recent work at Sannai Maruyama, the largest Jomon settlement yet investigated, occupied at differing rates of intensity over nearly two millennia from 3900 to 2300 BCE, where changes in lithic assemblages and low ratios of deer and wild boar in the faunal assemblages in the later stages of occupation indicate a shift to a largely plant diet, and potential over-hunting of larger animals around this long-lived settlement.[56]

---

54  L. Janik, 'Awaking the symbolic calendar: animal figurines and the conceptualisation of the natural world in the Jomon of northern Japan', in D. Gheorghiu and A. Cyphers (eds.), *Anthropomorphic and Zoomorphic Miniature Figures in Eurasia, Africa and Meso-America: Morphology, Materiality, Technology, Function and Context* (Oxford: Oxbow, 2010), 113–21; Kaner (ed.), *Power of Dogu*, 151.

55  H. Koike, 'Exploitation dynamics during the Jomon period', in Aikens and Rhee (eds.), *Pacific Northeast Asia in Prehistory*, 53–7.

56  J. Habu, 'Growth and decline in complex hunter-gatherer societies: a case study from the Jomon period Sannai Maruyama site, Japan', *Antiquity*, 317 (2008), 571–84.

The significance of different animals changes during the Yayoi period, when deer start to feature in material culture depictions. For example, one survey of 364 pictorial representations on Yayoi period bronze bells found 129 pictures of deer and just 18 of wild boar. The first evidence for the domesticated pig also comes from the Yayoi period and it can be differentiated from wild boar at a number of sites in western Japan.[57] Recent work has focused on identifying the genetic forebears of Japanese pigs.[58] Perforated pig jawbones have been found at sites including Nabatake and Karako-Kagi, suggesting that they were mounted on poles, as is found in the Chinese Neolithic. At Karako-Kagi, wild boar continued to be raised in captivity. Animal bones also featured in divinatory rituals during the Yayoi, in which hot sticks were pressed onto mainly scapula, in practices reminiscent of Chinese Shang dynasty oracle bones. Over 75 per cent of these bones were deer, followed by boar.[59]

Pigs along with dogs, which were domesticated early in the Jomon, were the main domestic animals kept during the Yayoi. Although there are small numbers of horse and cattle bones from Yayoi sites in western Japan, they are not present in significant numbers until the later Kofun period.[60] Hoofprints in a Kofun period field at Kuroimine, Gunma prefecture, are evidence for the raising of horses by this time. Bones of domestic fowl are found on sites from the Yayoi period, and by the beginning of the Kofun period roosters appear in the repertoire of ceremonial material culture, including wooden examples thought to have played a role in funerary rituals, perhaps to reawaken the dead, and ceramic *haniwa* figures placed on burial mounds, though there is no evidence that chickens were being extensively consumed.[61] Fishing continued to be important, with evidence for specialized octopus-trapping using pots common at many Yayoi coastal sites, along with new types of net sinkers. The introduction of wet rice farming led to a restructuring of the way faunal food resources were exploited, but they continued to be an important part of the diet, helping support the increased population.

---

57 Hudson, 'Rice, bronze and chieftans', 149–50.
58 E.g. T. Anezaki, 'Pig exploitation in the southern Kanto region, Japan', *International Journal of Osteoarchaeology*, 17 (2007), 299–308; G. Larson et al., 'Patterns of East Asian pig domestication, migration and turnover revealed by modern and ancient DNA', *Proceedings of the National Academy of Sciences*, 104 (2010), 1087–92.
59 Hudson, 'Rice, bronze and chieftans', 150–1; H. Harunari, *Yayoi jidai no hajimari (The Beginning of the Yayoi Period)* (Tokyo University Press, 1990), 86–9.
60 Hudson, 'From Toro to Yoshinogari', 76.
61 H. Ishino, 'Rites and rituals of the Kofun period', *Japanese Journal of Religious Studies*, 19 (1992), 191–216 (198).

## Who were the early farmers?

Many traditional textbooks propose that the current Japanese population can be divided into 'Jomon' type and 'Yayoi' type people, and much physical anthropological research has gone into identifying these different populations and relating them to other peoples across Asia and the Pacific, work now supported by genetic evidence.[62] Temple and Larsen identify a number of impacts that agriculture has on the biology of many of the inhabitants of the archipelago, based on study of the skeletal remains of 400 Jomon and 521 Yayoi individuals.[63] The increasingly starchy diet, reflecting the consumption of carbohydrates such as sticky rice and yams and tubers, results in higher incidences of dental caries, notably during the late and final Jomon and into the Yayoi. Evidence for nutritional stress, affecting for example the formation of dental enamel, decreases with the arrival of rice farming, probably related to the increasing predictability and stability of food supply afforded by rice farming, as against the seasonal availability of foods for much of the Jomon. As discussed above, episodes of natural disaster, including flooding, must have caused stress in different ways. Work in the field of 'toilet archaeology' indicates that Jomon and Yayoi communities were equally affected by parasites, which must have thrived in the relatively densely packed settlements.[64] Infectious diseases may have affected Jomon and Yayoi populations differently. Temple and Larsen argue that while the *frequency* of infectious diseases may have fallen during the Yayoi period, the *diversity* of such diseases likely increased as a result of migration, with new illnesses such as tuberculosis being introduced from the continent.[65] While instances of such diseases fell during the first stages of farming in the Yayoi, chronic infection then increased once certain population thresholds were reached, and as agricultural practices intensified and political authority became more centralized. It will be interesting to see how such studies relate to the rise and fall of large

---

62 M.F. Hammer et al., 'Dual origins of the Japanese: common ground for hunter-gatherer and farmer Y chromosomes', *Journal of Human Genetics*, 51 (2006), 47–58; K. Hanihara, 'Dual structure model for the population history of the Japanese islands', *Japan Review*, 2 (1991), 1–33.

63 D.H. Temple and C.S. Larsen, 'Bioarchaeological perspectives on systemic stress during the agricultural transition in prehistoric Japan', in E. Pechenkina and M. Oxenham (eds.), *Bioarchaeology of East Asia: Movement, Contact, Health* (Gainesville: University Press of Florida, 2013), 344–67.

64 A. Matsui et al., 'Palaeoparasitology in Japan – discovery of toilet features', *Memórias do Instituto Oswaldo Cruz*, 98, Supplement 1 (2003), 127–36.

65 Temple and Larsen, 'Bioarchaeological perspectives'.

communities such as Hie-Naka, and the population movements associated with port-of-trade types of settlement such as Nishijinmachi.

Hudson defines agriculture on social criteria 'as a socioeconomic system which is *expansionary*, *exploitative*, and is based on principles of *social exclusion*', and argues that the biological evidence for an influx of migrants at the start of the Yayoi period 'is some of the best from anywhere in the prehistoric world'.[66] Estimates of population growth in the period from the end of the Jomon through to the first centuries of the first millennium CE suggest a possible increase from 75,000 to 5.4 million people, and an average annual population increase of over 1 per cent.

Comparable approaches have been adopted in the study of the early development of the Japanese language.[67] It is thought that the mountainous topography of the archipelago fostered great linguistic diversity during the Jomon period, perhaps reflected in the diversity of Jomon pottery styles, although some Japanese archaeologists argue that Jomon peoples must have been able to communicate with each other. But this diversity did not survive the advent of farming. This is argued to have resulted from population movement associated with the expansion of farming – the farming peoples speaking Japonic, the prototype for modern Japanese – rather than the adoption of the new language by existing Jomon peoples.

## Conclusion

While the debate about the nature of Jomon cultivation is set to continue, fuelled by the increasing though still limited use of flotation and associated archaeobotanical techniques, it is clear that the introduction of paddy rice farming in the Japanese archipelago brought about significant change. This included a major restructuring of annual and everyday subsistence practices and investment in permanent facilities, namely the paddies themselves, whose construction, management, and maintenance took on monumental proportions and accompanying social significance. Both the introduction of wet rice farming in the early first millennium BCE and the subsequent spread of the Yayoi 'package' through western Honshu and Shikoku, and then into eastern Honshu, involved the movement of people and the spread of the Japonic language, the precursor of modern Japanese. But rice farming was

---

66  M. Hudson, 'Agriculture and language change in the Japanese islands', in P. Bellwood and C. Renfrew (eds.), *Examining the Farming/Language Dispersal Hypothesis* (Cambridge: McDonald Institute for Archaeological Research, 2003), 311, 312.

67  Hudson, 'Agriculture and language change'.

not spreading into unoccupied territories, and from the early farming hamlets of northern Kyushu to the pioneering agricultural settlements of northern Honshu there is evidence for a mixing of incoming traits with native practices rather than any straightforward replacement.

Rice farming was not, however, the only subsistence activity in which Japanese people from the Yayoi period onwards engaged. Hunting and gathering continued to be important activities. The relationships with animals changed over time as hunting became an elite pastime, represented in sets of *haniwa* figures on burial mounds in the fifth and sixth centuries. The *matagi* hunters of northern Japan have maintained the tradition of hunting large mammals.[68] And the exploitation of wild plant resources continues to the present day. Dry-field cultivation of grains such as wheat and millet has continued to provide an important component of the Japanese diet.

Domesticated animals did not play an important role in early agricultural societies in Japan. From the Yayoi period, horse and cattle were probably used mainly for cultivation and transportation as a means of supplementing labour, not for meat and milk or other secondary products as elsewhere in Eurasia. Domesticated pigs were kept from the Yayoi period, but their contribution to the Yayoi diet was limited.

This chapter has reviewed how changes in subsistence activities can be understood in the context of social and cultural developments in the archipelago during the Jomon, Yayoi, and Kofun periods. This long span of time witnessed many changes in subsistence practices. Broad-based foraging economies replaced large-game hunting in the early stages of the Jomon, which supported the development of relatively sedentary village communities, some of which, notably those in southern Kyushu, are remarkably early. By the middle Jomon, large regional centres were developing, mainly in eastern and northern Japan, acting as foci for regional exchange networks of commodities such as greenstones and obsidian. Along the Pacific coast, in particular, large shell middens appeared, indicating the intensive exploitation of marine resources, leading to pressure on those resources. Debate still surrounds the possibility of cultivation during the Jomon, and the limited evidence that does exist suggests that we need to redefine what is understood by cultivation among temperate foragers.

Although there are tantalizing finds of rice grains in the fabric of pottery vessels and some very early AMS dates for carbonized rice grains from

---

68 G.L. Barnes, 'Landscape and subsistence in Japanese history', in I.P. Martini and W. Chesworth (eds.), *Landscapes and Societies* (New York: Springer, 2010), 321–40.

northern Honshu,[69] there is widespread acceptance that paddy rice farming first became established in northwestern Kyushu in the first centuries of the first millennium BCE, introduced either from the Korean peninsula or direct from southern China. Rice farming appears to have spread out of this initial foothold only after several centuries, and there is now good evidence for paddy landscapes with associated irrigation systems from across the archipelago with the exception of Hokkaido. Rice agriculture appears with metallurgy (bronze and iron) and weaving, and the complex processes of which the introduction of these new technologies was part also saw a degree of population change, with migrants coming into Japan from the continent, and the formation of what was to become the Japanese language. Agriculture came to support the establishment of regional hierarchical societies controlled by a new class of elite leaders, who legitimated their power through a series of ritualized practices drawing on a new symbolic code based on agriculture, hunting, and warfare.

Rice farming is and was by no means the only subsistence practice in Japan. Continuing through the Yayoi period, hunting, gathering, and fishing and cultivation of a variety of crops sustained village communities. As regional societies became increasingly centralized, however, and population densities increased, so did the intensification of paddy agriculture. By the fifth century CE, centrally controlled large-scale land development was being undertaken by the authorities in the emerging central capital area. The remarkable discoveries of the well-preserved farming village at Kuroimine and the elite residential compound at Mitsudera in Gunma prefecture dating from the middle sixth century CE provide a vivid snapshot of the nature of rural settlement in central Japan, sealed by a catastrophic volcanic eruption. In eastern and northern Japan, outside the control of the emerging early Japanese state, different trajectories were followed in which a range of horticultural and agricultural activities were practised.[70]

Conrad Totman divides the narrative for the pre-industrial sections of his *History of Japan* into discussions of what he terms dispersed and intensive agriculturalists, with the transition during the medieval period, around 1250 CE, preceded by early and later foragers.[71] The archaeological record now demonstrates that there was an intensity to paddy rice farming in the Yayoi

69 S. Nakayama (ed.), *Nikkan ni okeru kokumotsu nogyo no kigen* (*Origin of Grain Agriculture in the Japanese Archipelago and the Korean Peninsula*) (Kofu: Yamanashi Prefectural Museum, 2014).

70 Crawford, 'Advances in understanding'.

71 C. Totman, *A History of Japan* (Oxford: Blackwell, 2000).

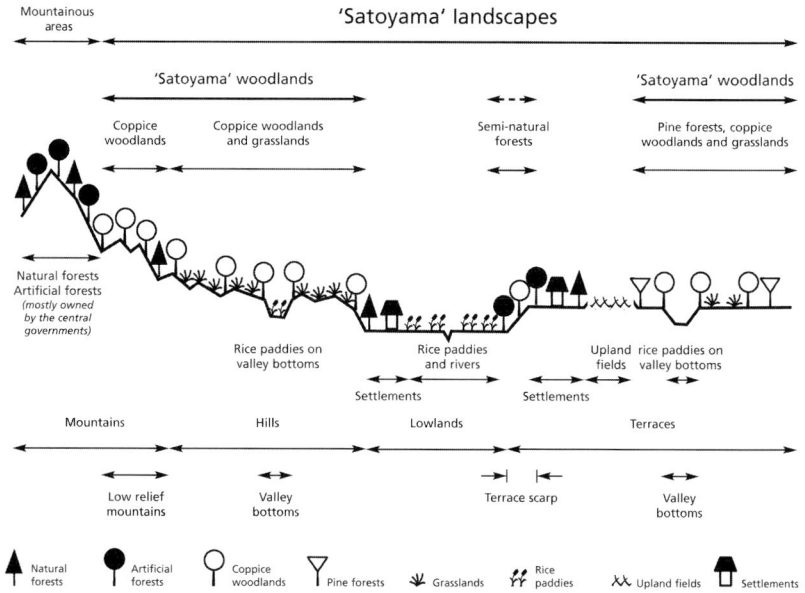

Figure 14.8 Model of the *satoyama* landscape.

and Kofun periods prior to 500 CE that reshaped the lives of the inhabitants of much of the archipelago. In the late nineteenth century, at the beginning of Japan's industrialization, over 80 per cent of the population were engaged in farming. By 1985 this proportion had dropped to 3.5 per cent, and is today even lower.[72] Rice-related rituals continue to be central to imperial ceremonial, and rice continues to be regarded as the staple Japanese foodstuff. And the range of subsistence practices accompanying paddy rice farming informs how Japanese people understand their own rural landscapes, now expressed in terms of *satoyama*, 'Japan's traditional and fragile landscape system ... comprising carefully managed coppice woodlands, villages strung along the base of hills and carefully tended paddy fields ... that made possible the sustainable interaction of humans and nature' (Figure 14.8).[73] Our understanding of the processes leading to agrarian societies increasingly draws on sophisticated understanding of human intellect, motivations, and practices in conjunction with climatic episodes, historical contingencies, and chance

72 E. Ohnuki-Tierney, *Rice as Self: Japanese Identities Through Time* (Princeton University Press, 1993), 17.
73 K. Takeuchi et al. (eds.), *Satoyama: The Traditional Rural Landscape of Japan* (Berlin: Springer, 2003).

coincidences of events.[74] The Japanese record can doubtless contribute to those debates.

For all of these reasons, the study of the archaeology of early agriculture in Japan merits attention on a global stage. Very few regions can boast the intensity of archaeological activity and the high-resolution archaeological record that Japan has developed from the later twentieth century.

# Further reading

Aikens, C.M. and T. Higuchi. *The Prehistory of Japan*. New York and London: Academic Press, 1982.

Akazawa, T. 'Cultural change in prehistoric Japan: receptivity to rice agriculture in the Japanese archipelago.' In F. Wendorf and A.E. Close (eds.), *Advances in World Archaeology*. New York: Academic Press, 1982. 151–211.

Barnes, G.L. 'Landscape and subsistence in Japanese history.' In I.P. Martini and W. Chesworth (eds.), *Landscapes and Societies*. New York: Springer, 2010. 321–40.

Crawford, G. 'Advances in understanding early agriculture in Japan.' *Current Anthropology*, Supplement 4, 52 (2011), S331–45.

Edwards, W. 'Buried discourse: the Toro site and Japanese national identity in the early postwar period.' *Journal of Japanese Studies*, 17 (1991), 1–23.

Habu, J. *Ancient Jomon of Japan*. Cambridge University Press, 2004.

Hanihara, K. 'Dual structure model for the population history of the Japanese islands.' *Japan Review*, 2 (1991), 1–33.

Hosoya, L.A. 'Sacred commonness: an archaeobotanical approach to Yayoi social stratification: the "Central Building Model" and the Osaka Ikegami site.' In K. Ikeya, H. Ogawa, and P. Mitchell (eds.), *Interactions Between Hunter-Gatherers and Farmers: From Prehistory to Present*. Osaka: National Museum of Ethnography, 2009. 99–178.

Hudson, M. 'Foragers as fetish in modern Japan.' In J. Habu et al. (eds.), *Hunter-Gatherers of the North Pacific Rim*. Osaka: National Museum of Ethnology, 2003. 263–74.

'From Toro to Yoshinogari: changing perspectives on Yayoi period archaeology.' In G.L. Barnes (ed.), *Hoabhinhian, Jomon, Yayoi and Early States: Bibliographic Reviews of Far Eastern Archaeology*. Oxford: Oxbow, 1990. 63–112.

'Rice, bronze and chieftains: an archaeology of Yayoi ritual.' *Japanese Journal of Religious Studies*, 19 (1992), 139–89.

*The Ruins of Identity: Ethnogenesis in the Japanese Islands*. Honolulu: University of Hawai'i Press, 1999.

Hudson, M. and G. Barnes. 'Yoshinogari: a Yayoi settlement in northern Kyushu.' *Monumenta Nipponica*, 46 (1991), 211–35.

Imamura, K. 'Jomon and Yayoi: the transition to agriculture in Japanese prehistory.' In D.R. Harris (ed.), *The Origins and Spread of Agriculture and Pastoralism in Eurasia*. Washington, DC: Smithsonian Institution Press, 1996. 442–65.

---

74 G. Barker, *The Agricultural Revolution in Prehistory: Why did Foragers Become Farmers?* (Oxford University Press, 2006).

Kaner, S. 'The western language Jomon.' In G.L. Barnes (ed.), *Hoabhinhian, Jomon, Yayoi and Early States: Bibliographic Reviews of Far Eastern Archaeology*. Oxford: Oxbow, 1990. 31–62.

Kidder, J.E. *Himiko and Japan's Elusive Chiefdom of Yamatai: Archaeology, History and Mythology*. Honolulu: University of Hawai'i Press, 2007.

Kobayashi, T. *Jomon Reflections: Forager Life and Culture in the Prehistoric Japanese Archipelago*. Oxford: Oxbow, 2005.

Matsui, A. and M. Kanehara. 'The question of prehistoric plant husbandry during the Jomon period in Japan.' *World Archaeology*, 38 (2006), 259–73.

Miyamoto, K. 'The East Asian contexts for the origins of agriculture in Japan.' In S. Kaner, L. Janik, and K. Yano (eds.), *Origins of Agriculture: Challenging Old Orthodoxies, Championing New Perspectives*. Cambridge: McDonald Institute for Archaeological Research, forthcoming.

Mizoguchi, K. *The Archaeology of Japan: From the Earliest Rice Farming Villages to the Rise of the State*. Cambridge University Press, 2013.

Nishida, M. 'The emergence of food production in Neolithic Japan.' *Journal of Anthropological Archaeology*, 2 (1983), 305–22.

Ohnuki-Tierney, E. *Rice as Self: Japanese Identities Through Time*. Princeton University Press, 1993.

Pearson, R. (ed.). *Ancient Japan*. Washington, DC: Arthur M. Sackler Gallery; Tokyo: Agency for Cultural Affairs, 1992.

Shoda, S. 'Radiocarbon and archaeology in Japan and Korea: what has changed because of the Yayoi dating controversy?', *Radiocarbon*, 55 (2010), 421–7.

Soumare, M. *Japan in Five Ancient Chinese Chronicles*. Fukuoka: Kurodahan Press, 2009.

Takahashi, R. 'Symbiotic relations between paddy-field rice cultivators and hunter-gatherer-fishers in Japanese prehistory: archaeological considerations of the transition from the Jomon age to the Yayoi age.' In K. Ikeya, O. Hidefumi, and P. Mitchell (eds.), *Interactions Between Hunter-Gatherers and Farmers: From Prehistory to Present*. Osaka: National Museum of Ethnology, 2009. 71–98.

Takeuchi, K., R.D. Brown, I. Washitani, A. Tsunekawa, and M. Yokohari (eds.). *Satoyama: The Traditional Rural Landscape of Japan*. Berlin: Springer, 2003.

Totman, C. *Japan: An Environmental History*. London: I.B. Tauris, 2014.

Tsude, H. 'Early state formation in Japan.' In J.R. Piggott (ed.), *Capital and Countryside in Japan, 300–1180: Japanese Historians Interpreted in English*. Ithaca, NY: East Asia Program, Cornell University, 2006. 13–53.

Wieczorek, A. and W. Steinhaus (eds.). *Zeit der Morgenröte: Japans Archäologie und Geschichte bis zu den ersten Kaisern*. Mannheim: Reiss-Engelhorn-Museen, 2004.

Yano, K. 'The introduction of wet rice cultivation into western Japan and its Jomon precursors.' In S. Kaner, L. Janik, and K. Yano (eds.), *Origins of Agriculture: Challenging Old Orthodoxies, Championing New Perspectives*. Cambridge: McDonald Institute for Archaeological Research, forthcoming.

# 15

# The Nara basin paddies, Japan

KEN'ICHI OKADA (TRANSLATED BY SIMON KANER)

The date and mode of the introduction of agriculture into the Japanese archipelago continue to be an area of vigorous debate. The early Japanese archaeological sequence is divided into 'Palaeolithic', 'Jomon', and 'Yayoi' periods, and the division between the Jomon and the Yayoi is defined by the presence of agriculture. Namely, the Jomon is regarded as being based on food procurement, while the Yayoi is seen as 'the period in which lifestyles based on food production appeared in Japan'.[1]

The technology of wet rice farming was introduced into Japan from the East Asian continent, firstly into northwestern Kyushu shortly after 1000 BCE. Some of the most extensive areas of prehistoric rice paddy discovered to date are in the Nara basin, although no paddy sites in this area yet extend as far back as 1000 BCE. These sites in the Nara basin are, however, very informative about the spread of rice farming through the western part of the Japanese archipelago, and about the associated transition from the Jomon to the Yayoi period of Japanese prehistory. The site of Kashiwara is one of the most important Jomon sites in the area, providing the ceramic chronological sequence for the end of the Jomon.[2] The enormous quantities of tools discovered at Karako-Kagi since the 1940s demonstrated unequivocally that the Yayoi period was agricultural.[3] Discoveries in the Nara basin have proved

---

1 M. Sahara, *Nogyo no kaishi to kaikyu shakkai no keisei* (*The Beginnings of Agriculture and the Formation of Agricultural Society*) (Tokyo: Iwanami Shoten, 1975); and see Chapter 14.
2 M. Suenaga, *Kashiwara*, Nara Ken Shiseki Meito Tennen Kinenbutsu Chosa Hokokusho 17 (Nara Prefectural Board of Education, 1961).
3 M. Suenaga et al., *Yamato Karako Yayoi shiki iseki no kenkyu* (*Research on the Yayoi Type Site at Yamato Karako*), Kyoto Teikoku Daigaku Bungakubu Kokogaku Kenkyu Hokoku 16 (Kyoto: Rinsen Shoten, 1976; 1st edn 1943).

that paddy facilities were present between 2,600 and 2,400 cal BP, in the early Yayoi period.

Rice paddy technology was not invented in the archipelago, but spread into Japan from the Chinese mainland through the Korean peninsula. Recent archaeological investigations in Nara prefecture are adding greatly to our understanding of the spread of rice farming through Japan, even though the Nara evidence postdates the initial arrival of wet rice farming into northwest Kyushu by several centuries. A number of new sites have been excavated, dating from the middle of the early Yayoi period, about 2,500 years ago. These excavations have revealed a massive area of planned rice paddy, over 25,000 m$^2$ in area, complete with the irrigation systems needed for its operation. Findings from these sites suggest that wet rice cultivation began in this area relatively suddenly, and continued despite a number of natural disasters. These sites therefore offer the possibility of understanding the conditions under which wet rice farming spread through this part of Japan.

## Early Yayoi rice paddies in Nara

The site of Karako-Kagi, mentioned above, is located in the central part of the Nara basin (Figure 15.1). Excavated repeatedly since 1936, it is regarded as a classic example of a Yayoi agricultural settlement, enclosed by ditches, with

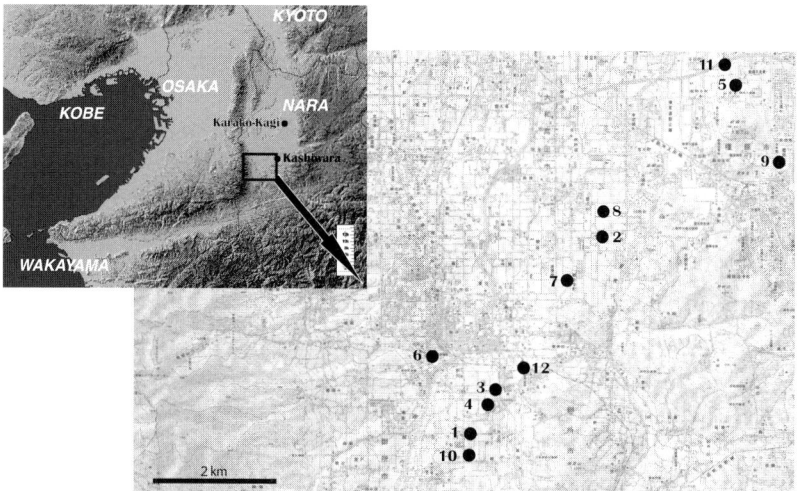

Figure 15.1 The distribution of final Jomon and early Yayoi sites in the southern Nara basin.
1. Shijo-shinano; 2. Jimyoji; 3. Kashiwara; 4. Kawanishi-nenarigaki; 5. Haginomoto;
6. Kannonji-honma; 7. Kamotsuba; 8. Tamade; 9. Saragi; 10. Imade; 11. Akitsu; 12. Nakanishi.

large buildings and bronze-working workshops, with clusters of rectangular burial enclosures (*hokei shukobo gun*) in the vicinity. No paddy fields, however, have been found associated with Karako-Kagi.

A number of large-scale excavations were recently undertaken in the southwestern Nara basin in advance of the Keinawa expressway linking Kyoto, Nara, and Wakayama, which crosses the basin from north to south. The area affected by the construction of the new road had been paddy since at least medieval times and, unlike many of the more urbanized parts of the region, had not been developed for industrial or commercial purposes. For this reason, very few large archaeological sites have been discovered to date. Evaluation surveys undertaken along the proposed route of the new road, however, demonstrated the presence of a series of major sites.

The first discovery of paddy remains in the Nara basin, at Haginomoto in Kashihara, was made in conjunction with the construction of this new road.[4] An area of rice paddy, some 1,800 m$^2$ in extent, was discovered sealed by layers of fine sands. This area was divided by 5 cm high ridges into small rectangular paddies, each about 2.5 × 4 m in area, what we would now identify as 'small-section paddies' (*shokukaku suiden*) (Figure 15.2). This type of paddy was also found at the Tamade site in Gose city, about 2.4 km southwest of Haginomoto.[5]

Here, middle and late Yayoi paddies formed an upper layer, beneath which were sealed early Yayoi paddies. Beneath this were discovered remains from the late final Jomon, including traces of buildings, burial pits, and pottery dumps (Figure 15.3). The early Yayoi paddies extended over 4,800 m$^2$ and formed two layers, separated by a layer of sand. As at Haginomoto, both layers at Tamade comprised small-section paddies. The long ridges were aligned parallel to the natural contours at 1.5 m intervals, with short ridges at right angles to the long ones every 3.5–5.5 m creating a series of small

---

4 Archaeological Institute of Kashihara, 'Haginomoto iseki: genchi setsumeikai shiryo (The Haginomoto site: materials from the onsite explanation)' (Nara kenritsu Kashihara Kokogaku Kenkyujo, 2008); N. Mitsuishi et al., 'Haginomoto iseki (Kawanishi-cho 5, 7–9 ku) (The Haginomoto site [Kawanishi town locations 5, 7–9])', in *Nara-ken Iseki Chosa Gaiho 2007 nendo* (*Summary of Excavations in Nara in 2007*) (Nara kenritsu Kashihara Kokogaku Kenkyujo, 2011).

5 Gose City Board of Education, 'Keinawa Jidoshado kankei iseki Tamade chiku. Hakkutsu chosa genchi setsumeikai shiryo (Sites along the Keinawa expressway: the Tamade location, materials for the onsite explanation of the excavation)' (Gose City Board of Education, 2009); M. Kimoto et al., 'Keinawa Jidoshado kanren iseki Hakkutsu Chosa Hokoku Heisei 21 nen chosa no gaiyo (Report of excavations of sites along the route of the Keinawa expressway: outline of research in 2009' (Gose City Board of Education, 2010).

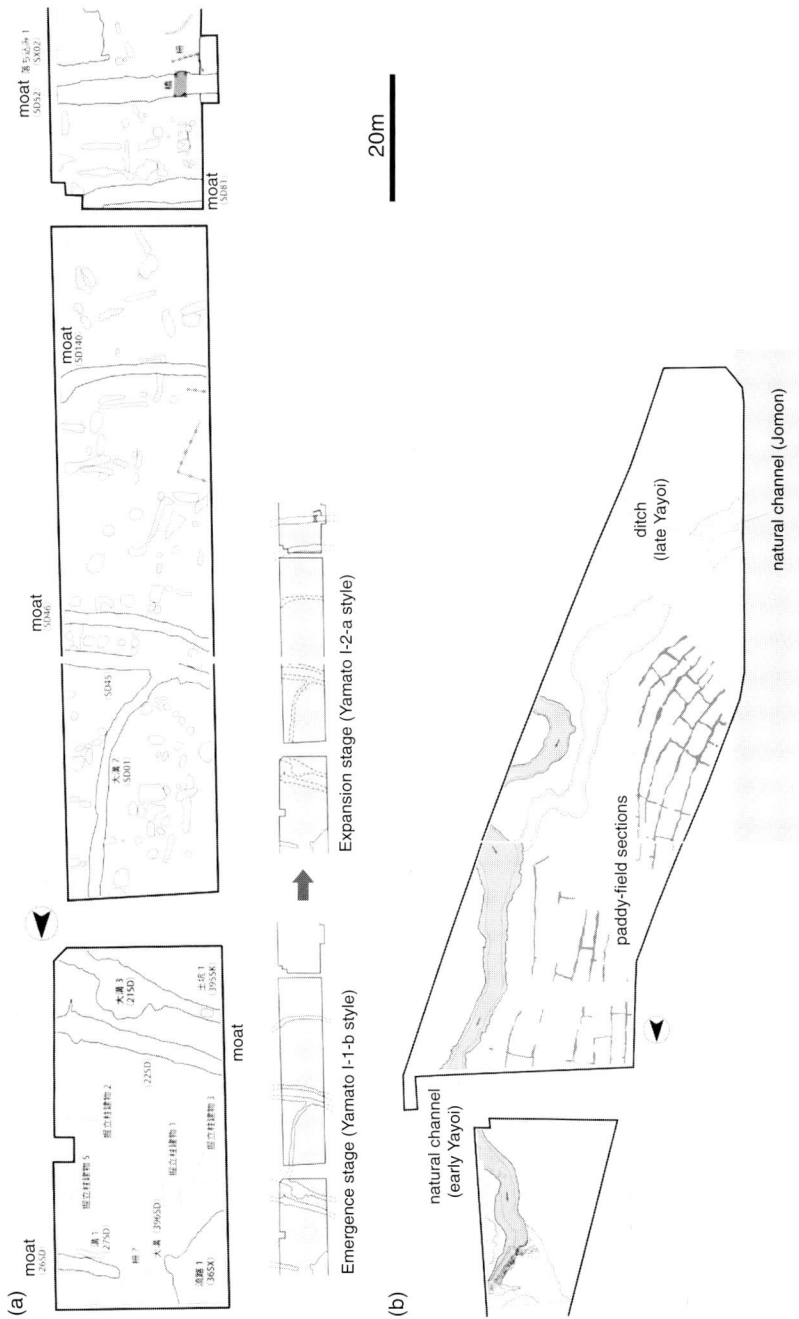

(a)

moat
SD52
落ちこみ 1
SX02

moat
SD51

moat
SX81

moat
SD140

moat
SD46

SD45

大溝 7
SD01

moat

大溝 3
215D

225D

土坑 1
395SK

大溝 1 396SD

掘立柱建物 5

掘立柱建物 2

掘立柱建物 1

掘立柱建物 3

溝 1
275D

柱穴

溝 2
26UF

溝道 1
365SX

Emergence stage (Yamato I-1-b style)

Expansion stage (Yamato I-2-a style)

20m

(b)

natural channel
(early Yayoi)

paddy-field sections

ditch
(late Yayoi)

natural channel (Jomon)

Figure 15.2 Early Yayoi paddy fields and settlement at (a) Kawanishi-Negarigaki, a moated circular settlement of the Early Yayoi period; and (b) Haginomoto, the first paddy fields of the Early Yayoi period found in the Ner basin.

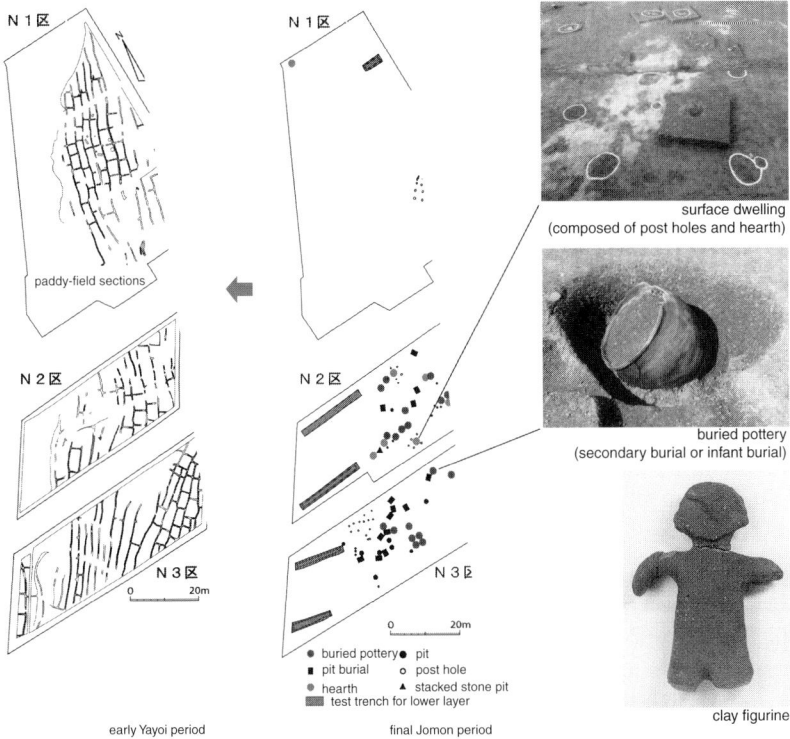

Figure 15.3 The transition from the final Jomon settlement to early Yayoi paddy fields at Tamade.

rectangular units. At Tamade the ridges of the later phase were reoriented by 90 degrees from the earlier phase.

This technique of constructing small-section paddies appears to have been designed to create as much flat area as possible in sloping and hilly terrain with the least effort. The ridges were carefully planned to ensure that the water irrigated all the paddies. It is significant that these ridges were realigned in the later phase. It is also thought that, following the abandonment of the late final Jomon settlement, the area was left for a while, and reclaimed for paddy for rice cultivation during the early Yayoi. Although we do not know how long the paddy was in operation during the Yayoi, the sand layer indicates that it was flooded at least once. The people working the paddies did not completely give up, however, and reconstructed their paddies, adjusting them to the changes in local topography wrought by the inundation. The discovery of these early Yayoi paddies in the Nara basin was followed by that of much larger-scale paddies and associated facilities which extended over an area of more than 25,000 m² at the Nakanishi-Akitsu site complex.

## Early Yayoi paddies at the Nakanishi-Akitsu site complex

The Nakanishi site is located 1.4 km southeast of Tamade (Figure 15.4, left). The site is on a gently sloping alluvial fan which extends to the north, and to the south lie the Kose hills. The southwestern edge of the site, and the highest point on the ridge, is occupied by the fifth-century keyhole-shaped mounded tomb of Murono-Miyayama, burial place of the powerful Katsuragi clan. To the west the Katsuragi River flows down to the plain, while the Manganji River rises to the south, carving a gentle valley to the northeast as it flows towards the Soga River.

Excavations at Nakanishi-Akitsu began in 2009 and are continuing (Figure 15.4). Twenty seasons of excavations have taken place to date at Nakanishi, with early Yayoi paddies investigated between the fourteenth and twentieth excavation areas, in conjunction with the construction of the Keinawa expressway. The tree-covered southernmost area of the site was investigated during the fifteenth season.[6] To the north of this, two phases of paddy construction, separated by a layer of sand as at Tamade, were revealed during the fourteenth, sixteenth, eighteenth, and twentieth seasons. The structure of the paddies was as seen at Tamade: a series of small units divided by larger and smaller ridges.[7]

---

6  K. Kikui, 'Nakanishi iseki dai 15 ji chosa (Fifteenth excavation of the Nakanishi site)', in *Nara-ken iseki chosa gaiho 2010 nendo* (*Summary of Excavations in Nara in 2010*) (Nara kenritsu Kashihara Kokogaku Kenkyujo, 2011).

7  K. Okada, 'Nakanishi iseki dai 14 ji chosa (Fourteenth excavation of the Nakanishi site)', in *Nara-ken iseki chosa gaiho 2009 nendo* (*Summary of Excavations in Nara in 2009*) (Nara kenritsu Kashihara Kokogaku Kenkyujo, 2010); Archaeological Institute of Kashihara, 'Nakanishi iseki dai 18 ji chosa – Yayoi jidai zenki suiden no chosa. Genchi setsumeikai shiryo (Eighteenth season of excavations at Nakanishi: research on early Yayoi paddy fields: materials for the onsite explanation)' (Nara kenritsu Kashihara Kokogaku Kenkyujo, 2011); J. Matsuoka and K. Okada, 'Nakanishi iseki dai 16 ji chosa (Sixteenth excavation at the Nakanishi site)', in *Nara-ken iseki chosa gaiho 2010 nendo* (*Summary of Excavations in Nara in 2010*); M. Motomura and S. Nakano, 'Nakanishi iseki dai 18 ji chosa (Eighteenth excavations at the Nakanishi site)', in *Nara-ken iseki chosa gaiho 2012 nendo* (*Summary of Excavations in Nara in 2012*) (Nara kenritsu Kashihara Kokogaku Kenkyujo, 2013).

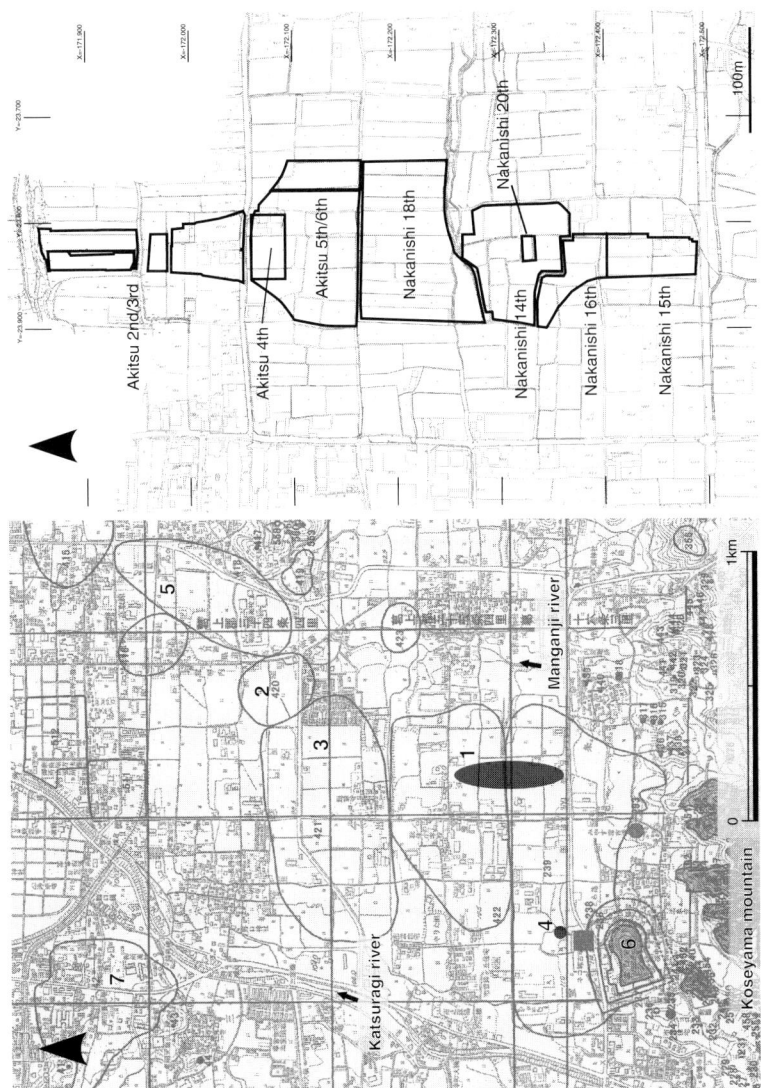

Figure 15.4 Location of the Nakanishi-Akitsu site complex: 1: Tamade; 2: Saragi; 3: Imade; 4: Nakanishi-Akitsu recent excavations (expanded plan on right); 5: Nakanishi, second excavation; 6: Murono-miyagama tomb; 7: Kamutsuba.

Immediately to the north of the eighteenth excavation area, three layers of early Yayoi paddies extend into Akitsu areas 5 and 6.[8] The northernmost part of the site, investigated in the fourth and fifth seasons, produced evidence for a large watercourse in the northeastern sector, but no clear traces of paddy, indicating that this was the northern limit of the paddy area.[9] The area of paddy therefore extended some 340 m north to south on either side of the valley, covering a total area exceeding 25,000 m². It is possible that the area of early Yayoi paddy extended over 100 m to the west, following the topography, and to the Manganji River in the east. If future research indeed proves this to be the case, then the total area of paddy at Nakanishi-Akitsu was between 50,000 and 100,000 m².

## Stratigraphy and date

The extensive paddies at Nakanishi-Akitsu all date to the early Yayoi period (2,600–2,400 cal BP). Stratigraphy and the dating of associated artefacts provide the basis for the chronology of the paddies.[10] Although the quantity of remains from the paddy soils was relatively low, the specific types of ceramics recovered indicate that the site dates from the late final Jomon (*tottaimon*-style pottery decorated with incised bands) to the late part of the early Yayoi (Yamato 1-2-b phase) (see Figure 15.6).[11] A thick deposit comprising sand and gravel indicative of inundation by flood extended over a wide area, sealing the paddies found in the fifteenth season in the southern part of the site, and reaching to the fifth and sixth excavation areas at Akitsu to the north. Slightly later pottery (Yamato II-1-a style from the end of the early Yayoi to the start of the middle Yayoi) was found above this flood deposit. The fourth excavation area at Akitsu produced pottery of the

---

8  K. Okada et al., 'Akitsu iseki dai 5 ji chosa (Fifth excavation of the Akitsu site)', in *Nara-ken iseki chosa gaiho 2011 nendo* (*Summary of Excavations in Nara in 2010*); K. Okada et al., 'Akitsu iseki dai 6 ji chosa (Sixth excavation of the Akitsu site)', in *Nara-ken iseki chosa gaiho 2012 nendo* (*Summary of Excavations in Nara in 2012*).

9  K. Okada et al., 'Akitsu iseki dai 4 ji chosa (Fourth excavation of the Akitsu site)', in *Nara-ken iseki chosa gaiho 2010 nendo* (*Summary of Excavations in Nara in 2010*).

10  See K. Kobayashi et al., 'Kawachi chiiki ni okeru Yayoi zenki no C14 nendai sokutei kenkyu (Research into C14 dating of the early Yayoi in the Kawachi area)', *Bulletin of the National Museum of Japanese History*, 139 (2008); S. Fujita and K. Mametani, 'Nara-ken ni okeru dokki hennen (Pottery chronology in Nara prefecture)', in *Nara ken no Yayoi doki shusei: honbunhen* (*Survey of Yayoi Pottery from Nara Prefecture: Texts*) (Nara kenritsu Kashihara Kokogaku Kenkyujo Kenkyu Seika 6, 2011).

11  Okada, 'Fourteenth excavation of the Nakanishi site'; Okada et al., 'Sixth excavation of the Akitsu site'.

Yamato 1-2-b and 11-1-a phases, with sherds of the later Yamato 11 and Yamato 111 phases above that.[12]

The chronology of the process of paddy development can be seen in the following sequence, extending back to the final Jomon. During the fourteenth and sixteenth seasons at Nakanishi, cultivated soils from the paddies were discovered that formed a palaeosol. The artefacts recovered from this soil were mainly *tottaimon* pottery from the second half of the final Jomon period.[13] From the silt or fine sand layers below this was unearthed pottery from the early-middle part of the final Jomon, with pottery from the middle-late Late Jomon from the sand and gravel layer under the silt or fine sand layer. The chronological order of the artefacts and stratigraphy therefore accorded with each other (Figure 15.5).[14] This indicates high levels of erosion and sedimentation activity from the later late Jomon to the middle final Jomon, becoming lower towards the end of the final Jomon, the soils formed at this time becoming the palaeosol. Paddies were constructed after the formation of this palaeosol. The same palaeosol was found immediately below the cultivated paddy soil in the fourth, fifth, and sixth excavation areas at Akitsu, but contained only a few artefacts. A large quantity of final Jomon *tottaimon* pottery was found in the palaeosol that extended along the watercourse, covered by a layer of gravel.[15] This *tottaimon* pottery was identified as belonging to *tottaimon* phases 2a to 3b, and in the absence of any Yayoi pottery, this layer is considered to have formed before the end of the final Jomon.

Therefore, unlike the results from the fourteenth and sixteenth seasons at Nakanishi outlined above, the findings from the fourth, fifth, and sixth seasons at Akitsu indicate that the thick gravel layer was formed through the erosion and sedimentation of the watercourse from the late final Jomon, and that it became the base of the soil. Paddies were constructed here after

---

12  Okada et al., 'Fourth excavation of the Akitsu site'.

13  At Location 14 of the Nakanishi site, over 3,000 rice (*Oryza sativa*) phytoliths per gram were recovered from paddy soils, though from the oldest layers this was 0, while large quantities of *Phragmites* and *Pleioblastus* phytoliths were recovered. J. Matsuoka and K. Okada, 'Nakanishi iseki dai 16 ji chosa (Sixteenth excavation at the Nakanishi site)', in *Nara-ken iseki chosa gaiho 2010 nendo (Summary of Excavations in Nara in 2010)*. Therefore it seems that the construction of paddy fields does not extend back to the final Jomon period.

14  Okada, 'Fourteenth excavation of the Nakanishi site'.

15  Okada et al., 'Fourth excavation of the Akitsu site'; Okada et al., 'Sixth excavation of the Akitsu site'.

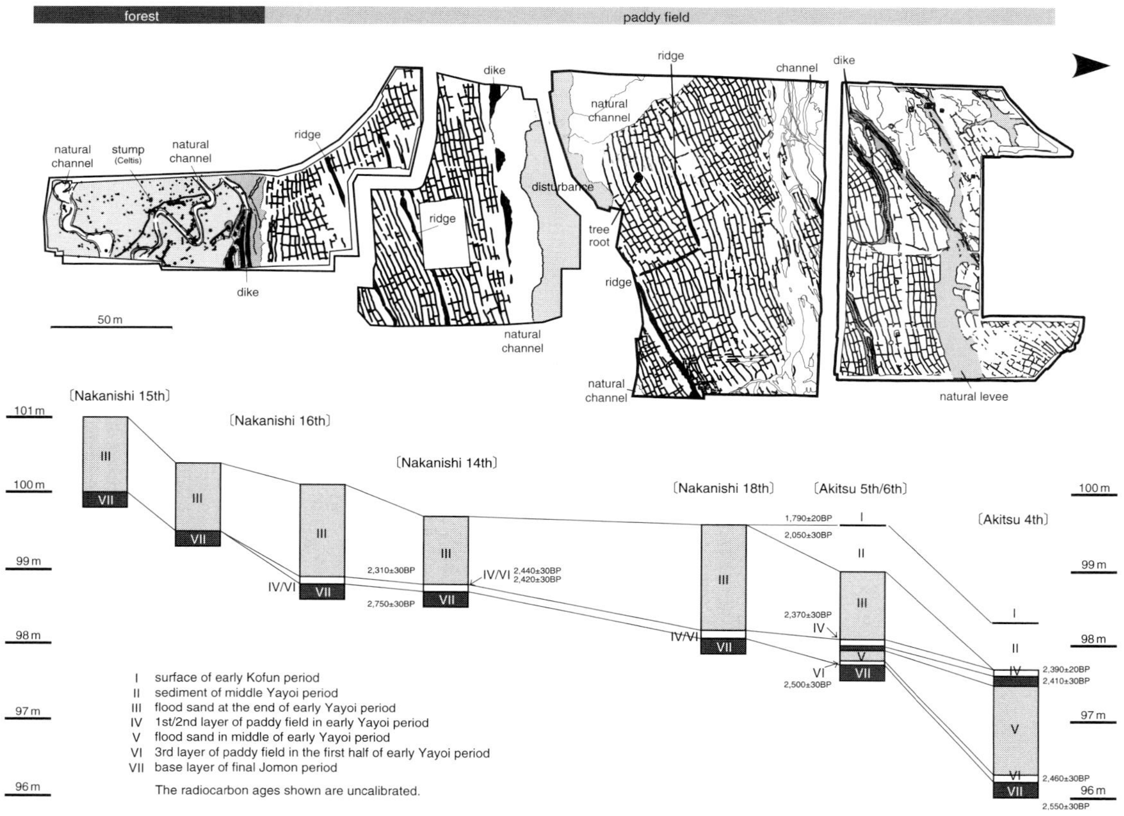

Figure 15.5 Plan and section of early Yayoi paddies at Nakanishi-Akitsu

this soil had formed. It is therefore inferred that the earliest paddies were not built until after the Yamato I-I-a phase of the early Yayoi period.[16]

In summary, the early Yayoi paddies at Nakanishi-Akitsu were used from the Yamato I-I-a to Yamato I-I-b phases. This is supported by radiocarbon dating of wood, seeds, and carbonized remains attached to pottery sherds,[17] and is similar in date to the Yamato I phase pottery from Karako-Kagi (Figures 15.6 and 15.7).[18]

## The village of paddy owners

The village where the people who built the paddies at Nakanishi-Akitsu lived has not yet been discovered. In the second excavation a ditch 1.1 m wide and 30 cm deep, dating from the early to the early middle Yayoi period, was found, however, to the north of the remains of the paddy, close to the Murono-Miyayama mounded tomb, where the elevation is a little higher.[19] Only a 1.6-metre-long section was excavated, but it produced numerous finds compared with the surrounding area. The pottery dating to the Yamato I-2 and II-I phases corresponded with the period of use of the paddy field. Fine sands and coarse sands with clay had accumulated above the ditch, and a layer dating to the Yamato III phase was identified above the sand layer. This indicated that the layer of sand deposited by the flood between the early and early middle Yayoi extended to the area near the Murono-Miyayama tomb. This is the only ditch from the early Yayoi period in the vicinity. Although the

16  *Tottaimon* 3b pottery of the end of the final Jomon and Yamato I-I-a pottery of the early Yayoi period have much in common, but there are also differing opinions on their precise relative chronology. I think that one follows the other. K. Okada, 'Kinki chiho Jomon banki doki hennen to Nara kenka kijun shiryo (The chronology of final Jomon pottery in the Kinki region and basic data for Nara prefecture)', in *Juyo bunkazai Kashiwara iseki shutsudohin no kenkyu (Research on Excavated Materials from the Important Cultural Property Kashiwara Site)*, Kashihara Kokogaku Kenkyujo Kenkyu Seika 11 (Nara kenritsu Kashihara Kokogaku Kenkyujo, 2011). Kawachi I-0 type pottery as found at the Saragun-Jori site in Osaka prefecture, from a purely typological perspective, seems to predate the Yamato I-I-a type – H. Morioka, 'Kinki chiiki (The Kinki region)', in *Koza Nihon no Kokogaku 5 Yayoi Jidai (jo) (Survey of Japanese Archaeology, vol. v: The Yayoi Period, Part 1)* (Tokyo: Aoki Shoten, 2011) – but there seems to be a temporal difference with the *Tottaimon* 3b (Nagahara type) which supports my contention. T. Nakao and W. Yamane, *Saragun-Jori iseki VIII (Saragun-Jori site VIII)* (Sakai: Osaka-fu Bunkazai Senta, 2009).

17  Matsuoka and Okada, 'Sixteenth excavation at the Nakanishi site'.

18  K. Kobayashi et al., 'Karako-Kagi iseki, Shimizukaze iseki hakkutsu shiryo no C14 nendai sokutei (C14 dating of excavated materials from Karako-Kagi and Shimizukaze)', in *Tawaramoto-cho bunkazai chosa nenpo (Annual Report on Cultural Properties Research in Tawaramoto Town)* (Tawaramoto Town Board of Education, 2006).

19  M. Kimoto, *Nakanishi iseki dai 2 ji hakkutsu chosa hokoku* (Gose-shi: Gose Gose-shi Kyōiku Iinkai, Heisei 2, 1990).

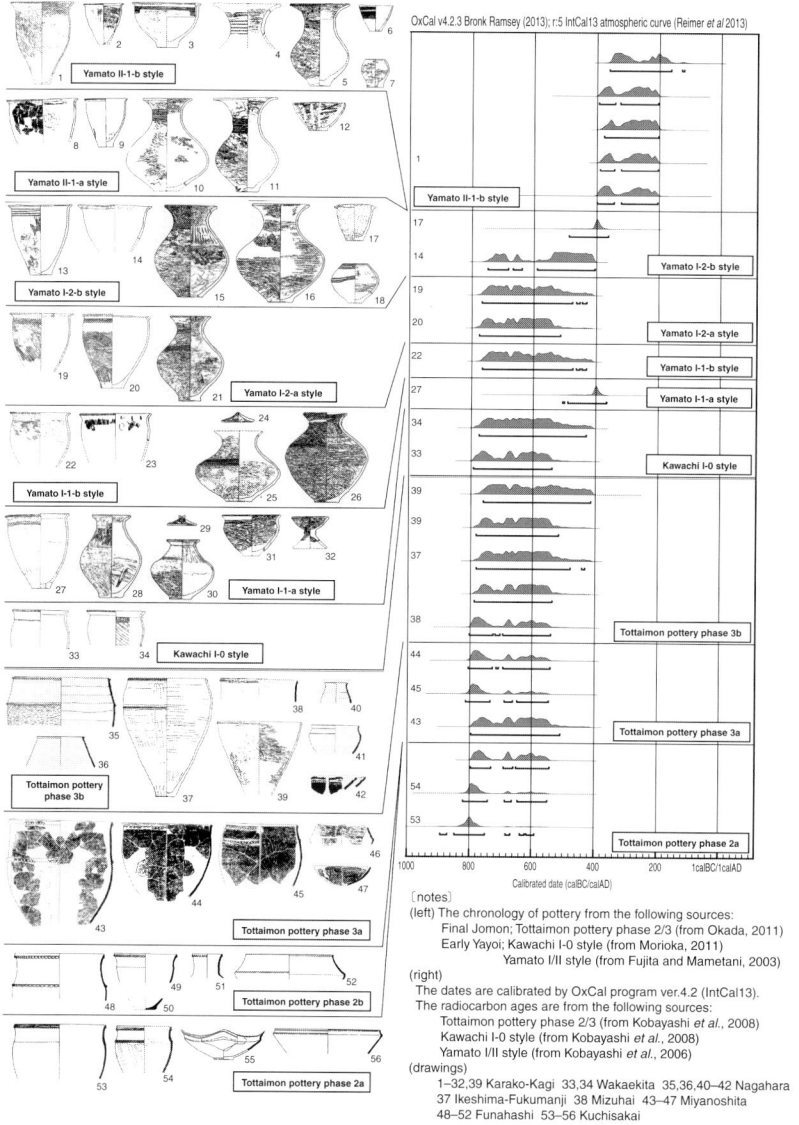

Figure 15.6  Final Jomon and early Yayoi pottery chronology and calibrated radiocarbon dates.

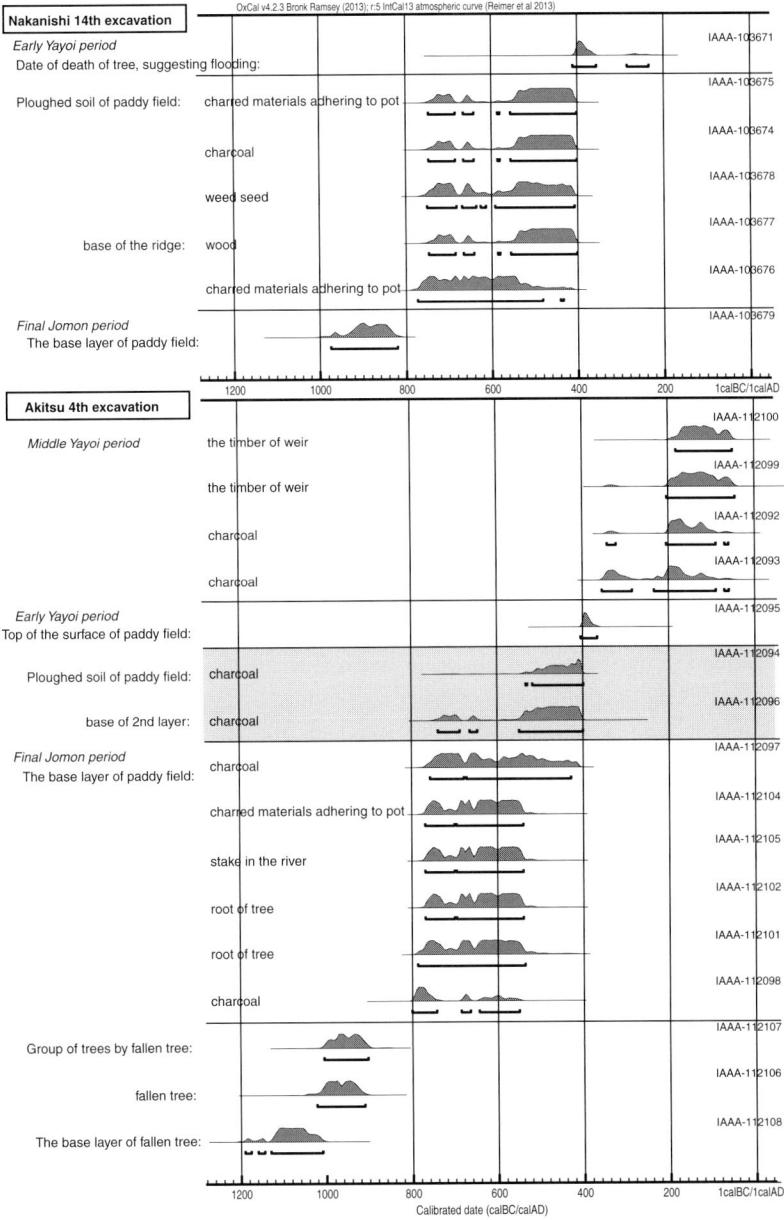

Figure 15.7  Calibrated radiocarbon dates from the paddy fields at Nakanishi-Akitsu.

nature of the ditch remains uncertain, I consider that it formed part of a moat enclosing the settlement of the people who built the paddies.

Traces of the village of the people who built the paddies at Haginomoto were discovered some 400 m north of the Haginomoto site, at Kawanishi-Nenarigaki.[20] This settlement was used for a relatively short period from the Yamato 1-1-b to 1-2-a phases, and was enclosed by a moat (Figure 15.2). The settlement extended across an area measuring 140 m north to south. Two buildings with their posts set in pits were identified within the enclosure, and there are also many other pits within the settlement area whose function has yet to be confirmed. The moat at Kawanishi-Nenarigaki was 1.0–2.5 m wide and 50–80 cm deep, and can be distinguished from other ditches running across the site. Many archaeological remains were found in all the ditches and the moat. Although the ditch at Nakanishi is shallower than the ditch in the second excavation area, the fact that it was over a metre wide and contained many artefacts supports the interpretation that it functioned as a moat enclosing a settlement area.

Another early Yayoi ditch-enclosed settlement was discovered at Shijo-Shinano, 3.5 km north of Haginomoto.[21] The settlement area was about 150 m long and 100 m wide, and was occupied from the Yamato 1-1-b phase and abandoned in the Yamato II phase. It seems that moat-enclosed settlements were relatively common at this time, and indeed I suggest that they were built every 3 to 4 km, the distance between the sites of Shijo-Shinano, Haginomoto, and Nakanishi. The distance between the paddy remains at Haginomoto and the moat at Kawanishi-Nenarigaki is 400 m, and the distance between the paddy at Nakanishi and the second excavation area is 500 m, about the same as at Haginomoto, further supporting the idea of the presence of a village in this location. It takes under ten minutes to walk this distance, probably less time than was required to walk from one side of the paddy to the other.

## Buried forest at Nakanishi-Akitsu

The Nakanishi site produced relatively few artefacts: a small number of pottery sherds and just a few stone reaping knives. Activity is shown by

---

20  T. Fukunishi (ed.), 'Kawanishi-nenarigaki iseki – Yayoi jidai zenki no kango shuraku no chosa (The Kawanishi-Nenarigaki site: investigation of an early Yayoi ditch-enclosed settlement)', *Nara kenritsu Kashihara Kokogaku Kenkyujo Chosa Hokoku*, 107 (2011).

21  M. Motomura (ed.), *Shijo-Shinano iseki (The Shijo-Shinano Site)*, Chosa Hokoku 100 (Nara kenritsu Kashihara Kokogaku Kenkyujo, 2007).

footprints preserved in the soils, but people did not leave their implements in the paddy fields. Rather than in the paddies themselves, discoveries of pottery and stone tools were concentrated in the forested area to the south of the fifteenth excavation area at Nakanishi (Figure 15.5 above).[22] The preserved remains of 265 trees were found, some of them still standing and others fallen, beneath the sandy flood deposits that covered the paddies. The majority were identified as *Morus australis*, *Camellia*, and *Acer*, which indicated a deciduous forest with occasional evergreen trees. The girth and age of the trees varied among species. *Quercus* subgen. *Cyclobalanopsis* (evergreen oak) were thick, while the *Cephalotaxus harringtonia* (cowtail pine) were slender. Assuming that all the trees died during the flood, we can observe the forest succession over the hundred years prior to the flood. In addition to natural disturbances, including the flood, this succession was influenced by human activities along the stream. A concentration of some thirty walnut shells (*Juglans mandshurica* var. *sachalinensis*) at the edge of the remains of the forest overlooking the paddies suggests the gathering of nuts. A number of stone tools, including arrowheads, flakes, and roughouts, indicates the hunting of animals such as wild boar. Stumps of *Celtis* (Japanese hackberry) over a metre in diameter tell of logging activities, for lumber. Between 40 and 50 per cent of the wooden implements from Kawanishi-Nenarigaki and Shijo-Shinano, contemporary with Nakanishi-Akitsu, were made of evergreen oak (*Quercus* subgen. *Cyclobalanopsis*), and it is probable that this wood was selected for logging from the outset.

## Paddy development and operation

Using data from historical sources it is possible to estimate Yayoi rice harvests. As described above, the paddy fields at Nakanishi were established and used during the early Yayoi period, after which they were abandoned. While their overall area, estimated as being as much as 100,000 m², seems very large given the limited time they were in use, how much rice could actually have been cultivated there? Research by a group led by Kaoru Terasawa suggests that paddy fields from the early to middle Yayoi could

---

22 Archaeological Institute of Kashihara, 'Nakanishi iseki hakkutsu chosa. Genchi setsu-meikai shiryo: Yayoi jidai zenki no suiden to satoyama (Excavations at Nakanishi: materials for the onsite explanation: early Yayoi period paddies and *satoyama*)' (Nara kenritsu Kashihara Kokogaku Kenkyujo, 2010); K. Kikui, 'Yayoi jidai zenki no suiden to shinrin – Nara-ken Gosho-shi Nakanishi iseki (Forests and paddy fields in the early Yayoi period – the Nakanishi site, Gose city, Nara prefecture)', *Kikan Kokogaku*, 115 (2011).

be expected to have yielded similar quantities to what are historically described as low-yield (*geden*) or very low-yield (*gegeden*) paddies.[23] In experiments carried out by Yukiko Kikuchi and Nobuaki Miyoshi, red-kernelled rice yields supported this estimate, although the results did vary depending on the kind of rice sown, the method of sowing (direct sowing or transplantation of seedlings), and the density of sowing.[24] According to Goichi Sawada, on whose research the estimates provided by the Terasawa group were based, *gegeden* produced the lowest yield from ancient paddies, calculated as 31.75 kg (0.244 *koku*) of unpolished rice (*genmai*) per *tan* (991.74 m²). This is close to the average yield achieved by the Kikuchi experimental group for directly sowed *tsutsu*-variety rice. *Geden* yielded twice as much as *gegeden*, i.e. 63.5 kg (0.488 *koku*) per *tan*. This value is also close to the average yield of *tsutsu* rice when densely planted during experiments. Whether or not the transplantation method was used during the early Yayoi remains under discussion. The remains of rice stubble found at Nakanishi-Akitsu indicate that the estimates should range between *gegeden* (lowest) and *geden* (highest).

One *tan* (991.74 m²) is equal to an area which yielded one *koku* (180 litres or 150 kg of rice). Very low-grade rice paddy (*gegeden*) was considered to yield one quarter of a *koku*, while the next grade up, low-grade paddy (*geden*), yields half of one *koku* of rice. If one *koku* of rice was normally consumed by an adult in a single year, then four *tan* of *gegeden* (3,966.96 m²) or two *tan* of *geden* were needed to supply sufficient rice for a year for one adult. We can then estimate the number of people that the paddies at Nakanishi would have supported: while 25,000 m² have been found so far, it is estimated that the total area of paddy is between 50,000 and 100,000 m², i.e. yielding enough rice to support a minimum population of 12.6 people, and a maximum of 25.21 people (50,000 m²), and between 25.21 and 50.42 people (100,000 m²). These figures remain speculative, however, as we do not know how much rice was actually consumed by individuals during the Yayoi period. Contemporary Japanese people consume on average 59 kilograms of rice in a year, as part of their mixed diet. On this basis, the number of people the Nakanishi paddies could support would double.

---

23 K. Terasawa and K. Terasawa, 'Yayoi jidai shokubutsushitsu shokuryo no kisoteki kenkyu – shoki nogyo shakai no zentei toshite (Basic research into the quantification of plant foods in the Yayoi period)', in *Kashihara Kokogaku Kenkyujo Kiyo* (*Proceedings of the Archaeological Institute of Kashihara*), vol. v (Nara kenritsu Kashihara Kokogaku Kenkyujo, 1981).

24 A. Kikuchi and N. Miyoshi, 'Yayoi jidai no Korne shukakurgo ni tsuite – fukugen suiden ni okeru jikken kokogakuteki kenkyu (On the amount of the rice harvest in the Yayoi period – reconstructing paddy fields on the basis of experimental archaeological research)', *Kodai*, 120 (2007).

## Population of the village

How many people worked on the paddy fields? The population of Nakanishi-Akitsu can be estimated based on the sites of similar size at Kawanishi-Nenarigaki and Shijo-Shinano. The number of houses at these sites, however, is not known, and so we must use the area of the enclosure as an indication of site size. We can use the site of Daikai in Hyogo prefecture as a model, where pit-dwellings were excavated within the moated area. During the early Yayoi at Daikai the moat was enlarged. Five pit-dwellings, eleven storage pits, and one wooden coffin burial were discovered. Assuming that all the buildings were occupied at one time, and on average five people lived in a single dwelling, then up to twenty-five people lived at the site. Hideto Morioka estimated that the average Yayoi village settlement comprised a small group of families, about twenty people in all, inhabiting four dwellings.[25] Hideji Harunari also estimated that most villages were relatively small, with a population of up to about thirty people.[26] The enclosed area of the Daikai site measured 65 × 35 m. The long axes of Kawanishi-Nenarigaki and Shijo-Shinano were 140 m and 150 m respectively, twice the dimensions of Daikai, suggesting a possible population twice that of Daikai. Such estimates may be too simplistic, however, as many moats were constructed at both Kawanishi-Nenarigaki and Shijo-Shinano.

## Rice and mountain vegetables

If the village at Nakanishi-Akitsu was of a similar scale and the population a maximum of forty to sixty people, the yield of rice previously estimated could not have supported the whole population of the village. If the paddy field was 50,000 m², the yield could not support the population. Only if the consumption of rice during the Yayoi period was much less, half that of the previous estimate, could the 50,000 m² of paddy field (assumed to produce a harvest comparable to the low-yield *geden* paddies) have supported the population. The Terasawa group estimated the amount of rice consumed per person per day based on the estimated rice yield. These estimates were *c.* 2 *go* (1 *go* = 180 cc) during the late Yayoi period, 1 *go* during the middle Yayoi period, and 0.2 *go* during the early Yayoi period. The Terasawa group concluded that the

25 Morioka, 'The Kinki region'.
26 H. Harunari, 'Kinki ni okeru Yayoi jidai no kaishi nendai (Chronology of the beginning of the Yayoi period in Kinki)', in T. Nishimoto (ed.), *Shin Yayoi Jidai no hajimari* (*New Beginnings of the Yayoi Period*), vol. 11 (Tokyo: Yuzankaku, 2007).

yield was much less than expected for Yayoi people, and that these small yields must have influenced the consumption of rice greatly, especially in the early and middle Yayoi period. Therefore people during the early Yayoi mainly depended on food sources other than rice for starch, such as millet, wheat and barley, beans, potatoes, and nuts.[27] It may be difficult to imagine, given the apparent scale of the large rice paddy field at Nakanishi, that people mainly depended on food other than rice, but it is easier to understand if we take into consideration the traces of human activities in the buried forest discovered next to the village.

## Before the construction of the paddy fields

Two pottery dumps from the *tottaimon* 3 phase at the end of the final Jomon period were excavated in the forest. The existence of these remains indicates that the village at this time was not far from the forest. Although the forest fauna then was different from that of the Yayoi period, we can be certain that the forest was exploited during the latter for hunting, gathering, and harvesting wood. They continued to utilize the forest space in similar ways to their Jomon forebears, even once the paddy fields were built in the early Yayoi period. The forest not only supplied food compensating for the small yield of rice from the paddies, but also provided various other resources, such as meat and timber.

There is evidence for how the forest was used at the end of the Jomon period, prior to the construction of the paddies. During the investigations at Nakanishi-Akitsu, buried forests were discovered in area 15 at Nakanishi that dated not only to the early Yayoi but also the final Jomon. Immediately beneath the earlier early Yayoi paddy layers on the southern bank of the waterway were found trunks of a variety of species of oak, including *Quercus* subgen. *Cyclobalanopsis*, *Quercus* Sect. *Cerris*, and *Quercus* Sect. *Prinus*.[28] On the northern bank a concentration of late final Jomon *tottaimon* phase 2 pottery was found, suggesting that people were living nearby at this stage. By contrast, the small number of artefacts from the south side of the river suggests that there was little settlement on this side. Just below the roots complete examples of stag beetle (*Prosopocoilus inclinatus*) were discovered. The ecological characteristics suggest that this was a liminal zone between mountains and exploited areas. The pollen analysis suggests that at area 6 of

27 Terasawa and Terasawa, 'Basic research into the quantification of plant foods'.
28 Okada et al., 'Fourth excavation of the Akitsu site'.

the Akitsu site there was very little woodland pollen, but a predominance of grass, notably *Artemisia* which favours cool and dry conditions, again suggesting a relatively open forest environment.[29] There were also quite high quantities of chestnut (*Castanea crenata*) away from the waterway on slightly higher ground, suggesting there were stands in the vicinity of the new paddies as well.

At the Kannonji-Honma site which spans the border between Kashihara and Gose cities, some thirty trunks of chestnut have been found buried in an old river course, dating from the middle part of the final Jomon.[30] A possible settlement with many artefacts, traces of buildings, and burials was located about 200 m south of this chestnut stand, and it seems that many materials were dumped in the watercourse.[31] These include many plant remains, in particular chestnuts, indicating that these were being exploited as food by the people living there. Some of the chestnut timbers had also been used for architectural purposes. Along with the evidence from Akitsu area 6 and Nakanishi area 14, it seems that from the end of the final Jomon to the early half of the early Yayoi, the environment into which rice paddies were being introduced had chestnut as an important component, which was being utilized for various purposes by the Jomon people there.

## The transformation of the landscape

What type of landscape provided the context for the development of the paddy fields at Nakanishi-Akitsu? On the relatively higher ground near the hills, there were stands of forest, while on the lower slopes paddy fields were newly established. We have seen above that the site was located between a river and a forest, on ground predominantly covered by grasses. In areas 4 and 6 at Akitsu, the black palaeosol sealed late final Jomon layers. Pollen

29  M. Kanehara, 'Akitsu iseki kaso ni okeru shokusei, kankyo no fukugen to taisekiso seisei kankyo no kento (Investigating the alleviated environments and reconstructing the environment and vegetation from the lower layer of the Akitsu site)', in *Nara-ken iseki chosa gaiho 2012 nendo* (*Summary of Excavations in Nara in 2012*).

30  K. Hiraiwa, 'Kashihara no rekishi wo saguru 17 (Exploring the history of Kashihara 17)', in *Heisei 20 nendo Maizo Bunkazai Hakkutsu Chosa Seikaten* (*Exhibition of the Results of Archaeological Excavations in 2009*) (Nara: Kashihara-shi Senzuka Shiryokan, 2010).

31  M. Motomura, 'Kannonji-Honma iseki – Keinawa Jidoshado (Kannonji 1 ku) (The Kannonji-Honma site – Keinawa expressway [Kannonji Location 1])', in *Nara-ken iseki chosa gaiho 2008 nendo* (*Summary of Excavations in Nara in 2008*) (Nara kenritsu Kashihara Kokogaku Kenkyujo, 2009); M. Okada (ed.), 'Kannonji Honma iseki 1 (Kannonji 111 ku) (Kannonji Honma 1 [Kannonji location 111])', in *Nara kenritsu Kashihara Kokogaku Kenkyujo Chosa Hokoku 113* (Nara kenritsu Kashihara Kokogaku Kenkyujo, 2013).

analysis suggests a relatively open forest with chestnut and oak.[32] Investigations at Nakanishi area 14 showed that black palaeosol which became the cultivated soil for the paddy field contained only small amounts of arboreal pollen but high densities of phytoliths of *Phragmites* and *Pleioblastus*.[33] This reconstructed landscape comprised unstable land, which fluctuated between wetland conditions when the groundwater level was high, and dry land with stands of bamboo. If it had been a stable wetland, it would have supported an ecosystem with high biodiversity, making it attractive to Jomon collectors, but during dry periods when it became just an arid riverbed, it was no longer so productive or useful. The introduction of the new agricultural techniques which transformed the local landscape would therefore not have been problematic in terms of previous subsistence activities. Indeed, the utilization of this landscape for rice paddy would have complemented the existing subsistence strategies. I consider this to be one reason for the rapid and smooth introduction of irrigated rice cultivation in the Nara basin (Figure 15.8).

## The background to the introduction of irrigated rice cultivation

There is no doubt that the introduction of irrigated rice cultivation was an epoch-making transition in the Japanese archipelago. It eventually provided a stable food supply and agricultural surplus, resulting in the distribution, accumulation, and concentration of wealth. This process was very important for the subsequent development of society and economy in Japan. The reasons for the introduction of rice farming were not as simple as agriculture being superior to what went before, which is how it is perceived by some, who regard rice farming as being a better way of life than hunting and gathering.

It is well known that during the Jomon period complex hunting-gathering societies developed supported by sophisticated techniques, including storage and the removal of bitter tannins from nuts. I consider that the technologies of Jomon culture facilitated the introduction of rice cultivation, along with its complex irrigation facilities, because there was no demerit to the pre-existing ways of life, and because rice farming could be accommodated within the

---

32 Kanehara, 'Investigating the alleviated environments'.
33 Matsuoka and Okada, 'Sixteenth excavation at the Nakanishi site'.

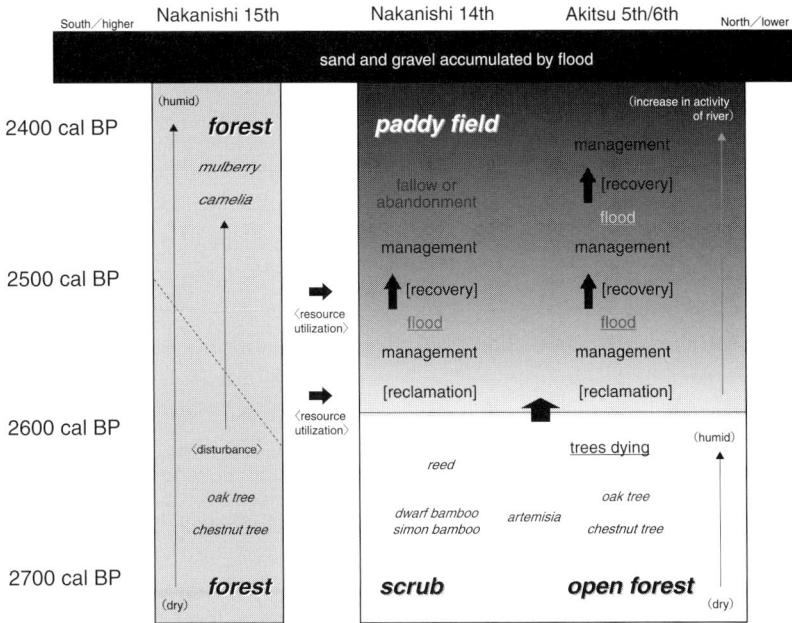

Figure 15.8 Transformation of the wild landscape to paddy field at Nakanishi-Akitsu.

range of existing social activities. In this regard, it is especially important to note that rice cultivation did not infringe on the various existing means of subsistence, and it neither replaced nor was it superior to these. No evidence has yet been discovered for any clash between the old and new economic activities.

The development of large rice paddies at Nakanishi-Akitsu at the start of the early Yayoi period does indeed seem to have been relatively sudden, but they were constructed using part of the landscape that was hardly used at the end of the final Jomon, as demonstrated by the absence of traces of Jomon activities from the palaeosol which become the basis for the creation of the paddy field. As mentioned above, it is likely that the area used was rather dry, dominated by grasses, becoming wet when the groundwater level was high. Therefore, the productivity of Jomon gatherers was low in this area and it was not much used, so that it was not problematic to transform it for these new economic activities.

However, the reclamation of land for large paddy fields and the building of irrigation facilities, along with the ongoing management of cultivated, land including the removal of undergrowth and weeding, represent an investment of labour not directly connected to the harvest. There must have been reasons why this was put into practice. Two reasons can be considered.

1. The continuity of cultivated land. The control and cultivation of useful plants were practised by interfering with the natural vegetation in the final Jomon period. An example is the development of a stand of chestnut trees at Kannonji-Honma during the middle final Jomon period.[34] Such chestnut stands were utilized not only for gathering nuts, but also for procuring timber. The continuous utilization of land led to the depletion of resources, so that it was usually necessary to leave the exhausted land until it recovered and to seek out new land to secure sufficient resources. In the case of rice paddies, however, it was possible to continuously make use of the same land. Even if the soil was exhausted after the harvest, through leaving sections of the paddy complex fallow it was possible to continue growing rice.[35] Namely, it was no longer necessary to wait for the natural recovery of the land. In this way rice cultivation and the cyclical use of land made the food supply more stable and predictable.

2. Storing capability and reproducibility of harvests. The idea of storing food developed during the Jomon period, as can be seen in the large numbers of storage pits for nuts, particularly in low wet areas. Similar nut storage pits existed in the Yayoi period, but the most common form of storage was for harvested rice brought into the village. The difference between the methods is in the form of storage, and the more important point is that storing nuts was just for consumption, while storing rice was for both consumption and seeds for sowing in the next year.

This reproducibility of harvest was very attractive. Jomon society longed for rebirth and held many kinds of ritual, including those involving *dogu* ceramic figures, examples of which were excavated at Kashiwara and Tamade. The main target of rebirth was of course human beings, but since many animal-shaped clay figurines were made, and are often found in conjunction with

---

34 Hiraiwa, 'Exploring the history of Kashihara 17'.
35 At Location 14 of the Nakanishi site, many paddy grasses were discovered (including *Scirpus, Monochoria vaginalis Presl* var. *Plantaginea Solms-Laub., Cyperaceae*). Matsuoka and Okada, 'Sixteenth excavation at the Nakanishi site'. It is possible that these grasses vary depending on how the paddy is managed.

accumulations of burnt animal bones and other remains, the natural resources which supported the society were also the focus of ideas of rebirth. The cyclical reproduction of natural resources could maintain and reproduce society, and human beings greatly influenced the cycle. Therefore, rice grains became symbolic of rebirth, and the storage of seed rice meant the control of rebirth by humans.

A number of impressions of seed rice on pottery dating from the late final Jomon period are known from sites in the Kinki area. While these impressions demonstrate the existence of rice, they do not prove that agriculture was yet being practised.

Twenty impressions of rice grains were found on a deep ceramic bowl of the *tottaimon* 2a phase from the Saragi site near Tamade.[36] Such a quantity of impressions indicates that this was more than an accident or that these were just miscellaneous grains. At present, there is no evidence of irrigated rice cultivation to the east of the Setouchi region (the area facing the Seto Inland Sea) during the later final Jomon period, but it is possible that seed rice itself was introduced to the Nara basin as the symbol of reproducible grains. It is proposed here that irrigated rice cultivation was introduced to these new areas from existing rice-producing areas, soon after the introduction of the grains themselves.

This chapter has tried to explain the processes of the introduction of irrigated rice cultivation at the transition from the Jomon period to the Yayoi, based on the detailed recent excavations in Nara prefecture. I have tried to present a model for the major changes that constituted the 'origins of agriculture' in the Nara basin. The investigation of the sites described here is still in progress and my hypotheses will no doubt have to be re-examined in the light of future research results.

## Further reading

Amino, Y. *Rethinking Japanese History*. Ann Arbor: University of Michigan Center for Japanese Studies, 2012.

Barnes, G.L. *State Formation in Japan: Emergence of a 4th-Century Ruling Elite*. Ann Arbor: University of Michigan Center for Japanese Studies, 1988.

Hudson, M. *The Ruins of Identity: Ethnogenesis in the Japanese Islands*. Honolulu: University of Hawai'i Press, 1999.

36 Y. Yonekawa et al., 'Keinawa Jidoshado Saragi chiku 2009 nendo (Excavations at the Saragi location on the route of the Keinawa expressway in 2009)', in *Nara-ken iseki chosa gaiho 2009 nendo (Summary of Excavations in Nara in 2009)*.

Kidder, J.E. *Himiko: The Elusive Kingdom of Yamatai.* Honolulu: University of Hawai'i Press, 2007.

Mizoguchi, K. *The Archaeology of Japan: From the Earliest Rice Farming Villages to the Rise of the State.* Cambridge University Press, 2013.

Totman, C. *Japan: An Environmental History.* London: I.B. Tauris, 2014.

# 16

# Early agriculture in Southeast Asia and the Pacific

HUW BARTON

Mainland Southeast Asia (MSEA) and island Southeast Asia (ISEA) form a complex geographic and political region consisting of eleven countries spread from India to China and New Guinea (Map 16.1). MSEA consists of Cambodia, Laos, Malaysia, Myanmar, Thailand, and Vietnam. The islands (ISEA) include the nations of Indonesia and the Philippines, Singapore, the Sultanate of Brunei, and East Timor. The island of Borneo, as well as being home to Brunei, also consists of the Federated States of Sarawak and Sahul and the Indonesian region of Kalimantan. Other large islands include Sumatra, Java, Sulawesi, Flores, Timor, Halmahera, and Seram. Island chains reach from the Philippines to Borneo via Palawan and also to the south through the Sulu archipelago. The Lesser Sunda Islands form a scattering of small islands along the 'ridge of fire' from the east coast of Java to Timor, providing an island-hopping route from Sumatra to the Moluccas, west of New Guinea.

The climate of this region ranges from humid subtropical to tropical from southern China into Vietnam, with lowland and montane evergreen forests, deciduous dipterocarp forests, limestone karst forests, littoral forests, and peatswamp and mangrove forests. These forest types are typical of much of the region, with deciduous dipterocarp forest replaced by evergreen mixed dipterocarp forests closer to the equator. Climates are affected to a greater or lesser extent by the intertropical convergence zone, creating strong seasonal changes in rainfall and cyclonic weather, especially along coastal regions.

Thailand is under the influence of the monsoon winds, having a northeast and southwest monsoon season with high periods of rainfall along the coasts, but areas of relatively dry climate in the interior on the leeward side of the mountains. Borneo is generally wet throughout the year with annual rainfall of over 3,000 mm along the northwest coast, but with more seasonal climes along the eastern coast of Kalimantan. The Lesser Sunda Islands have the driest climates in Indonesia, supporting a distinct biota on the other side of

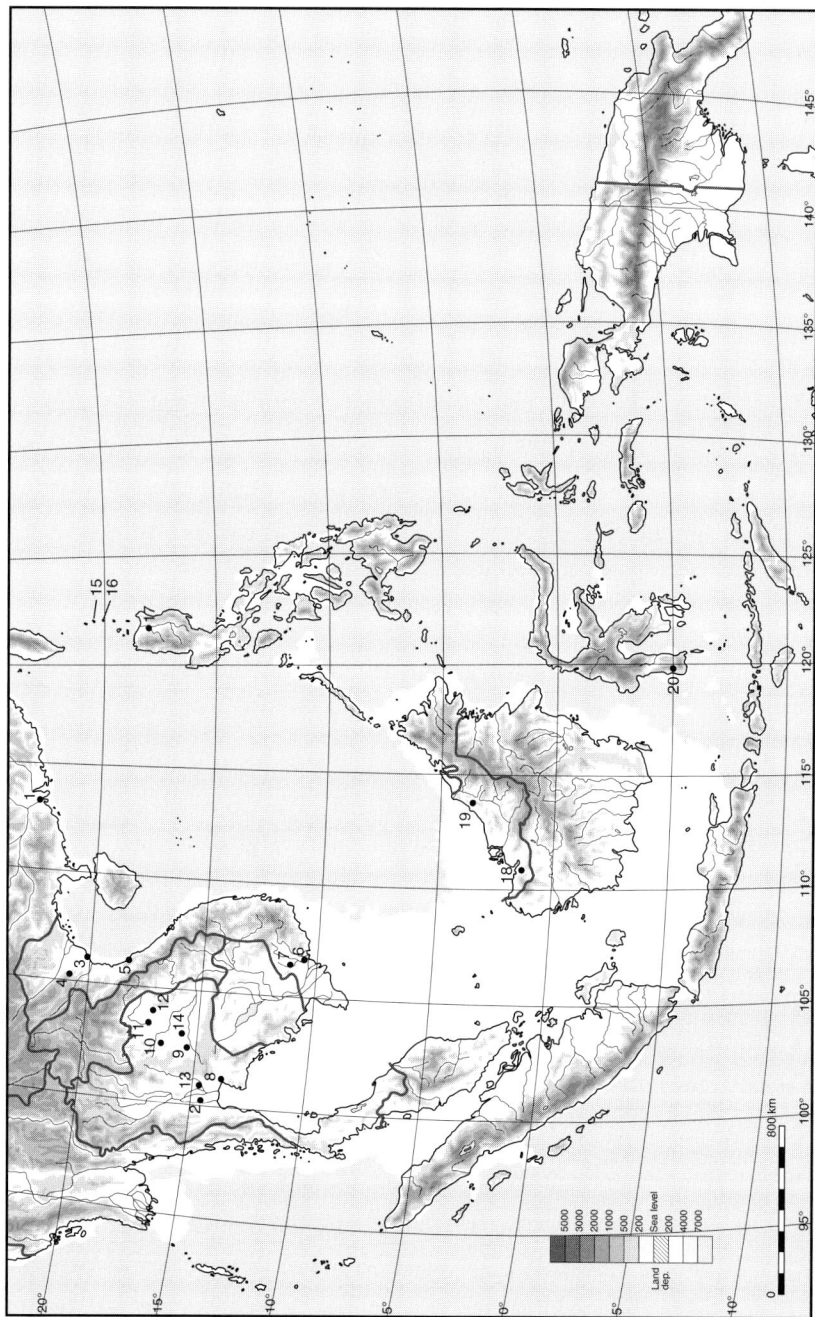

Map 16.1  Southeast Asia, showing the principal archaeological sites mentioned in Chapter 16: 1. Xincun; 2. Spirit Cave; 3. DaBut; 4. Phung Nguyen; 5. Tach Lac; 6. Rach Nui; 7. An Son 7. Loc Giang; 8. Kok Phanam Di; 9. Neon U-Loke; 9. Ban Lum Khao; 10. Non Nok Tha; 11. Ban Chiang; 12. Ban Na Di; 13. Nil Kham Maeng; 13. Nor Mak La; 13. Non Pa Wai; 14. Ban Non Wat; 15. Anaro; 16. Savidug; 16. Sunget; 17. Andarayan; 18. Gua Sireh; 19. Niah Cave; 20. Leang Burung; 20. Ulu Leang.

Webber's Line with deciduous forest, patches of dry thorny forest, and areas of savanna grassland.

The landforms of MSEA incorporate coastal, often swampy plains and interior flood-prone valleys, dissected by intervening uplands. The interiors of Thailand and Cambodia consist of large areas of lowland plains with the Khorat plateau to the north of Thailand and the Chao Phraya plains in the southwest. Several of the large islands such as Sumatra and Borneo support high interior ranges rising up from low, swampy coastal plains of lowland peat swamp and lowland dipterocarp rainforest. Several major rivers may have formed important routes from coastal regions inland and vice versa in prehistory, enabling rapid movements of population. By the colonial period, many of these big rivers, and their multitude of smaller branches, formed an arterial network of major trade routes carrying imported ceramics, bronze, scented woods, rattan, bird nests, and a multitude of other goods.

## Neolithic paradigms

The term 'Neolithic' is often used to describe cultural and technological changes across MSEA and ISEA during the mid-Holocene from c. 3000 BCE to c. 1500 BCE that included sedentism, the spread of agriculture, and the introduction of new materials (including pottery and polished stone tools) and new technologies (such as weaving with spindle whorls), along with domesticated pigs and chickens. Initially, it is argued, these communities spread south and west in China from villages along the lower Yangtze River, moving overland into the subtropical and tropical regions of MSEA and by sea routes into ISEA via Taiwan.[1] Originally this spread of cultures and materials was thought of as a 'package' of materials carried with migrant communities transforming or wiping out indigenous populations of hunter-gatherers as they moved into new landscapes.[2] However, as seen in Chapters 12 and 14, the 'package' is now more than a little disarticulated in time and space. Pottery first appears by 18,000 BP in China and Japan, though

---

1 P. Bellwood, *First Farmers: The Origins of Agricultural Societies* (Oxford: Blackwell, 2005); M.T. Carson et al., 'The pottery trail from Southeast Asia to Remote Oceania', *Journal of Island & Coastal Archaeology*, 8 (2013), 17–36; C. Higham, *The Archaeology of Mainland Southeast Asia: From 10,000 BC to the Fall of Angkor* (Cambridge University Press, 1989), and *Early Culture of Mainland Southeast Asia* (Bangkok: River Books, 2002); C. Higham et al., 'The prehistory of a friction zone: first farmers and hunter-gatherers in Southeast Asia', *Antiquity*, 85 (2011), 529–43; C. Zhang and H.-C. Hung, 'The emergence of agriculture in southern China', *Antiquity*, 84 (2010), 11–25.

2 Bellwood, *First Farmers*; J. Diamond and P. Bellwood, 'Farmers and their languages: the first expansions', *Science*, 300 (2003), 597–603.

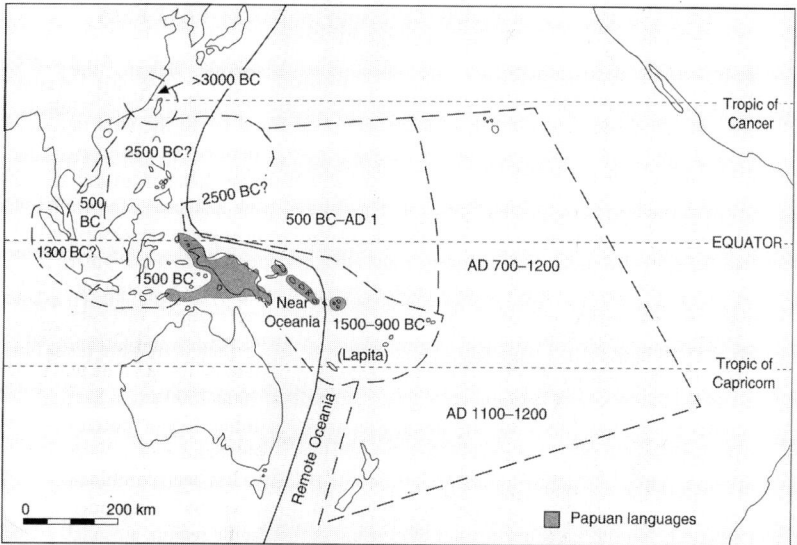

Figure 16.1 Peter Bellwood's model of the Austronesian dispersals of farmers from MSEA into ISEA.

it does not appear to spread widely across MSEA and ISEA until the mid-Holocene. Other items are also disarticulated from the original Neolithic 'package', including sedentism, which appears to predate farming among some coastal hunter-gatherer groups in southern China, Vietnam, and southern Thailand.[3] Ground-edge pebble axes occur in Vietnam several thousand years ahead of any evidence of farming.[4]

As envisaged by Peter Bellwood, the initial spread of agriculture was by peoples who were capable, driven, and brought with them an extremely flexible agricultural system that incorporated grains such as rice as well as the cultivation of root crops and trees (Figure 16.1).[5]

3 C. Higham, 'Mainland Southeast Asia from the Neolithic to the Iron Age', and K.S. Nguyen et al., 'Northern Vietnam from the Neolithic to the Han period', both in I. Glover and P. Bellwood (eds.), Southeast Asia: From Prehistory to History (London: RoutledgeCurzon, 2004), 41–67 and 189–201.

4 M.F. Oxenham et al., 'Skeletal evidence for the emergence of infectious disease in Bronze and Iron Age northern Vietnam', American Journal of Physical Anthropology, 126 (2005), 359–76.

5 P. Bellwood, 'Austronesian prehistory in Southeast Asia: homeland, expansion and transformation', in P. Bellwood et al. (eds.), The Austronesians: Historical and Comparative Perspectives (Canberra: Department of Anthropology, Australian National University, 1995), 96–111; Bellwood, First Farmers.

The early Austronesians began their ethnolinguistic career as subtropical coastal and riverine peoples with a Neolithic economy based on cereal and tuber cultivation and a set of domesticated animals. Their ethnographic descendants in island Southeast Asia managed to *create for themselves* a much wider range of subsistence economies, including rainforest foraging and collection-for-trade; sea nomadism; varied forms of both irrigated and rain-fed rice cultivation; shifting cultivation of cereals, fruits and tubers; and even palm exploitation . . .[6]

While compelling, this statement incorporates a number of key assumptions, some of which remain untested. First, it assumes a 'farming' mentality that is unique to a group of people, a sort of 'blueprint' for all forms of plant cultivation, that initially began with rice (see Chapter 12) but that is readily adapted to other forms of plant cultivation. Second, it wraps up two very different forms of plant cultivation, one based on the growth of annuals (rice and millets) and a very different approach that is based on the cultivation and management of perennials.[7] This latter system, broadly referred to as 'vege-culture', involves root crops, palms, and trees in a wide variety of practices, involving mobile hunter-gatherers as well as sedentary farmers. Important differences between cereal farming and vegecultural modes of plant cultivation is that the former involves clearance of vegetation to create spaces to grow cereal crops, whereas the latter is often embedded within existing vegetation structures – it is often described as a 'mimic' of forest structure – and can occur within forest with minimal clearance. The expansionist model of farming also attempts to accommodate modern-day observations that Austronesian languages are spoken by most of the cultural groups across MSEA and ISEA and that these peoples share Mongoloid (Asian) physical features.[8] Dates proposed for the arrival of Neolithic communities in MSEA include *c.* 3000 BCE, the late third millennium BCE,[9] and as late as *c.* 1650 BCE.[10]

---

6 Bellwood, 'Austronesian prehistory', 110 (italics mine).
7 H. Barton, 'The reversed fortunes of sago and rice, *Oryza sativa*, in the rainforests of Sarawak, Borneo', *Quaternary International*, 249 (2012), 96–104; H. Barton and T.P. Denham, 'Prehistoric vegeculture and social life in island Southeast Asia and Melanesia', in G. Barker and M. Janowski (eds.), *Why Cultivate? Anthropological and Archaeological Approaches to Foraging–Farming Transitions in Southeast Asia* (Cambridge: McDonald Institute for Archaeological Research, 2011), 17–26.
8 P. Bellwood, *The Prehistory of the Indo-Malaysian Archipelago* (Honolulu: University of Hawai'i Press, 1997).
9 F. Ripsoli, 'The incised and impressed pottery style of mainland Southeast Asia: following the paths of Neolithization', *East and West*, 57 (2007), 235–304.
10 C. Higham and T. Higham, 'A new chronological framework for prehistoric Southeast Asia, based on a Bayesian model from Ban Non Wat', *Antiquity*, 83 (2009), 125–44.

Using a maritime route into ISEA, occupation of the Philippines first occurred around 2000 BCE and arguably spread rapidly south into Borneo and Indonesia and east into Sulawesi and other islands en route to New Guinea.[11] Central to the expansionist argument is that no cultivation practices, or food production of any kind, existed before 3500 BCE in MSEA and ISEA.[12] As Neolithic communities expanded outwards, indigenous populations of hunter-gatherers were either pushed aside and ignored or absorbed as farmers moved along the coastlines and down the big riverine floodplains of MSEA and by various routes into the big islands of Borneo, Sumatra, and Java and the smaller archipelagoes of Micronesia. Ultimately these populations moved further eastwards to become part of the Lapita colonization of Near and Remote Oceania *c.* 1300 BCE.[13]

Rice, though today seemingly the dominant food plant geographically, is not the only major crop or food staple in the region.[14] Farming across MSEA and ISEA incorporates a wide range of approaches in the cultivation of rice, with the creation and maintenance of cleared fields within which a plant like rice is a mono-crop (wet and dry), as well as vegetative modes within polycultural (mixed planting) modes of plant propagation. Vegecultural systems are distinctly different from seed-based forms of cultivation and it has even been suggested that rice, at least in ISEA, was actively resisted (or certainly adopted only slowly) by indigenous groups, at least as a staple food crop, for millennia, and was more likely gradually grafted into pre-existing vegecultural forms of plant management and cultivation.[15]

Key plants for this indigenous 'agricultural' activity (and I use the word cautiously here, as defining cultivation outside of the use of cereal domesticates such as rice is problematic for reasons expanded on below) are roots and tubers such as taro and yams, sago palms, bananas, and bamboo. Proponents of this view accept the likelihood that vegetative modes of plant manipulation (including cultivation) are early and may have involved

11 P. Bellwood, 'Asian farming diasporas? Agriculture, languages, and genes in China and Southeast Asia', in M. Stark (ed.), *Archaeology of Asia* (Oxford: Blackwell, 2006), 96–118.
12 Bellwood, 'Asian farming diasporas?'
13 P. Bellwood and P. Koon, '"Lapita colonists leave boats unburned!" The question of Lapita links with island Southeast Asia', *Antiquity*, 63 (1989), 613–22.
14 Barton, 'Reversed fortunes'; G. Crawford, 'East-Asian plant domestication', in Stark (ed.), *Archaeology of Asia*, 77–95.
15 E.g. Barton and Denham, 'Prehistoric vegeculture'; H. Barton and V. Paz, 'Subterranean diets in the tropical rain forests of Sarawak, Malaysia', in T.P. Denham et al. (eds.), *Rethinking Agriculture: Archaeological and Ethnoarchaeological Perspectives* (Walnut Creek, CA: Left Coast Press, 2007), 50–77.

plants that have become domesticates as well as species that remain genetically wild today, including several different types of sago palm.[16]

The best evidence currently of an early vegecultural agriculture lies in the intermontane valleys of New Guinea at the site of Kuk Swamp (see Chapter 17). Here there is demonstrable evidence of plant cultivation from at least 10,000 years ago, possibly even swiddening,[17] and an even longer record of significant environmental manipulation of the vegetation in the highlands, involving clearance and fire in association with stone tools inferred to be digging tools dating from c. 25,000 years ago.[18] Identification of vegecultural propagation systems will require distinguishing, via proxy evidence, between what some may term systems of plant 'management' (practised by hunter-gatherers) as opposed to plant 'cultivation' (practised by farmers). To make matters worse, there is unlikely to exist any clear dichotomy between 'management' and 'cultivation'; rather there will be a multitude of variations in the intensity of practices involving different plants and different polycultural systems. Adding to these difficulties, many plants that are utilized as food staples, such as sago palms (e.g. *Metroxylon sagu Rott.*), are not considered 'domesticates', while those that are, e.g. *Musa* sp. (bananas), *Dioscorea alata*, and *Colocasia esculenta* (L.), have complex, unresolved domestication histories (see below).

## Mainland Southeast Asia

Post-Glacial hunter-gatherer populations were widely dispersed throughout the region. Group size was probably small, perhaps simply the family unit. The degree of residential mobility is unknown, but if communities were following game, such as wild pigs and deer, they are likely to have ranged widely, collecting other small game and tubers, nuts, and fruits.[19] Typical stone tool assemblages of MSEA from terminal Pleistocene sites consist of

16 Barton, 'Reversed fortunes'; A. Kjær et al., 'Investigation of genetic and morphological variation in the sago palm (*Metroxylon sagu; Arecaceae*) in Papua New Guinea', *Annals of Botany*, 94 (2004), 109–17.

17 T.P. Denham and S. Haberle, 'Agricultural emergence and transformation in the upper Wahgi valley, Papua New Guinea, during the Holocene: theory, method and practice', *The Holocene*, 18 (2008), 492–3.

18 S. Bulmer, 'Reflections in stone: axes and the beginnings of agriculture in the Central Highlands of New Guinea', in A. Pawley et al. (eds.), *Papuan Pasts: Cultural, Linguistic and Biological Histories of Papuan-Speaking Peoples* (Canberra: Pacific Linguistics, 2005), 387–450.

19 R. Shoocondej, 'Late Pleistocene activities at the Tham Lod rockshelter in highland Bang Mapha, Mae Hongson province, northwestern Thailand', in E.A. Bacus et al. (eds.), *Uncovering Southeast Asia's Past* (Singapore: NUS Press, 2006).

informal flake assemblages and characteristically flaked pebble tools, termed Hoabinhian. These are unifacially or bifacially flaked lenticular river pebbles, often flaked around the entire circumference of the piece, named after sites in northern Veitnam where they were first described.[20] Hoabinhian assemblages from the early Holocene appear to overlap at some locations in northern Veitnam with the earliest evidence of pottery and quadrangular stone adzes, though not in Thailand or peninsular Malaysia.[21]

Chester Gorman's excavations of Spirit Cave in 1965 and 1970, located in the uplands of northern Thailand, remain the best evidence of the subsistence practices of terminal Pleistocene foragers in MSEA. The site appears to have been initially occupied by at least 12,000 years ago, with occupation continuing over the next 6,000 years.[22] Botanical remains from layers dating to around 10,000 years ago yielded remains of about twenty-two genera of plants, including sources of gum, resins, and poisons.[23] Smashed fragments of the genus *Canarium* were by far the most common, but the assemblage also included Chinese water chestnut, *Trapa* sp., bottle gourd, *Lagenaria* sp., Pepper, *Piper* sp., and a type of cucumber, *Cucumis* sp.[24] The presence of *Lagenaria*, *Cucumis*, *Trapa*, and the legumes suggested to Gorman the possibility of horticulture rather than just simply plant-gathering.[25] Analysis of the faunal remains from Spirit Cave also revealed evidence of arboreal species and raised the possibility of the use of poisons (*Madhuca*, *Euphorbiaceae*) in association with ballistic weaponry.[26]

For the early Holocene there is good evidence from several coastal and inland regions in southern China, Vietnam, and Thailand of the existence of relatively sedentary groups of hunter-gatherers. Some of these groups appear to have been making and using simple pottery as well as making polished stone tools.[27] Sites of early pottery use date from 12,000–8,000 BP in southern China at the sites of Zengpiyan, Gexinqiao, Baida, and Kantun. Pottery

20 W.G. Solheim, 'Reworking Southeast Asian prehistory', *Paideuma*, 15 (1969), 125–39.
21 Bellwood, *Prehistory of the Indo-Malaysian Archipelago*; Higham, *Archaeology of Mainland Southeast Asia*.
22 C. Gorman, 'The Hoabinhian and after: subsistence patterns in Southeast Asia during the late Pleistocene and early Recent periods', *World Archaeology*, 2 (1971), 301–20 (301).
23 Higham, *Archaeology of Mainland Southeast Asia*, 53.
24 Gorman, 'The Hoabinhian'; D. Yen, 'Hoabinhian horticulture: the evidence and the questions from northwest Thailand', in J. Allen et al. (eds.), *Sunda and Sahul: Prehistoric Studies in Southeast Asia, Melanesia and Australia* (New York and London: Academic Press, 1977), 567–99.
25 C. Gorman, 'Hoabinhian: a pebble-tool complex with early plant associations in Southeast Asia', *Science*, 163 (1969), 671–3.
26 Higham, *Archaeology of Mainland Southeast Asia*, 53.
27 Higham et al., 'Prehistory of a friction zone'.

vessels from Zengpiyan are characteristically thick-walled and tempered with quartz grit.[28] The oldest pottery is either plain or combed with a multiple-toothed tool to form parallel rib-like striations over the surface. Later pottery is cord-impressed.[29] Recovered plant macro-remains reveal a diet of wild berries, nuts, and seeds, as well as some unidentified tubers.[30]

Early Neolithic occupation sites in MSEA date from the late third and first half of the second millennia BCE. For the most part, subsistence strategies are characterized by varying combinations and emphases on foraging and food production. There is no sweeping change towards farming, but rather a patchy uptake of food production, including rice and millets, and ongoing reliance on the gathering of local shellfish and plants and the hunting of game. It is generally thought that the first farmers in the region began moving southwards from southern China, northern Vietnam, and Thailand. In the southern region of Fujian the earliest rice remains are dated to 2870–2340 BCE, and from the Shixia site in northern Guandong province, deposits containing rice grains and stalks range from 3000–2500 BCE. A review of dated sites containing evidence of rice and millets by Zhang and Hung in southwestern China suggests that rice cultivation postdates 2500 BCE in that region, spreading further southwards into MSEA after 2300–2000 BCE.[31]

Along the southwestern subtropical coastline of Guandong province, the earliest sedentary communities are generally thought to have been pottery-using coastal hunter-gatherer-fisher communities living in post-built dwellings, burying their dead, and possessing a material culture characterized by sand-tempered pottery and stone tools, including grinding slabs and pestles, grooved pebbles, net weights, and pierced pebble sinkers for fishing.[32] At the coastal site of Xincun, Guandong province, a stone tool assemblage of pebble tools and grinding stones dating between 3500 and 2500 BCE was analysed for starch remains, as other approaches to recover archaeobotanical data had failed.[33] This study revealed a suite of plants, including sago palms, bananas, fern roots, freshwater roots, and Job's Tears.[34] It is not possible to determine whether these communities were engaged in any form of 'horticulture' or were still essentially foragers; however, the suite of plants

---

28  Ibid.; C. Zhang and H.-C. Hung, 'Later hunter-gatherers in southern China, 18000–3000 BC', *Antiquity*, 86 (2012), 11–29.

29  Zhang and Hung, 'Later hunter-gatherers'.   30  Ibid.

31  Zhang and Hung, 'Emergence of agriculture'.

32  X. Yang et al., 'Sago-type palms were an important plant food prior to rice in southern subtropical China', *PLoS ONE*, 8 (2013), e63148; Zhang and Hung, 'Later hunter-gatherers'.

33  Zhang and Hung, 'Emergence of agriculture'.   34  Yang et al., 'Sago-type palms'.

found here is consistent with known practices of swiddening and vegecultural cultivation elsewhere in MSEA. Evidence for domestic rice in the form of bilobate rice phytoliths was recovered from tool sediments dating to *c.* 2500 BCE,[35] but its low frequency arguably shows that this plant was not yet a major component of the subsistence system.

Evidence of a 'pre-Neolithic' emerges in Vietnam between around 11,000–7,000 BP along the Hong (Red) River. These sites are considered by some to be a late phase of the Hoabinhian, containing edge-ground axes and paddle-impressed cord-marked pottery.[36] The dead were buried within occupation sites, and sprinkled with ochre and sometimes with stone and shell ornaments.[37] Pottery appears more widely during the mid-Holocene in northern Vietnam at Da But cultural sites dating between 4500 and 2500 BCE, prior to the emergence of 'agriculture'.[38] Da But sites are generally characterized by large shell midden deposits, some degree of sedentism, burial of the dead, edge-ground pebble axes, pebble net sinkers, and very coarse sand-tempered, cord-marked pottery.[39] As with sites in coastal China such as Xincun, these communities are described as pre-Neolithic because they lack clear evidence of a shift in subsistence from hunting and gathering to agriculture, even though pottery and polished stone tools are present. Pottery and polished stone tools have also been found in some Hoabinhian assemblages inland in caves/rock shelters dating to 4200–2000 BCE, suggesting use of these technologies by more mobile communities of hunter-gatherers as well.[40] This has prompted the use of the term Pre-Neolithic Pottery-using Cultures (PNPC – distinct from the PPNC or Pre-Pottery Neolithic of the Near East) to describe cultural adaptations at this time.[41]

In northern Vietnam, sites of the Phung Nguyen Complex (2500/2000–1500 BCE) occur on raised terrain near freshwater streams along the lower reaches

---

35 Ibid.   36 Nguyen et al., 'Northern Vietnam'.   37 Ibid.

38 M.F. Oxenham and H. Matsumura, 'Man Bac: regional, cultural, and temporal context', in M.F. Oxenham et al. (eds.), *Man Bac: The Excavation of a Neolithic Site in Northern Vietnam* (Canberra: ANU E Press, 2011), 127–34.

39 Nguyen et al., 'Northern Vietnam'.

40 J.C. White, 'Emergence of cultural diversity in mainland Southeast Asia: a view from prehistory', in N. Enfield (ed.), *Dynamics of Human Diversity: The Case of Mainland Southeast Asia* (Canberra: Pacific Linguistics, 2011), 9–46.

41 Oxenham and Matsumura, 'Man Bac'. They use the term 'pre-Neolithic' because of the presumed lack of agriculture while pottery and edge-ground stone tools are present. This further complicates the use of the term Neolithic, as here it is positively identified by the presence of agriculture, while in the context of ISEA, M. Spriggs, 'Archaeology and the Austronesian expansion: where are we now?', *Antiquity*, 85 (2011), 510–28, defends the position that a Neolithic may be defined by the presence of pottery and polished stone tools, in the absence of agriculture.

of the Red River. Pottery at these sites is sand-tempered, ranging widely in colour from yellow to red to grey-black. Decoration is simple, consisting of incision on the neck, impressing, comb-marking, and cord-marking.[42] Other artefacts include clay spindle whorls, clay balls, quadrangular polished stone adzes, a few shouldered adze forms, stone arrowheads, stone bracelets, and ground stone (including pieces with linear grooves that may have been used for jewellery manufacture).[43] As with other early settlement sites, there is still no direct evidence for the cultivation of rice or of other crops.

The earliest known 'Neolithic' sites in southern Vietnam are located along the Vam Co Dong, Vam Co Tay, and Dong Nai drainage systems near the Mekong delta, and date from c. 2000 to 1500 BCE.[44] Early occupation sites appear in protected coastal or near-coastal locations with access to freshwater. Artefacts recovered include spindle whorls, bone harpoons for hunting, clay bow pellets, whetstones, stone bangles, barkcloth beaters, and a variety of polished stone adzes, primarily of quadrangular cross-sectional form with parallels from southern China and northeast and central Thailand, suggesting cultural connections to the north and west.[45] The site of Tach Lac, Ha Tinh province (3000–2700 BCE), also appears to have been occupied initially by pottery-using hunter-gatherers. Following a short hiatus in habitation, the pottery assemblage changes with the introduction of pedestalled and decorated pottery, quadrangular-sectioned and shouldered stone adzes, grinding stones, and bone artefacts c. 1500 BCE.[46]

Settlements such as those at An Son (2200–1200 BCE) and Loc Giang (2200 BCE) consist of raised platforms made from alluvial silts and loams, and at Rach Nui (1600–1200 BCE) foundations were laid with ceramics and shell lime mortar. While details of above-ground construction remain poorly understood, it is likely that ground-level habitations were constructed at An Son and Loc Giang, and perhaps ground-level and stilted houses were built on the raised platforms at Rach Nui. At Rach Nui light wooden fences (perhaps even daubed) were built around the margins of the platforms, to

42 P. Nguyen, 'Nguyen Ba Khoach', *Asian Perspectives*, 23 (1980), 23–53.    43 Ibid.
44 M. Nishimura and K.D. Nguyen, 'Excavation of An Son: a Neolithic mound site in the middle reach of the Vam Co Dong River, southern Vietnam', *Bulletin of the Indo-Pacific Prehistory Association*, 22 (2002), 101–9; P. Bellwood et al., 'An Son and the Neolithic of southern Vietnam', *Asian Perspectives*, 50 (2011), 144–74.
45 Bellwood et al., 'An Son'; Higham, 'Mainland Southeast Asia from the Neolithic to the Iron Age'.
46 P.J. Piper and M.F. Oxenham, 'Of prehistoric pioneers: the establishment of the first sedentary settlements in the Mekong delta region of southern Vietnam during the period 2,000–1,500 cal BCE' (forthcoming).

separate the house plots from surrounding communal activity spaces.[47] At An Son faunal remains indicate the presence of domesticated dogs and pigs from 2100 BCE. The presence of cut marks on the dog bones and their relatively haphazard pattern of discard throughout the site suggest they were primarily used as a source of food here. Analysis of the pig remains from An Son also identified a strong selection pattern of individuals two years and younger, suggesting the existence of a managed population.[48]

The emergence of the Neolithic in Thailand is currently dated approximately to the early to mid third millennium BCE[49] and is marked by increasing levels of sedentism, incised and impressed pottery, polished stone adzes, and domesticated pigs, chickens, and rice.[50] By the very end of the mid-Holocene, in the late third millennium BCE, mixed mortuary/occupation sites of settled societies that cultivated plants and raised domestic stock appear in several interior parts of MSEA.[51] By the late third/early second millennium BCE in southern Thailand, sites located near or on the coast are characterized by the presence of settled societies with a maritime adaptation, again without clear signs of agriculture.[52] Settlements at these sites are generally located on slightly elevated ground, adjacent to tracts of low-terrace soil in the middle course of tributary streams.[53]

The Khorat plateau in central Thailand contains a number of important early Neolithic sites ranging from relatively small low mounds (0.8 to 5 ha) up to defended settlements greater than 100 ha.[54] The plateau is bounded north and east by the Mekong River and contains floodplains, river terraces, flanking hills, and some igneous rocky outcrops. Sites were originally detected here based on pottery eroding from low mounds and the occasional discovery of human remains beneath settlements.[55] Key early Neolithic sites include Non Nok Tha, Ban Chiang, and Ban Na Di, and were excavated during the 1960s and early 1970s. Non Nok Tha is located at the confluence of two streams and was used as a burial ground from 3000/2500 until around 500 BCE.[56] The lowest levels included burials of adults and children with a

47 Ibid.
48 P.J. Piper et al., 'Early evidence for pig and dog husbandry from the Neolithic site of An Son, southern Vietnam', *International Journal of Osteoarchaeology*, 24 (2012), 68–78.
49 Higham, 'Mainland Southeast Asia from the Neolithic to the Iron Age'.
50 Higham, *Archaeology of Mainland Southeast Asia*.
51 White, 'Emergence of cultural diversity', 34.
52 Higham et al., 'Prehistory of a friction zone'.
53 Higham, *Archaeology of Mainland Southeast Asia*.   54 Ibid., 92.   55 Ibid., 96.
56 D.T. Bayard, 'Excavation at Non Nok Tha, northeastern Thailand, 1968', *Asian Perspectives*, 13 (1970), 109–43.

range of grave goods, including pottery, small polished quadrangular stone adzes, shell bracelets, shell disc beads, and a single bronze axe.[57] A practice of interring humans and animals emerges for the first time with the burial of a child interred with three pottery vessels; the rear limbs and jaw of a young pig were placed on the chest, and beyond the feet lay the remains of a dog.[58] Two additional burials were also found with complete and fragmentary animal remains and complex depositional patterns. One of these, Burial 14, contained the remains of a child interred with four complete cord-marked pottery vessels. After this the body was covered in a layer of smashed pottery sherds that appear to have been deliberately broken over the body. Rows of shell beads were placed around the body and a bone spatula was placed on the left thigh. An entire pig and the fore limb of a bovid were placed in the grave near the head, and the fore and rear limbs of a pig were placed on the shoulders and ankles.[59] This practice of human–animal burial was carried out at other similar sites, including Ban Non Wat (Figure 16.2).

Ban Chiang dates from 3500/3000 BCE to the start of the first millennium CE and is located in rolling lowlands near three streams. This site was excavated several times from 1967 up to 1975 to clarify issues of stratigraphy and allow specialists in soils, pollen, zoology, and physical anthropology direct access to the site. Excavations in 1973 by Nikhom Suthiragasa opened several squares, one of which contained a 4 m stratigraphic sequence. At the base he noted impressions of cloth, ash lenses, and rice remains.[60] Later excavations in 1974–5 by a combined team from the Thai Fine Arts Department and the University of Pennsylvania revealed several mortuary layers. The lowest contained various forms of polished, incised, and cord-marked wares in association with extended and inhumed burials.[61] Excavation also recovered rice remains that may predate 2500 BCE, but there is still disagreement about whether these represent domesticated or wild rices.[62]

An important transitional site in southern Thailand, Khok Phnom Di, appears to have supported populations of sedentary hunters and gatherers practising a mixed economy largely dependent upon foraging, with some evidence for agriculture in later phases.[63] Khok Phnom Di is now located c. 22 km from the coast but would have been situated on a coastal barrier near

57 Ibid.    58 Higham, *Archaeology of Mainland Southeast Asia*, 102.    59 Ibid., 102.
60 Ibid., 107.    61 Ibid., 111.
62 D. Yen, 'Ban Chiang pottery and rice: a discussion of the inclusions in the pottery matrix', *Expedition*, 24 (1982), 51–64.
63 Higham et al., 'Prehistory of a friction zone'.

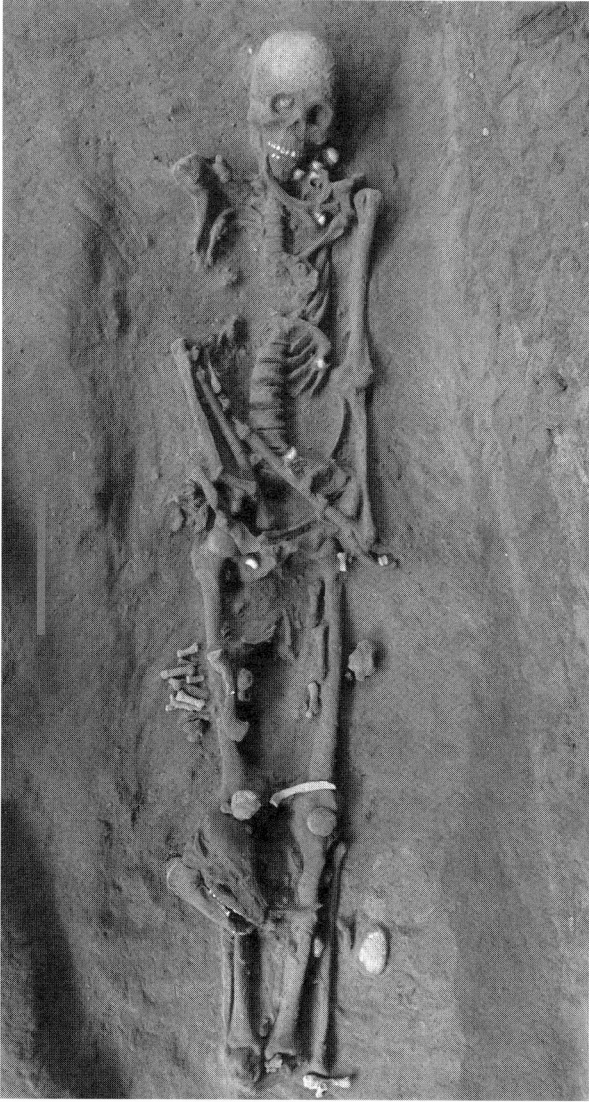

Figure 16.2 Burial 86 at Ban Non Wat, c. 1500 BCE: individual interred with pig remains, including pig skull placed on right lower limb.

estuary mangroves and areas of freshwater.[64] The earliest occupation in the area dates from 4710–3960 BCE, based on pollen and charcoal from cores

---

64 Higham, *Archaeology of Mainland Southeast Asia*, 67.

indicating raised levels of burning and an increase in grasses and weeds known to be associated with rice fields, but there is no direct evidence of rice cultivation at this time.[65] From *c.* 2000 to 1400 BCE Khok Phnom Di was used as a burial ground, with high quality pottery vessels, cord-marked or burnished; rice was present for the first time albeit in small quantities, otherwise subsistence remained heavily dependent on maritime resources.[66] By 1800–1700 cal BCE stone hoes appear in the archaeological sequence along with shell knives – associated with local cultivation of rice – and the first appearance of domestic dogs.[67] There is a complex mortuary history at this site. In the lowest stratigraphic level (Zone A) excavators recovered a total of 104 inhumations of men, women, and infants, associated with post holes, small hearths, and, apart from one shell bead, a complete lack of burial goods.[68] In Zone B there are some significant changes, including four rich graves that interred a woman and three infants. Other burials contained modest grave goods and there is evidence of several above-ground mortuary structures. Zone C contained no burials but was rich in pottery, pottery-making implements, and faunal remains.

The search for the earliest rice and for clues to the diet in general has remained a key research interest in the region and, with the development of new techniques such as isotope analysis, is revealing new complexities. Recent examination of isotopic records from sites in the upper Mun River valley in central Thailand shows non-linear uptake of $C_3$ plants (which include rice) from the second millennium BCE.[69] During this period rice is thought to have been cultivated in low-lying areas irrigated by rainfall.[70] The earliest Neolithic middens at Ban Non Wat contain evidence of rice chaff alongside freshwater fish bones, shellfish, and bones from wild game, including deer and wild bovids.[71] Isotope data were derived from human teeth, primarily from the site of Ban Non Wat but with contributions from Noen U-Loke, Ban Lum Khao, and Ban Chiang. The results for Ban Non Wat

---

65 L. Kealhofer and D.R. Piperno, 'Early agriculture in Southeast Asia: phytolith evidence from the Bang Pakong valley, Thailand', *Antiquity*, 68 (1994), 564–72; Higham, *Archaeology of Mainland Southeast Asia*, 67.

66 Bellwood, *Prehistory of the Indo-Malaysian Archipelago*, 256.

67 Piper et al., 'Early evidence for pig and dog husbandry'.

68 Higham, *Archaeology of Mainland Southeast Asia*, 71.

69 C.L. King et al., 'Economic change after the agricultural revolution in Southeast Asia?', *Antiquity*, 88 (2014), 112–25.

70 Ibid., 115.

71 A. Kijngam, 'The mammalian fauna', in C. Higham and A. Kijngam (eds.), *The Origins of the Civilization of Angkor*, vol. IV: *The Excavation of Ban Non Wat* (Bangkok: Fine Arts Department of Thailand, 2010), 189–97.

and Noen U-Loke indicated a gradual increase in the consumption of rice during the early Bronze Age, followed by a decline throughout the rest of the second millennium, with increased consumption again during the later Iron Age.[72] Associated with this intensification in rice consumption is an increase in moat building at some sites to retain water (possibly for rice cultivation) and an increase in the symbolic importance of rice, apparent in its inclusion in burials. Several iron hoes were also recovered from Iron Age burials at Ban Non Wat.[73] The increase in rice consumption during the Bronze Age is also seen at sites in the Sakon Nakhon basin such as Ban Chiang and Ban Na Di, but the later rise during the Iron Age does not occur, nor is there evidence of moat construction at these locations.[74]

As part of the Thailand Archaeometallurgy Project in southern Thailand, Weber et al. undertook detailed archaeobotanical investigations at three sites in the Khao Wang Prachan valley, southern Thailand – Non Pa Wai, Nil Kham Maeng, and Nor Mak La – dating from the second millennium BCE until the first millennium CE. They have recovered one of the largest samples of carbonized seeds in the region. Against expectation, from a total sample of 3,294 seeds they recovered fewer than 50 rice grains, and these were mostly from one site, Nil Kham Maeng. The majority of their samples consisted of millet (*Setaria italica*), some *Panicum* sp., and *Coix* sp.[75] AMS dating of seeds and charcoal at these sites was good, but complicated by issues of disturbance; however, they feel that the chronology indicates use of millets from the late third millennium BCE with no evidence of rice in the foodways at any of these sites until the first millennium BCE.[76] This again seems to indicate that while rice was present and possibly cultivated in the region by the second millennium BCE, it remained a minor component of the diet (Figure 16.3).

## Island Southeast Asia

Island Southeast Asia (ISEA) is often characterized as a region with local-scale, limited agriculture, or none at all, prior to the dispersal of East Asian agricultural practices focused on rice, other crop plants, and domesticated animals after *c.* 4,000 years ago.[77] There is no direct evidence of agriculture

---

72  King et al., 'Economic change'.    73  Ibid., 115.    74  Ibid.
75  S. Weber et al., 'Rice or millets: early farming strategies in prehistoric central Thailand', *Journal of Archaeological and Anthropological Sciences*, 2 (2010), 79–88.
76  Ibid.
77  Diamond and Bellwood, 'Farmers and their languages'; Bellwood, *First Farmers*. See also below.

Figure 16.3  Rice remains from 'Neolithic' sites in Thailand: (a) domesticated rice spikelet base from Khao Sam Kaeo TP43 US4, dating to 383–203 BCE (WK18769); (b) rice caryopsis from Khao Sam Kaeo TP57 US16, dating to 359–57 BCE (WK21175); (c) rice caryopsis from Ban Non Wat K500 4.2 GEN, direct AMS date of 441–203 BCE (BA121030); (d) rice caryopsis from Phu Khao Thong S7 US4, dating to 36 BCE to 125 CE (OXA26629).

(c)

2 mm

(d)

2 mm

Figure 16.3 (cont.)

prior to the purported Austronesian dispersal, but then there is no direct evidence of agriculture after this either. Until much later in the Holocene, there is no archaeology of 'agriculture' anywhere in ISEA.

Rice is first identified at the site of Andarayan in Taiwan as a few husk and stem inclusions in pottery fabric dated to 1700 BCE.[78] Rice husk remains in sediments and inclusions of rice in pottery from the cave site of Gua Sireh

---

78 B. Snow et al., 'Evidence of early rice cultivation in the Philippines', *Philippine Quarterly of Culture and Society*, 14 (1986), 3–11.

on the north coast of Borneo date to 2800–2100 BCE,[79] and rice remains from Leang Burung in Sulawesi date to *c.* 2000 BCE[80] and from Ulu Leang to between 100 and 1000 CE.[81] Rice grains from Maros Cave, Sulawesi, remain securely dated to 500 CE. To date, quantities of rice recovered from ISEA archaeological sites remain very small and primarily restricted to inclusions in pottery. To complicate matters, where rice has been identified, the species of rice has been inferred rather than demonstrated.[82] Domesticated rice, *Oryza sativa*, did not arrive into a region devoid of wild species of rice. There are many species of wild rice found growing in wetland areas (especially *O. rufipogon* – an important wild precursor of the domesticated rice complex in southern China) and in secondary forests.[83] Rice certainly moved out of Taiwan/MSEA during the early third millennium BCE, but in what context and for what purpose (i.e. was it primarily a food or a marker of status?) remains to be resolved.[84]

As mentioned above, the putative dispersal of East Asian agriculture, and other Neolithic characteristics, into ISEA is argued to have occurred from Taiwan or mainland China and is often linked to the spread of Austronesian languages.[85] The material culture of the early Neolithic in Taiwan, 4000–3000 BCE, consisted of cord-marked pottery, polished stone adzes, and slate spearheads, and by 3000 BCE included rice along with evidence of forest clearance.[86] Overall, pottery assemblages are seen as having strong links with southern China. Between 2500 and 1500 BCE elements of this cultural package, including the presence of domesticated pigs and chickens, occur south of Taiwan in the Philippines, Sulawesi, northern Borneo, and Halmahera. Early

79 P. Bellwood et al., 'New dates for prehistoric Asian rice', *Asian Perspectives*, 31 (1992), 161–70.
80 V. Paz, 'Rock shelters, caves, and archaeobotany in island Southeast Asia', *Asian Perspectives*, 44 (2005), 107–18.
81 F. Bulbeck, 'Ian Glover's contribution to the development of archaeology in island Southeast Asia', in B. Bellina et al. (eds.), *50 Years of Archaeology in Southeast Asia: Essays in Honour of Ian Glover* (Bangkok: River Books, 2010), 26–39.
82 See e.g. Yen, 'Ban Chiang pottery and rice'.
83 D.A. Vaughan, 'Biogeography of the genus *Oryza* across the Malay archipelago', *Rice Genetics Newsletter*, 8 (1991), 73–5.
84 See Barton, 'Reversed fortunes'; Barton and Denham, 'Prehistoric vegeculture'; B. Hayden, 'Rice: the first luxury food?', in G. Barker and M. Janowski (eds.), *Why Cultivate? Archaeological and Anthropological Approaches to Foraging–Farming Transitions in Southeast Asia* (Cambridge: McDonald Institute for Archaeological Research, 2011), 75–94; R. Hunter-Anderson et al., 'Rice as a prehistoric valuable in the Marianas Islands', *Micronesia*, 34 (1995), 69–89.
85 Bellwood, *Prehistory of the Indo-Malaysian Archipelago*, 117–24.
86 Bellwood, 'Austronesian prehistory', 107.

pottery decoration is varied, and consistently 'red-slipped' rather than cord-marked.[87]

The Batanes Islands lie on the northern edge of the tropics, 150 km from the southern tip of Taiwan and 200 km from the north coast of Luzon, Philippines. Human occupation of these islands dates from c. 2000 BCE and consists of red-slipped pottery in the earliest levels, but again there is no evidence of rice cultivation. By soon after 1500 BCE, at Sunget, Savidug, and Anaro, for the first time there is evidence of Taiwan nephrite and slate, domestic pigs and dogs, red-slipped and stamped pottery, pottery spindle whorls, side-notched stone net sinkers, and grooved and stepped trapezoidal stone adzes (Type 1A in Duff's 1970 catalogue) providing evidence for much stronger cultural links with Taiwan at this time.[88] A few waisted stone tools, interpreted as probably hoes, were also recovered from Itbayat, dating to c. 2000–1500 BCE.[89] Analysis of faunal material shows the presence of introduced pigs on the island of Sabtang by 1200 BCE and of dogs in Batanes by 500 BCE.[90]

Outside of Taiwan the evidence for rice agriculture rapidly diminishes, as does the cohesion of any 'monothetic' cultural package. As Matthew Spriggs notes, 'In much of the region we have generally fragmentary and poorly-dated Neolithic assemblages, often considerably disturbed, and a distribution of sites that are spread over nearly 2000 years from their first appearance 4000 years ago until c. 2300/2100 BP.'[91] Few assemblages contain the full suite of items that might be considered the classic Neolithic 'package' of, for example, red-slipped pottery, quadrangular stone adzes, slate adzes, certain forms of shell bead, spindle whorls, barkcloth beaters, and domesticated rice, pigs, and chickens. More typically, some elements are present (in varying quantities) while others are absent in the early levels or never appear at all.[92] Spriggs explains the apparent fragmentation of the Austronesian-borne cultural package throughout the region as the predictable result of negotiated transfers of items, ideas, and technologies between indigenous groups and migrants, where 'things' are accepted or rejected based on cultural interests

---

87 Ibid.

88 Ibid.; P. Bellwood and E. Dizon, 'The Batanes Islands and the prehistory of island Southeast Asia', in P. Bellwood and E. Dizon (eds.), *4000 Years of Migration and Cultural Exchange* (Canberra: ANU E Press, 2013), 235–9.

89 P. Bellwood and E. Dizon, 'Other portable artefacts from the Batanes sites', in Bellwood and Dizon (eds.), *4000 Years of Migration*, 123–48.

90 P.J. Piper et al., 'The terrestrial vertebrate remains', in Bellwood and Dizon (eds.), *4000 Years of Migration*, 169–200.

91 Spriggs, 'Archaeology and the Austronesian expansion', 517.   92 See ibid., table 1.

or particular environmental tolerances.[93] The spread of domesticated rice is also no longer seen as central to this purported demic expansion, where 'The real Neolithic "package" or process of "Neolithization" did not necessarily involve agriculture at all. But it certainly did involve pottery, its complex vessel forms and surface finish surely betokening new social relations; it certainly did involve a suite of shell artefacts with equally novel meanings, and also new technologies of cloth and barkcloth . . . One participated in this new world by speaking the new (Austronesian) language.'[94] In making this statement Spriggs shifts the focus of the Neolithic and of 'Neolithization' from the spread of systems of food production to the spread of new systems of social organization within which material things and technologies were embedded, but were not themselves the drivers of change. The clearest analogy for this must be the spread of Pama–Nyungan languages across a continent of hunter-gatherers in Australia during the mid-Holocene. It is hypothesized that this occurred in three waves, beginning around 5,000–4,000 years ago, moving down the east and west coasts of Australia and finally into the semi-arid and arid interior by 3,000–2,000 years ago.[95] What ultimately facilitates the language spread is not demic diffusion, but an attractive shift in social structures where small, endogamous, and inward-looking groups begin to participate in wider social worlds through new alliances facilitated by ceremony, exogamous marriage, and larger-scale exchange networks.[96] Possibly these new linkages provided new ways for individuals to acquire status and prestige within their own groups and in the eyes of rivals not yet participating in these new social arrangements. In the same way, Spriggs is suggesting that deeper social transformations may lie at the heart of an Austronesian spread of languages and of material objects across ISEA: an indigenous process of social transformation may have been just as important as the arrival of new material things. It might also be inferred that, while there may have been some degree of inter-island contact prior to contact with Austronesian migrants, plausibly extending back to the Pleistocene, the level of regional human interaction was significantly ramped up at this time.[97]

---

93 Ibid., 517.   94 Ibid., 523.
95 N. Evans and P. McConvell, 'The enigma of Pama–Nyungan expansion in Australia', in R. Blench and M. Spriggs (eds.), *Archaeology and Language II: Archaeological Data and Linguistic Hypotheses* (London: Routledge, 1989), 174–90.
96 Ibid., 184.
97 M. Donohue and T.P. Denham, 'Farming and language in island Southeast Asia: reframing Austronesian history', *Current Anthropology*, 51 (2010), 223–56; Spriggs, 'Archaeology and the Austronesian expansion'.

Niah Cave on the northwest coast of Borneo and its Neolithic cemetery sequence are a good example of a rich cultural sequence that shows – beyond the introduction of earthenware pottery – 'fragmentation' of the purported Austronesian Neolithic package outside Taiwan and the northern Philippines. The Neolithic cemetery at Niah is one of the largest in ISEA, certainly the largest single collection of human remains known in Borneo, with a cultural sequence that begins at least 45,000 years ago.[98] The Neolithic at Niah Cave is marked by the appearance of a series of inhumations and the beginnings of a long phase of burial dating from c. 3,500–3,300 BP (c. 1500 BCE) until c. 2,000 BP, following a significant hiatus of occupation of some 4,000 years.[99] The lithic assemblage already shows evidence of increasing levels of sedentism from c. 12,000 years ago with the introduction of pebble mortars and pestles and grinding stones.[100] During the mid-Holocene, the cave mouth seems to have been primarily a focus for burial, not a site of occupation, as it was up to the beginning of the Holocene.

Neolithic material culture includes earthenware pottery (mostly plain, paddle-made), polished quadrangular (Type 2A–D in Duff's 1970 catalogue) and lenticular stone adzes (though rare), pigmented shell (worked and unworked), some shell beads and arm-rings, metal-work, textiles, and burial furniture (Figure 16.4).[101] Ceramics were mostly recovered from the cemetery phase of the site and include a variety of vessel forms such as large and small jars, large urns, bowls, and bottles, as well as distinctive but rare double-spouted vessels.[102] Vessel decoration consists primarily of plain wares with some incised and impressed wares and some basket- and cord-marked ware, mostly paddle-impressed. Red-slipped pottery is absent from this site, and doesn't appear in later sequences either. Metal Age deposits dating from 2,000 years ago are similar and incised or impressed decoration is rare. Some rice remains were found as inclusions in 14 pottery sherds, though more than 1,500 pieces needed to be sampled in order to find this evidence.[103] It is

98 G. Barker et al., 'The "human revolution" in lowland tropical Southeast Asia: the antiquity of anatomically modern humans, and of behavioural modernity, at Niah Cave (Sarawak, Borneo)', *Journal of Human Evolution*, 52 (2007), 243–61.

99 L. Lloyd-Smith et al., '"Neolithic" societies c. 4,000–2,000 years ago: Austronesian farmers?', in G. Barker (ed.), *Rainforest Foraging and Farming in Island Southeast Asia* (Cambridge: McDonald Institute for Archaeological Research, 2013), 255–98.

100 H. Barton et al., 'Late Pleistocene foragers, c. 35,000–11,500 years ago', in Barker (ed.), *Rainforest Foraging and Farming*, 171–214.

101 Lloyd-Smith et al., '"Neolithic" societies', 272.   102 Ibid., 273.

103 G. Barker et al., 'Foraging–farming transitions at the Niah Caves, Sarawak, Borneo', *Antiquity*, 85 (2011), 492–509.

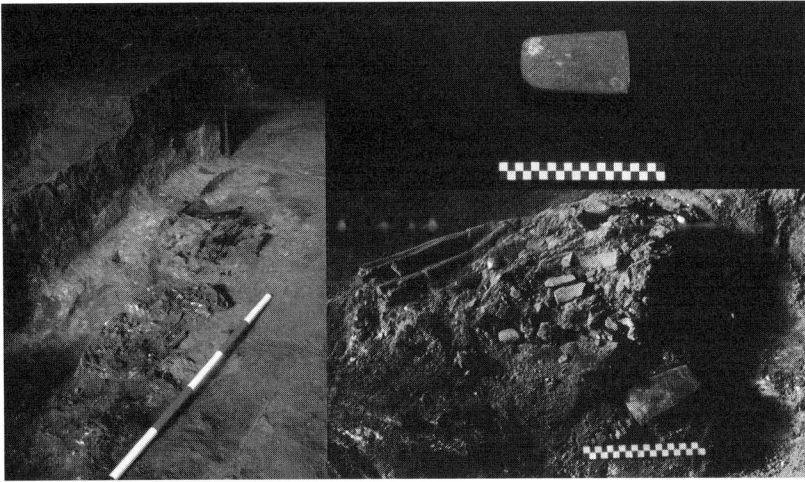

Figure 16.4 Niah Cave, flexed burial B205, looking northeast (left, scale = 1 m), with a close-up view (top right) showing a Neolithic polished quadrangular adze that was buried with it (bottom right, black and white scales in cm).

not until the Metal Age (late first millennium BCE) that rice husk is seen for the first time as pottery temper.

Krigbaum assessed the ratio of $C_3$ to $C_4$ from a sample of pre-Neolithic and Neolithic human remains to gauge changes in the diet at the site.[104] His results showed an increase in $C_3$ values from the Mesolithic (pre-pottery) to Neolithic (pottery) sample. Given the general absence of rice remains at this site, which otherwise yielded good overall organic preservation, the isotope values have been interpreted as showing a shift from closed-canopy living to a population spending more time in open, cleared environments, rather than a shift in diet towards $C_3$ plants such as rice. A gradual increase in the intensity of vegecultural modes of plant cultivation, perhaps towards forms of swidden-type cultivation seen at Kuk by 10,000 BP, may also explain these results.

Analysis of skull morphologies by Jessica Manser aimed to identify the presence of any significant shifts in skeletal features occurring as a result of new migrants entering the region.[105] Her analyses did not show any evidence

104 J. Krigbaum, 'Reconstructing human subsistence in the West Mouth (Niah Cave, Sarawak) burial series using stable isotopes of carbon', *Asian Perspectives*, 44 (2005), 73–89.
105 J. Manser, 'Morphological analysis of the human burial series at Niah Cave: implications for late Pleistocene–Holocene Southeast Asian human evolution', unpublished PhD thesis (New York University, 2005).

for this; rather they reflected a pattern of long-term continuity, with no statistically significant differences between pre-Neolithic and Neolithic populations.[106] Interestingly this reinforces the findings of Bulbeck twenty years earlier, who assessed a sample of human remains from MSEA and ISEA and also found no clear evidence of population replacement.[107]

## Lapita

Generally thought to derive from the red-slipped pottery tradition of ISEA, the phenomenon of Lapita pottery is yet another hotly contested archaeological expression of the 'Neolithic'.[108] Lapita is characterized by highly ornate dentate-stamped or incised pottery that is first seen in the Bismarck archipelago *c.* 3,300 BP, spreading rapidly from there into Near and Remote Oceania within about 200 years.[109] With the shorter timescale involved in its dispersal, Lapita appears far more coherent and 'monothetic' as evidence of Neolithic population migration.

A good example of what Lapita consists of, and may represent, is the fabulous and unique Lapita cemetery, Teouma, on the south coast of Éfaté, Vanuatu, dating from *c.* 3,300–3,200 BP. Interpreted as a burial site of the earliest colonists in the region, it consists of a rich assemblage of ornate dentate-stamped pottery in a variety of forms, including large carinated burial vessels, rare flat-bottomed vessels, cylinder stands, and double-rimmed forms.[110] Burials hint at elaborate pre- and post-burial rituals consisting of primary interment and some secondary burial. None of the burials have skulls in articulation with the body and there is evidence of skull removal and the reorientation and recombination of some individuals (Figure 16.5).[111]

The magnificent pottery of this site, though, is short-lived. Over the next two hundred years the pottery assemblage changes, with a dramatic restriction in vessel form and vessels that maintain little evidence for decoration apart from notching on the lip.[112] This decay of design systems over 200 to 300 years following the initial period of colonization is a pattern that seems to

---

106 Lloyd-Smith et al., '"Neolithic" societies', 289.
107 D. Bulbeck, 'A re-evaluation of possible evolutionary processes in Southeast Asia since the late Pleistocene', unpublished MA thesis (Canberra: Australian National University, 1982).
108 Bellwood and Koon, 'Lapita colonists'; Carson et al., 'Pottery trail'; Spriggs, 'Archaeology and the Austronesian expansion'.
109 Spriggs, 'Archaeology and the Austronesian expansion', 517.
110 S. Bedford et al., 'The Teouma Lapita site and the early human settlement of the Pacific Islands', *Antiquity*, 80 (2006), 812–28.
111 Ibid.   112 Ibid., 820.

Figure 16.5 Three skulls placed on the chest of a single burial at Teouma, Vanuatu.

be broadly repeated across all Lapita sites.[113] Clark and Murray suggest that 'The designs applied to Lapita ceramics, and probably to other objects, including the human body by tattooing, were more complex in the early migration phase, when computer simulation of colonization specifies intergroup contact, particularly for non-related marriage partners, was essential to demographic success.'[114]

It is hard to imagine that the rather short-lived phenomenon of Lapita pottery is in any way related to the first appearance of red-slipped pottery in the Batanes Islands some 800 years earlier.[115] Lapita peoples were originally thought to have practised some form of horticulture involving root crops such as yams and taros as well as utilizing nuts and other tree crops.[116] Recent isotopic studies of human remains from Teouma reveal far

---

113 G. Clark and T. Murray, 'Decay characteristics of the eastern Lapita design system', *Archaeology in Oceania*, 41 (2006), 107–17.

114 Ibid., 115.

115 But see Bellwood and Koon, 'Lapita colonists'; and Carson et al., 'Pottery trail'.

116 A. Crowther, 'Starch residues on undecorated Lapita pottery from Anir, New Ireland', *Archaeology in Oceania*, 40 (2005), 62–6; C. Gosden, 'Production systems and the colonization of the Western Pacific', *World Archaeology*, 24 (1992), 55–69; J. Hather, 'The archaeobotany of subsistence in the Pacific', *World Archaeology*, 24 (1992), 70–81; P. Matthews, 'Aroids and the Austronesians', *Tropics*, 4 (1995), 105–26.

greater dependence on protein sources (marine and terrestrial) than expected, suggesting that during early phases of island colonization people were not greatly reliant on horticulture.[117] From the Bismarcks colonists had to pass through populations of islanders that had inhabited New Ireland, New Britain, and the Solomon Islands since the late Pleistocene before stepping off into the unknown. Within 400 years they had reached Fiji.[118]

## Multiple domestication events: complex origins, multiple dispersals?

The following short review of the domestication of some Southeast Asian crops and pigs and chickens is discussed separately because it is a story that is not linked to the evidence at any one particular site or even any one region. Rather, the evidence suggests a history of multiple domestication 'events' and long-term human translocations of wild plants and animals, sometimes over long distances, ultimately leading to the emergence of phenotypes archaeologists identify as 'domesticates'. What is also implied is that the 'domestication' process is not fixed in time and space, but may be better viewed as processes that allow 'domestication' multiple times in multiple locations. It is certainly not best seen or explained as a process that had one clear point of origin from which all 'domesticates' later spread.

### Bananas

Most of the world's edible bananas derive from the Eumusa section and are either hybrids from *Musa acuminata* alone or have hybridized with *Musa balbisiana*.[119] Their pathway from wild plants to domestication occurred in ISEA and has involved the reduction of seed production and sterility of their fruit. Perrier et al. undertook a detailed analysis of DNA and ploidy levels in wild bananas from across Southeast Asia and Melanesia, showing that there is no single origin of domesticated *Musa* sp. The modern *Musa* banana has arisen from hybridizations between *M. acuminata* subspecies derived from

---

117  F. Valentin et al., 'Lapita subsistence strategies and food consumption patterns in the community of Teouma (Efate, Vanuatu)', *Journal of Archaeological Science*, 37 (2010), 1820–9.

118  T.P. Denham et al., 'Dating the appearance of Lapita pottery in the Bismarck archipelago and its dispersal to Remote Oceania', *Archaeology in Oceania*, 47 (2012), 39–46.

119  J. Kennedy, 'Pacific bananas: complex origins, multiple dispersals?', *Asian Perspectives*, 47 (2008), 75–94; X. Perrier et al., 'Multidisciplinary perspectives on banana (*Musa* spp.) domestication', *Proceedings of the National Academy of Sciences*, 108 (2011), 11311–18.

ISEA and western Melanesia.[120] The most likely vectors moving the banana over these vast distances are human beings, translocating plants, probably via vegetative propagation between islands. The antiquity of this activity is completely unknown, is likely to have occurred many times in the past (perhaps as a process it has never really ceased), and may well extend back into the Pleistocene. While it is the fruit that is eaten widely today – it can be eaten raw, baked, or roasted, used as a source of sugars, or even fermented – this may not necessarily have been the primary target of human interest. Bananas, like many species of palm, have a wide range of uses, with stem and leaves providing shelter and clothing, textiles, silage, rope, and cordage, and the stem of some varieties may also be eaten.[121]

### Taro and yams

Taro, *Colocasia esculenta* (L.), is another plant with a complex domestication history in ISEA that is now widely dispersed geographically and likely involved multiple domestication events in multiple loci as a result of long-term human engagement and movement.[122] Lebot considers it plausible that taro underwent multiple domestication events on either side of the Wallace Line from India, southern China, Melanesia, and northern Australia.[123] Taro, along with bananas, is one of the key plants associated with the earliest definitive agricultural levels at Kuk Swamp 6,400–7,000 years ago, but may also have been under cultivation as a wild plant as early as 10,000 years ago (see Chapter 17). The greater yam, *Dioscorea alata*, is another plant with a murky domestication history in this region. Some consider *D. alata* to be a true cultigen derived from several other species, while others[124] suggest that it might actually be a true species that has been brought into domestication more than once. A study of 'wild' and 'domesticated' yams in Africa shows the complexity of sorting out long-term human–plant interactions in the case of tubers. Scarcelli et al. undertook a genetic analysis of 'wild' (in

---

120 Perrier et al., 'Multidisciplinary perspectives', 11312.

121 S.C. Nelson et al., '*Musa* species (banana and plantain)', *Species Profiles for Pacific Island Agroforestry*, 15 (2006), 1–33; Perrier et al., 'Multidisciplinary perspectives'; R.C. Ploetz et al., 'Banana and plantain: an overview with emphasis on Pacific island cultivars', *Permanent Agriculture Resources, Hawaii, USA*, 27 (2007), 1–27.

122 V. Lebot, *Tropical Root and Tuber Crops: Cassava, Sweet Potato, Yams and Aroids* (Wallingford: CABI, 2009); P. Matthews and D.V. Nguyen, 'Taro: origins and development', in C. Smith (ed.), *Encyclopedia of Global Archaeology* (New York: Springer, 2014), 7237–40.

123 Lebot, *Tropical Root and Tuber Crops*.

124 E.g. V. Lebot, 'Biomolecular evidence for plant domestication in Sahul', *Genetic Resources and Crop Evolution*, 46 (1999), 619–28.

their terms) 'predomesticated' plants (*D. abyssinica* and *D. praehensilis*) that reproduced sexually from the forest with cultivated varieties (*D. cayenensis*, *D. rotundata*) that were vegetatively propagated.[125] They found that nearly half the samples (47 per cent) considered to be 'wild' contained genes from cultivated 'domesticated' yams and that fourteen samples could be considered genetically intermediate between the 'wild' and 'domesticated' plants. The mixture of genes from 'wild' and 'domesticated' varieties suggested ongoing hybridization, probably from feral plants abandoned in old fallows that have since returned to forest.[126]

## Pigs

Domesticated pigs first appear only at the end of the fifth millennium BP in peninsular Southeast Asia, in co-occurrence with the first evidence of sedentary agriculture.[127] Mitochondrial DNA sequences from wild, feral, and domesticated pigs in island Southeast Asia indicate that the basal lineages of *Sus scrofa* occur in the west of island Southeast Asia.[128] Two distinct haplotypes found in Chinese wild boar are shared by several East Asian domestic pigs and suggest multiple domestication events in mainland and possibly insular Southeast Asia.[129] Overall, the genetic evidence points to at least four separate, though possibly entangled, domestication pathways, one in India and three from wild boar populations that are indigenous to peninsular Southeast Asia.[130] Repeated human movement of domestic pigs, and also regional ancient population dispersals of wild boar, complicate the record.[131] For example, Larson et al. suggest that the current Pacific clade of domestic pigs was transported out of ISEA prior to a later population replacement in that region by new domestic pigs probably derived from central China.[132] Analysis of mitochondrial DNA sequences of domestic pigs

125 N. Scarcelli et al., 'Genetic nature of yams (*Dioscorea* sp.) domesticated by farmers in Benin (West Africa)', *Genetic Resources and Crop Evolution*, 53 (2006), 121–30.

126 H.D. Mignouna and A. Dansi, 'Yam (*Dioscorea* spp.) domestication by the Nago and Fon ethnic groups in Benin', *Genetic Resources and Crop Evolution*, 50 (2003), 519–28 (524).

127 Higham, *Early Culture of Mainland Southeast Asia*.

128 G. Larson et al., 'Worldwide phylogeography of wild boar reveals multiple centers of pig domestication', *Science*, 307 (2005), 1618–21.

129 Ibid., 1620.

130 G. Larson et al., 'Patterns of East Asian pig domestication, migration, and turnover revealed by modern and ancient DNA', *Proceedings of the National Academy of Sciences*, 107 (2010), 7686–91 (7690).

131 M. Fang and L. Andersson, 'Mitochondrial diversity in European and Chinese pigs is consistent with population expansions that occurred prior to domestication', *Proceedings of the Royal Society B*, 273 (2006), 1803–10.

132 Larson et al., 'Patterns of East Asian pig domestication', 7690.

in Vanuatu suggests a putative origin of the Pacific clade in coastal Southeast Asia, possibly Vietnam.[133]

## Chickens

Like the pig, the chicken appears to have complicated origins, involving a long history of human use and deliberate translocations of various landraces into different regions at different times. The chicken, *Gallus gallus domesticus*, is thought to derive from the Red Jungle Fowl, *Gallus gallus*, distributed across mainland Southeast Asia, Indonesia, and southern China, and was likely domesticated by at least 5,400 BP.[134] Mitochondrial DNA evidence indicates possible domestication events in southwestern China, Southeast Asia, and India.[135] The earliest archaeological remains of chickens outside China have been recovered at Khok Phnom Di, dated to around 4,000 years ago,[136] though it is not certain whether these remains are from the wild jungle fowl or a domesticate.

## Vegecultures of MSEA and ISEA

An important characteristic of agricultural systems in MSEA and ISEA is the diversity of approaches to cultivation broadly referred to as vegeculture. We do not yet have dates for the antiquity of these approaches, though as noted above, there is the possibility that some practices are quite ancient. Vegetative planting today is normally undertaken in cleared or semi-cleared areas referred to as 'swiddens'. And however 'agriculture' was introduced in MSEA and ISEA, swiddening is now one of the most widespread cropping systems in South and Southeast Asia, and remains dominant in Borneo and the hills of Thailand, Burma, Laos, Vietnam, Cambodia, and southwestern China.[137]

---

133 J.K. Lum et al., 'Recent Southeast Asian domestication and Lapita dispersal of sacred male pseudohermaphroditic "tuskers" and hairless pigs of Vanuatu', *Proceedings of the National Academy of Sciences*, 103 (2006), 17190–5 (17194).

134 D. Niu et al., 'The origin and diversity of Chinese native chicken breeds', *Biochemical Genetics*, 40 (2002), 163–74; A.A. Storey et al., 'Investigating the global dispersal of chickens in prehistory using ancient mitochondrial DNA signatures', *PLoS ONE*, 7 (2012), e39171.

135 Y.-W. Miao et al., 'Chicken domestication: an updated perspective based on mitochondrial genomes', *Heredity*, 110 (2013), 277–82; Storey et al., 'Investigating the global dispersal of chickens'.

136 Higham, *Early Culture of Mainland Southeast Asia*.

137 J.E. Spencer, *Shifting Cultivation in Southeastern Asia* (Berkeley: University of California Press, 1966), 4.

Swiddeners create forest patches in different ways, sometimes felling all timber, sometimes leaving tall timber, or even pollarding selected trees. Felled timber may be burned or left to rot in situ, and the newly cleared spaces planted with a mixture of annuals and perennials. Usually swiddens are left fallow for three to six years or even longer periods, during which time the vegetation is allowed to grow unchecked. By moving into a new patch, usually within a larger region following a cyclic schedule, the swiddener creates a meshwork of patches in different stages of regrowth. These patches may be anything from one to six years or even decades old, depending on family or village use of the landscape. These areas of secondary forest are not abandoned areas even though annuals are not planted; they represent important places for hunting and gathering plants.

Old swiddens provide food, medicines, materials for craft, fibres for clothing and rope, bark for walling houses or flooring or for the making of baskets, gums, resins for burning, mastics, caulking, incense, wood oils, dyes, hunting poisons, fuel, leaves for roofing, shingles, and wood for building and making tools, boats, and weapons.[138]

In this system, the swiddener manipulates and manages selected components of the forest, rather than radically transforming them, creating agricultural plots that mimic forest structure.[139] Harris considered that 'Swidden cultivation and fixed-plot horticulture ... come closer to simulating the structure, functional dynamics and equilibrium of the natural ecosystem than any other agricultural system man has devised.'[140]

In many parts of ISEA the swiddener is most definitely the partner of the rice farmer, providing food security as there are many factors in the tropics that may lead to failure of the rice crop, such as drought, pests, and severe weather.[141] Plants that are commonly intercropped within swiddens include millet (*Setaria italica*), Job's Tears (*Coix lachryma-jobi*), corn (*Zea mays*), and

138  K.J. Pelzer, 'Swidden cultivation in Southeast Asia: historical, ecological, and economic perspectives', in P. Kunstadter et al. (eds.), *Farmers in the Forest: Economic Development and Marginal Agriculture in Northern Thailand* (Honolulu: University Press of Hawai'i, 1978), 272.

139  Ibid.; D.R. Harris, 'Agricultural systems, ecosystems and the origins of agriculture', in P.J. Ucko and G.W. Dimbleby (eds.), *The Domestication and Exploitation of Plants and Animals* (Chicago: Aldine Press, 1969), 6; C. Geertz, *Agricultural Involution: The Process of Ecological Change in Indonesia* (Berkeley: University of California Press, 1963).

140  Harris, 'Agricultural systems', 6.

141  Barton, 'Reversed fortunes'; J. Prill-Brett, 'The Bontok: traditional wet-rice and swidden cultivators of the Philippines', in G.G. Marten (ed.), *Traditional Agriculture in Southeast Asia* (Boulder, CO: Westview Press, 1986), 54–84 (68).

Figure 16.6 Landscape view of a typical homegarden (behind house) showing polycultural nature of mixed plantings that grades seamlessly into a secondary, managed forest, that itself has regenerated from an older slash-and-burn field (identified by the low areas of vegetation in the image)

root crops such as taro (*Colocasia esculenta*) and yams (*Dioscorea alata, Dioscorea esculenta*) (Figure 16.6).[142]

## Conclusion

The history of early agriculture in MSEA and ISEA defies a simple summary. Within each region there are complex flows of materials, people, and ideas. It certainly does not make sense to speak of *the* Neolithic across the entire region. The ways in which people and things have moved about within Southeast Asia appear highly complex. In far southern subtropical China and northern Vietnam, pottery appears to have moved independently of agriculture, while design motifs and styles show similarities between these regions. Stone tools also appear to have their own trajectory, with the early appearance of ground stone axes towards the end of the Pleistocene in northern Vietnam – again in worlds apparently without agriculture. During the late Pleistocene and early Holocene, tropical coastlines of China, northern Vietnam, and southern Thailand may have been home to sedentary and semi-sedentary groups of pottery-using hunter-gatherer-fisher communities. These were peoples who engaged in complex mortuary rights, may have

142 Prill-Brett, 'Bontok', 68.

expressed status in their treatment of the dead, and had complex human–animal relationships. Pottery seems to play an important role in burial ritual across the region, being interred in graves as whole pots or smashed, used as primary and secondary burial containers, and at times ornately decorated.

Agriculture in MSEA is normally thought of as the practice of cultivating rice, but again, as the evidence from the Batanes Islands and central Thailand shows, rice appears to be a plant with a complex biography. The most comprehensive analysis of archaeobotanical evidence from the Khao Wang Prachan valley in central Thailand shows that millets rather than rice were the key crop and that rice does not figure as an important cultivar until the mid second millennium BCE. Bellwood has claimed that the Austronesian migrants were farmers in every sense of the word, just as proficient with the cultivation of rice as with the cultivation of root crops, tree crops, palms, and bananas. The nature of vegecultural plant propagation, though, is very different to plant cultivation and shares more in common with hunter-gatherer systems of in situ plant management than it does with the cleared fields of cereal cultivation. It seems more likely that rice was adopted into vegecultural systems indigenous to MSEA and possibly ISEA rather than being brought into a region as a 'package' of farming (rice and vegecultural practices) from China. Limited archaeological and palaeoecological data from Sarawak indicate the presence of significant landscape modification by at least 6,500 years ago that includes clearance and burning.[143] This is suggestive of a pre-Austronesian system of landscape management and manipulation, perhaps even of some form of swidden cultivation not too dissimilar to that seen at Kuk Swamp in the highlands of New Guinea from 10,000 years ago.

This is a rich region for new archaeological research. While long dominated by a particular view of technological and social change,[144] there seems much potential for new ideas and new approaches. Histories of plant and animal domestication again point to these complexities. The evidence for pig and chicken domestication seems to mirror that of bananas, taros, and yams, suggesting multiple loci of domestication from India and across ISEA. Human movement and translocation appear to have been an important element in the human–plant and human–animal interactions from which domestication has arisen. The nature of vegetative plant manipulation allows for multiple domestication events, as do the vast time depths of human, and indeed of hominin, occupation in this region.

---

143  S.E. Jones et al., 'Forest disturbance, aboriculture and the adoption of rice in the Kelabit highlands of Sarawak, Malaysian Borneo', *The Holocene*, 23 (2013), 1528–46.

144  E.g. Bellwood, 'Asian farming diasporas?'

The challenge for researchers of the present and future is to abandon long-held 'classic' terminologies of Mesolithic and Neolithic and of cultures reflected in the stamp of material things and of their languages. Rather than trying to make people fit into entangled concepts like pre-Neolithic pottery-using cultures or pottery-using Neolithic cultures independent of agriculture, or complex hunter-gatherers independent of rice agriculture, we should ignore the contradictions – which are of out own making – and instead explore the diversity for what it is and what it can teach us about the rich complexity of human adaptation in this remarkable part of the world.

## Further reading

Barker, G. et al. 'The "human revolution" in lowland tropical Southeast Asia: the antiquity of anatomically modern humans, and of behavioural modernity, at Niah Cave (Sarawak, Borneo).' *Journal of Human Evolution*, 52 (2007), 243–61.

Barker, G. and M. Richards. 'Foraging–farming transitions in island Southeast Asia.' *Journal of Archaeological Method and Theory*, 20 (2013), 256–80.

Barton, H., G. Barker, D. Gilbertson, et al. 'Late Pleistocene foragers, *c.* 35,000–11,500 years ago.' In G. Barker (ed.), *Rainforest Foraging and Farming in Island Southeast Asia.* Cambridge: McDonald Institute for Archaeological Research, 2013. 171–214.

Barton, H. and T.P. Denham. 'Prehistoric vegeculture and social life in island Southeast Asia and Melanesia.' In G. Barker and M. Janowski (eds.), *Why Cultivate? Anthropological and Archaeological Approaches to Foraging–Farming Transitions in Southeast Asia.* Cambridge: McDonald Institute for Archaeological Research, 2011. 17–26.

Bellwood, P. 'Asian farming diasporas? Agriculture, languages, and genes in China and Southeast Asia.' In M. Stark (ed.), *Archaeology of Asia.* London: Blackwell, 2006. 96–118.
 *First Farmers: The Origins of Agricultural Societies.* Oxford: Blackwell, 2005.
 *The Prehistory of the Indo-Malaysian Archipelago.* Honolulu: University of Hawai'i Press, 1997.

Bellwood, P., J.J. Fox, and D. Tyron. *The Austronesians: Historical and Comparative Perspectives.* Canberra: Department of Anthropology, Australian National University, 2005.

Bulmer, S. 'Reflections in stone: axes and the beginnings of agriculture in the Central Highlands of New Guinea.' In A. Pawley, R. Attenborough, J. Golson, and R. Hide (eds.), *Papuan Pasts: Cultural, Linguistic and Biological Histories of Papuan-Speaking Peoples.* Canberra: Pacific Linguistics, 2005. 387–450.

Donohue, M. and T.P. Denham. 'Farming and language in island Southeast Asia: reframing Austronesian history.' *Current Anthropology*, 51 (2010), 223–56.

Higham, C. *The Archaeology of Mainland Southeast Asia: From 10,000 BC to the Fall of Angkor.* Cambridge University Press, 1989.
 *Early Culture of Mainland Southeast Asia.* Bangkok: River Books, 2002.

Higham, C., X. Guangmao, and L. Qiang. 'The prehistory of a friction zone: first farmers and hunter-gatherers in Southeast Asia.' *Antiquity*, 85 (2011), 529–43.

King, C.L., A. Bentley, C. Higham, et al. 'Economic change after the agricultural revolution in Southeast Asia?' *Antiquity*, 88 (2014), 112–25.

Lebot, V. *Tropical Root and Tuber Crops: Cassava, Sweet Potato, Yams and Aroids*. Wallingford: CABI, 2009.

Nguyen, K.S., M.H. Pham, and T.T. Tong. 'Northern Vietnam from the Neolithic to the Han period.' In I. Glover and P. Bellwood (eds.), *Southeast Asia: From Prehistory to History*. London: RoutledgeCurzon, 2004. 189–201.

Paz, V. 'Rock shelters, caves, and archaeobotany in island Southeast Asia.' *Asian Perspectives*, 44 (2005), 107–18.

Piper, P.J., N. Amano Jr, S. Hsiu-Ying Yang, and T. O'Connor. 'The terrestrial vertebrate remains.' In P. Bellwood and E. Dizon (eds.), *4000 Years of Migration*. Canberra: ANU E Press, 2013. 169–200.

Spencer, J.E. *Shifting Cultivation in Southeastern Asia*. Berkeley: University of California Press, 1966.

Spriggs, M. 'Archaeology and the Austronesian expansion: where are we now?' *Antiquity*, 85 (2011), 510–28.

Torrence, R. and P. Swadling. 'Social networks and the spread of Lapita.' *Antiquity*, 317 (2008), 600–16.

White, J.C. 'Emergence of cultural diversity in mainland Southeast Asia: a view from prehistory.' In N. Enfield (ed.), *Dynamics of Human Diversity: The Case of Mainland Southeast Asia*. Canberra: Pacific Linguistics, 2011. 9–46.

Zhang, C. and H.-C. Hung. 'Later hunter-gatherers in southern China, 18000–3000 BC.' *Antiquity*, 86 (2012), 11–29.

# 17

# Swamp cultivators at Kuk, New Guinea

## Early agriculture in the highlands of New Guinea

TIM DENHAM

The idea of New Guinea as a centre of early agriculture and plant domestication is, at first glance, strange and confronting. The region does not seem to conform to global stereotypes of early agricultural development. Many of the supposed characteristics of 'Neolithic' cultures, such as pottery, were not present at the time agriculture developed. There was no cereal domestication; indeed, agriculture has traditionally been based on vegetative propagation rather than seed-based reproduction. Early agriculture in the New Guinea region also lacks many of the oft-associated, socially transformative aspects documented elsewhere, including large-scale and hierarchical political units, urbanism, and the so-called 'rise of civilization'.

Although New Guinea does not appear to fit traditional portrayals, multidisciplinary investigations at Kuk Swamp in the upper Wahgi valley have demonstrated that the island is a centre of early and, possibly, independent agricultural development.[1] The wetland at Kuk was periodically manipulated or drained for plant exploitation and cultivation throughout the Holocene. Claims for agriculture dating to c. 10,000 years ago are contentious, whereas evidence for the construction of mounds on the wetland margin and cultivation of bananas at c. 7,000–6,400 cal BP is robust. From approximately 4,500–4,000 years ago to the present, the wetland has been periodically drained, using ditches for cultivation. Other wetland sites

---

1 T.P. Denham, 'Early agriculture and plant domestication in New Guinea and island Southeast Asia', *Current Anthropology*, 52, Supplement 4 (2011), S379–95; T.P. Denham et al., 'Origins of agriculture at Kuk Swamp in the highlands of New Guinea', *Science*, 301 (2003), 189–93; J. Golson, 'The New Guinea highlands on the eve of agriculture', *Bulletin of the Indo-Pacific Prehistory Association*, 11 (1991), 82–91; J. Golson and P.J. Hughes, 'The appearance of plant and animal domestication in New Guinea', *Journal de la Société des Océanistes*, 36 (1980), 294–303; G.S. Hope and J. Golson, 'Late Quaternary change in the mountains of New Guinea', *Antiquity*, 69 (1995), 818–30.

with similar types of archaeological and palaeoecological evidence occur elsewhere in the highlands.[2]

Archaeological findings in the highlands corroborate genetic evidence indicating that New Guinea has been a significant centre of plant domestication. Several globally important subsistence and cash crops, including bananas and sugarcane, as well as possibly taro and yams, were initially domesticated in the New Guinea region.[3] Furthermore, the global significance of Kuk to agricultural history has been recognized: in 2008 it became Papua New Guinea's first UNESCO World Heritage Site.[4]

## Geographic setting

Kuk Swamp (hereafter 'Kuk') is located approximately 12 km northeast of Mount Hagen, the provincial capital, in Western Highlands province, Papua New Guinea. The archaeological site is located on the former Kuk Tea (subsequently Agricultural) Research Station, covering *c.* 280 ha. Although tropical, Kuk is located in the highlands (i.e. more than 1,200 m above sea level) at an altitude of *c.* 1,560 m. The valley has a lower montane, a humid climate with an average annual temperature of 19 degrees C, and annual rainfall of *c.* 2,700 mm.[5] Rainfall is primarily orographic with a slight dry season between May and June, although soil water content is usually sufficient for year-round plant growth.

Kuk forms part of the extensive wetlands carpeting the floor of the upper Wahgi valley. Based on altitude and without human intervention, the

2 T.P. Denham, 'Early to mid-Holocene plant exploitation in New Guinea: towards a contingent interpretation of agriculture', in T.P. Denham et al. (eds.), *Rethinking Agriculture: Archaeological and Ethnoarchaeological Perspectives* (Walnut Creek, CA: Left Coast Press, 2007), 78–108; T.P. Denham and S.G. Haberle, 'Agricultural emergence and transformation in the upper Wahgi valley during the Holocene: theory, method and practice', *The Holocene*, 18 (2008), 499–514; J. Golson, 'The Ipomoean revolution revisited: society and sweet potato in the upper Wahgi valley', in A. Strathern (ed.), *Inequality in New Guinea Highland Societies* (Cambridge University Press, 1982), 109–36; S.G. Haberle, 'The emergence of an agricultural landscape in the highlands of New Guinea', *Archaeology in Oceania*, 38 (2003), 149–58; J.M. Powell, 'The history of plant use and man's impact on the vegetation', in J.L. Gressitt (ed.), *Biogeography and Ecology of New Guinea*, vol. 1 (The Hague: Junk, 1982), 207–27.

3 V. Lebot, 'Biomolecular evidence for plant domestication in Sahul', *Genetic Resources and Crop Evolution*, 46 (1999), 619–28; X. Perrier et al., 'Multidisciplinary perspectives on banana (*Musa* spp.) domestication', *Proceedings of the National Academy of Sciences*, 108 (2011), 11311–18.

4 J. Muke et al., 'Nominating and managing a World Heritage Site in the highlands of Papua New Guinea', *World Archaeology*, 39 (2007), 324–38.

5 P.J. Hughes et al., 'Human induced erosion in a highlands catchment in Papua New Guinea: the prehistoric and contemporary records', *Zeitschrift für Geomorphologie*, Supplement, 83 (1991), 227–39; J.R. McAlpine et al., *Climate of Papua New Guinea* (London: Commonwealth Scientific and Industrial Research Organisation; Canberra: ANU Press, 1983).

vegetation of the lower valley slopes would be lower montane forest with a mixed canopy of *Castanopsis–Lithocarpus* spp., while the upper valley slopes would comprise upper montane forest dominated by *Nothofagus* spp. Today, the valley floor is a horticultural landscape of cultivated plots, grasslands, settlements, and planted stands of she-oak (*Casuarina oligodon*).

## A brief history of research

Preliminary research in several disciplines first signalled that agriculture had a long antiquity in the highlands of New Guinea. Ethnobotanical research in the Pacific suggested New Guinea was a centre of plant domestication.[6] Palaeoecological research documented major transformations and degradation of the lower montane forest in parts of the highlands by *c.* 5,000–4,000 years ago.[7] Archaeological excavations at other wetlands in the upper Wahgi valley uncovered evidence of agricultural practices, including wooden digging sticks and ditches, that were over 2,000 years old.[8]

The potential of Kuk to unravel the history of agriculture in the highlands was first indicated by finds unearthed during modern drainage of the wetland in 1969; subsequently, between 1972 and 1977, six major field seasons of multi-disciplinary research were directed by Jack Golson, with Philip Hughes as co-director from 1974.[9] Over 180 trenches or open area excavations were completed, and archaeological and stratigraphic recording occurred along more than 15 km of newly dug plantation drain (Figure 17.1). Small-scale fieldwork

---

6 J. Barrau, 'Introduction', in J. Barrau (ed.), *Plants and the Migrations of Pacific Peoples: A Symposium* (Honolulu: Bishop Museum Press, 1963), 1–6; D.E. Yen, 'The origins of Oceanic agriculture', *Archaeology and Physical Anthropology in Oceania*, 8 (1973), 68–85; see also J. Golson, 'Unravelling the story of early plant exploitation in highland Papua New Guinea', in Denham et al. (eds.), *Rethinking Agriculture*, 109–25.

7 J.M. Powell, 'The impact of man on the vegetation of the Mt Hagen region, New Guinea', unpublished PhD thesis (Canberra: Australian National University, 1970); Powell, 'History of plant use'; see also G.S. Hope and S.G. Haberle, 'The history of the human landscapes of New Guinea', in A. Pawley et al. (eds.), *Papuan Pasts: Cultural, Linguistic and Biological Histories of Papuan-Speaking Peoples* (Canberra: Pacific Linguistics, 2005), 541–54.

8 J. Golson et al., 'A note on carbon dates for horticulture in the New Guinea highlands', *Journal of the Polynesian Society*, 76 (1967), 369–71.

9 J. Allen, 'Prehistoric agricultural systems in the Wahgi valley: a further note', *Mankind*, 7 (1970), 177–83; J. Golson, 'Archaeology and agricultural history in the New Guinea highlands', in G. de G. Sieveking et al. (eds.), *Problems in Economic and Social Archaeology* (London: Duckworth, 1976), 201–20; J. Golson, 'No room at the top: agricultural intensification in the New Guinea highlands', in J. Allen et al. (eds.), *Sunda and Sahul: Prehistoric Studies in Southeast Asia, Melanesia and Australia* (New York and London: Academic Press, 1977), 601–38; J. Golson, 'New Guinea agricultural history: a case study', in D. Denoon and C. Snowden (eds.), *A Time to Plant and a Time to Uproot: A History of Agriculture in Papua New Guinea* (Port Moresby: Institute of Papua New Guinea Studies, 1981), 601–38.

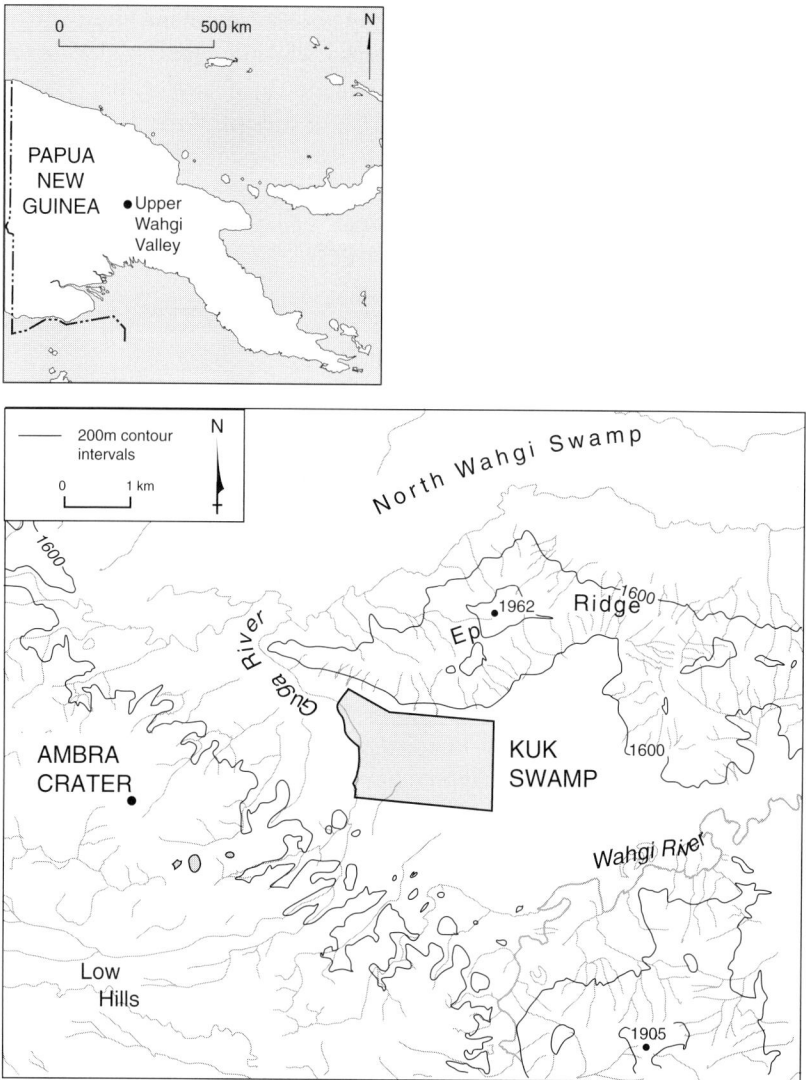

Figure 17.1 Maps showing (above) the location of Kuk in Papua New Guinea; and (below) Kuk Swamp within its landscape setting.

and site visits occurred until the Station was effectively abandoned by the national government in 1990. Archaeology at Kuk was complemented by what was at the time an innovative range of approaches, including agronomy; the application of macrofossils (seeds and wood) and microfossils (phytoliths, pollen, and microcharcoal) to archaeobotany and palaeoecology; thermoluminescence, ESR, and radiocarbon dating; and a range of stratigraphic investigations.[10]

The original claims for early agriculture derived from these investigations were not widely accepted, due to limited publication of the archaeological evidence; uncertainties regarding the mode of formation and function of archaeological features associated with early agricultural activities; a lack of palaeoecological evidence contemporary with early agricultural remains; and limited archaeobotanical evidence for the presence, use, and cultivation of plants.[11] As a result, renewed multidisciplinary research on early agriculture was initiated at Kuk in 1997 to clarify issues arising from previous work.

The archaeological excavations undertaken at Kuk in 1998 and 1999 were designed to determine the form and function of features and palaeosurfaces associated with the early periods of manipulation and drainage of the wetland, namely those predating *c.* 2,500 years ago. Analyses undertaken on associated artefacts and soil/sediment samples comprised:

- Radiocarbon dating (conventional and AMS) to improve the accuracy and resolution of the agricultural chronology.
- Intensive palaeoecological analyses (paired microcharcoal, phytolith, and pollen analyses, as well as entomology) to determine environmental

---

10 W.T. Bell, 'Thermoluminescence dating of cooking stones from the Kuk Tea Research Station site, New Guinea', *Archaeology and Physical Anthropology in Oceania*, 11 (1976), 51–5; Hughes et al., 'Human induced erosion'; M. Ikeya and J. Golson, 'ESR dating of phytoliths (plant opal) in sediments: a preliminary study', *ESR Dating and Dosimetry* (1985), 281–5; H. Polach et al., 'Radiocarbon dating: a guide for archaeologists on the collection and submission of samples and age-reporting procedures', in G. Connah (ed.), *Australian Field Archaeology: A Guide to Techniques* (Canberra: Australian Institute of Aboriginal Studies, 1983), 145–52; J.M. Powell, 'Plant resources and palaeobotanical evidence for plant use in the Papua New Guinea highlands', *Archaeology in Oceania*, 17 (1982), 28–37; J.M. Powell, 'Ecological and palaeoecological studies at Kuk 1: below the grey clay', unpublished manuscript, Kuk archive, Australian National University, 1984; J.M. Powell et al., *Agricultural Traditions in the Mount Hagen Area*, Department of Geography Occasional Paper 12 (Port Moresby: University of Papua New Guinea, 1976); S.M. Wilson, 'Phytolith analysis at Kuk, an early agricultural site in Papua New Guinea', *Archaeology in Oceania*, 20 (1985), 90–7.
11 T.P. Bayliss-Smith, 'People–plant interactions in the New Guinea highlands: agricultural hearthland or horticultural backwater?', and M. Spriggs, 'Early agriculture and what went before in island Melanesia: continuity or intrusion?', both in D.R. Harris (ed.), *The Origins and Spread of Agriculture and Pastoralism in Eurasia* (London: UCL Press, 1996), 499–523 and 524–37.

transformations associated with former practices, to differentiate anthropic from climatic components of vegetation history, and to obtain ecological signatures for key archaeological features and periods.

- Archaeobotanical analyses, including phytolith and starch granule residues from stone artefacts, to determine the presence, use, and cultivation of food plants.
- Mixed-method stratigraphic analyses (X-radiography, X-ray diffraction, and soil micromorphology) to characterize sedimentation and soil formation processes through time.[12]

Although archaeological excavations have not occurred at Kuk since 1999, multidisciplinary research continues on previously collected samples. These initiatives are designed to provide palaeoecological and use-wear records for periods of drainage during the last 2,500 years that are comparable to those established for earlier periods. Archaeobotanical investigations also continue on macrobotanical samples, including aroid seeds (histology and micro-scopy), and on tuber fragments (aDNA, AMS, and starch grain analysis).

## Stratigraphy

The stratigraphic model for Kuk was developed using a suite of analyses.[13] The mixed-method strategy was designed to disentangle and reconstruct a hierarchy

12 T.P. Denham, 'Environmental archaeology: interpreting practices-in-the-landscape through geoarchaeology', in B. David and J. Thomas (eds.), *Handbook of Landscape Archaeology* (Walnut Creek, CA: Left Coast Press, 2008), 468–81, and 'The Kuk morass: multi-disciplinary investigations of early to mid Holocene plant exploitation at Kuk Swamp, Wahgi valley, Papua New Guinea', unpublished PhD thesis (Canberra: Australian National University, 2003); Denham et al., 'Origins of agriculture at Kuk Swamp'; T.P. Denham et al., 'Reading early agriculture at Kuk (phases 1–3), Wahgi valley, Papua New Guinea: the wetland archaeological features', *Proceedings of the Prehistoric Society*, 70 (2004), 259–98; T.P. Denham et al., 'New evidence and interpretations for early agriculture in highland New Guinea', *Antiquity*, 78 (2004), 839–57; T.P. Denham et al., 'A multi-disciplinary method for the investigation of early agriculture: learning lessons from Kuk', in A. Fairbairn et al. (eds.), *New Directions in Archaeological Science*, Terra Australis 28 (Canberra: ANU E Press, 2009), 139–54; T.P. Denham et al., 'Contiguous multi-proxy analyses (X-radiography, diatom, pollen and microcharcoal) of Holocene archaeological features at Kuk Swamp, upper Wahgi valley, Papua New Guinea', *Geoarchaeology*, 24 (2009), 715–42; R. Fullagar et al., 'Early and mid-Holocene processing of taro (*Colocasia esculenta*) and yam (*Dioscorea* sp.) at Kuk Swamp in the highlands of Papua New Guinea', *Journal of Archaeological Science*, 33 (2006), 595–614; S.G. Haberle et al., 'The palaeoenviron-ments of Kuk Swamp from the beginnings of agriculture in the highlands of Papua New Guinea', *Quaternary International*, 249 (2012), 129–39.
13 Denham, 'Environmental archaeology', following M. Canti, 'A mixed-method approach to geoarchaeological analysis', in A.J. Barham and R.I. MacPhail (eds.), *Archaeological Sediments and Soils: Analysis, Interpretation and Management* (Institute of Archaeology, University College London, 1995), 183–90.

of site formation processes for different episodes of wetland inundation, tephra deposition, and soil formation during drier periods or following drainage for cultivation. The superimposition of depositional (sedimentary) and pedogenic (soil formation) processes was reconstructed for different stratigraphic units, with particular reference to periods of wetland manipulation and abandonment during the early and mid-Holocene (Figure 17.2).

Distinct stages in the development of each stratigraphic unit and archaeo-logical context were characterized and can be summarized in a generalized three-step model:

1. Original deposition – whether aeolian (tephra), alluvial (silts and clays), or autogenic (peat) – represented by inherited sedimentary stratification.
2. Anthropic and pedogenic alteration of the sediment and formation of archaeological deposits and palaeosols, respectively, including those associated with wetland manipulation, drainage, and cultivation.
3. Modification of archaeological contexts prior to and following burial through repeated periods of waterlogging and soil formation.

An ability to identify and characterize post-depositional modifications has proven essential for establishing the reliability of different contexts for archaeobotany, dating, and palaeoecology.

### Outline of conceptual framework

Numerous conceptual frameworks have been developed and applied to understand agricultural history at Kuk. Golson's early interpretations empha-sized ecology and efficiency and were expressed in neo-Boserupian terms, whereas later interpretations drew on Modjeska and Gorecki to develop more socially and politically oriented perspectives.[14] Subsequent interpreta-tions have variously interrogated the evidence using insights derived from human ecology and post-processual thought.[15]

---

14 Golson, 'No room at the top'; J. Golson and D. Gardner, 'Agriculture and sociopolitical organisation in New Guinea highlands prehistory', *Annual Review of Anthropology*, 19 (1990), 395–417; see also N. Modjeska, 'Production and inequality: perspectives from central New Guinea', in Strathern (ed.), *Inequality in New Guinea Highland Societies*, 50–108; and P. Gorecki, 'Human occupation and agricultural development in the Papua New Guinea highlands', *Mountain Research and Development*, 6 (1986), 159–66.

15 Respectively: T.P. Denham and H. Barton, 'The emergence of agriculture in New Guinea: continuity from pre-existing foraging practices', in D.J. Kennett and B. Winterhalder (eds.), *Behavioral Ecology and the Transition to Agriculture* (Berkeley: University of California Press, 2006), 237–64; and Denham, 'Early to mid-Holocene plant exploitation'; T.P. Denham, 'A practice-centred method for charting the emer-gence and transformation of agriculture', *Current Anthropology*, 50 (2009), 661–7.

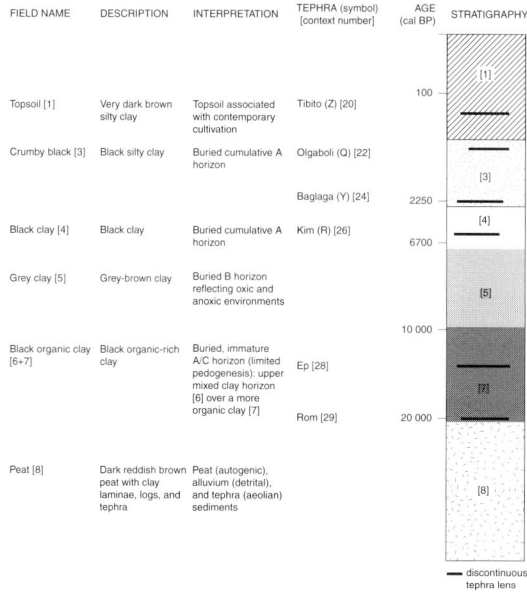

| FIELD NAME | DESCRIPTION | INTERPRETATION | TEPHRA (symbol) [context number] | AGE (cal BP) | STRATIGRAPHY |
|---|---|---|---|---|---|
| Topsoil [1] | Very dark brown silty clay | Topsoil associated with contemporary cultivation | Tibito (Z) [20] | 100 | [1] |
| Crumby black [3] | Black silty clay | Buried cumulative A horizon | Olgaboli (Q) [22] | | [3] |
| | | | Baglaga (Y) [24] | 2250 | |
| Black clay [4] | Black clay | Buried cumulative A horizon | Kim (R) [26] | 6700 | [4] |
| Grey clay [5] | Grey-brown clay | Buried B horizon reflecting oxic and anoxic environments | | | [5] |
| | | | | 10 000 | |
| Black organic clay [6+7] | Black organic-rich clay | Buried, immature A/C horizon (limited pedogenesis): upper mixed clay horizon [6] over a more organic clay [7] | Ep [28] | | [7] |
| | | | Rom [29] | 20 000 | |
| Peat [8] | Dark reddish brown peat with clay laminae, logs, and tephra | Peat (autogenic), alluvium (detrital), and tephra (aeolian) sediments | | | [8] |

▬ discontinuous tephra lens

Figure 17.2  Archaeostratigraphic model for the stratigraphy at Kuk.

At Kuk, agriculture in the past has been inferred using a triangulation method. In other words, the identification of agriculture is not dependent upon one type of evidence; rather, it is situated using multiple lines of evidence. These comprise archaeological remains associated with plant cultivation; archaeobotanical evidence for the presence, use, and cultivation of plants; and palaeoenvironmental records (palaeoecology, geomorphology, and sedimentology) documenting landscape changes accompanying the emergence and transformation of agriculture through time (Figure 17.3).

An evolving methodology focused on practices has been built upon this multidisciplinary approach. Practices are human actions in the past, including habitual modes of behaviour and dispositions, as well as individual idiosyncrasies.[16] Evidence of practices accumulates and becomes inscribed

16 J. Barrett, *Fragments from Antiquity: An Archaeology of Social Life 2900–1200 BC* (Oxford: Blackwell, 1994); M. Bruno, 'Practice and history in the transition to food production', *Current Anthropology*, 50 (2009), 703–6; Denham, 'Environmental archaeology'; S. Jussuret, 'Socializing geoarchaeology: insights from Bourdieu's theory of practice applied to Neolithic and Bronze Age Crete', *Geoarchaeology*, 25 (2010), 675–708, following P. Bourdieu, *The Logic of Practice*, trans. R. Nice (Cambridge: Polity Press, 1990).

| Definition | Evidence |
|---|---|
| Social dependence or involvement | Plant use with or without domestication (Archaeobotany)<br><br>Environmental transformation (Geomorphology, Palaeoecology, Sedimentology) ←——→ Cultivation practices (Archaeology) |
| Inferred | Documented |

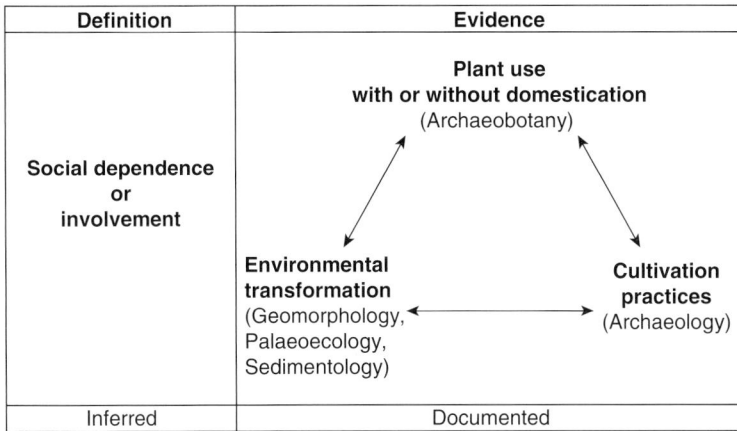

Figure 17.3 Schematic depiction of the conceptual and methodological bases for the interpretation of early agriculture in New Guinea.

within a landscape through time. The landscape is the appropriate scale of analysis and interpretation because it encapsulates everyday experience; in other words, it is a meaningful spatial scale for past human experience. Furthermore, the variability in plant exploitation practices across Papua New Guinea today, if symptomatic of the past, suggests that a landscape or regional approach to investigating agriculture should be adopted in order to avoid bringing together evidence of practices from different parts of the island that never actually co-occurred in the past.[17]

A chronology of practices can then be assembled for a landscape. Co-occurring practices can be brought together, or 'bundled', to interpret different forms of plant exploitation in the past (Figure 17.4). Perhaps the most crucial element of these reconstructions is archaeological and pedogenic evidence of former cultivation and archaeobotanical evidence of cultivated plants. Without this evidential grounding, the interpretation of cultivation and agriculture in the past, whether based solely on palaeo-ecology or on phenotypically 'domesticated' plant fossils, is largely inferential.

17 R.M. Bourke and T. Harwood (eds.), *Food and Agriculture in Papua New Guinea* (Canberra: ANU E Press, 2009); T.P. Denham, 'Envisaging early agriculture in the highlands of New Guinea: landscapes, plants and practices', *World Archaeology*, 37 (2005), 290–306; Denham, 'Early agriculture and plant domestication'.

Years (cal BP)

| Constituent practice | 50,000 | 10,000 | 1,000 | 100 | 0 | Form of plant exploitation |

Burning

Forest disturbance (axe/adze) — — — — → ground — — — — → metal

Tree exploitation

Digging — stone tools? — — — wooden digging stick

Tuber exploitation

Staking

Plot preparation

Planting

Mound construction

Ditch digging

*Casuarina* tree fallowing

Pig (*Sus scrofa*) rearing  ?

Fence construction  ?

Sweet potato (*Ipomoea batatas*) cultivation

Form of plant exploitation (right side):
Foraging
Shifting cultivation? (**plot preparation and planting**)
Intensive wetland/ (**mound construction**)
Intensive dryland/ wetland cultivation (**digging of ditches**)
Intensive wetland cultivation and drainage
Semi-permanent, rotational dryland cultivation (***Casuarina* tree fallowing**)
Intensive cultivation and pig husbandry (**sweet potatoes and pigs**)

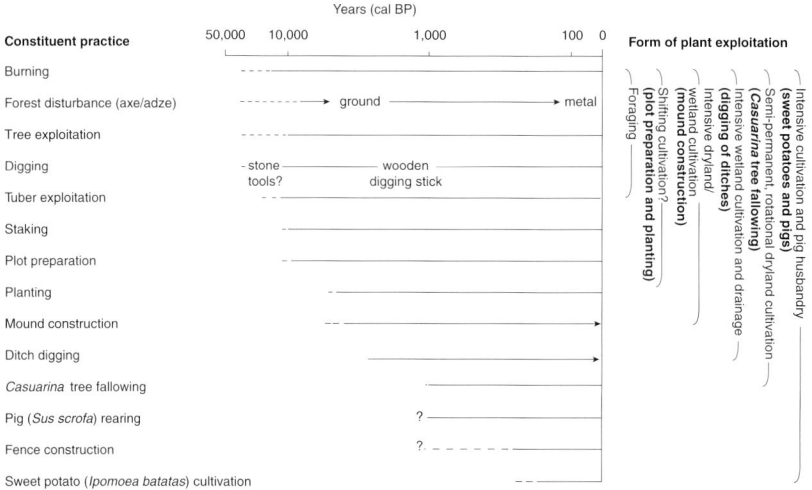

Figure 17.4 Chronology of practices and forms of plant exploitation in the upper Wahgi valley.

# Chronology of plant exploitation

## Life during the Pleistocene

People arrived in New Guinea at least 50,000–45,000 years ago, with evidence for occupation of the highlands from that time.[18] The colonists are presumed to have engaged in generalized patterns of behaviour, including landscape and plant management using fire; broad spectrum plant exploitation encompassing tree (nuts, fruits, and possibly forms of sago) and tuber exploitation; broad spectrum animal exploitation; and high degrees of mobility across land and presumably water. Early inhabitants of the upper Wahgi valley found a forested valley floor, with climatically induced fluctuations in the relative dominance of upper and lower montane forest species.

18 Denham and Barton, 'Emergence of agriculture in New Guinea'; M.-J. Mountain, 'Highland New Guinea hunter-gatherers: the evidence of Nombe rockshelter, Simbu, with emphasis on the Pleistocene', unpublished PhD thesis (Canberra: Australian National University, 1991); J.F. O'Connell and J. Allen, 'Pre-LGM Sahul (Pleistocene Australia–New Guinea) and the archaeology of early modern humans', in P. Mellars et al. (eds.), *Rethinking the Human Revolution: New Behavioural and Biological Perspectives on the Origin and Dispersal of Modern Humans* (Cambridge: McDonald Institute for Archaeological Research, 2007), 395–410; G.R. Summerhayes et al., 'Human adaptation and plant use in highland New Guinea 49,000 to 44,000 years ago', *Science*, 330 (2010), 78–81.

At Kuk, pollen records indicate burning, opening of the forest, and establishment of grassland patches for at least the last 20,000 years (Figure 17.5).[19] Although fires can be caused by lightning, an increasing part of the signal can be attributed to burning by people. More definitive traces of past human presence are represented by a possible hearth on the wetland margin dated to c. 30,000 years ago.

Early anthropic burning occurred from c. 40,000 cal BP in the Owen Stanley Ranges to the east and from c. 32,000 cal BP in the Baliem valley to the west.[20] Indeed, burning during the Pleistocene has been recorded in all the major intervening inter-montane valleys along the highland spine of the island: Telefomin, Haeapugua, and Wahgi valley; while similar records of burning are more limited in lowland New Guinea and in island Melanesia.[21]

Recurrent accounts portray pre-agricultural occupation of the highlands in the Pleistocene as temporary and based on hunting and the exploitation of seasonally producing *Pandanus* spp.[22] Putting aside issues related to hunting, which are less contentious, this scenario rests on two major assumptions, which are actually spatially and chronologically contingent, in that they do not apply to the highlands as a whole during the Pleistocene or last glacial maximum.

First, *Pandanus brosimos*, high altitude *Pandanus*, is often assumed to be seasonally producing and to have been the primary food plant at high

19  Denham et al., 'New evidence and interpretations'; Haberle et al., 'Palaeoenvironments of Kuk Swamp'.

20  Respectively: G.S. Hope, 'Environmental change and fire in the Owen Stanley Ranges, Papua New Guinea', *Quaternary Science Reviews*, 28 (2009), 2261–76; and S.G. Haberle et al., 'Environmental change in the Baliem valley, montane Irian Jaya, Republic of Indonesia', *Journal of Biogeography*, 18 (1991), 25–40.

21  Denham et al., 'New evidence and interpretations'; S.G. Haberle, 'Late Quaternary change in the Tari basin, Papua New Guinea', *Palaeogeography, Palaeoclimatology, Palaeoecology*, 137 (1998), 1–24; Haberle et al., 'Palaeoenvironments of Kuk Swamp'; G.S. Hope, 'The vegetational changes of the last 20,000 years at Telefomin, Papua New Guinea', *Singapore Journal of Tropical Geography*, 4 (1983), 25–33; Hope and Haberle, 'History of the human landscapes'; C. Lentfer et al., 'Natural and human impacts in a 35,000-year vegetation history in central New Britain, Papua New Guinea', *Quaternary Science Reviews*, 29 (2009), 3750–67.

22  S. Bulmer, 'Between the mountain and the plain: prehistoric settlement and environment in the Kair--onk valley', in J.H. Winslow (ed.), *The Melanesian Environment* (Canberra: ANU Press, 1977), 61–73; Golson, 'Ipomoean revolution revisited'; Hope and Golson, 'Late Quaternary change'; A.S. Fairbairn et al., 'Pleistocene occupation of New Guinea's highland and subalpine environments', *World Archaeology*, 38 (2006), 371–86; cf. T.P. Denham, 'Exploiting diversity: plant exploitation and occupation in the interior of New Guinea during the Pleistocene', *Archaeology in Oceania*, 42 (2007), 41–8.

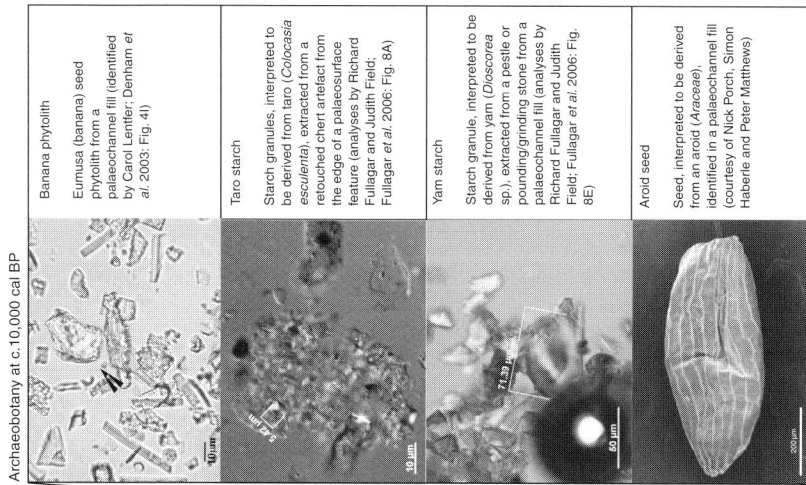

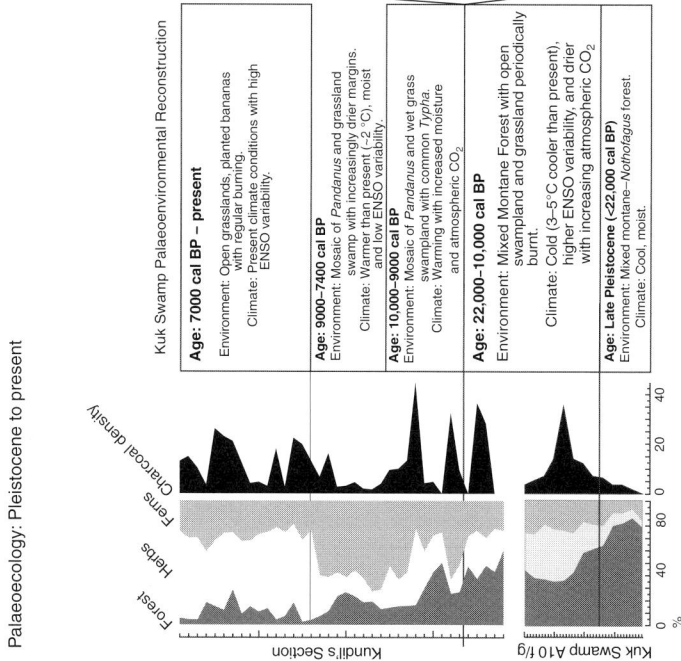

Figure 17.5  Archaeobotanical and palaeoecological information from Kuk: (left) summary pollen and microcharcoal diagram; (right) photomicrographs of phytoliths and starch grain residues from stone tools, and an electron micrograph of an aroid seed at Kuk dating to c. 10,000 years ago.

altitude, or in the highlands generally, during the Pleistocene. Nut produc-tion, or masting, in *P. brosimos* is not seasonally reliable and varies with climate. In weakly seasonal climates, such as the upper Wahgi valley, nut production is also weakly seasonal and discontinuous. Consequently, in this part of the highlands, *P. brosimos* would not have provided a predictable food source to facilitate seasonal occupation.

Second, the floors of highland valleys are assumed to have been carpeted with resource-depauperate *Nothofagus*-dominated forests following the downward altitudinal movement of vegetation communities during the LGM. Although true for some inter-montane valleys, pollen diagrams from the upper Wahgi valley are variable. At Kuk (*c.* 1,560 m), mixed lower montane forests persisted before, during, and after the LGM. In contrast, at the slightly higher altitude site of Draepi-Minjigina within the same valley (*c.* 1,890 m), mixed oak forests drop markedly and *Nothofagus* forests pre-dominate. The persistence of lower montane forest on the valley floor at Kuk is significant, because these forests are comparatively rich in faunal and floral resources, especially in comparison to *Nothofagus* forests that are relatively devoid of edible plant resources other than *P. brosimos*.[23]

The re-evaluation above suggests people did not just inhabit the highland interior of New Guinea on a seasonal basis. Such a model only applies to *Nothofagus* forests in more seasonal climates; it does not apply to the less seasonal parts of the highlands, such as the upper Wahgi valley, which continuously maintained a broader resource base.[24] In any case, people were mobile and ranged across the highlands and lowlands to access resources throughout the year. This highly mobile land-use patterning is evident in the Ivane valley where multiple open sites show that groups of foragers exploited high altitude *Pandanus* and lower altitude yams during the Pleistocene.[25]

### Transitions

Various models have proposed how people's plant exploitation practices changed around the Pleistocene–Holocene transition.[26] In general terms,

23  Golson, 'Ipomoean revolution revisited'; Hope and Golson, 'Late Quaternary change', 827; Powell, 'History of plant use', 219.
24  Denham and Barton, 'Emergence of agriculture in New Guinea'; Denham, 'Exploiting diversity'.
25  Summerhayes et al., 'Human adaptation and plant use'.
26  Golson, 'Ipomoean revolution revisited'; Hope and Golson, 'Late Quaternary change'; Denham and Barton, 'Emergence of agriculture in New Guinea'; Denham and Haberle, 'Agricultural emergence', following in a broad sense L. Groube, 'The taming of the

these models focus upon how people increasingly began to manage the landscape and the edible plant resources contained within it. For example at Kuk, in contrast to other highland locales, early Holocene warming and increased precipitation did not lead to forest encroachment and the replacement of grasslands; rather, rainforest advance was 'muted' and a mosaic of grassland and forest subject to episodic burning persisted.

Within the upper Wahgi landscape, people focused on areas where edible resources were potentially different and more abundant than under the forest canopy. These included disturbed gaps within the forest, such as landslides and tree falls; the disturbed patches people created; as well as ecotones, riparian corridors, and wetlands. Over time people increasingly maintained these environments and created new ones within the forest using fire and stone tools. The increased human intervention in the landscape was designed to increase resource density and the productivity of favoured species, primarily plants, but also presumably to hunt and gather the fauna attracted to and supported by the increased edible resources within those gaps and patches.

There are two significant transitions that contributed to the change from resource intensification to cultivation. First, people began to focus on, and to increasingly manage, certain types of plant for their diet, which led to deliberate planting. Second, people began to create new environments, or cleared plots, within the forest for planting.

Transition 1: At some point, people began to increasingly focus upon the management of individual species: starch-rich plants such as bananas (*Musa* spp.), taro (*Colocasia esculenta*), yams (*Dioscorea* spp.), and edible grasses, including sugarcanes (*Saccharum* spp.) and *pit-pit* (*Setaria* spp.); oil- and protein-rich palms and trees (*Pandanus* spp. and *Castanopsis* sp., respectively); and leafy vegetables. At this time, their dietary focus presumably shifted from broad spectrum hunting and gathering, or foraging, to more selective exploitation and management of caloric and oil- and protein-rich plants. Through time, people shifted from solely using burning and clearing to increase the density of favoured plants; they began to deliberately remove reproductively viable parts from plants growing in the landscape and to replant them in

rainforests: a model for late Pleistocene forest exploitation in New Guinea', D.R. Harris, 'An evolutionary continuum of people–plant interaction', and D.E. Yen, 'The domestication of environment', all in D.R. Harris and G.C. Hillman (eds.), *Foraging and Farming: The Evolution of Plant Exploitation* (London: Unwin Hyman, 1989), 292–304, 11–26, 55–75.

managed gaps and patches. Given the dominance of vegetative propagation in all forms of traditional horticulture in New Guinea, as well as the transplantation of seedlings, suckers, and cuttings in arboriculture, it is presumed that initial planting was based on a pre-existing awareness of the vegetative capacity of plants. Although the focus here is upon edible plants, the rationale for the earliest planting may not have been primarily food; it could as readily have been to establish boundary markers, gather materials or condiments, medicinal or ritual uses, and a host of other purposes.[27]

Transition 2: At a later time, people began to create and prepare plots within the forest, as well as in other environments, for planting. Initially, it may be envisaged, planting occurred within managed gaps and artificially created patches in order to supplement the density and range of resources – edible or otherwise. With time, people began to clear areas within the rainforest to create plots primarily for planting; thus, any increased resource density as a result of vegetation clearance or disturbance (characteristic of patches) was incidental and secondary to the plant resources obtained from deliberate planting (characteristic of plots). Plots were probably not clear-felled; large trees were probably left standing after being ring-barked or pollarded to provide shade and to assist soil retention. Minimal tillage can be envisaged, in which planting occurred by dibbling, or making a hole in the ground using a stick, planting, and then filling in by hand.

The archaeological, chronological, palaeoecological, and stratigraphic evidence for these two transitions is inevitably ambiguous. How is it possible to differentiate resource intensification from localized, small-scale relocation and planting within the landscape? How is it possible to differentiate patches with limited planting from plots with a greater degree of planting? These ambiguities are conceptual, in the sense that agriculture in New Guinea represents a dependence upon cultivated plants for food and not just food production or planting.[28] These ambiguities are also methodological, in the sense that the fragmentary and partial evidence could be interpreted in many ways. These issues are illustrated by wetland manipulation and plant exploitation at Kuk *c.* 10,000 years ago.

27 J.M. Powell, 'Ethnobotany', in K. Paijmans (ed.), *New Guinea Vegetation* (Amsterdam and Oxford: Elsevier, 1976), 106–83; and e.g. J. Kennedy, 'Bananas and people in the homeland of genus *Musa*: not just pretty fruit', *Ethnobotany Research and Applications*, 7 (2009), 179–97.

28 Denham, 'Early to mid-Holocene plant exploitation'; cf. B.D. Smith, 'Low-level food production', *Journal of Archaeological Research*, 9 (2001), 1–43.

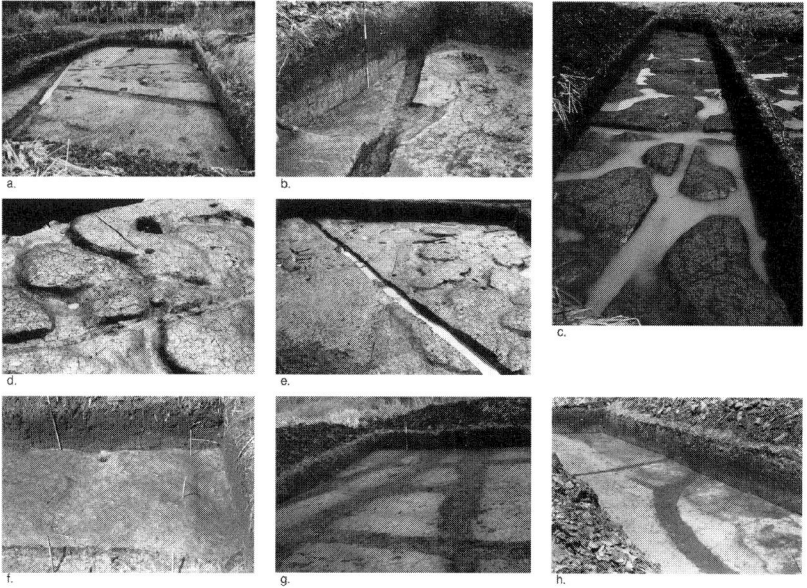

Figure 17.6 Archaeological features indicative of early agricultural practices at Kuk: general (a) and close-up (b) images of the early Holocene palaeosurface dating to *c.* 10,000 years ago; general (c) and close-up (d–e) images of the preserved bases of mounds and pit with post hole (f) dating to *c.* 7,000–6,400 years ago; triangular ditch junction (g; cross-cutting ditch in the centre of the image) and dendritic ditch junction (h) dating to *c.* 3,000–2,500 years ago.

## Ambiguities of practice, c. 10,000 years ago

Despite contrary claims, there is insufficient evidence to unambiguously determine that cultivation in prepared plots occurred on the wetland margin at Kuk *c.* 10,000 years ago.[29] There are, however, multiple lines of evidence suggestive of people clearing vegetation and exploiting starch-rich plants in a restricted area on the wetland margin at this time (Figure 17.6). These include:

1. Anthropic disturbance of montane forests using fire and presumably stone tools to maintain a mosaic of habitats in the landscape.
2. Localized clearance of vegetation and soil disturbance evident in the fills of an adjacent palaeochannel.

29 Denham, 'Early to mid-Holocene plant exploitation'; Denham et al., 'Reading early agriculture at Kuk'; Golson, 'Unravelling the story'.

3. Digging, possibly for planting and harvesting.
4. Possible staking of plants.
5. Modification of the palaeosurface to aid drainage within a cleared area.
6. Procurement and processing of starch-rich plants, including possibly taro (*Colocasia esculenta*) and a yam (*Dioscorea* sp.).[30]

To recap, this multidisciplinary evidence is insufficient to unequivocally state that these practices represent agriculture, i.e. cultivation within a plot, as they may as equally represent incidental planting within a maintained patch. Three key lines of evidence are ambiguous and require clarification. First, the extent of soil preparation is unknown, although immature A/C soil profiles are consistent with limited soil formation during short-lived locally drier conditions.[31] Given that minimal tillage is likely to have occurred, as it does in many forms of swidden cultivation in New Guinea today, additional evidence for soil preparation need not be present. Second, features and artefacts do not necessarily indicate planting, although they may be consistent with the anticipated range of archaeological remains associated with planting in a patch or plot. These include staking, digging, microtopographical manipulation for surface drainage, and processing of plants. Third, evidence for planting is suggestive, but ultimately equivocal. Although Musa section bananas (formerly Eumusa section), taro, and some yams are generally considered to be of lowland derivation, and are all present at Kuk *c.* 10,000 years ago, the precise altitudinal range of these plants in New Guinea at that time is uncertain.[32] Thus, it is not clear whether these plants were brought to the highlands for cultivation or were growing wild in the Kuk vicinity.

Conservatively, the multidisciplinary evidence for practices on the wetland margin at Kuk *c.* 10,000 years ago is suggestive of intensive use of the landscape and plants, but it does not necessarily reflect a way of life dependent upon the cultivation of food in plots. In terms of the two transitions identified above, there seems to be an emerging focus on starch-rich plants, perhaps growing locally (including taro, a yam, and possibly bananas), and there is evidence for the creation of patches or plots. Ultimately, though, evidence for planting is equivocal.

---

30 Denham, 'Kuk morass'; Denham et al., 'Reading early agriculture at Kuk'; Fullagar et al., 'Early and mid-Holocene processing of taro'; Haberle et al., 'Palaeoenvironments of Kuk Swamp'.
31 Denham et al., 'Contiguous multi-proxy analyses'.
32 Denham et al., 'New evidence and interpretations'; Hope and Golson, 'Late Quaternary change'.

## Swidden cultivation across the landscape

Something different started to occur within the upper Wahgi valley land-scape during the early Holocene.[33] Direct archaeological evidence of these practices is lacking from Kuk, but disturbance of the montane rainforest using fire and stone tools continued, and perhaps increased, on the valley floor to create a mosaic of expanding grasslands and disturbed montane forest, primarily composed of subcanopy taxa (Figure 17.5). Phytolith frequencies and intact phytolith chains indicate bananas were periodically common and are likely to have been planted locally. Additionally, people continued to exploit starch-rich plants, including taro and a yam. Taken together with increased erosion rates within the Kuk catchment, swidden cultivation is inferred to have been developed and practised on the valley floor during the early Holocene.

## Cultivation using mounds, 7,000–6,400 years ago

The earliest archaeological remains of former mounds used for cultivation date to c. 7,000–6,400 years ago on the wetland margin at Kuk (Figures 17.6c–f and 17.7 below). Mixed-method sedimentological investigations indicate that these mounds are artificial.[34] Mounded cultivation coincides with 'higher levels of burning, dramatic falls in *Pandanus* and other forest species, and dramatic increases in herbs, predominantly grasses', as well as locally drier conditions.[35] The more effective clearance of forests is associated with the use of ground stone axe-adzes from this time.[36] Grasslands maintained by burn-ing persisted until the late twentieth century in this landscape.[37]

Elevated phytolith frequencies of bananas are interpreted as representing cultivation within mounded plots as well as elsewhere in the landscape.[38]

---

33 Denham and Haberle, 'Agricultural emergence'; Denham et al., 'Origins of agriculture at Kuk Swamp'; Fullagar et al., 'Early and mid-Holocene processing of taro'; Haberle et al., 'Palaeoenvironments of Kuk Swamp'; Hughes et al., 'Human induced erosion'.

34 Denham, 'Kuk morass'; T.P. Denham, 'Archaeological evidence for mid-Holocene agriculture in the interior of Papua New Guinea: a critical review', *Archaeology in Oceania*, 38 (2003), 159–76; Denham et al., 'Contiguous multi-proxy analyses'.

35 Denham et al., 'Contiguous multi-proxy analyses', 735.

36 O.A. Christensen, 'Hunters and horticulturalists: a preliminary report of the 1972–4 excavations in the Manim valley, Papua New Guinea', *Mankind*, 10 (1975), 24–36.

37 Denham et al., 'New evidence and interpretations'; Haberle et al., 'Palaeoenvironments of Kuk Swamp'; M. Leahy, 'The Central Highlands of New Guinea', *Geographical Journal*, 87 (1936), 229–62; J.M.K. Sniderman et al., 'A late Holocene palaeoecological record from Ambra Crater in the highlands of Papua New Guinea and implications for agricultural history', *The Holocene*, 19 (2009), 449–58.

38 Denham et al., 'Origins of agriculture at Kuk Swamp'; Denham et al., 'New evidence and interpretations'; Haberle et al., 'Palaeoenvironments of Kuk Swamp'.

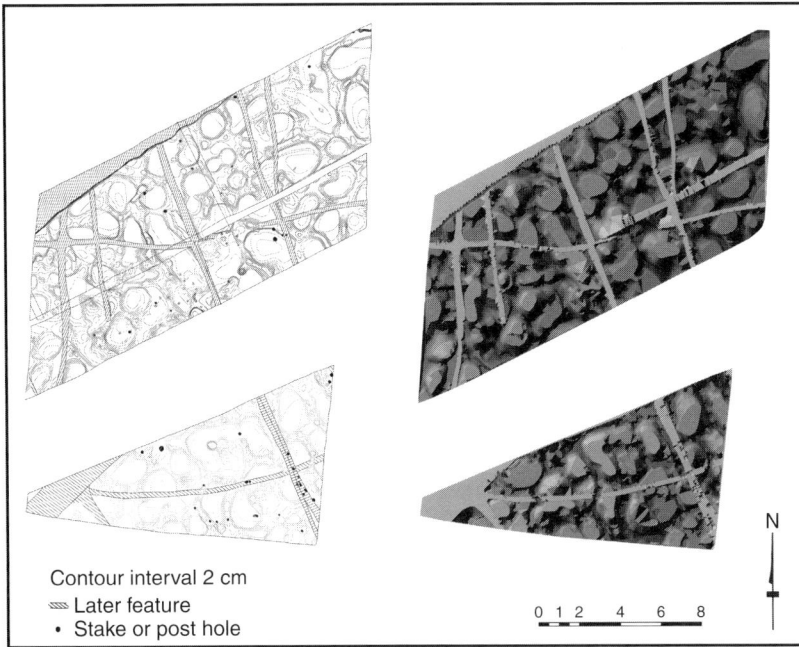

Figure 17.7 Digital representation of the preserved bases of mounds dating to *c.* 7,000–6,400 years ago.

Residues on stone tools recovered from features and soil/sediment associated with the mounds suggest continued exploitation of tuberous plants, including taro.[39] Consequently, the multidisciplinary evidence demonstrates cultivation of bananas, and presumably other plants, in specially prepared plots containing mounds. People would have been heavily reliant upon these cultivated plots because the surrounding landscape was degraded to anthropic grasslands maintained by burning; in other words, to a landscape with limited edible plant resources.

Golson originally considered the mounds to have enabled the cultivation of plants with different edaphic requirements: water-tolerant plants (such as taro) in the wetter areas between mounds, and water-intolerant plants (such as sugarcane, *Saccharum* spp.) on the drier raised islands. However, the diatom assemblages in the fills of features between mounds are suggestive

39 Fullagar et al., 'Early and mid-Holocene processing of taro'.

of damp conditions rather than standing water. Mounds were probably generalized innovations for cultivation in the colder altitudes of the highlands; namely, they provided slightly warmer growth environments for plants due to cold air drainage over and around the mound, as well as composting within its interior.[40] The innovation could have been adapted to wetland margins, as Golson envisaged, although it plausibly occurred on dryland slopes across the lower floor of the upper Wahgi valley around the same time, or earlier. Mound cultivation extended into wetlands when local conditions permitted, hence the variable dates for archaeological remains at Kuk, Mugumamp, and Warrawau.[41] Archaeological evidence of mounds is better preserved in the wetlands, where burial followed the return of wetter conditions and abandonment. On drier slopes any evidence has been destroyed through subsequent gardening, soil formation, and erosion.

## The advent of ditches, c. 4,500–4,000 years ago

Around 4,500–4,000 years ago, people began to construct ditches to drain Kuk and other wetlands (Figures 17.6g–h and 17.8). The earliest ditches at Kuk date to at least 4,000 years ago, and a wooden hastate-shaped spade was collected from a ditch at Tambul (2,170 m) and radiocarbon dated to c. 4,600–4,100 years ago.[42] Most drainage networks documented archaeologically are rectilinear and comprise straight ditches articulating at right angles, although curvilinear forms also occur.[43] The palaeosurfaces and palaeosols associated with these former field systems, especially the earlier ones, have mostly been reworked during subsequent periods of drainage and cultivation.

40 E. Waddell, *The Mound Builders: Agricultural Practices, Environment and Society in the Central Highlands of New Guinea* (Seattle: University of Washington Press, 1972).

41 Denham, 'Archaeological evidence for mid-Holocene agriculture'; J. Golson, 'Gourds in New Guinea, Asia and the Pacific', in S. Bedford et al. (eds.), *Fifty Years in the Field: Essays in Honour and Celebration of Richard Shutler Jr.'s Archaeological Career*, Monograph 25 (Auckland: New Zealand Archaeological Association, 2002), 69–78; E.C. Harris and P.J. Hughes, 'An early agricultural system at Mugumamp Ridge, Western Highlands province, Papua New Guinea', *Mankind*, 11 (1978), 437–45.

42 T.P. Denham, 'Agricultural origins and the emergence of rectilinear ditch networks in the highlands of New Guinea', in Pawley et al. (eds.), *Papuan Pasts*, 329–61; Denham et al., 'Origins of agriculture at Kuk Swamp'; Denham et al., 'Reading early agriculture at Kuk'; J. Golson, 'The Tambul spade', in H. Levine and A. Ploeg (eds.), *Work in Progress: Essays in New Guinea Highlands Ethnography in Honour of Paula Brown Glick* (Oxford: Peter Lang, 1997), 142–71.

43 Denham, 'Agricultural origins and the emergence of rectilinear ditch networks'; Golson, 'No room at the top'.

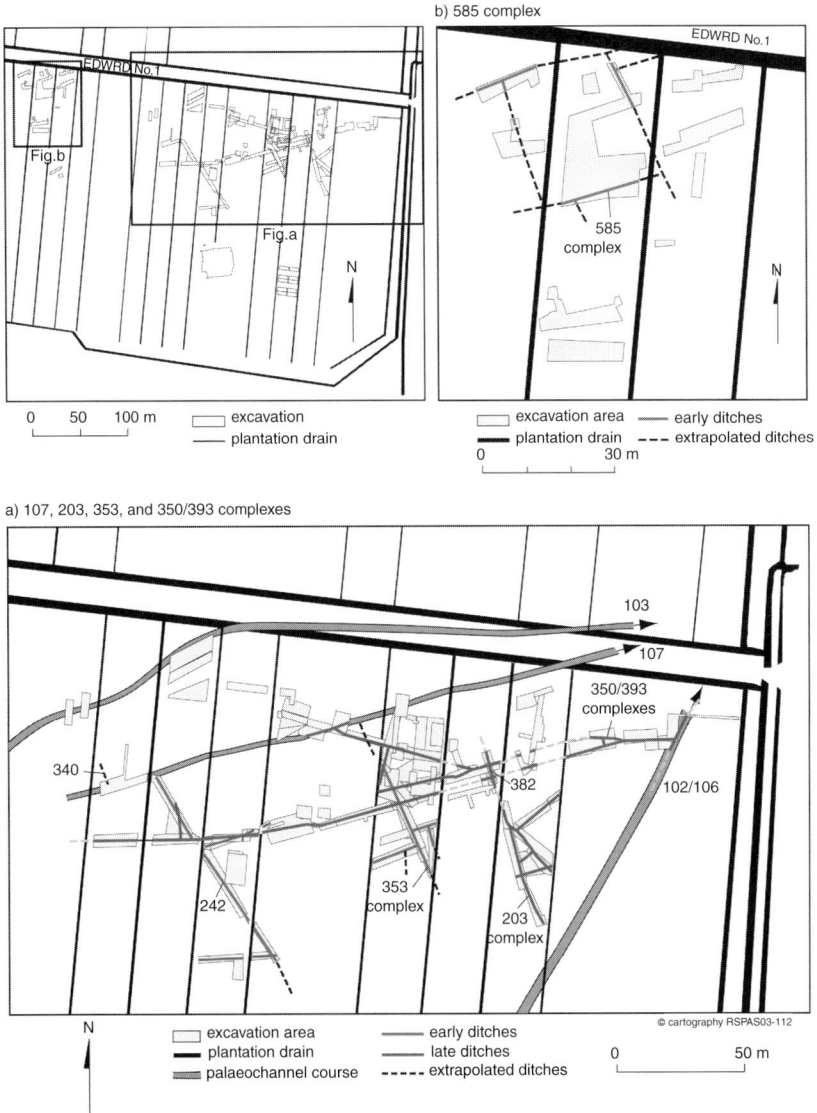

Figure 17.8 Plans of the oldest ditch networks exposed in excavation at Kuk: 'early' ditches date to c. 4,400–4,000 years ago, and 'late' ditches date to c. 3,000–2,500 years ago.

Ditches and ditch networks at Kuk have been grouped into a series of phases based on stratigraphic and tephro-chronological correlations;[44] the fills of only a few features have been radiocarbon dated. Although specific ditches and ditch networks show periods of use, abandonment, and in some cases re-use, a reliable and detailed chronology for drainage and cultivation has not yet been constructed for Kuk as a whole. The wetland was abandoned due to warfare and uncultivated at the time gold prospectors entered the valley in 1933,[45] and presumably there were periods of abandonment in the past. However, it has proven difficult to disentangle spatially variable use at different temporal scales; namely, to differentiate longer periods of abandonment possibly across the whole wetland from shorter periods of abandonment to fallow within a mosaic of plots that are in various stages of cultivation across the wetland.

Despite these chronological uncertainties, ditches did become more widespread within the highlands from c. 2,750–2,150 years ago, given synchronous occurrence at Kuk, Haeapugua, Kana, and Warrawau then, and subsequently at numerous sites. Around that time, wooden digging sticks and spades, stone artefacts, and archaeobotanical remains become more common. These include remains of wax gourd (*Benincasa hispida*) at Kana.[46]

---

44 T.P. Bayliss-Smith, 'The meaning of ditches: interpreting the archaeological record using insights from ethnography', in Denham et al. (eds.), *Rethinking Agriculture*, 126–48; T.P. Bayliss-Smith and J. Golson, 'Wetland agriculture in New Guinea highlands prehistory', in B. Coles (ed.), *The Wetland Revolution in Prehistory* (Exeter: Prehistoric Society and Wetland Archaeological Research Project, 1992), 15–27; T.P. Bayliss-Smith and J. Golson, 'A Colocasian revolution in the New Guinea highlands? Insights from phase 4 at Kuk', *Archaeology in Oceania*, 27 (1992), 1–21; T.P. Bayliss-Smith and J. Golson, 'The meaning of ditches: deconstructing the social landscapes of drainage in New Guinea, Kuk, phase 4', in C. Gosden and J. Hather (eds.), *The Prehistory of Food: Appetites for Change* (London: Routledge, 1999), 199–231; T.P. Bayliss-Smith et al., 'Archaeological evidence for the Ipomoean revolution at Kuk Swamp, Papua New Guinea', in C. Ballard et al. (eds.), *The Sweet Potato in Oceania: A Reappraisal* (University of Sydney, 2005), 109–20; S. Coulter et al., 'The geochemical characterisation and correlation of locally distributed late Holocene tephras layers at Ambra Crater and Kuk Swamp, Papua New Guinea', *Geological Journal*, 44 (2009), 568–92; Golson, 'Ipomoean revolution revisited', and 'No room at the top'; J. Golson et al. (eds.), *10,000 Years of Gardening at Kuk* (Canberra: ANU E Press, forthcoming).

45 J. Ketan, *An Ethnohistory of Kuk* (Port Moresby: National Research Institute, 1998).

46 P. Matthews, 'Identification of *Benincasa hispida* (wax gourd) from the Kanae archaeological site, Western Highlands province, Papua New Guinea', *Archaeology in Oceania*, 38 (2003), 186–91; J. Muke and H. Mandui, 'In the shadows of Kuk: evidence for prehistoric agriculture at Kana, Wahgi valley, Papua New Guinea', *Archaeology in Oceania*, 38 (2003), 177–85; see also Golson et al., 'Note on carbon dates'.

## Ongoing elaborations

Evidence for drainage and cultivation at Kuk and other wetlands includes sequential agronomic innovations that continue to the present, such as *Casuarina* tree-fallowing and the introduction and adoption of the pig (*Sus scrofa*) and sweet potato (*Ipomoea batatas*). Although some innovations have had only minor impacts, others have transformed agriculture as well as highland societies.

The planting of *Casuarina* in fallow land fixes nitrogen and increases carbon in the soil, thereby enriching it for subsequent cultivation.[47] Seedlings of *Casuarina oligodon* are transplanted into plots near the end of the cropping cycle and left to grow for eight to twelve years before being felled, ring-barked, or pollarded for firewood and timber. Archaeobotanical evidence suggests *Casuarina* tree-fallowing was practised at Kuk within the last 1,000 years,[48] with palaeoecological evidence suggestive of slightly earlier development elsewhere in the highlands.[49] Today, *Casuarina* tree-fallowing is still only practised in a restricted geographic area of the highlands.

Pigs are an Asian domesticate thought to have been introduced to New Guinea within the last 3,500 years; they were uncommon in the highlands until the last 1,500 years.[50] Sweet potato is a South American domesticate introduced to the Pacific by Polynesians, although generally considered a post-Magellan introduction to New Guinea.[51] In the early twentieth century highland societies were heavily reliant on sweet potato cultivation for carbo-hydrate, although they were only variably dependent upon pig rearing for protein. Sweet potato is considered to have greatly increased the productivity of highland agricultural systems previously based on taro, bananas, and some yams. Pig rearing could feasibly have alleviated protein deficiency in many highland societies, although pigs were primarily used as valuables in exchange networks and for feasting rather than for regular daily consumption. Ethnographically observed 'big-men' societies in the highlands are

47 R.M. Bourke and B. Allen, 'Village food production systems', in Bourke and Harwood (eds.), *Food and Agriculture in Papua New Guinea*, 193–269 (245–7).

48 Denham, 'Kuk morass'; Powell, 'Plant resources'.

49 S.G. Haberle, 'Prehistoric human impact on rainforest biodiversity in highland New Guinea', *Philosophical Transactions of the Royal Society B*, 362 (2007), 219–28.

50 A. Sutton et al., 'Archaeozoological records for the highlands of New Guinea: a review of current evidence', *Australian Archaeology*, 69 (2009), 41–58.

51 Golson, 'No room at the top'; see C. Roullier et al., 'Historical collections reveal patterns of diffusion of sweet potato in Oceania obscured by modern plant movements and recombination', *Proceedings of the National Academy of Sciences*, 110 (2013), 2205–10.

thought to postdate the introduction and widespread adoption of intensive sweet potato cultivation and pig rearing.

## Implications of the Kuk research

The multidisciplinary evidence from Kuk has established the New Guinea region as an early centre of agricultural development and plant domestication. This research has led to the development of a contingent approach to early agriculture; namely, interpretations of early agriculture need to be developed in terms of the practices and resources in different regions of the world, rather than according to a 'one size fits all' template. Such an approach has more general applicability and can assist with characterizing current chronological and geographic disparities between the evidence for plant domestication and cultivation in some regions of the wet tropics, such as the lowland neotropics.[52]

The research at Kuk also has far-reaching implications for understanding the long-term history of regions beyond New Guinea. Foremost among these, the cultivation of bananas at Kuk c. 7,000–6,400 years ago has provided a geographic and chronological anchor for genetic and phytogeographic interpretations of the domestication and dispersal of most significant cultivar groups of this plant.[53] These interpretations track west from New Guinea, around the Indian Ocean, and terminate in West Africa over 2,000 years ago.[54] Similar geodomestication pathways have yet to be reconstructed for other New Guinea domesticates, including breadfruit (*Artocarpus altilis*), sago (*Metroxylon sagu*), sugarcane (*Saccharum officinarum*), and some taro and yam varieties.

The westward dispersal of vegetatively propagated plants from New Guinea, such as those listed above, indicates dispersal under forms of cultivation that are currently undocumented archaeologically.[55] Plants dispersed

---

52 D.R. Piperno and D.M. Pearsall, *The Origins of Agriculture in the Lowland Neotropics* (San Diego: Academic Press, 1998).

53 Perrier et al., 'Multidisciplinary perspectives on banana'.

54 T.P. Denham and M. Donohue, 'Pre-Austronesian dispersal of banana cultivars west from New Guinea: linguistic relics from eastern Indonesia', *Archaeology in Oceania*, 44 (2009), 18–28; H. Rangan et al., 'Environmental history of botanical exchanges in the Indian Ocean world', *Environment and History*, 18 (2012), 311–42; E. De Langhe, 'The establishment of traditional plantain cultivation in the African rain forest: a working hypothesis', in Denham et al. (eds.), *Rethinking Agriculture*, 361–70.

55 T.P. Denham, 'From domestication histories to regional prehistory: using plants to re-evaluate early and mid-Holocene interaction between New Guinea and Southeast Asia', *Food and History*, 8 (2010), 3–22.

across a mosaic of landscapes in island Southeast Asia that included forms of cultivation. The exact timing and cultural associations of these dispersals are uncertain, as are the forms of agriculture with which they are associated. The eastward dispersal of these plants from New Guinea and the forms of agriculture with which they are associated are clearer, because they are associated with the colonization of Remote Oceania. However, the historical processes through which plant domesticates from New Guinea became important subsistence and commercial crops across vast regions of the wet tropics in the Old World, as well as parts of the New World, remain to be elicited.

Plants have also dispersed eastwards from Southeast Asia and been incorporated into cultivation practices in the highlands of New Guinea in the distant past. The wax gourd and probably the bottle gourd were grown in the highlands at least 2,000 years ago. Additionally, in the mid twentieth century, kudzu (*Pueraria lobata*), an Asian domesticate, was reported to be grown in parts of the highlands.[56] Consequently, plant movements into and out of the New Guinea region are nothing new. Similar processes have been ongoing for millennia. These plant movements have the potential to shed considerable light on inter-regional connections during the Holocene, as well as subsequent transformations in cultivation practices and social life.

## Further reading

Allen, J. 'Prehistoric agricultural systems in the Wahgi valley – a further note.' *Mankind*, 7 (1970), 177–83.

Bayliss-Smith, T.P. 'The meaning of ditches: interpreting the archaeological record using insights from ethnography.' In T.P. Denham, J. Iriarte, and L. Vrydaghs (eds.), *Rethinking Agriculture: Archaeological and Ethnoarchaeological Perspectives*. Walnut Creek: Left Coast Press, 2007. 126–48.

'People–plant interactions in the New Guinea highlands: agricultural hearthland or horticultural backwater?' In D.R. Harris (ed.), *The Origins and Spread of Agriculture and Pastoralism in Eurasia*. London: UCL Press, 1996. 499–552.

Bourke, R.M. and T. Harwood (eds.). *Food and Agriculture in Papua New Guinea*. Canberra: ANU E Press, 2009.

Brookfield, H.C. 'The ecology of highland settlement: some suggestions.' *American Anthropologist*, 66 (1964), 20–38.

Christensen, O.A. 'Hunters and horticulturalists: a preliminary report of the 1972–4 excavations in the Manim valley, Papua New Guinea.' *Mankind*, 10 (1975), 24–36.

56 J.B. Watson, '*Pueraria*: names and traditions of a lesser crop of the Central Highlands, New Guinea', *Ethnology*, 3 (1968), 1–5.

Denham, T.P. 'Agricultural origins and the emergence of rectilinear ditch networks in the highlands of New Guinea.' In A. Pawley, R. Attenborough, J. Golson, and R. Hide (eds.), *Papuan Pasts: Cultural, Linguistic and Biological Histories of Papuan-Speaking Peoples*. Canberra: Pacific Linguistics, 2005. 329–61.

'Archaeological evidence for mid-Holocene agriculture in the interior of Papua New Guinea: a critical review.' *Archaeology in Oceania*, 38 (2003), 159–76.

'Early agriculture and plant domestication in New Guinea and island Southeast Asia.' *Current Anthropology*, 52, Supplement 4 (2011), S379–95.

'Early to mid-Holocene plant exploitation in New Guinea: towards a contingent interpretation of agriculture.' In T.P. Denham, J. Iriarte, and L. Vrydaghs (eds.), *Rethinking Agriculture: Archaeological and Ethnoarchaeological Perspectives*. Walnut Creek: Left Coast Press, 2007. 78–108.

'Envisaging early agriculture in the highlands of New Guinea: landscapes, plants and practices.' *World Archaeology*, 37 (2005), 290–306.

'The Kuk morass: multi-disciplinary investigations of early to mid Holocene plant exploitation at Kuk Swamp, Wahgi valley, Papua New Guinea.' Unpublished PhD thesis (Canberra: Australian National University, 2003).

Denham, T.P. and H. Barton. 'The emergence of agriculture in New Guinea: continuity from pre-existing foraging practices.' In D.J. Kennett and B. Winterhalder (eds.), *Behavioral Ecology and the Transition to Agriculture*. Berkeley: University of California Press, 2006. 237–64.

Denham, T.P., J. Golson, and P.J. Hughes. 'Reading early agriculture at Kuk (phases 1–3), Wahgi valley, Papua New Guinea: the wetland archaeological features.' *Proceedings of the Prehistoric Society*, 70 (2004), 259–98.

Denham, T.P. and S.G. Haberle. 'Agricultural emergence and transformation in the upper Wahgi valley during the Holocene: theory, method and practice.' *The Holocene*, 18 (2008), 499–514.

Denham, T.P., S.G. Haberle, and C. Lentfer. 'New evidence and interpretations for early agriculture in highland New Guinea.' *Antiquity*, 78 (2004), 839–57.

Denham, T.P., S.G. Haberle, C. Lentfer, et al. 'Origins of agriculture at Kuk Swamp in the highlands of New Guinea.' *Science*, 301 (2003), 189–93.

Fullagar, R., J. Field, T.P. Denham, and C. Lentfer. 'Early and mid-Holocene processing of taro (*Colocasia esculenta*) and yam (*Dioscorea* sp.) at Kuk Swamp in the highlands of Papua New Guinea.' *Journal of Archaeological Science*, 33 (2006), 595–614.

Golson, J. 'The Ipomoean revolution revisited: society and sweet potato in the upper Wahgi valley.' In A. Strathern (ed.), *Inequality in New Guinea Highland Societies*. Cambridge University Press, 1982. 109–36.

'The New Guinea highlands on the eve of agriculture.' *Bulletin of the Indo-Pacific Prehistory Association*, 11 (1991), 82–91.

'No room at the top: agricultural intensification in the New Guinea highlands.' In J. Allen, J. Golson, and R. Jones (eds.), *Sunda and Sahul: Prehistoric Studies in Southeast Asia, Melanesia and Australia*. New York and London: Academic Press, 1977. 601–38.

'Unravelling the story of early plant exploitation in highland Papua New Guinea.' In T.P. Denham, J. Iriarte, and L. Vrydaghs (eds.), *Rethinking Agriculture: Archaeological and Ethnoarchaeological Perspectives*. Walnut Creek, CA: Left Coast Press, 2007. 109–25.

Golson, J., T.P. Denham, P.J. Hughes, P. Swadling, and J. Muke (eds.). *10,000 Years of Gardening at Kuk*. Canberra: ANU E Press, forthcoming.

Golson, J. and P.J. Hughes. 'The appearance of plant and animal domestication in New Guinea.' *Journal de la Société des Océanistes*, 36 (1980), 294–303.

Groube, L. 'The taming of the rainforests: a model for late Pleistocene forest exploitation in New Guinea.' In D.R. Harris and G.C. Hillman (eds.), *Foraging and Farming: The Evolution of Plant Exploitation*. London: Unwin Hyman, 1989. 292–304.

Lebot, V. 'Biomolecular evidence for plant domestication in Sahul.' *Genetic Resources and Crop Evolution*, 46 (1999), 619–28.

Powell, J.M. 'The history of plant use and man's impact on the vegetation.' In J.L. Gressitt (ed.), *Biogeography and Ecology of New Guinea*, vol. 1. The Hague: Junk, 1982. 207–27.

'Plant resources and palaeobotanical evidence for plant use in the Papua New Guinea highlands.' *Archaeology in Oceania*, 17 (1982), 28–37.

Powell, J.M., A. Kulunga, R. Moge, et al. *Agricultural Traditions in the Mount Hagen Area*. Department of Geography Occasional Paper 12. Port Moresby: University of Papua New Guinea, 1976.

Yen, D.E. 'The domestication of environment.' In D.R. Harris and G.C. Hillman (eds.), *Foraging and Farming: The Evolution of Plant Exploitation*. London: Unwin Hyman, 1989. 55–75.

'The origins of Oceanic agriculture.' *Archaeology and Physical Anthropology in Oceania*, 8 (1973), 68–85.

# 18

# Early agriculture in sub-Saharan Africa
## to *c.* 500 CE

PAUL J. LANE

This chapter provides a review of the current state of knowledge of early agriculture in sub-Saharan Africa from its inception in different regions to *c.* 500 CE. 'Agriculture' is used here in its broadest sense to imply any and all forms of food production, including subsistence systems largely reliant on the cultivation of crops (glossed here as 'farming', although this took many forms, from shifting cultivation to horticulture and even forest gardening), those that rely primarily on tending livestock (referred to here as either 'herding' or 'pastoralism'), and those that entail a broadly balanced combination of farming and herding (termed 'agropastoralism' here). As the following discussion highlights, such broad categories mask considerable diversity and tend to simplify often quite complex systems of food production. Arboriculture, for example – as perhaps best indicated by the exploitation of oil palm in and at the margins of the rainforest belt but also evident in the savanna parklands of West Africa and in parts of the dry *nyika* hinterland of the East African coast – provided an important component of many agricultural systems from quite an early date.

Co-existence of different food production systems in the same landscape often enhanced food security and risk-reduction strategies. Their co-existence also required mediation by different groups of human participants through a complex of social relations and exchange mechanisms. The spread of agriculture throughout sub-Saharan Africa also entailed considerable population movement, although perhaps more often in the form of incremental spread than actual intentional migration, due in no small part to the uneven distribution of soils, vegetation complexes, and rainfall regimes that were suited to either crop cultivation or livestock herding or some combination of these with foraging, fishing, and hunting. The farming and herding communities that moved into new areas brought with them their own social and material practices and had their own languages, all of which would have diverged from those among the pre-existing autochthonous hunter-fisher-forager populations that already inhabited these areas, thereby creating quite diverse ethnolinguistic mosaics and social landscapes. That both immigrant and autochthonous populations interacted, exchanged goods and services, incorporated elements of each other's practices and beliefs, and also inter-married, is well attested by linguistic and genetic histories and the material archaeological record. That at times these relationships and interactions were fraught with tension and even hostility also seems probable, and can perhaps be inferred from elements of the material record – especially where traces of physical violence have survived, quite literally, embodied and embedded in human remains. It is also worth bearing in mind that even though different agricultural systems were well established across most of sub-Saharan Africa by *c.* 500 CE, and even more so by the end of the first millennium CE, there remained many vibrant hunter-gatherer populations from the rainforest to the Kalahari and from West to East Africa for centuries afterwards, such that their living descendants are still found in many parts of the continent to this day.

With a few notable exceptions, the nature and significance of these inter-actions have only relatively recently become a feature of archaeological research. Moreover, because of the common problems of equifinality that often limit interpretation of archaeological records, determining their precise nature at different times and in different places in the past remains quite challenging methodologically, analytically, and even in theoretical terms. Equally hard to define, perhaps even more so, are the processes of domes-tication, how and why it occurred in different localities, what mechanisms were involved, and how it may be identified from archaeological and palaeoecological traces.

## Beginnings of food production

Pastoralism was the earliest form of food production in sub-Saharan Africa, developing first in North Africa *c.* 8,000 years ago,[1] and gradually spreading southwards during the early to mid-Holocene while rainfall across the Sahara was significantly higher than it is today. Two consequences of these higher rainfall regimes were the presence of numerous sources of permanent surface

---

[1] A. Gautier, 'Animal domestication in North Africa', in M. Bollig et al. (eds.), *Aridity, Change and Conflict in Africa: Proceedings of an International ACACIA Conference held at Königswinter, Germany, October 1–3, 2003* (Köln: Heinrich-Barth-Institut, 2007), 75–89.

water, and comparatively lush savanna-like vegetation, providing ideal conditions for groups of mobile, cattle-centred, ceramic-using societies. By the fifth millennium BCE these were present across Chad and areas further east, where they encountered groups of complex hunter-gatherer-fishers, many of which were also ceramic-using, in the western Sahara.[2] By the late fifth to early fourth millennium BCE cattle-keeping societies had spread to the southern edges of the western Sahara, as attested by finds from Adrar Bous in the Ténéré desert of Niger (Map 18.1).[3] With the onset of drier conditions after *c.* 2500 BCE linked to changes in the position of the intertropical convergence zone, groups began moving southwards, especially along the better-watered river valleys and drainage systems, which had become, with the increasing aridity and reduction in swampy conditions that favoured malaria- and trypanosomiasis-bearing vectors, more hospitable to pastoralists.

Overall, the initial food-producing societies practised a broad spectrum economy, but to varying degrees, as signalled by the different proportions of wild to domestic taxa, the relative abundance of different species, and variety of fish represented in faunal assemblages at different sites. These indicate that domesticated cattle and small stock were present from the mid third millennium BCE in the Tilemsi valley (Figure 18.1), some 80–85 km north of Gao, Mali; from around 2200 BCE in the eastern inland Niger delta, Mali, at Windé Koroji Ouest; and from *c.* 1600 BCE at Kobadi and Kolima Sud.[4] Domestic livestock are also present at several pioneer settlements along the Tichitt-Oulata-Néma escarpment in Mauritania by *c.* 2200 BCE (see Chapter 19). In the lower Tilemsi valley, although domestic taxa are abundant, wild resources, including water-dependent species, remained important, along with fish and shellfish. At Kobadi, on the other hand, there is evidence for the presence of specialist fishing communities by the early second millennium BCE and a more uniform subsistence repertoire. Further south and east in northern Burkina Faso, sites dated to between 2200 and 1000 BCE, and associated with highly mobile Late Stone Age (LSA) groups, contain some sparse evidence for the cultivation of pearl millet, along with the exploitation

---

2 R. Kuper and S. Kröpelin, 'Climate-controlled Holocene occupation in the Sahara: motor of Africa's evolution', *Science*, 313 (2006), 803–7.

3 J.D. Clark and D. Gifford-Gonzalez (eds.), *Adrar Bous: Archaeology of a Central Saharan Granitic Ring Complex in Niger* (Tervuren: Royal Museum for Central Africa, 2008).

4 K.C. MacDonald and R.H. MacDonald, 'The origins and development of domesticated animals in arid West Africa', in R.M. Blench and K.C. MacDonald (eds.), *The Origins and Development of African Livestock: Archaeology, Genetics, Linguistics and Ethnography* (London: UCL Press, 2000), 127–62; K. Manning, 'A developmental history of West African agriculture', in P. Allsworth-Jones (ed.), *West African Archaeology: New Developments, New Perspectives* (Oxford: Archaeopress, 2010), 43–52.

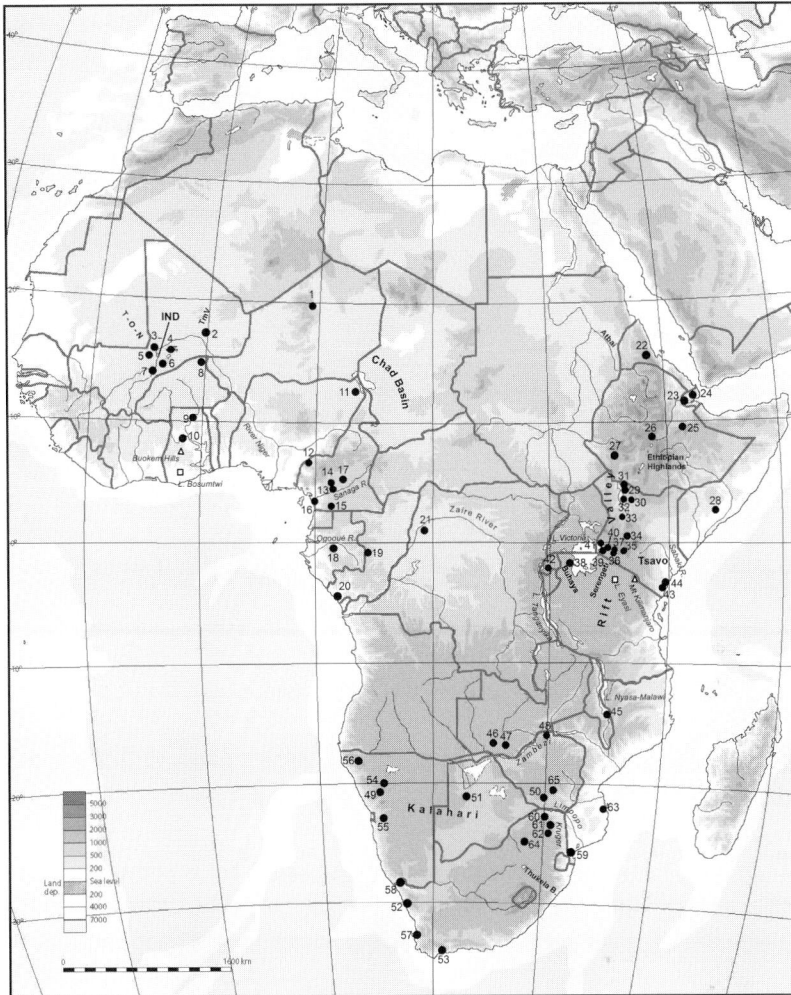

Map 18.1  1. Adrar Bous; 2. Korkorichinikat; 3. Windé Koroji Ouest; 4. Windé Koroji Ouest; 5. Kobadi; 6. Kolima Sud; 7. Ti-N Akof; 8. Laga Oda; 9. Asa Koma; 10. FeJx3; 11. Gogoshiis Qabe; 12. Handoga; 13. Asmara; 14. Kumali; 15. Dongodien; 16. North Horr; 17. Ilert; 18. Jarigole; 19. Lokori; 20. Ol Ngoroi; 21. Enkapune ya Muto; 22. Birimi; 23. K6; 24. Jenne-jeno; 25. Zilum; 26. Ngamuriak; 27. Sugenya; 28. KM2 & 3; 29. Gogo Falls; 30. Wadh Lang'o; 31. Usenge 3; 32. Kabusanze; 33. Mgombani; 34. Panga ya Saidi; 35. Shum Laka; 36. Oliga; 37. Nkang; 38. Abang Minko; 39. Bwambé-Sommet; 40. Nanga Eboko; 41. Toubé 1; 42. Abéké; 43. Tchissinga West; 44. Leopard Cave; 45. Bambata Cave; 46. Toteng; 47. Spoegrivier; 48. Blombos Cave; 49. Geduld; 50. Mirabib; 51. Orunwange 95/1; 52. Kasteelberg Hill; 53. Jakkalsberg; 54. Situmpa; 55. Matola; 56. Happy Rest; 57. Klein Africa; 58. Silver Leaves; 59. Nkope Hill; 60. Kalundu; 61. Kadzi; 62. Chibuene; 63. Broederstroom; 64. Mabveni, Zimbabwe; IND = Inland Niger Delta sites.

475

Figure 18.1  Cattle burial from basal levels at Karkarichinkat Nord, Mali, *c.* 2600 BCE.

of a range of wild fruits (as at the site of Tin-Akof) from as early as *c.* 1800 BCE,[5] but lack direct evidence for the presence of domesticated livestock until the start of the Christian era.[6]

The arrival of these groups in the West African Sahel is attested archaeologically by the presence of distinctive bifacially retouched projectile points broadly the same as examples found widely distributed across the Sahara.[7] In places, these stone points are associated with distinctive geometrically decorated ceramics similar to types from broadly contemporary sites in the eastern and south-central Sahara. Ultimately, three distinct material culture traditions emerged, as reflected in the variations between ceramic and stone-tool assemblages, although they have overlapping geographic distributions. These are the Kobadi tradition centred on the Azawad, Mema, and Gourma regions; the Tichitt tradition present along the Tichitt-Oulata-Néma escarpment and in

5  K. Neumann et al., 'Early food production in the Sahel of Burkina Faso', *Berichte des Sonderforschungsbereichs*, 268 (2000), 327–34.

6  P. Breunig, 'Pathways to food production in the Sahel', in P. Mitchell and P.J. Lane (eds.), *The Oxford Handbook of African Archaeology* (Oxford University Press, 2013), 555–70.

7  Ibid.

the Mema; and the Windé Koroji (or Tilemsi) tradition present in Tilemsi and the Gourma.

The West African Sahel has also long been known as a locus of the domestication of pearl millet (*Pennisetum glaucum*). Based on the distribution of its wild ancestor (*P. glaucum violaceum*), Harlan argued that in contrast to the domestication of Southwest Asian cereals such as emmer, einkorn, and barley, it is unlikely that initial domestication of African cereals such as pearl millet and sorghum was restricted to a single, primary centre, and instead there were most likely several independent episodes of domestication of pearl millet across the West African Sahel.[8] This has been confirmed by more recent research. Currently, the oldest finds of millet in this region come from a sample of excavated sites in the Karkarichinkat region of the lower Tilemsi valley, northern Mali, where they have been dated to between *c.* 2600 and 2000 BCE (Figure 18.2).[9] Within five hundred years or so of these initial occurrences, the cultivation of pearl millet was widespread across the Sahel, with well-dated evidence, in the form of actual plant remains or crop impressions on pottery, now known from various sites. These include several sites in the Dhar Néma, Mauritania, by *c.* 1700 BCE, along with a number of other sites in the Dhar Tichitt and Dhar Walata, and Ounjougou (Bandiagara escarpment, Mali), by *c.* 1700–1500 BCE. The numerous grinding stones found at certain sites, such as those in Dhar Néma, also highlight the significance of grains in local diets, although not all of these need have been morphologically 'domestic' species. Towards the close of the second millennium BCE, pearl millet was also being cultivated quite widely in northeastern Nigeria in the Chad basin.[10]

As in the West African Sahel, livestock herding, particularly cattle, was practised in northeastern Africa somewhat earlier than crop cultivation, as attested at the Laga Oda rock shelter in the Ethiopian highlands and the open-air site of Asa Koma near Lake Abhé, Djibouti, both dating to around 2000 BCE.[11] Other early finds are known from various third- and second-millennium BCE Sudanese Atabi sites near the modern-day border with

8  J. Harlan, 'Agricultural origins: centers and non-centers', *Science*, 174 (1971), 468–74.

9  K. Manning et al., '4500-year-old domesticated pearl millet (*Pennisetum glaucum*) from the Tilemsi valley, Mali: new insights into an alternative cereal domestication pathway', *Journal of Archaeological Science*, 38 (2011), 312–22.

10  S. Kahlheber and K. Neumann, 'The development of plant cultivation in semi-arid West Africa', in T.P. Denham et al. (eds.), *Rethinking Agriculture: Archaeological and Ethnoarchaeological Perspectives* (Walnut Creek, CA: Left Coast Press, 2007), 320–45.

11  M. Curtis, 'Archaeological evidence for the emergence of food production in the Horn of Africa', in Mitchell and Lane (eds.), *Oxford Handbook of African Archaeology*, 567–80.

Figure 18.2 SEM image of the domestic pearl millet rachis and involucre from Er Neg, lower Tilemsi valley, Mali, *c.* 2000 BCE.

Eritrea, many of which also include caprine remains; site FeJx 3 on Lake Besaka in the Ethiopian Rift Valley and Gobedra, Ethiopia, both date to *c.* 1500–500 BCE; and the Gogoshiis Qabe rock shelter, Somalia, dates to between 2300 and 1000 BCE.[12] At both Asa Koma and Laga Oda, the cattle remains were associated with large assemblages of wild fauna (and freshwater fish in the case of Asa Koma), and material culture assemblages typical of earlier foraging populations, suggesting both sites represent the beginnings of localized adoption of food production by autochthonous groups. The same seems to be the case at the site of Handoga (Djibouti), where the earliest cattle remains, dating to the second millennium BCE, made up a very tiny proportion of the overall faunal assemblage, which was dominated by wild terrestrial fauna and fish.[13] Evidence for such continuities was largely lacking at FeJx 3, and certain material traces suggest that the site was occupied by early immigrant herders or agropastoralists.

12 S. Brandt, 'The upper Pleistocene and early Holocene prehistory of the Horn of Africa', *African Archaeological Review*, 4 (1986), 41–82.
13 H. Grau, 'Handoga: site d'habitat de pasteurs nomades?', *Archeologia Paris*, 159 (1981), 55–9.

In contrast to cattle, on current evidence both sheep and goats were incorporated into food-producing economies rather later, although dates for the first occurrence of caprines are variable. These range from the late second millennium BCE at Gogoshiis Qabe, early to mid first millennium BCE on Ancient Ona tradition sites around Asmara, Eritrea,[14] and *c*. 100 CE at Kumali rock shelter, southwest Ethiopia.[15] The general trend, which has some similarity to that documented for the western Sahel, thus seems to have been an initial introduction of domesticated cattle and their adoption among some pre-existing hunter-gatherer-fishers, followed by a later adoption of small stock and corresponding diminishing contributions of wild species to overall diet and subsistence strategies.

Regarding crop cultivation, the Ethiopian highlands are known to have been a centre of local plant domestication, including the African cereal tef, and enset (a starchy, banana-like tuber), but also coffee (*Coffea arabica*), noog (*Guizotia abyssinica*), probably finger millet, and possibly sorghum. There is little direct evidence for crop cultivation during the second millennium BCE, although there is indirect evidence for the exploitation of indigenous wild grasses from Laga Oda rock shelter contemporary with the herding of domesticated cattle.[16] The domestication of local species may well have derived from the intensification of such practices, and the presence of grinding equipment attests to their processing (Figure 18.3).

Domestic livestock (cattle and caprines) were also present in the Lake Turkana basin, northern Kenya, by *c*. 2200 BCE, associated with at least two new pottery types (Nderit and Ileret). These new material and subsistence traditions are regarded conventionally as marking the commencement of the Pastoral Neolithic. This material occurs in conjunction with a microlithic-based LSA stone tool technology at sites such as Dongodien, North Horr, and Ileret.[17] Obsidian, probably obtained locally, now became the preferred raw material, and this period also witnessed the first appearance of stone bowls made from lava, pumice, and similar 'soft' rocks. In the same general vicinity of northern Kenya, new forms of inhumation burial marked by large stone

14 P.R. Schmidt, 'Variability in Eritrea and the archaeology of the northern Horn during the first millennium BC: subsistence, ritual, and gold production', *African Archaeological Review*, 26 (2009), 305–25.

15 E.A. Hildebrand et al., 'The Holocene archaeology of southwest Ethiopia: new insights from the Kafa Archaeological Project', *African Archaeological Review*, 27 (2010), 255–89.

16 J.D. Clark and G.R. Prince, 'Use-wear in later Stone Age microliths from Laga Oda, Haraghi, Ethiopia, and possible functional interpretations', *Azania*, 13 (1978), 101–10.

17 J. Barthelme, *Fisher-Hunters and Neolithic Pastoralists in East Turkana, Kenya* (Oxford: British Archaeological Reports, 1985).

Figure 18.3 *In situ* andesite grinding stone associated with carbonized barley seeds (in burned soil and charcoal below) from the Ancient Ona Culture site of Ona Gudo, Asmara plateau, Eritrea, *c.* 800–400 BCE.

monoliths, as at Jarigole and Lokori, similarly appear between *c.* 3000 and 2000 BCE (Figure 18.4).[18] Although none of the known examples are directly associated with settlements, one possible interpretation of these sites is that they functioned as 'gathering places' for various ritual practices aimed at reinforcing social networks between different mobile and possibly widely dispersed communities.

These changes in the archaeological record support the hypothesis of population migration into the Lake Turkana basin and the case for these newcomers bringing with them livestock (domesticated outside the region) and new ways of exploiting the landscape. The available historical linguistic

18 K.M. Grillo and E.A. Hildebrand, 'The context of early megalithic architecture in eastern Africa: the Turkana basin, *c.* 5000–4000 BP', *Azania*, 48 (2012), 193–217.

Figure 18.4 Lothagam West (GeJi10) Pastoral Neolithic pillar site, West Turkana, Kenya.

evidence suggests these migrant communities may have spread in small groups from South Sudan, Ethiopia, and possibly Somalia, and some were speakers of proto-Southern Cushitic languages. The apparent independent evolution in East Africa of the allele associated with lactase persistence some 7,000–3,000 years ago likewise lends support to such arguments, especially as its very rapid spread is consistent with genetic models of population migration.[19] The geographic distribution of various disease vectors, especially tsetse fly, would have constrained initial settlement to certain areas and restricted southward movement until the development of more disease resistant herds and/or new strategies had been adopted for manipulating habitats so as to limit infection.[20] Other factors may well have played a role, however, and it is clear that these pioneer communities interacted with autochthonous LSA hunter-gatherer-fishers.

Further south in the central Rift Valley and eastern highlands of Kenya, the earliest traces of domestic livestock typically first occur in rock shelters associated with LSA hunter-gatherers around *c.* 2500–2000 BCE, as attested at sites such as Ol Ngoroi (Figure 18.5) on the Laikipia plateau and Enkapune

Figure 18.5 Ol Ngoroi rock shelter, Lolldaiga hills, Kenya.

19 S.A. Tishkoff et al., 'Convergent adaptation of human lactase persistence in Africa and Europe', *Nature Genetics*, 39 (2006), 31–40.

20 D. Gifford-Gonzalez, 'Animal disease challenges to the emergence of pastoralism in sub-Saharan Africa', *African Archaeological Review*, 18 (2000), 95–139; D.K. Wright, 'Frontier animal husbandry in the Northeast and East African Neolithic: a multiproxy palaeoenvironmental and palaeodemographic study', *Journal of Anthropological Research*, 26 (2011), 213–44.

ya Muto in the central Rift.[21] Domesticated caprines were also present at several sites around Lake Victoria by c. 2400–2150 BCE, although only in small numbers and on sites associated with LSA Kansyore hunter-fisher-gatherers.[22] Further south and east, evidence for the presence of specialized pastoralist economies is documented at several sites in the Tsavo and middle Sabaki River areas of southeast Kenya by c. 1800–1700 BCE;[23] the Maasai Mara, southwestern Kenya, by c. 1200–100 BCE; and in open woodlands and grasslands on the Serengeti plains, the western slopes of Mt Kilimanjaro, and around the Lake Eyasi basin, Tanzania, by the mid to late first millennium BCE.[24]

## Consolidation of food production

Following initial adoption of domesticated plant and animal species, and their integration into pre-existing hunting and gathering subsistence strategies, subsequent millennia witnessed the local domestication of a number of other key crops.

In West Africa these included cowpea (*Vigna unguiculata*) and oil palm (*Elaeis guineensis*), both by c. 1700 BCE, African rice (*Oryza glaberrima*), Bambara groundnut (*Vigna subterranea*), and the baobab tree (*Adansonia digitata*) between c. 1000 and 500 BCE, and fonio (*Digitaria exilis*) by the mid first millennium CE.[25] Around the forest margins, West African yams (*Dioscorea* spp.) were almost certainly domesticated by c. 2000–1500 BCE (and, if using historical linguistic reconstructions as a guide, perhaps significantly earlier),[26] although direct archaeobotanical evidence is scarce. A wide range of other tubers, roots, vines, and leafy greens were also cultivated or otherwise 'managed' on a routine basis, along with several tree species, including *Parkia biglobosa* (locust bean tree, or néré; exploited for its fruit, from which a fermented condiment is made, and its seed pods) and *Vitellaria paradoxa* (shea or karité; although used for firewood and

---

21 P.J. Lane, 'Trajectories of pastoralism in northern and central Kenya: an overview of the archaeological and environmental evidence', in M. Bollig et al. (eds.), *Pastoralism in Africa: Past, Present and Future* (Oxford: Berghahn, 2013), 104–43.

22 P. Lane et al., 'The transition to farming in eastern Africa: new faunal and dating evidence from Wadh Lang'o and Usenge, Kenya', *Antiquity*, 81 (2007), 62–81.

23 Wright, 'Frontier animal husbandry'.

24 M.E. Prendergast, 'Hunters and herders at the periphery: the spread of herding in eastern Africa', in H. Jousse and J. Lesur (eds.), *People and Animals in Holocene Africa: Recent Advances in Archaeozoology* (Frankfurt: Africa Magna, 2011), 43–58.

25 D. Fuller and E.A. Hildebrand, 'Domesticating plants in Africa', in Mitchell and Lane (eds.), *Oxford Handbook of African Archaeology*, 503–21.

26 R.M. Blench, 'Using linguistics to reconstruct African subsistence systems: comparing crop names to trees and livestock', in Denham et al. (eds.), *Rethinking Agriculture*, 408–38.

charcoal, the shea tree is mostly prized for its nuts, which can be processed to produce butter for cooking and cosmetics).

Botanical remains recovered from a number of sites in the West African forest zone likewise indicate a continuing importance of wild resources, including *Digitaria*, hackberry (*Celtis*), incense tree (*Canarium schweinfurthii*), and oil palm (*Elaeis guineensis*). More active husbandry of the latter (for which there is plentiful evidence in the form of charred macro-remains from numerous Kintampo sites, increasing in frequency over time), leading ultimately to its domestication,[27] has also been inferred from sharp increases in its pollen signature and related evidence for forest clearance (as oil palm is shade intolerant, it does not fare well in thick forest) in sediment cores from Lake Bosumtwi, Ghana, around 1500 BCE, and 800 BCE in the Niger delta region. Increased regional aridity owing to climate change during the period *c.* 2500–1400 BCE, which triggered the marked decline in tree cover and corresponding expansion of savanna vegetation referred to as the 'Dahomey Gap',[28] may have also further encouraged the spread of oil palm.

Alongside this evidence for oil palm arboriculture, the cultivation of pearl millet is attested in Kintampo contexts (Figure 18.6) dated to between *c.* 1740 and 1130 BCE at the site of Birimi, northern Ghana.[29] Across the savanna zone, new crops were also added to this repertoire, including locally domesticated species such as cowpea (*Vigna unguiculata*), African rice (*Oryza glaberrima*), fonio (*Digitaria exilis*), and yam (*Dioscorea* sp.). With the exception of cowpea (attested archaeologically from several rock shelters in the Buokem hills, central Ghana, from *c.* 1830–1590 BCE, and also at K6, where it may have been used as animal fodder), the earliest securely dated evidence for these is significantly later. Sorghum, likely domesticated further north and east, was also cultivated in the drier areas, although again direct evidence for its presence is comparatively late (in Senegal, for instance, sorghum is not attested in archaeological contexts until around the BCE/CE transition).[30]

27 A.L. Logan and A.C. D'Andrea, 'Oil palm, arboriculture, and changing subsistence practices during Kintampo times (3600–3200 BP, Ghana)', *Quaternary International*, 247 (2012), 63–71.

28 M.A. Sowunmi, 'The beginnings of agriculture in West Africa: botanical evidence', *Current Anthropology*, 26 (1985), 127–9; U. Salzmann and P. Hoelzmann, 'The Dahomey Gap: an abrupt climatically induced rain forest fragmentation in West Africa during the late Holocene', *The Holocene*, 15 (2005), 190–9.

29 A.C. D'Andrea and J. Casey, 'Pearl millet and Kintampo subsistence', *African Archaeological Review*, 19 (2002), 147–73.

30 A.C. D'Andrea et al., 'Early domesticated cowpea (*Vigna unguiculata*) from central Ghana', *Antiquity*, 81 (2007), 686–98; S. Kahlheber and K. Neumann, 'The development of plant cultivation in semi-arid West Africa', in Denham et al. (eds.), *Rethinking Agriculture*, 320–46.

Figure 18.6 Terracotta 'cigars' from Birimi, Ghana – this artefact form is especially diagnostic of the Kintampo culture.

Regionally, the particular crop and livestock repertoires varied considerably, depending on local ecological conditions and the distribution of the wild ancestors of the key domesticates. As agriculture became more widespread, especially in the savanna regions, local types and hybrids also evolved. Sanga cattle, a crossbreed between local African taurine cattle and South Asian humped zebu (which were present on the continent by at least the mid first millennium CE and possibly earlier), and the breeds of fat-tailed sheep common in East and southern Africa, are perhaps the best-known examples, although many other local breeds of cattle, sheep, and goat are known, among them the various West African shorthorn cattle breeds, including N'Dama, Baoulé, and Somba. Breeds of dwarf sheep and goats are also known, especially in forested zones but also further north. The earliest examples of dwarf goats, dated to the second millennium BCE, come from Kintampo sites in Ghana, with rather more recent occurrences known from sites further north, including Jenne-jeno (Mali) and the Gajiganna phase III site of Zilum (Nigeria).[31] Particular characteristics of many of these dwarf species are their greater tick resistance and tolerance to disease, such as trypanosomiasis and theileriosis, and their ability

---

31 V. Linseele, *Archaeofaunal Remains from the Past 4000 Years in Sahelian West Africa: Domestic Livestock, Subsistence Strategies and Environmental Change* (Oxford: Archaeopress, 2007).

to thrive in drier habitats and withstand recurrent drought. Moreover, the genesis of these local breeds and manipulation of their habitats were critical to the eventual southward spread of livestock across the continent (and hence the 'domestication' of the landscapes they inhabited), and likely explains the timing of the initial introduction of different species into specific regions.[32]

In East Africa after *c.* 1500 BCE, early pastoralist sites tend to become larger in extent and begin to display a remarkable degree of material, economic, and spatial variability. Two broad cultural traditions, known as the Savanna Pastoral Neolithic and Elementeitan, can be discerned partly in terms of material culture differences, settlement locations, and herd management strategies.[33] Ground stone artefacts, including axes, adzes, 'horn straighteners', and stone bowls (Figure 18.7), accompany flaked stone industries, principally on obsidian. In general terms, faunal assemblages from both Elementeitan and Savanna Pastoral Neolithic sites tend to indicate a commitment to cattle and sheep/goat pastoralism among both societies. By *c.* 1000 BCE at least some herding communities, as at Ngamuriak and Sugenya in the Maasai Mara (Kenya), were able to sustain a subsistence pattern dependent almost exclusively upon domestic stock, which may have been facilitated in

Figure 18.7 Example of a Pastoral Neolithic stone bowl, from site GvJh73, central Rift Valley, Kenya.

32 Gifford-Gonzalez, 'Animal disease challenges'.   33 Lane, 'Trajectories of pastoralism'.

part by the emergence of a bimodal rainfall regime around this time. There is, nonetheless, some internal diversity and differing degrees of dependence upon domestic herds, ranging from a generalized pattern of hunting, fishing, gathering, and herding to specialized livestock production, in both traditions.

From *c.* 500 BCE onwards, evidence for early farming communities, which are also associated with the first use of metal in the region, begins to appear in the archaeological record, initially to the west of Lake Victoria in parts of modern-day Rwanda, Burundi, and Uganda, then from *c.* 200 CE to the east of Lake Victoria in western, central, and coastal Kenya, and northern and coastal Tanzania. By 500–700 CE, these farming communities occupied most of East Africa except the arid and semi-arid regions, including the northern and central Rift Valley and adjacent areas further south. Historical linguists believe these communities were also the first speakers of proto-Eastern Bantu (also referred to as 'Mashariki') to have occupied the region, having spread originally from a proto-Bantu 'homeland' in northern Cameroon and southern Nigeria. Archaeologists have sought to classify the ceramics associated with these early farming communities (EFC; also referred to as the Early Iron Age or EIA) principally in terms of formal and stylistic variations. Since at least some of the chronologically later types are found further south and/or east of the earliest dated EFC ceramics, this has tended to reinforce a view that the expansion of EFCs across the region was, principally, as a consequence of population growth and subsequent settlement migration and that, in turn, this provided the primary mechanism by which Eastern Bantu languages and knowledge of metal-working were introduced into southern and east-Central Africa.

As they expanded their geographic range, these early farming communities would have encountered both hunter-gathering (associated with LSA material traditions) and early herding societies (associated with Pastoral Neolithic traditions). The influence of Central Sudanic and Eastern Sahelian speakers on the EFC Mashariki populations during the last millennium BCE is particularly clearly attested by a wide range of Sudanic and Sahelian loanwords in Eastern Bantu languages for livestock, cereals, various economic practices, and certain items of material culture.[34] Equally, exchange and interaction between EFC LSA and Pastoral Neolithic 'groups' can be demonstrated archaeologically at a number of sites.[35]

---

34 C. Ehret, *An African Classical Age: Eastern and Southern Africa in World History, 1000 BC to AD 400* (Charlottesville: University of Virginia Press, 1998), 47–53.
35 P.J. Lane, 'The "moving frontier" and the transition to food production in Kenya', *Azania*, 39 (2004), 243–64.

Figure 18.8 *In situ* Urewe hemispherical bowl and dimple-based pot from site LOL-13, Lolui Island, Uganda.

From an archaeological perspective, the earliest dated sites associated with the adoption of iron metallurgy and crop cultivation are those at which Urewe ware (Figure 18.8), named after the type site close to the Yala River in western Kenya, occurs. The earliest Urewe sites all lie to the west of Lake Victoria and are especially concentrated around Buhaya in Tanzania and the Kivu-Rusizi River region in Rwanda/Burundi. Radiocarbon dates suggest an initial appearance here between the eighth and sixth centuries BCE. Urewe ware had a fairly wide distribution across much of Rwanda, Burundi, and neighbouring parts of southwestern Uganda, western Kenya, and northwestern Tanzania.[36] Urewe ware sites are also closely associated with the first appearance of iron-working in the Great Lakes region and considerable

36 C.Z. Ashley, 'Towards a socialised archaeology of ceramics in Great Lakes Africa', *African Archaeological Review*, 27 (2010), 135–63.

research effort has been directed at elucidating the origins and nature of this technology. Archaeological evidence from excavated sites such as KM2 and KM3, near Kemondo Bay (Tanzania), for instance, in conjunction with the results of experimental and ethnographic studies, indicate that EFC smelters had a sophisticated knowledge of the physical and chemical processes involved, and by the first millennium CE were capable of generating furnace temperatures high enough to produce carbon steel.[37]

It is generally assumed that EFC populations were mixed farmers, who placed rather more emphasis on crop cultivation than on herding, and this is suggested by a preference for settlement locations close to better-watered areas along the intersection between submontane forest and woody savanna. Actual evidence for subsistence strategies from Urewe sites is quite rare, however. Important exceptions are the sites of Gogo Falls and Wadh Lang'o in South Nyanza, and Usenge 3 in North Nyanza, all in western Kenya, from which evidence for the exploitation of both cattle and small stock has been recovered. Recent excavations at various sites in Rwanda also provide important new data of relevance to understanding early agricultural practices in the region, including remains of pearl millet, sorghum, and legumes (most probably cowpea) from the site of Kabusanze, dated to *c.* 380–420 CE and associated with classic Urewe ceramics.[38] Direct evidence for the cultivation of different pan-African native crops is also known from the open air site of Mgombani (dated to *c.* 660–890 CE), southern Kenya, and Panga ya Saidi, a large limestone cave in the nearby Dzitsoni uplands likely occupied by terminal LSA hunter-gatherers. Both sites have yielded grains of domesticated sorghum, pearl millet and finger millet, and baobab seeds, while pulse seeds of *Vigna* sp. (possibly cowpea) were recovered from Mgombani.[39]

## Cultivating the rainforest

The nature, inception, and rate of spread of agriculture in Central Africa, especially in areas now covered by tropical rainforest, is based on quite patchy data sets. Nonetheless, there is sufficient evidence to allow a reasoned

---

37 P.R. Schmidt and S.T. Childs, 'Innovation and industry during the early Iron Age in East Africa: the KM2 and KM3 sites of northwestern Tanzania', *African Archaeological Review*, 3 (1995), 53–94.

38 J.D. Giblin and D.Q. Fuller, 'First and second millennium AD agriculture in Rwanda: archaeobotanical finds and radiocarbon dates from seven sites', *Vegetation History and Archaeobotany*, 20 (2011), 253–65.

39 R. Helm et al., 'Exploring agriculture, interaction and trade on the eastern African littoral: preliminary results from Kenya', *Azania*, 47 (2012), 39–63.

reconstruction of the key developments and drivers of change. Two separate phases can be identified: an initial Stone-to-Metal phase marked by the presence of ceramics associated with polished stone axes and hoes between *c.* 1500 BCE and 100 CE; and an overlapping early Iron Age, signalled archaeologically by the first evidence for iron-working and new styles and forms of ceramics, between *c.* 400 BCE and 1000 CE. Research has shown that the presence of ground stone artefacts such as axes and hoes is not always a good indicator of the presence of food producers (in many cases they may be a far better indicator of terminal LSA hunter-gatherers), and that some pre-farming communities also made pottery (as for example at Shum Laka rock shelter, northwestern Cameroon). Nevertheless, the marked increase in sites across the Congo basin after *c.* 600 BCE and the introduction of new technologies likely signal demographic increase and southward migration of incipient slash-and-burn agriculture. From the distribution of 'Stone-to-Metal Age' (SMA) sites (i.e. those associated with initial adoption of iron metallurgy in conjunction with continued widespread use of stone tools), the main migration routes seem to have been from south-central Cameroon eastwards along the northern boundaries of the rainforest, and southwards along the Atlantic seaboards of what are now Equatorial Guinea, Gabon, and Congo, with some eastward movement along the Ogooué River as far as modern-day Lopé (central Gabon), between *c.* 800 and 300 BCE. The homogenous nature of the pottery over this entire strip implies that this was a single cultural group, as also suggested by the restricted settlement preference during this phase for hilltops and other dominant positions along river courses.[40]

This southward movement may well have been facilitated by forest fragmentation as a consequence of the weakening of the Atlantic monsoon from around 1500 BCE. A few hundred years later, more extensive forest regression appears to have triggered the southward movement of a new group of people with knowledge of iron metallurgy as well as farming, who were speakers of proto-Western Bantu languages. The earliest of these sites, at Oliga in southern Cameroon, is dated to the mid first millennium BCE. Subsequent expansion by these metal-using communities across areas already occupied by the makers of Malongo ceramics and further inland across areas that now lie within the forest zone was fairly rapid between *c.* 600 BCE and 100 CE. There followed a decline in settlement and possibly even a 'population crash' leading to the abandonment of large parts of the interior, perhaps

---

40 R. Oslisly et al., 'Climatic and cultural changes in the West Congo basin forests over the past 5000 years', *Philosophical Transactions of the Royal Society B*, 368 (2013), 20120304.

as a result of environmental impacts triggered by widespread forest-burning associated with charcoal production and slash-and-burn agriculture.[41]

It is likely that yams were an important component, and perhaps also millet and even banana, as possibly documented at the site of Nkang, situated *c.* 70 km northwest of Yaoundé, Cameroon, dated to between 800 and 350 BCE.[42] Recent work in southern Cameroon indicates that pearl millet was being cultivated at Abang Minko and Bwambé-Sommet by around 400–200 BCE in an area that currently lies within the forest zone, along with the exploitation of a range of forest-based plant resources, including oil palm and the edible nut *Canarium schweinfurthii*. The cultivation of Bambara ground-nut is also attested at the nearby site of Akonéte.[43] Both pearl millet and Bambara groundnut are savanna crops that originated further north and are adapted to drier conditions than those that currently prevail in southern Cameroon. This would imply that annual average rainfall was lower than today when these sites were occupied. In turn, this might explain why, even if banana/plantain were being cultivated a few centuries earlier further north at Nkang, they were not recovered on the more southerly sites.[44]

As at Nkang, much of the available evidence concerning subsistence strategies in Central Africa comes from pits. These are especially common on sites dating to between 900 BCE and 600 CE, and some are associated with LSA/Stone-to-Metal Age traditions, while others clearly have an EIA affiliation. Most pits are typically between 1.5 and 3 m deep and contain mixed ceramic, stone, and on occasion metal assemblages (hence an EIA affiliation), along with the remains of oil palm and *Canarium* and other edible nuts. Their distribution extends across the forest zone from the Atlantic coasts of Cameroon, Congo, and Gabon to as far north as Nanga Eboko, central Cameroon. Faunal remains at these sites are rare, although ovicaprids are known from Nkang and Toubé 1 (Gabon). The evidence from several rock shelters on the other hand, including Shum Laka and Abéké (Cameroon),

---

41 J. Maley and P. Brenac, 'Vegetation dynamics, palaeo-environments and climatic changes in the forests of western Cameroon during the last 28,000 years BP', *Review of Paleobotany and Palynology*, 99 (1998), 157–87; R. Oslisly and L. White, 'Human impact and environmental exploitation in Gabon during the Holocene', in Denham et al. (eds.), *Rethinking Agriculture*, 347–60.

42 C. Mbida et al., 'Evidence for banana cultivation and animal husbandry during the first millennium BC in the forest of south Cameroon', *Journal of Archaeological Science*, 27 (2000), 151–62.

43 K. Neumann et al., 'First farmers in the Central African rainforest: a view from southern Cameroon', *Quaternary International*, 249 (2012), 53–62.

44 K. Neumann and E. Hildebrandt, 'Early banana in Africa: the state of the art', *Ethnobotany Research and Applications*, 7 (2009), 353–62.

points to a reliance on wild species,[45] while the exploitation of marine shellfish is documented at some of the coastal sites in Gabon and the Republic of Congo. In the latter, several Ceramic LSA sites, such as Tchissinga West on the Loango coast, are dated to between *c.* 1300 and 100 BCE, with deep pits filled with carbonized oil palm nuts and occasional flat grinding stones and distinctive globular-necked jars. EIA sites, distinguished by the presence of a very different style of ceramics and the presence of iron artefacts and slag, first appear in this area around 100 BCE;[46] however, other than evidence for the exploitation of oil palm, no direct material evidence for subsistence practices has been recovered from either category of site on this part of the coast. Extensive surveying along the main river channels in the Zaire basin has also documented a range of similar sites, although with their own distinctive ceramic styles, that suggest an initial establishment of farming communities in these areas between *c.* 800 and 100 BCE.[47]

## Early herding and farming in southern Africa

The transition to food production in southern Africa commenced around 2,300 to 1,800 years ago. As in other parts of the continent, the transition was likely triggered in part by the southward movement of groups of farmers (generally considered to have entered the region from two directions, the northwest and the northeast, and to have been speakers of early Eastern Bantu languages) and herders (thought by some to have been speakers of a proto-Khoekhoe language, who entered the region from the Lake Nyasa-Malawi/Lake Tanganyika corridor). However, it is also clear that LSA hunter-gatherers in the region were regularly exploiting wild grasses and other plants for food and so may well have been predisposed to the adoption of cereal agriculture without much incentive for changing other cultural practices.

The first herders kept mostly sheep with some cattle in certain localities, and in a few instances also goats. Evidence for the presence of domestic livestock has been recovered from a number of sites across southern Africa dated to around the BCE/CE transition, and in a few localities somewhat

45 P. Lavachery, 'The Holocene archaeological sequence of Shum Laka rock shelter (Grassfields, western Cameroon)', *African Archaeological Review*, 18 (2001), 213–47.
46 J. Denbow, 'Pride, prejudice, plunder and preservation: archaeology and the re-envisioning of ethnogenesis on the Loango coast of the Republic of Congo', *Antiquity*, 86 (2012), 383–408.
47 M.K.H. Eggert, 'Central Africa and the archaeology of the equatorial rainforest: reflections on some major topics', in T. Shaw et al. (eds.), *The Archaeology of Africa: Food, Metals and Towns* (London: Routledge, 1993), 289–329.

Figure 18.9  View across early herder settlement areas, Kasteelberg Hill, South Africa.

earlier. The earliest known examples come from the recently investigated Holocene levels at Leopard Cave, in the Erongo mountains, central west Namibia, where caprine remains associated with a large, mixed terrestrial wild fauna have been directly dated to *c.* 300–40 BCE.[48] Other sites yielding the remains of domestic sheep include Bambata Cave, southwestern Zimbabwe; Toteng, northern Botswana, *c.* 50 BCE; and several in South Africa, including Spoegrivier, *c.* 100 BCE, and Blombos Cave, *c.* 40 CE.[49] Other Namibian sites yielding caprine remains that are likely to be of an early date include Geduld, Mirabib, and Orunwanje 95/1, although none of these remains have been directly dated. Among the South African sites, several localities on Kasteelberg Hill (Figure 18.9), roughly 140 km north of Cape Town, and the site of Jakkalsberg close to the mouth of the Orange/Gariep River, have yielded large assemblages of domestic stock, in both cases associated with thin-walled ceramics and dated to around the mid first millennium CE.[50] In contrast, at

48  D. Pleurdeau et al., '"Of sheep and men": earliest direct evidence of caprine domestication in southern Africa at Leopard Cave (Erongo, Namibia)', *PLoS ONE*, 7 (2012), e40340.
49  K. Sadr, 'A short history of early herding in southern Africa', in Bollig et al. (eds.), *Pastoralism in Africa*, 171–97.
50  K. Sadr, 'The Neolithic of southern Africa', *Journal of African History*, 44 (2003), 195–209.

many of the other sites wild terrestrial species, and in the case of coastal sites shellfish and seals, dominate the faunal assemblages. In the light of such trends, along with other ambiguities in the available data, there has been considerable debate over whether all of the sites with evidence for the presence of domestic livestock were indeed inhabited by herders, with some arguing that certain sites were more likely occupied by forager populations who had obtained livestock by some means. Sadr, in particular, has questioned the universal attribution of various material culture signatures (such as thin-walled ceramics, fine-line rock-paintings of sheep, the comparatively large variants of ostrich eggshell beads, and even aspects of the stone toolkits) to 'pastoralist' proto-Khoekhoe.[51] He has also argued that the generally low percentages of livestock remains relative to wild taxa on these sites more likely suggests a subsistence strategy involving a mix of goat herding and regular hunting and gathering.

In contrast to the early herding populations, the early farming communities (EFC) of southern Africa were typically restricted to the moister eastern and southeastern parts of the region, where rainfall is restricted to the austral summer months. Within this large area, certain ecological zones were unsuited to farming, often because of low rainfall but also because of other factors, including topography, soil characteristics, vegetation cover, and wildlife density. Most of these areas were already inhabited by autochthonous LSA hunter-gatherers, and in many cases these groups continued to exploit the natural resources of these locales and co-existed alongside farming communities. As has been illustrated by archaeological research in areas such as the Thukela basin in KwaZulu-Natal, the nature of these relationships was quite variable across both space and time, ranging from symbiosis and clientship to serfdom, marginalization, and even outright hostility.[52]

EFC sites are typically signalled in the archaeological record by the first appearance of pottery, at least on the eastern side of the region, and evidence for the use of iron (and in some cases also copper). As in East Africa, because of this close association with the introduction of iron-smelting technology, this phase is often referred to as the Early Iron Age, or EIA, commencing in this region around 200 CE and lasting to the ninth or tenth century CE. Ceramic typologies in association with radiocarbon dates for the first occurrence have been used to reconstruct the southward spread of EFCs. EFC ceramics are all attributed to the Chifumbaze Complex, comprising two major traditions: the

---

51 K. Sadr, 'An ageless view of first millennium CE southern African ceramics', *Journal of African Archaeology*, 6 (2008), 103–29.

52 A.D. Mazel, 'People making history: the last ten thousand years of hunter-gatherer communities in the Thukela basin', *Southern African Humanities*, 1 (1989), 1–168.

Urewe tradition, originating in East Africa, and the Kalundu tradition, which possibly originated in Angola. Urewe tradition ceramics are further divided into two branches (Kwale and Nkope), with Kwale occurring along the Indian Ocean seaboard and its hinterland between southern Kenya and Durban (South Africa), whereas Nkope ceramics are found on EFC sites in central and western Tanzania, Malawi, Zambia, Zimbabwe, and northern South Africa. The earliest manifestations of these traditions in the region date to between *c.* 350 BCE and 300 CE, and include the sites of Situmpa (Zambia, Nkope branch, *c.* 290 BCE to 70 CE), Benefica (Angola, Kalundu tradition, *c.* 250 CE), and Matola (Mozambique, Kwale branch, *c.* 350 BCE to 255 CE).

Key early sites include Happy Rest (fourth to seventh centuries CE) and Klein Africa in South Africa (fifth to sixth centuries CE), and evidence from both points to subsistence economies based on stock-keeping and the cultivation of sorghum, millet, and pulses. At Happy Rest, ovicaprines outnumber cattle and, to judge from the slaughter patterns, were normally raised to near adulthood. Hunting was also important at many EFC sites, including many in the area of the Kruger National Park. Overall, the faunal assemblages from a great many of the earliest farming sites in the region (among them Nkope Hill, Malawi, *c.* 530 CE, and Kalundu, Zambia, *c.* 540 CE), as well as from some second or third phase EFC sites, such as Kadzi (Zimbabwe, *c.* 770 CE) in the middle Zambezi valley, are dominated by wild species. Where domesticated species are present, ovicaprines tend to be significantly more common than cattle – a situation which does not change until late in the first millennium CE, and then only at some sites.[53]

On the eastern side of the region, 'Matola / Silver Leaves' ware (*c.* 350 BCE to 430 CE) represents the earliest archaeological expression of these pioneer farmers in coastal Mozambique, southeastern Zimbabwe, Swaziland, and a westward-trending extension across Limpopo province (South Africa) as far as southeastern Botswana. These groups expanded southwards along what is now coastal KwaZulu-Natal, preferentially settling areas that today receive more than 800 mm of rain a year and / or are close to iron ore sources. Most were mixed agropastoralists, although there is local and regional variation. In coastal Mozambique and KwaZulu-Natal, shellfish were an important element in local diets, as were various gathered wild seeds, fruit, and nuts. Whereas cattle and small stock are represented in faunal assemblages, so too are wild fauna, as at Chibuene (*c.* 600–900 CE, southern

---

53 S. Badenhorst, 'Subsistence change among farming communities in southern Africa during the last two millennia: a search for possible causes', in S. Badenhorst et al. (eds.), *Animals and People: Archaeozoological Papers in Honour of Ina Plug* (Oxford: Archaeopress, 2008), 215–28.

Mozambique).[54] Local pollen signatures there also point to some small-scale clearance or vegetation in the general area,[55] which may have been used for cultivation or grazing, but overall the scale of agriculture at and around the site seems to have been limited during this initial pioneering phase. On Mzonjani sites further south there seems to have been a much greater reliance on ovicaprines, along with the cultivation of African cereals, including sorghum and millet, pulses, and cucurbits.[56] In areas away from the coast, including the Limpopo valley and Northern Transvaal (Gauteng), there is similar evidence for mixed herding and cultivation of cereals, from sites such as Silver Leaves (*c.* 420–545 CE) and Broederstroom (*c.* 550–700 CE). There are also several material indicators on many EFC sites that further point to the importance of crop cultivation, most obviously the upper and lower grinding stones found on most sites and sometimes in considerable quantities, and frequent remains of grain bins (e.g. Mabveni, south-central Zimbabwe) and storage pits (e.g. Broederstroom, South Africa).

## Conclusion

The development and spread of farming and herding in sub-Saharan Africa were long drawn-out and uneven processes spanning up to five millennia with many stops and starts. They entailed the domestication of several different crop species; the modification and manipulation of ecological niches to better suit the needs of farming and herding; the nurturing of new cross-breeds, hybrids and varieties better adapted to distinctively African ecological conditions; and the exploitation of a vast array of other plant species that seemingly have not undergone significant morphological change as a consequence. Over the longer term, the history of agriculture on the continent also involved the adoption of a wide range of 'exotic' species from other parts of the globe; and, as critically, the spread of various African domesticates to other parts of the world.[57] However, relative to many other continents, sub-Saharan Africa's standing as an area for researching the origins and spread of farming remains

---

54 S. Badenhorst et al., 'Faunal remains from Chibuene, an Iron Age coastal trading station in central Mozambique', *Southern African Humanities*, 23 (2011), 1–15.

55 A. Ekblom et al., 'Land use history and resource utilisation from AD 400 to the present, at Chibuene, southern Mozambique', *Vegetation History and Archaeobotany*, 23 (2014), 15–32.

56 T. Maggs and V. Ward, 'Early Iron Age sites in the Muden area of Natal', *Annals of the Natal Museum*, 26 (1984), 105–40.

57 J.A. Carney and R.N. Rosomoff, *In the Shadow of Slavery: Africa's Botanical Legacy in the Atlantic World*, (Berkeley: University of California Press, 2009); D. Fuller and N. Boivin, 'Crops, cattle and commensals across the Indian Ocean: current and potential archaeobotanical evidence', *Études Océan Indien* 42/43 (2009), 13–46.

low within the global archaeological community, often because of a presumed absence of 'primary' centres of domestication south of the Sahara. This is unfortunate given the diversity of sources available and that the origins of food production in sub-Saharan Africa followed a different trajectory to these in most other regions with the adoption of domestic animals typically preceding the adoption of food crops. Moreover, the subsequent histories of food production offer numerous opportunities for novel theoretical insights into a range of topics from the creation and maintenance of ethnic mosaics across moving and stable frontiers, the drivers of agricultural intensification and the ecological impacts of the adoption of farming to the reconstruction of ideological structures and patterns of descent, propositions concerning 'landscape domestication' and even whether morphological change is always the most salient marker of 'domestication'.[58] However, given the momentum of current research, as outlined here, this situation may be set to change.

## Further reading

Badenhorst, S. 'Descent of Iron Age farmers in southern Africa during the last 2000 years.' *African Archaeological Review*, 27 (2010), 87–106.

Blench, R.M. 'Using linguistics to reconstruct African subsistence systems: comparing crop names to trees and livestock.' In T.P. Denham, J. Iriarte, and L. Vrydaghs (eds.), *Rethinking Agriculture: Archaeological and Ethnoarchaeological Perspectives*. Walnut Creek, CA: Left Coast Press, 2007. 408–38.

Blench, R.M. and K.C. MacDonald (eds.). *The Origins and Development of African Livestock: Archaeology, Genetics, Linguistics and Ethnography*. London: UCL Press, 2000.

Breunig, P. 'Pathways to food production in the Sahel.' In Mitchell and Lane (eds.), *Oxford Handbook of African Archaeology*, 555–70.

Casey, J. 'The Stone to Metal Age in West Africa.' In Mitchell and Lane (eds.), *Oxford Handbook of African Archaeology*, 599–610.

Curtis, M. 'Archaeological evidence for the emergence of food production in the Horn of Africa.' In Mitchell and Lane (eds.), *Oxford Handbook of African Archaeology*, 567–80.

de Maret, P. 'Archaeologies of the Bantu expansion.' In Mitchell and Lane (eds.), *Oxford Handbook of African Archaeology*, 627–43.

Denbow, J. *The Archaeology and Ethnography of Central Africa*. Cambridge University Press, 2014.

Eggert, M.K.H. 'Central Africa and the archaeology of the equatorial rainforest: reflections on some major topics.' In T. Shaw, P. Sinclair, B. Andah, and A. Okpoko (eds.), *The Archaeology of Africa: Food, Metals and Towns*. London: Routledge, 1993. 289–329.

Ehret, C. *An African Classical Age: Eastern and Southern Africa in World History, 1000 BC to AD 400*. Charlottesville: University of Virginia Press, 1998.

---

58 K. Neumann, 'The romance of farming – plant cultivation and domestication in Africa', in *African Archaeology: A Critical Introduction*, Stahl, A. B. (ed.), (Oxford: Blackwell, 2005), pp. 249–75.

Fuller, D. and E.A. Hildebrand. 'Domesticating plants in Africa.' In Mitchell and Lane (eds.), *Oxford Handbook of African Archaeology*, 503–21.

Gifford-Gonzalez, D. 'Animal disease challenges to the emergence of pastoralism in sub-Saharan Africa.' *African Archaeological Review*, 18 (2000), 95–139.

Gifford-Gonzalez, D. and O. Hanotte, 'Domesticating animals in Africa: implications of genetic and archaeological findings.' *Journal of World Prehistory*, 24 (2011), 1–23.

Huffman, T.N. *Handbook to the Iron Age: The Archaeology of Pre-colonial Farming Societies in Southern Africa*. Scottsville: University of KwaZulu-Natal Press, 2007.

Jousse, H. and J. Lesur (eds.). *People and Animals in Holocene Africa: Recent Advances in Archaeozoology*. Frankfurt: Africa Magna, 2011.

Kusimba, C. and S.B. Kusimba (eds.). *East African Archaeology: Foragers, Potters, Smiths and Traders*. Philadelphia: University of Pennsylvania Museum of Archaeology and Anthropology, 2003.

Lane, P.J. 'Trajectories of pastoralism in northern and central Kenya: an overview of the archaeological and environmental evidence.' In M. Bollig, M. Schnegg, and H.-P. Wotzka (eds.), *Pastoralism in Africa: Past, Present and Future*. Oxford: Berghahn, 2013. 104–43.

Lesur, J. *Chasse et élevage dans la Corne de l'Afrique entre le Néolithique et les Temps Historiques*. Oxford: Archaeopress, 2007.

MacDonald, K.C., R. Vernet, M. Martinon-Torres, and D.Q. Fuller. 'Dhar Néma: from early agriculture to metallurgy in southeastern Mauritania.' *Azania*, 44 (2009), 3–48.

Manning, K. 'A developmental history of West African agriculture.' In P. Allsworth-Jones (ed.), *West African Archaeology: New Developments, New Perspectives*. Oxford: Archaeopress, 2010. 43–52.

Marshall, F.B. and E.A. Hildebrand. 'Cattle before crops: the beginnings of food production in Africa.' *Journal of World Prehistory*, 16 (2002), 99–143.

Mazel, A.D. 'People making history: the last ten thousand years of hunter-gatherer communities in the Thukela basin.' *Southern African Humanities*, 1 (1989), 1–168.

Mitchell, P.J. *The Archaeology of Southern Africa*. Cambridge University Press, 2002.

Mitchell, P.J. and P.J. Lane (eds.). *The Oxford Handbook of African Archaeology*. Oxford University Press, 2013.

Neumann, K., K. Boesten, A. Höhn, et al. 'First farmers in the Central African rainforest: a view from southern Cameroon.' *Quaternary International*, 249 (2012), 53–62.

Oslisly, R., L. White, I. Bentaleb, et al. 'Climatic and cultural changes in the West Congo basin forests over the past 5000 years.' *Philosophical Transactions of the Royal Society B*, 368 (2013), 20120304.

Phillipson, D.W. *African Archaeology*. 3rd edn. Cambridge University Press, 2005.

Sadr, K. 'A short history of early herding in southern Africa.' In M. Bollig, M. Schnegg, and H.-P. Wotzka (eds.), *Pastoralism in Africa: Past, Present and Future*. Oxford: Berghahn, 2013. 171–97.

Stevens, C.J., S. Nixon, M.A. Murray, and D.Q. Fuller (eds.). *The Archaeology of African Plant Use*. Walnut Creek, CA: Left Coast Press, 2014.

Wadley, L. 'Gender in the prehistory of sub-Saharan Africa.' In D. Bolger (ed.), *A Companion to Gender Prehistory*. Oxford: Wiley-Blackwell, 2012. 313–32.

Wright, D.K. 'Frontier animal husbandry in the Northeast and East African Neolithic: a multiproxy palaeoenvironmental and palaeodemographic study.' *Journal of Anthropological Research*, 26 (2011), 213–44.

# 19

# The Tichitt tradition in the West African Sahel

KEVIN C. MACDONALD

The enigmatic Tichitt civilization has remained relatively unheralded in world archaeology despite its place as one of sub-Saharan Africa's earliest complex societies. It is perhaps best known as an early case study for cereal domestication in the Sahel. In 1976 Patrick Munson published evidence based on preserved grain impressions in pottery temper which appeared to show the incipient domestication of millet (*Pennisetum glaucum*) around 1100 BCE. Subsequent work has demonstrated that domestic millet was in fact already present in this region before that date, and that its domestication may have already taken place in regions to the north or east (see below). More remarkable are the Tichitt tradition's complex of large, proto-urban dry-stone masonry settlements, associated with burial monuments, which show a particular concentration along the Tichitt and Walata escarpments, but which exist further to the south in the Tagant and Néma escarpment ranges. The spatial distribution and layout of these settlements have drawn the attention of a host of scholars since the initial work of Munson.[1] Here we will explore the economic evidence for the Tichitt tradition, the nature of its social complexity, and the implications of its ultimate expansion further to the southeast into the margins of the middle Niger (Figure 19.1).

## Tichitt: agricultural origins

The highlands of southeastern Mauritania form a broad semicircle around the Hodh depression, with an array of escarpments from west to east: Dhar

---

[1] P.J. Munson, 'The Tichitt tradition: a late prehistoric occupation of the southwestern Sahara', unpublished PhD thesis (University of Illinois at Urbana-Champaign, 1971), and 'Archaeological data on the origins of cultivation in the southwestern Sahara and their implications for West Africa', in J.R. Harlan et al. (eds.), *Origins of African Plant Domestication* (The Hague: Mouton, 1976), 187–209.

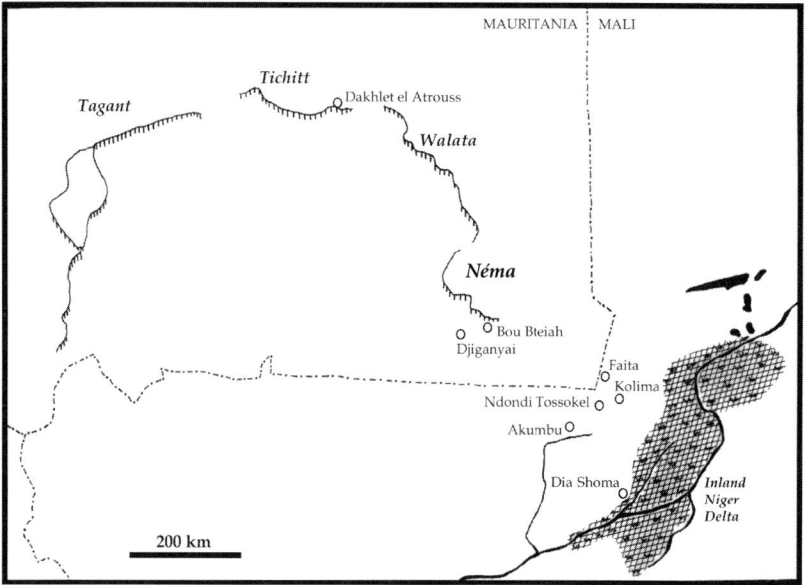

Figure 19.1 The Tichitt tradition: a regional map.

Tagant, Dhar Tichitt, Dhar Walata, and Dhar Néma. The Hodh was filled with lakes during the Holocene optimum, but after 4000 BCE there was a gradual regression, with permanent surface waters fading around 1000 BCE.[2] It was during this time of climatic degradation that the Tichitt tradition (as it was dubbed by Patrick Munson) arose. Munson's initial arguments for the origins of sedentism, agriculture, and complexity in the region turned upon a local version of the classic 'oasis hypothesis', whereby decreasing availability of water and stands of wild grain led to the establishment of millet domestication, villages, and territoriality.[3] However, ongoing research at Tichitt tradition sites has shown that this equation is not as straightforward as was originally supposed.

Prior to the time of Tichitt, the region was populated by diffuse groups of mobile herders and hunter-gatherers. This period has alternatively been referred to as pre-Tichitt, Tichitt phase 1, or the Akreijit phase. Pre-Tichitt sites are small, relatively superficial localities, essentially temporary camp-sites (Figure 19.2). Once thought to represent dispersed hunter-gatherer

2 R. Vernet, *Préhistoire de la Mauritanie* (Nouakchott: Centre Culturel Français A. de Saint-Exupéry; Paris: Sépia, 1993).

3 V.G. Childe, *The Most Ancient East* (New York: Knopf, 1929).

Figure 19.2 The pre-Tichitt site of Bou Bteiah, situated on a rocky outcrop within a vast plain – ideal for monitoring herds or wild game movements.

populations separated from Tichitt by a brief hiatus,[4] they are now understood to have been both pastoral and continuous with Tichitt itself. On the basis of new faunal data from excavations in the Dhar Néma region, there is evidence that the pre-Tichitt economy was a generalized one, combining pastoralism with hunting and fishing.[5] While no evidence of domestic cereals has yet been recovered, the notion of a hiatus between pre-Tichitt and Tichitt is contradicted by a continuous occupational sequence from Djiganyai, a settlement mound in the Dhar Néma region, linking pre-Tichitt and Tichitt elements (Figure 19.3).[6] In Munson's original study, the pre-Tichitt phase was left undated and a single determination on bivalve shells from a 'beach' associated with pre-Tichitt ceramics was dismissed, at 3,700 ± 130 BP (2290 to 1920 BCE), as being too recent.[7] However, it is now becoming apparent that pre-Tichitt does in fact immediately precede Tichitt at c. 1900 BCE. From Bou Khzama II, Person et al. have dated a pre-Tichitt midden context to

4 Munson, 'Archaeological data'.
5 A. Person et al., 'Les sites du Néolithique final du Dhar Néma (Mauritanie): relations peuplement – environnement', in C. Descamps and A. Camara (eds.), *Senegalia: études sur le patrimoine ouest-africain: Hommage à Guy Thilmans* (Saint-Maur: Sépia, 2006), 297–307; K.C. MacDonald et al., 'Dhar Néma: from early agriculture to metallurgy in southeastern Mauritania', *Azania*, 44 (2009), 3–48.
6 MacDonald et al., 'Dhar Néma'.    7 Munson, 'Tichitt tradition', 184–6.

Figure 19.3  Excavations at Djiganyai in 2000.

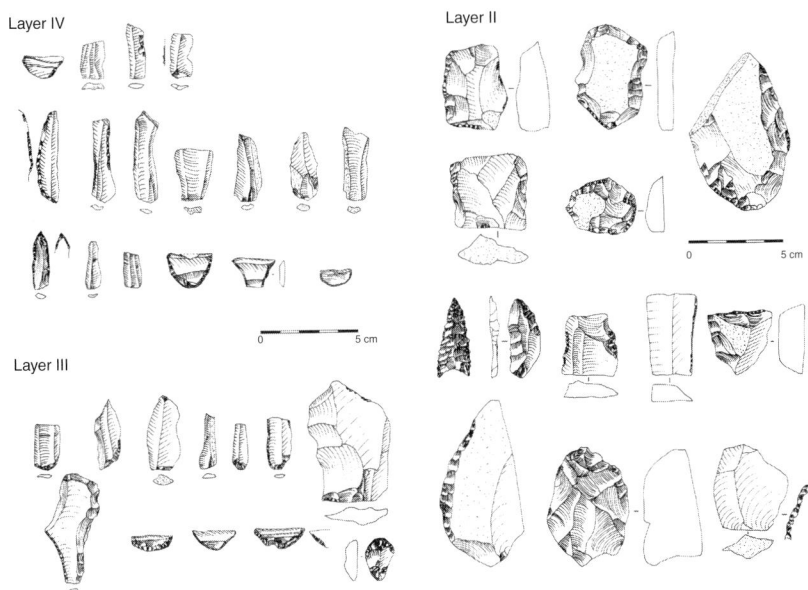

Figure 19.4 Pre-Tichitt to Tichitt lithics from the sequence at Djiganyai.

3,765 ± 35 BP (2280–2130 BCE),[8] and at Djiganyai pre-Tichitt materials occur in stratigraphy directly below early Tichitt materials and have been dated to 3,550 ± 40 BP (1950–1770 BCE).[9]

It is important to note that, although a change in fabric occurs in pre-Tichitt to Tichitt ceramics (sand to chaff temper), the forms and thicknesses of pre-Tichitt ceramics closely resemble those of early Tichitt and they share a number of other decorative motifs (including cord-wrapped roulettes and stylus incisions). Regarding lithic sequences, geometric microliths gradually decrease and projectile points increase, suggesting a gradual transformation rather than a rupture or hiatus between pre-Tichitt and early Tichitt (Figure 19.4).[10] In terms of economy, to understand the origins of Tichitt subsistence systems one must first better understand pre-Tichitt, which up until now has been almost unstudied. Unfortunately at this point, as pre-Tichitt ceramics do not feature external grain impressions and as suitable

8 A. Person et al., 'Environnement et marquers culturels en Mauritanie sud-orientale: le site Bou Khzama (DN4), premiers resultants et approche biogéochimique', in A. Bazzana and H. Bocoum (eds.), *Du Nord au Sud au Sahara: cinquante ans d'archéologie française en Afrique de l'Ouest et au Maghreb* (Paris: Sépia, 2004), 195–213.
9 MacDonald et al., 'Dhar Néma'.   10 Ibid.

Figure 19.5 Domestic millet impressions in a Tichitt tradition potsherd.

deposits have not been sampled, we can only speculate about its cultivation activities.

For the Tichitt tradition itself, research on grain impressions embedded in its potsherds has intensified since the 1990s (Figure 19.5). The direct AMS dating of organics in these sherds has pushed back the advent of domestic millet at Dhars Tichitt, Walata, and Néma to around 3,500 BP (c. 1900–1700 BCE).[11]

11 S. Amblard, *Tichitt-Walata, République Islamique de Mauritanie: civilisation et industrie lithique* (Paris: ADPF, 1984); D.Q. Fuller et al., 'Early domesticated pearl millet in Dhar Néma (Mauritania): evidence of crop-processing waste as ceramic temper', in R.T.J. Cappers (ed.), *Fields of Change: Progress in African Archaeobotany* (Groningen: Barkhuis, 2007), 71–6; MacDonald et al., 'Dhar Néma'.

In other words, the cultivation of domestic millet was taking place from the very beginning of the Tichitt sequence. The questions must then be posed: when and where did the western Sahel's 'agricultural revolution' occur?

Regardless of whether African millet domestication was multicentric or from a common source, new finds from the Tilemsi valley suggest that Tichitt's was not the pristine domestication that it was once supposed to be. Domestic millet remains from Karkarichinkat Nord in Mali's Tilemsi valley have been dated to between 2500 and 2000 BCE, and Manning speculates that the presence of non-shattering rachises on her specimens pushes initial domestication dates back still further.[12] Based upon Fuller's findings that non-shattering rachises evolved gradually – over a millennium or more[13] – we may still be looking for the cereal domestication process in what is now the Sahara around 3000 BCE or earlier. Certainly by around 1900 BCE domestic millets in West Africa were widespread, with specimens from northern Ghana[14] and the Gourma/Bandiagara region of Mali.[15] Tichitt cultivation was thus either part of a much wider process which was sweeping the Sahel at the time, or we may yet find roots of a longer, contiguous process of agricultural innovation in Mauritania. Still, it remains tempting to hypothesize that the material transition from pre-Tichitt to Tichitt (c. 1900 BCE) corresponds with increasing sedentism and the addition or introduction of intensive millet farming to what had previously been a mobile pastoral economy.

## Tichitt complexity: settlement sequence and expansion

Africa's mid-Holocene pastoral societies were no strangers to flares of social complexity. Monumental tumuli and long-distance trade in prestigious

---

12 K. Manning, 'A developmental history for early West African agriculture', in P. Allsworth-Jones (ed.), *West African Archaeology: New Developments, New Perspectives* (Oxford: Archaeopress, 2010), 43–52 (46); K. Manning et al., '4500-year-old domesticated pearl millet (*Pennisetum glaucum*) from the Tilemsi valley, Mali: new insights into an alternative cereal domestication pathway', *Journal of Archaeological Science*, 38 (2011), 312–22.

13 D.Q. Fuller, 'Contrasting patterns in crop domestication and domestication rates: recent archaeobotanical insights from the Old World', *Annals of Botany*, 100 (2007), 903–24.

14 A.C. D'Andrea et al., 'Archaeobotanical evidence for pearl millet (*Pennisetum glaucum*) in sub-Saharan West Africa', *Antiquity*, 75 (2001), 341–8.

15 K.C. MacDonald, 'The Windé Koroji complex: evidence for the peopling of the eastern inland Niger delta (2100–500 BC)', *Préhistoire Anthropologie Méditerranéennes*, 5 (1996), 147–65; S. Ozainne et al., 'Developing a chronology integrating archaeological and environmental data from different contexts: the late Holocene sequence of Ounjougou (Mali)', *Radiocarbon*, 51 (2009), 457–70.

polished stone objects (beads, axes, and stone arm-rings) are amply demonstrated across the Sahara from 4000 BCE.[16] Tichitt forms a more durable and sedentary expression of such social disequilibria. Its socioeconomic trajectory has been researched and debated for decades, with Munson's work at Dhar Tichitt during the late 1960s followed by that of new researchers there and in nearby regions.[17] Chronology has, however, been a perennial problem, partly because the deflated nature of many key sites yields only occasional 'cuts' or sediment traps with datable organics, though chaff-tempering of the majority of Tichitt ceramics facilitates the AMS dating of pottery. Munson's initial eight-phase sequence has now been reduced to three or four developmental phases, although Amblard-Pison prefers to opt out of chronological ordering given the current state of the evidence.[18] Here, it is argued that the Tichitt ceramic and architectural chronology supports a four-phase developmental sequence.

### Pre-Tichitt: phase 1 (Akreijit phase), c. 2600–1900 BCE

See the section above ('Tichitt: agricultural origins') for a discussion of this phase.

### Early Tichitt: phases 2 and 3 (Khimiya/Goungou phases), c. 1900–1600 BCE

Originally viewed as a mobile, pre-agricultural period for Tichitt pastoralists,[19] we now know that domesticated pearl millet (*Pennisetum glaucum*) was farmed during this period.[20] However, a degree of continued mobility is

16 K.C. MacDonald, 'Before the empire of Ghana: pastoralism and the origins of cultural complexity in the Sahel', in G. Connah (ed.), *Transformations in Africa: Essays on Africa's Later Past* (London: Leicester University Press, 1998), 71–103.

17 Munson, 'Archaeological data'; A.F.C. Holl, *Economie et société Néolithique du Dhar Tichitt (Mauritanie)* (Paris: Éditions Recherches sur les Civilisations, 1986); Vernet, *Préhistoire de la Mauritanie*; M. Ould Khattar, 'Les sites Gangara, la fin de la culture de Tichitt et l'origine de Ghana', *Journal des Africanistes*, 65 (1995), 31–41; MacDonald et al., 'Dhar Néma'; S. Amblard-Pison, *Communautés villageoises Néolithiques des Dhars Tichitt et Oualata (Mauritanie)* (Oxford: British Archaeological Reports, 2006); Person et al., 'Les sites du Néolithique final du Dhar Néma'.

18 Munson, 'Archaeological data'; Vernet, *Préhistoire de la Mauritanie*; MacDonald et al., 'Dhar Néma'; K.C. MacDonald, 'Betwixt Tichitt and the IND: the pottery of the Faïta Facies, Tichitt tradition', *Azania*, 46 (2011), 49–69; Amblard-Pison, *Communautés villageoises Néolithiques*.

19 Munson, 'Archaeological data'.

20 S. Amblard, 'Agricultural evidence and its interpretation on the Dhars Tichitt and Oualata, south-eastern Mauritania', in G. Pwiti and R. Soper (eds.), *Aspects of African Archaeology: Papers from the 10th Congress of the Pan-African Association for Prehistory and Related Studies* (Harare: University of Zimbabwe Publications, 1996), 421–7; MacDonald et al., 'Dhar Néma'.

implied by the fact that most well-stratified dates for Tichitt's distinctive dry-stone architecture fall in subsequent periods. This was thus very much a formative stage in the advent of Tichitt territoriality and social hierarchy.

### Classic Tichitt: phases 4 to 6 (Nkahl/Naghez/Chebka phases), c. 1600–1000 BCE

Classic Tichitt represents a major socioeconomic transformation during which most of Tichitt's main population centres developed. As well as the expansion of vast settlements of conjoined clusters of stone-walled compounds across Dhars Tichitt and Walata, and as far afield as Dhar Tagant,[21] this period also saw the Tichitt tradition enter the Méma region of the middle Niger, initially perhaps only as dry season pastoral visitors, but ultimately as permanent settlers.[22] For Dhar Tichitt itself a four-tier settlement hierarchy is proposed,[23] ranging from hamlets (about 2 ha) through villages (≤10 ha) and district centres (about 15 ha) to regional centres (about 80 ha). Each district centre may have 'administered' between 3 and 20 villages and hamlets, while the regional centre of Dakhlet el Atrouss-I features 540 stone-walled compounds, most of them containing stone pillar granary foundations and several dwellings made of perishable materials (straw, mats, wattle-and-daub, etc.) (Figure 19.6). Dakhlet el Atrouss-I is arranged in 26 compound clusters, perhaps relating to lineage quarters, with some large outlying walled areas, either for keeping livestock or protecting the soil of garden areas. Surrounding and within the site are well over 100 unexcavated tumuli.

### Late Tichitt: phases 7 and 8 (Arriane/Akjinjeir phases), c. 1000–400 BCE

Tichitt's final centuries were ones of dispersal and decline. Tichitt tradition settlements now expand beyond the core Tichitt-Walata-Néma region as the Dhars and the Hodh basin empty out.[24] Remaining settlements are smaller

---

21 Ould Khattar, 'Les sites Gangara'.

22 K.C. MacDonald, 'A view from the south: sub-Saharan evidence for contacts between North Africa, Mauritania and the Niger, 1000 BC–AD 700', in A. Dowler and E.R. Galvin (eds.), *Money, Trade and Trade Routes in Pre-Islamic North Africa* (London: British Museum Press, 2011), 72–82.

23 A.F.C. Holl, 'Late Neolithic cultural landscape in southeastern Mauritania: an essay in spatiometrics', in A.F.C. Holl and T.E. Levy (eds.), *Spatial Boundaries and Social Dynamics: Case Studies from Food-Producing Societies* (Ann Arbor, MI: International Monographs in Prehistory, 1993), 95–133.

24 Ould Khattar, 'Les sites Gangara'; MacDonald, 'Betwixt Tichitt and the IND'; MacDonald et al., 'Dhar Néma'.

Figure 19.6  Plan of Dakhlet el Atrouss-I.

and situated in more defensible positions. Munson viewed these changes as a result of environmental collapse and Berber incursions aided by iron weaponry.[25] These ideas receive some support from recent studies of early North African trade which reveal an increasing number of central Saharan Berber agricultural and entrepôt sites from the fifth century BCE onwards and mounting evidence for a limited slave trade.[26] Stylistic affinities in late Tichitt pottery assemblages and the local advent of iron metallurgy may also indicate syncretism with incoming Berber groups during this period.[27]

## Tichitt: sociopolitical definition

Tichitt has been identified as West Africa's first large-scale complex society: a 'chiefdom'[28] or even an 'incipient state'.[29] Today, neither of these terms sits

25 P.J. Munson, 'Archaeology and the prehistoric origins of the Ghana empire', *Journal of African History*, 21 (1980), 457–66.
26 E.g. D. Mattingly, 'The Garamantes of Fezzan: an early Libyan state with trans-Saharan connections', in Dowler and Galvin (eds.), *Money, Trade and Trade Routes*, 49–60.
27 MacDonald et al., 'Dhar Néma'.
28 A.F.C. Holl, 'Background to the Ghana empire: archaeological investigations on the transition to statehood in the Dhar Tichitt region (Mauritania)', *Journal of Anthropological Archaeology*, 4 (1985), 73–115.
29 Munson, 'Archaeology and the prehistoric origins of the Ghana empire'.

well with a growing Africanist scepticism towards the utility of such con-trived and imported social evolutionary categories.[30] Let us instead simply consider Tichitt's characteristics at its apogee (c. 1600–1000 BCE).

As noted above, a number of settlements from Tichitt and Walata were massive, exceeding the area of many middle Niger urban sites at the apogee of the empires of Ghana and Mali. Unfortunately, there is as yet no fine-grained chronological information on exactly when and how such settle-ments expanded – we only know that most dates positively associated with such architecture fill a 600-year span: 1600–1000 BCE. Evidence for Tichitt's active co-ordination of long-distance trade networks is equivocal, with beads of semi-precious stone (carnelian and amazonite) recovered in limited volumes from Tichitt sites.[31] Holl suggests that such items moved as tribute or prestige goods up and down Tichitt's hierarchy of settlements.[32] Putting these uncertainties to one side, in our present state of knowledge, the most striking aspect of Tichitt is the strong settlement hierarchy along the Tichitt and Walata escarpments, coupled with the spread of distinctive settlements and/or ceramics across Dhar Néma, Dhar Tagant, and ultimately into the middle Niger.[33] Also of interest, classic Tichitt's stone-walled settle-ments do not seem designed for defence, but rather to demarcate space, most probably lineage space, with some inequalities visible between the catchments of settlements and groupings of compounds within settlements.[34] Such settlements also often feature large enclosures without internal features – probably the base of cattle kraals. Taken together, this indicates a society with internal competition for cattle wealth and territory, perhaps gradually expanding due to seasonal needs for pasture. However, aspects of ritual are also evident, notably the concentration of hundreds of tumuli in the Dhar Tichitt escarpment, compared to barely a dozen in the extensively surveyed and prehistorically well-populated Dhar Walata.[35] Is this a regional difference in mortuary practice or part of a larger ideological phenomenon marking out Dhar Tichitt as an ideological centre of gravity, perhaps an ancestral locality that made it an indispensable dwelling-place for élites? Resolving such speculation will require the systematic investigation of

---

30 S.K. McIntosh (ed.), *Beyond Chiefdoms: Pathways to Complexity in Africa* (Cambridge University Press, 1999).
31 MacDonald, 'A view from the south'.  32 Holl, 'Late Neolithic cultural landscape'.
33 Ibid.; MacDonald, 'Betwixt Tichitt and the IND'.
34 Holl, 'Background to the Ghana empire', and 'Late Neolithic cultural landscape'.
35 Amblard-Pison, *Communautés villageoises Néolithiques*.

Tichitt's tumuli, research which should also at last clarify the social structures of the Tichitt tradition.

## The middle Niger legacy of the Tichitt tradition

Although a gap of almost 500 years divides the last dated vestiges of Tichitt and the earliest possible advent of the historical empire of Ghana (or Wagadu), there has long been speculation that there is some form of connection between the two.[36] Most importantly, the Soninke peoples who founded Ghana/Wagadu are seen as descendants of the Tichitt diaspora, although this largely linguistic speculation had no archaeological support until the 1990s.[37] Bit by bit, largely through the presence of distinctive Tichitt tradition ceramics at the northern margins of the middle Niger and in the lowest layers of the region's great tell sites, connections have become apparent.

Classic Tichitt ceramics (decorated largely with cord-wrapped roulettes) – termed Faïta pottery in Mali – occur at small levée-top sites beside the ancient Méma floodplain of the middle Niger, particularly in an area known locally as 'Ndondi Tossokel' (Figure 19.7). These single-component sites, although eroding, feature small intact middens containing cattle bone, broken pottery, and worked, imported stone (largely phthanite siltstone from the Mauritanian Dhars, used for both chipped and polished implements).[38] The forms of polished implement at the early Faïta sites conform to Amblard's typology of polished stone axes and rings from Tichitt.[39] Assemblages identical to those from Ndondi Tossokel also occur atop Saberi Faïta, the last inselberg of the Tichitt chain, situated on the Mauritanian border with Mali. Spread over 6 ha, this site also features grinding equipment, and remnants of stone walling, which is absent from early Faïta sites along the Méma floodplain. Such Tichitt assemblages in the middle Niger have their earliest direct date at the site of Kolima-Sud, a deeply stratified floodplain site, where Faïta pottery and imported stone co-occur with ceramics of local fisherfolk from c. 1300 BCE.[40] As has been extensively argued elsewhere, this site was

---

36 See Munson, 'Archaeology and the prehistoric origins of the Ghana empire'.
37 K.C. MacDonald, 'Tichitt-Walata and the middle Niger: evidence for cultural contact in the second millennium BC', in Pwiti and Soper (eds.), *Aspects of African Archaeology*, 429–40.
38 K.C. MacDonald, 'Socio-economic diversity and the origins of cultural complexity along the middle Niger (2000 BC to AD 300)', unpublished PhD thesis (University of Cambridge, 1994), and 'Tichitt-Walata and the middle Niger'.
39 Amblard, *Tichitt-Walata*.   40 MacDonald, 'Socio-economic diversity'.

Figure 19.7 Classic Tichitt rim forms from Ndondi Tossokel, in the middle Niger.

first occupied by local fisherfolk,[41] and subsequently had an additional season-al presence of Tichitt-derived pastoralists, as witnessed by the appearance of classic Tichitt pottery, cattle remains, phthanite, and cattle figurines.

Tichitt pottery's only qualitative difference from that of the Mauritanian Dhars and the early Faïta Facies is that of temper: grog and bone temper dominates chaff in the latter, instead of vice versa. The explanation for this is probably tied to access, or lack thereof, to crop processing waste. As it has been hypothesized that early Faïta represents the seasonal presence of a transhumant pastoral segment from the Mauritanian Dhars in the middle Niger floodplain,[42] they would hardly have had access to millet chaff in this ecologically unsuitable area.

Around 900 BCE, a broad settlement transformation took place in the middle Niger. Instead of a seasonal pastoral presence with ephemeral camps and/or short-term co-occupations with fisherfolk (as at Kobadi and Kolima-Sud), this extension of the Tichitt tradition began to make its own

41 K.C. MacDonald, 'Invisible pastoralists: an inquiry into the origins of nomadic pastor-alism in the West African Sahel', in C. Gosden and J. Hather (eds.), *Prehistory of Food: Appetites for Change* (London: Routledge, 1999), 333–49.
42 MacDonald, 'Socio-economic diversity', and 'Invisible pastoralists'.

more permanent settlements. These ranged from the 10 ha site of Kolima Sud-Est, with rammed-earth architecture, dated to *c.* 900–400 BCE,[43] to the founding layers of the tell complexes at Akumbu.[44] Further south, in the Macina region, there is one of Mali's most ancient urban tells, Dia Shoma, where Tichitt ceramics appear in the first occupation phase of 800–0 BCE alongside earthen architecture and iron metallurgy.[45]

In sum, the Tichitt diaspora may be found at the base of the middle Niger's urban civilization whose basis lies in the first-millennium BCE layers of tells like Akumbu and Dia. Indeed, in the waning days of the Tichitt tradition in the Mauritanian Dhars, a major settlement centre of 12 to 20 ha already existed at Dia Shoma.[46] Thus, perhaps the continuity between Dhar Tichitt and middle Niger civilization – from which the empires of Ghana and Mali would arise – is not so far-fetched as it once seemed. Tichitt, and its role in the advent of Sahelian West African civilization, merits much more attention than it has heretofore received, and it may still be justly said that only a spoonful of soil has been sifted along the middle Niger and Mauritanian escarpments for every heaped shovel-full along the Nile.

## Further reading

Amblard-Pison, S. *Communautés Villageoises Néolithiques des Dhars Tichitt et Oulata (Mauritanie)*. Oxford: British Archaeological Reports, 2006.

Holl, A.F.C. 'Background to the Ghana empire: archaeological investigations on the transition to statehood in the Dhar Tichitt region (Mauritania).' *Journal of Anthropological Archaeology*, 4 (1985), 73–115.

'Late Neolithic cultural landscape in southeastern Mauritania: an essay in spatiometrics.' In A.F.C. Holl and T.E. Levy (eds.), *Spatial Boundaries and Social Dynamics: Case Studies from Food-Producing Societies*. Ann Arbor, MI: International Monographs in Prehistory, 1993. 95–133.

MacDonald, K.C. 'Before the empire of Ghana: pastoralism and the origins of cultural complexity in the Sahel.' In G. Connah (ed.), *Transformations in Africa: Essays on Africa's Later Past*. London: Leicester University Press, 1998. 71–103.

43 S. Takezawa and M. Cissé, 'Domestication des céreales au Méma, Mali', in S. Sanogo and T. Togola (eds.), *Proceedings of the 11th Congress of the PanAfrican Association for Prehistory and Related Fields* (Bamako: Institut des Sciences Humaines, 2004), 105–21.

44 MacDonald, 'Socio-economic diversity', 92.

45 R. Bedaux et al., 'The Dia Archaeological Project: rescuing cultural heritage in the inland Niger delta (Mali)', *Antiquity*, 75 (2001), 837–48; R. Bedaux et al. (eds.), *Recherches archéologiques à Dia dans le delta intérieur du Niger (Mali): bilan des saisons de fouilles 1998–2003* (Leiden: CNWS, 2005).

46 Bedaux et al., 'Dia Archaeological Project'; Bedaux et al. (eds.), *Recherches archéologiques à Dia*.

'Betwixt Tichitt and the IND: the pottery of the Faïta Facies, Tichitt tradition.' *Azania*, 46 (2011), 49–69.

'Invisible pastoralists: an inquiry into the origins of nomadic pastoralism in the West African Sahel.' In C. Gosden and J. Hather (eds.), *Prehistory of Food: Appetites for Change*. London: Routledge, 1999. 333–49.

MacDonald, K.C., R. Vernet, M. Martinon-Torres, and D.Q. Fuller. 'Dhar Néma: from early agriculture to metallurgy in southeastern Mauritania.' *Azania*, 44 (2009), 3–48.

Manning, K. 'A developmental history for early West African agriculture.' In P. Allsworth-Jones (ed.), *West African Archaeology: New Developments, New Perspectives*. Oxford: Archaeopress, 2010. 43–52.

Munson, P.J. 'Archaeological data on the origins of cultivation in the southwestern Sahara and their implications for West Africa.' In J.R. Harlan, J.M.J. de Wet, and A.B. Stemler (eds.), *Origins of African Plant Domestication*. The Hague: Mouton, 1976. 187–209.

'Archaeology and the prehistoric origins of the Ghana empire.' *Journal of African History*, 21 (1980), 457–66.

Ould Khattar, M. 'Les sites Gangara, la fin de la culture de Tichitt et l'origine de Ghana.' *Journal des Africanistes*, 65 (1995), 31–41.

Vernet, R. *Préhistoire de la Mauritanie*. Nouakchott: Centre Culturel Français A. de Saint-Exupéry; Paris: Sépia, 1993.

# 20

# Early agriculture in the Americas

DEBORAH M. PEARSALL

## Crops of the Americas and the geography of domestication

At the time of European contact in the fifteenth century CE, millions of people throughout the Americas lived in agriculturally based societies. Some practices and foods were millennia old; others coalesced late in prehistory. Domestication and agriculture did not arise everywhere, however, nor did all societies take an agricultural route. Distributions of wild ancestors, genetic studies of American crops, and archaeology give us snapshots of the geography of plant domestication (Figure 20.1) and of the diversity of crops grown (Table 20.1).

Today our understanding of the ancestry and areas of origin of a few crops is quite good, while for others little has changed since the 1970s, when one of the first comprehensive overviews, *Crops and Man*, was written by Jack Harlan.[1] Economically important crops are more likely to have been studied by agronomists and plant geneticists. For example, decades of debate and study of the only widespread American grain, maize, and its related wild species leave little doubt that wild *Zea mays* subsp. *parviglumis*, Balsas teosinte, gave rise to maize in a single domestication.[2] Balsas teosinte grows today in the deciduous tropical forests of southern and western Mexico, making this region the likely area of origin. How early Native farmers achieved the dramatic transformation of teosinte to maize is still being studied, but it was likely a process of a few thousand years that combined conscious and unconscious selection targeting seed dispersal, seed size,

---

1 J.R. Harlan, *Crops and Man* (Madison, WI: American Society of Agronomy, 1975).
2 E.S. Buckler IV and N.M. Stevens, 'Maize origins, domestication, and selection', in T.J. Motley et al. (eds.), *Darwin's Harvest: New Approaches to the Origins, Evolution, and Conservation of Crops* (New York: Columbia University Press, 2006), 67–90.

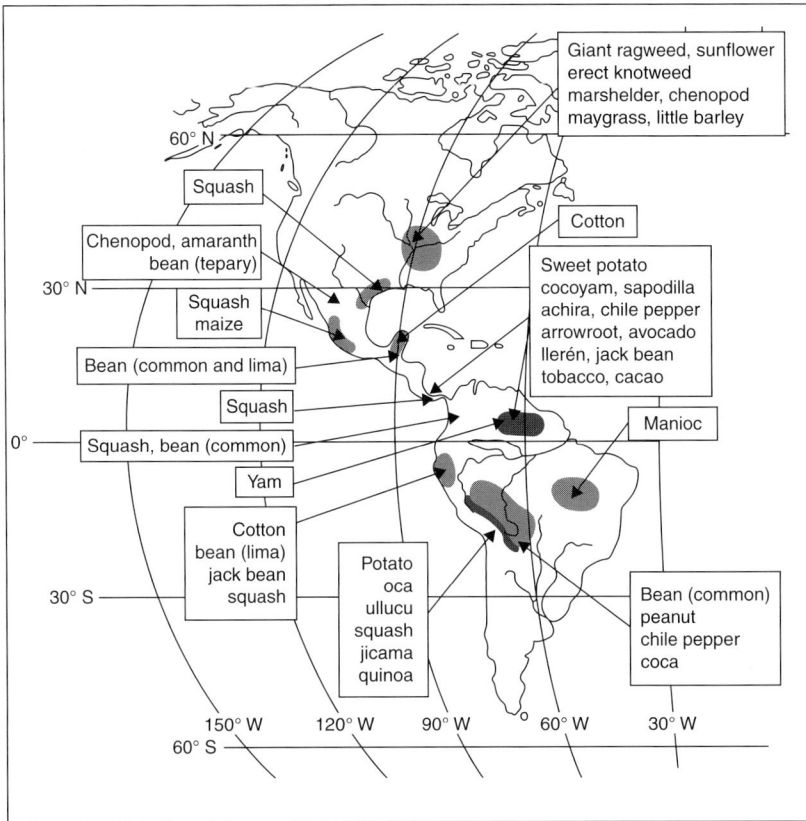

Figure 20.1 Likely areas of origin for selected crops of the Americas.

photoperiod, and starch production. Of the lowland root and tuber crops (arrowroot, cocoyam, llerén, manioc, sweet potato, yam), only productive and undemanding manioc is well studied. The primary stable crop for millions of people worldwide, mostly the poor of tropical countries, manioc was domesticated from *Manihot esculenta* subsp. *flabellifolia* on the southern border of the Amazon basin.[3] For many other crops, from fruit trees to roots and tubers to pseudocereals, we know only the broad geographic range of their likely area of origin. Seasonal environments, especially forests and forest fringes, were key habitats for domestication in the Americas.[4]

3 B.A. Schall et al., 'Evolution, domestication, and agrobiodiversity in the tropical crop cassava', in Motley et al. (eds.), *Darwin's Harvest*, 269–84.
4 D.R. Piperno and D.M. Pearsall, *The Origins of Agriculture in the Lowland Neotropics* (San Diego, CA: Academic Press, 1998).

Table 20.1 A short list of crops of the Americas.

**'Pseudocereals', grains, oil seeds**

| | |
|---|---|
| amaranth | *Amaranthus caudatus* (Andes), *A. cruentus* (Mexico) |
| cañahua | *Chenopodium pallidicaule* |
| chenopod | *Chenopodium berlandieri* var. *jonesianum* (North America), *C. berlandieri* subsp. *nuttaliae* (Mexico) |
| erect knotweed | *Polygonum erectum* |
| giant ragweed | *Ambrosia trifida* |
| little barley | *Hordeum pusillum* |
| maize | *Zea mays* |
| marshelder | *Iva annua* var. *macrocarpa* |
| maygrass | *Phalaris caroliniana* |
| quinoa | *Chenopodium quinoa* |
| sunflower | *Helianthus annuus* var. *macrocarpus* |

**Legumes (pulses)**

| | |
|---|---|
| bean, common | *Phaseolus vulgaris* |
| bean, lima | *Phaseolus lunatus* |
| bean, tepary | *Phaseolus acutifolius* |
| bean, runner | *Phaseolus coccineus* |
| jack bean | *Canavalia ensiformis, C. plagiosperma* |
| lupine | *Lupinus mutabilis* |
| peanut | *Arachis hypogaea* |

**Squashes and gourd**

| | |
|---|---|
| bottle gourd | *Lagenaria siceraria* |
| squash | *Cucurbita pepo, C. argyrosperma* (=*C. mixta*), *C. moschata, C. maxima, C. ficifolia* |

**Roots and tubers**

| | |
|---|---|
| Achira | *Canna edulis* |
| arrowroot | *Maranta arundinacea* |
| cocoyam | *Xanthosoma sagittifolium* |
| jicama | *Pachyrrhizus ahipa* |
| llerén | *Calathea allouia* |
| manioc | *Manihot esculenta* |
| oca | *Oxalis tuberosa* |
| potato | *Solanum tuberosum* |
| sweet potato | *Ipomoea batatas* |
| ullucu | *Ullucus tuberosus* |
| yam | *Dioscorea trifida* |

**Fruit trees**

| | |
|---|---|
| achiote | *Bixa orellana* |
| avocado | *Persea americana* |
| black sapote | *Diospyros digyna* |
| cacao | *Theobroma cacao* |

Table 20.1 (cont.)

| | |
|---|---|
| ciruela de fraile | *Bunchosia armeniaca* |
| guava | *Psidium guajava* |
| lucuma | *Pouteria lucuma* |
| pacae | *Inga* species |
| papaya | *Carica papaya* |
| peach palm | *Bactris gasipaes* |
| pepino | *Solanum muricatum* |
| sapodilla | *Manilkara achras* |
| soursop, custard apple | *Annona* sp. |
| tree tomato | *Cyphomandra betacea* |
| yellow sapote | *Pouteria campechianum* |
| yellow, red mombin | *Spondias* sp. |
| **Spices, stimulants, fibre** | |
| chile peppers | *Capsicum annuum, C. baccatum, C. frutescens/C. chinense, C. pubescens* |
| coca | *Erythroxylum coca, E. novogranatense* |
| cotton | *Gossypium barbadense, G. hirsutum* |
| tobacco | *Nicotiana rustica, N. tabacum* |

More basic research, especially collection of wild related species and traditional crop varieties, is needed to understand the ancestry of many crops, and the pace of extinction, habitat loss, and loss of indigenous knowledge is accelerating. Based on available data, plant domestication in the Americas was characterized by multiple, independent domestications of species in useful genera in North, Central, and South America.[5] We see this pattern for pseudocereals, legumes, chiles, squashes, tobacco, cotton, and a number of fruit trees. Plants needed for nutritionally balanced meals were domesticated multiple times in diverse settings. For example, where land can be farmed in the Americas, there is a domesticated legume or pulse to thrive there, from peanuts, adapted to moist lowland environments, to the cold-tolerant lupine and the versatile common bean.

Tracing the domestication of root and tuber foods is especially challenging, since only manioc and potato are well studied. Each of those crops emerged in a single region/centre. Whether this pattern characterizes root and tuber domestication in general is unknown; archaeological data hint at multiple domestications (or the very early spread) of some root and tuber crops. Better understanding of the geography of plant domestication could

5 Ibid.

provide valuable insights into the nature of early social networks in the Americas.

## The early history of domestication

The early history of plant domestication begins in lower Central America and northwestern South America (Map 20.1), and is known in large part from microfossil evidence (phytoliths, starch grains, pollen). Human occupation of the neotropics began in the late Pleistocene, and by 10,900–9400 BCE people occupied diverse environments and in some cases modified them by fire.[6] Burning of forests and small-scale land clearance is dated to 11050 BCE* at Lake La Yeguada in Panama, for example. Arrowroot was the earliest domesticate there, dating to 7800 BCE* at the Cueva de los Vampiros site and 5800 BCE* at Aguadulce. By 5800 BCE* maize and gourd were introduced to Panama and llerén and squash were present, and manioc was introduced shortly thereafter.

Plant domestication began before 8500 BCE in southwest coastal Ecuador. Squash phytoliths were recovered from terminal Pleistocene and early Holocene strata at Vegas sites.[7] Phytoliths recovered from the earliest levels are from wild squash, with domesticated-size squash phytoliths directly dated to 9840–8555 BCE.[8] Other Vegas crops included gourd and llerén, and maize was introduced just before 5800 BCE*. Maize continued to be grown at Real Alto and Loma Alta, two Valdivia tradition farming villages (4500–2250 BCE), along with cotton, jack bean, achira, manioc, chile pepper, llerén, and arrowroot.[9] Agriculture in coastal Ecuador remained broad-based for many millennia, incorporating wild/managed tree fruits as well as annual crops.[10]

Domesticated arrowroot dates back to 9250–8500 BCE* at the San Isidro site in the Colombian Andes, where starch was identified on a pounding tool.[11] Palms and avocado were also present, but whether domesticated or

---

6 Ibid. All dates are calibrated C14 dates. An * indicates that the calibration was estimated graphically from the published non-calibrated date.

7 Piperno and Pearsall, *Origins of Agriculture*.

8 D.R. Piperno and K.E. Stothert, 'Phytolith evidence for early Holocene *Cucurbita* domestication in southwest Ecuador', *Science*, 299 (2003), 1054–7.

9 K. Chandler-Ezell et al., 'Root and tuber phytoliths and starch grains document manioc (*Manihot esculenta*), arrowroot (*Maranta arundinacea*), and llerén (*Calathea* sp.) at the Real Alto site, Ecuador', *Economic Botany*, 60 (2006), 103–20.

10 D.M. Pearsall, *Plants and People in Ancient Ecuador: The Ethnobotany of the Jama River Valley* (Belmont, CA: Wadsworth/Thomson Learning, 2004).

11 Piperno and Pearsall, *Origins of Agriculture*.

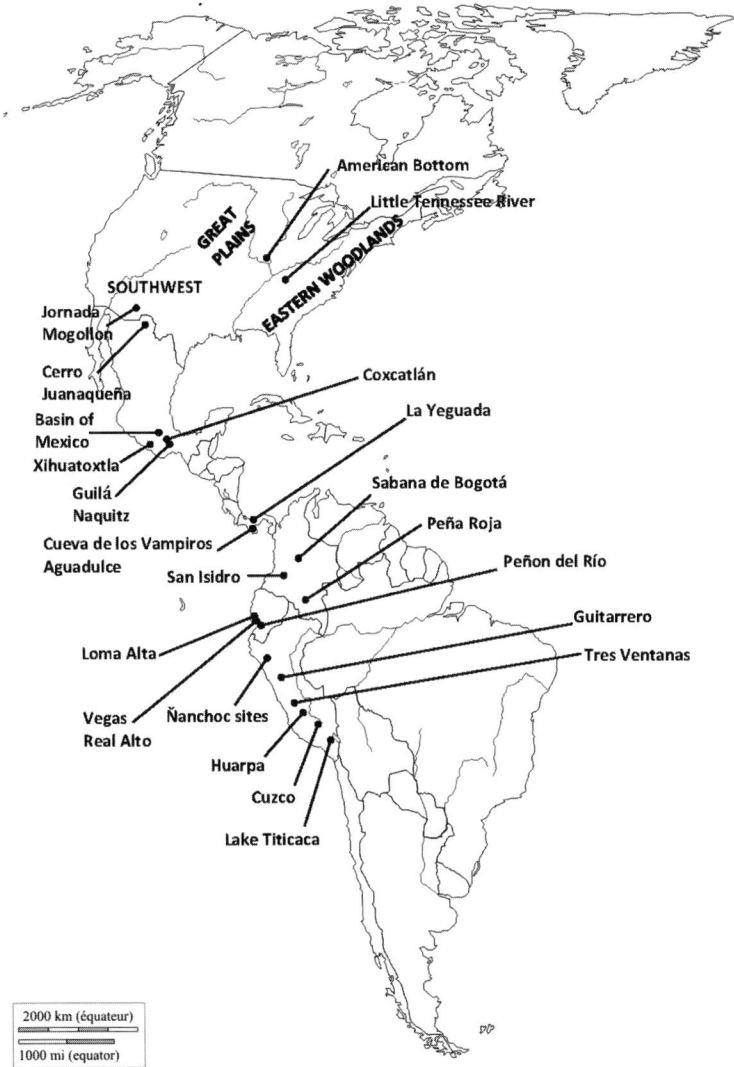

Map 20.1 Early agricultural sites and regions in the Americas.

wild/managed is unknown. Pollen records documented maize in association with forest clearance and disturbance beginning at 7250 BCE* in one core, and in several sequences from 5500 BCE* and after. Palm and domesticated squash, llerén, and gourd were directly dated to 8250–6500 BCE* at the Peña Roja site in eastern Colombia.

At sites in the Nanchoc valley of northern Peru, initial direct dates on domesticates with primitive morphologies, including manioc and peanut, were modern, but new direct dates document squash at 8283 BCE, peanut at 6538 BCE, and cotton at 4113 BCE, and confirm early occurrence of manioc.[12] Starch from bean and pacae seeds, squash flesh, and peanut was recovered from dental calculus of teeth dating from 7163–5744 BCE.[13] Domestication may be equally ancient in the central Peruvian sierra, but dating ambiguities exist for important sites. Oca, chile pepper, lucuma, and common and lima beans were recovered from Guitarrero Cave in strata dated 9250–8500 BCE*, but beans were directly dated as much younger.[14] Several root crops were recovered from Tres Ventanas Cave in equally ancient strata, but one was directly dated to 5800 BCE*. Domestication of a diverse array of local Andean tubers, pulses, and quinoa was likely underway before 5800 BCE*.[15]

The best-known data on early domestication in Mesoamerica come from two caves, Coxcatlán and Guilá Naquitz, each located in the semi-arid highlands of central Mexico. The excellent preservation of crop remains in these dry sites, and in the case of Coxcatlán, its historically early excavation and thorough publication, have long influenced perceptions of the history of plant domestication. Maize, squash, and bottle gourd first appear at Coxcatlán during the Coxcatlán phase, 5800–4400 BCE*; by the end of the phase, tree fruits were present whose dispersal and maintenance depended on humans.[16] Another squash, common bean, tepary bean, and chile pepper appeared over the next 2,000 years. The supposed antiquity of domesticates in the Coxcatlán sequence has largely not stood up to direct dating of crop remains, however. Coxcatlán-phase maize was directly dated to 3600 BCE, common beans 300 BCE, and tepary beans 440 BCE.[17] Only bottle gourd was as ancient as expected from site stratigraphy. Guilá Naquitz Cave also

---

12  T.D. Dillehay et al., 'Preceramic adoption of peanut, squash, and cotton in northern Peru', *Science*, 316 (2007), 1890–3.

13  D.R. Piperno and T.D. Dillehay, 'Starch grains on human teeth reveal early broad crop diet in northern Peru', *Proceedings of the National Academy of Sciences*, 105 (2008), 19622–7.

14  L. Kaplan and T.G. Lynch, '*Phaseolus* (Fabaceae) in archaeology: AMS radiocarbon dates and their significance for pre-Columbian agriculture', *Economic Botany*, 53 (1999), 261–72.

15  D.M. Pearsall, 'Plant domestication and the shift to agriculture in the Andes', in H. Silverman and W.H. Isbell (eds.), *Handbook of South American Archaeology* (New York: Springer, 2008), 105–20.

16  C.E. Smith, Jr, 'Plant remains', in D.S. Byers (ed.), *The Prehistory of the Tehuacan Valley*, vol. I: *Environment and Subsistence* (Austin: University of Texas Press, 1967), 220–5.

17  Bean dates from Kaplan and Lynch, '*Phaseolus* in archaeology'; maize dates from A. Long et al., 'First direct AMS dates on early maize from Tehuacan, Mexico', *Radiocarbon*, 31 (1989), 1035–40.

documents early domesticated squash, maize, chile pepper, and bottle gourd.[18] Squash (*Cucurbita pepo*) was directly dated to 8000–6000 BCE and maize to 4250 BCE.[19]

Recent research at Xihuatoxtla shelter in the central Balsas River valley, southwest Mexico, has now documented early maize in the dry tropical forest setting of its wild ancestor.[20] Maize phytoliths were recovered from site sediments, and maize starch and phytoliths from grinding stones, dating to 6700 BCE. Domesticated squash was also present. From the Balsas region maize spread first through the lowlands; it is documented, for example, at 5100–5000 BCE in a sediment core on the Gulf Coast, and maize pollen and/or phytoliths document the crop in southern Pacific coastal Mexico, Pacific coastal Guatemala, northern Belize, and Honduras by 3500 BCE.[21] Maize was carried south through the tropical lowlands prior to this time, however, as it is documented earlier in Panama, Colombia, and Ecuador.

Early domestication in the Americas took place in the context of changing climatic conditions, namely increasing warmth and moisture.[22] The earliest crop records in the northern tropics fall within the northern thermal maximum (8500–3400 BCE), a period wetter than present, some prior to a reversal to colder, drier conditions (6300–5800 BCE: maize, arrowroot), others at the end or shortly after that reversal (squash, llerén, manioc). Domestication was earlier in the southern tropics, with arrowroot, llerén, squash, and gourd present before the southern thermal maximum (8000–5500 BCE). The list of domesticates in the southern tropics expands greatly during the thermal maximum and the millennia during which ENSO (El Niño – Southern Oscillation) was weak (6800–3800 BCE: maize, peanut, cotton, *Phaseolus*, jackbean, achira, manioc, chile, potato). Domesticates were moved during

18 C.E. Smith, Jr, 'Preceramic plant remains from Guilá Naquitz', in K.V. Flannery (ed.), *Guilá Naquitz: Archaic Foraging and Early Agriculture in Oaxaca, Mexico* (Orlando, FL: Academic Press, 1986), 265–74.

19 B.D. Smith, 'The initial domestication of *Cucurbita pepo* in the Americas 10,000 years ago', *Science*, 276 (1997), 932–4; D.R. Piperno and K.V. Flannery, 'The earliest archaeological maize (*Zea mays*, L.) from highland Mexico: new accelerator mass spectrometry dates and their implications', *Proceedings of the National Academy of Sciences*, 98 (2001), 2101–3.

20 D.R. Piperno et al., 'Starch grain and phytolith evidence for early ninth millennium BP maize from the central Balsas River valley, Mexico', *Proceedings of the National Academy of Sciences*, 106 (2009), 5020–4.

21 Piperno and Pearsall, *Origins of Agriculture*.

22 D.M. Pearsall and P.W. Stahl, 'The origins and spread of early agriculture and domestication: environmental and cultural considerations', in J.A. Matthews (ed.), *The Sage Handbook of Environmental Change*, 2 vols. (Los Angeles, CA: Sage, 2012), vol. II, 328–54.

this warm interval: for example, maize from west Mexico into Central and South America, and manioc from the southern edge of the Amazon to Peru (with peanut), Ecuador, and Panama. Too little is known of the areas of origin of many crops to trace early movements; many early finds are starch or phytolith residues from artefacts, and artefacts of comparable ages have not been studied from possible areas of origin.

The history of plant domestication begins in temperate North America between 3200 and 1785 BCE, when native squash, chenopod, marshelder, and sunflower were domesticated in the Eastern Woodlands, and maygrass, erect knotweed, little barley, and giant ragweed were grown and moved outside their native ranges.[23] Variation exists in the relative importance of native crops and wild plants, with American Bottom populations (Mississippi floodplain near St Louis) producing the largest quantities of native crops over the longest time period. Acorn use was often higher in regions with less reliance on native crops.[24] Maize was incorporated into indigenous crop husbandry in the Eastern Woodlands around 300 BCE.[25] For the better part of a millennium maize was one food in a broad diet, until its transformation into a staple crop between 800 and 1200 CE. Directly dated maize macro-remains and cooking residues place the crop in the Midwest and Northeast at about the same time.[26]

Maize was introduced from Mexico into the Southwest by 1600 BCE or somewhat earlier, just prior to the late Archaic or early Agricultural period (1500 BCE to 0–500 CE), and by the end of the period had transformed food-ways based on native plants.[27] With the widespread adoption of maize came substantial habitations with storage features. Maize, beans (common and tepary), and pepo squash form the core of Southwestern agriculture, with cotton and bottle gourd also introduced early, and other beans and squashes later arrivals. Wild native annuals, commonly used during the early middle

23 B.D. Smith and C.W. Cowan, 'Domesticated crop plants and the evolution of food production economies in Eastern North America', in P.E. Minnis (ed.), *People and Plants in Ancient Eastern North America* (Washington, DC: Smithsonian Books, 2003), 105–25.

24 C.M. Scarry, 'Patterns of wild plant utilization in the prehistoric Eastern Woodlands', in Minnis (ed.), *People and Plants*, 50–104.

25 Smith and Cowan, 'Domesticated crop plants'.

26 J.P. Hart et al., 'Extending the phytolith evidence for early maize (*Zea may* spp. *mays*) and squash (*Cucurbita* sp.) in central New York', *American Antiquity*, 72 (2007), 563–83.

27 L.W. Huckell, 'Ancient maize in the American Southwest: what does it look like and what can it tell us?', in J.E. Staller et al. (eds.), *Histories of Maize: Multidisciplinary Approaches to the Prehistory, Biogeography, Domestication, and Evolution of Maize* (Amsterdam and London: Elsevier Academic Press, 2006), 97–107.

Archaic (prior to 1500 BCE), remained a component of diet through the Pueblo IV/Classic period.[28]

In the Great Plains, during the Archaic (3500–500 BCE) plant foods included native annuals, fleshy fruits, nuts, roots, and grasses.[29] The earliest directly dated domesticates are squash (2218–2142 BCE), marshelder (628–609 BCE), and maize (813–878 CE), which was likely introduced earlier. Woodland populations (500 BCE to 800–900 CE) were more sedentary, ceramics were introduced, and cultivated plants were increasingly used. The maize-based Plains Village tradition (900–1600 CE) developed out of this foundation. Maize was also a widespread component of diet from 700–1600 CE in the eastern Canadian prairies and adjacent boreal forests.[30]

## Early food-producing societies

What was life like in early mid-Holocene food-producing societies of the Americas? Several examples illustrate the range of variation that existed and also commonalities, such as reduction in mobility and emergence of villages. At Real Alto, Ecuador, one of the earliest American agricultural villages, inferences can be drawn concerning social organization, ritual activities, and emerging political complexity. Other examples of early food-producing societies will be drawn from Mesoamerica and the desert borderlands of the southwest United States and northwest Mexico.

There are many ethnographically documented combinations of domesticated, managed, and wild plants used by non-agricultural societies, i.e. those that do not depend on domesticates for a substantial part of their diet.[31] The length of time between the appearance of domesticates and agriculture is variable, with cases of a long period of low-level food production, such as in Eastern North America (4,000-year separation between domestication of native crops and dependence on maize). But it can be difficult to gauge the contribution of domesticated plants to past diet.[32] *Presence* of domesticates is not the same as *dependence* on domesticates; different kinds of food may

28 L.W. Huckell and M.S. Toll, 'Wild plant use in the North American Southwest', in Minnis (ed.), *People and Plants*, 37–114.
29 M.J. Adair, 'Great Plains paleoethnobotany', in Minnis (ed.), *People and Plants*, 258–346.
30 M. Boyd et al., 'Reassessing the northern limit of maize consumption in North America: stable isotope, plant microfossil, and trace element content of carbonized food residue', *Journal of Archaeological Science*, 35 (2008), 2545–56.
31 B.D. Smith, 'Low-level food production', *Journal of Archaeological Research*, 9 (2001), 1–43.
32 D.M. Pearsall, 'Investigating the transition to agriculture', *Current Anthropology*, 50 (2009), 609–13.

become incorporated into the archaeological record in different ways (e.g. foods with robust inedible parts survive as charred macro-remains, tubers as starch or phytolith residues on tools). There is a tendency to assume that roots and tubers, squashes, legumes, and tree fruits were not staples in early food-producing systems, and to equate agriculture with maize as a staple crop.[33] But many root and tuber crops are equal to or exceed maize in caloric production, and when such resources are available, agriculture may follow quickly after domestication.

In southwest coastal Ecuador, domesticated plants are first documented during the early mid-Holocene Vegas tradition.[34] All Vegas sites but one are very small – dense scatters of lithic debris, likely associated with ephemeral structures. Site 80 is distinctively different: covering an area of over 2,000 m², it served as a base camp for the seasonally mobile population, who buried their dead there.[35] Thus, prior to the appearance of villages in coastal Ecuador, a dispersed community began to link themselves to place via ancestors. One burial is distinctive: a female burial in a small structure, suggesting an early, central role for women in community and ceremonial life. Site locations – along seasonal streams – indicate that plant cultivation had already begun to shape the interactions of people and landscape.

Following a brief hiatus, life in southwest Ecuador was transformed during the Valdivia period (4400–1400 BCE).[36] Valdivia is one of the earliest ceramic traditions of the Americas; the earliest Valdivia sites are among the first villages of the Americas; by the time of the middle Valdivia, the Real Alto site had grown to be a town, one of the earliest in the Americas.

Household and community structure at Real Alto provide insights into Valdivia society.[37] The earliest village was small (150 m across), and circular or

---

33 J. Iriarte, 'New perspectives on plant domestication and the development of agriculture in the New World', in T.P. Denham et al. (eds.), *Rethinking Agriculture: Archaeological and Ethnoarchaeological Perspectives* (Walnut Creek, CA: Left Coast Press, 2007), 167–88.

34 Piperno and Pearsall, *Origins of Agriculture*; Piperno and Stothert, 'Phytolith evidence'.

35 K.E. Stothert, 'Expression of ideology in the formative period of Ecuador', in J.S. Raymond and R.L. Burger (eds.), *Archaeology of Formative Ecuador* (Washington, DC: Dumbarton Oaks Research Library and Collection, 2003), 337–420.

36 J.G. Marcos, 'A reassessment of the Ecuadorian Formative', in Raymond and Burger (eds.), *Archaeology of Formative Ecuador*, 7–32; J.A. Zeidler, 'The Ecuadorian Formative', in Silverman and Isbell (eds.), *Handbook of South American Archaeology*, 459–88.

37 J.E. Clark et al., 'First towns in the Americas', in M.S. Bandy and J.R. Fox (eds.), *Becoming Villagers: Comparing Early Village Societies* (Tucson: University of Arizona Press, 2010), 205–45; J.G. Marcos, 'The ceremonial precinct at Real Alto: organization of time and space in Valdivia society', unpublished PhD thesis (University of Illinois at Urbana-Champaign, 1978); J.A. Zeidler, 'Social space in Valdivia society: community patterning and domestic structure at Real Alto, 3000–2000 BC', unpublished PhD thesis (University

U-shaped, with 12–15 houses. Houses were small (8.4 m²) single-family dwellings, giving a total population of 50–60 people. The village grew until by the end of the early Valdivia it had doubled in size, and was occupied by 150–250 people. The village plan continued to reflect a division of space into domestic (outer ring of houses) and public (interior plaza) domains; no structures for public ritual were present.

In the middle Valdivia, Real Alto grew into a town, 400 m across and U-shaped or rectangular. Average house size increased to 102 m² extended-family dwellings, and population grew to 1,800. Community structure also changed, with the construction of two ceremonial mounds (Fiesta and Charnal House mounds) facing each other across the central plaza. The mounds divided the plaza into two segments, creating several levels of potential segmentation/opposition within the community. While there is no direct evidence of who participated in and who led ceremonies, most researchers argue that ritual life at Real Alto included shamanism.[38] Shamanic practices of tropical forest agriculturalists include rituals focused on life-cycle issues of women (puberty, pregnancy), curing, and divination. Shamans also keep a community's ceremonial calendar, and provide leadership in both the domestic and sacred realms.

Over time at Real Alto, distinctive rituals became formalized within structures built on platform mounds, two to four social groups existed in the town, and family structure changed to extended families, with house clusters suggesting increased emphasis on descent group.[39] Two sizes of extended-family house existed, indicating differences in relative social standing of households, but there was no evidence of differential access to resources. Neither were there differences in grave goods, but some individuals were treated differently after death.[40] Most individuals were buried next to or in wall trenches of domestic structures. The Charnal House mound had a concentration of burials in a very different context: an adult female was buried in a tomb under the threshold, with nearby male and juvenile burials

of Illinois at Urbana-Champaign, 1984); Stothert, 'Expression of ideology'; Marcos, 'Reassessment of the Ecuadorian Formative'.

38 D.W. Lathrap et al., *Ancient Ecuador: Culture, Clay and Creativity, 3000–300 BC* (Chicago: Field Museum of Natural History, 1975); J.G. Marcos, *Real Alto: la historia de un centro ceremonial Valdivia* (Guayaquil: Escuela Superior Politécnica del Litoral; Quito: Corporación Editora Nacional, 1988); P.W. Stahl, 'Hallucinatory imagery and the origin of early South American figurine art', *World Archaeology*, 18 (1986), 134–50; Stothert, 'Expression of ideology'.

39 Zeidler, 'Social space in Valdivia'.

40 Marcos, 'Ceremonial precinct at Real Alto'; Marcos, 'Reassessment of the Ecuadorian Formative'.

within the structure. The inference is burial of a woman in the apical role for a corporate kin group. The Fiesta mound also represented a distinctive context: large pits within a series of paired structures contained evidence of feasting activities, such as broken drinking vessels and exotic sea food. The inference is social competition through feasting: ritual to attract and retain group members.

The transformation of Real Alto from village to town during the middle Valdivia period represented significant changes in social relationships, and ritual feasting, led perhaps by shamans, helped create and maintain the new social order. While there are hints of differences in social standing, access to more labour (acquired by attracting followers through feasting), rather than prestige goods, seems to be the key element of status differences: labour to put more fields into production, to water long-growing root crops during the dry season, or to grow an extra maize crop in an *albarrada* (water catchment feature).

The first farmers of western Mexico were small groups of cultivators who likely shifted settlements seasonally.[41] Xihautoxtla shelter, where early maize was identified, was repeatedly visited by small groups who stayed for several weeks or more. They used unmodified river cobbles and stone slabs as grinding tools, and manufactured chipped stone tools. Two contemporary sites in the region lack grinding stones, suggesting that different sets of activities were carried out there. Palaeoenvironmental data from nearby lakes indicate that lacustrine environments were used by Archaic period inhabitants of the region, including, perhaps, for cultivating plants on the lake edge. Population mobility appears to decline over time with the emergence of food production in Mexico. In the highland Tehuacan valley, for example, researchers argue on the basis of site locations, numbers, and sizes that semi-sedentary camps (i.e. occupied for two or three seasons) appear in the Riego phase (7500–6000 BCE*) and small sedentary sites by the Abejas phase (4500–2750 BCE*).[42] By 2000 BCE, sedentary villages appear widely in Mesoamerica, marking the beginning of the Formative period (2000 BCE to 250 CE), which represents the time when agriculture, village life, and ceramic production came together.[43]

---

41 A.J. Ranere et al., 'The cultural and chronological context of early Holocene maize and squash domestication in the central Balsas River valley, Mexico', *Proceedings of the National Academy of Sciences*, 106 (2009), 5014–18.

42 R.S. MacNeish et al., 'The archaeological reconnaissance', in R.S. MacNeish et al. (eds.), *The Prehistory of the Tehuacan Valley*, vol. V: *Excavations and Reconnaissance* (Austin: University of Texas Press, 1972), 341–495.

43 T.G. Powis, 'Formative Mesoamerican cultures: an introduction', in T.G. Powis (ed.), *New Perspectives on Formative Mesoamerican Cultures* (Oxford: Archaeopress, 2005), 1–14.

The late Archaic through early Formative was a period of change in Mesoamerica, from sparse populations of low-level food producers to settled agriculturalists and growing populations.[44] The southwest Pacific coasts of Mexico and Guatemala provide contrasting views of life during this transition. Large shell mounds, dating to 5500–1800 BCE, are highly visible Archaic sites in coastal Mexico. These sites have been interpreted as seasonal occupations of foragers who harvested estuarine resources, and perhaps used some domesticated plants. Pollen, phytolith, and charcoal data from environmental cores adjacent to sites now document that sustained slash-and-burn farming, incorporating maize, took place between 2700 and 1800 BCE.[45] Farming settlements were likely located inland, away from saline and seasonally inundated soils, and now buried beneath stream alluvium. The inference is that populations of farmer-foragers with reduced mobility lived in base camps near the best agricultural land, with seasonal settlements near rich estuarine resources.

This rich coastal environment extends into Pacific coastal Guatemala, where there is a 6,000-year palaeoenvironmental record of human occupation.[46] Evidence for anthropogenic fire survives from the late Archaic, and microfossil evidence indicates that maize, squash, and cotton were cultivated and arboreal species managed by non-sedentary peoples before the appearance of the first permanent villages. The lack of late Archaic sites indicates that populations were more mobile than those of coastal Mexico; the overall scarcity of crop remains suggests a low level of food production, with fire used to encourage useful wild plants and to attract animals.

Recent research in the desert borderlands of northwest Mexico and the southwest United States indicates that Archaic populations who grew domesticated plants were less mobile than previously thought.[47] Early farming systems were very diverse in this region, incorporating flood, water-table, run-off, irrigated, dry, and rain-fed farming systems, with nearly all early

---

44 R.G. Lesure, 'Early social transformations in the Soconusco', in R.G. Lesure (ed.), *Early Mesoamerican Social Transformations: Archaic and Formative Lifeways in the Soconusco Region* (Berkeley: University of California Press, 2011), 1–24.

45 D.J. Kennett et al., 'Pre-pottery farmers on the Pacific coast of southern Mexico', *Journal of Archaeological Science*, 37 (2010), 3401–11.

46 M. Blake and H. Neff, 'Evidence for the diversity of late Archaic and early Formative plant use in the Soconusco region of Mexico and Guatemala', in Lesure (ed.), *Early Mesoamerican Social Transformations*, 47–66.

47 G.J. Fritz, 'The transition to agriculture in the desert borderlands: an introduction', in L.D. Webster et al. (eds.), *Archaeology Without Borders: Contact, Commerce, and Change in the US Southwest and Northwestern Mexico* (Boulder: University Press of Colorado, 2008), 25–33.

systems focused on alluvial lands with naturally replenished soils.[48] In south-east Arizona, for example, maize, bean, cotton, and amaranth were grown before evidence of canals, terraces, and larger and more permanent settlements appears.[49] Eventually there is large labour investment in canals and terraces, suggesting reduced mobility and increased territoriality.

There were differences in the rates at which foraging populations in the desert borderlands were transformed into farming ones. For example, the population of the Cerro Juanaqueña site in Chihuahua, Mexico, made significant investments in agriculture by 1200 BCE, while the nearby Jornada Mogollon region did not undergo this transition until 1000 CE.[50] Cerro Juanaqueña is the earliest known *cerros de trincheras* site (complex of hilltop terraces, rock rings, and stone walls). The terraces served as living surfaces, while farming took place in the floodplain of the Rio Casas, below the site. Maize was found in 60 per cent of features, suggesting it was a dietary staple; there were also large numbers of worn grinding stones, possible domesticated amaranth, and wild chenopod and other seeds. This suggests a population that was relatively sedentary: the Rio Casas floodplain offered a lower risk and higher return rate for maize agriculture than was possible in the Jornada Mogollon region, where more mobile populations relied on productive wild resources (especially shrubs and mesquite).

## Agricultural practices and domestication of landscapes

Agriculture led to landscape transformations in the Americas, the scale of which varied across time and place. Fire was an important, early management tool. Other practices that changed landscapes include management of water (through irrigation, water catchment features, construction of raised and ditched fields) and soil (through terracing, formation of black earths, fallow regimes).

By the time of European contact, anthropogenic landscapes existed throughout the Americas. For example, the Gulf Coast and piedmont of

---

48 J.B. Mabry and W.E. Doolittle, 'Modeling the early agricultural frontier in the desert borderlands', in Webster et al. (eds.), *Archaeology Without Borders*, 55–70.

49 J.B. Mabry, 'Changing knowledge and ideas about the first farmers in southeastern Arizona', in B.J. Vierra (ed.), *The Late Archaic across the Borderlands: From Foraging to Farming* (Austin: University of Texas Press, 2005), 41–83.

50 R.J. Hard and J.R. Roney, 'The transition to farming on the Río Casas Grandes and in the southern Jornada Mogollon region', in B.J. Vierra (ed.), *Late Archaic across the Borderlands*, 141–86.

Mesoamerica, where Cortés came inland, was a productive patchwork of cultivation interspersed with managed forests and scrublands.[51] Well-drained lands (hill slopes and constructed terraces) were cultivated in the rainy season, and in the dry season margins of wetlands were farmed as water receded or was drained away. Tree crops such as cacao were cultivated in special plots as well as being part of managed forests and house gardens. In the semi-arid basins of the central highlands, the upper slopes remained in forest, while rain-fed agriculture was practised on lower slopes, constructed terraces and floodwater and irrigation cultivation along watercourses and terraced basin floors, and wetland cultivation on poorly drained basin soils.

Landscapes were also significantly transformed in Southwest and Eastern North America, and intensive practices (i.e. those requiring high labour inputs) were used in both regions.[52] In the Southwest both stream floodplains and upland slopes were farmed. Irrigation systems that supplemented summer rainfall and sometimes permitted a second crop were found in many river valleys. Slopes were modified for agriculture by construction of terraces (to increase soil depth and water retention) and check dams (to slow and spread water run-off).

Historical accounts of farming in the Eastern Woodlands suggest that selective burning and clearance had created a productive mosaic of cultivated fields, successional growth, semi-permanent open areas, and open forests.[53] There are accounts of cropping for extended periods of time, with brief fallows and localized burns to control weeds (in-field burning).[54] Fields varied in size, including very large fields, and systems that approached annual cropping. Raised fields, ridged fields, and hilled fields were known and house gardens were common, but slope modification has not been identified. The first farmers of the Eastern Woodlands appear to have targeted floodplain environments. In the lower Little Tennessee River valley, for example, human impact on bottomland forests, as shown by increases in disturbance-favoured species, increased after the appearance of squash and gourd.[55] Over time, lower terraces as well as active floodplains were farmed. Minimal forest

---

51 T.M. Whitmore and B.L. Turner II, 'Landscapes of cultivation in Mesoamerica on the eve of the conquest', *Annals of the Association of American Geographers*, 82 (1992), 402–25.

52 W.E. Doolittle, 'Agriculture in North America on the eve of contact: a reassessment', *Annals of the Association of American Geographers*, 82 (1992), 386–401.

53 W.M. Denevan, 'The pristine myth: the landscape of the Americas in 1492', *Annals of the Association of American Geographers*, 82 (1992), 369–85.

54 Doolittle, 'Agriculture in North America'.

55 P.A. Delcourt et al., 'Holocene ethnobotanical and paleoecological record of human impact on vegetation in the Little Tennessee River valley, Tennessee', *Quaternary Research*, 25 (1986), 330–49.

clearance occurred in upland forests until nearly the time of Euro-American settlement.

Prior to European contact, farming throughout the Americas was carried out exclusively by hand tools and human labour; draught animals and the traction plough are post-contact. There were two broad classes of farming tool: digging or planting sticks and spade-like implements, with a blade in the same plane as the handle; and hoes or mattocks, with a blade set at an angle to the handle.[56] The wooden digging or planting stick was wedge-shaped and used to make planting holes or to turn the soil. The tip was fire-hardened or sometimes the tool was tipped with stone. In the Andes the foot-plough or *chaqui-taclla* brought the foot of the cultivator into use to turn heavy sod (Figure 20.2). Hoes or mattocks were used for cultivating around crops; blades were made of wood, stone, or bone scapulas. In Mesoamerica and western South America tools were sometimes tipped with copper or bronze. The steel machete is used today for clearing brush and felling trees; prehistorically, wooden and stone tools were used for cutting and clearing.[57] Stone axes, made by hafting a shaped, sharpened stone to a wooden handle, smashed wood fibres, more rarely cutting through them. Cutting was supplemented by girdling and firing, with the largest trees often left standing. Clubs or 'swords' made of hard wood were used to remove undergrowth and for weeding. Other traditional approaches to weed control included mulching, shading out weeds with cover crops, and in-field burning.

While examples of the 'hard technologies' of agriculture (i.e. permanent field features, discussed below) are well preserved in the Americas, 'soft technologies', the essential practices for manipulating the field environment, leave little to no archaeological evidence.[58] Adding organic fertilizer to soil (i.e. bird guano, fish, animal dung, mucking, composting) was likely a pre-historic practice, as was planting on anthropogenic soils ('black earths', former settlement sites). Fire was an important agricultural technology.[59] Traditional farmers use fire in combination with forest clearing to create and maintain openings for sun-demanding crops; fire removes debris, kills pests, and returns nutrients to the soil via ash deposition. Cropping patterns are

56 R.A. Donkin, *Agricultural Terracing in the Aboriginal New World*, Viking Fund Publications in Anthropology 56 (Tucson: University of Arizona Press, 1979).

57 W.M. Denevan, *Cultivated Landscapes of Native Amazonia and the Andes* (Oxford University Press, 2001).

58 Ibid.   59 Denevan, 'The pristine myth', and *Cultivated Landscapes*.

Figure 20.2 Drawing of a foot-plough by Felipe Guaman Poma from his *El Primer Nueva Coronica y Buen Gobierno*.

known from ethnographic accounts and some historical records.[60] The literature gives the impression that mixed cropping (polyculture) dominates traditional farming, but there are many variations, including companion planting (e.g. corn–beans–squash: each crop provides benefits to the others), agroforestry (combining annual and perennial crops with tree crops), zonation (different species in blocks or rings within fields), and planting that is nearly monocropping (fields dominated by one crop, with a few individuals of others). There are many examples of environmental zonation, where fields are dispersed across microhabitats, for example the verticality that characterizes traditional Andean agriculture, and planting the floodplains of major rivers, where crops are matched to microrelief, soil, and differential flooding. Native agriculturalists in the Americas also practise crop rotation (changing crops year to year in a field), sequential planting (one crop after another in a field), and fallowing (allowing land to rest, to restore fertility and combat weeds and pests).

Water management was essential to prehistoric agriculture in many parts of the Americas, and transformed landscapes. In desert coastal Peru, for example, early farmers cultivated self-watering alluvial lands along rivers and their outflows, and locations where short ditches or embankments could guide water.[61] Intensification and expansion of agriculture depended on irrigation. Canal irrigation was practised in South America from southern coastal Ecuador to central Chile, in intermontane Andean valleys, the Altiplano of southern Peru/northern Bolivia, and some valleys along the Caribbean. In Peru, canal irrigation is documented in twenty-five to thirty coastal valleys, with the largest system and area irrigated on the north coast, dating to 1000 CE.[62] Small-ditch irrigation began by 4500–3400 cal BCE in the Nanchoc valley.[63]

Irrigation was also critical to agriculture in the Southwest United States.[64] Early farmers planted well-watered alluvial lands; rain-fed farming was practised only rarely in the region, in higher elevations with sufficient rainfall. Historical accounts indicate that stone and brush weirs and earthen berms were built to slow and divert water from streams, springs, and flood run-off. Rock terraces built on hillsides slow run-off, trap sediment, and create

---

60 Denevan, *Cultivated Landscapes*.   61 Ibid.; Pearsall, 'Plant domestication'.

62 M.E. Moseley, *The Incas and their Ancestors: The Archaeology of Peru*, 2nd edn (London: Thames & Hudson, 2001).

63 T.D. Dillehay et al., 'Preceramic irrigation canals in the Peruvian Andes', *Proceedings of the National Academy of Sciences*, 102 (2005), 17241–4.

64 Mabry and Doolittle, 'Modeling the early agricultural frontier'.

planting surfaces. Canal irrigation dates back to 1250–400 BCE* in the southern and central parts of the Southwest. Irrigated farming likely required shifting field locations/fallow cycles to replenish nutrients and to avoid salinization. The roughly contemporaneous dates from the American Southwest and Mesoamerica (see below) suggest independent development of water management systems.

Development of water management technology began during the Formative in Mesoamerica.[65] Practices included use of floodwater and run-off, springs, and upland and valley-bottom perennial stream systems. Floodwater and run-off systems were the most common, dating to 1200 BCE and later in numerous locations. Features include dams, canals, ditches, drains, artificial ponds and reservoirs, raised fields, terraced fields, and ridged fields. Much less common were spring-fed systems (770 BCE), upland perennial stream systems (300 BCE), and valley-bottom systems (1050 BCE). A deep-water well dated to 7900 BCE, possibly used for hand irrigation, has been identified at a site in the Tehuacan valley. Most of the familiar kinds of water control system were developed along with the emergence of villages throughout Mesoamerica between 1200 and 1000 BCE. There is considerable variability in the scale of early systems, but horizontal, kin-based organization is inferred.

The development of agriculture in the Andean highlands was linked to the creation of productive agricultural lands through landscape modification. The basic forms were irrigation, terracing, and raised fields.[66] Irrigation supplemented rainfall, and was practised in many inter-Andean valleys, with extensive systems in larger basins with expanses of land. Irrigation canals are common in the Lake Titicaca basin, where canals associated with raised fields carried water away from the lake. Irrigated bench terraces at Huarpa near Ayacucho date from 200 BCE to 600 CE.

Terraces, flat planting surfaces created on slopes, are mostly found in arid and semi-arid highlands in the Americas, and in the driest areas are associated with irrigation.[67] The most northerly zone of terracing stretches from south-western Colorado through to the Sierra Madre of western Mexico. The distribution is quite dispersed, and consists of cross-channel terraces across narrow drainages. There are discontinuous zones of terracing in Mesoamerica,

65 J.A. Neely, 'Mesoamerican Formative period water management technology: an overview with insights on development and associated method and theory', in Powis (ed.), *New Perspectives*, 127–46.
66 Denevan, *Cultivated Landscapes*.   67 Donkin, *Agricultural Terracing*.

including the basins of central and southern Mexico and western Guatemala, with few terraces south of Guatemala until the Andes. Forms include cross-channel terraces, contour terraces, and valley-floor terraces. In higher elevations frost hazard is alleviated in part by terracing, since crops can be grown above frost-prone valley bottoms.

Terracing extended discontinuously in South America from Venezuela to Chile and northwest Argentina, with heavy concentrations of irrigated terraces in southern Peru, including around the Inca capital Cuzco and northern Bolivia.[68] Expanses of rain-fed terraces occur in the eastern Peruvian Andes and southern Ecuador. Sloping-field terraces, in which retaining walls running across a slope accumulated soil and controlled run-off, were the most common type. Bench or staircase terraces were long, narrow expanses of level, deep soil held by high stone retaining walls. Terraces altered field microclimates, optimizing production, reducing risk, and permitting cropping in unfavourable settings. Both unirrigated and irrigated terraces have been dated as early as 2400 BCE in Peru, with large terracing systems dating to 600 CE and later.

Raised fields are artificially elevated earthworks that improve drainage and provide planting surfaces in wetlands.[69] Such fields, called *chinampas*, were an important component of agriculture on the fringes of lakes in the Basin of Mexico, for example. Formed of lake mud, aquatic vegetation, and domestic refuse, *chinampas* did not float, but some seed beds were in the form of movable rafts. *Chinampa* fields were usually narrow, but could be quite long, and were often planted along the edges with trees.[70] Some 12,000 ha of *chinampas* helped feed the population of the Aztec capital. Earlier, buried *chinampa* systems have been documented by remote sensing in the northern Basin of Mexico. Raised-field systems occur elsewhere in highland Mexico, as well as in the lowlands of the Mexican Gulf Coast, northern Belize, and Guatemala. Swampy land can also be cultivated by digging ditches to drain away water, rather than building up soil.

The largest expanses of raised fields in the Andean highlands are in the Sabana de Bogotá (Colombia), northern Ecuador, and the Lake Titicaca basin.[71] In the Lake Titicaca region, from 600–1200 CE the Tiwanaku state supported dense populations in a region marginal for agriculture through

---

68 Denevan, *Cultivated Landscapes*.   69 Ibid.
70 C.T. Morehard, 'Mapping ancient *chinampa* landscapes in the Basin of Mexico: a remote sensing and GIS approach', *Journal of Archaeological Science*, 39 (2012), 2541–51.
71 Denevan, *Cultivated Landscapes*.

raised-field technology and selection of nutritious local crops like potato, quinoa, and lupine.[72] Approximately 25,000 ha of raised fields were built on flat or gently sloping land. Fields functioned for thermal protection, provided higher fertility through mucking, and retained water in droughts and drained it in floods. Earlier, smaller field systems date to 1500–200 BCE in the region.[73]

In the South American lowlands, large expanses of raised fields are located in northern Colombia (earliest 800 BCE), the coast of French Guiana (1000 CE), and the Guayas basin (southwest Ecuador).[74] In Ecuador, research at the Peñon del Rio complex discovered buried fields dating from 500 BCE to 500 CE beneath larger, visible fields constructed after 500 CE. Maize phytoliths were identified from both early and late fields.[75] Raised fields supported intensive agriculture in this region of large-scale flooding and tidal influx.

Areas of the Amazon basin preserve evidence of intentional and non-intentional farming practices that transformed environments into productive, domesticated landscapes.[76] In addition to anthropogenic burning, already discussed, other elements of transformation included human settlements and their associated gardens; creation of mounds (domestic, ceremonial, burial), forest islands in savannas and wetlands, ring ditch sites, and raised fields; creation of black earths (resulting from domestic debris and large quantities of charcoal that may have been deliberately added); creation of paths, trails, and roads, including extensive systems of raised causeways; fisheries management; and agroforestry (culling non-economic species and replacing them with useful ones). Many of these practices were ancient and persistent in the Amazon.

---

72 A. Morris, 'The agricultural base of the pre-Incan Andean civilizations', *Geographical Journal*, 165 (1999), 286–95; J.W. Janusek and A.L. Kolata, 'Top-down or bottom-up: rural settlement and raised field agriculture in the Lake Titicaca basin, Bolivia', *Journal of Anthropological Archaeology*, 23 (2004), 404–30.

73 C.L. Erickson, 'The dating of raised-field agriculture in the Lake Titicaca basin, Peru', in W.M. Denevan et al. (eds.), *Pre-Hispanic Agricultural Fields in the Andean Region* (Oxford: British Archaeological Reports, 1987), 373–84.

74 Denevan, *Cultivated Landscapes*; S. Rostain, 'Agricultural earthworks on the French Guiana coast', in Silverman and Isbell (eds.), *Handbook of South American Archaeology*, 217–33.

75 D.M. Pearsall, 'Evidence for prehistoric maize cultivation on raised fields at Peñon del Rio, Guayas, Ecuador', in Denevan et al. (eds.), *Pre-Hispanic Agricultural Fields*, 279–95.

76 C.L. Erickson, 'Amazonia: the historical ecology of a domesticated landscape', in Silverman and Isbell (eds.), *Handbook of South American Archaeology*, 157–83.

## American agriculture in worldwide perspective

New data, especially plant microfossils (phytoliths, starch grains, pollen), demonstrate that agriculture is as old in the American tropics as in the early Old World primary centres.[77] Plant domestication began in the early Holocene, and the longer-term environmental changes that accompanied the Pleistocene–Holocene transition can be considered the ultimate causal factors behind the development of food production. The identification of proximate causation in specific cases is much more conjectural, as cultural and environmental factors are difficult to disentangle, especially given the limitations of the archaeological record.

In the American tropics, early food producers were semi-sedentary to sedentary, occupying alluvial or wetland-edge habitats. Groups appear to have been organized at the level of family or hamlet, with no evidence for social complexity. Expansion of forests in the neotropics during the early Holocene changed plant distributions, closing formerly open woodlands and altering edge habitats favoured by many starch-rich root and tuber species. Among the human responses indicated by the record of early agriculture are creating and maintaining open habitats for favoured plants, altering mobility patterns as resources expanded or contracted, changing diet in response to changing availabilities of foods, and increasing densities of desirable plants and animals by cultivation/management. The record indicates that in the early Holocene there were frequent and dispersed plant domestications: some were advantageous and early domesticates spread, sometimes widely, through social interactions among foragers and horticulturalists. Cultivation was small-scale, in well-watered settings.

Increasingly productive crops fuelled population growth, which led to the spread of societies dependent on agriculture into new habitats, and creation of built environments for farming. This last is the most visible threshold of the process, having left its mark throughout the Americas on the landscape, in sediment cores, and in numbers of sites. Agriculture eventually spread into all suitable environments in the Americas, with landscape modification and crop improvements opening up or increasing the potential of previously unsuitable or geographically limited environments. With clear evidence that the roots of plant domestication lay in the early Holocene, the challenge now facing us is to expand the palaeoenvironmental and archaeological

---

77 Piperno and Pearsall, *Origins of Agriculture*; Pearsall and Stahl, 'Origins and spread of early agriculture'.

records of this process, and to better understand people–plant interrelationships during the late Glacial period.

# Further reading

Bermejo, J.E.H. and J. León (eds.). *Neglected Crops: 1492 from a Different Perspective*. Rome: Food and Agriculture Organization of the United Nations, 1994.

Blake, M. and H. Neff. 'Evidence for the diversity of late Archaic and early Formative plant use in the Soconusco region of Mexico and Guatemala.' In R.G. Lesure (ed.), *Early Mesoamerican Social Transformations: Archaic and Formative Lifeways in the Soconusco Region*. Berkeley: University of California Press, 2011. 47–66.

Boyd, M., T. Varney, C. Surette, and J. Surette. 'Reassessing the northern limit of maize consumption in North America: stable isotope, plant microfossil, and trace element content of carbonized food residue.' *Journal of Archaeological Science*, 35 (2008), 2545–56.

Byers, D.S. (ed.). *The Prehistory of the Tehuacan Valley*, vol. 1: *Environment and Subsistence*. Austin: University of Texas Press, 1967.

Chandler-Ezell, K., D.M. Pearsall, and J.A. Zeidler. 'Root and tuber phytoliths and starch grains document manioc (*Manihot esculenta*), arrowroot (*Maranta arundinacea*), and llerén (*Calathea* sp.) at the Real Alto site, Ecuador.' *Economic Botany*, 60 (2006), 103–20.

Clark, J.E., J.L. Gibson, and J. Zeidler. 'First towns in the Americas: searching for agriculture, population growth, and other enabling conditions.' In M.S. Bandy and J.R. Fox (eds.), *Becoming Villagers: Comparing Early Village Societies*. Tucson: University of Arizona Press, 2010. 205–45.

Denevan, W.M. *Cultivated Landscapes of Native Amazonia and the Andes*. Oxford University Press, 2001.

Denham, T.P., J. Iriarte, and L. Vrydaghs (eds.). *Rethinking Agriculture: Archaeological and Ethnoarchaeological Perspectives*. Walnut Creek, CA: Left Coast Press, 2007.

Dillehay, T.D., J. Rossen, T.C. Andres, and D.E. Williams. 'Preceramic adoption of peanut, squash, and cotton in northern Peru.' *Science*, 316 (2007), 1890–3.

Donkin, R.A. *Agricultural Terracing in the Aboriginal New World*. Viking Fund Publications in Anthropology 56. Tucson: University of Arizona Press, 1979.

Erickson, C.L. 'The dating of raised-field agriculture in the Lake Titicaca basin, Peru.' In W.M. Denevan, K. Mathewson, and G. Knapp (eds.), *Pre-Hispanic Agricultural Fields in the Andean Region*. Oxford: British Archaeological Reports, 1987. 373–84.

Hard, R.J. and J.R. Roney. 'The transition to farming on the Rio Casas Grandes and in the southern Jornada Mogollon region.' In B.J. Vierra (ed.), *The Late Archaic across the Borderlands: From Foraging to Farming*. Austin: University of Texas Press, 2005. 141–86.

Harlan, J.R. *Crops and Man*. 2nd edn. Madison, WI: American Society of Agronomy, 1992.

Hawkes, J.G. *The Potato: Evolution, Biodiversity, and Genetic Resources*. Washington, DC: Smithsonian Institution Press, 1990.

Huckell, L.W. and M.S. Toll. 'Wild plant use in the North American Southwest.' In P.E. Minnis (ed.), *People and Plants in Ancient Western North America*. Washington, DC: Smithsonian Institution Press, 2004. 37–114.

MacNeish, R.S., M.L. Fowler, A. Garcia Cook, et al. (eds.). *The Prehistory of the Tehuacan Valley*, vol. v: *Excavations and Reconnaissance*. Austin: University of Texas Press, 1972.

Minnis, P.E. (ed.). *People and Plants in Ancient Eastern North America.* Washington, DC: Smithsonian Institution Press, 2003.

Motley, T.J., N. Zerega, and H. Cross (eds.). *Darwin's Harvest: New Approaches to the Origins, Evolution, and Conservation of Crops.* New York: Columbia University Press, 2006. 67–90.

Pearsall, D.M. *Plants and People in Ancient Ecuador: The Ethnobotany of the Jama River Valley.* Belmont, CA: Wadsworth/Thomson Learning, 2004.

Pearsall, D.M. and P.W. Stahl. 'The origins and spread of early agriculture and domestication: environmental and cultural considerations.' In J.A. Matthews (ed.), *The Sage Handbook of Environmental Change.* 2 vols. Los Angeles: Sage, 2012. vol. ii, 328–54.

Piperno, D.R. and T.D. Dillehay. 'Starch grains on human teeth reveal early broad crop diet in northern Peru.' *Proceedings of the National Academy of Sciences,* 105 (2008), 19622–7.

Piperno, D.R. and D.M. Pearsall. *The Origins of Agriculture in the Lowland Neotropics.* San Diego, CA: Academic Press, 1998.

Piperno, D.R., A.J. Ranere, I. Holst, J. Iriarte, and R. Dickau. 'Starch grain and phytolith evidence for early ninth millennium BP maize from the central Balsas River valley, Mexico.' *Proceedings of the National Academy of Sciences,* 106 (2009), 5020–4.

Raymond, J.S. and R.L. Burger (eds.). *Archaeology of Formative Ecuador.* Washington, DC: Dumbarton Oaks Research Library and Collection, 2003.

Sauer, J.D. *Historical Geography of Crop Plants: A Select Roster.* Boca Raton, FL: CRC Press, 1993.

Silverman, H. and W.H. Isbell (eds.). *Handbook of South American Archaeology.* New York: Springer, 2008. 157–83.

Simmonds, N.W. and J. Smartt (eds.). *Evolution of Crop Plants.* 2nd edn. Essex: Longman Scientific & Technical, 1995. 383–8.

Stone, D. (ed.). *Pre-Columbian Plant Migration.* Papers of the Peabody Museum of Archaeology and Ethnology 76. Cambridge, MA: Harvard University Press, 1984.

Webster, L.D., M.E. McBrinn, and E.G. Carrera (eds.). *Archaeology Without Borders: Contact, Commerce, and Change in the US Southwest and Northwestern Mexico.* Boulder: University Press of Colorado, 2008.

# Nanchoc valley, Peru

## TOM D. DILLEHAY

Archaeologists have long hypothesized the causes of the transition from foraging to food production. Beginning with Childe, the theoretical conception of the transition has often been one of transformative change, in which a force such as demographic growth or environmental variation caused the population to elect to produce food. Later theories, such as Rindos's co-evolutionary model, identified selection rather than population-level forces as the means by which the transition occurred.[1] More recently, human behavioural ecology theory has similarly focused on social and economic issues that shape individual decisions, but identified fitness-related goals as the primary impetus that directs human choice.[2] Fundamentally, behavioural ecology assumes that human decision-making is formed by evolution. It also emphasizes the structure and variability of the environment in the success or failure of human strategies. Most archaeologists investigating the shift to food production cautiously employ various aspects of these and other approaches, adapting them to the variable conditions in their particular study area. This is the approach our research team has taken in examining the emergence of food production in northern Peru during the early to middle Holocene period.

Determining the environmental stimuli and constraints of subsistence practices and especially food production in the Central Andean region of South America from excavated archaeological contexts involves the analysis of palaeoecological data drawn from various disciplines, including macrobotanical and microbotanical remains and habitat-specific vertebrate (e.g.

1 V.G. Childe, *Man Makes Himself* (London: Watts, 1936); D. Rindos, *The Origins of Agriculture: An Evolutionary Perspective* (Orlando, FL: Academic Press, 1984).
2 See e.g. B. Winterhalder and D.J. Kennett (eds.), *Behavioral Ecology and the Transition to Agriculture* (Berkeley: University of California Press, 2006); and D.R. Piperno, 'The origins of plant cultivation and domestication in the New World tropics: patterns, process, and new developments', *Current Anthropology*, 52, Supplement 4 (2011), S56–78.

rodents, birds, and reptiles) and invertebrate remains (e.g. molluscs, snails, insects).[3] Faunal and floral evidence for early mixed foraging and horticultural economies also includes the study of relative frequencies of different non-domesticated and domesticated species. In addition, the domestication and adoption of certain plant foods are common proxies for both intensification and risk-management processes aimed at sustaining growing populations. The presence of nutritious cereals, such as quinoa in the Andes, versus more bulk productive species, such as corn, potatoes, and beans, is a direct indicator of the intensity of food production.

These exemplary types of palaeoecological and subsistence knowledge are essential to understanding the evolution of early food-producing societies. Furthermore, the size and rate of growth of early human populations had important ramifications for the production of food surplus, and the development of later, more complex, hierarchically structured urban societies with a stratum of elites at the apex. To closely examine these aspects of the past, the archaeological record of technology, economy, social organization, and demographic structure of early populations is significant. Based on analogies with a range of ethnographic and historical cases, it is possible that the socioeconomic organization of emergent food-producing societies corresponds to common-pool resource institutions, communal land use, and 'the commons'.[4] Understanding the long-term histories of such institutions as communal resource use requires archaeological evidence of how such forms of socioeconomic organization were created, maintained, and changed and what environmental and social parameters influenced the decision-making of these societies.

Some of the best-documented palaeoecological and archaeological evidence for the early adoption of cultigens and food production in South America comes from the multiple, closely juxtaposed resource zones of the western slopes of the Andes in northern Peru (Figure 21.1), where plant macro- and micro-remains, the latter from starch grains, phytoliths, pollen, and the calculus of human teeth, reveal the presence of several

---

3 E.g. D.M. Pearsall, 'Plant food resources of the Ecuadorian Formative: an overview and comparison to the Central Andes', in J.S. Raymond and R. Burger (eds.), *Archaeology of Formative Ecuador* (Washington, DC: Dumbarton Oaks Research Library and Collection, 2003), 213–57; D.R. Piperno, 'Prehistoric human occupation and impacts on neotropical forest landscapes during the late Pleistocene and early/middle Holocene', in M.B. Bush and J.R. Flenley (eds.), *Tropical Rainforest Responses to Climatic Change* (Berlin and New York: Springer, 2007), 193–218; Piperno, 'Origins of plant cultivation'.

4 E. Ostrom, *Governing the Commons: The Evolution of Institutions for Collective Action* (Cambridge University Press, 1990).

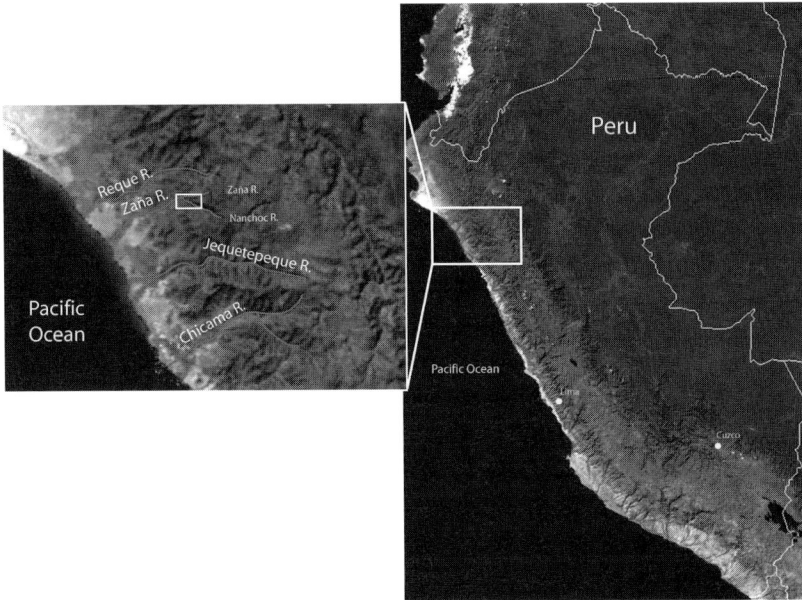

Figure 21.1 Location map of the Nanchoc valley in Peru

important food crops. In the Nanchoc valley, located at 1,500–1,800 m above sea level, major crops were adopted between 10,000 and 7,000 years ago, including squash (*Cucurbita moschata*), peanuts (*Arachis* sp.), common bean (*Phaseolus*), pacay, a tree fruit (*Inga feuilleei*), quinoa (*Chenopodium*), coca (*Erythroxylum novogranatense* var. *truxillense*), and industrial cotton (*Gossypium*). Macrobotanical remains and the bones of various large and small animal species from excavated sites in the valley provide evidence for the shift from broad-spectrum subsistence to an agricultural economy in a seasonally dry tropical montane forest flanked by thorny scrub and humid forests on the western slopes of the Andes.[5] The evidence indicates that by 6,500 years ago an effective agricultural system exploiting small but fertile alluvial patches along the Nanchoc River and employing a wide range of wild and domesticated seed, tree, vegetable, and root crops provided balanced, nutritious, and stable diets to the inhabitants of the valley.[6]

---

5 D.R. Piperno and T.D. Dillehay, 'Starch grains on human teeth reveal early broad crop diet in northern Peru', *Proceedings of the National Academy of Sciences*, 105 (2008), 19622–7.
6 T.D. Dillehay (ed.), *From Foraging to Farming in the Andes: New Perspectives on Food Production and Social Organization* (Cambridge University Press, 2011).

## Environmental parameters

There are three significant environmental drivers that potentially affected early food production in the Nanchoc valley during the early to middle Holocene period. First, increased seasonal moisture between 10,000 and 7,000 BP produced several results amenable to incipient crop use in the valley. Previously arid landscapes became less dry, resulting in the presence of greater surface vegetation similar to the patchy tropical forested slopes in the region today.[7] Second, episodic El Niño and flood intensity increased, beginning as early as 5,000 years ago. However, between 7,000 and 4,000 years ago, higher precipitation levels were also linked to a significant increase in temperature. Third, changes in the sea level also had an impact on regional climatic conditions, with shifting prevailing winds altering temperatures and precipitation rates, resulting in more arid conditions after 7,000 BP, despite intermittent El Niño floods.

In the Nanchoc valley, the intensified adoption of cultigens primarily took place between 7,000 and 4,000 BP, roughly the peak period of aridity during the hypsithermal.[8] Although local palaeoecological data from the valley do not reflect a period of severe aridity, a warm, usually dry environment did exist. How stable or unstable these conditions were is not known. It is probable that some foraging and incipient horticultural groups shifted in and out of an increased reliance on plant foods as they found themselves in varying climatic, subsistence, and/or social crises. In addition to environmental parameters, it is also probable that social conditions, such as settlement dispersion or aggregation, shared technological inventions, and cultural transmission of new ideas and experiences, were important factors determining economic and dietary choices in the valley. In these and other cases, we know that some terminal Pleistocene hunters and gatherers solved nutritional and seasonal scheduling problems associated with non-domesticated plant foods by continuing to rely on large and small game animals and, in some cases, a few cultivated plants (i.e. squash, *Cucurbita moschata*) while likely coping with short-term climatic changes.[9]

---

7 See P.J. Netherly, 'An overview of climate in northern South America from the late Pleistocene to the middle Holocene', in Dillehay (ed.), *From Foraging to Farming*, 76–99.

8 T.D. Dillehay et al., 'Preceramic adoption of peanut, squash, and cotton in northern Peru', *Science*, 316 (2007), 1890–3; T.D. Dillehay et al., 'Preceramic irrigation canals in the Peruvian Andes', *Proceedings of the National Academy of Sciences*, 102 (2005), 17241–4; Dillehay (ed.), *From Foraging to Farming*.

9 Dillehay (ed.), *From Foraging to Farming*.

Figure 21.2 The location of Las Pircas sites on the alluvial fans of the Nanchoc valley.

Although we do not fully comprehend why particular environmental locations were selected over others in the Nanchoc valley, a few semi-sedentary settlements appear early in the interiors of small *quebrada* or alluvial fans around 9,000 BP. These are locations inferred to be the most suitable settings for food production, because they contain some of the richest soils and they are characterized by the presence of small intermittent streams that provide seasonal run-off water for archaeologically documented household garden plots (Figure 21.2).

## The cultural sequence of the Nanchoc valley

Preserved charcoal from excavated house remains and garden plots was suitable for radiocarbon assays, which provide a chronology for several phases of human occupation from the late Pleistocene to the middle Holocene period (*c.* 11,500–5,000 BP). Three archaeological phases in the valley have been recorded.[10]

The early El Palto phase (*c.* 11,500–10,000 BP) is associated with a pattern of scheduled, possibly seasonal movements between coastal and upland

10 Ibid.

locations in northern Peru, where various plants, animals, and seafood were available during all or at different times of the year. Regional and local variation in stone tools, dated around 10,000 BP, and the use of small domestic structures (Figure 21.3) and local raw lithic material suggest the economic exploitation of circumscribed local territories (primarily alluvial fans drained by small streams) and possibly semi-sedentism by Paijan settlers. Domesticated squash (*Cucurbita moschata*) was adopted at this time. The constriction of territory, reduced mobility, and localization of population continued and accelerated past 9,000 BP into the following Las Pircas and Tierra Blanca phases. In some areas of the valley, this pattern of resource exploitation began to change between 9,000 and 7,000 years ago when people of the Las Pircas phase began to settle more permanently on selected alluvial fans.

Las Pircas foragers began a permanent or perhaps sedentary life at higher elevations between 9,000 and 7,000 BP, with small organized settlements, burial of the dead, domestic circular houses, subtle social differences in the artefact inventory, and small garden plots near their homesteads (Figure 21.4). Unifacial stone tools, a varied ground stone technology, simple food storage, and a food economy based primarily on the exploitation of a wide variety of plants and animals dominated the technology. Las Pircas sites yielded wild and cultivated squash, *Chenopodium* (e.g. quinoa), peanut, yucca, manioc, and several unidentified fruits. Low frequencies of exotic materials (e.g. marine shell, carved stingray spines, quartz crystals, and raw stone material) suggest minor contact with distant coastal and highland areas. Las Pircas sites are generally interpreted as small-scale ephemeral occupations, roughly similar to ethnographic foraging groups.

During the Tierra Blanca phase (7,000–5,000 BP), settlements aggregated closer to the valley floor and its fertile soils. House styles changed (from small circular to larger, multiple-room rectangular: Figure 21.5), cotton, beans, and coca were added, and residents constructed an artificial agricultural system associated with irrigation canals and sedentism. (Corn does not appear in the local archaeological record until about 4,000 years ago.) Although exotics disappeared, the separation of public and private or domestic space was pronounced, as evidenced by dual, stone-lined, multi-tiered earthen mounds at the Cementerio de Nanchoc site in the valley (Figure 21.6). At this site, lime was produced in a controlled, presumably public ritual context for probable use with coca leaves and/or as a food supplement (Figure 21.7). The mounds were located on an alluvial fan separated from but also accessible by all households. For reasons not fully understood, sedentism and food

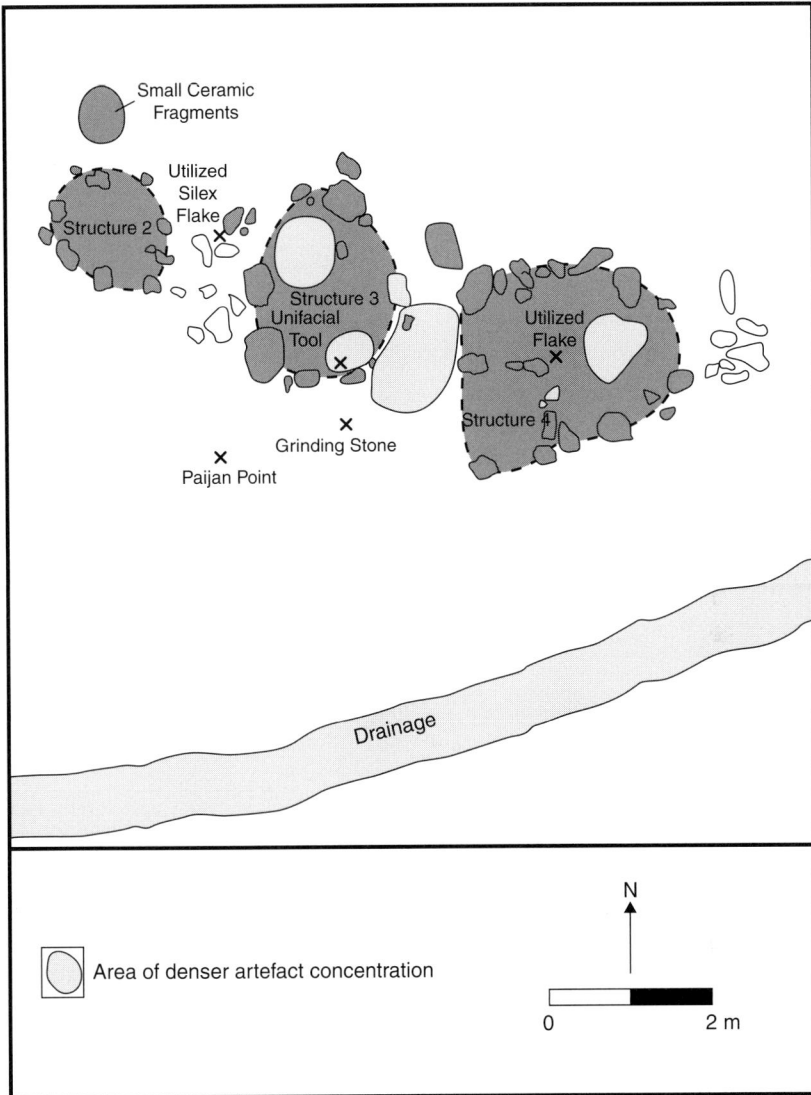

Figure 21.3 Schematic drawing of Paijan house remains dated around 10,000 BP.

production did not occur everywhere in this valley during this phase. Some groups continued practising a mobile foraging way of life well after more cultigens were introduced into the area. Between 6,000 and 5,000 BP, farmers and foragers co-existed and were co-dependent on one another.

Figure 21.4 The remains of an excavated Las Pircas house.

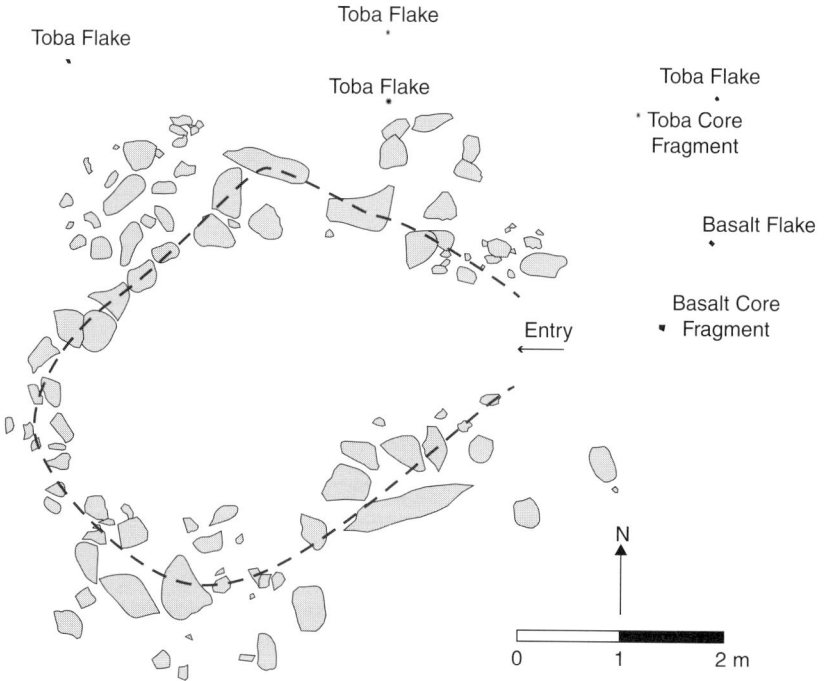

Toba Flake

Toba Flake

Toba Flake

Toba Flake

Toba Core
Fragment

Basalt Flake

Basalt Core
Fragment

Entry

N

0    1    2 m

Figure 21.5 The foundation of a rectangular-shaped Tierra Blanca house form.

Figure 21.6 Outline of the two mounds at the Cementerio de Nanchoc site.

Figure 21.7 Coca leaves excavated from a Tierra Blanca house floor.

There is widespread evidence that the transition from foraging to food production in parts of the valley altered aspects of the material culture. For instance, there is evidence for increased utilization of food crops in association with changes in grinding stone tools, houses, and storage pits, which appear to be a direct product of food production. It is possible to equate changes in house form or design with functional changes in the subsistence regime. For instance, circular forms of the Las Pircas phase are associated with a semi-sedentary to incipient sedentary life and with a broad-spectrum economy focused on foraging and a few food crops. However, in the Tierra Blanca phase, the reverse occurs, with the rectangular house form associated primarily with plant food production and secondarily with foraging.

Though people still relied on foraging for some subsistence means during the Tierra Blanca phase, the rich resources of the seasonally dry tropical forest, combined with food crops (i.e. squash, beans, yucca, avocado, chile pepper, peanut, quinoa), allowed for a more settled way of life.[11] During this period, several new sociocultural traits were developed: planning and decision-making, risk management, communal land use, resource sharing between different groups, and technological innovation. And this happened during the peak aridity of the hypsithermal between 7,000 and 4,000 BP.

In summary, in some localities of the valley, the palaeoecological and archaeological analyses relate climatic and environmental change to specific stone tool industries, dietary regimes, site and house forms, food crops, and differential human responses. Between 11,000 and 10,000 BP, there occurred a compression of terminal Pleistocene and later early Holocene people into several circumscribed habitats from the coastal plains to the mountain slopes of the Nanchoc valley. This probably led to increased contact and promoted the later development of more complex social relationships evidenced during the following Las Pircas and Tierra Blanca phases. There is archaeological evidence that terminal Pleistocene and early Holocene groups began to decrease their mobility, aggregate, and establish more permanent camps at the edge of the dry thorn forest near active springs equidistant from the desert coast to the west and the seasonally dry forests to the east. These sites were highly localized, as indicated by the presence of local lithic raw material and various floral and faunal foods indigenous to the seasonally dry environment. Sites of the following Las Pircas and early Tierra Blanca phases, dated between 9,000 and 5,000 BP, were associated with a more stable environment,

11  Ibid.

albeit increasingly more arid, and with more prolonged social contact and exchange. This led to enhanced conditions for population growth and greater cultural complexity, as evidenced by the presence of large and numerous grinding stones, irrigation canals and increased crop production, and permanent domestic structures forming small, aggregated household communities.

The development of more permanent and extensive forms of sedentism and small, complex food-producing societies in the Nanchoc valley and in a few other areas on the coast and in the highlands occurred between 5,000 and 3,500 BP. During this period, maritime and agricultural villages on the coast increased in size, and the first large-scale monumental, non-domestic architecture appeared in the form of stone platform mounds and small ceremonial pyramids. A few examples are the sites of Huaca Prieta, Alto Salaverry, Aspero, Huaynuna, Caral, and Garagay.[12]

## Public architecture, community organization, and food production

Communal construction projects are noted for the Nanchoc valley during the middle Holocene period. These include agricultural earthworks (i.e. canals and fields) and possible ceremonial mounds that are associated with the rise of crop production. Mound-building was restricted to the small teardrop-shaped structures at the site of Cementerio de Nanchoc.[13] The moundsites represent one of the earliest public architectural expressions in the Central Andes and, of particular relevance, can be situated within the local settlement system. The mounds produced evidence of lime production, which is believed to have been associated with the consumption of coca leaves. The archaeological record of both Las Pircas and Tierra Blanca households shows evidence for heating calcium-bearing limestone to produce lime as an alkali, used in historic times and today to extract alkaloids from coca leaves. Coca leaves (*E. novogranatense* var. *truxillense*) and precipitated lime were preserved in the floors of several houses. Two radiocarbon

---

12 M.S. Aldenderfer, *Montane Foragers: Asana and the South-Central Andean Archaic* (Iowa City: University of Iowa Press, 1998); W. Creamer et al., 'Archaeological investigation of late Archaic sites (3000–1800 BC) in the Pativilca valley, Peru', *Fieldiana Anthropology*, 40 (2007), 1–78; P. Kaulicke (ed.), 'El período Formativo: enfoques y evidencias recientes. Cincuenta años de la Misión Arqueológica Japonesa y su vigencia, Primera parte', *Boletín de Arqueologia PUCP*, 12 (2008), 'Segunda parte', 13 (2009); M.E. Moseley, *The Incas and their Ancestors: The Archaeology of Peru* (New York: Thames & Hudson, 2001); J. Quilter, 'Late preceramic Peru', *Journal of World Prehistory*, 5 (1991), 387–438.

13 Dillehay, *From Foraging to Farming*.

dates on the leaves indicate that coca chewing in the valley began at least 7,000 years ago.[14]

The horticultural landscape of the Las Pircas phase is characterized by the presence of short feeder ditches taking water from the upper reaches of small streams at the headwaters of alluvial fans, which flowed into small garden plots adjacent to fifteen to twenty houses. A more intensified and communal organization of agriculture in the valley occurred during the subsequent Tierra Blanca phase. This phase is defined by the presence of more than twenty-five households that correspond to small communities linearly aggregated downslope on the alluvial fans near a 2.5 km long irrigation canal that watered the fertile floodplain of the river valley. That is, a major settlement transformation took place from one phase to the other, with the Tierra Blanca people shifting from small stream-irrigated horticulture on alluvial fans to canal-irrigated floodplain agriculture. At the smallest scale, these changing domestic and communal food production landscapes of the valley were linked exclusively to local sociopolitical conditions, rather than to a larger valley-long polity or centralized authority. At the largest scale, the organization of agriculture by local communities is reflected in a 'legible' landscape,[15] one that eventually became familiar to non-local communities that adopted similar food production practices in similar alluvial and river-bottom landscapes. At a small or large scale, these landscapes are records of alternative ways to communally create, transform, and manage resources, and of different concepts of the relationship between nature and culture.

In summarizing the interdisciplinary data from the Nanchoc valley, small-scale changes combining short-distance environmental moves, development of irrigation and crop technologies, and continued reliance on some hunting and gathering, in a specific mixed environmental setting among various households of small, dispersed, and aggregated communities, made significant socioeconomic advances and held a magnetic potential for causing change elsewhere in the region. Interdisciplinary research on the specific and small-scale environmental setting of the Nanchoc valley allowed us to pinpoint specific human and palaeoecological parameters as people not only adjusted to local climate changes over a long period of time but also transformed their social and economic practices to benefit from them. The collective evidence shows that similar developments were not taking place in neighbouring areas as far away as 2–5 km within the same valley, where

---

14 Ibid.

15 J. Scott, *Seeing Like a State: How Certain Schemes to Improve the Human Condition Have Failed* (New Haven, CT: Yale University Press, 1999).

similar suitable climatic and environmental conditions existed. Although spatially extensive foraging sites of hunters and gatherers characterized other alluvial fans during this same period, neighbouring groups made decisions to stay primarily with a foraging life. Although we cannot point directly to climate changes as spurring these social and cultural changes, there must have been choices and preferences by local communities in responding to them, with some groups deciding to change, others possibly deciding to move elsewhere, and others maintaining a status quo.

## The adoption and spread of food production

Although the introduction of domesticates happened relatively early in places like the Nanchoc valley in the Central Andes, aggregated household village formation based on agricultural surplus developed a few millennia afterwards. There was an apparent lag in the widespread adoption and intensification of agriculture. We know that the ancient human occupation in the Nanchoc valley was long-lived and coincided with a shift towards more arid conditions in the climate by at least 7,000 BP. Climatic change resulting in this shift sparked this particular opportunity for sustained agriculture on a small scale in the valley, resulting in semi-sedentism to sedentism at certain alluvial fans. This new dependence on crop production did not stimulate its immediate adoption in neighbouring areas with a similar climate. Given the current database, it seems rather clear that the exploitation of plant and animal species and the shift to food production in this case study do not fit into a simple unilinear sequence.

Returning to the opening theme of this study, our work in the valley attempted to examine the factors that were involved in decisions to forage or produce food. This approach allowed us to assess the relative importance of variables that contributed to the spread of food production. The expectations of our research drove us to assess the costs associated with food production, and to hypothesize a probable sequence for the transition to food production in association with early to middle Holocene settlements, as well as the later geographic expansion of farmers in the region.

Furthermore, our research built on the study of plant and animal remains in archaeological sites, and attempted to model the specific decisions that individual communities made concerning the procurement or production of specific crop foods. At the core, our interpretations assume that communities chose to either forage or farm based upon perceived greater returns. This interpretation made use of economic concepts that are critical to understanding adaptive decision-making in the context of food production, such as the marginal value of resources, and opportunity costs (e.g. when does the value of a cultivated resource decline, and how does the amount of labour, time, and competing opportunities factor into the decision to farm at any given time?). These concepts allow for an interpretation that anticipates future (as opposed to immediate) returns, examines the varying value of foods or resources in the context of an unpredictable future, and allows for the assessment of long-term and short-term returns on different kinds of labour expenditures (e.g. hunting, gathering, gardening). These notions are critical to understanding the context of human decision-making that involved food production in the valley. We believe that the low energy requirements for early gardening in this seasonally dry forest would have made food production appear as the best option, as a small plot of irrigated land could produce a relatively high yield following a single growing season.

We also hypothesize that in the centuries that followed the initial adoption and development of food production, both foragers and food producers weighed the option of procuring food from a greater distance, which apparently was the case with food producers, as evidenced by the increased presence of exotic cultigens at Tierra Blanca sites.[16] Similarly, the Tierra Blanca food producers continued to engage in occasional foraging, which perhaps entailed travelling longer distances. This likely narrowed their foraging options to high-ranked prey, as suggested by the increased presence of deer bones in the Tierra Blanca sites.

A final critical aspect of our work focused on the expansion of food producers into new environments, such as the interiors of larger alluvial fans and especially the fertile and more expansive floodplain downvalley near the coast. This expansion appears to have been density dependent, and reflects population growth and the limited capacity of Tierra Blanca floodplain farming to support a burgeoning population. The expansion of food producers must also have been associated with the recruitment of new fertile niches, such as the generation of large tracts of alluvium following major El Niño events. We expect that in this density-independent scenario, population expansion would have occurred after the landscapes of the alluvial fans and narrow upvalley floodplains had been significantly altered and maximized for production. There is no current evidence to indicate that the single densely populated core that once occurred in the mountainous up-valley Nanchoc

16  Dillehay, *From Foraging to Farming.*

area during the early to middle Holocene period ever developed again in the region. After 5,000 BP a more widely dispersed agricultural population developed. This pattern intensified after 4,000 BP, when larger monuments and agricultural villages appeared in the valley and the wider region for the first time.

## Further reading

Aldenderfer, M.S. *Montane Foragers: Asana and the South-Central Andean Archaic*. Iowa City: University of Iowa Press, 1998.

Childe, V.G. *Man Makes Himself*. London: Watts, 1936.

Creamer, W., J. Haas, and A. Ruiz. 'Archaeological investigation of late Archaic sites (3000–1800 BC) in the Pativilca valley, Peru.' *Fieldiana Anthropology*, 40 (2007), 1–78.

Dillehay, T.D. *From Foraging to Farming in the Andes: New Perspectives on Food Production and Social Organization*. Cambridge University Press, 2011.

Dillehay, T.D., H.H. Eiling, Jr, and J. Rossen. 'Preceramic irrigation canals in the Peruvian Andes.' *Proceedings of the National Academy of Sciences*, 102 (2005), 17241–4.

Dillehay, T.D., J. Rossen, T.C. Andres, and D.E. Williams. 'Preceramic adoption of peanut, squash, and cotton in northern Peru.' *Science*, 316 (2007), 1890–3.

Kaulicke, P. (ed.). 'El período Formativo: enfoques y evidencias recientes. Cincuenta años de la Misión Arqueológica Japonesa y su vigencia, Primera parte. *Boletin de Arqueologia PUCP*, 12 (2008).

'El período Formativo: enfoques y evidencias recientes. Cincuenta años de la Misión Arqueológica Japonesa y su vigencia, Segunda parte. *Boletin de Arqueologia PUCP*, 13 (2009).

Moseley, M.E. *The Incas and their Ancestors: The Archaeology of Peru*. New York: Thames & Hudson, 2001.

Netherly, P.J. 'An overview of climate in northern South America from the late Pleistocene to the middle Holocene.' In T.D. Dillehay (ed.), *From Foraging to Farming in the Andes: New Perspectives on Food Production and Social Organization*. Cambridge University Press, 2011. 76–99.

Ostrom, E. *Governing the Commons: The Evolution of Institutions for Collective Action*. Cambridge University Press, 1990.

Pearsall, D.M. 'Plant food resources of the Ecuadorian Formative: an overview and comparison to the Central Andes.' In J.S. Raymond and R. Burger (eds.), *Archaeology of Formative Ecuador*. Washington, DC: Dumbarton Oaks Research Library and Collection, 2003. 213–57.

Piperno, D.R. 'The origins of plant cultivation and domestication in the New World tropics: patterns, process, and new developments.' *Current Anthropology*, 52, Supplement 4 (2011), S56–78.

'Prehistoric human occupation and impacts on neotropical forest landscapes during the late Pleistocene and early/middle Holocene.' In M.B. Bush and J.R. Flenley (eds.), *Tropical Rainforest Responses to Climatic Change*. Berlin and New York: Springer, 2007. 193–218.

Piperno, D.R. and T.D. Dillehay. 'Starch grains on human teeth reveal early broad crop diet in northern Peru.' *Proceedings of the National Academy of Sciences*, 105 (2008), 19622–7.

Quilter, J. 'Late preceramic Peru.' *Journal of World Prehistory*, 5 (1991), 387–438.

Rindos, D. *The Origins of Agriculture: An Evolutionary Perspective*. Orlando, FL: Academic Press, 1984.

Scott, J. *Seeing Like a State: How Certain Schemes to Improve the Human Condition Have Failed*. New Haven, CT: Yale University Press, 1999.

Winterhalder, B. and D.J. Kennett (eds.). *Behavioral Ecology and the Transition to Agriculture*. Berkeley: University of California Press, 2006.

# 22

# Early agricultural society in Europe

ALASDAIR WHITTLE

## A first walk across Neolithic Europe

Anyone crossing Europe in the fifth or fourth millennium cal BCE would have encountered landscapes busy with people and their animals, and seen over and over again many signs of human activity. Clearances in woodland, garden cultivations, and some areas of pasture would have been recurrent; numerous settlements would have been visible in most regions, except in the uplands;[1] people would have been out and about nearly everywhere (Figure 22.1), not only in and around the places where they lived, going about their everyday tasks, but also more widely in what has been called the taskscape,[2] tending herds and flocks of animals; and a traveller would have met other people on the move, some over considerable distances,[3] carrying sometimes by boat but often on foot the many objects and materials which by now were circulated between different areas of the continent.

A walk across Europe, however, would not have been the same in 4500 cal BCE as in 3500 cal BCE, and the experience of a wanderer would have varied quite markedly from place to place; this was not a static, timeless world, but one with its own distinctive history. In southeastern Europe, for example, new things and practices, very probably brought initially by new people, but perhaps also rapidly adopted by indigenous people, had appeared as far back as the seventh millennium cal BCE; novelties included pottery, houses, crops,

1 A. Whittle, *Europe in the Neolithic: The Creation of New Worlds* (Cambridge University Press, 1996); A. Jones (ed.), *Prehistoric Europe: Theory and Practice* (Chichester: Wiley-Blackwell, 2008); C. Fowler et al. (eds.), *The Oxford Handbook of Neolithic Europe* (Oxford University Press, forthcoming); J. Robb and O.J.T. Harris (eds.), *The Body in History: Europe from the Palaeolithic to the Future* (Cambridge University Press, 2013).
2 T. Ingold, *The Perception of the Environment: Essays in Livelihood, Dwelling and Skill* (London: Routledge, 2000).
3 D. Gronenborn, 'Fernkontakte aus dem nördlichen Europa während der bandkeramischen Kultur', in P. Kalábková et al. (eds.), *PANTA RHEI: Studies on the Chronology and Cultural Development of South-Eastern and Central Europe in Earlier Prehistory* (Bratislava: Comenius University, 2010), 561–74.

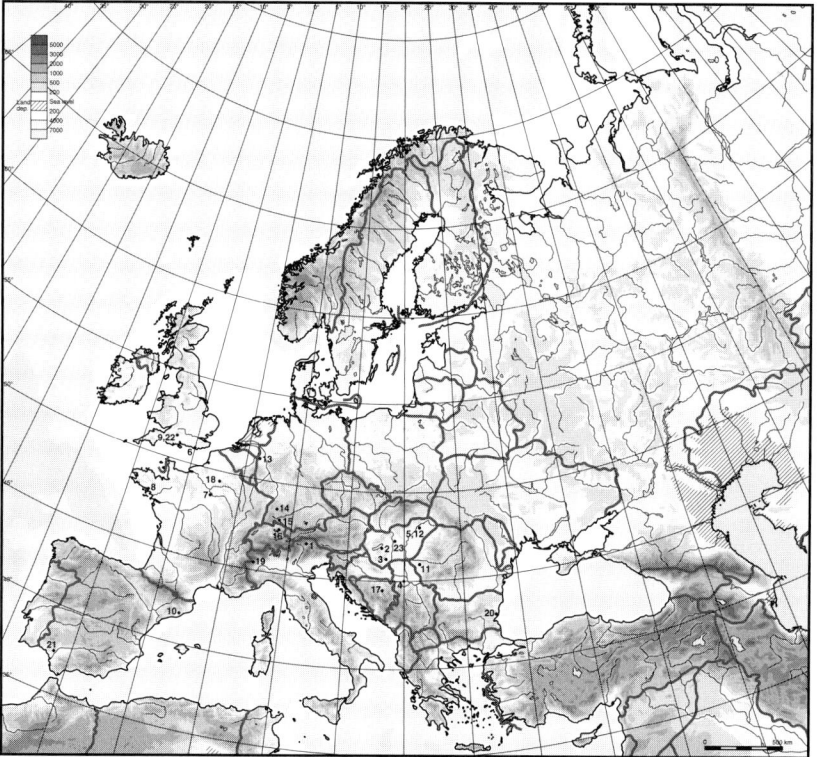

Map 22.1 Europe, showing the principal archaeological sites mentioned in Chapter 22:
1. Iceman; 2. Balatonszárszó-Kis-erdei-dűlő; 3. Alsónyék-Bátaszék; 4. Vinča-Belo Brdo;
5. Tiszapolgár-Basatanya; 6. Whitehawk; 7. Passy; 8. Locmariaquer; 9. Durrington Walls;
10. La Draga; 11. Uivar; 12. Csőszhalom-Polgár; 13. Aldenhoven; 14. Vaihingen;
15. Hornstaad-Hörnle; 16. Arbon Bleiche; 17. Okolište; 18. Cuiry-lès-Chaudardes; 19. Monte
Viso; 20. Varna; 21. Valencina de la Concepción; 22. Stonehenge; 23. Budakalász.

and domesticated animals. In western Hungary, to take just one example, scattered communities of the Starčevo culture had come into the territory of dispersed (and archaeologically here nearly invisible) hunter-gatherers by around 6000 cal BCE,[4] to be in turn succeeded by more numerous and larger settlements of the Linear Pottery culture (or LBK)[5] from after 5500 cal BCE; excavations in advance of motorway construction on the south side of Lake

---

4 E. Bánffy, *The 6th Millennium BC Boundary in Western Transdanubia and its Role in the Central European Neolithic Transition* (Budapest: Institute of Archaeology, Hungarian Academy of Sciences, 2004).

5 After *Linearbandkeramik* in German, denoting the characteristic decorated pottery.

Balaton revealed a village at Balatonszárszó-Kis-erdei-dűlő[6] with numerous substantial post-framed longhouses of a style widely found in central parts of western Europe in the later sixth millennium cal BCE.[7] By 4500 cal BCE, even larger settlements of the Lengyel culture were coming to an end, for example at the remarkable agglomeration at Alsónyék-Bátaszék (Figure 22.2), where again excavations in advance of road building have given a slice across a settlement some 1.5 km by 800 m in extent, showing in the portion investigated over 100 post-framed houses (slightly smaller than their LBK predecessors, also present on this site), frequent pits both large and small, and getting on for 2,500 individual graves, dispersed across the settlement space in groups probably linked to household neighbourhoods.[8] Alsónyék was what archaeologists call a flat settlement, but not far away to the east and southeast there were many settlement mounds or tells, where repeated occupation over many generations on the same spot had produced increasingly visible accumulations of settlement remains, successive inhabitants and users literally sitting on top of the residues and histories of their forebears. A famous example is Vinča-Belo Brdo in Serbia (Figure 22.3), beside the Danube just south of Belgrade, where probably over 7 m of deposit formed between approximately the middle of the sixth and the middle of the fifth millennium cal BCE.[9] At some time around 4500 cal BCE the main occupation of Vinča-Belo Brdo came to an end, and many other tells followed suit, around this time or subsequently.[10] By roughly 3500 cal BCE, the nature of settlement in the Carpathian basin, and widely through many parts of southeastern Europe as a whole, had changed quite markedly, with on the whole smaller, and more dispersed, occupations, and with burial grounds in some phases and areas more visible archaeologically (Figure 22.4) than the places of the living.[11]

6  T. Marton and K. Oross, 'Reconstructing space in a familiar world: the formation of late LBK settlements in central Transdanubia', in J.K. Kozłowski (ed.), *Interactions Between Different Models of Neolithization North of the Central European Agro-Ecological Barrier* (Kraków: Polska Akademia Umiejętności, 2009), 51–73.

7  For a review of an enormous literature, see P. Bickle and A. Whittle (eds.), *The First Farmers of Central Europe: Diversity in LBK Lifeways* (Oxford: Oxbow, 2013).

8  A. Osztás et al., 'Alsónyék-Bátaszék: a new chapter in research of the Lengyel culture', *Documenta Praehistorica*, 39 (2012), 377–96.

9  W. Schier, 'The relative and absolute chronology of Vinča: new evidence from the type site', in F. Draşovean (ed.), *The Vinča Culture, its Role and Cultural Connections* (Timişoara: Museum of Banat, 1996), 141–62.

10 T. Link, *Das Ende der neolithischen Tellsiedlungen: ein kulturgeschichtliches Phänomen des 5. Jahrtausends v. Chr. im Karpatenbecken* (Bonn: Habelt, 2006).

11 P. Raczky and Z. Siklósi, 'Reconsideration of the Copper Age chronology of the eastern Carpathian basin: a Bayesian approach', *Antiquity*, 87 (2013), 555–73.

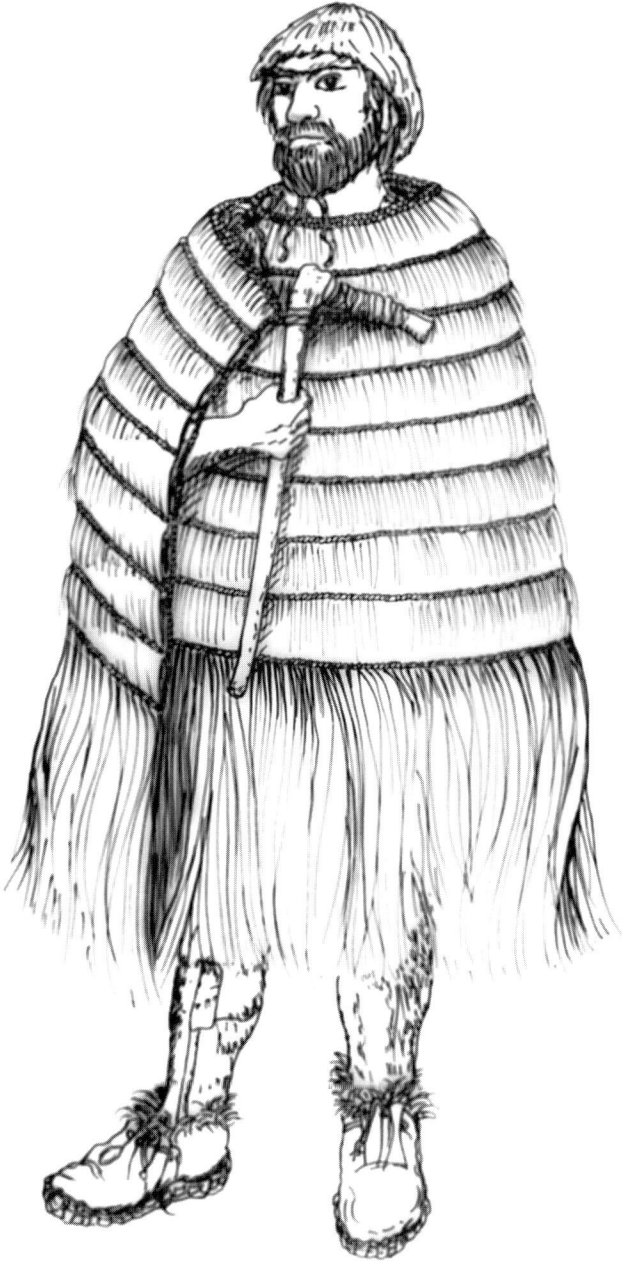

Figure 22.1 Reconstruction of the Alpine Iceman, dated to the later fourth millennium cal BCE.

Figure 22.2 Houses of the Lengyel culture at Alsónyék-Bátaszék, Hungary, dating to the earlier fifth millennium cal BCE.

Further north, in central and western Europe, what our traveller would have seen was rather different. New things, practices, and ideas had appeared in the middle of the sixth millennium cal BCE with the LBK culture. A long-running debate continues here too about the identity of the people involved, whether incomers or locals or a mixture of the two; current research on aDNA appears at the moment to tip the balance back to a predominance of incomers,[12] but the issue is complicated and the necessary research far from complete. Longhouse settlements of the LBK had been widespread between approximately 5500 cal BCE to after 5000 cal BCE, found on fertile soils through the river valleys of the region. Following a period of changes, perhaps even involving some kind of decline or even crisis and hiatus in some areas,[13]

12 M.-F. Deguilloux et al., 'European Neolithization and ancient DNA: an assessment', *Evolutionary Anthropology*, 21 (2012), 24–37.
13 A. Zeeb-Lanz, 'Gewaltszenarien oder Sinnkrise? Die Grubenanlage von Herxheim und das Ende der Bandkeramik', in A. Zeeb-Lanz (ed.), *Krisen – Kulturwandel – Kontinuitäten: zum Ende der Bandkeramik in Mitteleuropa* (Rahden: Marie Leidorf, 2009), 87–101.

Figure 22.3  The section excavated by Miloje Vasić at the tell of Vinča-Belo Brdo, in 1933.

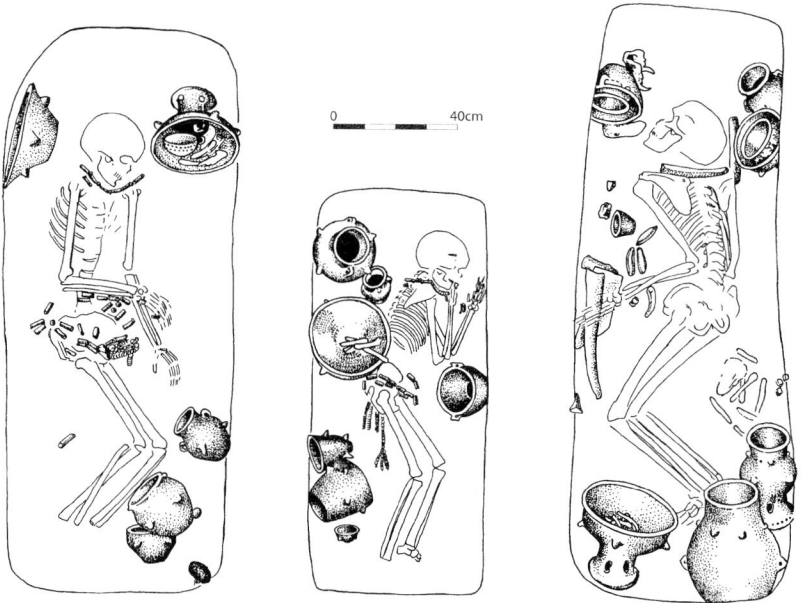

Figure 22.4  A portion of the burial ground at Tiszapolgár-Basatanya.

longhouse settlement continued to roughly the middle of the fifth millennium cal BCE; during this long period, there were hunter-gatherers to the north, on the North European Plain, around the Baltic and away northwards, to the west, in the Rhine–Meuse estuary, on the fringes of the Paris basin, and in northwest France, and to the south, in the Alpine foreland. By around 4500 cal BCE, the last longhouses were being built (see Chapter 23), and from the later fifth millennium cal BCE onwards much altered. New things, practices, and ideas spread further, bringing changed ways into Brittany (probably in the first half of the fifth millennium cal BCE), the Alpine foreland from around 4300 BCE, and into southern Scandinavia and Britain and Ireland from just before 4000 cal BCE onwards.[14] In many areas a very different world came into existence. Settlements are regularly elusive in the archaeological record, though not everywhere. We know of a short, early burst of house construction in Ireland, for example, probably from the late thirty-eighth into the thirty-seventh century cal BCE;[15] and there is an enduring and puzzling contrast between the wonderfully preserved settlements of the Alpine foreland (Figure 22.5), with their detailed biographies revealed by dendrochronological analysis of house timbers, and the relative dearth of structures elsewhere.[16] In some kind of compensation, while the places of the living come and go in the archaeological record, various constructions are much more prominent. Ditched, banked, and palisaded enclosures are one characteristic sign, presumably of communal effort, and were probably more used for periodic assembly, exchange, and shared ritual, and sometimes also for defence, than for permanent occupation (Figure 22.6). These 'monuments' had a long history across the Paris basin and environs, the Rhineland, and points east,[17] but recent research has shown a surprisingly short *floruit* in southern Britain, where new enclosure constructions can now be dated between the late thirty-eighth and mid thirty-sixth centuries cal BCE.[18] The

---

14 A. Whittle and V. Cummings (eds.), *Going Over: The Mesolithic–Neolithic Transition in North-West Europe* (Oxford University Press for the British Academy, 2007).

15 G. Cooney et al., 'Ireland', in A. Whittle et al., *Gathering Time: Dating the Early Neolithic Enclosures of Southern Britain and Ireland* (Oxford: Oxbow, 2011), 562–669.

16 P. Pétrequin, 'Lake dwellings in the Alpine region', and R. Ebersbach, 'Houses, households, and settlements: architecture and living spaces', both in F. Menotti and A. O'Sullivan (eds.), *The Oxford Handbook of Wetland Archaeology* (Oxford University Press, 2013), 253–67, 283–301; D. Hofmann, 'Living by the lake: domestic architecture in the Alpine foreland', in D. Hofmann and J. Smyth (eds.), *Tracking the Neolithic House in Europe: Sedentism, Architecture, and Practice* (New York: Springer, 2013), 197–227.

17 N. Andersen, *Sarup*, vol. 1: *The Sarup Enclosures* (Moesgaard: Jysk Arkæologisk Selskab, 1997).

18 Whittle et al., *Gathering Time*.

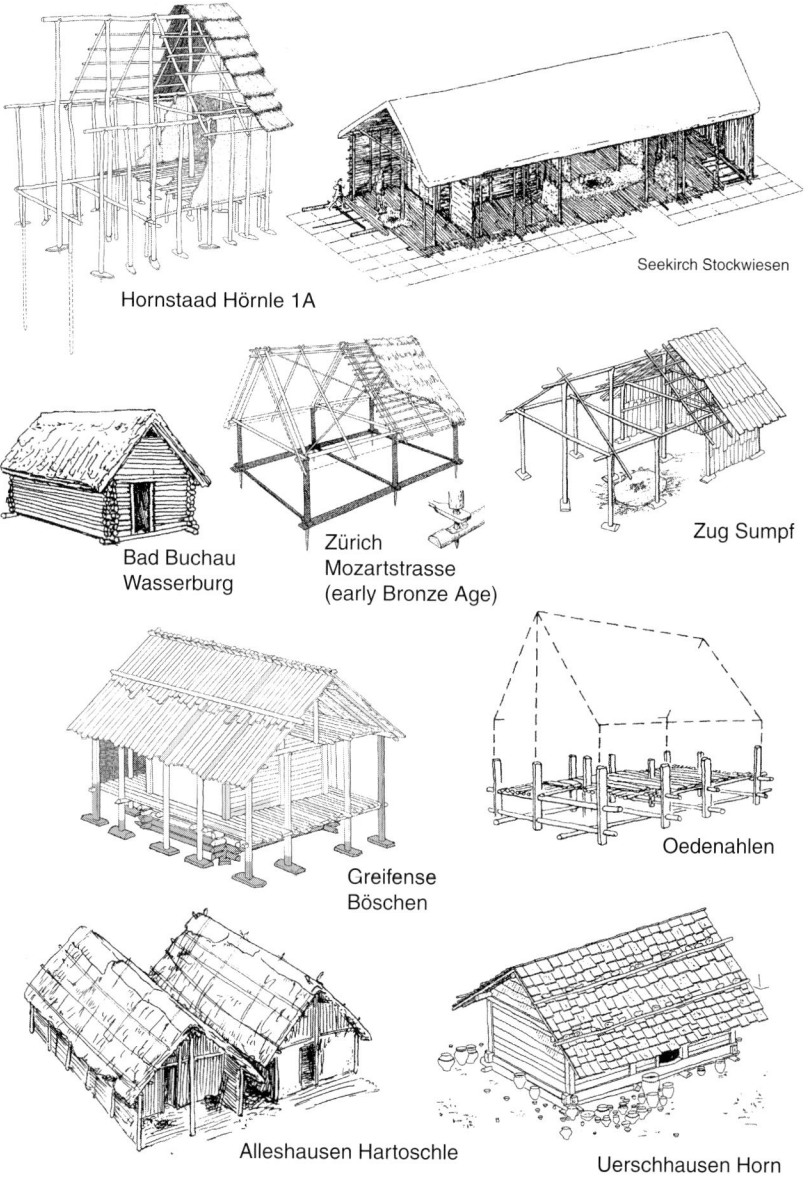

Hornstaad Hörnle 1A

Seekirch Stockwiesen

Bad Buchau
Wasserburg

Zürich
Mozartstrasse
(early Bronze Age)

Zug Sumpf

Greifense
Böschen

Oedenahlen

Alleshausen Hartoschle

Uerschhausen Horn

Figure 22.5 Varieties of houses in the Alpine foreland.

Figure 22.6 Reconstruction of the causewayed enclosure at Whitehawk, Sussex.

other recurrent but very varied form of monument was the mound or cairn containing burials, often in some kind of inner structure. These too had a long and complicated history. Elongated earthen mounds covering varied burials, at Passy and other sites in the Paris basin, and perhaps overlapping with the last longhouses in that region, are one candidate for an early stage of development, monumentalizing the idea and memory of the house and formalizing it by association with the dead.[19] Long and round cairns in Brittany (Figure 22.7), with both closed cists and chambers accessible by linking passages (*tertres tumulaires* and so-called passage graves), are another candidate for an early date.[20] Other variations on the theme follow widely in the early fourth millennium cal BCE in Britain and Ireland, perhaps mainly from about 3800 cal BCE, and in northern Germany and southern Scandinavia; surprisingly short biographies have recently been shown for both southern British and northern German examples, and this raises again the question of the social significance of the people whose remains were accumulated

19 A. Thomas et al., 'Unpacking burial and rank: the role of children in the first monumental cemeteries of western Europe (4600–4300 BCE)', *Antiquity*, 85 (2011), 772–86.
20 S. Cassen (ed.), *Autour de la Table: explorations archéologiques et discours savants sur des architectures mégalithiques à Locmariaquer, Morbihan (Table des Marchands et Grand Menhir)* (Nantes: Laboratoire de recherches archéologiques, CNRS, and Université de Nantes, 2009).

Figure 22.7 The monument complex at Locmariaquer, Morbihan, Brittany, including the Er Grah long cairn, stone row with the fallen Grand Menhir Brisé, and the passage grave of La Table des Marchands.

together in these structures.[21] In the southern British case, by about 3500 cal BCE a passing observer would have seen a fascinating mixture of old and new forms: the latest innovation in the form of linear *cursus* monuments, some enclosures still in use, and the occasional long barrow or chambered tomb still being built in archaic style.[22]

Similar contrasts could be drawn in the Mediterranean world, though in a brief chapter like this the reader will have to forgive incomplete and selective coverage. New things and practices spread in the early sixth millennium cal BCE (with comparable debates about the people involved), and there was a somewhat diverse settlement record across the sixth and fifth millennia cal BCE in Italy, southern France, and Iberia.[23] Varied burial monuments then appeared in Iberia, for example, probably from the later fifth millennium cal BCE onwards, first chambered tombs or dolmens, then rock-cut tombs, and *tholoi* from the late fourth millennium cal BCE or the start of the third.[24] There was again no single history. Ditched enclosures are found in southeast Italy as early as the sixth millennium cal BCE, while those in southern France of the later fifth millennium cal BCE, for example in the upper Garonne valley, share many features with those further north at this time.[25] Nor were these disconnected worlds. Beads found in early monuments in Brittany, for example, made of a greenstone called variscite, were very probably of Iberian origin.[26]

---

21  A. Bayliss and A. Whittle (eds.), 'Histories of the dead: building chronologies for five southern British long barrows', *Cambridge Archaeological Journal*, 17, Supplement 1 (2007), 1–147; D. Mischka, 'The Neolithic burial sequence at Flintbek LA 3, north Germany, and its cart tracks: a precise chronology', *Antiquity*, 85 (2011), 742–58; P. Chambon and J. Leclerc (eds.), *Les pratiques funéraires Néolithiques avant 3500 av. J. C. en France et dans les régions limitrophes* (Paris: Société Préhistorique Française, 2003).

22  Whittle et al., *Gathering Time*.

23  J. Robb, *The Early Mediterranean Village: Agency, Material Culture and Social Change in Neolithic Italy* (Cambridge University Press, 2007).

24  L. García Sanjuán et al. (eds.), *Exploring Time and Matter in Prehistoric Monuments: Absolute Chronology and Rare Rocks in European Megaliths / Explorando el tiempo y la material en los monumentós prehistóricos: cronología absoluta y rocas raras en los megalitos europeos. Menga: Journal of Andalusian Prehistory*, Monograph 1 (Seville: Andalusian Government, 2011).

25  M. Gandelin, *Les enceintes chasséennes de Villeneuve-Tolosane et de Cugnaux dans leur contexte du Néolithique moyen européen* (Toulouse: Centre de Recherches sur la Préhistoire et la Protohistoire de la Méditerranée; École des Hautes Études en Sciences Sociales, 2011).

26  J.A. Linares Catela and C. Odriozola Lloret, 'Cuentas de collar de variscita y otras piedras verdes en tumbas megalíticas del suroeste de la Península Ibérica: cuestiones acerca de su producción, circulación y presencia en contextos funerarios', in García Sanjuán et al. (eds.), *Exploring Time and Matter*, 335–69.

All these features, from numerous people on the ground and repeated occupations of place, from innumerable houses and the rich arrays of accompanying material culture, from gardens and herds, to monumental accumulations and constructions including tells, enclosures, and tombs, were all part of the new world with agriculture which came into being in Europe from the seventh millennium cal BCE onwards. We should not deny hunter-gatherers their own history, nor rob them of an undoubted ability, when they so chose and when the circumstances enabled them, to build, to maintain occupation of place, to use their dead to mark place and territory, and to construct elaborate worldviews.[27] We should also be very careful not to create too rigid distinctions between hunter-gatherers and early farmers. But most of the European examples of this kind of elaboration among hunter-gatherers (such as in the Danube Gorges in the late seventh millennium cal BCE or in the western Baltic in the fifth millennium cal BCE)[28] belong to periods of probably intense contact with farming communities. In this sense, the examples presented so far, albeit briefly, are among the consequences of the introduction of agriculture into Europe.

That claim needs to be put into context, in three important ways. It was not only agriculture, in the form of the cultivation of cereals and the husbandry of cattle, sheep and goats, and pigs, that produced this changing world; we could think of agriculture as a necessary but insufficient condition by itself for producing all the changes visible in the archaeological record. Second, while it can seem attractive to think of a 'package' of new things and practices, it is evident from even this initial survey that there was much diversity across time and space. The challenge now is to forget past theoretical divides, including 'science wars', and to unify economic and demographic with social, conceptual, and symbolic dimensions of what we choose to call the Neolithic way of life; it was farmers who operated early farming, and farmers could be diverse in their values, goals, and worldviews. Third, I believe that the overall trajectory of the development of the Neolithic in Europe is actually a surprising one, which does not show steady linear development from the seventh to the third millennia cal BCE, in either economic or social dimensions, and it has taken a long time for European

27  R.J. Kelly, *The Lifeways of Hunter-Gatherers* (Cambridge University Press, 2013).
28  D. Borić, 'Adaptations and transformations of the Danube Gorges foragers (*c.* 13,000–5500 cal BC): an overview', in R. Krauß (ed.), *Beginnings – New Research in the Appearance of the Neolithic between Northwest Anatolia and the Carpathian Basin: Papers of the International Workshop 8th–9th April 2009, Istanbul* (Rahden: Marie Leidorf, 2011), 157–203; L. Larsson, 'Mistrust traditions, consider innovations? The Mesolithic–Neolithic transition in southern Scandinavia', in Whittle and Cummings (eds.), *Going Over*, 595–616.

Neolithic research to come to terms with this. This lack of steady development is a characteristic not confined to the Neolithic period, but one which in my view spills on into the Bronze Age in Europe, though full coverage of that story would take up more space than is available here.[29]

Neolithic Europe has by now seen well over a century of research, and the pace of investigation shows no sign of slackening. Modern infrastructural changes, including road building, have given many opportunities for investigations on a scale far larger than normally possible in purely research conditions, and the battery of techniques still being developed, including, for example, high resolution geophysical survey, isotopic and genetic analysis, and formal chronological modelling, enables many more detailed insights than were available to previous generations of researchers. There is thus no shortage of things to report, and a chapter of this kind can only hope to give a selective impression of the dynamic nature of research. To illustrate my three points above, I will discuss three principal, linked themes, those of community, making a living, and worldviews, and will round things off with my view of what happened in Neolithic histories in Europe.

## Community

When I try to stand back from the enormous array of detail for local and regional situations and sequences, what strikes me again and again about the evidence for Neolithic Europe is the recurrence of communal activity, shared effort, and mutual engagement. I immediately need to qualify this, to allow for both diversity and change, but the sense of shared lives is everywhere very strong. An agricultural life was not one to embark on alone. I will look at questions of community especially through settlements, with particular emphasis on houses and households, with a glance at material culture and some burial practices. But in stressing community, I also want to keep open the possibility of internal difference, as one of the dynamics in rates and kinds of change may have been a tension between competing values.

Time after time, we come across evidence for groups of houses.[30] This simple statement also instantly needs qualification. Some regions and periods are 'house-rich', such as southeastern Europe from the seventh to the fifth millennia cal BCE, or central and parts of western Europe from the later sixth to the mid fifth millennium cal BCE, or the Alpine foreland from the late fifth

29 C. Prescott and H. Glørstad (eds.), *Becoming European: The Transformation of Third Millennium Northern and Western Europe* (Oxford: Oxbow, 2012).
30 Hofmann and Smyth (eds.), *Tracking the Neolithic House*.

to the third millennium BCE, while others are 'house-poor', such as much
of western Europe in the fourth and third millennia cal BCE. There are real
issues of visibility to deal with, in that absence of evidence is not necessarily
evidence of absence. Fragile house floors and walls recently recovered from
the mid-third-millennium cal BCE context of Durrington Walls in southern
Britain,[31] or the unexpected waterlogged structures of the later sixth millennium at La Draga in northeast Spain,[32] make the point well. Even within
generally house-rich areas, such as southeastern Europe, there are differences
in local and regional sequences. Some sites in Greece and Bulgaria have
groups of buildings from early on, while further north into the Balkans early
phases generally seem to have smaller and less concentrated groupings of
structures;[33] with new investigations on a bigger scale, this impression
too is changing, witnessed by discoveries in the Starčevo phase at Alsónyék
of ovens, as well as very large pits and burials, even though the ground plans
of buildings themselves were not recovered.[34] In other situations, houses
were a marker of community from the outset. The earliest LBK in central
Europe, beginning in the mid sixth millennium cal BCE, already had substantial post-framed longhouses, which from a date conventionally set at
about 5300 cal BCE became even larger.[35] In Ireland, and arguably to some
extent in Britain as well, solidly built and sometimes quite large rectangular
houses were part of the process of the initial establishment of a new way
of life, but were not found further into the sequence, disappearing after a
surprisingly short time.[36]

Houses also varied considerably in their size, layout relative to neighbours,
continuity from phase to phase, and duration.[37] Virtually all identifiable

31 M. Parker Pearson, *Stonehenge: Exploring the Greatest Stone Age Mystery* (London:
Simon & Schuster, 2012).
32 A. Palomo et al., 'Harvesting cereals and other plants in Neolithic Iberia: the assemblage
from the lake settlement at La Draga', *Antiquity*, 85 (2011), 759–71.
33 J. Chapman, 'Meet the ancestors: settlement histories in the Neolithic', in D. Bailey et al.
(eds.), *Living Well Together? Settlement and Materiality in the Neolithic of South-East and
Central Europe* (Oxford: Oxbow, 2008), 68–80.
34 E. Bánffy et al., 'Early Neolithic settlement and burials at Alsónyék-Bátaszék', in
J.K. Kozłowski and P. Raczky (eds.), *Neolithization of the Carpathian Basin: Northernmost
Distribution of the Starčevo/Körös Culture* (Kraków: Polish Academy of Sciences; Budapest:
Institute of Archaeological Sciences of the Eötvös Loránd University, 2010), 37–51.
35 H. Stäuble, *Häuser und absolute Chronologie der ältesten Bandkeramik* (Bonn: Habelt, 2005).
36 J. Smyth, *Settlement in the Irish Neolithic: New Discoveries at the Edge of Europe* (Oxford:
Oxbow, 2014).
37 J. Müller, 'Dorfanlagen und Siedlungssysteme: die europäische Perspektive:
Südosteuropa und Mitteleuropa', in Badisches Landesmuseum, *Jungsteinzeit in
Umbruch: die 'Michelsberger Kultur' und Mitteleuropa vor 6000 Jahren* (Karlsruhe:
Badisches Landesmuseum, 2010), 250–7.

buildings were rectangular (setting aside a long-running debate about whether some pits were used in early phases in southeastern Europe as a kind of semi-subterranean structure), often with one or two subdivisions or rooms. Some structures with two storeys are known. On both tells and flat settlements in southeastern Europe houses are normally rather uniform in size, rarely exceeding 15 m in length. In that area they are often set out in more or less straight rows, though the precision of layout varies. Concentric arrangement is also known, as in the uppermost levels of the tell at Uivar in western Romania, and throughout the tell layers at Csőszhalom-Polgár in northeast Hungary (the northernmost tell in Europe), both from the earlier fifth millennium cal BCE. Both sites illustrate a combination of uses of buildings. Each has the vertical accumulation of its tell, but with an accompanying flat settlement.[38] At Csőszhalom, the houses in the flat settlement (here often about 12 m long) are set out in very rough rows, but share the same linear alignment, while those on the tell are concentrically arranged, a difference without doubt deliberate, and backed by contrasts in the nature of the finds and deposits in each.

In the developed LBK, from about 5300 cal BCE, groupings of generally larger longhouses are found, though smaller buildings are included in the range of structures. These can often be in excess of 20 m long, and structures over 30 m long are not that uncommon, though they may have been locally pre-eminent.[39] The size and layout of settlements varied; it is tempting to use the modern vocabulary of hamlets and villages, but this is dangerous and does not encompass all the diversity evident. Some sites were small, with just a handful of buildings in use at any one time, and in some settings such groupings occur in ribbon-like settings along streams, classically in the case of the valleys of the Merzbach[40] and Schlangengraben on the Aldenhoven plateau in northwest Germany, while others are more concentrated, as at Vaihingen in southwest Germany.[41] Even in any one local situation there

---

38 P. Raczky and A. Anders, 'Late Neolithic spatial differentiation at Polgár-Csőszhalom, eastern Hungary', in Bailey et al. (eds.), *Living Well Together*, 35–53; F. Draşovean and W. Schier, 'The Neolithic tell sites of Parţa and Uivar (Romanian Banat): a comparison of their architectural sequence and organization of social space', in S. Hansen (ed.), *Leben auf dem Tell als soziale Praxis* (Bonn: Habelt, 2010), 165–87.

39 J. Pechtl, 'A monumental prestige patchwork', in D. Hofmann and P. Bickle (eds.), *Creating Communities: New Advances in Central European Neolithic Research* (Oxford: Oxbow, 2009), 186–201.

40 J. Lüning and P. Stehli (eds.), *Die Bandkeramik im Merzbachtal auf der Aldenhovener Platte* (Köln: Rheinland-Verlag, 1994).

41 A. Bogaard et al., 'Towards a social geography of cultivation and plant use in an early farming community: Vaihingen an der Enz, south-west Germany', *Antiquity*, 85 (2011), 395–416.

may be variation, since in the Merzbach valley what is probably the earliest occupied place, Langweiler 8, went on to become by far the largest local grouping of buildings. There is a very active debate about how LBK settlements were laid out, and there may be no single answer. One model, long dominant, proposes the independence of individual buildings, each set within its own working space or yard, with yards also combined in neighbourhoods or wards. This model is bound up with the view, in turn based on the close study of changing motifs on decorated pottery, that no one LBK building was occupied for more than about twenty-five years (despite the use of oak for the characteristic rows of posts), producing a dozen or more 'house generations' in the case of the Aldenhoven plateau and seventeen or eighteen in the case of Vaihingen.[42] This has been challenged by an alternative model of rows, though this may work better in parts of central Europe than elsewhere; longer durations have also been proposed.[43] A further rather attractive variation is the idea of varying neighbourhood clusters.[44] Whatever the outcome of such debate, the classical problem remains of the absence of preserved house floors or occupation levels, finds only generally surviving in any quantity in the LBK context in accompanying pits. It is very hard, therefore, to estimate how many people inhabited an LBK longhouse. The yard model is normally accompanied by the view that only a rather modest-sized nuclear or small extended family filled the LBK longhouse, but in that case the routine 'over-build' is puzzling compared to the structures found in southeastern Europe.

In the Alpine foreland, the good conditions of preservation show a range of constructions, including buildings raised on stilts to sit above wet lake edges, but again these are all rectangular. Just occasionally, buildings occur in ones and twos, and often one or two structures can be shown by dendrochronological analysis to have been built a year or two before others joined them, but the normal pattern is small groups of houses; there is evidence in some areas that by the later fourth millennium BCE some settlements were larger than in earlier generations. Alpine foreland houses were rather

---

42 J. Lüning, 'Bandkeramische Hofplätze und die absolute Chronologie der Bandkeramik', in J. Lüning et al. (eds.), *Die Bandkeramik im 21. Jahrhundert* (Rahden: Marie Leidorf, 2005), 49–74.

43 O. Rück, 'New aspects and models for Bandkeramik settlement research', in Hofmann and Bickle (eds.), *Creating Communities*, 159–85.

44 L. Czerniak, 'House, household and village in the LBK of Little Poland', in L. Amkreutz et al. (eds.), *Something Out of the Ordinary? Interpreting Diversity in the Early Neolithic Linearbandkeramik of Central and Western Europe* (Cambridge University Press, forthcoming).

regular in size, again not often exceeding 10–12 m in length, and often close set, both in almost grid-like patterns and in rows, both single and spaced out.[45] One of their most surprising features is their brevity of use. We can certainly call their occupants farmers, though especially in early centuries they exploited plenty of red deer alongside cattle, pigs, and cereals,[46] and we might expect buildings to signify sustained sedentary existence. It may be, however, that it was occupation of locality that endured in this cultural context, rather than individual settlements. The duration of settlements in some cases gradually lengthened with the passage of time, but repeatedly we find evidence for durations, especially but by no means only in earlier centuries, of not more than ten to fifteen years. The brief occupations of both Hornstaad-Hörnle 1A and Arbon Bleiche 3 were brought to an end by fire,[47] perhaps in both cases accidentally, and other endings may have been due to variations in lake levels, but there are plenty of other instances where no specific cause can be identified. It seems unlikely that long-term permanence of particular buildings was planned or anticipated here, and a very different mindset can be proposed, difficult though that is to envisage from a modern, western perspective.[48]

These few examples do not of course exhaust the evidence available across Europe, but even this selection underlines the general observation that over and over again we see people living together. Was this always in the same way? Two kinds of evidence suggest not. Some of these communities may have been more important than others. Size and prominence have been suggested to be important factors. Notions of alliances and networks of connection and mutual support are attractive models for dispersed communities, but certain players and places may have held more cards than others. There is a recurrent idea that tells were significant locales, as a visible demonstration of continuity and ancestry, which the recent investigations

45 Ebersbach, 'Houses, households, and settlements'.
46 E.G. Schibler et al., Ökonomie und Ökologie neolithischer und bronzezeitlicher Ufersiedlungen am Zürichsee: Ergebnisse der Ausgrabungen Mozartstrasse, Kanalisationssanierung Seefeld, AKA/Pressehaus und Mythenschloss in Zürich (Zürich: Kantonsarchäologie; Fotorotar, 1997).
47 B. Dieckmann et al., 'Die Befunde einer jungsteinzeitlichen Pfahlbausiedlung am westlichen Bodensee', in Landesamt für Denkmalpflege, Siedlungsarchäologie im Alpenvorland IX (Stuttgart: Theiss, 2006), 8–275; S. Jacomet et al. (eds.), Die jungsteinzeitliche Seeufersiedlung Arbon-Bleiche 3: Umwelt und Wirtschaft (Frauenfeld: Departement für Erziehung und Kultur des Kantons Thurgau, 2004).
48 D. Hofmann, 'Living by the lake: domestic architecture in the Alpine foreland', in Hofmann and Smyth (eds.), Tracking the Neolithic House, 197–227.

of contemporaneous flat settlements only serve to underline.[49] Some of the larger LBK settlements have been picked out as 'central places', perhaps with specific roles in the distribution of raw materials such as stone and flint that needed to be imported into areas occupied.[50] Simply keeping numbers of people together may have been significant, in providing shared labour and – in a world now with plenty of evidence for interpersonal, and from time to time intergroup, violence and conflict[51] – the means of collective defence.

There is also intriguing new evidence for difference within settlements. We should not forget cases already mentioned like Uivar and Csőszhalom, though it might be argued there that the tells had a specialized ritual role within a unified social setting. But were householders on the tells in some way superior to those below? At the tell of Okolište in Bosnia, neighbouring houses in the earlier fifth-millennium levels, set in rows, appear to have had different associated activities, some concentrating on agricultural production, others on craft production, and yet others on hunting.[52] Does this hint at internal difference, or should the notion of household in fact be distributed across several buildings? Something similar is apparent at the late LBK settlement of Cuiry-lès-Chaudardes in the Aisne valley, in northern France, where the remains of cattle and pigs were found preferentially in the pits flanking larger longhouses, which were grouped more centrally, while the remains of wild game, including red deer and boar, were associated with smaller houses, more on the periphery of the site.[53] At Vaihingen in southwest Germany, analysis of site layout, pottery decoration, and plant remains has been combined to suggest groupings of houses, perhaps constituting something like clans. It is argued that these not only had varying connections regionally and beyond to other areas of settlement, part of the complicated networks and affiliations of LBK existence, but also had

49 J. Chapman, 'Places as timemarks: the social construction of prehistoric landscapes in eastern Hungary', in J. Chapman and P. Dolukhanov (eds.), *Landscapes in Flux: Central and Eastern Europe in Antiquity* (Oxford: Oxbow, 1997), 209–30.
50 J. Petrasch, 'Zentrale Orte in der Bandkeramik?', in J. Eckert et al. (eds.), *Archäologische Perspektiven: Analysen und Interpretationen im Wandel* (Rahden: Marie Leidorf, 2003), 505–13.
51 R. Schulting and L. Fibiger (eds.), *Sticks, Stones, and Broken Bones: Neolithic Violence in a European Perspective* (Oxford University Press, 2012).
52 J. Müller et al. (eds.), *Okolište 1: Untersuchungen einer spätneolithischen Siedlungskammer in Zentralbosnien* (Bonn: Habelt, 2013).
53 L. Hachem, *Le site Néolithique de Cuiry-lès-Chaudardes – I: de l'analyse de la faune à la structuration sociale* (Rahden: Marie Leidorf, 2011).

differential access to the best local soils; probably all the households and people involved were cultivating the same plants in broadly the same kind of way, but with subtle differences in how they could do this.[54] In a wider study of diet and lifetime mobility in the LBK, it has been found that men buried with stones adzes are more likely to have been born and to have spent their lives locally, suggesting in another way the potential importance of access to and perhaps control of prime resources.[55]

In the mid to later fifth millennium cal BCE in central Poland (see also Chapter 23), it has been suggested that trapezoidal longhouses, at the very end of the longhouse tradition, may have been individually more independent economically, which is partly reflected in the greater space around each structure, though these buildings did still form larger and smaller clusters.[56] Finally, in the later fourth-millennium BCE context of Arbon Bleiche 3 on the Bodensee, two broad groupings are apparent within the closely set rows of near-identical houses; it is worth dwelling on the exceptional detail here.[57] Some houses (1–4, 8, 20, and 24) had considerably more remains of wild animals than others (such as 7 and 23). The largest quantities of deer were recovered from houses 3, 8, 20, and 24; wild cattle were very frequent in houses 3, 8, and 20; while houses 8 and 20 yielded additional concentrations of brown bear, marten/polecat, badger, and otter bones. Domestic cattle were dominant in the northern excavated part of the village, while domestic pigs were more frequent in the southern part, closer to the lakeshore. Sheep and goats were kept in both the northern and the southern parts (though they were present in bigger numbers only in certain houses). In addition, pottery of a style common at the eastern end of the Alps (the Boleráz style of the Baden culture) was more frequent in the lakeward and central parts of the excavated area; other pottery was in local style. In addition, in the landward part, pike, perch, and particularly fish of the carp family dominated; these were obviously caught in fixed nets close to the shore,

54 Bogaard et al., 'Towards a social geography of cultivation'; A. Bogaard, *Plant Use and Crop Husbandry in an Early Neolithic Village: Vaihingen an der Enz, Baden-Württemberg* (Bonn: Habelt, 2012).

55 Bickle and Whittle (eds.), *First Farmers of Central Europe*.

56 A. Marciniak, 'The society in the making: the house and household in the Danubian Neolithic of the central European lowlands', in T. Kerig and A. Zimmermann (eds.), *Economic Archaeology: From Structure to Performance in European Archaeology* (Bonn: Habelt, 2013), 47–63.

57 Jacomet et al. (eds.), *Die jungsteinzeitliche Seeufersiedlung Arbon-Bleiche 3*. It appears now that the precise date of the settlement may need revision, though probably not the brevity of its occupation (Urs Leuzinger, pers. comm.).

which was also confirmed by finds of net sinkers. Whitefish dominated in the lakeward part of the village; these had to be caught from boats on the open water using trawled nets, without net sinkers. People here lived close together, but house by house they were not all doing the same things.

Rich arrays of material culture are typical of Neolithic settlement across Europe. There may have been a general relationship between the increased quantities of things and the more settled nature of existence, but specific circumstances suggest variations. In house-poor areas, pottery for example may have been made seasonally or for special gatherings, rather than have been available in every context throughout the year; wells in the LBK show that people used wooden and birch bark vessels as well as clay contain-ers. Pottery was probably mainly made and used locally, though there are plausible examples of imports from neighbouring and also from time to time more distant areas. Conversely, many things were brought in from varying distances, including a wider range of flint and other flakeable stone, and hard stone for adzes and axes. One of the most spectacular examples recently studied has been the fine jadeitite axes produced from specific boulders high in the western Italian Alps (Figure 22.8), starting in the later sixth and continuing into the earlier fourth millennium cal BCE, which were then moved, by exchange or other means, widely into central and western Europe.[58] Copper was also produced from restricted sources in increasing quantities in southeastern Europe by the fifth millennium cal BCE, with specific mines identified, and the technology gradually spread westwards.[59] A copper axe was carried by the Iceman, born south of the Alps in the later fourth millennium cal BCE,[60] and copper finds were significant in southern Iberia by the end of the fourth and into the third millennium cal BCE.[61] Some of the graves in the mid fifth millennium cal BCE cemetery at Varna on the Black Sea coast of Bulgaria show developed metallurgy in the form of

---

58 P. Pétrequin et al. (eds.), *Jade: grandes haches alpines du Néolithique européen. V<sup>e</sup>et IV<sup>e</sup>millénaires av. J.-C.* (Besançon: Presses Universitaires de Franche-Comté, 2013).

59 C. Strahm, 'L'introduction de la metallurgie en Europe', in J. Guilaine (ed.), *Le Chalcolithique et la construction des inegalités* (Paris: Errance, 2007), 49–71; A. Dolfini, 'The emergence of metallurgy in the central Mediterranean region: a new model', *European Journal of Archaeology*, 16 (2013), 21–62; B.W. Roberts, 'Production networks and consumer choice in the earliest metal of western Europe', *Journal of World Prehistory*, 22 (2009), 461–81.

60 S. Bortenschlager and K. Öggl (eds.), *The Iceman and his Natural Environment: Palaeobotanical Results*, The Man in the Ice 4 (Vienna and New York: Springer, 2000).

61 M. Cruz Berrocal et al. (eds.), *The Prehistory of Iberia: Debating Early Social Stratification and the State* (New York: Routledge, 2013).

Figure 22.8 One of the boulders high in the western Italian Alps from which jadeitite axes were quarried: a block of rough jadeitite, at Vallone Porco, at 2,400 m above sea level; Mont Viso is in the background.

heavy cast copper tools, alongside technically simpler copper rings, needles and awls, and beaten sheet goldwork.[62]

Things both connected and defined people. Two traditional approaches can be noted. An important one has been to seek spatial regularities and associations in successive phases, using the resulting 'cultures' as a signature of shared identity in any one region and time, with population displacements and replacements a favourite past explanation of periodically abrupt changes in style. The other conventional approach has been to pick out particular objects and categories as both valuables (variously on the basis of distance from source, rarity, and the labour involved in manufacture) and individual possessions. Fine stone axes, and things in copper and gold, have been recurrent candidates, and a narrative is often presented of increasing differentiation through time. Neither approach should be lightly dismissed. It has been tempting to set aside old-fashioned 'culture history', since the narratives in question are often based largely on pottery, and the areas in question are regularly so large that it is hard to envisage a single, bounded identity within them. When mapped, or set in chronological tables, the boundaries between cultures can seem hard and fast, but this is rarely the case on the ground. I believe that in many ways the materiality of Neolithic existence bound people together more than it set them apart, creating a sense of familiarity and security. Even where there are discernible differences in detail, such as within Vaihingen and Arbon Bleiche, community was maintained, even if for varying periods of time. Likewise, the jadeitite axes and rings in impressively large early monuments in Brittany, or the profusion and concentration of copper and gold at Varna, can obviously be taken as evidence of unequal access to desirable objects. It is not always easy, however, to pin down questions of possession and ownership. Varna stands out as an exception in its regional and wider setting,[63] and several of its most abundantly furnished graves were cenotaphs. Jadeitite axes in Britain, possibly with the status of ancestral heirlooms brought by incomers, have very rarely been found in specific contexts (one was beside a trackway across wetland in Somerset, another in front of a chambered tomb in southwest Scotland). It is rather rare in general to find major accumulations of objects in single contexts, so

62  I. Ivanov, 'Die Ausgrabungen des Gräberfeldes von Varna', in A. Fol and J. Lichardus (eds.), *Macht, Herrschaft und Gold: das Gräberfeld von Varna und die Anfänge einer neuen europäischen Zivilisation* (Saarbrücken: Moderne Galerie des Saarland-Museums, 1988), 49–65.

63  J. Chapman, 'From Varna to Brittany via Csőszhalom: was there a "Varna" effect?', in A. Anders and G. Kulcsár (eds.), *Moments in Time: Papers Presented to Pál Raczky on his 60th Birthday* (Budapest: L'Harmattan, 2013), 323–35.

I believe that even where valuables were desired and acquired, it was also important to give them away.

Similar tensions can also be seen in the last dimension of communality briefly to be discussed here, that of mortuary practices. The archaeologically visible dead of any one place and time were regularly treated in very similar ways. That varied through time, for example from diverse and scattered burials in and around settlements in southeastern Europe (but not, so far, much in Greece), to the emergence in the late sixth and fifth millennia cal BCE, especially in the eastern Balkans, of separate cemeteries. Such burial grounds were a feature of the LBK in its developed phase probably from around 5300 cal BCE onwards, and of its successors in the fifth millennium cal BCE, with collective barrows and tombs emerging in western Europe, as already noted, from the fifth millennium cal BCE onwards, becoming numerous especially in the fourth. Whether as individual burials in cemeteries, or collective deposits within formal, monumentalized tombs, there is again a strongly communal feel to these practices. Even by the later fourth millennium cal BCE in northern France, a date by which some models would predict more pronounced social difference, there was repeated deposition of individual corpses, largely without grave goods, in above- and below-ground chambers (*allées sépulchrales* and *hypogées*), forming substantial collectivities (often with more than a hundred people), perhaps over quite short periods of time.[64]

We also have to deal again with questions of visibility and internal difference. Not everyone may be represented in cemeteries or monuments. Even the largest LBK burial grounds, with numbers of graves in the low hundreds, are unlikely to include the whole population,[65] and the same may apply with many collective tombs. So in both cases we could be looking at pre-eminent individual members or groupings within the local community, such as particular families, households, or lineages, though there could be yet other dimensions such as sodalities or ritualized associations cross-cutting purely local community; isotopic studies of lifetime mobility show mixtures of locally and non-locally born people.[66] Valencina de la Concepción, above the Guadalquivir River near Seville in southwest Spain, nicely illustrates some of these challenges in the late fourth to earlier third millennium cal

---

64 P. Chambon, *Les morts dans les sépultures collectives Néolithiques en France: du cadavre aux restes ultimes* (Paris: CNRS, 2003).

65 P. van de Velde, 'Much ado about nothing: Bandkeramik funerary ritual', *Analecta Praehistorica Leidensia*, 29 (1997), 83–90.

66 E.g. Bickle and Whittle (eds.), *First Farmers of Central Europe*.

BCE. With an estimated area of over 400 ha, Valencina stands out locally and regionally. While there are settlement features principally in the form of pits, with some evidence for copper-working, many of the known features are to do with disposal of the dead. These include some of the most remarkable megalithic monuments of Iberia, such as the large dolmens and *tholoi* of La Pastora, Matarrubilla, and Montelirio.[67] Other mortuary contexts include artificial caves and simple pits. In all these settings, successive deposition of individuals was made, forming various collectivities. Was this a place for everyone, or was it, perhaps more plausibly, a dominant locale, with particular groups or lineages able to control or otherwise acquire exotic materials, including here not only copper but also African and eastern Mediterranean ivory,[68] for deposition in the most prominent monuments?

## Making a living

Around 7000 cal BCE there were hunter-gatherers everywhere across Europe; by soon after 4000 cal BCE, very few of these remained, principally in the eastern Baltic and points north. Some farmers hunted, as already noted; the Körös culture of the earlier sixth millennium cal BCE on the Great Hungarian Plain, where conditions of preservation are remarkably good, shows hunting of wild game, fowling, fishing, and shellfish collection, but undoubtedly the main resources exploited were cereals and sheep (and goats).[69] Later on, elsewhere, wild animals may have become important as a symbolic category in their own right, and hunting as a sport or marker of gendered identity may also have been significant. There is still room for improvement in the application of appropriate recovery techniques, including sieving and flotation, especially in conditions of rescue or contract archaeology, when time pressures can squeeze best practice; in that scenario, it is perhaps the recovery of plant remains that suffers most. Nor is there any justification for thinking that we know all there is to find out about subsistence. It is only recently that analysis of fatty acids or lipids in pottery has opened the way to

67 M.E. Costa Caramé et al., 'The Copper Age settlement of Valencina de la Concepción (Seville, Spain): demography, metallurgy and spatial organization', *Trabajos de Prehistoria*, 67 (2010), 87–118.

68 T.X. Schuhmacher et al., 'Sourcing African ivory in Chalcolithic Portugal', *Antiquity*, 83 (2009), 983–97.

69 A. Bogaard et al., 'Archaeobotanical evidence for plant husbandry and use', and L. Bartosiewicz, 'Mammalian bone', both in A. Whittle (ed.), *The Early Neolithic on the Great Hungarian Plain: Investigations of the Körös Culture Site of Ecsegfalva 23, County Békés* (Budapest: Institute of Archaeology, Hungarian Academy of Sciences, 2007), 421–45, 287–325.

understanding the use of dairy products. The research has shown this practice from unexpectedly early dates, back to the earlier sixth millennium cal BCE in the Carpathian basin and to the later sixth in central Europe; it was also present in Anatolia in the seventh millennium cal BCE.[70] Even this exciting result leaves many questions, since the ability to digest milk after weaning ('lactase persistence') is restricted, and it may be that it was some time after the initial development of milking that the necessary genetic mutation spread more widely among the population (see Chapter 6). In that case, early use of dairy products was probably mainly in the form of cheese and other processed products. There is enormous scope too for further studies of dentition, since different diets will leave different traces, and of health in general. Generally it is hard not to see Neolithic subsistence as successful, but detailed studies show plenty of examples of episodes of stress and disease in the life histories of individuals,[71] and life tables, for example from the central Mediterranean, suggest life expectancy of little over forty years.[72]

That Neolithic communities subsisted largely on cereals and animal products is not therefore in doubt. Even though perhaps a specialized figure, accustomed to high altitude, the Iceman from the southern Alps in the later fourth millennium cal BCE had eaten cereals as part of his last meal or meals.[73] This broad result is shown over and over again from excavations right across Europe, though there were phases now and then when wild resources were still important. The pattern is not unvarying. For example, crop variety seems to have declined as cultivation spread to the west, with fewer cereal species and fewer associated legumes,[74] and sheep were replaced by cattle as the key animal, not only in central Europe, but also in the Carpathian basin.[75] The challenge now is to understand the balance of resources, and the

---

70 O.E. Craig et al., 'Did the first farmers of central and eastern Europe produce dairy foods?', *Antiquity*, 79 (2005), 882–94; R.P. Evershed et al., 'Earliest date for milk use in the Near East and southeastern Europe linked to cattle herding', *Nature*, 455 (2008), 528–31; M. Salque et al., 'Earliest evidence for cheese making in the sixth millennium BC in northern Europe', *Nature*, 493 (2012), 522–5.

71 E.g. L. Fibiger, passim, in Bickle and Whittle (eds.), *First Farmers of Central Europe*.

72 Robb, *Early Mediterranean Village*.

73 J.H. Dickson et al., 'The omnivorous Tyrolean Iceman: colon contents (meat, cereals, pollen, moss and whipworm) and stable isotope analyses', *Philosophical Transactions of the Royal Society B*, 355 (2000), 1843–9; W. Groenman-van Waateringe, 'The Iceman's last days: the testimony of *Ostrya carpinifolia*', *Antiquity*, 85 (2011), 434–40.

74 S. Colledge and J. Conolly (eds.), *The Origins and Spread of Domestic Plants in Southwest Asia and Europe* (Walnut Creek, CA: Left Coast Press, 2007); A. Kreuz, 'Die Vertreibung aus dem Paradies? Archäobiologische Ergebnisse zum Frühneolithikum im westlichen Mitteleuropa', *Bericht der Römisch-Germanischen Kommission*, 91 (2012), 23–196.

75 Bartosiewicz, 'Mammalian bone'; D. Orton, 'Both subject and object: herding, inalienability and sentient property in prehistory', *World Archaeology*, 42 (2010), 188–200.

organization, scale, and goals of production, and to examine critically how and whether things changed markedly or significantly through time; the conventional expectation is of linear intensification, but I believe that more subtle developments were a key ingredient of Neolithic histories.

The model of intensive, prolonged cultivation in fixed, relatively small gardens, rather than in extensive fields or in shifting plots managed by slash-and-burn techniques, is persuasive and seems demonstrable whenever the appropriate recovery techniques provide the weed assemblages which decide the issue.[76] We have already seen probable variety in the situation at LBK Vaihingen, and it can be inferred that gardens were maintained in the Alpine foreland while particular settlements came and went; nonetheless there is also evidence for cycles of woodland use in parts of the Alpine foreland, so we perhaps have to be cautious in applying the same fixed-plot model everywhere, at all times.[77] Larger and more extensive systems of stone walls of the earlier fourth millennium cal BCE, sharing a common axis across the landscape, have been found preserved beneath blanket peat in Co. Mayo, western Ireland, but are probably largely to do with animal management rather than cereal cultivation.[78] Neither pollen analysis nor features of excavated settlements (for example for storage) suggest a marked increase in the scale of cultivation through time. We should note, however, the evidence for ploughing from the fourth millennium cal BCE, in the form of preserved criss-cross marks in the subsoil beneath covering barrows, and the models and representations of paired cattle. This may be significant, but we cannot be sure that animal traction was not harnessed earlier than this, and the means by which earlier gardens were cultivated is likewise unknown. So one model could be of recurrent, relatively small-scale but productive

76 A. Bogaard, *Neolithic Farming in Central Europe: An Archaeobotanical Study of Crop Husbandry Practices* (London: Routledge, 2004); Kreuz, 'Die Vertreibung aus dem Paradies?'; W. Schier, 'Extensiver Brandfeldbau und die Ausbreitung der neolithischen Wirtschaftsweise in Mitteleuropa und Südskandinavien am Ende des 5. Jahrtausends v. Chr.', *Prähistorische Zeitschrift*, 84 (2009), 15–43.

77 M. Rösch et al., 'Spätneolithische Landnutzung im nördlichen Alpenvorland: Beobachtungen – Hypothesen – Experimente', and A. Billamboz and J. Köninger, 'Dendroarchäologische Untersuchungen zur Besiedlungs- und Landschaftsentwicklung im Neolithikum des westlichen Bodenseegebietes', both in W. Dörfler and J. Müller (eds.), *Umwelt – Wirtschaft – Siedlungen im dritten vorchristlichen Jahrtausend Mitteleuropas und Südskandinaviens* (Neumünster: Wachholtz, 2008), 301–15, 317–34; Ebersbach, 'Houses, households, and settlements'; N. Bleicher, *Altes Holz in neuem Licht: archäologische und dendrochronologische Untersuchungen an spätneolithischen Feuchtbodensiedlungen Oberschwabens* (Stuttgart: Theiss, 2009).

78 S. Caulfield, 'The Neolithic settlement of north Connaught', in T. Reeves-Smyth and F. Hamond (eds.), *Landscape Archaeology in Ireland* (Oxford: British Archaeological Reports, 1983), 195–215.

cultivation, carried out by individual households, which varied in detail but did not significantly intensify over time.

Getting at scale is even harder with herds and flocks. One obvious model is again of household-based ownership and management – perhaps linked closely to gardens, not least for manuring – early on of flocks of sheep and later of herds of cattle. Isotopic studies are beginning to reveal something of the detail of animal movement, at differing distances from settlements, for example in southwest Germany in the LBK.[79] There would be advantages in household co-operation to maintain larger herds and to spread risks, but evidence already reviewed suggests plenty of difference among the residues associated with individual structures, so that it is unwise to envisage the community operating as a single, unified whole. Other studies suggest further ways of breaking down the generalized picture. Body-part representation and bone treatment suggest in both central Poland in the LBK and southern England in the earlier fourth millennium cal BCE that sheep may have been used for more routine consumption, while cattle may have been reserved for feasting.[80] While the balance between cereals and animal products is extremely difficult to establish, we may envisage a mainly 'domestic mode of production', as Marshall Sahlins called it,[81] and allow for variation among both households and communities. It is tempting to see an increase in the scale of herds and flocks over time,[82] with live animals a both visible and audible testament to prowess and success, and their meat a main attraction at communal feasts and gatherings; those with the biggest herds, or more willing to slaughter prized beasts, would have gained most reward. But again it is very difficult to quantify this; one recent study of causewayed enclosures in southern Britain, in whose ditches cattle remains are prominent, suggests that in fact numbers of animals being consumed at any one time were probably quite small.[83]

I believe therefore that we should be suspicious of claims for simple trends towards intensification and increased scale over time. One version of this, the so-called 'secondary products revolution', has been widely cited, and still attracts many adherents. According to this, milk, wool, traction in the form of

---

79 C. Knipper, *Die räumliche Organisation der Linearbandkeramischen Rinderhaltung: naturwissenschaftliche und archäologische Untersuchungen* (Oxford: Archaeopress, 2011).

80 A. Marciniak, *Placing Animals in the Neolithic: Social Zooarchaeology of Prehistoric Farming Communities* (Institute of Archaeology Publications, University College London, 2005); D. Serjeantson, 'Food or feast at Neolithic Runnymede?', in D. Serjeantson and D. Field (eds.), *Animals in the Neolithic of Britain and Europe* (Oxford: Oxbow, 2006), 113–34.

81 M. Sahlins, *Stone Age Economics* (Chicago: Aldine Press, 1974).

82 Orton, 'Both subject and object'.  83 Whittle et al., *Gathering Time*.

wheeled vehicles and ploughs, and alcohol and other drugs came into Europe from the fourth millennium as a set of secondary innovations from the Near East and the eastern Mediterranean.[84] Now, it is clear that these can be assigned to various dates. Milk came in earlier, as we have seen, and wool probably later; the jury is out on the chronology of ploughs and the exploitation of animal traction, though wheeled vehicles do seem genuinely to appear in both the Carpathian basin and the Alpine foreland in the fourth millennium;[85] even then, we have to specify what effect small carts could have had on production. My own view therefore is that agricultural production remained largely household-based. Beyond the needs of survival, which were on the whole successfully met, the goals of production were to meet the social obligations of hasehold and community. In any situation, there were likely to be differences and variations, as more and more studies are showing, a possibility not confined to later situations. It is very hard to link the scale or control of production to, say, the possession of particular valuables or the ability to mobilize labour for communal efforts of monument construction, in specific instances, though this is not implausible; correlations between the possession of stone adzes and local isotopic signatures in the LBK should be borne in mind. But it seems unlikely that particular households, lineages, communities, or other social groupings were in the end able to so control the means of production that ownership of land or surplus became held by a minority in society as a whole.

## Worldviews

So there were all those communities, some living closely together in groupings of houses, and others still tightly connected even though they were more dispersed across their landscapes; population increased in many areas, and great communal acts of construction were undertaken; and people worked in gardens

---

84 A. Sherratt, 'Plough and pastoralism: aspects of the secondary products revolution', in I. Hodder et al. (eds.), *Pattern of the Past: Studies in Honour of David Clarke* (Cambridge University Press, 1981), 261–305; H.J. Greenfield, 'The secondary products revolution: the past, the present and the future', *World Archaeology*, 42 (2010), 29–54; V. Heyd, 'Growth and expansion: social, economic and ideological structures in the European Chalcolithic', in M.J. Allen et al. (eds.), *Is there a British Chalcolithic? People, Place and Polity in the Later 3rd Millennium* (Oxford: Oxbow, 2012), 98–114; A. Marciniak, 'The secondary products revolution: empirical evidence and its current zooarchaeological critique', *Journal of World Prehistory*, 24 (2011), 117–30.

85 W. Schier, 'Jungneolithikum und Kupferzeit in Mitteleuropa (4500–2800 v. Chr.)', in Badisches Landesmuseum, *Jungsteinzeit in Umbruch*, 26–36.

with their crops and moved around their local and wider taskscapes with their animals. How did these people see the world, and what were their values?

Archaeologists have often struggled to come up with satisfactory answers to these questions. This has been partly because of a perception that dimensions of past lives like worldview must be less accessible than, say, the workings of the agricultural economy; partly due to a preference for characterizations based on aspects of social differentiation such as rank and status; and partly because of the obviously great diversity of the evidence, which perversely often results in monolithic explanations. To try to get round some of these difficulties, I want here to risk some generalizations.

One way to start could be to compare hunter-gatherers and farmers. The social anthropologist Alan Barnard has sketched a series of differences, in which hunter-gatherers value immediate consumption, sharing, followership, and deference to the will of the community; they classify everyone as kin, think of the land as sacrosanct and primordial, regard people as free individuals, and equate natural equality with social harmony, with strong sanctions against anti-social behaviour; farmers, by contrast, value accumulation, saving for oneself and dependants, leadership, high status, and initiative; they divide up society by means of kinship and groupings such as tribes, regard land as sovereign and associated with alienable wealth or political authority, see people as sacrosanct, and esteem inequality, equating it with the ability to accumulate, achieve, and compete.[86] There is much to debate here, not least the immediate dangers from the scale of generalization. Not all hunter-gatherers are the same, and early farmers were no less diverse; in both cases it is important to keep open, as already seen in this chapter, the possibility of differences, contrasts, and tensions within any one situation; and the timescales over which such transformations are effected can be very long indeed.[87] One of the attractions of his scheme, however, is the claim that elements of the hunter-gatherer mode of thought, as he calls it, can perfectly well be maintained even when the technology of subsistence has altered – as in the southern African context which Barnard has studied, where people turned to small-scale cultivation and stock-keeping.

---

86 A. Barnard, 'From Mesolithic to Neolithic modes of thought', in Whittle and Cummings (eds.), *Going Over*, 5–19.

87 K.V. Flannery and J. Marcus, *The Creation of Inequality: How our Prehistoric Ancestors Set the Stage for Monarchy, Slavery, and Empire* (Cambridge, MA: Harvard University Press, 2012).

A further useful way to think about the worldview of early farmers is through their sense of time. For the purposes of this discussion, Neolithic temporality can be seen as mutually constituted by futures, presents, and pasts. Clearances, gardens, herds, and flocks can all be seen as obvious investment in the future; possession of land and place were also part of the agricultural ideology of continuity. The Alpine foreland example in particular has shown how permanence and impermanence of residence and place may be relative, but in this case possession and use of the land normally endured. In other cases, strikingly with the tells of southeastern Europe, the future was written generation by generation in the maintenance of pre-eminent places. The future need not be seen as confined to the technology of agricultural life. Material culture, too, served as a forward-looking projection of identities; not just in dramatic instances like the winning of jadeitite from high Alpine locations or copper from underground seams, but also in the making and firing of mundane pots, materiality was partly about what was to come.

Life also goes forward in the rolling present, and Neolithic existence was rich in connections and performances, routine and episodic. Mostly it would seem that people lived well together, day to day, and year to year, and the important new evidence for interpersonal and intergroup violence[88] in fact serves to underline that general claim. There is no indication yet that episodes of violence, for example in the late LBK, were concentrated in boundary situations, so rather we could think of an endemic level of competition and a periodic tendency for normal dispute-solving mechanisms to break down. Networks of connection and alliance must normally have maintained peaceful relations. An ethic of co-operation and perhaps sharing must have enabled the maintenance of large aggregations of settlement which lack signs of differentiated houses or spaces within them. Beautiful things were acquired but often given away; desirable animals were sacrificed for feasts, in which a single large beast could have fed hundreds of people.[89]

Tracking the past was also characteristic of early farmers in Europe. Demonstration of the fact of past possession served as legitimation in the present, and for the future. This took different forms. Tells in southeastern Europe have nicely been dubbed 'ancestral timemarks',[90] though that still leaves us puzzling over how to characterize contemporary flat settlements. Houses themselves could be seen as a vehicle of descent, the idea of 'house societies', first formulated by Claude Lévi-Strauss, being increasingly

---

88 Schulting and Fibiger (eds.), *Sticks, Stones, and Broken Bones*.
89 Marciniak, *Placing Animals in the Neolithic*.   90 Chapman, 'Places as timemarks'.

borrowed by Neolithic specialists.[91] If that is too abstract or too loose a fit with the anthropological model, then the concrete example of LBK long-houses illustrates the blending of past and present; as older buildings decayed, after whatever span of use, they normally seem to have been left alone to decay while successors were created around them. Grave by grave and in accumulating clusters or rows, cemeteries beside settlements inscribed the past into the ground. Over wide swathes of western Europe, from Scandinavia to the central and western Mediterranean, people created complex visions (and perhaps cults) of the past through burial monuments; some of their architectural features may have memorialized the deep past, for example in the mimicking of earlier longhouses in the form of barrows and cairns, though the dead accumulated in such constructions normally belong to the immediate past. Remembered forebears were perhaps later transformed into remote ancestors.

## What happened in Neolithic histories

Control of future, present, and past, no less than of agricultural production itself, could have enabled difference to emerge. Some households within communities, and some communities compared to others, could have had access to better land and resources and could have produced more. Unreciprocated gifts and generosity could have created unbalanced social relations. Some people could have been more charismatic, more able to command the respect necessary to mobilize labour for communal enter-prises, and more skilled at patching up disputes as well as more adept at provoking them in the first place. A recent near-global survey has charted some of the many ways in which, over the long term, social inequality could be created, though it has also rightly stressed the inbuilt resistance to the emergence of difference.[92] The account, however, largely left out Europe. That is a pity, as both the timescales and character of social change in prehistoric Europe seem different to many other situations. The adoption of agriculture had many consequences in Europe, some of which this chapter has attempted to sketch. Differences among people and their communities were one of these, but no single, linear trajectory of increasing social inequality can easily be tracked. In my view, the range of values held in

---

91 R.A. Beck, 'The durable house: material, metaphor and structure', in R.A. Beck (ed.), *The Durable House: House Society Models in Archaeology* (Carbondale: Center for Archaeological Investigation, Southern Illinois University, 2007), 3–24.
92 Flannery and Marcus, *Creation of Inequality*.

common by Neolithic people in Europe provided checks and balances against tendencies in the direction of competition, acquisitiveness, and inequality. It seems no accident, for example, that the displays of what we would call wealth in the Varna cemetery took place in the mid fifth millennium cal BCE, shortly before the old order of the tell system began to unravel,[93] and I have hinted at other cycles of increasing tension and dissolution.[94]

Clear, directional change has often been a major expectation of Neolithic history; the longer things went on, the more society was seen to become more hierarchical: stepping towards the modern. In this view, the third millennium is a particularly important hinge. Someone on the move across Europe even as late as around 2800 cal BCE, however, would have seen, in my view, a complicated mixture of changes, continuities, and the old ambiguities. Take the great settlements at the heart of Orkney,[95] or the early constructions at Stonehenge,[96] or corded ware burial grounds in central Europe,[97] or the end of the Baden culture cemetery at Budakalász near the Danube in northern Hungary,[98] or the continuing settlements of the Alpine foreland.[99] If these involved, in part, dominant individuals or pre-eminent lineages, these were not new phenomena, and the evident collectivities and communalities would also have been familiar to previous generations. More complex, detailed, precise, and regionalized narratives are now required.

## Further reading

Bailey, D., A. Whittle, and D. Hofmann (eds.). *Living Well Together? Settlement and Materiality in the Neolithic of South-East and Central Europe*. Oxford: Oxbow, 2008.

93 D.W. Anthony, 'The rise and fall of Old Europe', in D.W. Anthony with J.Y. Chi (eds.), *The Lost World of Old Europe: The Danube Valley, 5000–3500 BC* (Institute for the Study of the Ancient World at New York University and Princeton University Press, 2010), 28–57.

94 A. Whittle, 'Unexpected histories? South-east and central Europe', in Fowler et al. (eds.), *Oxford Handbook of Neolithic Europe* (forthcoming).

95 A.M. Jones, *Prehistoric Materialities: Becoming Material in Prehistoric Britain and Ireland* (Oxford University Press, 2012).

96 Parker Pearson, *Stonehenge*.

97 E. Neustupný, 'Kultura se šňůrovou keramikou', in E. Neustupný et al. (eds.), *Archeologie pravěkých čech*, vol. IV: *Eneolit* (Prague: Archeologický ústav AV ČR, 2008), 124–47; A. Muhl et al., *Tatort Eulau: ein 4500 Jahre altes Verbrechen wird aufgeklärt* (Stuttgart: Theiss, 2010); V. Heyd, 'Families, prestige goods, warriors and complex societies: Beaker groups of the 3rd millennium cal BC along the upper and middle Danube', *Proceedings of the Prehistoric Society*, 73 (2007), 327–79.

98 M. Bondár and P. Raczky (eds.), *The Copper Age Cemetery of Budakalász* (Budapest: Pytheas, 2009).

99 Pétrequin, 'Lake dwellings in the Alpine region'.

Bickle, P. and A. Whittle (eds.). *The First Farmers of Central Europe: Diversity in LBK Lifeways*. Oxford: Oxbow, 2013.

Bogaard, A. *Neolithic Farming in Central Europe: An Archaeobotanical Study of Crop Husbandry Practices*. London: Routledge, 2004.

   *Plant Use and Crop Husbandry in an Early Neolithic Village: Vaihingen an der Enz, Baden-Württemberg*. Bonn: Habelt, 2012.

Bortenschlager, S. and K. Öggl (eds.). *The Iceman and his Natural Environment: Palaeobotanical Results*. The Man in the Ice 4. Vienna and New York: Springer, 2000.

Chambon, P. *Les morts dans les sépultures collectives Néolithiques en France: du cadavre aux restes ultimes*. Paris: CNRS, 2003.

Chapman, J. and P. Dolukhanov (eds.). *Landscapes in Flux: Central and Eastern Europe in Antiquity*. Oxford: Oxbow, 1997.

Colledge, S. and J. Conolly (eds.). *The Origins and Spread of Domestic Plants in Southwest Asia and Europe*. Walnut Creek, CA: Left Coast Press, 2007.

Cruz Berrocal, M., L. García Sanjuán, and A. Gilman (eds.). *The Prehistory of Iberia: Debating Early Social Stratification and the State*. New York: Routledge, 2013.

Flannery, K.V. and J. Marcus. *The Creation of Inequality: How our Prehistoric Ancestors Set the Stage for Monarchy, Slavery, and Empire*. Cambridge, MA: Harvard University Press, 2012.

Fowler, C., J. Harding, and D. Hofmann (eds.). *The Oxford Handbook of Neolithic Europe*. Oxford University Press, forthcoming.

Greenfield, H.J. 'The secondary products revolution: the past, the present and the future.' *World Archaeology*, 42 (2010), 29–54.

Hofmann, D. and P. Bickle (eds.). *Creating Communities: New Advances in Central European Neolithic Research*. Oxford: Oxbow, 2009.

Hofmann, D. and J. Smyth (eds.). *Tracking the Neolithic House in Europe: Sedentism, Architecture, and Practice*. New York: Springer, 2013.

Ingold, T. *The Perception of the Environment: Essays in Livelihood, Dwelling and Skill*. London: Routledge, 2000.

Jones, A. *Prehistoric Materialities: Becoming Material in Prehistoric Britain and Ireland*. Oxford University Press, 2012.

   (ed.). *Prehistoric Europe: Theory and Practice*. Chichester: Wiley-Blackwell, 2008.

Kelly, R.J. *The Lifeways of Hunter-Gatherers*. Cambridge University Press, 2013.

Marciniak, A. *Placing Animals in the Neolithic: Social Zooarchaeology of Prehistoric Farming Communities*. Institute of Archaeology Publications, University College London, 2005.

Parker Pearson, M. *Stonehenge: Exploring the Greatest Stone Age Mystery*. London: Simon & Schuster, 2012.

Prescott, C. and H. Glørstad (eds.). *Becoming European: The Transformation of Third Millennium Northern and Western Europe*. Oxford: Oxbow, 2012.

Robb, J. *The Early Mediterranean Village: Agency, Material Culture and Social Change in Neolithic Italy*. Cambridge University Press, 2007.

Robb, J. and O.J.T. Harris (eds.). *The Body in History: Europe from the Palaeolithic to the Future*. Cambridge University Press, 2013.

Schulting, R. and L. Fibiger (eds.). *Sticks, Stones, and Broken Bones: Neolithic Violence in a European Perspective*. Oxford University Press, 2012.

Serjeantson, D. and D. Field (eds.). *Animals in the Neolithic of Britain and Europe*. Oxford: Oxbow, 2006.

Smyth, J. *Settlement in the Irish Neolithic: New Discoveries at the Edge of Europe*. Oxford: Oxbow, 2014.

Whittle, A. *Europe in the Neolithic: The Creation of New Worlds*. Cambridge University Press, 1996.

Whittle, A. and V. Cummings (eds.). *Going Over: The Mesolithic–Neolithic Transition in North-West Europe*. Oxford University Press for the British Academy, 2007.

Whittle, A., F. Healy, and A. Bayliss. *Gathering Time: Dating the Early Neolithic Enclosures of Southern Britain and Ireland*. Oxford: Oxbow, 2011.

# 23

# Pioneer farmers at Brześć Kujawski, Poland

PETER BOGUCKI AND RYSZARD GRYGIEL

The earliest farmers of central Europe are among the most studied prehistoric societies in the world, yet they still confront archaeologists with many questions and challenges. For nearly forty years, we have investigated farming communities from the sixth and fifth millennia BCE in a part of northern Poland known as Kuyavia (in Polish, Kujawy) that lies along the Vistula River (in Polish, Wisła) south of the modern cities of Toruń and Bydgoszcz. Around a town called Brześć Kujawski, the earliest farmers left a remarkable record of their presence, including traces of houses, burials, and pits containing pottery, stone tools, animal bones, and charred seeds, while the impact that they had on the local environment is revealed by the study of sediments and pollen cores.

The landscape of Kuyavia is defined by its glacial heritage. It is a flat plain covered by morainic clay and glacial outwash lying between two east–west glacial meltwater valleys. Languid slow-moving streams run in troughs left by meltwater running under ice sheets that covered the area until 20,000 years ago. Retreating glaciers left behind blocks of ice that became embedded in post-Glacial sediments. When the chunks of stagnant ice melted, they left small basins that became lakes and ponds. Many basins have filled with peat and other biogenic sediments, so the modern cultivated landscape of Kuyavia masks the environmental variation present when the first farmers arrived.

Millennia of erosion and ploughing have left the traces of Neolithic settlement in Kuyavia lying just below the modern surface. The plough zone is scraped off to reveal the lower portions of prehistoric features, including pits, post holes, bedding trenches of houses, and graves. We know that the surface on which the prehistoric occupants of these sites trod was probably a few dozen centimetres higher, but what remains permits us to reconstruct the outlines of houses and find the graves of their occupants. The lower parts of pits contain enough rubbish in the form of pottery, stone tools and chipping

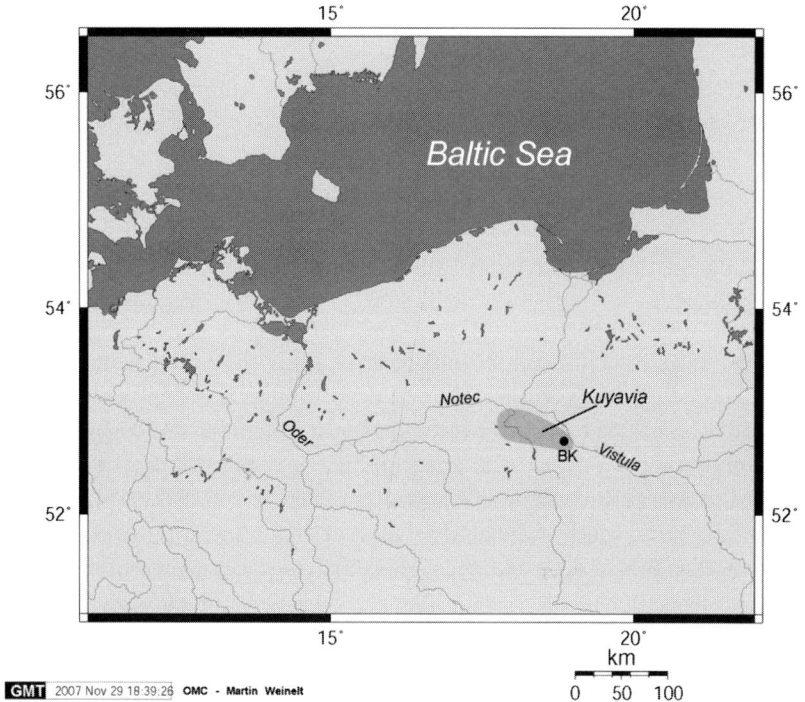

Map 23.1 North-central Europe showing location of Kuyavia and Brześć Kujawski (BK).

waste, animal bones, and seeds to permit the reconstruction of the material world of the Neolithic farmers and to study their economy.

We were not the first to excavate at Brześć Kujawski. In the spring of 1933, a young researcher at the Archaeological Museum in Warsaw, Konrad Jażdżewski, gazed out the window of an attic room in an agricultural school just outside Brześć Kujawski. He had come to rescue a late Neolithic grave found in the school's field. Across a road and a lake lay a low ridge of gravel and clay. 'Something must be there,' he thought, and a few days later, his initial inspection of the site revealed pottery and ground stone tools. The museum director allowed Jażdżewski to remain longer, and by summer his excavations began to yield spectacular results.

Jażdżewski discovered traces of Neolithic longhouses and burials at Brześć Kujawski.[1] Unlike the rectangular longhouses first found at Köln-Lindenthal

---

1 K. Jażdżewski, 'Cmentarzyska kultury ceramiki wstęgowej i związane z nimi ślady osadnictwa w Brześciu Kujawskim', *Wiadomości Archeologiczne*, 15 (1938), 1–105 (93).

in Germany in the early 1930s, the houses at Brześć Kujawski had bedding trenches that ran around their perimeter in a long trapezoidal outline. Posts set into these trenches formed the walls. Many house outlines overlapped, indicating that structures were replaced multiple times. Among the houses were graves holding crouched skeletons with copper ornaments. Jażdżewski called the people who built these houses and were buried among them the 'Brześć Kujawski Group', but before radiocarbon dating, it was unclear how they fitted in with other early farming societies in central Europe.

World War II interrupted Jażdżewski's research at Brześć Kujawski. In 1976, the authors arrived under the auspices of the Museum of Archaeology and Ethnography in Łódź, Poland, to pick up where Jażdżewski left off.[2] Archaeological methods had improved since World War II, and our aim was to excavate carefully to obtain charcoal for radiocarbon dating and to recover animal bones and charred seeds to study the subsistence economy. During the 1950s and 1960s, analysis of Jażdżewski's finds had shown that the Brześć Kujawski Group were not the only Neolithic inhabitants of the site. An earlier farming society, known as the Linear Pottery culture (also called the *Linearbandkeramik* or LBK), had also lived there. Thus the story of early Neolithic farming settlement in Kuyavia involves not one, but two, societies, the first during the second half of the sixth millennium BCE, the second in the middle of the fifth millennium BCE.

## Linear Pottery pioneer farmers

Along the northern periphery of central Europe, Linear Pottery farmers established settlements on the North European Plain along the lower Oder and Vistula.[3] Linear Pottery settlement areas of the North European Plain formed 'exclaves' of the larger zone in upland central Europe occupied by these agriculturalists. One such exclave is found in Kuyavia, where clusters of Linear Pottery sites lie on low fingers of land beside glacial landforms such as shallow lakes and valleys.

One settlement cluster is found around Brześć Kujawski (Figure 23.1), where a string of Linear Pottery sites follows a complex of shallow troughs left by subglacial channels running approximately 20 km east–west from the

---

2 P. Bogucki and R. Grygiel, 'Early farmers of the North European Plain', *Scientific American*, 248 / 4 (1983), 104–12 (106).

3 P. Bogucki, 'Neolithic dispersals in riverine interior central Europe', in A. Ammerman and P. Biagi (eds.), *The Widening Harvest: The Neolithic Transition in Europe: Looking Back, Looking Forward* (Boston: Archaeological Institute of America, 2003), 249–72 (259–62).

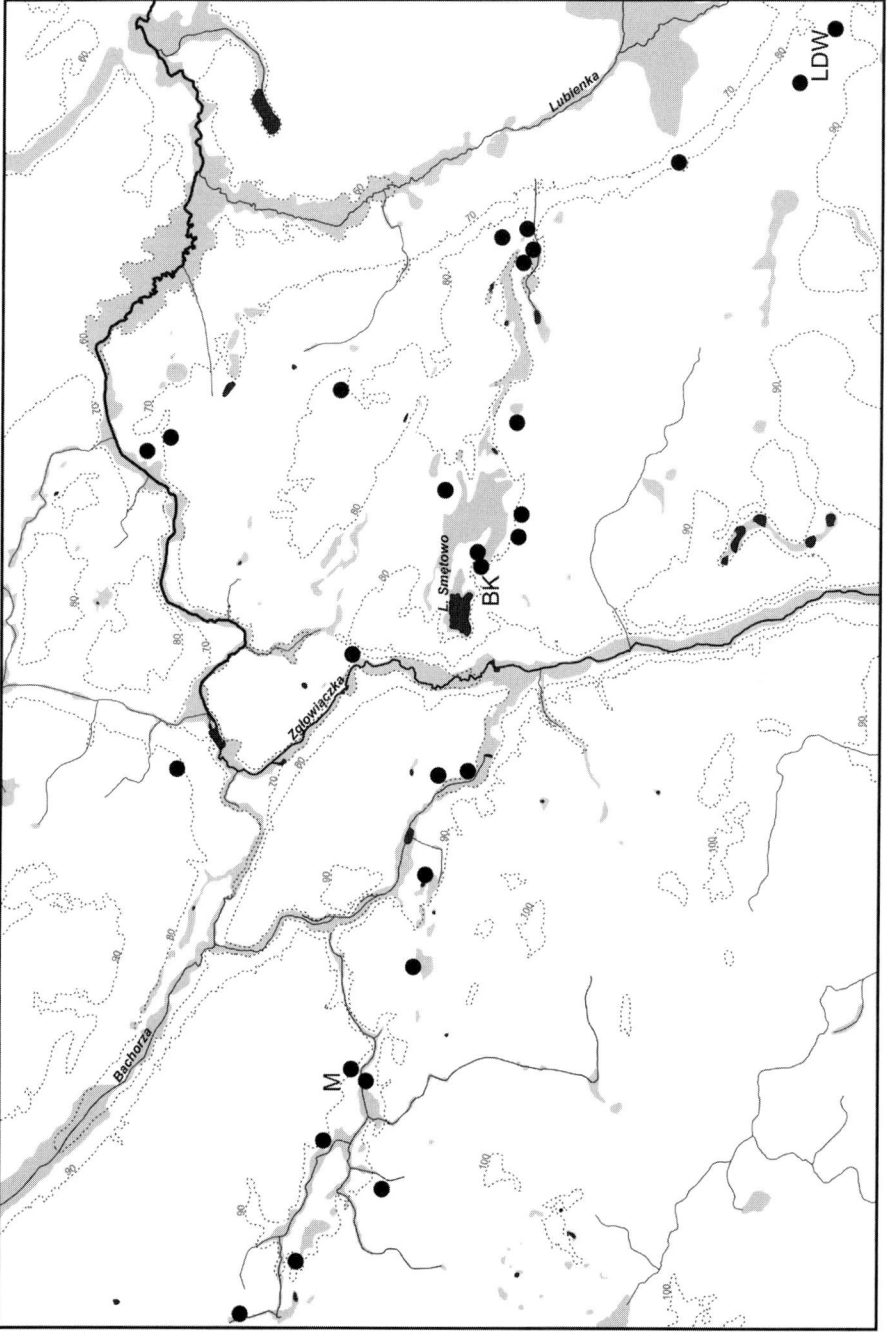

Figure 23.1 Map of Linear Pottery settlement near Brześć Kujawski. M – Miechowice; BK – Brześć Kujawski; LDW – Ludwinowo.

edge of the Vistula valley into the interior of the Kuyavian moraine plateau.[4] The preference of Linear Pottery farmers for relic glacial landforms is typical of their settlement on the North European Plain. Not only were these the main elements in the lowland hydrological network but they also provided openings in the forest that could be enlarged for settlements and fields.

Among nearly thirty sites, several localities stand out. On the edge of the Vistula valley, a complex of sites near Kruszyn was found recently during rescue excavations for the A1 motorway. Nearby is Ludwinowo, where an extensive settlement excavated by Joanna Pyzel has yielded traces of many pits and thirteen houses.[5] The row of sites at the eastern edge of the Kuyavian moraine continues through Smólsk and Nowa Wieś. A multi-period Linear Pottery settlement with houses is found 8 km to the west, at Brześć Kujawski, along with many smaller sites nearby. About 10 km further west, across the Zgłowiączka River, a large Linear Pottery settlement with two structures is found at Miechowice, and several kilometres beyond that lies a settlement with a house at Zagajewice.

The Linear Pottery occupations around Brześć Kujawski exhibit several important characteristics. First, their principal archaeological features are large pits, often elongated, that are filled with rubbish. Second, post-hole patterns at several sites define rectangular structures. House 3 at Brześć Kujawski measures 6 × 3 m, with a bedding trench at the northern end (Figure 23.2), while the two structures at Miechowice and one at Zagajewice are approximately 8 × 7 m. At Ludwinowo, aside from one anomalously large structure over 47 m long, the other twelve houses average 18 × 6 m.[6] Although it is possible that the elongated pits are features associated with additional houses whose post holes have eroded away, large concentrated settlements with dozens of longhouses over 20 m long, on the scale of Bylany, Elsloo, or Köln-Lindenthal, have yet to be found. Finally, many – but not all – Linear Pottery sites were occupied later by people of the Brześć Kujawski Group.

4  R. Grygiel, *Neolit i Początki Epoki Brązu w Rejonie Brześcia Kujawskiego i Osłonek* (*The Neolithic and early Bronze Age in the Brześć Kujawski and Osłonki Region*), 2 vols. (Konrad Jażdżewski Foundation for Archaeological Research, Museum of Archaeology and Ethnography, Łódź, 2004–8), vol. i, 113–19.

5  J. Pyzel, 'Preliminary results of large scale emergency excavations in Ludwinowo 7, comm. Włocławek', in R. Smolnik (ed.), *Siedlungsstruktur und Kulturwandel in der Bandkeramik: Beitrage der internationalen Tagung 'Neue Fragen zur Bandkeramik oder alles beim Alten?!'* (Dresden: Landesamt für Archäologie, 2012), 160–6.

6  Ibid.

Figure 23.2 Linear Pottery structure at Brześć Kujawski 3/4.

Calibrated radiocarbon dates place Linear Pottery settlement in the Brześć Kujawski region and Kuyavia generally between 5400 and just after 5000 BCE.[7] Such dating is supported by the ceramic evidence, which corresponds to the detailed sequences available from the upland zone. At Smólsk, twenty-one unbroken or slightly damaged ceramic vessels were found at the bottom of a well 6 m deep. The forms and decoration of these vessels correspond to the oldest Linear Pottery style in Poland, the so-called 'Zofipole' style, another indication of very little delay between Linear Pottery settlement in the upper Vistula drainage and its first appearance in Kuyavia. Many Kuyavian settlements contain pottery with the classic 'music-note' motif in which incised lines are interrupted with dots (Figure 23.3), c. 5300/5200 BCE, while other features contain pottery dating to the end of the sixth millennium BCE. Some sites were occupied multiple times. For example, at Brześć Kujawski, there were at least two separate episodes of Linear Pottery occupation.

We believe that Linear Pottery pioneer farmers reached Kuyavia from several directions, based on different types of ceramics found at their sites.[8] Some came from the region of southern Poland known as Małopolska, around

7 Grygiel, *Neolit i Początki Epoki Brązu*, vol. I, 633–43.　8 Ibid., vol. I, 617–27.

594

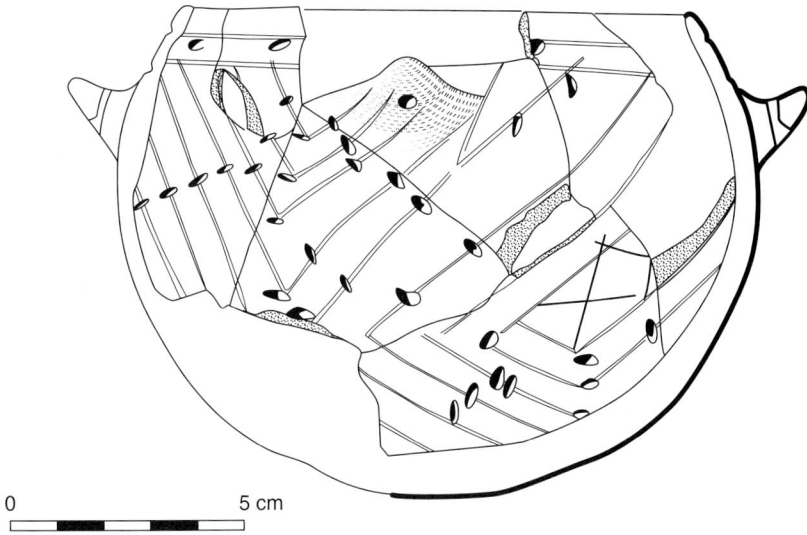

0                    5 cm

Figure 23.3  Linear Pottery vessel from Falborz.

the modern city of Kraków, probably travelling down the Vistula valley. Others seem to have come from Silesia, along the upper Oder River, presumably arriving across the plains and outwash valleys of central Poland. Still other pottery reflects connections with central Germany along the Elbe and Saale rivers. The Dutch archaeologist P.J.R. Modderman once characterized the Linear Pottery culture as having 'diversity in uniformity', and the heterogeneity of its pottery in the small area around Brześć Kujawski reflects this variety among pottery motifs which superficially appear to be very similar.

Flint tools used by the Linear Pottery culture in Kuyavia are made primarily from the 'chocolate' flint found in the Holy Cross mountains of central Poland and flint from Jurassic deposits near Kraków. Sickle gloss on many blades attests to their use in cutting grain and reeds. Ground stone tools, ranging from flat axes to high 'shoe-last' celts, were often made from amphibolite of Silesian origin. In order to get the most use from them, ground stone tools were frequently resharpened, leaving most of them considerably reduced from their original size.

Animal bones are superbly preserved in Kuyavian clay and gravel.[9] Linear Pottery animal bone collections in Kuyavia consist almost entirely of

9  P. Bogucki, *Early Neolithic Subsistence and Settlement in the Polish Lowlands* (Oxford: British Archaeological Reports, 1982), 57–63.

domestic animals, and among domestic animals, cattle comprise the over-whelming majority, almost always over 70 per cent. Sheep and goats make up under 20 per cent of most collections, while pig bones are very scarce. This pattern is consistent with most Linear Pottery faunal samples in central Europe, although it is somewhat extreme in its representation of cattle in relation to other species. Cattle clearly played a large part in the economy of the Linear Pottery settlements of Kuyavia.[10]

An unusual characteristic of Kuyavian Linear Pottery sites is that they have yielded an abundance of pottery fragments with small perforations. Such sieve sherds appear to be more common than in other regions, and one of us proposed many years ago that they were used for separating curds from whey in the manufacture of cheese. Recent analysis by Mélanie Salque of sieve sherds from Brześć Kujawski, Miechowice, and Ludwinowo has shown that many contain residues from milk fats, thus supporting the dairying hypothesis.[11]

Analysis of samples of carbonized plant remains by Aldona Bieniek has shown that the Linear Pottery farmers in the Brześć Kujawski area grew primarily emmer and einkorn wheat, probably as a mixed crop in small gardens that included typical field weeds found throughout Neolithic central Europe.[12] Peas and flax seeds were found at several sites, while poppy was identified at Smólsk. Poppy seeds have hitherto been confined to Linear Pottery sites in western Europe, and their discovery in Kuyavia marks the easternmost find of poppy in central Europe during the sixth millennium BCE. Smólsk is one of the sites whose pottery indicates western connections, so the presence of poppy is important corroboration of such affiliation.

Conspicuously absent from Linear Pottery sites in the Brześć Kujawski area are burials. At the moment, the only graves that can be attributed to a Linear Pottery occupation are a fragmentary skeleton of a child from Miechowice, two possible Linear Pottery burials at Brześć Kujawski, and two graves from Ludwinowo. This situation stands in sharp contrast to the large Linear Pottery cemeteries found at sites like Aiterhofen in Bavaria, Nitra in Slovakia, and Elsloo in Holland, as well as numerous settlement burials at sites like Vaihingen an der Enz in southwestern Germany. Two possible

---

10 Grygiel, *Neolit i Początki Epoki Brązu*, vol. 1, 544–77.

11 M. Salque et al., 'Earliest evidence for cheese making in the sixth millennium BC in northern Europe', *Nature*, 493 (2013), 522–5.

12 A. Bieniek, 'Neolithic plant husbandry in the Kujawy region of central Poland', in S. Colledge and J. Conolly (eds.), *The Origins and Spread of Domestic Plants in Southwest Asia and Europe* (Walnut Creek, CA: Left Coast Press, 2007), 327–42 (335).

explanations arise. One is that we have yet to find the Linear Pottery cemeteries of Kuyavia, although with excellent preservation of bone in the glacial clay, they should be recognizable if they exist. The other is that Linear Pottery occupations were so transient that in any single generation the few individuals who died were not sufficient to constitute an archaeologically visible cemetery. Isolated graves can be easily missed in the countryside or disturbed beyond recognition by subsequent settlement on the same site.

Many years ago, we characterized the Linear Pottery settlement in Kuyavia as having a 'tactical' nature, in that it represented relatively short-term occupations by pioneer groups still in the process of identifying the best locations for farming settlement.[13] We continue to hold this view. While it is clear from abundant evidence of cultivation and the amount of archaeological materials that Linear Pottery farmers established durable settlements along the Kuyavian lakes and valleys, the limited evidence for structures and the rarity of burials suggest that the habitations did not last more than a few years, certainly not longer than a generation or two. In only one case, at Brześć Kujawski, is there possible evidence for the secondary enlargement of a Linear Pottery house. Palaeoenvironmental research also indicates that although cereal pollen and some indicators of disturbed habitats appear in the pollen record at this time, significant environmental changes attributable to Neolithic settlement did not occur until later. It seems that the forest recovered quickly from small-scale clearances for fields and settlement, and the grazing of livestock did not have a great effect on the regeneration of the forest cover.

## Frontier households of the Brześć Kujawski Group

After 4700 BCE, following an apparent hiatus in settlement of several centuries, Brześć Kujawski Group settlements belonging to the Lengyel culture appear across Kuyavia (Figure 23.4).[14] These communities are clearly from the same Danubian tradition as the Linear Pottery culture, with their long-house architecture and contracted burials having clear antecedents in the Neolithic communities of upland central Europe. Sites of the Brześć Kujawski Group lie in the same landscape zones, and often at the same locations, as Linear Pottery settlements from several centuries earlier. They are far more numerous, larger, and of much longer duration.

13 P. Bogucki, 'Tactical and strategic settlements in the early Neolithic of lowland Poland', *Journal of Anthropological Research*, 35/2 (1979), 238–46 (242).
14 Grygiel, *Neolit i Początki Epoki Brązu*, vol. II, 1995–2009.

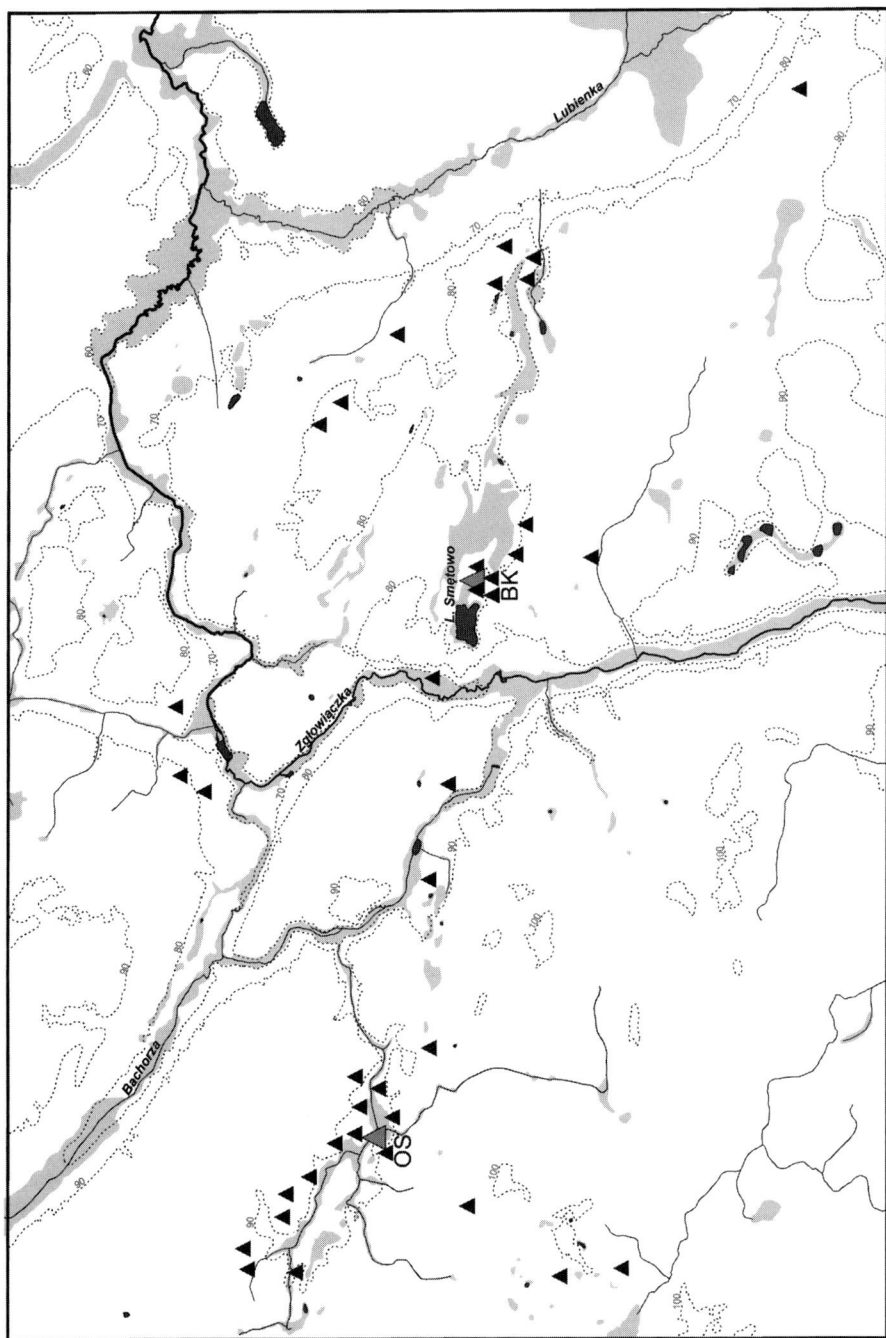

Figure 23.4  Map of sites of the Brześć Kujawski Group near Brześć Kujawski, with major settlements indicated by large triangles. BK – Brześć Kujawski; OS – Osłonki.

Figure 23.5 Excavation plan of the Brześć Kujawski Group settlement at Osłonki.

Two large settlements lying 8 km apart stand out in the area that we have studied: Brześć Kujawski and Osłonki.[15] Both settlements cover several hectares with dozens of longhouses and burials and are surrounded by multiple smaller settlements. Just northeast of Brześć Kujawski lies a slightly smaller settlement at Pikutkowo, while further east settlements of the Brześć Kujawski Group have been found at Smólsk and Kruszyn along the route of the A1 motorway. Near Osłonki, other settlements of the Brześć Kujawski Group include Miechowice, Konary, and Zagajewice.

A large settlement of the Brześć Kujawski Group contains several types of archaeological feature: longhouses with distinctive trapezoidal plans; large pits from which clay was dug to plaster the houses, and smaller pits dug for unknown reasons; unusual bathtub-shaped features in the interiors of many houses; burials; and, in the case of Osłonki, a ditch-and-palisade system (Figure 23.5). Due to the fact that many houses and pits overlap, it is possible to define three major phases of settlement of the Brześć Kujawski Group. The first, or 'early', phase begins before 4500 BCE. Small longhouses mark the establishment of farmsteads during this phase. It is followed by the 'classic' phase between c. 4500 and 4300 BCE, during which the settlements saw their most elaborate development, with large longhouses and rich burials. Finally,

---

15 R. Grygiel and P. Bogucki, 'Early farmers in north-central Europe: 1989–1994 excavations at Osłonki, Poland', *Journal of Field Archaeology*, 24/2 (1997), 161–78 (162).

Figure 23.6 Houses and other features of the Brześć Kujawski Group at Miechowice; note oval features within each house.

a late phase continues until about 4000 BCE, whereafter the Brześć Kujawski Group fades from the scene.

Perhaps the most striking features of the Brześć Kujawski Group are its trapezoidal longhouses, of which dozens are now known from settlements across Kuyavia (Figure 23.6). They are usually between 20 and 40 m in length along an axis running roughly northwest–southeast, 5–8 m wide at the southeast end and 3–5 m wide at the northwest end. Rather than digging an individual hole for each upright structural post, Brześć Kujawski house-wrights dug a continuous bedding trench around the perimeter of each structure. Posts were set closely together in this trench palisade-style. Impressions in the bottoms of trenches indicate that many posts were logs split lengthwise. Gaps between posts were filled with clay daub, taken from pits next to each house. We do not know how the roofs were constructed, although the assumption is that they were pitched along the main axis of the house. It is also difficult to determine where the entrances were.

Enigmatic bathtub-shaped pits are found in many, but not all, longhouses of the Brześć Kujawski Group, usually at the centre of the house near the eastern wall. After we first noticed them at Osłonki, subsequent examination of house plans from other sites indicated that they are ubiquitous. Their shape and size are inappropriate for food storage (which was probably high in the rafters away from rodents and vermin), and they contain almost no artefacts, bones, or seeds. Yet they are so consistent a feature of many houses that they evidently had a culturally patterned significance for the Brześć Kujawski Group.

The large clay-pits served as the source of daub for plastering houses and making pottery. They were made haphazardly as people dug out the clay they needed, resulting in many nooks, crannies, and even burrows. These pits then functioned as both traps for artefacts and other debris as well as the locations of deliberate rubbish disposal, all the while silting up by erosion from surrounding surfaces. In some places, dense concentrations of broken pottery, chipped stone, animal bones, and seeds are found, while elsewhere the fill contains almost nothing.

Brześć Kujawski pottery comes in several basic forms, including carinated bowls and tall-necked amphorae. Surface decoration is much reduced from that seen in the Linear Pottery culture and commonly consists only of rows of fingernail impression around the rims and waists of vessels. Handles and appliquéd knobs are also common ornaments. The ceramics of the Brześć Kujawski Group are distinctive for their mica temper.

Flint-workers of the Brześć Kujawski Group found that they could make most of their tools from the local Baltic erratic flint. Whenever possible, however, they were happy to use imported flint, including the 'chocolate' flint from the Holy Cross mountains, Jurassic flint from the Kraków uplands, and even Volhynian flint from the southeastern corner of Poland. Blades made from 'chocolate' flint were preferred for working hard materials such as bone and antler. Local erratic rocks were also used for making most ground stone tools. An assemblage of ground stone tools from a feature interpreted as a lumberjack's hut at Kuczyna, halfway between Brześć Kujawski and Osłonki, reflects various stages in the life of stone axes, from pre-form to exhausted tool.[16]

At Osłonki, a massive ditch system delimits the western side of the settlement, which was otherwise surrounded by water.[17] The surviving depth of the ditch often reaches 2 m or more. It was presumably coupled with a bank made from the excavated soil which has since been eroded and ploughed away. The Osłonki ditch is not continuous, with gaps suggesting entrances through it, although passage would have been complicated by the

---

16 R. Grygiel, 'The household cluster as a fundamental social unit of the Brześć Kujawski group of the Lengyel culture in the Polish lowlands', *Prace i Materiały Muzeum Archeologicznego i Etnograficznego (seria archeologiczna)*, 31 (1986), 43–334 (220–38).

17 Grygiel and Bogucki, 'Early farmers in north-central Europe', 170.

palisade running behind it. The ditch was not part of the original settlement layout, but rather was cut through spots where earlier houses had stood, suggesting that something happened to require fortification of the settlement. Burials in the ditch-fill indicate that it had started to silt up already during the life of the settlement.

Some of the richest information about the inhabitants of settlements like Brześć Kujawski and Osłonki comes from dozens of burials. Burials of the Brześć Kujawski Group were contemporaneous with their houses, so there is no possibility that the function of the sites alternated between settlement and cemetery. Instead, these two functions were integrated, so the dead were very much a part of the living settlement. Although at first glance the burials of the Brześć Kujawski Group appear to be distributed throughout its settlements, closer examination reveals that many occur in small clusters of two to nine graves, often lined up side by side. These micro-cemeteries clearly reflect memories of ancestors and the digging of new graves alongside theirs, and we can assume they must have been marked somehow on the surface.

Most graves contain skeletons in a crouched position with arms drawn up to the chest (Figure 23.7). During the early and middle phases of the Brześć Kujawski Group, males were always buried on their right side and the females on their left, with heads pointing towards the south or southeast. We do not know the reason for this practice, but clearly it reflected an important fundamental value that divided along gender lines. During the late phase of occupation, burials were more haphazard and did not conform to such strict rules. They are flexed, extended, or on their backs, oriented in almost every direction. Most graves contain single skeletons, but double and triple burials have occasionally been noted.

Accompanying many skeletons are artefacts. Many male graves have flint blades or axes made from red deer antlers, while female graves often contain copper ornaments, shell beads, stone beads, and bone arm-rings. More will be said about the antler axes below, but it is clear that they were a mark of masculinity. The shell beads are round, perforated disks cut from the valves of river mussels of the genus *Unio* which were then strung into hip belts. The number of beads in some belts runs into the thousands. Stone beads were less numerous and were made from marble-like calcite. Bone arm-rings were brassards worn on the upper arms, decorated with rows of small triangular incisions. A burial may contain multiple ornaments of different materials, or it may contain none at all.

The copper artefacts found at Brześć Kujawski and Osłonki represent the earliest known use of copper in this part of Europe, around 4500 BCE.

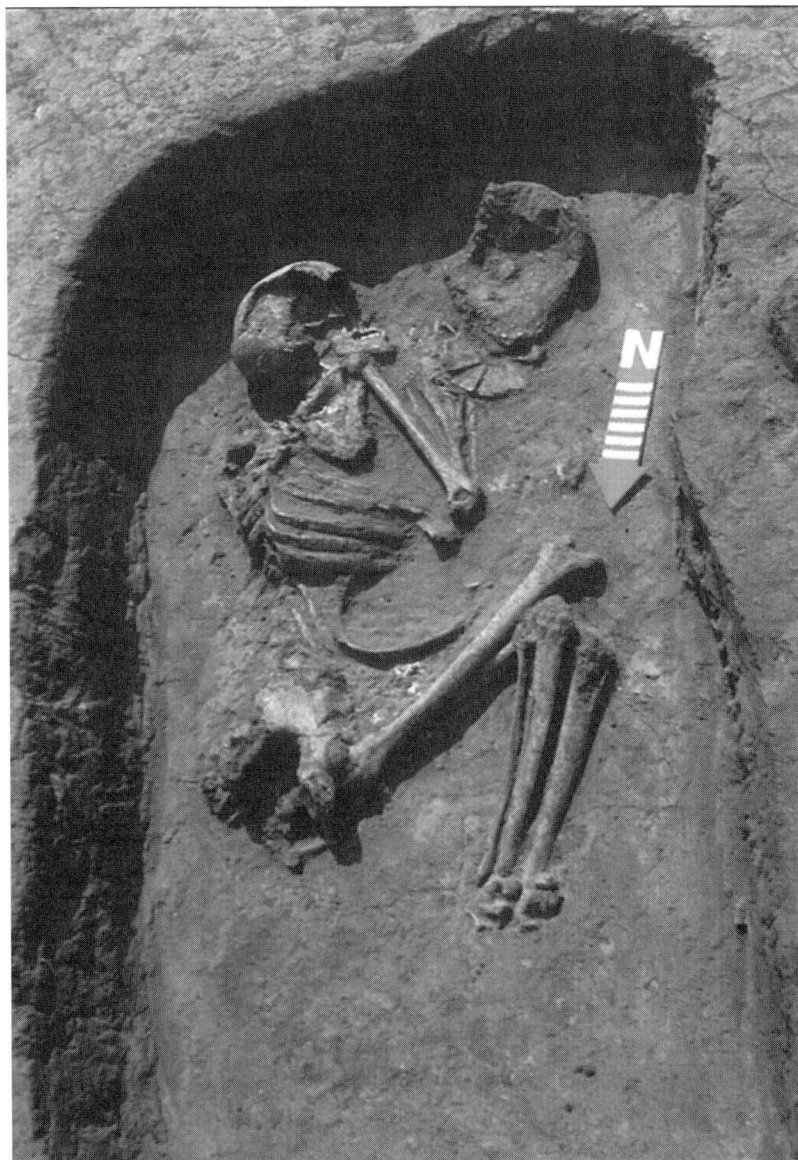

Figure 23.7 Burial of the Brześć Kujawski Group with copper artefacts at Osłonki.

Although the copper source has not yet been conclusively established, a trail of similar artefacts leads to the eastern Alps, hundreds of kilometres away. It was smelted, hammered into ribbons and sheets, and then shaped into beads, pendants, and head ornaments. Some burials had lavish displays of copper, while others had none. After a short period of availability around 4500 BCE, the copper supply was cut off, and the later burials do not contain metal ornaments. Despite the settlements being only 8 km apart, the copper at Osłonki has a different trace element signature from that at Brześć Kujawski.[18] Graves at Osłonki have much more elaborate copper displays than those at Brześć Kujawski, including complicated compositions of pendants and beads, and even a diadem of small copper strips.

Antler axes known as 'T-axes' found in Brześć Kujawski graves deserve special mention. They are made from sturdy beams of red deer antler, either from hunted animals or from shed antlers. After removing the base and brow tine with a combination of cutting and snapping, the tines and crown were removed. A hole was drilled through the location where the bez tine had been cut off, presumably to accept a wooden handle, and the snapped end was ground to a sharp edge. We know that the axes were made at Brześć Kujawski and Osłonki because we have found by-products of axe manufacture like severed bases and tines. In the male graves where they were found, they are often positioned such that if a handle had survived it would have been held by the corpse.

Skeletons from Brześć Kujawski, Osłonki, and other sites have been studied by anthropologists Emilia Garłowska and Wiesław Lorkiewicz.[19] Poor diets and hard labour took a toll on the early farmers. Cribra orbitalia, lesions in eye sockets caused by anaemia, was found in 80 per cent of children at Osłonki and persisted in 20 per cent of adults. Enamel hypoplasia, caused by dietary stress while dental crowns are forming in childhood, is found in many individuals. Bone modifications caused by habitual squatting are found on lower limbs, while Schmorl's nodes on vertebrae also reflect biomechanical stress. Teeth were used for more than chewing food: transverse grooves on lower incisors resulted from drawing string or thread repeatedly across the front of the mouth.[20] Grooves occur almost always on women's teeth, so this activity was gender-specific.

---

18 Grygiel, *Neolit i Początki Epoki Brązu*, vol. II, 1934–5.   19 Ibid., vol. II, 1811–50.
20 W. Lorkiewicz, 'Nonalimentary tooth use in the neolithic population of the Lengyel culture in central Poland (4600–4000 BC)', *American Journal of Physical Anthropology*, 144 (2011), 540–2.

Many skeletons bore traces of violence (Figure 23.8).[21] Among male skeletons, nearly a third had traces of traumatic injury 'above the hat line' caused by blows to the skull. Sometimes the individual survived, but in many cases the blow was lethal, often penetrating the skull. Victims of violence were not only adult men. At Osłonki, one grave contained skeletons of an adult female 25–35 years old, a child about 10 years old, and a child 4–6 years old. The woman and the older child were killed by blows to the head with a pointed round object 45 mm across, matching antler axes used by Neolithic farmers in this region.

The animal economy of the Brześć Kujawski Group is well known from relatively large collections of animal bones studied by Peter Bogucki and Daniel Makowiecki.[22] In marked contrast to the cattle-heavy Linear Pottery animal economy, Brześć Kujawski faunal samples are characterized by many more sheep and goats, often accounting for between 30 and 40 per cent of the identified specimens, and generally between 10 and 30 per cent pigs. Cattle were still the most important domestic species, comprising 40 per cent or more of most collections, but the diversification of the animal economy represents a change from the previous millennium. Wild mammals are better represented in the economy of the Brześć Kujawski Group than in the Linear Pottery diet, with a small but noticeable percentage of red deer and roe deer at every site. Other hunted mammals include wild horse, wild pig, beaver, otter, and bear. The people of the Brześć Kujawski Group also made extensive use of fish, birds, and turtles.

Settlements of the Brześć Kujawski Group also yielded a richer array of palaeobotanical data than their Linear Pottery precursors. Analysis of carbonized plant remains collected from Osłonki, Miechowice, and neighbouring sites by Aldona Bieniek shows heavy cultivation of wheat and some barley, with wheat chaff representing over 80 per cent of the botanical remains.[23] An extensive list of wild plant species contains both field weeds harvested along with the cereals as well as some gathered plants. An unusual feature of the botanical assemblages at Osłonki, Konary, and Miechowice is the presence of an unusually large number of grains and awns of feathergrass, *Stipa pennata*. Feathergrass is a xerothermic species typical of dry grasslands rather than

21 W. Lorkiewicz, 'Skeletal trauma and violence among the early farmers of the North European Plain: evidence from Neolithic settlements of the Lengyel culture in Kuyavia, north-central Poland', in R. Schulting and L. Fibiger (eds.), *Sticks, Stones, and Broken Bones: Neolithic Violence in a European Perspective* (Oxford University Press, 2012), 56–67.

22 P. Bogucki, 'Animal exploitation by the Brześć Kujawski Group of the Lengyel culture', in Grygiel, *Neolit i Początki Epoki Brązu*, vol. II, 1581–704 (1684–5).

23 Bieniek, 'Neolithic plant husbandry', 328–33.

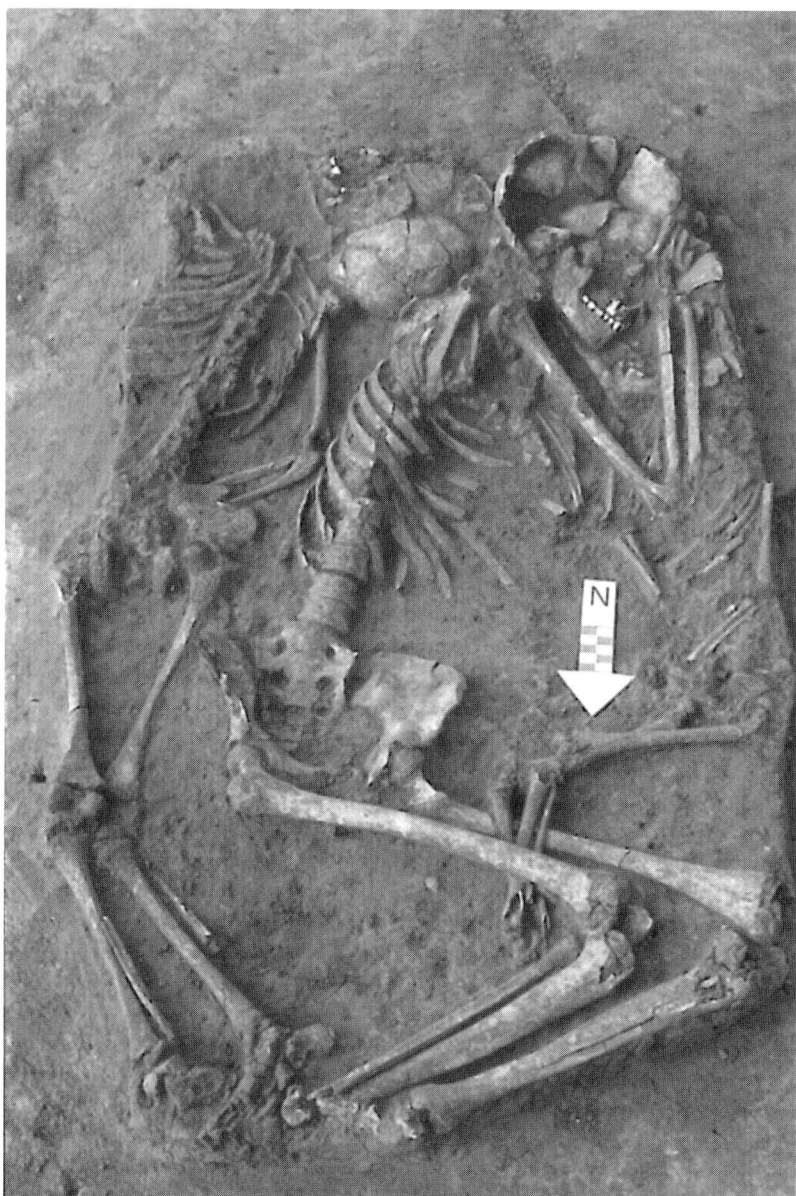

Figure 23.8 Multiple burial with victims of violence at Osłonki; the adult female at the centre and the older child on the left were killed by blows to the head, while the cause of death of the younger child on the right cannot be determined with certainty.

closed deciduous forests. It is unlikely that the feathergrass, whose use is unknown, would have been brought from a great distance, so its abundance at the sites of the Brześć Kujawski Group suggests the presence of open, dry habitats in the vicinity, either natural or anthropogenic.

Multiple lines of evidence studied by Dorota Nalepka, Bolesław Nowaczyk, and others have enabled us to assess the environmental impact of the settlement of the Brześć Kujawski Group at Osłonki and the neighbouring settlements of Miechowice and Konary, where three basins left by post-Glacial melting of stagnant ice filled with biogenic sediments.[24] Sandy deltas and lenses in the sediments suggest that loose soil from nearby cleared land washed or was blown into the basins, which were shallow lakes during the fifth millennium BCE. Additional mineral material and charcoal particles in the sediments reflect extensive activity around the shorelines of the lakes, while the presence of terrestrial snails among the mollusc samples also indicates delivery of soil from nearby land surfaces into the basins. At the same time, samples of *Cladocera*, or water fleas, shift from being dominated by species that flourish at low nutrient levels to those that require high nutrient levels, suggesting the dumping of human and animal wastes into the lakes. Such indicators of human activity, apparently lacking during the Linear Pottery occupation at Miechowice, indicate the pronounced and sustained effect of occupation by the Brześć Kujawski Group.

At the same time, this impact appears to have been localized in space and time. Although the pollen record during the period of the most pronounced disturbance is interrupted due to the corrosion of pollen grains by mineralization of the sediments, it resumes after a hiatus to reflect relatively unchanged composition of the surrounding forests. Eventually, the inflow of soil from surrounding land surfaces ended, and the *Cladocera* samples were again dominated by species that have lower nutrient requirements. During the middle of the fifth millennium BCE, however, the people and animals living at Osłonki, Miechowice, and Konary modified the landscape in the immediate environs of their settlements to trigger distinct signals in the palaeoecological record.

On the basis of the rich archaeological finds at Brześć Kujawski, Osłonki, and other sites, we can begin to reconstruct the Neolithic frontier society that flourished in Kuyavia during the fifth millennium BCE. Its basic unit of residence and decision-making was the household that occupied a longhouse,

---

24 P. Bogucki et al., 'Multiproxy environmental archaeology of Neolithic settlements at Osłonki, Poland, 5500–4000 BC', *Environmental Archaeology*, 17/1 (2012), 45–65 (60–3).

buried its dead in nearby graves, and left its rubbish in the adjacent pits.[25] At any one time, several households could be found at large settlements like Brześć Kujawski and Osłonki, while smaller settlements like Miechowice and Pikutkowo may have been home to one or two. While we do not know the exact composition of a household, we assume that members of several generations lived under the same roof. As households moved through their developmental cycle, some longhouses were enlarged or rebuilt.

Over time, new households formed, requiring construction of more long-houses and beginning the cycle anew, while others faded away and houses were abandoned. The many longhouses at Brześć Kujawski and Osłonki indicate that these settlements persisted over multiple household develop-mental cycles, even if houses may have been intermittently demolished and rebuilt. Such duration of settlement is also reflected in the many burials found at Brześć Kujawski, Osłonki, and other sites. We have characterized such long-term commitments to particular settlements as reflecting a 'stra-tegic' choice of prime locations for pursuing an agricultural economy char-acterized by intensive cultivation of cereals and a mixture of livestock, supported by fishing and hunting.[26]

Despite the abundance of grave goods in some burials, which suggests social differentiation, we do not see unequivocal signs of persistent hierarchy or institutionalized leadership in the Brześć Kujawski Group. Rather, this society can be characterized as 'transegalitarian', meaning that distinct but transient asymmetries in household status waxed and waned over time, depending on success (or lack of it) in achieving prestige. Households may have joined together into factions to advance common interests, perhaps allied against other such communities or outside groups.

Everyday life was difficult, as shown by the skeletal evidence for nutri-tional stress and hard work. Life was also violent, as is often the case in frontier communities. We have already mentioned the traces of lethal trauma on many skeletons, some of which appear to have been inflicted with antler T-axes. Furthermore, some houses of the classic phase at both Osłonki and Brześć Kujawski show signs of having been destroyed by fire and then either rebuilt or abandoned. At Osłonki, the fortification ditch was constructed after one such episode around 4300 BCE. The presence of antler axes and archery equipment in male graves suggests that they were

25  P. Bogucki and R. Grygiel, 'The household cluster at Brześć Kujawski 3: small-site methodology in the Polish lowlands', *World Archaeology*, 13/1 (1981), 59–72 (63–8).
26  Bogucki, 'Tactical and strategic settlements', 243.

recognized for their abilities in combat. Perhaps internal stresses and contentious asymmetries in status led to conflicts between factions that eventually contributed to the decline of the Brześć Kujawski Group.

The people of the Brześć Kujawski Group maintained long-distance contacts with other farming communities to the south and west. Their procurement of copper and calcite followed a chain of connections leading through Silesia and Bohemia, while their high-quality flint was obtained from sources in southern and southeastern Poland. Shared cultural practices such as longhouses and contracted burials, as well as common ceramic styles, situate the Brześć Kujawski Group firmly within the Danubian world established by the Linear Pottery culture a millennium earlier.

At the same time, however, Kuyavia lies along the borderland that separated the Danubian world from the foragers of the Baltic basin.[27] Antler T-axes like those made at Osłonki and Brześć Kujawski and used in various activities, including homicide, before being placed in male burials, were popular throughout the Mesolithic world of the fifth millennium BCE (Figure 23.9). Bone ornaments decorated with rows of incised triangles are also found in the Baltic basin. Kuyavia would have been only a few days by canoe on low-energy streams from the Baltic coast, so it is likely that foragers

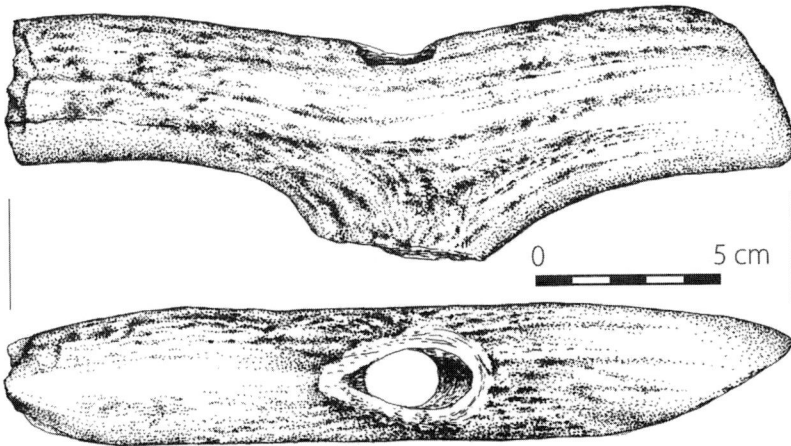

Figure 23.9 Antler 'T-axe' of the Brześć Kujawski Group from Osłonki.

27 P. Bogucki, 'The Danubian–Baltic borderland: northern Poland in the fifth millennium BC', in H. Fokkens et al. (eds.), *Between Foraging and Farming: An Extended Broad Spectrum of Papers Presented to Leendert Louwe Kooijmans*, Analecta Praehistorica Leidensia 40 (Leiden University Press, 2008), 53.

and farmers were aware of each other. The appearance of domestic cattle at sites in the southwestern Baltic at the end of the fifth millennium BCE shows that this borderland was porous rather than a barrier.

An enduring mystery, however, involves the end of the Brześć Kujawski Group and the eventual transformation of Neolithic society in the Polish lowlands to that known as the Funnel Beaker culture, characterized by very different settlement and burial practices. The violent episode around 4300 BCE marked the beginning of a decline in which burial practices were liberalized and some of the smaller settlements were abandoned, but it did not cause an immediate end to the Brześć Kujawski Group. One possibility is that intensive local land use was not sustainable, although that does not provide an entirely satisfactory explanation due to the fact that the environment quickly rebounded. Perhaps the old Danubian model simply did not satisfy an increasingly heterogeneous population, and the Funnel Beaker model was more acceptable in the long run.

Nonetheless, the impact of the Brześć Kujawski Group cannot be underestimated. Its settlements, which persisted across multiple generations, represent the first successful farming communities of the North European Plain, with an economy based on intensive cultivation and a mix of livestock species that took advantage of bountiful Kuyavian conditions. Its legacy lived on in the eventual transformation of indigenous forager societies of the North European Plain and perhaps in the oft-noted parallels between its longhouse architecture and earthen long barrows of the Funnel Beaker culture found nearby. Yet there is still much to be learned, and future generations of archaeologists will find that studying the Brześć Kujawski Group holds many challenges and rewards.

## Further reading

Bieniek, A. 'Neolithic plant husbandry in the Kujawy region of central Poland.' In S. Colledge and J. Conolly (eds.), *The Origins and Spread of Domestic Plants in Southwest Asia and Europe*. Walnut Creek, CA: Left Coast Press, 2007. 327–42.

Bogucki, P. 'Tactical and strategic settlements in the early Neolithic of lowland Poland.' *Journal of Anthropological Research*, 35 (1979), 238–46.

    *Early Neolithic Subsistence and Settlement in the Polish Lowlands*. Oxford: British Archaeological Reports, 1982.

    'Neolithic dispersals in riverine interior central Europe.' In A. Ammerman and P. Biagi (eds.), *The Widening Harvest: The Neolithic Transition in Europe: Looking Back, Looking Forward*. Boston: Archaeological Institute of America, 2003. 249–72.

'Animal exploitation by the Brześć Kujawski Group of the Lengyel culture.' In Grygiel, *Neolit i Początki Epoki Brązu*. vol. II, 2008, 1581–704.

'The Danubian–Baltic borderland: northern Poland in the fifth millennium BC.' In H. Fokkens et al. (eds.), *Between Foraging and Farming: An Extended Broad Spectrum of Papers Presented to Leendert Louwe Kooijmans*. Analecta Praehistorica Leidensia 40. Leiden University Press, 2008. 51–65.

Bogucki, P. and R. Grygiel. 'The household cluster at Brześć Kujawski 3: small-site methodology in the Polish lowlands.' *World Archaeology*, 13 (1981), 59–72.

'Early farmers of the North European Plain.' *Scientific American*, 248/4 (1983), 104–12.

Bogucki, P., D. Nalepka, R. Grygiel, and B. Nowaczyk. 'Multiproxy environmental archaeology of Neolithic settlements at Osłonki, Poland, 5500–4000 BC.' *Environmental Archaeology*, 17/1 (2012), 45–65.

Grygiel, R. 'Household cluster as a fundamental social unit of the Brześć Kujawski Group of the Lengyel culture in the Polish lowlands.' *Prace i Materiały Muzeum Archeologicznego i Etnograficznego (seria archeologiczna)*, 31 (1986), 43–334.

*Neolit i Początki Epoki Brązu w Rejonie Brześcia Kujawskiego i Osłonek (The Neolithic and Early Bronze Age in the Brześć Kujawski and Osłonki Region)*. 2 vols. Łódź: Konrad Jażdżewski Foundation for Archaeological Research, Museum of Archaeology and Ethnography, 2004–8.

Grygiel, R. and P. Bogucki. 'Early farmers in north-central Europe: 1989–1994 excavations at Osłonki, Poland.' *Journal of Field Archaeology*, 24 (1997), 161–78.

Jażdżewski, K. 'Cmentarzyska kultury ceramiki wstęgowej i związane z nimi ślady osadnictwa w Brześciu Kujawskim.' *Wiadomości Archeologiczne*, 15 (1938), 1–105.

Lorkiewicz, W. 'Nonalimentary tooth use in the Neolithic population of the Lengyel culture in central Poland (4600–4000 BC).' *American Journal of Physical Anthropology*, 144 (2011), 538–51.

'Skeletal trauma and violence among the early farmers of the North European Plain: evidence from Neolithic settlements of the Lengyel culture in Kuyavia, north-central Poland.' In R. Schulting and L. Fibiger (eds.), *Sticks, Stones, and Broken Bones: Neolithic Violence in a European Perspective*. Oxford University Press, 2012. 51–76.

Pyzel, J. 'Preliminary results of large scale emergency excavations in Ludwinowo 7, comm. Włocławek.' In R. Smolnik (ed.), *Siedlungsstruktur und Kulturwandel in der Bandkeramik: Beitrage der internationalen Tagung 'Neue Fragen zur Bandkeramik oder alles beim Alten?!'* Dresden: Landesamt für Archäologie, 2012. 160–6.

Salque, M., P. Bogucki, J. Pyzel, et al. 'Earliest evidence for cheese making in the sixth millennium BC in northern Europe.' *Nature*, 493 (2013), 522–5.

# Index